# THE ART
# OF BEING HUMAN

*Fourth Edition*

# THE ART
# OF BEING HUMAN

## THE HUMANITIES
## AS A TECHNIQUE
## FOR LIVING

**Richard Paul Janaro**
*New World School of the Arts*

**Thelma C. Altshuler**
*Miami-Dade Community College*

HarperCollins*CollegePublishers*

Acquisitions Editor: Lisa Moore
Development Editor: Marisa L. L'Heureux
Project Coordination and Text Design: Lachina Publishing Services, Inc.
Production/Manufacturing: Michael Weinstein/Paula Keller
Cover Design: Kay Petronio
Cover Photo: *Two Dancers* by Henri Matisse, 1937-1938. © 1993
   Succession H. Matisse, Paris/ARS, NY. Private Collection.
Photo Researcher: Rosemary Hunter
Compositor: Lachina Publishing Services, Inc.
Insert Printer: New England Book Components/R. R. Donnelley &
   Sons Company
Printer and Binder: R. R. Donnelley & Sons Company
Cover Printer: The Lehigh Press, Inc.

THE ART OF BEING HUMAN, Fourth Edition

Copyright © 1993 by Richard Paul Janaro and Thelma C. Altshuler

Library of Congress Cataloging-in-Publication Data

Janaro, Richard Paul.
    The art of being human : the humanities as a technique for living
  / Richard Paul Janaro, Thelma C. Altshuler. — 4th ed.
        p.   cm.
    Includes bibliographical references and index.
    ISBN 0-06-500282-2 (student ed.). — ISBN 0-06-500283-0
 (teacher ed.)
        1. Conduct of life.   2. Humanities.   I. Altshuler, Thelma C.
 II. Title.
 BJ1581.2.J36   1993                                      92-21354
 170′.44—dc20                                             CIP


 92  93  94  94  9  8  7  6  5  4  3  2  1

*This book is dedicated to the memory of our mothers*
*Jane and Rae*

# Brief Contents

# Contents

# Preface

This fourth edition of *The Art of Being Human* is, like its predecessors, an introduction to the humanities. It contains much that appears to have been successful with students and instructors and much that is new, reflecting the enlarged scope of our interests and concerns, inspired for the most part by the many letters we have received and by the students in our classes.

Part One, "Makers of the Humanities," is genre-oriented—dealing, as in previous editions, with the visual arts, music, theater, motion pictures, philosophy, and the art of critical thinking. Part Two, "Themes of the Humanities," continues the interdisciplinary approach that has been popular and has come to be, we believe, the trademark of this project. Many of the themes have been retained, and previous users will find, once again, chapters on mythology, love, happiness, coping with death, and freedom.

Our purpose continues to be *to suggest ways in which the humanities can become the personal possessions of free individuals, who can use them to shape their own lives into works of art.* For this reason we examine genre and theme.

The advantage of the thematic approach is that one does not have to restate the history of Eurocentered humanities or, for that matter, *male*-centered humanities. Though a chronological list of prominent names can still be found at the beginning of the book, this is not a record of exclusively Western civilization. Our treatment of myth is not confined to the Greeks and the Romans, for example. If love is seen in a Western context, we are at least partially concerned with gender definition and sex roles, a subject that is certainly multicultural. Similarly, happiness, death, and freedom are issues that we all face, regardless of what religion or ethnic background we represent.

The application of the humanities to the lives of individual students is what this book is about. So, once again, critical thinking in everyday life is given a chapter of its own that shows the importance of withholding hasty judgments, recognizing contexts, rejecting aimless digressions, and detecting hidden assumptions behind what people say and write. This chapter concludes Part One, "Makers of the Humanities," a placement that further underscores our intention to make the student's own future life the central concept of this book: for the critical-thinking human being is a participant in, not simply an observer of, the humanities.

In doing a book that strives to keep the humanities vital and fresh, we face the continual problem of keeping pace with all that is happening in the arts and in critical thought. If these were less tumultuous times, we might have been able to take more leisurely strides in our revisions, but such is far from the case! Readers and reviewers, as well as students, have cared enough to make many suggestions for changes in the text itself; and if years of involvement in the teaching of the humanities have taught us anything, it is that we must remain open to new ideas, new approaches, new ways of seeing. They have taught us to approach everything, including our book, without a rigid mind-set, but with a willingness to entertain even opposing viewpoints, and a need to learn that is as strong as the need to teach. This book would not be this book if each edition did not contain an abundance of new material.

## What's New?

Much of our learning has originated in the questions of students who are concerned about the exclusion of certain groups from traditional humanities studies and also about the future of the planet because of the damage that has been done to the environment. The present edition of *The Art of Being Human* contains two entirely new chapters, which have been inspired by student interest in those topics.

One new chapter, "**Society Versus the Humanities,**" looks at artists who have had a hard time getting themselves recognized for a number of reasons: racism, sexism, the political climate, and censorship from government or the moral majority. The conflict between the expressive needs of the artist and the needs of the culture at large often becomes itself the subject of a given work. The conflict may also manifest itself in other themes—as, for example, in Arthur Miller's *The Crucible*, in which the focus is on human rights in a repressive society. The chapter explores whether society tries to still or at least control the voice of the artist. It also suggests other, often-raised questions: "Why are so few women and minorities represented in this course?" "How has the group outside the establishment been depicted in the arts?" and "How *have* radical beliefs been suppressed?" And this new chapter examines social repression, particularly as it continues to be practiced through the stereotyping of ethnicity and gender. The new chapter opens the door for classroom discussions of these important and timely issues, which tie into a dominant motif in this text: the confluence of cultures in American society and the importance of representing more than a Eurocentered picture of the humanities.

The second new chapter, "**Nature in the Humanities,**" constitutes, to the best of our knowledge, the first textbook treatment of environmentalism as a major concern of the arts. Our students are confronting the bleak possibility of a future without any of the animal species we now know, a future spent indoors to escape intolerable ultraviolet rays. They are keenly interested in the environmental crisis, with signs of true dismay that previous generations have betrayed them. We hope they will be excited to discover that, as early as in Shakespeare, the humanities have given high priority to the preservation of the natural world.

Readers will also note that the entire book has a different appearance. The format has changed, and we believe very much for the better. There is a larger trim size and abundantly more art than was possible in the previous edition. Before, much of the artwork was concentrated in Chapter 2, "The Visual Artist." In this edition each discipline and each theme in the humanities is illustrated by artworks from every age. The additional art will, we trust, strengthen the interdisciplinary "feel" of the text. As in the first and second editions, but missing from the third, there is an insert containing reproductions in color of the paintings we insist *cannot* be studied in black and white. We hope the reader will find that we have been judicious in our selection of works that belong here.

## *Publisher's Note:* Supplementary Materials

| Resources | Available from |
| --- | --- |
| • Instructor's Edition with bound-in Instructor's Manual written by the authors | HarperCollins |
| • Audiocassette of world music, discussed in the Instructor's Manual | HarperCollins |
| • Art slide package specifically designed to complement this text | SANDAK ( 1-800-343-2806 ) |
| • *The Art of Being Human* telecourse package, including the text and 30 half-hour programs | Miami-Dade Community College Auxiliary Services Contact Cindy Elliott, 305-237-2158 |
| • Study Guide written by the authors to aid students taking the telecourse and using the text | HarperCollins |

## Acknowledgments

In gratitude do we acknowledge the correspondence from students, instructors, and general readers as well as the most helpful reviews written by those who have seen the manuscript in various stages of preparation:

Phyllis Asnien, Lakeland Community College
Eric Engdahl, California State University at Hayward
Milton E. Ford, Grand Valley State University
E. B. Hannum, University of South Alabama
Richard W. Wilhelmi, University of Mary
Mary Ellen Young, Lakewood Community College

We offer particular thanks to an extraordinary support team from Harper-Collins: Lisa Moore, our insightful senior editor, who oversaw the project with stern but loving care; Marisa L. L'Heureux, our painstaking and oh-so-patient developmental editor; and Rosemary Hunter, who worked above and beyond the call of duty to gather together the richly abundant artwork, relieving us of a nearly insurmountable responsibility. Gratitude to Jane Weiner of the New World School of the Arts staff for her generous gift of time and her insights into antisocial computers. Many thanks also go to Robert Olander and Nancy Tenney of Lachina Publishing Services, who were charged with the final preparation of the manuscript. Both of them displayed keen sensitivity to the spirit of the text and a true understanding of its mission. We hope the final result justifies the time and patience that the team has given to this endeavor.

Richard Paul Janaro
Thelma C. Altshuler

# *Chronological List of Names*

The names of those who appear in this book recur in connection with their contributions to human thought and accomplishment. We furnish the following chronological list as a helpful reminder of the order in which they were born.

| | |
|---|---|
| Homer | 9th century B.C. |
| Thales | 640-546 B.C. |
| Anaximander | 611-547 B.C. |
| Gautama | 563-483 B.C. |
| Sophocles | 496-406 B.C. |
| Euripides | 480-460 B.C. |
| Socrates | 469-399 B.C. |
| Aristophanes | 448-380 B.C. |
| Aristippus | 435-356 B.C. |
| Plato | 427-347 B.C. |
| Aristotle | 384-322 B.C. |
| Epicurus | 342-270 B.C. |
| Augustine, St. | 354-430 |
| Epictetus | 1st-2d centuries, A.D. |
| Anselm, St. | 1033-1109 |
| Aquinas, St. Thomas | 1225-1274 |
| Dante Alighieri | 1265-1321 |
| Giotto di Bondone | 1266-1337 |
| Van Dyck, Jan | 1370-1440 |
| Joan of Arc | 1412-1431 |
| Leonardo da Vinci | 1452-1519 |
| Machiavelli, Niccolò | 1469-1527 |
| Copernicus, Nicholas | 1473-1543 |

| | |
|---|---|
| Michelangelo Buonarroti | 1475 - 1564 |
| Calvin, John | 1509 - 1564 |
| Cervantes Saavedra, Miguel de | 1547 - 1616 |
| Galileo Galilei | 1564 - 1642 |
| Shakespeare, William | 1564 - 1616 |
| Descartes, René | 1596 - 1650 |
| Milton, John | 1608 - 1674 |
| Racine, Jean | 1639 - 1699 |
| Newton, Sir Isaac | 1642 - 1727 |
| Molière ( Jean-Baptiste Poquelin ) | 1622 - 1673 |
| Swift, Jonathan | 1667 - 1745 |
| Congreve, William | 1670 - 1729 |
| Pope, Alexander | 1688 - 1744 |
| Voltaire ( François Marie Arouet ) | 1694 - 1778 |
| Hume, David | 1711 - 1776 |
| Rousseau, Jean Jacques | 1712 - 1778 |
| Smith, Adam | 1723 - 1790 |
| Kant, Immanuel | 1724 - 1804 |
| Goya, Francisco | 1746 - 1828 |
| Bentham, Jeremy | 1748 - 1832 |
| Sheridan, Richard B. | 1751 - 1816 |
| Blake, William | 1757 - 1827 |
| Beethoven, Ludwig van | 1770 - 1827 |
| Hegel, Georg Wilhelm Friedrich | 1770 - 1831 |
| Paine, Thomas | 1771 - 1809 |
| Byron, George Gordon, Lord | 1788 - 1824 |
| Schopenhauer, Arthur | 1788 - 1860 |
| Shelley, Percy B. | 1792 - 1822 |
| Keats, John | 1795 - 1821 |
| Shelley, Mary Wollstonecraft Godwin | 1797 - 1851 |
| Emerson, Ralph Waldo | 1803 - 1882 |
| Hawthorne, Nathaniel | 1804 - 1864 |
| Mill, John Stuart | 1806 - 1873 |
| Darwin, Charles | 1809 - 1882 |
| Dickens, Charles | 1812 - 1870 |
| Kierkegaard, Søren | 1813 - 1855 |
| Thoreau, Henry David | 1817 - 1862 |
| Brontë, Emily | 1818 - 1848 |
| Marx, Karl | 1818 - 1883 |
| Melville, Herman | 1819 - 1891 |

| | |
|---|---|
| Queen Victoria | 1819-1901 |
| Ibsen, Henrik | 1828-1906 |
| Dickinson, Emily | 1830-1886 |
| Manet, Edouard | 1832-1883 |
| Twain, Mark (Samuel Langhorne Clemens) | 1835-1910 |
| Whistler, James McNeill | 1834-1903 |
| Peirce, Charles | 1839-1914 |
| James, William | 1842-1910 |
| Nietzsche, Friedrich | 1844-1900 |
| Edison, Thomas Alva | 1847-1931 |
| Gogh, Vincent van | 1853-1890 |
| Shaw, George Bernard | 1856-1950 |
| Veblen, Thorstein | 1857-1929 |
| Dewey, John | 1859-1952 |
| Housman, A. E. | 1859-1936 |
| Barrie, James | 1860-1937 |
| Robinson, Edwin Arlington | 1869-1935 |
| Gandhi, Mohandas K. | 1869-1948 |
| Lenin, V. I. | 1870-1924 |
| Russell, Bertrand | 1872-1970 |
| Mondrian, Piet | 1872-1944 |
| Jung, Carl | 1875-1961 |
| Frost, Robert | 1875-1963 |
| Griffith, D. W. | 1875-1948 |
| Ravel, Maurice | 1875-1937 |
| Einstein, Albert | 1879-1955 |
| Spengler, Oswald | 1880-1936 |
| Teilhard de Chardin | 1881-1955 |
| Picasso, Pablo | 1881-1973 |
| Joyce, James | 1882-1941 |
| Modigliani, Amedeo | 1884-1920 |
| Sennett, Mack | 1884-1960 |
| Lawrence, D. H. | 1885-1930 |
| O'Keeffe, Georgia | 1887-1986 |
| Anderson, Maxwell | 1888-1959 |
| O'Neill, Eugene | 1888-1953 |
| Hitchcock, Alfred | 1889-1980 |
| Prokofiev, Serge | 1891-1953 |
| Huxley, Aldous | 1894-1963 |
| Wilder, Thornton | 1897-1975 |

# THE ART
# OF BEING HUMAN

*Mary Cassatt,* Peasant Mother and Child *(c. 1895) (Gift of Alfred E. Hamill. The Art Institute of Chicago, All Rights Reserved)*

# Introduction: To Be Human

The humanities have been vital to the curriculum of higher learning ever since there have been colleges and universities. In times past the students who took a humanities course as a "distribution requirement" seldom asked for a definition of the subject. Didn't everybody know that the course would deal with the important painters, composers, poets, philosophers, novelists, and playwrights? They expected the instructor to provide a list of who these people were, and they knew that "the List" had been drawn up years ago and agreed to by well-educated minds throughout the world.

Many of the names on the List remain. They are still worth our time, still have much to give. Could one have a humanities course without Michelangelo, Shakespeare, Beethoven, or Picasso? But nothing on earth is nonnegotiable, including the List. It must, of course, be continually reevaluated to include contributions too long ignored and new names that shouldn't have to wait a hundred years for the slow process of universal consent to their inclusion.

To begin with—and let us start on a totally honest note—the List was the creation of a male-dominated, Eurocentric cultural tradition, which believed that the humanities were to be defined as the finest expressions of the human soul and that this soul was a legacy from Western European society: Greece, Rome, Spain, France, England, Germany, and, finally (and often reluctantly), the United States. It was also a male legacy. Earlier in this century books about the humanities defined it as the study of *man*: man's hopes, fears, dreams, and ideals; man's most noble thoughts. With scarcely a thought that things might be otherwise, those who wrote about and taught the humanities continually referred to "man's upward strivings" or "when man first walked upright" or "man's finest hour."

They would have said they were of course including women in what was meant to be a generic reference to humanity. Yet the List didn't include many women, nor would students have been likely to find many contributors of different ethnic backgrounds.

The humanities can still be defined as *the cumulative expressions of humanity's finest moments: the ideas, the songs, the poems and plays, the statues, the soaring buildings, the ballerina's longest leap*. But it should be clear that the great moments when human beings find meaning in life and are able to freeze it in a form so that it is always there for us . . . these wonderful moments can happen anytime, anywhere, to any person (see Plate 1, following page 72).

A casual glance through the chapters that follow might give the impression that the traditional List lives on and that you are about to embark upon yet one more journey into the past glories of Western civilization.

The "greats" are all here, it is true. To ignore them would be to imply that they are not worth studying. Surely *the past has its rights*. Whatever the circumstances that made Western philosophy and art what it is, the thinkers and the ar-

*Surely the past has its rights. (Ewing Galloway, N.Y.)*

*Thomas Gainsborough,* Robert Andrews and His Wife: *Held fast by the times and customs within which they were reared. (In the collection of G. W. Andrews, photo courtesy of the National Gallery, London)*

tists should not be blamed for the glaring absence of female and multiethnic contributions as the "tradition" developed. As those who might have distinguished themselves were trapped by barriers beyond their power to remove, so too were the "greats" held fast by the times and customs within which they were reared.

Do not believe for one moment, however, that in all cases the individual works of the humanities merely reflect the period that gave rise to them. In our quest for a fresh way of looking at the humanities, we found some interesting surprises: an unexpected plea in Shakespeare for treating the earth with love and kindness; extraordinary and still-vital significance in Mary Shelley's *Frankenstein*, once known as the distant ancestor of the great horror films; surrealistic elements in an eighteenth-century painter's works that might have made Salvador Dali wince.

We do not make mention of side roads along the well-traveled thoroughfare of the Western tradition just to be "different." Nor for that reason do we include myths from non-Western cultures. We do not include the contributions of Mary Cassatt and Georgia O'Keeffe only because they are women. We include the work of everyone who we think can shed light on the intellectual and emotional nature of that most complex of species: *the human being*. Not to seek as wide a spectrum as possible would be to give the false impression that the light of humanness is the sole possession of a very few gifted souls.

This last statement brings us to the underlying reason for the book that lies before you. One more text that traces the historical development of the humanities—whether purely Western or more global—is not needed. There are many excellent scholars of the humanities who have given us major studies of both kinds.

Our intention has been to demonstrate that the humanities are indeed, as our subtitle puts it, a "technique for living." In the end, what matters, as far as we, the authors, are concerned, is not the possession of some facts about important works of art, philosophy, and drama; important concepts in religion; or important

*Edgar Degas,* Prima Ballerina: *What humanity does besides taking care of basic needs. (The Louvre. Photo: Giraudon/Art Resource)*

*"All that beauty was enough even for me. I would often walk around the lake by myself, and I would not be thinking about my past unhappiness. . . . I was only watching the birds who floated above the lake, then landed ever so lightly on the water that no ripples appeared."*

*Amy Tan*
The Kitchen God's Wife

theories of what history means. What matters is what these things mean to each of us, personally and internally. Not to recognize that one's life can be changed dramatically and infinitely for the better by encounters with the humanities is to miss the point of why they exist to begin with, for the makers of the humanities were people like us, with a particular hunger, a particular need. As human beings ourselves, we can identify with the drive to give expression to pain and joy and with the wonder of realizing something.

Creativity and thought are the exclusive birthright of no one; they are part of the gift of being born human. Noting what some people have done with their gift is a great incentive to explore the landscapes of our innermost selves and to recognize the power we may have to find the means of extending ourselves into space like a visual artist, of singing our own songs, of acting out our own dramas, of speaking out our own philosophy loud and clear and finding ways to make others listen.

This text is about the art of being human—not an exploration of the biological details of being human and not a scientific analysis of human behavior. We do not seek to understand, only to love and to appreciate what humanity does *besides* taking care of basic needs. Why do you sing as you walk along? Why do you draw flowers on your note pad while the professor is lecturing? Why do you sometimes feel you want to leap like a dancer? Why do you sometimes sit and look at the sea, which seems so timeless, and ask yourself whether time is real after all? In these things we practice the art of being human.

---

*Humanities*

---

The cumulative artistic and intellectual achievements of humanity. The artistic and intellectual experiences of those who appreciate but do not themselves create. A study of those achievements and the critical process by which they can best be understood. The humanities are, in other words, three things:

*A body of work;*

*A way of life filled with joyous moments of thought and esthetic pleasure;*

*An academic discipline devoted to studying the important expressions of the human spirit through which our existence is made richer and more meaningful.*

---

Like any art, the art of being human can always be better, can it not? We need only find more and more inspiration in the works of those who have been successful in making art of their lives. This inspiration is, really, what this book is about and the reason why the List is never finished, never fully adequate, always to be reexamined.

After the wheel has been invented, after we have learned to build shelters and bridges and mountain tunnels, and after we know how to pay the rent, we eventually have to leave our work behind and think about what else we are here for. Some, alas, never do that, and maybe they are a little unhappy about their lives without quite knowing why.

*David Hockney,* A Bigger Splash: *We define the good life in terms of concrete assets. (The Tate Gallery/Art Resource)*

## The Humanities and Economics

There is a strong reason why many find they have little or no time for the humanities. Apart from the obvious cause—the List itself, which may be resented because it excludes so much—there is the brutal reality of economics. The need to earn a living, the need to better oneself, the need to find a secure "place in the sun" often assume the top priority.

Even in our early years *marketability* is the magic word. We say of men and women, "What are they worth?" Nearly everyone understands this question to be a fiscal one. So is, "What have they done with their lives?" From the moment we are born, we accumulate equity (or fail to); woe to the wretch who attains the age of 65 and has "nothing"—meaning no bank accounts, no property, no investments, no collections of durable goods, and no means to purchase sleek cars and fashionable clothes—to show for having lived. When the question of a person's worth arises, one rarely hears comments like "He is a caring person and has so much to offer" or "She not only paints but keeps an extraordinary journal in which she tries to capture every subtle moment of experience." A person's worth, more often than not, is related to his or her total marketability, his or her ability to acquire concrete assets.

One reason we define the good life in terms of concrete assets is that there are not enough of them. Economists offer us the following as the law of life: *Our wants are insatiable, but our resources are limited*. If the good things of life were not scarce, they would not cost money; if the good things became abundant, this situation alone would be enough to alter human nature. If the need for money were suddenly to disappear, many, many people would wonder what to do with themselves. They might also find, to their confusion, that with such abundance, the good things weren't as good as they once seemed.

The humanities are a storehouse of good things, and they are not affected by money. With respect to the humanities, we could say that *resources are unlimited, but average wants are too quickly satisfied*. Ironic, isn't it? Just the reverse of what happens in economics. With the humanities one is never poor except by choice.

Yes, it can be argued that recordings are relatively expensive, as are books; theater and concert tickets can go for astronomical prices. But radio is not expensive. Museums are often free. Art galleries do not charge admission for browsing. Library cards are available on demand. Community theaters and local orchestras charge far less than their professional counterparts and can be just as inspired. The creative expressions of humanity are there if they are really needed.

Cost is not the factor that inhibits many from taking advantage of these creative works, some of the few unlimited resources left on earth. Take the case of Woodrow Tatlock, an upstanding man of his community, who served Conley and Sons, Hardware, Inc., faithfully for 35 years, then retired and spent his golden years promising himself that he would at last visit the National Gallery, go to the Metropolitan Opera, and read all those books his late wife used to tell him about. He never found the time, of course.

On his deathbed he is reported to have murmured that he was sorry for all the missed opportunities. Some assumed he was talking about the humanities. Or was it about his career at Conley and Sons?

The few people who gathered at his funeral—his sons, their wives and children, a couple of neighbors—all said that Mr. Tatlock had been a good man,

*With respect to the humanities, we could say that resources are unlimited, but average wants are too quickly satisfied.*

which is sometimes another way of saying that one has passed on without significant net worth. What else was there to say? That Mr. Tatlock had not made the most of every minute while he was alive? That he might have opened himself to the wonders of being human—but chose not to?

## Gifts of the Humanities

Mr. Tatlock's life would have been better had he devoted some time to the humanities. He would have spent time in the company of great minds who had asked questions about how the universe began, whether there is a God, and who decides on the validity of moral values. He would have been used to the beautiful products of creative minds, which have given and are still giving us the music, the dance, the paintings, and the literature that complete our humanness. He would have understood that even though science and technology are slowly opening all of nature's locked doors and are helping us to live longer, the humanities are still where we go to help us decide how to make the most of our lives. Science has invented tranquilizers; the humanities bring us true peace.

*Science has invented tranquilizers; the humanities bring us true peace.*

The humanities, at least temporarily, quiet the anxieties we feel when we find ourselves drifting, wondering what to do next, asking ourselves why we are here and what we are doing with our lives. Unlike characters in novels and plays, most of us "real" people exist discontinuously, fragmentarily. If we weren't so busy trying to keep up with daily work or school schedules, we might be anxious even more of the time, but there are plenty of those moments when we feel uncentered, unconnected. Yes, we must get to a certain destination, but once there, what do we do? And after we leave, where do we go?

On a day-to-day basis, with obligations to fulfill and tasks to be done, we may have the illusion of being involved in richly significant stuff, but the sad truth is that we really do not *know*. We haven't the time to freeze-frame the onward motion of our lives and do periodic evaluations. Let me see, am I heading in a particular direction? Is this where I want to be?

In Willy Russell's 1981 play *Educating Rita*, the heroine, a 26-year-old hairdresser taking a course in Britain's Open University, is fascinated to discover that the protagonist of Ibsen's play *Peer Gynt* is searching for the meaning of life. Such a thing has never occurred to her, "because you see, where we live, there is no meaning to life." Pushed to the wall, many of us might say as much (or as little).

Not that life is required to have a meaning. It's just that the makers of the humanities keep finding meaning, and their insights often help us make sudden sense of experience. As we mature, we carry with us so many of these insights, encased in memorable language; we also derive comfort from the knowledge that others have the same confusions, feel the same pain and longing that we do. A gift of the humanities is the cumulative human mind that all can share who wish to. In one of Anton Chekhov's plays a character suddenly says, "Any idiot can face a crisis. It's this day-to-day living that wears you out." Through the humanities, we discover that somebody else agrees with something we just found out we always knew.

*Through the humanities, we discover that somebody else agrees with something we just found out we always knew.*

The poet Robert Frost describes the time his narrator stopped by a neighbor's woods on a snowy evening and felt the sudden rightness of all things, being face to face with pure beauty—a moment when no explanation is needed for being alive. But the moment cannot last. One cannot escape from time and obligations. The narrator must move on, as the last three lines of the poem suggest:

*For I have promises to keep,*
*And miles to go before I sleep,*
*And miles to go before I sleep.*[1]

For millions of readers this little poem has said it all. The rare times come unexpectedly. Life is heightened. We need nothing more. Then we go home, and finally we die, and perhaps we never visit that place again. Again a poet has told us something we know from the moment we're old enough to think about death, but we never knew it *in quite this way*. Unless we are talking about philosophy or speculative science, the meanings we derive from the humanities have been ours all along—just put in a way we hadn't thought of.

The humanities are therefore like little lights twinkling way off in a dark bay. We look, and we know where we are.

We don't need words. When a piece of music hits just the right chord, when a singer glides effortlessly into the right note, when a dancer pirouettes into the waiting arms of her partner and he lifts her as if she were light as a bird, when a figure skater leaps into a triple axel and lands perfectly, losing not a moment of continuity—at such times the world needs no further justification; we are stopping by a neighbor's woods on a snowy evening.

*Form and meaning are two gifts from the humanities.*

The humanities thus have for us the gift of form. Form is the *significant arrangement of the parts*. We can experience moments of form in our day-to-day lives when suddenly, for no apparent reason, things fall into place. Or, lacking such moments naturally, we can go find them in music, art, sculpture, literature, or theater; in a park with paths and arrangements of flowering shrubs; or in the backyard of somebody who took a little time to place rocks in just the right relationship to each other and put a lounge chair in the cool shade of just the right tree.

Having the time for moments of meaning and moments of beauty (and often they are the same!) has many positive effects, though of all the wonders of life, the humanities have the least obligation to provide a payoff. Still, we can say that it is there. People who have acquired the habit of stopping by woods are less likely to act on sudden, thoughtless impulses. True, they will probably not ever see *the same* woods again, but they know how to freeze-frame their lives and draw a deep breath until things fall into place for them once more.

*Learning how to be a critical thinker is another gift.*

This ability to slow down, to keep life from rushing over one like an avalanche, is the hallmark of the *critical thinker*, the person who can stand back and look life in the eye whenever it starts to get confusing, who can keep cool and delay reacting until all the parts of a situation fall into place. In the long run, this capacity may be the greatest gift of all. The critical thinkers are the ones who have taken all their other gifts and made art of their lives. They know how to talk, how to listen, how to mull over what they have heard, and they know what to do. They are the levelheaded people we need as leaders and intelligent followers; they are task-makers and task-achievers.

At the conclusion of Anne Rice's novel *The Witching Hour* (1990), the main character sums up his belief in human power in this way:

". . . I do believe in the final analysis that a peace of mind can be obtained in the face of the worst horrors and the worst losses. It can be obtained by faith in change and in will and in accident; and by faith in ourselves, that we will do the right thing, more often than not, in the face of adversity.

*Dorothea Lange,* Migrant Mother, California, 1936: *"Faith in ourselves . . . in the face of adversity." (The Library of Congress)*

"For ours is the power and the glory, because we are capable of visions and ideas which are ultimately stronger and more enduring than we are."[2]

The humanities have redirected the evolutionary process, and have left their own tracks along with the footprints of *Homo sapiens*. There is no going back. Humanity may be many things. It is the only species that has killed as a way of solving a problem. It is the only species that has ever understood the environment as well as destroyed it. It is the only species that has tried so desperately to give meaning to life as well as committed suicide in startling numbers. But it is also the species that has made the universe over in its own image and created beauty, truth, justice, and goodness. It has made quite a habitat for itself, despite the terrible things it is capable of doing to its surroundings. Heaven *has* been brought to earth, and the doors are always open for those who want to live there. The humanities have made that much possible.

*Humanity is also the species that has made the universe over in its own image and created beauty, truth, justice, and goodness.*

## Notes

1.  From "Stopping by Woods on a Snowy Evening" from *The Poetry of Robert Frost*, edited by Edward Connery Lathem. Copyright 1923, ©1969 by Holt, Rinehart and Winston. Copyright 1951 by Robert Frost. Reprinted by permission of Henry Holt and Company, Inc.

2.  Anne Rice, *The Witching Hour* (New York: Alfred A. Knopf, 1990), 964.

# *Makers of the Humanities*

The humanities are the accumulated works of great minds and creative artists as well as the private expressions and creative needs of each one of us. To study the humanities is to study a well-known tradition, to explore less celebrated but no less significant contributions, and to relate the study to ourselves—to our thinking, to our emotions, and to our growing awareness of what it means to be human, to be alive in what is sometimes a very puzzling world.

The first half of this book talks about individual disciplines within the humanities: visual art, music, philosophy, and so on. In each case we, the authors, make an effort to assist you in making a personal inventory of needs and preferences.

The hope is that you will gain in self-knowledge. Without this, the art of being human cannot be practiced.

The first step is to recognize that each of us shares a fundamental something with the stars of the humanities tradition—the people on the List that we mentioned in the Introduction. That something is a dual personality. Each of us has to some degree a logical, orderly, law-abiding self—and a spontaneous, often rebellious, yet imaginative and exciting self. We need to understand this duality before we can properly begin our study.

*Jean-Honore Fragonard*, Satyr Pressing Grapes Beside a Tiger *(1774) (Gift of Mr. and Mrs. Robert J. Hamman in honor of Suzanne Folds McCullagh. The Art Institute of Chicago, All Rights Reserved)*

# 1

# Apollo
and Dionysus

## Overview

The heroine of a recent comic novel[1] has been telling her male companion that she must leave. She is attending a conference on world problems, and the main speaker is scheduled to go on. Still, she is attracted to the young man, who tells her:

> "Good. Do that. But if you're interested in experiencing the world as a better place, then stay here with me."

> "Oh yeah? That'd be fine—maybe for you and me, but how about the rest of humanity?"

> "A better world has gotta start somewhere. Why not with you and me?"

*Apollo*
*reason*
*order*
*clarity*
*moderation*
*analysis*
*control*


*Dionysus*
*passion*
*spontaneity*
*instinct*
*frenzy*
*faith*
*excess*

Their conversation illustrates two approaches to life that philosophers and psychologists have described in a way first spelled out by a nineteenth-century German philosopher, Friedrich Nietzsche (1844 - 1900). In *The Birth of Tragedy*, Nietzsche tells his readers that an emotional response to theater, even to a classical tragedy, is far better than a purely intellectual response. To contrast the two possible reactions to drama—the emotional and the rational—the philosopher reacquainted his readers with the names of two ancient Greek gods: Apollo, the god of truth and light, logic and order; and Dionysus, the god of fertility, spontaneity, sexuality, and emotional exultation. Nietzsche complains that classical tragedy has for too long been taught in an *Apollonian* fashion, with emphasis on structure and meaning. What *he* saw in tragedy was a thrilling experience in theater that appealed to the senses and the feelings; he saw a *Dionysian* event.

Since Nietzsche, historians of the humanities have used these terms to represent the polarities of reason and emotion that can be found throughout the arts and philosophy as well as in the real world of human experience.

In the quotation at the start of this chapter, the young woman's goals appear to be lofty, universal, and purposeful. She is concerned about humanity in the abstract, not about her immediate desires and feelings. The young man's approach is personal, centered on his need for gratification and living in the moment. The woman is engaged in long-range planning. At this point she is Apollonian; he, Dionysian.

The Apollonian spirit is scientific and critical; by emphasizing reason, it offers assurance that the universe is intelligible. More than that, it demands that intuition be held in check by the clear light of rationality. An Apollonian person delights in connections that can make sense out of apparently unrelated phenomena.

*Michelangelo,* David: *An Apollonian David. (Alinari/ Art Resource NY)*

The Dionysian spirit is found in abundance in the humanities. It is the moving force behind most of the world's great music, dance, poetry, theater, and visual art. The Dionysian person is not afraid of trusting hunches and intuition, of expressing deep-rooted emotion. The Dionysian is responsive to the folk wisdom of people who have never read a book but who instinctively know how to survive in this world. Dionysians feel that they know how to get the most out of life. Throughout this book we shall be running into examples of this outlook and its frequent conflicts with Apollonianism.

This chapter deals with these polarities as we find them in individuals, in government and law, in the arts, and in education. The book as a whole, like most books, is Apollonian in that it has a certain structure and is divided into chapters, each of which deals with a certain subject. But it has its Dionysian strains. We want you, the reader, to experience the excitement of the arts as well as to think critically about them and about yourself. We want you to be open-minded, willing to reverse yourself, willing to trust the opinions of others even if they do not at first seem rationally founded, willing to take on the adventure of living with the fullness of both mind and heart, of both intellect and the senses.

Our hope is that conscious recognition of these extremes will lead you to a balance between the two: long believed to represent the ideal mode of living.

*The truth was felt by instinct here,—*
*Process which saves a world of truth and time.*

*Robert Browning*

## Personal Temperament

Scholars, almost invariably Apollonian, make classifications. This period in history, they say, was the "Age of Reason," that of "Romance," one age paving the way for a dominant idea in the next. Yet, within each "age" characterized in Apollonian course outlines, people continued to live their own lives within families, with little regard for intellectual pronouncements. As children develop, their parents observe that one child seems to be naturally neat, another untidy; one aggressive, the other timid; and so forth. These temperamental differences are apparent to anyone who knows the children, without regard to historical period. The toys change— wood, plastic, or electronic—but the responses of the children who play with them and the variety of individual temperaments do not always follow the historical designation of a period.

Labels give a false picture of uniformity. The majority of Athenian contemporaries of Socrates did not engage in dialogues exploring ultimate principles, and in the time when poets proclaimed their willingness to die for love, prosaic tasks, such as floor sweeping and bill paying, continued to be performed. Historical periods, in the eyes of historians, are stable units of time. Real life is not so easily categorized.

But historical labels address the human need for order, for the assurance that "history" is very real, that the "onward" course of humanity is interpretable. We can use the labels so long as we keep reminding ourselves that they can be misleading and are often legitimately subject to debate. Just when did the Renaissance start? At the stroke of midnight in the year 1400? Were there not thousands of human beings who never even *knew* that they were living through a renaissance?

Nonetheless, as the gulf in time widens between us and the death of Nietzsche, we look back with growing admiration at those remarkable labels that the philosopher has given us, for if people are not always "modern" in the historian's sense, they *do* appear to oscillate between the extremes of order and disorder. They can even be said to gravitate closer to one or the other pole, making very broad personality distinctions meaningful.

*Donatello, David: A Dionysian David. (Alinari/Art Resource)*

## Ways of Observing

Walking in a forest, the Apollonian would derive pleasure from recognizing the kinds of plants growing there, not just naming them but comparing the shapes and textures of their parts. It would be a delight to observe that a tiny fragment of a fern had the structure of a giant plant seemingly unrelated to it. Such recognition reassures the Apollonian of the order in a planned universe. Botanical information would be available to the scientist, who is also Apollonian. But even the casual Apollonian walker, unaware of species or genus, can and does notice, group, and compare. The Apollonian walk is a way of seeing and thinking with care and reflection.

Walking in the same forest, the Dionysian would feel the cool air, touch leaves, smell fragrances, sit, run, or climb, without the need to analyze sensations and feelings. The experience would be worthwhile for its own sake. With no need to discover order, real or assumed, the Dionysian accepts what comes. There is no need to debate with the Apollonian (who tends to win debates, as well as succeed in other language-related activities). The Dionysian becomes part of nature in a way envied by Apollonians (who may rush back to their desks and compose poems about fortunate savages they claim to admire).

The simple act of walking in a forest may change according to different sensibilities. The two described do not, of course, exhaust the possibilities. We have seen that the Apollonian remains aware, while the Dionysian simply experiences without thinking about it. The Dionysian moving through the forest derives as much delight from this venture as the more controlled Apollonian gains from keeping an alert mind throughout the walk.

Using the distinctions Nietzsche has provided, we can identify a consciousness that falls exactly in the middle, a person who moves so routinely that there is no memory of having been in a forest at all. This is also the consciousness—shared at *some* point by all of us—that becomes accustomed to taking a certain path in a daily trip from one point to another. *All* trips seem to be the same, with no sense of novelty and hence no need to notice or to mentally record the scene, no desire to open one's senses—to hear unfamiliar sounds, touch unusual surfaces, and look at what the filter of overlapping leaves does to sunlight. The routine walk leaves the individual unaware of either sensibility, unable to enjoy life from either the Apollonian or the Dionysian perspective.

## Leisure

The Sabbath has been a major contribution to human development. Observing the commandment "Remember the Sabbath day, to keep it holy," the early Hebrews decreed that no work should be done on a day set aside for rest and study. So important was the Sabbath that nothing, not even a recent death in the family, was allowed to interfere with the "keeping" of the special day. Whether tied to religion or not, the practice serves to change the rhythm of the week and prevents work from completely dominating us.

In recent years, emphasis has been on the *Dionysian* weekend, a time for eating, drinking, loud music, "getting away from it all." With a slight hint of the Puritan work ethic and its long-standing prescription that fun has to be earned, advertisements encourage pleasure and weekend abandon, accompanied by a deliberate rejection of thought and control. Popular jingles remind us that we deserve pleasure without thought.

Advertisements may encourage Dionysian activities, but not all responses are purely Dionysian responses. The Apollonian at play remains in control, knowing when to quit, willing to spend the weekend mowing the lawn and doing household repairs before retiring to an evening of television watching or reading. The Apollonian is always aware of the consequences and is thus unwilling to risk a hangover and the regret that might follow spontaneous outbursts. The "pure" Dionysian at play is, of course, a descendant of the original followers of Dionysus—or Bacchus—in his guise as the god of wine, devotion to whom required drunken revelry and riotous orgy. Drink loosens the tongue, making us say and enjoy hearing remarks that the "daytime self" would find foolish. Dionysian drinking is a group activity, democratic in its rejection of rank, title, or ceremony, as has been demonstrated by many an office Christmas party. When junior clerk faces chief executive officer the following Apollonian week, both, now sober, may be frantically trying to recall how much the refreshments contributed to regrettable intimacy: "Did I really say that?" "Will somebody hold me to that promise?"

*The Apollonian at play remains in control, knowing when to quit, willing to spend the weekend mowing the lawn and doing household repairs.*

## Food

The Dionysian approach to food has nothing to do with diet, health, or moderation. Those who cook the food may require Apollonian skills painstakingly acquired. But those who eat it can indulge in gastronomical pleasures without concern, permitting no prohibitions of any kind. "Go on, you only live once," says the Dionysian host urging a friend to eat forbidden fat or sugar. In eating to excess and indulging in pent-up food fantasies, the weekend Dionysian is likely to reject all rules of nutrition. A deliberate lawbreaker, the Dionysian gives in to madness that may bring eventual regret but, for now, seems worthwhile. This breaking of diet represents more than the weakness of someone who would like to obey but lacks the will to do so. It is also a challenging of Apollonian medical authorities, a desire for the suspension of rules. When we read about a celebration of the 100th birthday of someone who brags about having outlived the doctor who put him on a restricted diet, we have met a worshipper of the god of good luck, another Dionysian deity. There is a Dionysian delight in the deliberate disregarding of physicians, nutritionists, and the other advisors who insist we do only what is good for us.

### Sex

*Many more women now have the freedom that comes with self-support . . . yet many still assume a man must be older, taller, earn more, weigh more, be the "right" race, class, and religion, better educated, and so on. In other words, we are still looking for forms of security, strength, and social approval that we no longer need . . .*

*Gloria Steinem*

In sexual matters the direct confrontation between Apollo and Dionysus is crashingly evident. Moral standards, taboos against premarital and extramarital sex and interracial alliances, and even, in some cases, legal restrictions governing the approved manner of having sex can all be regarded as Apollonian. But we are now living in the aftermath of the sexual revolution of the 1960s. "Living together" as an alternative to marriage is widely accepted, as are same-sex relationships, even when they include wedding ceremonies and the adoption of children. The demand for freedom of sexual preference is certainly Dionysian, but the Apollonian response is to warn against indiscriminate and incautious indulgence without proper safeguards.

The pro-life/pro-choice debate can be Apollonian on both sides. Both offer rational arguments, often divided by the definition of when life can properly be said to begin. In addition, Apollonians are likely to cite the social cost of unwanted children, while Dionysians develop arguments attacking the irrationality of legislating personal lives. Both sides have their calm, reflective proponents, as well as their passionate orators. Both can be Dionysian, appealing to the emotions of listeners and readers.

The campaign for sexual freedom can also become an Apollonian force seeking to impose Dionysian rules to undo the ravages of sexual repressiveness. Suppose a low-keyed, conservative visitor accidentally showed up at a nude beach. Urged to strip, the visitor could well resist and demand the right to hide his or her body. "Take your clothes off, have *fun*!" might be not only the exhortation, but the commandment. Those who refuse excess in whatever form are made to feel unwelcome by an appeal for conformity to nonconformity—a stance that appears to be a clear expression of Apollonianism.

## A Way of Understanding the Humanities

Apollonian and Dionysian outlooks may be seen in diverse elements of human life. They are also apparent in their impact on the arts. The basic difference, according to Nietzsche, is in the extent to which morality is imposed on artistic purpose and in the effect on audiences. Living during the Victorian era, Nietzsche was particularly sensitive to the predominant moral approach, which emphasized the *good* a work of art should accomplish in terms of edifying subject matter, with lessons designed to improve the values and ideals of audience or reader. This section will examine the possibility that the humanities can be, at will, either Apollonian or Dionysian.

## Poetry

Dionysian literature would seem to be a contradiction in terms. After all, even the most chaotic-appearing novel and the most disorganized poem are *about* an experience, and words are required to communicate it. We comprehend the emotions, but an artist is recording them, thus placing the reader at one remove from the event itself. Apollonianism in literature is cited by Nietzsche as an orderly expression of distanced emotion, which, no matter how well done, is no substitute for the actual experience of living.

Still, even within literature, the two forces appear to exist, with order, morality, and submission to authority on one side, disorder and revolt against authority on the other. Two poems help to illustrate: John Milton's "On His Blindness" and A. E. Housman's "The Laws of God, the Laws of Man." Both originate in despair and a Dionysian urge to rebel. Milton says:

> *When I consider how my light is spent*
> *Ere half my days, in this dark world and wide,*
> *And that one talent which is death to hide,*
> *Lodged with me useless, though my soul more bent*
> *To serve therewith my Maker, and present*
> *My true account, lest he returning chide:*
> *"Doth God exact day-labor, light denied?"*
> *I fondly ask; but Patience, to prevent*
> *That murmur, soon replies, "God doth not need*
> *Either man's work or his own gifts; who best*
> *Bear his mild yoke, they serve him best. His state*
> *Is kingly. Thousands at his bidding speed*
> *And post o'er land and ocean without rest:*
> *They also serve who only stand and wait."*

The first seven and a half lines of the poem reveal a Dionysian-like impatience to accomplish, but it is actually the Apollonian need to leave a mark, certain that human achievement will have lasting results. This is a theme found in much literature. Theme itself is an Apollonian element, and the humble obedience to God, urged in the final line, is also Apollonian, though it might seem not to be. In its calm assertion that there is a tangible purpose in waiting, Milton's sense of a creative void is not antireason.

It can even be argued that no poem adhering to the formal requirements of meter and rhyme can be Dionysian. But—and here is the paradox—we must accept the possibility of there being a totally Dionysian *idea* sitting (sometimes uneasily) within an ordered context. The result is poetic tension: the calm of poetic form in subtle conflict with an emotional explosion longing to take place. The experience of that tension is essentially Dionysian, as this poem by A. E. Housman (1859-1936) illustrates. Though the poet does not explode, he is clearly not content with the Apollonian:

*The laws of God, the laws of man,*
*He may keep that will and can;*
*Not I: let God and man decree*
*Laws for themselves and not for me;*
*And if my ways are not as theirs*
*Let them mind their own affairs.*
*Their deeds I judge and much condemn,*
*Yet when did I make laws for them?*
*Please yourselves, say I, and they*
*Need only look the other way.*
*But no, they will not; they must still*
*Wrest their neighbour to their will,*
*And make me dance as they desire*
*With jail and gallows and hell-fire.*
*And how am I to face the odds*
*Of man's bedevilment and God's?*
*I, a stranger and afraid*
*In a world I never made.*
*They will be master, right or wrong;*
*Though both are foolish, both are strong.*
*And since, my soul, we cannot fly*
*To Saturn nor to Mercury,*
*Keep we must, if keep we can,*
*These foreign laws of God and man.*[2]

*Much poetry can be described as Apollonian for holding in check Dionysian emotions.*

What so often happens is that the artist, like Housman, hearing the subterranean whispers of unbridled Dionysian passions, seeks in Apollonian form—here, the regularity of the rhythmic and rhyme patterns—a way of controlling his or her emotions (see Plate 2 following page 72). Otherwise, if he or she is completely carried away by them, by what right does he or she claim to be an artist to begin with? Is there not something fundamentally Apollonian in the very *idea* of a work's aspiring to the status of art and the artist to a place in human memory? Can such a place be reserved for the millions of us who *do* give free rein to our emotions, often regretting the fact the next day and surely very seldom leaving something of note behind?

The question we have raised leads in turn (which is an Apollonian thought progression, of course) to the larger issue of how Dionysian a work can become in form as well as content and still deserve the designation of art. Were Housman to be completely Dionysian in approach, he would have splattered the words all over the page, even as many modern artists splatter their paint, introducing nonsense terms and utilizing an irrational syntax that disorients the reader.

## Music

On the one hand, we could argue that music by its very nature is essentially Dionysian. Its appeal is to the emotions, not the intellect. On the other hand, music, like poetry, has formal characteristics that act as potential restraints on uncontrolled passion. It too has underlying rhythm and frequently a principle of repetition that, like rhyme, keeps the artist from becoming lost in the labyrinth of the unconscious. With music, we face the same question posed in relation to poetry: How Dionysian can we become without saying we have left the domain of art?

Designations in music must be tentative, at best, since much music that is now considered highly formal and highly traditional, such as the symphonies of Beethoven, was in its time often viewed with a certain amount of distrust. The dissonant seventh chords introduced by Beethoven would surely have been called Dionysian by early-nineteenth-century critics, but they are now comfortably ensconced within the archives of classicism. Time and tradition often lend an air of Apollonian respectability to what was once outrageous and shocking.

Serious, or concert, music of all periods except our own may generally and safely be termed Apollonian. Even the drawn-out emotionalism of Tchaikovsky and the extreme romanticism of Richard Strauss do not violate the principles of musical form. By the time of Tchaikovsky and Strauss, from the latter half of the nineteenth century to the early years of the twentieth, music was expected to have a more direct assault upon the emotions without losing all perspective. Orchestral poems, like *Manfred* and *Don Quixote*, allow the composer more freedom in developing his or her themes than did earlier forms, but we can note the use of repeated themes, which keep the experience turning back upon itself, giving it shape and direction.

Often we mistake a Dionysian "message" for pure Dionysianism in music. A case in point is Ravel's popular *Bolero* (1928), originally written as a ballet and the source of a near riot upon the occasion of its first performance. The insistent theme, endlessly repeated with increasingly pronounced rhythmic underpinnings, seems to be encouraging the listener to throw aside all restraint and surrender to an orgiastic, completely irrational state. No doubt the visual impact of a distinctly un-Victorian dance had something to do with the near riot at the premiere. But nothing more Apollonian can be imagined than a piece of music that is a continual restatement of, not even a variation on, just one theme and has a boldly identifiable rhythm. A real-life Dionysian orgy is characterized by totally innovative—nonrepeated—behavior and an absence of regular rhythm, an absence of things that remind the Apollonian self to take care.

We are living at a time of near-extreme Dionysianism in behavior, hence one in which the arts are filled with adventurous experiments in rule breaking. We would suppose that certain uncontrolled forms of rock can be considered Dionysian, if only because they continue to set new records in decibels, loudness usually interfering with our ability to put experience into any kind of perspective. Perhaps, by supporting the rock movement, we are really saying we are afraid to think, afraid to face some unpleasant realities about ourselves and our times.

But the music of the Beatles, which, like that of Beethoven, shocked a good many purists in the beginning, now begins to take on the glow of high respectability. Many of their songs, at first dismissed as mere ear-splitting nonsense, have shown themselves to be highly structured pieces, built firmly on recognized musical principles. Many traditionalists in music education use "Eleanor Rigby" as an almost classic example of syncopation, the principle by which the main theme plays against, not with, the underlying rhythm.

Conservative adults tend to believe that all rock music is a dangerous lure, debasing the minds of both listeners and dancers. At one time, even jazz was considered detrimental, partly because its origins were outside the mainstream of white-dominated power, and partly because its appeal, like that of liquor, aimed at passions considered base. Today, jazz has become an art form, an accepted Apollonian art form, which has achieved the respectability of being a part of university curricula, listed in the catalogs and studied for credit. Jazz has recognized and teachable styles and patterns as well as a place in history.

*Ravel's* Bolero, *which seems at first to be Dionysian, is basically Apollonian in form and structure. The music of the Beatles also turns out to be highly structured.*

By the same token, there has developed a musicology of rock, a tradition with influences and styles now being analyzed seriously by music students. We may have even reached the point at which the apparent abandon of so-called punk rock is a sociological, not an artistic, event, a point at which we can tell the difference between the two yet regard "punk" with Apollonian seriousness.

## Drama

So we find ourselves, in critically Apollonian fashion, returning to the same question: How Dionysian may a work of art be in form as well as in spirit? This issue is paramount in drama, an ancient art form, which seems absolutely to depend on repeated and recognizable characters, portents of things to come, and an obligatory climax in which conflicting forces inevitably collide and some resolution is reached.

But Nietzsche's original designation of the Apollonian and the Dionysian grew out of a discussion of drama, specifically, Greek tragedy. Aware that the birth of tragedy lay in primordial rituals (such as that of human sacrifice), which were anything but Apollonian, Nietzsche argued that by emphasizing the moral lessons to be learned from tragedy, early critics like Aristotle had taken the form out of its primitive—and, for Nietzsche, far more exciting—context. By concentrating on what was to be *learned* from tragedy, later critics ignored the excitement of the play in favor of schematic patterns that ultimately instructed audiences in the proper way to behave. In their eyes, so Nietzsche believed, tragedy became a pale replica of basic human passions.

*Oedipus Rex*, often considered the perfectly structured and therefore representatively Apollonian tragedy, can be viewed in two contrasting ways. In addition to its geometrically designed plot, which brings the hero ever closer to the truth of his birth and incestuous marriage (see Chapter 4 for a fuller discussion), the play can be seen as having a decidedly Apollonian moral theme: *Mortals should not try to outwit fate.*

But we must not forget that Freud and his disciples saw in *Oedipus* a drama of the titanic struggle between the forces of organized society and the unconscious Oedipal desire of the male for his mother. Freud saw primitive myth in the drama, and so did Nietzsche, who, like the first of the psychoanalysts, was responding to the restraining effects of Victorian morality.

For Nietzsche it was decidedly wrong to be concerned with morality to an extent that made no allowance for the strong emotions a tragedy unleashes. These emotions, which we mention in Chapter 4, were considered dangerous by Aristotle. Over the centuries dramatic criticism has stressed the importance of the calming effect that takes place in tragedy following the catastrophe. In both Greek and Shakespearean tragedy, moral order reasserts itself after emotion has run its course. If the fallen hero is the king or queen, a new and rational ruler comes upon the scene. We leave the theater satisfied, our Apollonian selves assured that chaos does not reign.

*Eugene O'Neill and Tennessee Williams were seldom capable of rational discourse about their plays. They appear to have relied on instincts far below the rational surface.*

But can we say that every Greek tragedian looked to the Aristotelian norms for guidance? Or that Shakespeare left his theatrical kingdoms in reestablished order for any reason beside political ones? (Shakespeare wrote for the company that was supported by the royal house itself!) May not Nietzsche have a point when he says that drama is essentially Dionysian in that it constitutes a living, direct experience, as opposed to the secondary experience of literature?

*Hans Hofmann,* Effervescence *(1944): Highly obscure formal principles. (University Art Museum, University of California at Berkeley; gift of the artist)*

Significantly enough, many contemporary dramatists have resisted the efforts of critics to interpret and explain their work and to criticize it on intellectual and moral grounds. Eugene O'Neill (1888 - 1953) and Tennessee Williams (1912 - 1983), two of the most formidable forces in American theater, were seldom capable of rational discourse about their plays. They appear to have relied on instincts far below the rational surface.

Williams, in particular, was obsessed with the very theme of Apollo versus Dionysus. Coming as he did from a background of Old South (Apollonian) gentility, he enjoyed creating plays about the destructive effects of suppressed passion. While we could argue that his themes were actually Apollonian *statements* and that his strongest plays—*A Streetcar Named Desire* (1947) and *Cat on a Hot Tin Roof* (1955)—owe their audience success to an unerring sense of structure that is Greek-like in its mounting intensity, we can also not fail to see that Williams's most powerful scenes, such as Stanley Kowalski's rape of Blanche DuBois in *Streetcar*, unleash white-hot emotion that sears the viewer.

Unlike poetry, drama contains the additional element of an actor's living presence. Even in highly symbolic plays, the living actor will duplicate real-life emotion. Anger is anger, whether it occurs in a highly realistic play, like *Cat on a Hot Tin Roof*, or a German expressionistic work in which both set and characters represent ideas. Engulfed by the emotions pouring forth from the stage, audiences seldom ask themselves, "What is the playwright trying to tell us?" Of, if they do, they may sense that something is missing from the experience.

On the other hand, much contemporary theater may be perceived as going "too far"; at least, it does to the Apollonian inside us. Like some modern art and music that seems to be working from highly obscure formal principles, modern theater sometimes goes out of its way to be unusual to the point of being unidentifiable. There has even been a performance at which the audience was blindfolded and forced to sit in terror while bodies and other objects tumbled over it and deafening music drowned out any screams that might have been uttered. Dionysianism is always there to support the interests of those who wish to rebel against all authority, even that of art itself.

Tolerance for the unfamiliar in art will be a persistent theme in this book. But we must not rule out the possibility that the nonfamiliar, having been given its say, may still be dismissed as nonart. Some formal principle, however eccentric, appears to be necessary. This, of course, may subsequently be discovered, as has been the case with the music of the Beatles. But think how confusing it will be for future humanities teachers to say to their classes, "The world of art contains art itself and its own opposite, that which lacks art." How unanswerable might be the question, "Then are we to consider *everything* as belonging to the world of art?" To measure the artistry of some recent events calling themselves drama, we might suppose a high admission price to be a "logical" yardstick for the critic to use.

*Think how confusing it will be to say to a class, "The world of art contains art itself and its own opposite, that which lacks art."*

## The Arts as Revolutionary Forces

In the late 1960s the most popular show on Broadway was the musical *Hair*, which was proudly passed off as a show without a book. Almost—but, we hasten

*Grant Wood,* American Gothic *(1930): The arts as a means of expressing revolutionary ideas. (Friends of American Art Collection. Courtesy of The Art Institute of Chicago, All Rights Reserved)*

to add, *not completely*—devoid of plot and transitions from song to song, *Hair* managed to bubble along just below the conscious level, its lyrics often not quite making rational sense. But its music was loud and insistent, and at the end of the evening, the audience was invited to come up onto the stage and join the cast in wild dancing. The show was a huge financial success, meaning that its high-priced appeal went far beyond the audience of young revolutionaries, whose movement was the original inspiration. Respectable executives and their spouses, often dressed to the teeth, let themselves go in the final dance. It began to look as if the Apollonian Establishment were quite ready to let down its own hair and get back to Dionysian basics.

Whether the off-center effects of *Hair* were coldly calculated and its destiny as a monumental money-making enterprise carefully sculpted, the case has been made many times for the arts as being properly revolutionary in nature and purpose. Both Karl Marx and Mao Zedong were advocates of this view. So was, much earlier, Jean-Jacques Rousseau (1712-1778), who, in commenting on the function of drama, insisted that to obtain committed revolutionaries, it was necessary to inflame them, to show a wrong and to leave it unresolved, thus allowing audiences to stream out of a theater and into the streets with the determination to do something in real life rather than be tranquilized by the leveling-off of emotions onstage. The ending would be played out in physical action, in the rallies and riots that would put into play the Dionysian elements deliberately ignored by scholars and critics such as Aristotle.

*Rousseau believed the purpose of art was to provoke rather than soothe, to show an injustice and then reach an abrupt, unsatisfying ending.*

For Rousseau the purpose of art was to provoke rather than soothe, to show an injustice, to draw the audience to the side of one clear victim and then reach an abrupt, unsatisfying ending. If the wrongdoer were not brought to justice, audiences would remain indignant. They would not be allowed the calming luxury of sighs and tears in witnessing a victim's death and release from suffering, nor be calmed by a philosophical acceptance of disappointment as a part of living. They would simply be aroused and left at a peak of emotion.

The contemporary labor organizer Cesar Chavez successfully employed this technique in his presentation of plays about the hardships suffered by Mexican migrant workers. In his Teatro Campesino, Chavez typically showed a poor man brutally deceived, first by those he paid to guide him across the border, then by the supervisors under whom he worked long and arduous hours for almost no compensation. The plays at the Teatro Campesino never had resolved endings. Instead, they encouraged an aroused audience, usually on its feet, to demand immediate social action.

Teachers of the humanities have tended to resist the revolutionary aspect of the arts, carefully separating artistic works from those considered propagandistic or blatantly didactic. The controversy continues. We may be assured that people will always use the arts as a means of expressing revolutionary ideas. If they are successful, as was Clifford Odets when his 1930s play *Waiting for Lefty* was the direct cause of a massive taxidriver strike, who are we to say that their intention has not been Apollonian; that they have not had the formal purpose of effecting social change through an artistic medium, not street violence; and that, being successful, their work does not deserve to be recognized as art?

*Art that deliberately seeks to provoke social action may be Apollonian in philosophical intent and in form, but Dionysian in spirit.*

## Religion

Religion seems to be just Apollonian, requiring a regular routine of worship, obedience to authority, distrust of emotion, and often consciousness of a stern, demanding God. But religion can be Dionysian, too, in its appeal to feeling and the senses. It was this Dionysian impulse that Nietzsche praised when he contrasted the Apollonian Judeo-Christian beliefs of his own time with the pagan beliefs of the past. The Greek god Prometheus, he pointed out, stole fire from Zeus and gave it to humanity because he believed Zeus to be unfair in trying to prevent this wonderful resource from reaching Earth. The myth encourages sympathy with humanity against the tyranny of Zeus. But the disobedience of Adam and Eve in gaining knowledge of good and evil is, in Hebrew scriptures, regarded as worthy of punishment. It is time, said Nietzsche, to give credit to the Dionysian side of human life and to stop the emphasis on human sin and God's mercy.

The Apollonian approach to religion has been found in a variety of forms: in commandments and restrictions; in rules for clothing and diet as well as ritual observances; in the orderly rhythm of celebrations; in the quiet design of simple places for worship as well as in gigantic cathedrals; in sermons emphasizing social conscience; and in prescribed, planned responses from the congregation. But Apollonian religion, like Apollonian government, can become repressive.

In Nathaniel Hawthorne's *The Scarlet Letter* (1850), the heroine, Hester Prynne, was required by the community to wear the letter *A*, which proclaimed her an adulteress. The Puritan community of New England regarded the application of God's laws to be of public concern rather than a matter for the private conscience of each person. Social condemnation was a means of assuring adherence to law. In his novel, Hawthorne portrays the disgrace of the sinner, who has borne a child by a man other than her husband, and the unrelenting inner agony of the adulterer, who is the town minister himself, able to hide the sin from everyone except God. In Puritanism, God *and* community are unyielding, avenging forces.

New England Puritanism was a branch of Protestantism, which began in the Reformation in part out of protest against Catholic ritual, denounced as excessive and sensual—hence, we would say, Dionysian. Protestant worship was based on the Bible as a holy book read by each congregant, rather than on the authority of priests and other interpreters of God's law. Worship was held in plain, undecorated churches, without incense, images, or processions of church dignitaries. Nor were there parades and street dancing to celebrate a holiday or honor a martyred saint. Puritans abolished Christmas decorations as pagan practice. Secular activities on the Sabbath were strictly forbidden. Today, some areas that restrict business enterprises from operating on Sundays in predominantly Protestant communities or on Saturdays in the nation of Israel are evidence that Puritan values are not restricted to any one religion.

Apollonian religion can have a positive impact as well. Religious rituals, experienced from week to week, have a steadying effect. They reestablish the broken rhythms of our lives. Whether we always accept every belief espoused by a given sect, the process itself of attending a church, of hearing old rules repeated— good rules to guide the lives of reasonable human beings, set forth by many wise individuals—cannot be lightly dismissed. Hawthorne's world of grim, austere Puritans is one extreme. It is found, we must remember, on the pages of a novel. We should not make the mistake of regarding the community aspect of every religion as being potentially repressive, a denial of human rights.

The Apollonian approach to religion includes morality, an insistence on distinguishing between right and wrong. Often the distinction is hard and fast— and unalterable. Nietzsche was opposed to the imposition of moral values from a central religious authority. For him, rigid morality weakened a society, preventing

*Hawthorne's* The Scarlet Letter *shows us the stern repressiveness of extreme Apollonianism in religion.*

*Gianlorenzo Bernini,* Ecstasy of Saint Teresa: *Religion can be Dionysian. (Alinari/Art Resource)*

strong energies from seeking a healthy outlet. Apollonians in religion frequently cite extreme Dionysian examples to support their disapproval. True, over the years Dionysian worship has involved uninterrupted, often orgiastic dancing, repeated chants, the removal of sin through animal sacrifice, and the ritualistic use of hallucinatory drugs.

Dionysian religious practice includes ceremonies that spring from feeling and instinct, not reason. It also includes an emphasis on fellowship rather than moral instruction, on the giving of love more than the categorization of sins. The mystical elements within the Judeo-Christian mainstream tradition can be termed Dionysian, and so can the traditional stories and songs that demonstrate simple, humble faith, as opposed to the intellectual grasp of large realities. Even the most dedicated Apollonian is likely to find warmth and comfort in the popular carol of "The Little Drummer Boy," who could give the baby Jesus only the "rum-a-tum-tum" of his drum rather than the costly gifts of the royal visitors.

A similar tale exists in Jewish tradition. The story is of a boy who was unable to read prayers; nevertheless his father took him to pray on Yom Kippur, the holiest day of the year. The boy took his flute out of his pocket and played it during the concluding prayers. Everyone heard it. The father was ashamed, but the pious leader, the Baal Shem Tov, said, "This child's flute has lifted up all our prayers. Through the strength of his yearning he played his heart's note perfectly. This was very dear to God, and all our prayers were accepted for his sake."

Ritual is often Dionysian in its appeal to the senses and the emotions, in its dramatic rather than literary representation of a basic element of belief. Consider the phases of the Easter season. First comes the revelry of Mardi Gras as the last fling before the restrictions of Lent. *Carnival* (a word derived from the Latin

*Some Dionysian elements in religion: the simplicity of "The Little Drummer Boy"; Mardi Gras; Easter Sunday.*

words for "farewell to meat") offers unrestrained merriment, costumes, pageantry, parades. Then come the somber days of restriction, symbolically purifying the believer for the celebration that is to come. In many churches, Good Friday means a dark place of worship, all sources of beauty shrouded, windows covered. Then, on Easter Sunday, light streams through stained glass windows; the church is at its most resplendent, and members of the congregation in bright new clothes sing hymns of celebration. Countless people flock to the churches at such festive times, seeking, if nothing else, an emotional uplift.

The Apollonian/Dionysian conflict often comes about through efforts to change practice and belief from within. Attempts at modification of old, established religious customs can be met with bitter resistance, as recently happened with the introduction of jazz masses and the singing of folk-rock hymns on once-hallowed altars.

Rebellion against orthodoxy is also found in the practice of "Santeria," a religion that originated some time ago in Africa and came to the United States via the islands of the Caribbean. Outwardly practicing Catholicism, the religion of their masters, slaves working in Cuba combined, or "syncretized," elements of polytheism with the saints of their new religion. In the synthesis, certain gods were "assigned" to cure certain parts of the body, and medicine men assisted in the rituals associated with the cures. Along with therapy, this blend of religions offered freedom from moral restrictions. The lovesick sufferer, lusting for someone already married, could seek help in the form of love potions and magic words, the Santerian gods not being guardians of traditional virtue.

For Nietzsche, this departure from morality would have provided a necessary counterbalance. We have already spoken of the contrast between the Greek and Hebrew approaches to human defiance of deity. The Greek myth encourages sympathy for Prometheus, benefactor of humanity. In Genesis, the disobedience of Adam and Eve is punished by banishment from Eden, and eventually by death. Both Jews and Christians are *instructed* to regret this fall from Paradise and to wait—in different ways—for deliverance from human suffering. The Promethean act of defiance was thus heroic, grand, emotionally stirring; that of Adam and Eve, a shameful lesson. Nietzsche feared that the Apollonian emphasis on sin would mean the triumph of all that was tame, cerebral, and passive in our nature.

## Apollo and Dionysus in Education

Almost nowhere in the personal experience of the average person are Apollonian and Dionysian factors likely to be as evident as they are in schools and colleges, for education itself as a process is always destined to be a showdown between the two forces. On one hand, education aims at the growth and unfolding of the individual, which can be Dionysian matters. If students were allowed to fully explore their creative potential, to develop in any chosen direction, without regard for the requirements of their teacher, local school board, parents, and society, they would be following a purely Dionysian course. But even before the creative potential of a kindergarten pupil or a first-grader is ever perceived—in fact, often before the child has entered school—certain Apollonian expectations have been impressed upon the pupil. For example:

> The pupil must learn to behave.
> The pupil must remain confined for long hours.

*In religion, Nietzsche feared, the Apollonian emphasis on sin would mean the triumph of all that was tame, cerebral, and passive in our nature.*

*The ideal condition would be, I admit, that men should be right by instinct; but since we are all likely to go astray, the reasonable thing is to learn from those who can teach.*

*Sophocles*

The pupil must show the results of certain teaching methods.
The pupil must therefore learn things that he or she may not want to
  learn.
Others know better than the pupil what is worth doing.

## The Lower Grades

Many problems arising in earlier years of education can be attributed to the imbalance between Apollo and Dionysus. Whether the problems were understood in precisely these terms or not, about half a century ago sweeping changes began to be made. Educators recognized the need to allow pupils more Dionysian freedom to learn who they were and what they wanted to become. Experimental schools sprang up everywhere, many of which developed reputations for overpermissiveness and abandonment of the three Rs. Typical of these early Dionysian classrooms would be sessions in which pupils banged objects together in a "rhythm band," got together in little groups to act out plays (which were really unconscious fantasies in disguise), and engaged in finger painting, much to the detriment of their clothes, the other children, and the classroom floor.

Most elementary schools, however, have sought to maintain a balance between excessive order and unbridled freedom. Educational theory, which is basically Apollonian, demands organization, planning, the writing of objectives, and the development of ways to measure a pupil's growth. Some teachers are overly Apollonian, insisting upon the lesson plan to the exclusion of all else, even when a given lesson appears not to be working. Others allow for Dionysian free spirits, with the result that they always seem to be running to catch up with their own objectives.

Schools tend to be top-heavy with administration, which is a very Apollonian entity. The teacher is answerable to the principal, the local school board, the PTA, the county overseers—ultimately to the state department of education. The extreme Dionysian has a hard time bringing pupils into line and getting them ready for the battery of tests that come along frequently, not to mention for classroom observers.

Schools are Apollonian in their insistence upon ordered rituals, from flag salutes to the straight-line march along the corridors to the cafeteria or the playground. Even where permissiveness reigns in a particular classroom, the schools themselves are often run like army training camps. Pupils must have a pass if they are found walking through the halls. They may not be many minutes late, if at all. They usually may not rise from their seats at will or talk to their classmates.

Since children are too young to comprehend the why's behind the subjects they study, they must do a great deal of rote learning, which is Apollonian, too. They must memorize the spelling and meaning of words as well as the multiplication tables. They must learn the capitals of every state and country and what crops are grown in the "black earth region."

Critics of excessive Apollonianism in education cite the fact that pupils become memorization machines at too early an age to defend themselves. After a time, pupils become exasperated with meaningless rote learning and start rebelling. The rebellious stage, say the critics, begins in junior high school. It soon becomes obvious to students that, even though requirements are many, it is not necessary to shine in order to get by.

It also becomes obvious that as students "put out" less and less, the Apol-

*If this pupil happens to be of so wayward a disposition that he would rather listen to a fictitious tale than to the narrative of some fine voyager or a wise conversation, . . . I see no other remedy but that his governor should . . . bind him prentice to a pastry-cook in some good town, though he were the son of a duke.*

*Montaigne*

lonian demands, while still there, do not have to be taken seriously. The classroom has become so artificial, say the critics, that few teachers are able to convince students to apply themselves. The content of most classes is irrelevant to students' lives.

The charge is also made that schools in Western society are dominated by a *white*, middle-class Apollonian system. The value system of the dominant culture determines what is to be studied, and how. Grammar workbooks may ask students to analyze sentences like the following:

> Mother and Jeff have gone to the shopping center to buy vinyl upholstery cleaner, and Jeff will polish the station wagon in the afternoon.
> After returning from a 14-day Caribbean cruise, Grandmother felt completely rejuvenated and no longer required the services of her psychiatrist.
> Father came home from the office looking very tired after a full day of business conferences and was in no mood whatever to learn that Eddie had been swimming in the deep end of the pool without permission.

Apollonian critics, on their part, charge that efforts to make the lower grades "relevant" usually end in disaster. They contend that changing grammar workbooks to make them reflect a multiethnic social base does not motivate students to learn how to spell, write, and speak any more effectively than they did before. Often, they say, their hands are tied. The pressures are Dionysian rather than Apollonian. Parents are becoming less and less concerned, having already given up. School administrators are afraid of having so many students fail that the newspapers will do an exposé; hence the better part of valor is to pretend that standards are important but to let students get away with anything.

*One educator reports that teachers in a certain school district "study the twenty-eight characteristics of 'effective teaching'—which they are then expected to demonstrate in each lesson."*

*Lynn V. Cheney*

## High Schools and Colleges

In the secondary schools and in institutions of higher learning, the Apollonian/ Dionysian conflict becomes acute. High school teachers often inherit students who, having become alienated from school long ago, are barely literate. The recourses are few:

> Using remedial programs with long hours of drill and rote learning.
> Abandoning classical educational ideals and taking students "wherever they are."
> Attempting to rekindle interest in school through innovative strategies, like games and self-paced studies.

Those who cling to the Apollonian hope of raising the literacy of their students often forgo teaching the real subject itself in favor of having a "tight ship" in which the students perform decently on objective tests. Those who want to make education a profound and meaningful experience often forgo literacy and the students' ability to perform well on tests in favor of excitement in the classroom.

The degree to which a college leans toward Apollo or toward Dionysus depends upon the prestige of the institution. The pillars of education—Ivy League colleges in the United States and the distinguished institutions of Europe and Latin America—are likely to be strongly Apollonian, requiring long hours of study and the passing of rigorous examinations. Colleges and universities of more recent vintage—especially the community colleges—are likely to be more experimental and to allow for Dionysian exploration. At the same time, some teachers in these institutions, deeply feeling the stigma attached to an "upstart" college with no reputation, can become ruthlessly Apollonian in their demands.

In schools given over to the free exercise of both Apollonian and Dionysian educational principles, understandable confusion reigns. Students come from a calculus class in which there is no room for personal expression to an experimental English class in which finger painting is an acceptable substitute for a theme. Some teachers within a given department acquire a reputation for being "tough" (hence Apollonian), while others are known for grading on a generous curve, accepting substitutions for last night's assignment, and allowing students to steer a discussion away from the homework so that they never find out who was prepared and who was not. While a student might want to learn something substantial, the temptation to enroll in a Dionysian class may be irresistible because, since no clear objectives have been stated, most people receive high grades.

No easy solution presents itself. The Apollonian college with its traditions and high standards may be paying little attention to the real needs of students as human beings. The Dionysian teacher with a "like me, like me at any cost!" approach may be paying little attention to the real needs of human beings as students.

*Some teachers in experimental Dionysian institutions, feeling the stigma attached to an "upstart" college, become ruthlessly Apollonian.*

## Apollonian Rules and Dionysian Feelings

Theory is Apollonian; practice is Dionysian. The rules are Apollonian, whether for calculus, a bridge game, or living in an organized society. Every classroom must have its rules of operation. Not even a Dionysian creative unfolding can take place in a totally disorganized atmosphere.

But the flow of life is itself Dionysian, as is the willingness to adapt to new and unfamiliar circumstances. Education must allow time for experimentation, exploration, and the discovery of possibilities that may lie dormant within the student.

A rigid objective test is Apollonian all the way, particularly when answers are either true or false. But a critical essay about a poem, a novel, or a painting is also Apollonian when the teacher insists that the writer actually deal with the work in question and not respond to it on a purely personal level.

Apollonian discussions relate to theme, color, use of language, historical effect, similarity in the works of two artists, growth from one period to another in the work of the same artist, use of a particular technique of fiction, symbolism, and the influence of certain key events in an author's life on his or her work. Apollonian analysis is critically detached and objective, maintaining perspective at all times. It is fundamental to the Western tradition, which venerates rationality and clear-sightedness.

We may argue that becoming objective and clear-sighted is a fundamental right. If students are encouraged to express themselves haphazardly at too early a stage in their growth, they are likely to have less and less to say later. For expression to be full there must be a command of words and practice in putting one word after another in some kind of meaningful sequence. Otherwise, scattered, impressionistic discourse becomes the only means of communication. ("How I Feel About the French Revolution" as a theme topic is surely more personal than historical!)

*Disciplined Apollonian approaches to learning are important for success in life, but students also want Dionysian warmth, good humor, and flexibility in their teachers.*

At the same time, as educators of the Apollonian perspective point out, the Dionysian promise can be misleading and ultimately cruel. If students are granted excessive subjective license, if the statement "Shakespeare has nothing to offer as far as I'm concerned" is allowed to stand unchallenged, students may be sent into the world unprepared for reality, for society never has been and never will be dominated by Dionysus. What does it profit a student to go through many years of school receiving high grades for undocumented, undefended opinions based on feelings, only to discover that in the Apollonian world such feelings are irrelevant to others?

But the truth of the matter probably is that the purely Dionysian teacher does not exist. Authority is authority, when all is said and done, and often those teachers who claim to be facilitating student learning by keeping quiet have developed subtle tricks to bring about certain predetermined results. Not to share these techniques with students—allowing students to imagine that they are developing freely and according to their own true natures—can be fostering a very dangerous delusion.

There seems no genuine alternative but to provide students with both Apollonian and Dionysian approaches in the classroom. Such influences will thus enable and motivate students to take responsibility for what happens to them in higher education. The awareness that disciplined Apollonian approaches to learning are important for success in life should motivate students to seek out the most demanding and challenging courses and teachers available. Yet as students meet these challenges, they will recognize the value of Dionysian warmth, good humor, and flexibility in their teachers. Students and teachers alike should recognize that the classroom need not imitate the world, but neither is the world going to be a very meaningful place without some principles to take into it.

# Glossary

**Apollonian:** Derived from Nietzsche's symbolic use of the name of the Greek god of light and truth, Apollo, to describe a psychological condition, the term can be either a noun—meaning "one who must have order and discipline in his or her life"—or an adjective, referring to the orderly, rational component in a person, a society, or a work of art.

**carnival:** From the Latin *carne vale*, "farewell to the flesh," this term originally referred to a medieval festival before Lent, highlighted by all manner of Dionysian excess. Its most notable present-day counterpart is Mardi Gras.

**Dionysian:** Derived from Nietzsche's symbolic use of the name of the Greek god of wine and vegetation, Dionysus, to describe a psychological condition, the term as a noun means "one who enjoys excess in pleasurable activities" or "one for whom intuition and spontaneity predominate," and as an adjective refers to the spontaneous or creative components in a person, a society, or a work of art.

**polarities:** Derived from the idea of natural poles (North and South; positive and negative), these are explanations for principles of alternation that appear to pervade the universe. Cyclical theories of history (e.g., Marxism) are based on certain types of polarities. In this chapter they are the Apollonian and Dionysian components, which apparently keep succeeding each other within a given personality, culture, or period of time.

# Notes

1. Tom Robbins, *Still Life with Woodpecker* (New York: Bantam Books, 1980).
2. "The Laws of God, the Laws of Man" from *Last Poems* by A. E. Housman. Copyright 1922 by Holt, Rinehart and Winston, Inc. Copyright 1950 by Barclays Bank Ltd. Reprinted by permission of Henry Holt and Company, Inc.

# Suggested Reading

Bly, Robert. *Iron John*. Reading, Mass.: Addison-Wesley, 1990. Bly claims that contemporary males are being denied the chance to realize the full potential of their manhood because its mythology is not being handed down to them. Of special relevance to this chapter is the Dionysian myth of the Wild Man.

Brecht, Bertolt. *The Caucasian Chalk Circle*, in *Parables for the Theater: Two Plays by Bertolt Brecht*. Minneapolis: University of Minnesota Press, 1947. The struggle between the Apollonian legal order and the Dionysian plea for bending the law is illustrated in this comic drama.

Golding, William. *Lord of the Flies*. New York: Coward, McCann, 1962. The Apollonian nature is the superficial trapping of civilization; humanity is fundamentally Dionysian, savage and destructive. At least this is the underlying premise of this celebrated novel about a group of upper-class English schoolboys who manage to survive a plane crash on a remote island.

Hawthorne, Nathaniel. *The Scarlet Letter*. 1850. The classic novel shows the stern repressiveness of extreme Apollonianism in American Puritanism.

Kazantzakis, Nikos. *Zorba the Greek*. Tr. Carl Wildman. New York: Simon & Schuster, 1952. Perhaps the ultimate novel about an Apollonian/Dionysian relationship. Zorba is a modern incarnation of Dionysus himself—passionate, irresistible, and irresponsible. His Apollonian friend is a British poet—sober, methodical, puritanical, and, in Zorba's opinion, incapable of being happy.

Mann, Thomas. *Death in Venice*. Tr. H. Lowe-Porter. New York: Vintage Books, 1964. The hero, a man with a repressive Apollonian moral sense, travels to Venice, a city of Dionysian sensuality. He unfolds in ways he cannot fully comprehend or deal with, and the imbalance inside him leads to tragedy.

Nietzsche, Friedrich. *The Birth of Tragedy*. Tr. Francis Golffing. Garden City, N.Y.: Doubleday & Co., 1956. Nietzsche's study of tragedy is probably the most significant since that of Aristotle, and in it he attacks the traditional Aristotelian view that the moral (i.e., Apollonian) element is the most important aspect in a tragedy. Nietzsche would have us appreciate the Dionysian qualities (those that arouse passion and excitement) in tragedy as well as in the other arts.

Pirsig, Robert. *Zen and the Art of Motorcycle Maintenance*. New York: Morrow, 1979. Already a modern classic, this intriguing autobiography of a human intellect makes profound comments about the Apollonian life.

Twain, Mark. *The Adventures of Huckleberry Finn*. 1884. Considered by many to be *the* great American novel, Twain's masterpiece gives us a hero who sums up the Dionysian side of the American character: its restlessness and unwillingness to be fenced in by authority.

*Marcel Duchamp,* Nude Descending a Staircase, No. 2 *(Philadelphia Museum of Art, Louise and Walter Arensberg Collection)*

# The Visual Artist

2

I have wanted to give the impression of a way of life quite different from that of us civilized people. Therefore I am not at all anxious for everyone to like it or to admire it at once.

*Vincent van Gogh, to his brother, Theo, in reference to* The Potato Eaters

Do you think I know what art is? Do you think I'd think anybody knew, even if they said they did? Do you think I'd care what anybody thought? Now if you ask me what we're trying to do that's a different thing.

*Georgia O'Keeffe*

Learn by heart the forms to be found in nature, so that you can use them like the notes in a musical composition. That is what these forms are for. Nature is a marvellous chaos, and it is our job and our duty to bring order into that chaos and—to perfect it.

*Max Beckmann*

Art is what the artist does.

*Robert Thiele*

37

# *Overview*

The people just quoted are all artists, and their sentiments allow for a wide range of definitions on the subject of art. Note, however, that only one—the last artist cited—makes a direct definition *statement*, and note that this statement seems deliberately, almost coyly, to be begging the question. But that, we might as well recognize, is the right of artists, so why resist? They are never going to come clean and tell us what *really* goes on in their minds—why one artist insists on stretching an enormous curtain from one mountain to another in Colorado and audaciously calling it art; why another spends months working on a sculpture he calls *Giant Ice Bag*, which looks like nothing else but a—giant ice bag!

The most precise and memorable definitions of art usually come from those who teach but do not create art. This pattern is hardly unique; we seldom find composers clearly defining music or poets stating categorically that "a poem is . . ." Most creators—not just those in the visual arts—seem to shy away from analysis, interpretation, and in some extreme cases, even praise. Artists either know (like Michelangelo) that they are titans and will be remembered for all time, or else they find (like van Gogh) that the question of fame is a matter of indifference to them. Artists who have completely revolutionized the form and scope of art (like Picasso) may nod politely in the direction of public taste, but in their hearts they know the public is going to have to catch up with what they are doing—and will someday be able to appreciate their work, however critics choose to define it.

The reader who prefers precise definitions of art can find them in any number of excellent sources, sources that present a chronological survey of the visual arts in their historical contexts. Since the present text aims at offering insights into the utilization of the humanities as a means of enhancing the quality of life, we are less concerned with defining what art *is* than with suggesting by way of representative examples what art can *do*. In this context Leonardo da Vinci and Georgia O'Keeffe are not so far from each other. The former is Renaissance, the latter contemporary, true; but both will survive, both will still be around a century from now—not because they fit certain definitions, but because what they left behind is still functioning to make human existence a happier thing.

Regrettably, many people avoid museums and galleries because they remember sterile classroom environments, stale memorized lists, and boring true-false tests. If the visual arts are to be living and vital components of our personal worlds, then we must first establish a true link between ourselves and the artists. What aspect of humanness do we and the artists share? Each of us must ask: What is there in *me* that can best relate to what is hanging over there on that wall or towering above me on the Sistine Chapel ceiling? If we do not begin by looking inward, we shall go through life with the uneasy feeling that the people who sign their names in the lower right-hand corner are just plain different from us: strangers as silent as the marble halls of the museums.

*Many people avoid museums and galleries because they remember sterile classroom environments, memorized lists, and true-false tests.*

## Let Me See!

Why do children in cars, buses, or trains always demand to sit by the window? For that matter, why do they make this demand on planes, when there is nothing to

*Claes Oldenburg,* Giant Ice Bag: *A sculpture that looks like nothing else but a giant ice bag. (Courtesy Thomas Segal Gallery, Boston)*

look at but clouds? There is a chance, of course, that there will be mountains or strange cities visible from that height. The probabilities don't matter. Children are new to the world, and instinctively they want to take in as much of it as they can. Old people in apartments along crowded city streets like to kneel on chairs and look out the window for hours on end. Integral to the experience of being alive is looking at things. Those who have been blind from birth substitute touching or listening. The point is that we spend much of our lives just looking around for no immediately practical reason, except one: *we have to.*

## Seeing with the Right Brain

Sitting next to a window, looking out at a street, or slowing to a crawl on the freeway to ogle at somebody fixing a tire or getting a ticket may be all some of us have left from our earliest childhood passion for seeing. (Recall the ecstatic look on the faces of babies when they first master the art of looking.) What happened to this passion? One answer is that as we mature and life grows more inwardly complex for us, we forgo "just looking" because we have learned it serves no real purpose. We start looking only at the things and the people that are important to our specialized existences, and even in that, we see only what we have to. One hears unhappy reports of men or women in an office not being able to conjure up the image of their spouse's face. We even pass by old friends without recognition because we haven't *needed* to remember what they looked like.

The process of selective seeing begins long before we report for our first job. Most of us remember what happened when an elementary school teacher asked us to draw a house. We made the generic drawn house (three rectangles with a triangle roof), just as we made stick figures to represent people. We made

*An artist is a dreamer consenting to dream the actual world.*

*George Santa*

the *symbol* of a house, because it was easier than trying to reproduce the real thing. We made the symbol of a face, the symbol of a person. Most of us don't draw what we see because we have forgotten how to look. The artist paints a sun that has radiance, depth, and color shadings. The rest of us draw something like this:

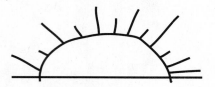

Such a drawing could just as easily be a porcupine peeking from behind a fence.

In recent years there has arisen a totally new school of thinking about artistic talent. This new way of thinking is an offshoot of medical research into what is called *hemispheric asymmetry*. As everyone knows, just like a globe of the earth, the brain is divided into two hemispheres. The brain's hemispheres, which are separated as well as connected by an intricate network of nerve fibers, the *corpus callosum*, really make up two complete brains, right and left, one acting as a backup to the other. In the case of a severe injury to either brain, the other can get the whole job done, given sufficient rehabilitation time. Rehabilitation in this case means the transference of functions from one brain to the other. Patients who do not recover all of their functions after a stroke have suffered damage to both sides.

But now the question is: What does a normal person do with two brains? The new research hypothesizes that, over the thousands of years during which the human brain has been developing, the two hemispheres have each come up with their own individual specialties. In other words, while either one can be the entire brain, if necessary, both hemispheres in a normal person work together, each contributing something the other lacks. Thus the phrase *hemispheric asymmetry* means having two halves that are *not* the same.

The left hemisphere seems to handle abstractions, concepts, and all forms of symbolism, including language. The right hemisphere seems to specialize in intuition and creativity—whatever cannot be verbalized.

Exponents of this new school of thinking point out that we have developed into a left-brain-dominated society. The dominant hemisphere controls the reverse side of the body. Thus most of us are right-handed and use our right foot to start walking or running. There are also the unfavorable connotations of the word *left*, going back to the origin of the word *sinister* from the Latin word for "left side." Also, *right* connotes "correct" or "true."

Betty Edwards, a California art teacher, has produced some extraordinary results after persuading beginning students that anyone can draw who can see. She has detailed these in a book called *Drawing on the Right Side of the Brain*. Edwards believes that those who say they have no artistic ability do so because they *see* with their left brains. They abstract from their familiar surroundings. Hence, if asked to draw a quick picture of a man driving a car, invariably they produce a stick figure. Is this *all* they can do? Edwards's answer is that stick figures are symbolic of human beings and therefore controlled by the left brain.

Visual artists also engage in selective *practical vision* when the need arises. They might even draw a stick figure of someone who seems visually uninteresting. But they will stop suddenly in the midst of a business transaction or a casual lunch with friends and engage in another kind of selective vision, one that is "impractical" or perhaps right-brained. It might be a stain on the waiter's jacket—the way the different colors flow into each other or the design they make against the white background. There is never any warning. Those of us who have artist friends will often find them sketching away furiously on a tablecloth or napkin, even as we are sharing an extremely personal confidence, hearing them occasionally mumble, "Is that a fact?"

Edwards refers to this sudden shift into the right brain as the "R-mode of consciousness." She has found systematic methods by which her students can block off the interference of the L-mode. Anyone, she contends, may alter the stimuli to which the left brain normally responds with its customary abstraction. For example, if we wish to reproduce an object in a magazine ad—say, a bottle of cleaning fluid—we can turn the ad upside down and draw exactly what we see. The new stimulus will be strange and unfamiliar, forcing us to see rather than to abstract. If we cannot readily identify the stimulus, we must reproduce it faithfully, not symbolically. Symbolic vision involves the exclusion of details, a cumulative process that separates us further and further from reality the older we become.

Another trick is to draw negative space, that is, the space surrounding an object. If we are asked to draw the bottle of cleaning fluid, our first impulse, after the panic subsides, is to concentrate on the bottle itself, which we might call positive space—space with something in it. But our left brain quickly loses interest in positive space unless what it contains is of immediate practical significance. Concentrating on negative space forces us, again, to respond to an unfamiliar stimulus.

Artists transferring to canvas what is directly before them—a person, a landscape, or an object—often squint toward their subjects, as though to isolate them from familiar surroundings or to turn them into unfamiliar stimuli. They are breaking up the dense reality the rest of us think we are seeing, but in reality are not.

Just as musicians must learn to like silence and solitude before they can appreciate musical sound, so too must aspiring visual artists take the time to walk in silence and look at what is there to be seen, without left-brain preconceptions—to look as though without prior knowledge of the subject or a prior commitment to accept, reject, or be indifferent. Those of us who are unable to walk as artists and see as artists receive an unexpected gift: the works themselves, which present to us a world that may be at once familiar and strange, or one that looks not at all like the reality we stopped seeing years ago.

What is ironic is our frequent rejection of art on the grounds that we can't tell what we are looking at. Would it make any difference if we could?

*Now open your eyes and focus on whatever you observed before—that plant or leaf or dandelion. Look it in the eye, until you feel it looking back at you. Feel that you are alone with it on Earth! That it is the most important thing in the universe, that it contains all the riddles of life and death. It does! You are no longer looking, you are seeing.*

*Frederick Franck*

| *Left Brain* | *Right Brain* |
| --- | --- |
| Logic | Intuition |
| Speech | Nonverbalism |
| Mathematics | Music |
| Reading | Experience |
| Concern for time | Independence of time |
| Stress on individualism | Empathy with others |

## The Urge to Imitate

Visual artists are always seeing. Sometimes they are preoccupied and don't realize they are seeing. Sometimes they *will* exchange confidences with you, holding onto everything you say, making intense eye contact so that, for all you know, you and you alone are all that matters at that moment in time. Out of the corner of their eye, however, they are unconsciously watching that profusion of color in the tie that man is wearing. The mind of the artist is a storehouse of images, colors, shapes, and lines.

Some of us who are not visual artists may nonetheless possess the skill of seeing as artists do—to a degree at least. Who has not been walking with friends and, in the midst of a stimulating argument, suddenly shushed everyone so they could catch the last streaks of a sunset? Then the walk and the argument continue as though they had never been interrupted. The memory of the argument is still vivid the next day. The auburn and gray ribbons that floated silently across the horizon are forgotten. But not for the artist, who may one day paint that scene exactly as remembered, or months or years later suddenly produce an inviting canvas with auburn and gray clouds peeking over a tent in the woods recalled from another experience of seeing.

Most of us see, at the most, briefly, and let it go at that. Visual artists have the need to do more than just see. They have to imitate what they see or have seen, either directly or broken into pieces of experience and reconstructed on canvas or in plaster or metal or wood.

Everyone has some desire to imitate what others say or do, or how they look. Someone describing a visit to the chimpanzee area of the zoo is likely to do an exaggerated imitation of a chimp as opposed to giving a purely verbal account of the event. Little children imitate their parents by dressing up in their clothes, repeating what they say to each other, and playing house. Long ago Aristotle said that "the instinct of imitation is implanted" in us from childhood. He used this premise to explain the phenomenon of drama, which the Greeks invented.

Greek actors did not imitate life directly. They wore masks and stilts so that they could be seen in large outdoor amphitheaters with twenty thousand people watching. They chanted poetic lines and danced, even as actors in today's musical theater interrupt the action to sing or dance. Nonetheless, this is imitation in the same way that visual artists are imitating life when they place colors and geometric shapes on a canvas.

In movies and theater today we are accustomed to acting that is so realistic we sometimes forget we are not watching reality but the imitation of it. Some paintings look as "real" as photographs, while much photography is made to look like painting. Some photographers have developed techniques of so altering a negative in the development process that nobody would guess the final product began in a camera.

Artists imitate what they see, but often their field of vision is inside their minds. The romantic poet Samuel Taylor Coleridge (1772-1834) wrote a great deal about imagination, something everyone experienced but no one could explain. The artist in particular, he believed, lived in two worlds and often could not tell them apart.

*O pure of heart!    thou need'st not ask of me*
*What this strong music in the soul may be!*

*What, and wherein it doth exist,*
*This light, this glory, this fair luminous mist,*
*This beautiful and beauty-making power.*[1]

We doubt you have ever seen a child who did not possess imagination in abundance. Children vividly describe encounters with strange visitors. They carry on long conversations with playmates their parents cannot see. In the process of acculturation, by which we learn to conform to the rules and regulations of family, school, business, and law, we gradually forget the lost world of childhood. Artists, however, do not; often they run afoul of the "adult" world as much as children do. Often those who have forgotten how to see and how to imitate will tell artists just what art is supposed to be.

Michelangelo (1475 - 1564), whose surname was Buonarroti but who has achieved the rare distinction of being remembered by his first name only, nonetheless struggled hard to achieve lasting fame on his own terms. He painted and sculpted the human body in the full glory of its nakedness, much to the displeasure of church authorities. Hired by Pope Julius II to carve the statues for the latter's tomb, he was continually told that his work was not adequate, that it did not suit the Pope's needs. Whether he could have met those needs had he chosen or knew no other way to be a sculptor than his own, we cannot know for sure. The project, however, was never completed. Michelangelo had a way of not finishing work that was not exactly what he wanted to do.

## Styles of Visual Art

Take someone with no prior history of museum-going to the opening of a new show at a small gallery, one very much into the latest trends in the art world, and you are likely to be bombarded with questions like "What is that supposed to be?" or "What am I supposed to be getting out of this?" If, however, you take the same person to a traveling exhibition of recognized masterworks by seventeenth-century Dutch landscape painters, you may notice a very different reaction. There will be interest or boredom, but *there will probably not be confusion*.

Without, perhaps, using the term *imitation*, the casual art viewer knows all about it, and expects imitation in art to be similar to the performance of a professional impersonator, who must sound exactly like the subject. A landscape recognized because the real place has been visited is likely to win instant approval.

As we shall see, there was a period in time when the precise transference of a scene was all the rage in the art world, and painters were judged according to their accuracy. Art historians, critics, and art lovers understand that realism is a *style*, not a requirement, of art. It was highly appropriate in the seventeenth and eighteenth centuries, but it is far less so at the present time. Art students will often be found sitting about the campus, sketch pads in hand, learning how to draw a close approximation of a tree or a building. It is understood, however, that such exercises do not represent the totality of their responsibility to visual art. Instructors know that, as they mature, the students will develop their own styles. They will be judged not as their trees or buildings were graded, but on the freshness of their vision: the vitality of color, the dynamic energy of line, the esthetic appeal of total form, which marks a new visual event, not the repetition of what others have done before.

In the case of style, as with art as a whole, exact definition is elusive. But

*Often those who have forgotten how to see and how to imitate will tell artists just what art is supposed to be.*

when Georgia O'Keeffe says, "Now if you ask me what we're trying to do that's a different thing," she is really talking about her style. The style of O'Keeffe, so readily identifiable, is what she is doing on the canvas (see Plate 3, following page 72).

O'Keeffe loved three things about the visual world above all others: its colors, shapes, and textures. When she first arrived from her home in Sun Prairie, Wisconsin, to study at the famous Art Institute of Chicago, she was a shy teenager, no doubt awed by the big city and its cosmopolitan galleries. This was in 1905, at the start of this century, when, as usually accompanies the dawning of a new period of time, artists of all disciplines became eager to break away from the past and experiment with new styles and techniques. O'Keeffe was bombarded with exciting ideas about what constitutes art and what an artist should be doing.

What came with her, tucked away in her unconscious, was her love for simple shapes and extremely bright colors.

> . . . she recalls seeing light on a red, white, and black patterned quilt before she could walk, and, as a toddler, the soft, smooth shapes made by buggy wheels in the dust—they looked good enough to eat![2]

When she was 20, O'Keeffe moved to New York and there came in contact with the most fashionable artists of the day, many of them exhibited in the studio of photographer Alfred Stieglitz, the man she was eventually to marry. But Stieglitz and his sophisticated circle had less influence on the maturing young girl than did a teacher named Arthur Dow, who was himself under the strong influence of Oriental art.

In the principles of Oriental art O'Keeffe found a style she could immediately understand, respond to, and imitate; it loved color also, and bold, simplified shapes, often imitated on canvas in a few masterly brush strokes. Later, when her esthetic and emotional differences with Stieglitz made her marriage seem less idyllic than it had once been, O'Keeffe left New York, which had never been her artistic home, and moved to the Southwest. In the undulating hills, the orange, craggy rocks, the snow-tipped mountains, and the exotic flowers, she found the constant visual stimulation she had been denied in drab (by comparison) New York. Her most famous works date from after this move, as she developed one of the most famous art styles of this century: flowers bursting from their stems, mountains, canyons, the infinite sky with its continually changing colors, the bleached skulls of dead animals—all transferred to canvases that were first painted stark white so that the electric colors and the proud shapes would stand out in sharp relief. Anyone who has traveled through the Southwest can tell from a simple glance at an O'Keeffe work what imitation means, and what style is. *It is the unique manner in which an artist shows us how he or she sees the world. It is the unique manner in which an artist shows what he or she loves to see.*

Critics and historians of art do us a service by carefully studying an artist's style and pointing out to us what we should be looking for. Most of the time artists themselves would be at a loss to tell you what and how to see. They know they *must* do whatever it is they do. An art critic looks at an artist's work the way the artist looks at the world: seeing what many of us would otherwise miss. The art historian's job is to show us how styles, though unique to each artist, often gravitate toward each other in particular times and places, creating schools and movements. We have the same phenomenon in music. Certain patterns of sound, certain kinds of harmonies, and certain ways instruments are used tend to be—as we look

*Condemning an artist's style is something akin to defaming a person's character or personality.*

*I am the most curious of all to see what will be the next thing that I will do.*

*Jacques Lipchitz*

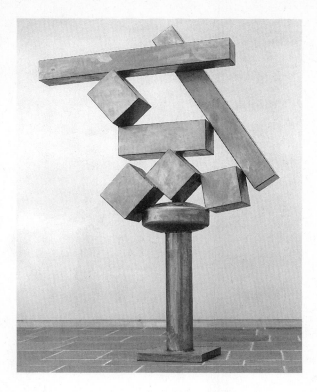

back—characteristic of particular times and places. No composer today can sound like Mozart, nor will the work of any visual artist look like that of van Gogh. If such unlikely similarities ever occurred, critics would immediately advise the upstart to find a new style.

None of what we have said means that artists are always happy about the stylistic demands placed on their work. Often a distinct conflict arises when an artist says, "This is what I do in art," and the art world replies, "Find another way to show what you are seeing." Condemning an artist's style is something akin to defaming a person's character or personality. But "Don't use such language" or "Don't be gay" or "Don't wear your hair so long" are not uncommon ways the world has of criticizing an individual's style of existing.

O'Keeffe did not win immediate acceptance, especially after her departure from New York. Nonconformists seldom do. Not that O'Keeffe appears to have made an aggressive effort to be a nonconformist. She seems to have cared more about preserving the things she saw and the way she saw them than she did about rave reviews or financial gain. Such steadfast commitment to one's own style of being often results (if one happens to be an artist) in important changes, new directions, or expanded definitions of art. A place was finally made for O'Keeffe in art history.

## Classicism

The terms *classical* and *classic* can be confusing to the student of the humanities. A *classic* is usually a work of literature or a drama or a popular song that continues to be read, performed, or sung long after its first appearance. It is not connected to

*Poseidon of Artemision:* Classical *thus denotes strength and durability. (National Museum of Athens. Bildarchiv Foto Marburg/Art Resource)*

any particular period of time. *Classical*, on the other hand, denotes both a period and a definite set of characteristics. In visual art it is a reference to the sculpture and architecture, primarily, of the so-called Golden Age of Athenian civilization: the fifth century B.C.

One of the first things that come to mind when we think of classical art is that it lacks color, because indeed so much of it was involved with stone: statues, buildings, and bas-reliefs (scenes and figures carved on the outside of temples and public edifices). *Classical* thus denotes strength and durability. Visit Athens today or the Elgin Marbles in the British Museum, and you will find that the long-ago past still comes to life in stone.

The purpose behind classical art was threefold. First, it was intended to beautify the city of Athens, which under the apparently inspiring leadership of Pericles developed the very *idea* of what a city was all about: a place in which enlightened human beings could enjoy their existence, surrounded by beautiful things. Second, it was meant to embody and thus keep alive Greek religion and mythology, because through them the Athenians could trace their ancestry back to the gods themselves. Third, it imparted a feeling of *cultural immortality*. How, the Athenian citizen may have asked, can such a place, carved as it is out of stone, be anything *but* immortal? Classical art thus has political ramifications as well. If Athens exists forever, so too will its significance to the unenlightened world.

The characteristics of classical art grow out of its purposes. To begin with, *it is nonemotional*. Artists who could do sculptures or bas-reliefs were probably regarded as expert artisans—well paid and respected, surely, but without allowances being made for their temperament and their need to serve their own vision.

Classical artists clearly worked for the good of the city, not their own expressive needs. They owed whatever talent they possessed to the common cause, to the beautification of the surroundings in much the same way that expert gardeners are hired today to serve not their own, perhaps offbeat, notions of landscaping but the esthetic needs of those who pay them. The sculptor's reputation as an artisan, not an artist, lasted for a long time. As late as the sixteenth century Leonardo da Vinci would reject the free offer of a large block of Carrara marble on the grounds that he was an artist, not a sculptor, suggesting that it be given instead to that eager worker Michelangelo. The latter, noting the marble was flawed, took it anyway and carved the *David*.

There are many classical elements in Michelangelo's work. His figures, except for the female nudes created for the Pope's tomb, are idealized, perfect—that is, harmonious—in shape and proportion. But he added something else that we seldom find in classical art: passion.

Emotion finds its way into Athenian art in the century following the Golden Age. Figures and scenes were depicted in a more realistic fashion, especially in moments of sensuality and in the agony of death throes. The Romans, who were not very original when it came to art, imitated the style of the classical period but were also heavily influenced by the realism of later centuries. The *Laocoön* is a Greek sculpture of the first century B.C., depicting in graphic detail the anguish of a father and his two sons as they are being strangled by sea serpents. The figures, you will note, are not idealized or shown in harmonious proportions.

Pure classical art can be called *geometric*, reflecting the classical belief that behind the visible world of the senses there lay a perfectly ordered universe comprehensible only to the intellect. Mathematical relationships were understood to be symbols of this ideal world. The geometric harmony of Athenian buildings and statues was meant to bring the ideal into the everyday life of the inhabitants.

*Classical artists worked for the good of the city, not their own expressive needs.*

*Laocoön. (Vatican Museum. Lauros-Giraudon/Art Resource)*

Of special significance is the widespread classical use of the *golden section*, or what Leonardo would call the *divine proportion*. The great fifth-century mathematician Euclid formulated the law of the golden section, which, simply stated, is this: the ratio between two sides of a plane figure must be such that the smaller segment is to the larger what the larger is to the sum of both. The numerical value of the ratio is approximately 1 to 1.68. The most popular geometric figure embodying Euclid's law is the rectangle, known, as we should expect, as the golden rectangle. If the width is 1, the length must be 1.68, and the length by itself will have the stated relationship to the sum of the width and the length.

Euclid's law was widely known in his time, and many found themselves looking for examples in nature, architecture, and mathematics. One belief, apparently borne out in actual experiments, was that if asked to divide a stick at the most esthetically pleasing point, people invariably marked the division that split the stick into two segments that illustrated the principle. (You might wish to see whether the experiment still works.) Recent blueprints of the probable floor of the Parthenon, constructed two centuries before Euclid, indicate that the architects had incorporated the golden section into their design, though they probably did not know it.

The golden section is also found throughout Roman ruins, in medieval cathedrals, on the pages of illuminated manuscripts from the Middle Ages, and almost everywhere in Renaissance art and architecture. Its appeal has never been fully explained, only confirmed, but the golden section remains a significant example of the esthetic pleasure that is universally derived from the classical style.

Finally, classicism rests on the assumption that *form is meaning*. The gods

*Euclid discovered the ratio, but whoever designed the Parthenon 200 years earlier seems to have known about it too.*

*A page from* The Book of Kells, *a medieval manuscript showing the pervasive use of the golden section. (Trinity College, Dublin. The Green Studio, Ltd.)*

and goddesses and mythological scenes depicted in these works were probably less important—to the Athenians—than the esthetic enjoyment they derived from the relationships among the parts.

Classical art, not having been born out of emotional upheaval, cannot be expected to create such a response in the viewer. This is in sharp contrast to the erotic art found in the Orient, which was intended to arouse definite feelings of sensuality in the viewer. We learn a valuable lesson here: esthetic pleasure has one universal constant—its value to us for its own sake. But it has various guises. Sometimes, as with classicism, it is smooth and serene. At other times, as with much contemporary art and music, it is filled with strong emotion. In other words, esthetic experience is not necessarily accompanied by sensations of tranquillity or of excitement. Look for a while at the photograph of Michelangelo's *David* (Chapter 1, page 16), a very early work of the artist that shows considerable classical influence and less of the throbbing emotion the sculptor was eventually to capture in marble. Though David is about to slay the giant Goliath, his face displays a definite sense of repose. Now look at the photograph of an earlier *David* by the sculptor Donatello (1386-1466) (in Chapter 1, page 18). This David has a sensuality about him that was very much in keeping with the emerging Renaissance. Michelangelo, sculpting his *David* a century later, was still looking back to the geometric calm of the classical past.

## Realism

The term *realistic* is widely and liberally used to describe styles not only of visual art but of acting, writing, and even thinking. We need not dwell on the probability that the meaning is hardly the same in all disciplines. Nor would critics specializing in the same discipline necessarily apply the label to the same work and for the same reasons.

To simplify what could be an endlessly complex matter, we will use the term, as it relates to visual art, to mean an artist's intent to imitate what is being seen or remembered or imagined so as to create within a viewer the illusion of a real person or event. Realism is a style of art using whatever techniques are available for bringing about accuracy of vision and replication of it on canvas or whatever medium the artist employs. If the intent of the artist is to create the illusion of reality, then the viewer, looking at the work, has every right to expect the illusion to be maintained.

On the other hand, the viewer may be wrongly assuming an intent to be realistic. Look at *The Actor* (Plate 4 following page 72) by Pablo Picasso (1881-1973), considered by many critics to be the premier artistic genius of the entire twentieth century. No viewer would have much trouble assuming the artist wanted us to recognize the figure as that of a human being. Furthermore, if one knew the title of the painting, one would nod and say, "Yes. I can see that he's an actor. The elaborate hand gesture and the hip stance are appropriate ways of depicting an actor." But if the viewer's expectations were fixed on realism, how to explain the dominant use of the rose color? Or the fact that the physical proportions of the figure are neither geometrically perfect, as in classicism, or faithful to the truth of human appearances? And what are the two mysterious hands protruding from behind the fragment of a set?

Picasso's intent obviously cannot be realism, and the artist cannot be held accountable for "inaccuracy." Doing our research, we discover that *The Actor* was completed over a two-year period in 1904-1905, during which time the artist seemed to be enamored of the rose color, which is so evident in his works of this time that the early years of the century have come to be called his "rose period." Regardless of how one actually feels about this painting, rejection on the grounds that "people don't look like that" is not justified.

The drawing below is a reproduction of a drawing found on the wall of the cave at Altamira, Spain. The dominant figure is that of a female bison, while the sketched head in the background is presumed to be that of a black bull. The intent of the cave artist is clear enough: to imitate the appearance of the animals. One theory is that Paleolithic artists drew pictures of animals whose meat was central to their diet. Another is that early people believed they would gain control of the hunt by having their artists draw the animals that were to be killed. In any event, we have to consider cave drawings as attempts at realism and indeed must accept them as realistic within the limits of the techniques and tools available.

During the Middle Ages visual art was almost exclusively religious in nature. The intent of artists was to imitate what they imagined heaven, the Holy Family, angels, and saints to look like. If you will scrutinize the photo of a twelfth-century painting of the Madonna on page 51, you will note that the Madonna and Child are flat, two-dimensional figures who bear no resemblance to real human beings. Yes, you may well ask, but have we not just said that the artist wanted to show heavenly beings? Indeed that was the intent, but we can deduce from early Renaissance religious paintings, in which figures are three-dimensional and do resemble human beings, that artists had to imagine heaven from what they knew of earth. The point we are making is this: medieval artists were attempting realism in the human face and form but lacked the technique to achieve it.

*We have to accept cave drawings as realistic within the limits of the techniques and tools available.*

*A cave drawing from Altamira, Spain. (Courtesy Department Library Services, American Museum of National History)*

*A twelfth-century Madonna and Child: Artists imitating what they imagined the Holy Family to look like. (Alinari/Art Resource)*

Now look at the *Alba Madonna* of Raphael (1483-1520), a contemporary of both Leonardo and Michelangelo who painted the work in 1510. Though the face of the child is a little more mature and knowing than is appropriate for his age, many critics have argued that the discrepancy arises not from a lack of technique but from the artist's intent to show the infant Christ as already having surpassed other children in wisdom and maturity. The face of the other child is clearly more realistic. In any case, Raphael painted at a time when the technique of perspective had already been invented, allowing artists to create the illusion of three-dimensionality on a two-dimensional plane.

Perspective in art means that figures are accurately sized relative to each other and to a background in order to come closer to an exact imitation of how the eye sees. The example we are always given is that of parallel railroad tracks, which remain straight in reality but which, to a given observer standing in one spot, will appear to converge; thus they are always painted as convergent lines. If painted otherwise, the artist would have to lose the right to call his or her work realistic. The study of optics becomes of crucial importance in the development of realism as a style; from it artists learned to draw figures in the background as smaller than those in the foreground, though in real life they might be the same

*Raphael,* The Alba Madonna *(1510). (Courtesy of the National Gallery of Art, Andrew W. Mellon Collection)*

height. Plate 5 (following page 72) shows *Meeting at the Golden Gate* by Giotto di Bondone (1266-1337), a thirteenth-century Florentine painter generally credited with having invented the technique of perspective.

By almost universal critical consensus the quintessential Renaissance painting is Leonardo's *The Last Supper* (Plate 6, following page 72), a mural for which the artist was commissioned in 1495 by the church of Santa Maria del Grazie in Milan. It occupies the entire wall of the refectory, and, though the paint is fading and the plaster cracked, visitors continue to be astonished when they enter the refectory today and experience the illusion that the room extends into the painting and continues on to the wall of the painted room in which Christ and the disciples are having their last supper together.

Surely the work is a triumph of perspective, but this is only one of the painting's extraordinary features. Leonardo was also a pioneer in the use of *chiaroscuro*, a technique of representing the contrast or interplay between light and shadow. Chiaroscuro, especially as further refined by Rembrandt in the seventeenth century, revolutionized the art of realistic painting, because it enabled artists to imitate the subtle (and often unnoticed) ways in which the real world strikes the eye. Look at Plate 6 and you will notice that the figures have blurred edges. They do not stand out one from the other or each from the background in bold outline. We do not see such bold outlines, and Leonardo knew it.

But such new techniques enabled artists to do more than give the illusion of a real event. Chiaroscuro in particular is a powerful technique by which artists can show us what is happening "beneath the surface"—something akin to the technique actors use to suggest what we call the "subtext," or what is going on inside the minds of the characters.

The fame of *The Last Supper*, however, probably rests upon the intense drama of the scene and the haunting beauty of the Christ figure in the middle. Advanced courses in play directing still require students to analyze the way Leonardo places his figures so that, while we see each of them in detail (except for Judas, the betrayer, who is wrapped in shadows), we cannot help but fix our vision on Christ. No matter how hard we try to concentrate on the disciples on either side, our eyes inevitably return to the place Leonardo wants them to be.

As for Christ, can we call the portrait realistic? In one sense, yes. We see before us a human being, recognizable in his inward sorrow, though the painting has faded to such a degree that one shudders to think the time may come when little of the figure will be visible.

In another sense it is not realistic, but not because Leonardo did not know how to imitate the human form accurately. In order to represent Christ as both human and divine, without resorting to the two-dimensional medieval halo that generally looks as if it were glued to the top of the head, Leonardo had to infuse this human being with divine properties. How does he do this? We are not quite sure, and there is always the possibility that we see divinity because we expect to find it. In any case, who could *not* find it? Notice the arms resting on the table in a gesture of peace and resignation, in sharp contrast to the anxiety-filled hand gestures of the others. Notice the anguish on the faces of the disciples, in sharp contrast to the calm, stoic expression of Christ. The hour of betrayal is near, and so is the inescapable agony of death on the cross. If you look as closely as possible at the face, you cannot fail to see the mysterious complexity of divine emotion: resignation, sorrow, forgiveness. No artist can imitate divine emotion from a real-life model. Leonardo goes beyond realism.

And so he does in his other masterpiece, the *Mona Lisa* of 1503-1505, which must rank as the portrait of portraits. Surely none has elicited as much controversy, mainly centering on that mysterious smile. One reason art critics have written volumes on the subject is that Renaissance realism tends to be *heightened* realism, *The Last Supper* being a colossal example, as is the *David* of Michelangelo, which looks like a real person but is at the same time idealized. One does not find *anyone* smiling in Renaissance portraits, because the intent of the artist is supposed to be the imitation of a real person idealized in the classical mode. (Even today don't we try to look our best when we gather together in the photographer's studio for the family portrait, and don't we often blame the photographer when Cousin Joe comes out looking 20 years older?)

There must have been something about Mona Lisa Giaconda, the wife of a Florentine merchant, which intrigued Leonardo—something about the personality of the woman that made the artist, consciously or otherwise, put more on the canvas than geometric perfection. One critic has suggested that we look at the painting by first covering the left side of the face, then the right. Presumably we see two different personalities: the one, that of a warm, sensuous woman; the other, that of an unemotional aristocrat. Another has said that Leonardo in this work has revealed the ambiguity of all faces. Yet another has attributed the complexity of the expression to the artist's incredible success in combining two styles, classicism and realism, as though the intent to idealize holds in check the intent to expose the woman's inner self. What we see, therefore, is psychological truth attempting to free itself from classical rigidity.

*The mysterious smile on Mona Lisa's face is unique for the Renaissance. One does not find* anyone *smiling in Renaissance portraits.*

*Leonardo da Vinci,* Mona Lisa: *Psychological truth attempting to free itself from classical rigidity. (The Louvre. Alinari/Art Resource)*

## *Terribilitá*: The Resistance of the Medium

What is true of Leonardo in *The Last Supper* and the *Mona Lisa* is very much the key to a full understanding of the genius of Michelangelo. We have already seen that the *David* combines both intense realism and classical perfection, but in this case we can say the classicism "wins out." David's passion for the task he is about to undertake is very much subdued by the classical sense of serenity.

What Shakespeare is to the theater and Beethoven is to music, Michelangelo is to the art of sculpture. While realism is indeed possible in this challenging form, the medium itself—stone, marble, iron, copper—makes doubly difficult an artist's intent to imitate minute details. How much easier to stay with classical idealism and be general rather than specific, serene rather than passionate.

Indeed the work of the youthful Michelangelo is classical, for at a very young age he was taken in as a sculptor's apprentice and trained to make religious statues. In his early twenties he was offered the famous block of Carrara marble we have already mentioned. Knowing that it was flawed, that Leonardo had somewhat arrogantly turned it down, and that it was 17 feet long, the artist was impassioned to create the most monumental piece of sculpture the world had ever seen. Stories of the four days it took to move the giant, as it was called, through the streets of Florence, lined with unbelieving citizens, are now legendary.

Even earlier, between 1498 and 1500, Michelangelo had done a *Pietá*, depicting the dead Christ lying across the lap of a grieving Mary. The folds of the dress alone would have been enough to challenge any sculptor even *without* having to worry about the emotions of the figure of Mary. As he grew older and gained in repute far and wide, he continued to challenge himself to do what had never been done either in marble or in paint. This passion gave to his work an unmatched intensity, but always held in check by the classicism in his training. This peculiar blend, found in his mature works like the statue of *Moses*, the epic paintings on the ceiling of the Vatican's Sistine Chapel, and *The Last Judgment* (which covers the entire altar wall of the chapel), has been called by some critics *terribilitá*, an Italian term for which there is no precise English equivalent. A visit to the chapel reveals the meaning at once, however. The word describes passion that is somehow frozen by the medium, yet nonetheless is alive and throbbing. Since so much about Michelangelo's long life is known, it is clear that the passion sprang from the artist's inner turmoil as he strained to imitate a vision that was fully visible only to himself.

In the case of the Sistine ceiling, legend says there was much physical suffering as well. When Pope Julius asked Michelangelo to cover the huge expanse with a series of discrete paintings on religious themes that would present a unified effect, the artist accepted not despite but *because* of the near impossibility of the task. He would have to lie flat on a scaffold for hours at a time with paint dripping on his face. Nor was he working on canvas. The medium was fresco, watercolors and wet plaster that when dry combine with the paints to form a wholly new kind of material, one whose texture creates a vivid sense of immediacy. To create such an immediacy in so sublime a place—and to do it lying on his back, high in the air! Did ever an artist's medium resist so mightily?

The project took four years. Though millions of visitors have passed below it, gazing up in awe at the incredible number of human and divine figures dominated by the central piece, *The Creation of Adam*, one wonders whether Michelangelo himself ever experienced a true sense of profound satisfaction. Could *any* artist whose genius drives him to such a challenge? A modern novelist has given the following fictional account of the physical beating Michelangelo may have endured (though art historians tend not believe it). The artist worked with his legs

> drawn up tight against his belly for balance, his eyes a few inches from the ceiling, until the unpadded bones of his buttocks became so bruised and sore he could no longer endure the agony. Then he lay flat on his back, his knees in the air, doubled over as tightly as possible against his chest to steady his painting arm. Since he no longer bothered to shave, his beard became an excellent catchall for the constant drip of paint and water. No matter which way he leaned, crouched, lay or knelt, on his feet, knees or back, it was always in strain.[3]

Genius propels the artist into a struggle with the impossible. The struggle leads to suffering, which in turn flares into passion, which somehow—nobody knows how—becomes embedded in the paint, the plaster, the marble. This is *terribilitá*. It is a style, of course, but not one an artist may arbitrarily choose to work in. The genius and the unceasing drive must be there, the obsession that will not allow the artist to rest or indeed to enjoy life.

Michelangelo lived to be 89 and continued working almost to the moment of death. He had to. Looking back upon his body of work, he realized he had destroyed a goodly portion of it out of anger with himself for not being able to imitate the visions inside him. He had almost destroyed the *Pietá Rondanini*, an old

*. . . we must recognize the emergence of Michelangelo as one of the great events in the history of Western man.*

*Kenneth Clark*

man's version of the Holy Family's agony with an emphasis this time on the face of Christ, no longer the youthful, serene, almost feminine Christ of the earlier *Pietá*, but a man who has suffered greatly. The old Michelangelo understood suffering well.

In many of his letters and in his poetry the artist continually expressed the conviction that his work was not for the multitude, not for the critics, but for God only. There is little reason to doubt Michelangelo believed this implicitly, that he attempted to judge his work as though to determine its worthiness for God. One suspects the artist knew why his media resisted him so mightily. He was asking them to do tasks meant for an ultimate critical approval.

When the medium is so evidently unyielding—like the marble used to create the *David*—and when the artist's conquest of it is so clear, humanity takes another step forward. But, of course, much time has passed since the 17-foot block succumbed to a superior, a *human* force. Today's art world accepts many media that classical artists would not have recognized. At contemporary exhibits one finds butcher's wrapping paper, bits of broken glass, sand glued to canvas, plastic, tar, coat hangers, nails, tin cans, rusty used mufflers, and so on. Today's artists and sculptors are not trying to equal or improve on Michelangelo. They seek to leave their own signatures upon the world—in language they understand.

A critic recently commented that where anything is possible, nothing matters. Some would contend that when the range of media is extended to include everything, then the domain of art becomes weakened. Are we too permissive when we allow the artist to say, "Art is what the artist does"? Are we entitled to ask who decides who is an artist? Defining something has meant placing certain limits around it. Michelangelo is a supreme example of someone who worked within excruciating limits. Many believe the tension produced by the struggle between the artist's passion and the limits of the medium is indeed the true ingredient of *all* art.

*That in thy holy footsteps I
    may tread:
The fetters of my tongue do
    thou unwind,
That I may have the power
    to sing of thee,
And sound thy praises
    everlastingly.*

    *Michelangelo Buonarroti*

*Michelangelo,* The Creation of Adam: *Genius propels the artist into a struggle with the impossible. (Sistine Chapel. Alinari/Art Resource)*

What we must grasp essentially is that there exists an ancient rivalry between the artist and the medium. The medium does not surrender willingly to the hands of the artist. This much is true no matter what kind of art we're speaking of. The blank paper in the typewriter stares up at the novelist, daring her or him to find—somehow, somewhere—just the right words in just the right order. The sonnet's structure hangs there in the memory of the poet, daring him or her to fill it with new images and new sounds that seem miraculously to require just 14 lines. The legs of human beings were never meant to do what the ballet dancer commands them to do. Ivory keys coldly reflect overhead stage lights—so still, and offering no help to the pianist.

The paradox of art, however, is that the achievement often seems effortless. Olympic ice-dancing champions glide in perfect balance across the silver-blue ice—he lifting, she perfectly still and weightless. The dancer-swan extends from the fingertips of the prince and pirouettes faster and faster until she becomes a white blur, then stops instantly. Not a motion is wasted.

## Goya: The Limitations of Realism

In the seventeenth century the art of portrait painting reached sublime heights very close to the peaks achieved by Leonardo. The Dutch master Rembrandt (1606 - 1669) is famous for the physical as well as the psychological realism of his portraits, both of individuals, including himself at various stages of his life, and of groups. He found the inner beauty behind the careworn exterior of aged subjects, and he refined the technique of chiaroscuro to such an extent that it has become the single most identifying element in his work. To look at a Rembrandt painting is to see such a contrast between light and dark that we are tempted to believe the source of light must be external to the painting.

Other artists of the period grew marvelously adept at landscapes as well as portraits. Critics and art historians generally agree that Rembrandt and his seventeenth-century colleagues carried realism in visual art as far as it could go. With perspective, light, and color shading so mastered, we should expect new generations of artists to seek new kinds of imitation, perhaps to imitate what the mind (the right brain?) sees only in dreams and fantasies.

Dominant among the innovators was Spain's major artist of the late eighteenth century: Francisco Goya (1746 - 1828). His early work is characterized by realistic landscapes depicting the natural beauty of the Aragon countryside in which he was nurtured and portraits of astonishing vitality, with finely detailed, almost photographic likenesses of his subjects. Though Goya was little known when he came to Madrid, the cultural center of Spain, he soon grew in popularity among the aristocracy, largely because of his skill in portraiture. After a time the need of the artist to express his inner drives and emotions became paramount, and he risked fame and fortune to satisfy that need.

In Goya's time realistic painting was a profession, but it could turn into downright hackwork, luring many artists to the style because of the money that could be made. An artist had only to study the established techniques carefully, spend a few years in apprenticeship copying the style of a master, and then develop a sophisticated, professional approach of his own. Little of his own personality had to go into the work. After a while, professionalism in this sense failed to suffice for Goya. His eyes began to turn inward. There were many things about the society—especially the high society in which he walked with ease as "one of us"—

*Rembrandt,* Self-Portrait: *Physical as well as psychological realism. (Courtesy of the National Gallery of Art, Mellon Collection)*

that went against the grain of a young man who was, after all, a country boy at heart. He felt a burning need to paint not what his employers wanted him to see, but what he saw in society, what he saw in the faces of the rich and the arrogant. He needed to paint his feelings. Goya personalized the concept of the artist's style. In one sense Leonardo and Michelangelo had already done this, but their strong roots in classical idealism had kept their passions in check. Not so with Goya.

The artist within was essentially a cynic, and Goya could not keep cynicism out of his work. His "portrait" of royalty, *The Family of Charles IV*, completed in 1800, best illustrates Goya's mood at the time his motivation as an artist was beginning to change.

The family is shown standing in a gallery: the king, the queen, and the young aristocrats of varying ages and sizes. In Rembrandtian style, there is light coming into the gallery from some undefined source beyond the canvas. There is just enough light to illuminate the faces. Certainly they do not represent the idealization of royalty that artists were normally paid to create. Goya showed the family not at its best, but at its worst. The youngest children have bizarre, almost paranoiac expressions. Perhaps for the very first time an artist has captured the less-than-enviable lifestyle of children who are not so much spoiled and pampered as enslaved to certain behaviors. The queen seems insensitive to them, indeed to just about everything. She is posing foolishly, as though she were not very bright and has a naive conception of what regal bearing is all about. The king is equally silly-looking, and there is also a trace of sadness in his face, a sense of now-unremembered, occasional happy times in a youth he never really had. We know that the children will grow up and be very much like their father.

The fact that the royal family must have been pleased with the portrait—after all, they did accept it and did not throw the artist out of the palace—remains one of the ironies in art history. Were the king and queen so vain or so blind to reality that they never noticed Goya's insulting approach? If so, then the artist was probably right in his assessment of the court of Madrid. His style became even darker, more pessimistic.

The invasion of Spain by Napoleon during the first decade of the nineteenth century did not help Goya's disposition much. The ravages of war, the inhumanities human beings were capable of inflicting on each other, depressed him further. In two of his masterpieces, *The Second of May* and *The Third of May*, Goya dramatized the theme of war's cruelty. In the latter painting we see the execution of several Spaniards by Napoleon's firing squad. Realistic detail has been minimized. There is pure fear on the faces of the condemned men, and those who are about to fire the guns are lacking in any expression. Nothing in the painting detracts from the overwhelming presence of fear. It would be hard for many viewers to ascribe beauty to the work.

Because of Goya's originality, his innovative artistic techniques, and the total range of his work, his significance in the history of art is assured. However, his later paintings, especially *Saturn Devouring His Children* (see Plate 7, following page 72), seem unpleasant, if not hideous, to many viewers. They raise even now, as they surely did then, questions of the legitimacy of art that seems less than beautiful, that affects many viewers negatively, provoking feelings of outrage and horror.

Contemporary art that intentionally disturbs the viewer is so commonplace that many of Goya's descendants would consider us impertinent if not foolish to ask whether art always has to be beautiful. They would contend that art by virtue of its artistry *is* beautiful, no matter what its subject matter or technique; that it is a beautiful experience to observe the creative personality in the act of

*A modern perspective is that art by virtue of its activity is beautiful, no matter what the subject matter or technique.*

*Francisco Goya,* The Third of May, 1808: *Nothing in the painting detracts from the overwhelming presence of fear. (The Prado, Madrid)*

self-assertion. Above all, if art is conquering the medium, breaking through limitations, then what, one might further ask, is not beautiful about the astonishing feat of capturing on canvas those elusive passions that also define our humanness?

## Impressionism

Despite innovators like Goya and the romantic departures from realism that we see in the work of visionaries like William Blake and J. M. W. Turner (see Chapter 15), realistic landscapes and portraiture continued to be popular styles. The royal family of Spain may have been pleased with Goya's version of how they looked, but those who could afford it generally demanded a kind of flattering realism, and those who liked to decorate their homes with landscapes also tended to want paintings with readily identifiable subjects.

With the invention of the camera in the mid-nineteenth century, realistic painting became less fashionable and a good deal less profitable. A new style of art was needed, one that would do what photography could not. The new artists scorned realism in favor of art that offered a fresh new way of imitating the world.

*The invention of photography had much to do with turning artists away from realism. They sought to do what the camera could not.*

In France, Edouard Manet (1832-1883) provided a comprehensive rationale for the new style. A painting, he said, should not imitate the superficial appearances of things. Nor should it be valued for what it says about the subject. Instead, a painting should be valued totally for itself; it is an *event*: an experience of color, shapes, and lines. It bears some relationship to the familiar world; that is, the world acts as the starting point. The artist sees a family, for example, enjoying a picnic by a lake. He or she transfers the scene to canvas as a continuum of light in its various hues and shadings, shapes blending in with each other, brightness blending in with shadows.

This new style at last found a name when Claude Monet (1840-1926) exhibited his painting entitled *Impression: Sunrise* (see Plate 8, following page 72). The subjective visions that became the content for the *impressionists* affected the viewer with the emotion felt by the artist. Color burst upon canvas in a profusion never before known. Artists experimented feverishly with new combinations of colors and new brushstroke techniques. The race was on to see who could approximate most closely the subtleties of visual consciousness. The new challenge posed by the medium required the blending of innumerable colors and shadings into a unified emotional effect.

*Impressionism was one segment of a late-nineteenth-century revolution that emphasized subjectivity and sensuality in art, music, and literature.*

The latter half of the nineteenth century was dominated by similar revolutions in all of the French arts. The impressionism of Monet, Manet, Renoir, Degas, and Pissarro had a musical counterpart in the 12-tone scale, the indeterminant rhythms, and the unfamiliar harmonies of Claude Debussy; a literary counterpart appeared in the psychological prose-poetry of Marcel Proust, the sensuous, subjective novels of André Gide, and the haunting verse of Baudelaire, Mallarmé, and Rimbaud, who found words for inner states never acknowledged before, let alone articulated. This emphasis on subjectivity seemed to some critics an overindulgence in the self and a too-easy surrender to sensuality as the dominant concern of personal experience. Others hailed it as a breakthrough, as a freeing of the artist from the rigid formalism of artistic media. Painting need not tell a realistic story; poetry could open new vistas to the imagination; music could introduce new and strange sounds; the novel could be something other than a narrative of cause and effect in the external world. Those who shook their heads and said that standards in the arts were disappearing often called the revolution "decadent."

*Mary Cassatt,* The Bath *(1891):
A vantage point above the scene
to disengage the viewer from the
normal way of looking. (Robert
A. Waller Fund. The Art Institute
of Chicago, All Rights Reserved)*

What *really* happened is that artists were imposing their will upon their medium and altering the medium; but, in so doing, they were setting up new barriers, new challenges for themselves. The foremost American impressionist was James McNeill Whistler (1834-1903), who painted the famous portrait of his mother in 1871. Though the work is universally admired for the subject matter, though reproductions have sold in the millions and are probably as omnipresent as "Home Sweet Home" embroidery samplers, most people are unaware that the painting's full title is *Arrangement in Black and Gray: The Artist's Mother.* Whistler used his mother as a subject—a woman in a particular setting, in a complex of color, shape, light, and shadow—to be experienced as a total event. The point is that the artist was not satisfied merely with doing justice to his mother's image, or even her personality, but, rather, sought to convey each and every segment of a certain moment in time, when a particular human being sat in a particular way, in a visual context that the artist captured.

Similarly, the work of another American, Mary Cassatt (1845-1926), illustrates the artist's concern for visual experience as an event of color and design rather than content. *The Bath* shows a woman bathing a young girl, but, though our natural inclination is to be charmed by a loving relationship between mother and child, love and tenderness are not the point here. We do not even know *who* the woman is. She could be the maid. Her identity does not matter. The impressionist wants to share with us visual events we probably miss in our daily experience. Cassatt even chooses a vantage point above the scene in order, perhaps, to disengage the viewer from the normal way of looking. From an elevated perspective, background and foreground attain an equality. The wall behind the woman and the child, the pitcher of water, the rug—each is as meaningful as the human figures. So are the stripes and the texture of the woman's outfit. The new artists thus liberated viewers from having to ask the traditional questions, like "Does she really look like that?" and "What is the artist trying to tell us about this person (or this place)?" The appropriate questions now became, "What happens on the canvas?" or better still, "What is the effect and how does the artist achieve it?"

Impressionism and related movements in the arts took hold so strongly on both sides of the Atlantic that, as we might expect, the altered medium soon became as authoritative as the traditions it replaced. Newer artists emerged who began to resist slavish imitation and go their own ways. The label *postimpressionism* has been coined by art historians as a convenient way of referring to the work of van Gogh and others, but we must remember that the label does not identify a specific group with common characteristics. The postimpressionists shared only the need to use their medium to define themselves. Of this group Vincent van Gogh (1853-1890) was surely the most original and the most intense.

Van Gogh remains the prototype of the artist who creates entirely for himself. His style was so strange in its time that the few critics who ever took notice of his work were generally baffled, having nothing with which to compare it. He lived most of his life in abject poverty, supported in part by his brother, Theo, who believed in van Gogh's genius and stood by him even when his work was denounced and ridiculed. Only one of the artist's paintings was ever sold during his lifetime. Tragically, he committed suicide before his fortieth birthday.

In fact, van Gogh is the prototype of the artist for whom art becomes the last outpost of being itself. Totally alienated in this world, totally misunderstood by almost everyone except his brother, rejected twice as a suitor (once with a vehement cry of "No, never, never!"), hovering much of the time on the thin border between functional rationality and insanity (eventually to cross the border, never to return), he survived as long as he did mainly because of his work. Small wonder that the viewer of his paintings becomes enveloped in a completely altered version of reality. What obligation did the artist feel toward an everyday world through which he passed as a stranger?

*Van Gogh's lines and bright colors virtually scream from the canvas. His art comes as close to sound as is possible in a silent medium.*

*Vincent van Gogh,* The Night Cafe *(1888): The viewer of van Gogh's paintings becomes enveloped in a completely altered version of reality. (Yale University Art Gallery, Bequest of Stephen Carlton Clark, B.A. 1903)*

In works such as *Sunflowers, Wheatfield with Crows,* and *Starry Night* (see Plate 9, following page 72), which have become priceless since van Gogh's death, the viewer witnesses a brushstroke method that has become utterly identified with its creator: a short, stabbing technique, as opposed to a flowing line, that makes the entire canvas appear to be throbbing with energy. His rational mind seldom under control, van Gogh abandoned himself to the sensuous impact of life's forms and colors, absorbing them fully and converting them into a heightened reality—an explosion of pure feeling transferred to color, shapes, and paint textures. The one critic who within van Gogh's lifetime found the work praiseworthy used a singularly appropriate term to describe it: insolent. Van Gogh's lines and bright colors virtually scream from the canvas. His art comes as close to sound as is possible in a silent medium.

*What obligation did van Gogh feel toward an everyday world through which he passed as a stranger?*

That van Gogh achieved no fame or recognition in his lifetime does not mean the artist deliberately withdrew into himself, deliberately flouted artistic tradition. Strange as his behavior may have been at times, he can also be described as an innocent. At an early stage of his development he remarked to his brother that he enjoyed making "childish drawings" to pass the time (and, one suspects, as a refuge from the world of social relationships in which he was ill at ease). The child in van Gogh never left him. What art historians now describe as a bold and revolutionary technique was presumably the only technique he knew. In lucid moments his innocence manifested itself in a wide-eyed confidence that someday his works would do very well in the marketplace.[4]

*. . . a short, stabbing technique, as opposed to a flowing line, that makes the entire canvas appear to be throbbing with energy.*

As we move into the current century, however, we find artists blatantly insisting on refashioning art to suit themselves, demanding that society follow *them*.

## Art as Alteration

The work of van Gogh and the impressionists, we can see at a glance, does not imitate reality as it is. Even the often intensely psychological self-portraits of Rembrandt and his fellow Dutch masters are impeccably accurate in the transference of minute details from the subject to the canvas. They acknowledge a responsibility to what we might term *the world as it is commonly perceived*, or literally, *the world of common sense*. For this reason we have placed them among the *realists* in the world of visual art. The impressionists did not transfer the minute details. Perhaps they did not even see them. They abstracted from a scene the components of the visual event that seemed important to them for whatever reason. Yet though their canvas transforms the world into a subjective experience of color and form, we have no trouble knowing it *is* the world with which we are familiar. We know the world on the canvas looks *different*, but it is still recognizable.

Much of the visual art produced throughout the twentieth century, however, must be taken not as the imitation of a visual event seen by an artist, but as an event in itself—something an artist has done (remember "Art is what the artist does"?); something that may resemble the world and the people we know, but not necessarily; or something that may embody the artist's feelings about life, art, love, politics, or injustice, but not necessarily. In fact, the only basis for saying yes or no to a great deal of modern art is that the viewer is affected in some way, that he or she recognizes that this event on the wall or over in that corner occupies space in a significant manner. (There are even artists and critics who will argue that the viewer's being affected in some way is really irrelevant. Art is something an artist does, and liking or disliking it is the viewer's problem, not the artist's.)

*The only basis for saying yes or no to a great deal of modern art is that the viewer is affected in some way or that this event on the wall or over in that corner occupies space in a significant manner.*

In this final section we are not proposing to argue the pros and cons of visual art that does not imitate so much as *add to* our surroundings. We wish only to identify it as a phenomenon with many supporters, a phenomenon that very often has undeniable impact and power, and should not be scorned or ignored until it has been experienced. Accepting the unfamiliar with an open mind is one of the fundamental lessons of the humanities.

*Accepting the unfamiliar with an open mind is one of the fundamental lessons of the humanities.*

Much modern art appalls those who insist upon defining art. Edward Kienholz (b. 1927) is an artist who has dazzled some and befuddled others. Here is one critic's description of *Still Live—1974*, one of his more controversial—what is the word?—achievements? audacities?

> Inside a barricaded space an armchair sits in front of "a black box mechanism containing a live cartridge and a random timer triggered to fire once within the next 100 years." After eight years, it still hasn't gone off. Viewers foolish enough to want to sit in this "hot seat" must sign a waiver. Kienholz told me, with some scorn and disbelief, that at the opening almost a dozen people did.[5]

What entitles *Still Live* to be considered art? When the live cartridge finally goes off and the work no longer justifies its name, will it still be art? An even more intense question: If someone were sitting in the hot seat when the cartridge fired and the mechanism became a death machine, would it still belong to the world of art? Or does it not belong to that world even now because of what it is? And finally: What *is* it?

*Kienholz's armchair and black box might well be beautiful to some. Others would argue that a work of art doesn't have to be beautiful.*

No doubt a great many people might dismiss the last question as irrelevant because *Still Live*, being a potential instrument of destruction, cannot be considered beautiful. But it may be risky anyway to insist upon beauty as the deciding characteristic a would-be work of art must possess. Philosophers and art critics alike have debated for centuries over the meaning of beauty, particularly over the crucial question of whether something *has* beauty in the same sense that a plant has flowers, or whether it is only *perceived* as having beauty. If the latter is the case, then no universal standards can exist to determine the beautiful, and Kienholz's armchair and black box might well be beautiful to some. Still others would argue that a work of art doesn't *have* to be beautiful, no matter how we define the word.

## Picasso

With Pablo Picasso (1881-1973) we have an artist whose life spanned a good portion of the entire twentieth century and whose bountiful innovations changed the nature of visual art for all time. He worked in so many styles in addition to the one for which he is most famous, cubism, that the doors to innumerable options are now open to those artists who have come after him. One might be able to present a course on modernism in visual art based exclusively on his work.

A professor of philosophy, on the first day of his course in "Contemporary Thought," asked class members to name any three figures who have had the greatest impact on the century. Various philosophers were named, no doubt because the responders believed they were on safe ground naming philosophers in a philosophy class. The professor then smiled and gave his own list: Freud, Einstein, and Picasso. Questions were raised about the third name.

The professor said that what great poets did for human language, great composers for sound, great scientists for the conquest of disease and the knowledge of our universe, Picasso did for the range of human visual experience. Picasso has given us totally new ways of seeing and, in capturing on canvas what he himself saw, has added new forms and colors to our human environment. Easily on a par with Leonardo and Michelangelo, Picasso was a genius of sublime proportions who has influenced not only the direction of art and sculpture, but architecture, drama, and literature as well. It is not too much to say that had Picasso never existed, the modern world would neither look nor "feel" quite as it does.

We have already said that imitation, the driving force behind all visual art, includes altering, but no amount of verbal explanation can help you fully comprehend what "altering" means in Picasso's work. One needs to experience as much Picasso as possible. If originals are not readily accessible, there are many, many art history books to look through as well as magnificent coffee-table volumes devoted exclusively to the artist.

Looking at a work typical of Picasso's cubist period, one is likely to see recognizable shapes, but only in the sense that we "recognize" stick figures as being intended to stand for human figures. A Picasso man or woman might have an angularly shaped head with one eye here, another there; a nose like an arc; or, as in his famous *Three Musicians* (1921), a mouth in the shape of an hourglass. When cubism burst upon the art scene in the early twentieth century, some critics and art lovers thought it was intended to be funny. What else could be the point of doing paintings and sculptures that were not totally abstract—that is, comprised of shapes, colors, and lines that looked like nothing but themselves—but, rather, were depictions of people and things that at the same time looked like no people or things ever seen before?

An important influence on the development of cubism may have been the explorations of optical science into the true nature of the eye and the way we see. It began to be understood that our *minds*, not our eyes, see things as whole and distinct entities. If vision alone could be separated from the entire complex of the experience we call seeing, if we could stop for a fleeting instant and catch just what the eyes are looking at, then the world would look something like the disembodied, often floating shapes that we find on the canvases of Picasso.

Picasso and fellow cubists discovered that we actually see objects as *events* extending over a given period of time, no matter how rapid. The eye, moreover, is in continual motion and observes a thing from continually shifting viewpoints. From where we sit or stand we *think* we are looking from one particular and fixed vantage point. Both realistic paintings and photographs foster the misconception that such a thing exists as a fixed observer with a stable field of vision. As one critic said:

> [The cubist] wished to present the total essential reality of forms in space, and since objects appear not only as they are seen from one viewpoint at one time, it became necessary to introduce multiple angles of vision and simultaneous presentation of discontinuous planes. This of course shatters the old continuity of composition imposed by the Renaissance single viewpoint.[6]

What the critic means by "simultaneous presentation of discontinuous planes" can

*It is not too much to say that had Picasso never existed, the modern world would neither look nor "feel" quite as it does.*

be easily understood from a careful study of *Guernica*, a mural painted in 1937 for the Spanish pavilion at the Paris World's Fair and now widely considered Picasso's masterpiece as well as one of the great art works of all time.

Picasso's *Guernica* presents the essence of one of the most inhumane events of this century: the German air force's so-called saturation bombing of Guernica, the cultural center of the Basque region in northern Spain and a stronghold of the Loyalist troops during the Spanish Civil War. The town was destroyed in a few minutes by one of the deadliest and most massive air strikes ever mustered by one nation against another, during which not only Loyalist soldiers but hundreds of civilian men, women, and children were massacred. Picasso, up to that time an artist with no political leanings, wanted the mural, for which he had been commissioned, to make a universal statement about the true horror of war. Without cubism, a style that can present simultaneously things that happen over a period of time, how could he have shown the world the total scene of devastation? What would a realist have done facing such a challenge?

In *Guernica* we can feel the tremendous impact that Picasso has had not only upon art but upon our entire civilization. In addition to giving us new viewing experiences, he has made events accessible to the imagination that might otherwise have remained abstract to anyone not at the scene to experience them as they occurred. Advanced motion picture technology has made possible a work such as Oliver Stone's *Platoon* (1986), the heightened realism of which brings viewers into direct confrontation with modern infantry war as it actually is. But viewers always have the recourse with movie realism to divorce themselves from what they are seeing, or, we might say, to recognize that the blood and gore they are witnessing in such massive amounts is not after all *really* real. The style of *Guernica*, as well as the eloquent silence that is art, makes us less likely to turn away from what it shows. That is, by not pretending to photographic realism, it achieves truth rather than reality, as reality is normally understood to be. Picasso's enduring greatness lies in the fact that he found a new pathway to truth, even as Freud was doing with the inner world and Einstein was doing with the physical universe.

*By not pretending to photographic realism,* Guernica *achieves truth rather than reality.*

## The Abstract and the Surreal

The impressionists transferred into their work their subjective way of seeing the world along with the emotions inspired by their inner experiences. Much of Picasso's work appears to be experimentation with innovation for the sheer joy of the creative process. At the same time, no one can deny the emotional impact of his masterpiece, *Guernica*; while we can never tell whether the artist has felt the same emotion we derive from viewing the work, Picasso must have been well aware that the mural would never be looked at for design and composition alone. In the twentieth-century revolution in the visual arts we find another rationale for doing art: *a work of art exists to add beauty to the world, and visual beauty arises from visual form, not emotion.*

We have become so accustomed to emotional responses when we see a play or movie, read a novel, and listen to music that we have difficulty conceiving of an experience in art that does not ask us to feel anything. You no doubt understood the concept of classicism, but our average encounter with the arts is likely to be filled with emotion, not the classical ideal of perfection. Reports of "My

*Pablo Picasso,* Guernica *(1937): Without cubism, how could Picasso have shown the world the total scene of devastation? (The Prado, Madrid)*

handkerchief was soaked when I left the theater" are usually taken as signs of approval.

In the worlds of both visual art and concert music, however, there are strong proponents of *un*emotionalism: people who profoundly believe that excellence in art and music is defined according to the artist's mastery of the rules governing the medium, that both art and music are media of presentation, not of expression. They maintain that emotion is in the heart of the beholder, but the artist is in no way accountable if the experience he or she has created leaves the viewer or listener cold.

Much contemporary visual art is called *abstract* for the obvious reason that the emphasis on design, composition, and color has led artists away from the need either to represent the real world accurately or to express their feelings on canvas. That an emotional significance may be there for a viewer anyway is not the same as *requiring* it to be there.

Abstractionism in art, according to its supporters, also resists interpretation. Once an interpretation is made, once the painting or sculpture appears to justify our sense that meaning is present, then, they fear, we will continue to establish meaning as a principal criterion by which a work of art is judged.

At an exhibition of works by Wassily Kandinsky (1866 - 1944), a young woman was overheard asking what a certain painting was "supposed to be." After studying the work intently for several minutes, the woman's friend suddenly cried, "Why, it's two electric light bulbs!" The previously baffled viewer smiled, nodded, and voiced high-level approval of the painting. For many, the ability to recognize *anything* from the familiar world constitutes an interpretation. This critical standard is almost universal: "It's good if you know what it is and bad if you don't."

Having abandoned the study of law for that of art, the young Kandinsky came under the heavy influence of van Gogh and his French compatriot Paul Gauguin, who had made his reputation from painting the lush vegetation and exotic

*For many modern artists, neither emotion nor meaning is a necessary ingredient of their work.*

*Wassily Kandinsky,* Black Lines *(1913): Kandinsky distinguished between beauty and any other kind of significance a painting might have. (Guggenheim Museum, New York. Gift of Solomon R. Guggenheim. Photo: Robert E. Mates, copyright The Solomon R. Guggenheim Foundation)*

natives of Tahiti. But Gauguin (1848-1903) may have unknowingly taken some steps toward abstractionism in the sense that his so-called primitive style of painting was one that presented a few key shapes in bold outline while eliminating minute details. Though his scenes are recognizable as imitations of the real world, Gauguin's work has no ties with realism (see Plate 10, following page 72).

Like many other modern artists, Kandinsky distinguished between beauty and any other kind of significance a painting might have:

> He argued that in order to speak directly to the soul and avoid materialistic distractions, it was preferable to use an art based solely on the language of color. Free from references to a specific reality, color could become like music, beautiful for its interrelationships of tones and intensities.[7]

*The 1913 exhibition of new artists at the Sixty-ninth Regiment Armory in New York is still considered the most important single art show ever held in this country.*

The new abstract directions in visual art generally came from the leading art centers of Europe, especially Paris, the city to which young American art students were flocking in the early part of this century. But New York had its own agenda and timetable, its own burning need to be respected as a hub of modernism. In 1913 an exhibition of new works by European artists was mounted at the Sixty-ninth Regiment Armory, still considered the most important single art show ever held in this country, if not anywhere in the world. In addition to Kandinsky, many American viewers saw for the first time the work of van Gogh, Gauguin, and Picasso.

One cannot say that the new work was unanimously acclaimed and received with open arms. The pieces by Picasso and the other cubists were denounced, and the room in which they were displayed was nicknamed the Chamber of Horrors. But one work by far caused the biggest uproar and controversy, bringing instant fame to its creator. This was *Nude Descending a Staircase, No. 2* (see the frontispiece for this chapter), and the artist was Marcel Duchamp (1887-1968), who had developed an abstractionist style by which he moved from an actual model through successive stages of reduction until all that was left from reality was the sense of descending movement and the *hint* of a human figure. Duchamp, in other words, abstracted from a real scene only those elements that interested him as an artist, excluding everything else because he had signed away his responsibility—and thus his obligation—to make his work resemble something a viewer could instantly recognize.

Of course, you may well argue, we *can* recognize what is going on in the painting once we know its title. But titles like *Untitled* and *Study* are not uncommon in modern art, as if artists not only care very little about what we recognize but actually take precautions against having interpretation interfere with the act of what we may call "pure viewing." The Dutch artist Piet Mondrian (1872-1944) went further than Duchamp in the abstraction process, moving so far from reality that not even the *suggestion* of a reference to it exists. *Composition*, with its characteristic Mondrian title (see Plate 11, following page 72), is a painting of austere and absolute simplicity in which all dynamic motion is absent; a work in which colors, shapes, and lines sit serenely in geometric relationships that defy the viewer to interpret them. Mondrian can be called a "classic abstractionist" in that his beautifully ordered designs evoke the same sort of serenity found in classical art. Incidentally, Mondrian was very fond of rectangles. To our knowledge no one has taken the trouble to measure their dimensions in the total body of his work. It would be interesting to see whether, consciously or otherwise, he ever used the golden section.

*The room that contained pieces by Picasso and other cubists was nicknamed the Chamber of Horrors.*

Modernism, however, implies rebellion against traditional styles and reasons for creating art. We should not expect that abstractionists created their own empire and their own rules. Other artists have gone their own way—not often back to the representation of the familiar world, at least not back to the pride that used to come from the amazing skill of transferring it in minute detail to canvas, but instead to the representation of a new world opened up earlier in the century, what we might call the *unfamiliar* world.

Greatly influenced by the explorations of Sigmund Freud (see Chapter 16) and Carl Jung (see Chapter 11) into the uncharted regions of the unconscious mind and the phenomenon of dreams as well as by intense efforts to define and analyze the sources of neurotic and more extreme forms of antisocial behavior, some artists were not satisfied with the untroubled, geometric niceties of a Mondrian and developed new styles that allowed them to bring the often nightmarish land of the unconscious into two- and three-dimensional existence.

*Modernism in art is a representation of the unfamiliar world, often the uncharted regions of the unconscious mind.*

*Surrealism* became the most popular of the "dream imitation" styles, and its major exponent has been Salvador Dalí (1904-1989). As the label implies, surrealism bears some relationship to the real world, about as much as dreams do. We find ourselves walking down a familiar street that suddenly turns into a place we think we've never been. We're set on accomplishing a task that suddenly doesn't matter anymore. Sometimes we see others from our own point of view, and sometimes we take on a different persona altogether, even looking at ourselves in the process of doing something.

Dalí, as you might suppose, won his fair share of ardent supporters, the inevitable group of viewers scratching their heads in perplexity, and a goodly number of detractors, who continue to see his work as a fraudulent, insincere attempt to capitalize on Freudian psychology, which was trendy among artists and writers in the 1920s and 1930s. But psychiatrists themselves have often found his work to be a fascinating case study of a uniquely neurotic personality who used his art as therapy. If you look carefully at *Inventions of the Monsters* (Plate 12, following page 72), you will see a dream landscape with both frightening and erotic shapes. Even if the artist's intention was to cash in on a trend, one might well ask where the figures *came* from, if not from Dalí's innermost self.

Perhaps a more significant question is to ask whether the projections of a neurotic artist add beauty to our world or whether beauty in *any* form is even an issue anymore. If Dalí were here to be questioned, might he not say, "Art is what the artist does, and I am an artist"?

## New Kinds of Realism

The need as well as the skill to imitate the familiar world is so deeply rooted in the long history of visual art that our expectation of finding realistic work in modern galleries would not be disappointed. What you're thinking is correct, however— modern realism is seldom "straight." The artist almost always has an ulterior motive. Today, realism is not a reversion to a traditional style. It serves the artist's need to show us something about our world and what is happening to it.

Edward Hopper (1882-1967) emerged out of the Depression years of the 1930s. His subjects are almost-deserted streets of American cities and forlorn, lonely, unhappy Americans, such as the three hunched figures sitting in a late-night diner in his famous *Nighthawks* (see page 374 in Chapter 13). The old saying about the exchange rate between a picture and many words is quite appropriate for Hopper. Though the Depression produced fiction and drama of considerable note, a Hopper painting communicates much about the disenchanted awakening from the American Dream. We can without difficulty make up pitiful stories to go with each of his hard-luck characters. Hopper represents the modern realist as observer of the contemporary scene, and his work offers yet one more purpose served by visual art: *to make us aware—painfully if necessary—of our time.* Though Hopper left us more than a quarter of a century ago, we cannot say our world has improved. Perhaps the difference would be that the diner would have closed by now because the lonely street has become unsafe. No doubt there are new Hoppers to show us *that*.

If South Africa is an example, artists by the score are motivated by the need to show and to make strong comments about the world in which they find themselves. Though the struggle against apartheid has been raging for decades and is still far from won, one positive note has been the growth and expansion of art communities as both black and white artists raise their voices in protest. Contemporary South African art is realism of perception, if not always of execution. Influenced by so many earlier styles of this century, artists such as Mandla Emmanuel Sibanda, who lives in Soweto, are experimenting in a variety of traditions. His 1987 painting *Zabalaza* (see Plate 13, following page 72) depicts angry protesters storming through the flames from an explosion. We have no trouble identifying who these people are and what is happening; at the same time, the artist, probably to impose some uniqueness born of his artistic nature, prefers to work in a neo-impressionistic mode. Or perhaps his intention is to intensify our awareness of the violence amid which the population lives and dies. The artist's comment on the painting is this:

> After the uprisings of 1976 until now we are still struggling for our freedom—so these determined young men are fighting no matter

*Edward Hopper's work is realism as social commentary. South African art of today is realism of perception, not execution.*

> how hard it is—running through burning flames, boiling soil. It is
> tough, but nothing will stop us from fighting.[8]

Perhaps no totally realistic representation of a single scene could have done what the artist clearly intended: to capture on one canvas a terrifying image of the whole conflagration. This is not a street, not a neighborhood; this is South Africa in flames.

Another purveyor of a special kind of realism is Duane Hanson (b. 1925), who burst upon the international art scene a couple of decades ago with some sculptures that almost redefined the medium. Neither classical nor abstract, they offered the sometimes frightened (and relatively few) visitors to his first gallery— an old garage—the shocking experience of what we might call "superrealism." Entering the "studio" through a squeaking and rusty door, one was greeted by a life-sized figure of a young girl hanging from a cross, the victim of a savage crime. In an adjoining alcove one gasped at the horrifying sight of another young girl, lying nude on a bed, pairs of blood-stained scissors thrust into her stomach, her open eyes still showing the terror she experienced before death mercifully came. Across from this sculpture lay the bloody figure of a young man, the twisted wreckage of his motorcycle beside him. As if believing the shock of the exhibit was not yet strong enough, Hanson capped off the evening with the piece that brought his work to the attention of the Whitney Museum, New York's premier showcase for what is new and significant in visual art: bloody corpses of handsome young men on a Vietnamese battlefield. One of the viewers was heard to whisper, "The technique is marvelous, but would you want this in your *house*?"

*Visitors to Duane Hanson's first gallery—an old garage—were greeted by a life-sized figure of a young girl hanging from a cross, the victim of a savage crime.*

After achieving almost instant notoriety, Hanson embarked on a second phase in which his sculptures were still superrealistic but not as frightening—at least not overtly so, but perhaps more alarming in a subtle sort of way. These works, like *Supermarket Lady*, imitate the dismal lifestyle of the American middle class, so accurate down to the last-minute detail as to spare us nothing. Hanson's realism here may well have been influenced by the soulless accuracy with which human robots are constructed in the Disney theme parks, the ones that smile vacuously at you and deliver life-affirming platitudes with all the warmth of the welcoming voices at modern airports.

Superrealism—need we say it?—does not exist to show off its technique, though many cannot get past their dazed astonishment. It is social and moral criticism of our times, our national values (or lack of them), and our apparently bleak future. That art can and does have a definite impact, that it *can* make a difference, is an easily testable assumption. You have only to look carefully at *Supermarket Lady* and ask whether *this* is how life should be. Clearly, the artist wants us to ponder this question.

Of special interest to our discussion in this final section is the collection of items in the woman's shopping cart: the sack of dog food; the TV dinners, which tell us where the art of dining has gone to; the giant box of tea bags. There are contemporary realists who focus on just such things, and not to make a statement about our culture; they do it because the things are considered legitimate objects of art in themselves.

Sometimes artists don't even bother to use a medium; that is, they bypass the time-consuming labor of imitation in favor of giving us the real thing. Often called "found" art, this style—if we can stretch the coverage of the term—brings old scrubbing boards, air-conditioning filters, and automobile mufflers into the

*Some modern art is not what artists do, but what they find.*

*I don't think it's very useful to open wide the door for young artists; the ones who break down the door are more interesting.*

*Paul Schrader*

galleries and museums. Thus art becomes not only what artists do, but what they find. No one can say found art is not the last word in realism, and it is defended on the grounds that it takes an artistic personality to spot "just the right thing." Found art also has democratic roots. The artists of this new tradition almost always find simple, pedestrian objects that have never been considered beautiful. There is even an exquisite documentary called *Junkyard*, in which the camera moves silently from one piece of junk to another; yet somehow the total effect is definitely an esthetic one.

One artist who has taken the lowliest of objects, the most overlooked and scorned items of everyday "stuff," and given them places of honor in prestigious museums and art centers is the sculptor Claes Oldenburg (b. 1929), so famous for what he has done with his undistinguished subjects that he has been placed at the very top of a whole new category designated as *pop art*. At the beginning of this chapter we mentioned the *Giant Ice Bag*, which the artist created for the United States pavilion at the 1970 World's Fair in Osaka, Japan. The sculpture not only imitates the reality of an ice bag, but does so with soft material that breathes in and out by means of a mechanism inside it. Why bother struggling, says the modern realist, to create the illusion of soft folds when you can simply *employ* soft folds?

Soft sculpture has occupied much of Oldenburg's time. Not content with using soft material where it realistically belongs, he has wittily been fashioning the illusion of hard objects out of soft textures, thus reversing the centuries-old sculptural tradition. Among the objects chosen for immortality through art that he has given us are a hamburger, a typewriter, and a toilet. No less than the Art Institute of Chicago has given a place of honor to Oldenburg's tall sculpture of a toothbrush,

*Duane Hanson,* Supermarket Lady: *So accurate down to the last-minute detail as to spare us nothing. (Courtesy of Duane Hanson)*

PLATE 1
*Frida Kahlo,* The Love Embrace of the Universe, the Earth (Mexico), Diego, Me and Senor Xolotl *(1949) (Oil on canvas, 27½" x 23¾". Private Collection, Mexico City. Photograph by Jorge Contreras Chacel/Courtesy of Centro Cultural Arte Contemporaneo, Mexico City)*

PLATE 2
*Jackson Pollock,* One (Number 31, 1950) *(1950) (Oil and enamel on unprimed canvas, 8'10' x 17'5⅝'. Collection, The Museum of Modern Art, New York. Sidney and Harriet Janis Collection Fund, by exchange)*

PLATE 3
*Georgia O'Keeffe,* White Canadian Barn, No. 2 *(1932) (Oil on canvas, 12" x 30". The
Metropolitan Museum of Art, The Alfred Stieglitz Collection, 1964). (64.310)*

PLATE 4
*Pablo Picasso,* The Actor
*(1905) (Oil on canvas, 76⅜" x
44⅛". The Metropolitan Museum
of Art, Gift of Thelma Chrysler
Foy, 1952) (52.175)*

PLATE 9
*Vincent van Gogh,* The Starry Night *(1889) (Oil on canvas, 29" x 36¼". Collection,*
*The Museum of Modern Art, New York. Acquired through the Lillie P. Bliss Bequest)*

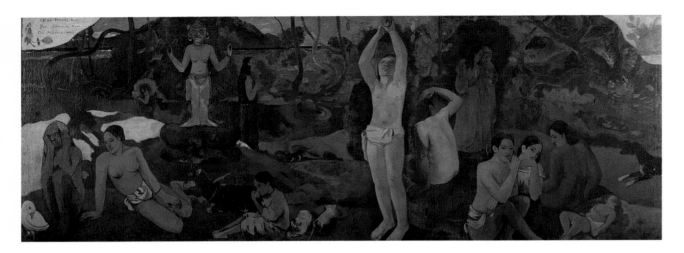

PLATE 10
*Paul Gauguin,* Where Do We Come From? What Are We? Where Are We Going?
*(Museum of Fine Arts, Boston. Photo: George M. Cushing)*

PLATE 11
*Piet Mondrian,* Composition
with Red, Green, Blue and Black
*(Stichting Beeldrecht, Haags
Gemeentemuseum)*

PLATE 14
*Christo*, Surrounded Islands *(Photo: G. Gorgoni/Sygma)*

*Andy Warhol,* 100 Cans *(1962):
The painting is both funny and
frightening. (Albright-Knox Art
Gallery, Buffalo, New York. Gift
of Seymour H. Knox, 1963)*

which uses both hard and soft materials. Whether the artist has found beauty or humor in his subjects we will allow the viewer to decide.

Worthy of mention relative to the pop art tradition is Andy Warhol (1928–1987), who catapulted to fame with a realistic painting depicting row upon row of Campbell's beef noodle soup as a "tribute" to mass culture. The painting is both funny and frightening (when one reflects on the number of choices and what this tells us about our culture). Warhol's inspiration and roots are obviously in commercial art. Another of his well-known works gives us 50 images of Marilyn Monroe, the Hollywood glamour queen of the 1950s, some distinct, some blurred, but all showing the same face.

As if we were not facing complexity enough in dealing with *modernism* in visual art, we no sooner catch our breath than we discover there is such a thing as *postmodernism*. This broad-based introductory chapter is hardly the place in which to attempt an in-depth analysis of all that this label encompasses. Rather, let us use a zoom lens and look at one particular example of a style that has been designated as postmodern, and it will be easy to see how it grows out of what has gone before.

An artist who calls himself Christo (b. 1935) neither copies reality nor uses found objects as his medium. Rather, he is the one to whom we were referring at the start of this chapter—the artist who "insists on stretching an enormous curtain from one mountain to another in Colorado and audaciously calling it art." We were, of course, being facetious. Christo is not particularly audacious, but he is a hard-working, dedicated professional artist who has found a way of expressing himself that is unique. He is a *realist who alters at the same time*. Perhaps he thought to himself that the logical next step would be not to imitate reality but to

*Christo is the modern artist
who does not imitate but
changes reality. He has
wrapped an entire building
in cloth and surrounded the
islands of Biscayne Bay in
Miami with vast sheets of
flamingo-colored plastic,
much to the dismay of art
purists and environmentalists.*

make creative changes in real places; the artist helping nature out, so to speak. Hence the *Valley Curtain* in the Rockies.

Before Christo alters, he studies the location, decides on what kind of alteration he will make, the kind of textures and colors he will employ, and how the finished whole will fit into the visual context of the scene. He has wrapped an entire building in cloth, done the same to one of the bridges in Paris, and surrounded the islands of Biscayne Bay in Miami with vast sheets of flamingo-colored plastic (see Plate 14, following page 72), much to the dismay of art purists and environmentalists.

Purists have argued that what Christo does cannot be called true art, since it is never created to last. On the other hand, we could say the same about yet another species of postmodernism, usually labeled *performance art*, whose purpose is to create an event for a group of onlookers. One performance artist is Canadian Les Levine (b. 1935), who has hacked a piano to bits with an ax and shoveled seven truckloads of dirt about an empty art gallery by the light of seventy votive candles. Clearly, all of these artists belong in some way to the tradition of contemporary realism because what they make happen is in fact really happening.

Whether some or all of it is worth doing is, of course, a question that you, a student of the humanities growing familiar with many of today's tendencies, must decide privately. Since we seem to be moving at a very accelerated pace (a tradition topples only to be replaced by another before a wide public is even aware of it), we find ourselves at a time when the very nature and purpose of visual art must be reexamined and redefined. Prestigious art critics and historians often disagree about which artist and which style—if indeed any at all—will survive tomorrow's reviews of new art shows.

Throughout this book we continually urge you not necessarily to like everything, but to know as much as possible about what is going on. Only then will you have collected the resources for making carefully considered choices among a rich variety of options.

# Glossary

*chiaroscuro:* A way of using paints (or pencil or charcoal) to reproduce the interplay of dark and light in the real world.

*classicism:* A reference to the formal qualities of art and architecture in ancient Greece and Rome.

*cubism:* A movement in modern art, epitomized by Picasso, in which the artist breaks down the field of vision into all of its discontinuous segments or in which the artist shows a number of visual events taking place simultaneously (as in Picasso's *Guernica*).

*golden section:* Also known as the "divine proportion"; once thought to be an immensely beautiful relationship between two sides of a rectangle, such that the smaller is to the larger what the larger is to the sum of both. The ratio is approximately 1 to 1.68.

*hemispheric asymmetry:* The theory that each of us is dominated by either the left brain, which spe-

cializes in logic and language, or the right brain, which governs imagination and creativity.

*imitation:* In this chapter, the transference of what is experienced either outside or inside the artist to a medium of art. It can mean a faithful reproduction of the real world, but is not limited to this definition.

*impressionism:* A mid-nineteenth-century movement in art; to some extent, a response to the invention of photography, wherein the attempt to be realistic is abandoned, and instead, artists project onto canvas a subjective experience of the world as colors and forms.

*perspective:* The technique of rendering, on a plane or a curved surface, objects as they appear to the eye; developed and refined during the early Renaissance in Italy.

*postimpressionism:* An extremely broad term used by art historians to refer to art of the late nineteenth and early twentieth centuries that is not impressionistic as such, not realistic, yet not abstract like modern art. The work of van Gogh belongs to this category.

*realism:* In this chapter, the reproduction of the familiar world as precisely as the available technique will allow. The term is not limited to a specific historical period. Even cave drawings can be considered early attempts at realism.

*surrealism:* A technique in contemporary art, epitomized by Salvador Dalí, in which what the viewer is looking at bears as much relationship to the familiar world as dreams do.

terribilitá: An Italian word used by critics and art historians to describe the quality of passion that Michelangelo was able to impart to a statue.

## Notes

1. Samuel Taylor Coleridge, "Dejection: An Ode," in *The New Oxford Book of English Verse* (Oxford: Oxford University Press, 1972), 547.
2. Jan Garden Castro, *The Art and Life of Georgia O'Keeffe* (New York: Crown, 1985), 1.
3. Irving Stone, *The Agony and the Ecstasy* (New York: Doubleday, 1961), 529–530.
4. Van Gogh must have been clairvoyant, for in 1987 his painting *Sunflowers* sold at auction for $38.5 million.
5. John Perreault, "Forging Ahead: A Sculpture Conference Diary," *Village Voice*, September 21, 1982, 84.
6. Gardner's *Art Through the Ages*, 7th ed., revised by Horst de la Croix and Richard G. Tansey (New York: Harcourt Brace Jovanovich, 1980), 819.
7. Bruce Cole and Adelheid Gealt, *Art of the Western World* (New York: Summit Books, 1989), 271.
8. Sue Williamson, *Resistance Art in South Africa* (New York: St. Martin's Press, 1989), 121.

## Suggested Reading

Adams, Henry. *Mont-Saint-Michel and Chartres.* Cambridge, Mass.: Riverside Press, 1933. In this elegantly written "travelogue," Henry Adams takes the reader back to the twelfth and thirteenth centuries to participate in the events surrounding the construction and life of these French architectural wonders.

Buonarroti, Michelangelo. *I, Michelangelo, Sculptor: An Autobiography through Letters.* Ed. Irving and Jean Stone. New York: New American Library of World Literature, 1964. A fascinating psychological and spiritual self-portrait materializes in this collection of letters and poems of the sculptor to his family, friends, the Medici, popes, artists, and business associates.

Castro, Jan Garden. *The Art & Life of Georgia O'Keeffe.* New York: Crown Publishers, 1985. A wonderful collection of color reproductions, along with an almost novel-like presentation of O'Keeffe's development as an artist and the sometimes inhibiting effects of her marriage to the photographer Alfred Stieglitz.

Cole, Bruce, and Adelheid Gealt. *Art of the Western World.* New York: Summit Books, 1989. A generously illustrated book written to accompany the PBS series of the same title; with an introduction by the series host, Michael Wood.

Edwards, Betty. *Drawing on the Right Side of the Brain.* Los Angeles: J. P. Tarcher, 1979. Practical exercises for people who think they can't draw.

Herrera, Hayden. *Frida: A Biography of Frida Kahlo.* New York: HarperCollins, 1991. For years the wife of famous muralist Diego Rivera was overshadowed by her husband's fame. This book gives her what the author considers to be her rightful place in modern art.

Janson, H. W. *History of Art.* 4th ed. Englewood Cliffs, N.J.: Prentice-Hall, 1991. A beautifully illustrated classic, which traces Western art from early cave paintings to the present.

McCarthy, Mary. *The Stones of Florence.* New York: Harcourt Brace Jovanovich, 1959. A nicely illustrated description of the past and present of the Italian city, often called a living museum.

Richardson, John, with Marilyn McCully. *A Life of Picasso, Vol. I, 1881–1906.* New York: Random House, 1991. This may become the definitive account of the life and work of the artist generally considered the giant of the twentieth century. It traces his early career and prepares the reader for an understanding of the development of cubism.

*Jean Antoine Watteau,* Mezzetin *(The Metropolitan Museum of Art, Munsey Fund, 1934)*

# Music: Sound and Silence

3

## Overview

Music is the shaped sounds between silences. Listening to music is more than just a pleasant way to spend time. Music is almost as necessary for survival as food or language. In a sense, music is both, translated into sound.

Human beings live in the midst of an *unplanned audio environment*. No one knows just when a jet will streak overhead or brakes will squeal or a screaming mob will turn the corner. The dawn of human time may have been a bit quieter, but hostile mammoths were probably sending forth horrendous bellows when it occurred. Anyway, the past scarcely matters in this regard. Today the majority of the world's population exists at the mercy of unwanted sound, audio pollution as damaging to mental health as air and water pollution are damaging to physical health.

*I have often regretted my speech, never my silence.*

*Publius Syrus*

As art has altered our visual surroundings, adding forms and colors that were not there before, so too has music altered our audio surroundings. We have options: the sound of a stick being dragged along a wrought-iron fence, the wrap-around rhythms of a supermarket amplifier, a rock band, a Beethoven symphony.

The gift that music offers us as one of our most treasured resources for living is *variety*—a wealth of sounds and forms, making possible a wide range of experiences. Limiting ourselves to one specific *kind* of music is as detrimental to growth as not experiencing variety in all of the other arts—or indeed in life itself.

Music as an art is made up of a number of separate elements. It can be produced by instruments, each with its own sound, or by the human voice. It cannot be produced by nature, though some musical sound imitates nature. Flutes can sound like birds. The string section of an orchestra, playing a certain part of Jean Sibelius's *Tapiola*, sounds almost exactly like wind in a deep forest.

*Too often we stay with what is comfortable and familiar, unwilling to stray into alien territories.*

The sounds of music can be loud or soft. They can be heard by themselves or in combinations. In music of any age or culture, sounds must be experienced in a sequence, usually with underlying rhythmic patterns. Instrumental notes and human voices can accompany each other, or work together to constitute a sound unity new to nature.

People who won't allow themselves to experience the variety that music has to offer usually have never taken the time and trouble to listen—*really listen*—perhaps because they are not sure what to listen *for*. This chapter will first separate the musical experience into its component parts; then it will provide some insight into a number of contrasting forms that the experience can assume.

## Musical Elements

Music may have begun as imitation of certain aspects of the audio environment: people making bird sounds or raindrop patters or animal noises. Maybe the reason was as simple as the need for better communication. Our language is filled with words that sound like what they define: *Crash! Boom! Bang!* More subtle is a word like *soar*, which makes us think of a hang glider climbing into the sky or an eagle floating high above a mountain.

The next stage may have been born in that moment when a man, a woman, or a child chose to imitate a sweet sound for the sake of doing just that, not for communication; when somebody said, *Why wait for the lovely and soothing call of a morning bird when I can sing myself?*

The basic element of music is a *tone*, a single sound that may imitate an actual sound in the audio environment or may be only imagined in the human mind—a *perfection* of sound that cannot exist in reality, but *can* be produced by the human voice or by an instrument invented to make it. The discovery of tone might be described as the beginning of the human victory over the unplanned audio environment. When tones are written down, they are called notes; they are the building blocks of musical art.

### The Scale

Early humans found they could make a number of different tones. Some were high, some were low. They could not have known what made the difference, that the lower the frequency of sound-wave vibrations, the lower the tone, and vice versa. But sooner or later they happened upon an arrangement of tones from low to high in a definite progression, and that was the beginning of music. The music of Western culture rests upon the foundation of the eight-tone progression we call the *scale*, and, as everyone knows, the tones are named *do-re-me-fa-so-la-ti-do*. As notes, they are called C-D-E-F-G-A-B-C. The eight tones are separated by *intervals*, which are the differences in frequency of vibrations as we go up or down the scale. We also know that a singer or an instrument may go up or down a whole or a half interval. Going up a half is represented on paper as a sharp ( ♯ ); going down a half, as a flat ( ♭ ). The standard scale contains eight full tones and five half tones, or sharps and flats ( depending upon whether one is going up or down ). The art of music has its roots in the way tones are arranged in a certain sequence. Of course, the scale is the fundamental sequence, but it is only the first of an infinite number of possibilities.

*The scale is the fundamental sequence, but it is only the first of an infinite number of possibilities.*

No one can be sure what instrument first produced tones in a sequence from low to high. However, we *do* know that the Greeks either invented or made widespread use of the *monochord*, probably a very remote ancestor of the guitar and mandolin. The monochord was a simple, rectangular wooden box with an opening on top and a single string tightly stretched across the opening. A movable bridge, probably made of wood, could be pressed down at certain points along the string, dividing it so that one side was held taut while the other could vibrate. An early version of the basic scale was probably the result. It is highly likely that the Greeks, with their passion for form and order, created a musical system of tones spaced at regular intervals. We know that Pythagoras, the great mathematician, was fascinated by musical sequences and their relationship to numerical sequences. The word *music* itself derives from the Greek *mousike*, which means "the art of the muse."

One prominent theory is that the art of *mousike* came into being as a means of perfecting the art of poetry. A melodic accompaniment to the epic chant-

*Greek vase,* Nude Youth Playing Double Flute to Two Men: *A perfection of sound that cannot exist in reality. ( The Metropolitan Museum of Art, Rogers Fund, 1906 )*

ing (or possibly singing) of heroic poetry was probably very popular. Perhaps the desired effect on the listener was the illusion that the Muse herself was present. We know that Plato was so charmed by this art that in his *Republic* he rated music as the very highest kind of education he would want in an ideal state. He maintained that experience in listening to music would liberate the spirit of pure reason within the soul, since music offered an ideal arrangement of meaningful sounds. To inhabit a realm of pure musical beauty was the same thing as inhabiting a realm of pure thought.

## Rhythm

Since no Greek musical manuscripts have survived, we can only speculate on what their music actually sounded like. We see no reason not to hazard a guess that music, along with sculpture, theater, and philosophy, reached high levels of sophistication during the Golden Age, which spanned the fifth and fourth centuries B.C. We know that the choral passages in the great tragedies were sung. We know that music was used to enhance ceremonial occasions, such as sporting events and the honoring of heroes. We know about the wild dancing orgies held in connection with the worship of Dionysus, god of fertility.

We also know that rhythm was the underlying factor in much of the music. There are written accounts of it, and moral distinctions were made. Certain rhythms were held to be appropriate for inspirational ceremonies because of their uplifting effect on the soul, while other rhythms—certainly those of the orgies—were deemed immoral, conducive to uncontrolled, licentious behavior.

We have said that music began with the discovery of tones, but this does not mean rhythm by itself could not have preceded tone, scale, and the earliest instruments. Most likely, a rat-a-tat pounding of sticks and stones was an early factor in human development, used to mark occasions of great solemnity and rituals of all kinds that bound groups together. Very young children left to their own devices can be observed rat-a-tatting with blocks or just with their hands, their beat becoming more pronounced and regular as they grow. Moving to a beat—in short, *dancing*—may be older than singing, though one can imagine occasions on which the two spontaneously erupted together.

Chapter 1 analyzed two contrasting aspects of human culture and human personality: the Apollonian and the Dionysian, after the Greek gods whose legendary characteristics inspired the philosopher Nietzsche to use these terms as labels to identify patterns of human thought, passions, and behavior. The Apollonian half of human beings, as we saw, enjoys order; the Dionysian half can exult in frenzy and disorder. Neither side is sufficient by itself. Civilization advanced with Apollonian order, but without Dionysian spontaneity, it can become rigid and uncreative. Dancing to Dionysian rhythms must be a very ancient means of putting Apollonian control temporarily to sleep, of releasing one's inhibitions. Mesmerized by the rhythm, one is apt to lose rational consciousness and become driven by forces buried deep in the human unconscious.

Rhythm usually is an alternation between stress and unstress. It acquires its different forms according to the pattern of alternation used. A familiar rhythm is that of the waltz, created from a stressed beat followed by two unstressed beats. Also described as a "stately" rhythm, it is far more Apollonian than it is Dionysian, and was thus suitable for the aristocrats of nineteenth-century ballrooms. The minuet as well as the time-honored fox-trot, which we still find at country club

*Dancing to Dionysian rhythms must be a very ancient means of putting Apollonian control temporarily to sleep.*

*Rhythm usually is an alternation between stress and unstress. It acquires its different forms according to the pattern of alternation used.*

dances, are based on Apollonian (that is, rigid and repetitive) rhythms. So are the marches used for funeral and graduation processions. Apollonian rhythms are probably what the Greeks called "uplifting to the soul."

Contemporary generations, which enjoy bouncing on a dance floor to the beat of rock bands, evidently find Dionysian liberation a satisfying escape from the Apollonian demands of their workplace or their school. Far from being new and trendy, rock rhythms probably stretch back to the dawn of humanity, and may well have bonded the group together in a collective, joyous release of pent-up energy. If civilization advanced along an Apollonian route, Dionysian rhythms were no doubt heard along the way. Moving to Dionysian (less formal, less rigid) rhythms keeps us in touch with our wild natures.

In formal musical art, such as that of concert pieces or popular, nonrock songs (musical theater or country), the rhythmic underpinning is usually quite pronounced and tends to remain unchanged either for the whole work or large portions of it. We might almost say that rhythm is the mortar that holds the work together, that gives coherence to a collection of sounds. In a symphony a change in rhythm is a major event, often very exciting to the listener. It opens up new possibilities, new directions, but then the new rhythm must continue the job of holding the piece together.

Our discussion to this point can be summarized as follows: *When musical tones met up with the ancient human passion for rhythm, a new force was born, which provided a way for human emotions to be expressed and released.*

Once rhythm was discovered, it probably never left musical art. Even the *plainsong*, a chant sung by medieval monks and clerics, has a rhythm, albeit hard to detect because there are so many stressed tones and those not stressed tend to be very delicately sung. When a relatively modern composer like Claude Debussy (1862-1918) seems to be lacking in rhythm, the reason is that the untrained ear cannot detect the subtle changes in stress marked by a very subdued percussion section. In the famous *Bolero* by Debussy's compatriot and fellow impressionist Maurice Ravel (1875-1937) the underlying rhythm is so pronounced that it virtually constitutes the entire piece.

Some composers attempt to be totally arrhythmic; that is, they avoid all regular alternations of stress and unstress, seldom repeating a pattern so that the listener will not become accustomed to it. In this manner the listener is kept off guard, presumably on edge, and the piece aspires to create a mood of agitation and emotional instability. Whether this is done because the composer wishes to be "different" or to make some kind of statement through the music, the reality is that nonrhythm is a *kind* of rhythm. Even if a composer insisted on having every tone stressed, the result would be a kind of rhythm.

So the issue is not what does or does not constitute rhythm but why music cannot exist without it. What is the magic it weaves inside us? One can speculate at great length, of course. We are conceived in rhythm, born in rhythm; parents clap their hands to make us happy. The universe itself throbs with rhythms. Current theories regarding the origins of the universe include the belief that before there were atoms and molecules, before there were material particles at all, the cosmos was made up of infinitesimally tiny strings whose rhythmic vibrations brought the first matter into being. We also have the rotation of the earth, the alternation of the seasons, night and day, birth and death. Want to go on? How about order and disorder, Apollo and Dionysus, belief and doubt, joy and sorrow?

Rock percussionist Mickey Hart of the Grateful Dead recently said, "Rhythm

*Far from being new and trendy, rock rhythms probably stretch back to the dawn of humanity, and may well have bonded the group together in a collective, joyous release of pent-up energy.*

*We are conceived in rhythm, born in rhythm. . . . The universe throbs with rhythms.*

is at the very center of our lives." If you were to ask someone which musical element they could most easily dispense with, "rhythm" would most probably *not* be the reply.

## Melody

As popularly understood, melody is the part we remember of a song or a symphonic movement. If nothing is remembered beyond a "babble" of instruments and a great deal of percussion, chances are many would ask, "What happened to the melody?"

About half a century ago Hollywood produced one of its classic tear-jerkers, a film called *The Great Lie*, in which a concert pianist, too busy with her worldwide appearances to raise her child, allows another woman to be a temporary foster mother, only to discover she has permanently given up her right to be a parent. Overwhelmed with grief, she plunges obsessively into her career, an act symbolized by the woman's sitting at the piano and pounding out the bold opening chords of Tchaikovsky's Piano Concerto no. 1. Now, what the audience remembered most about the film *was*, in fact, those chords and the beautiful melodic line that follows them. Many of the so-called big bands of the era made popular arrangements of the chords and the melody; Tchaikovsky was suddenly on top of the charts. The melody then was further debased into a song called "Tonight We Love." When the Boston Pops announced it was performing the concerto with a well-known pianist, the evening was immediately sold out. Unquestionably many people passed through the hallowed portals of Symphony Hall for the first time in their lives, and not a few must have been confused when the concerto lasted far longer than the three-minute duration of "Tonight We Love." To make matters worse, the beloved melody, which had come to *mean* Tchaikovsky for thousands, is never again heard in the concerto after the opening moments.

A great many music lovers prefer this composer to that one because of a number of tonal sequences that fall pleasantly on the ear and become associated with the composer, all other intricacies of the music becoming forgotten. They do not define melody so much as impose requirements upon it. That is, they wait for a sequence of sounds that they like and that is almost always repeated. Failing to hear such a sequence, they denounce the work as being "unmelodious." Contemporary operas are particularly vulnerable to harsh criticism on the grounds that they lack melodies people can remember; they lack the sort of famous arias that bring people back year after year to *Carmen, La Traviata*, and *The Marriage of Figaro*. Seldom does one read in a review that "the major melody of the piece is an unfamiliar sequence of sounds that fall disturbingly upon the ear." One is told there is melody, or there is not. In other words, by definition a melody has to sound beautiful. The unfamiliar in music is never going to be described as beautiful; it is "weird," "bizarre," or, at best, "strangely effective"—as though one were saying, "Somehow it works, even without melody."

In fact, however, the melody in a piece of music is the *sequence of lead tones that are distinguishable from supporting tones*. In a piano piece the tones that are produced by the left hand—that is, those in the lower registers—are generally referred to as *the bass*, and they serve to support or provide harmony for the tones produced by the right hand in the higher registers, which are considered the *melody*, or the *melodic line*. But even this broad definition does not apply in many, many instances. Sometimes the composer requires the pianist to play the melody with the left hand in the lower register, while the right hand supports in the higher register. When there is *no* support or even when the sole instrument is a drum, then the melody is whatever tones we hear. Music of the Far East often strikes the untrained ear as a monotonous succession of tones that never are broken into clearly separated sequences; hence it is said, "There is no melody to it." What we must remember is that all music contains melody, and sometimes nothing but! The composer is the one who decides when one melody ends and another begins.

The so-called beauty of melody is clearly a matter of historical period and cultural heritage. Those whose ancestral roots are in the Western European tradition and who have grown up with a love of concert music tend to define melody as it is found in the work of composers such as Mozart, Beethoven, Schubert, Tchaikovsky, Brahms, and so on. You will note that all but one is German; it is no coincidence that concertgoers who demand "melody" often mean sequences of tones that were at one time characteristically German in nature.

What "characteristically German" musical sound actually *means*, however, is one of the many unsolved mysteries in the humanities. A listener hearing the String Quartet in C, op. 76, no. 3, of Franz Josef Haydn would immediately think that the famous melody in the second movement sounds "unmistakably" German. It even became the song "Deutschland, Deutschland über Alles," which the Nazis used as their anthem. A musicologist could analyze the tones and tell us that the particular configuration in the final line is heard frequently in Mozart and Beethoven also, stamping their work as "characteristically" German.

French concert music sounds unmistakably French. Is it the sensuality in the melodic line? Russian music of the late nineteenth and early twentieth century tends to be bold and strident. Is it speaking in revolutionary tones? American concert music, such as that by Aaron Copland or Virgil Thomson, seems to use melodies that sound just right on a trumpet or a fiddle, to have long passages in which melodies seem to meander like lonesome cowboys wandering the endless plains. In other words, *it is probably not going too far to say that the sound image of a culture derives from its melodic lines*.

*The sound image of a culture derives from its melodic lines.*

Since the American musical heritage comes from the Western European, hence romantic, melody, we are accustomed to some identifying characteristics. Romantic melody—as in Tchaikovsky's *Romeo and Juliet* Overture—constitutes a sequence of tones that *must* be repeated several times. This is also called a *theme*, and often it is not only beautiful to the ears but comes to stand for something in the work. The memorable melody in *Romeo and Juliet* stands for the passion of the two young lovers. Near the end we hear it repeated in a minor key, representing their deaths.

A second characteristic of romantic melody is its evocation of images that have great impact on our senses: sunsets; water lilies floating quietly on a pond; thunderstorms (as in Beethoven's Sixth, or *Pastoral*, Symphony, or American Ferde Grofé's *Grand Canyon* Suite); the sounds of traffic (as in George Gershwin's *An American in Paris*); a lovely face half glimpsed through a lace curtain (as in Debussy's *The Girl with Flaxen Hair*).

The third—and the major—characteristic is feeling. Somehow certain sequences of tones communicate love, sorrow, joy, foreboding, regret, longing, or the fascination with the unknown. Many composers, for example, have told us in their melodies what death *sounds* like. Listen to Schubert's song "Death and the Maiden" or Richard Strauss's tone poem *Death and Transfiguration* for contrasting sound images of the final moment.

*Many composers have told us in their melodies what death sounds like.*

*classical: form and order
romantic: personal style and
feelings*

Music that we label *classical* (from the seventeenth and eighteenth centuries) was not supposed to be an expression of the composer's emotion. Form and order were its intentions. With the transition to romanticism in music (in the late eighteenth century), composers claimed the right to put their style, personality, and feelings into their music. How emotion is communicated nonverbally or without the facial expressions and bodily attitudes of a human being in front of us we can never know for sure, but the fact remains that *much music is what emotion sounds like*. Nor is the phenomenon limited to the Western European tradition. Every culture appears to know how its emotions are translated into musical sound. Melodies that have no emotional resonance for one person may evoke the strongest kind of feeling in someone else.

Music that is labeled *modern* belongs to the early part of the twentieth century and represents, among other things, a moving away from traditional romantic characteristics. Listen to Igor Stravinsky's *Rite of Spring* (discussed in Chapter 10), and you will know what "modern" means. Yet, while the melodies are certainly not romantic and the emotions are not easily understood, one perceives they are there.

*Minimalism, a school of
postmodern music, rejects
the idea that music is
supposed to produce an
emotional state inside the
listener.*

Concert music of our time is often called *postmodern*, and it is often identifiable by its clearly nonromantic approach to melody and its often painstaking avoidance of emotion. Minimalism, a school of postmodern music, rejects the idea that music is supposed to be an expression of the composer's inner life or that it is supposed to produce an emotional state inside the listener. Postmodern composers want to create "pure" music, which, like the colors and designs of the postmodern visual artist, reflect the composer's mastery of the discipline.

Listening to a new work that does not wish to evoke feeling can be a strange and baffling experience. How can we enjoy ourselves when what we are hearing lacks "warmth" or "soul"? But we must remember this: Like other arts, music is what it can and will be. We have the right to turn away, of course, as we have the right to turn away from any stranger. Yet we also possess the freedom to make friends.

## Harmony

In Eastern music, tones are normally played by themselves, that is, without *harmony*, the simultaneous production of tones by voices or instruments other than those that produce the dominant melodic line. So accustomed are we to hearing simultaneous tones that we tend to take harmony for granted, but like romantic melody, harmony has historical and cultural roots.

*In medieval music, harmony
would have been inappro-
priate. Prayers were sung in
unison, to sound like one
voice.*

During the Middle Ages, for example, a great deal of music was used in the churches and monasteries as a complement to the act of worship. Emphasis was placed on song as a means of communicating with God. These sung prayers are known as *plainsong* and were intended to be produced by numbers of priests and monks, acting as one voice asking God for mercy and forgiveness. Harmony created by units of voices singing different tones would have been out of place, since the understanding was that humanity was completely unified in being sinful and undeserving of salvation except through God's mercy.

As the Renaissance moved after 1400 from one European country to another, bringing with it a resurgence of the belief in human worth, in the glories of life on earth, and in the infinite possibilities of the individual, music, *secular* music, assumed a key place in the new pleasure-oriented scheme of things. The Renaissance emphasized enjoyment during one's brief stay on earth, and music could fill leisure hours with many joys. The royal courts all had musicians on hand. Scarcely an hour of the day went by without the sounds of lute, recorder, or oboe, playing sometimes alone but often in small consorts. Renaissance composers explored the harmonious interweaving of different instruments and voices, as if to say that music should be the contribution of a number of individuals, each adding to life's enjoyment, each with a musical statement to make. Harmony is the enhancement of musical beauty that occurs when individuals work together.

Renaissance harmonic experimentations brought forth a new art form: *opera*. In this, human voices sang melodic lines with orchestral accompaniment; what they sang told a story, so that dramatists and poets could add their own statements, the whole becoming a rich and complex visual tapestry and festival of sound. The Renaissance, having moved away from the somber religious view that this world is a vale of tears and only heaven can give us joy, believed in constructing a human heaven right here.

*Renaissance composers explored the harmonious interweaving of different instruments and voices.*

The Renaissance ideal of music as a major contributing force to what we nowadays call the "quality of life" has remained a permanent component of our cultural tradition. Whether composers use their music as an outlet for personal feelings; whether they try to make political or philosophical statements through tones, not words; or whether they seek only to create "pure" music that is not a personal expression—all of *us* use music as an enhancement of life, as a sometimes gracious and elegant, sometimes pulsating complement to existence.

Church music continued to be written, to be sure, most notably by Johann Sebastian Bach (1685-1750), who is discussed in a later section; but the Renaissance brought with it an outpouring of musical possibilities: new sounds, new instruments, and, as we have seen, new forms. Western music would never be the same as it was before the Renaissance. Combinations of instruments became *the orchestra*, which grew in size and complexity; as it did, composers were inspired to explore the range of the new instruments. By the eighteenth century the *symphony*, a musical form in separate units, or movements, became a concert staple. Major aggregations of musicians became known as *symphony orchestras*, and these steadily increased in numbers as Haydn, Mozart, Beethoven, Brahms, and, late in the nineteenth century, Mahler wrote works that required more and more players. One of Mahler's major works is titled *The Symphony of a Thousand* because it involves literally that many musicians and singers. Tchaikovsky's *1812 Overture* needs, in addition to a massive orchestra, any number of cannons being fired as the music reaches its climax. Beethoven's Ninth Symphony is now performed by an enormous orchestra of at least a hundred and fifty musicians in addition to a chorus of perhaps two hundred.

*By the eighteenth century the symphony, a musical form in separate units, or movements, became a concert staple.*

Musical harmony, especially in the glorious complexities of the great symphony orchestras, has become a model of human society at its most ideal. It requires every musician to pull together for one common purpose. No one sound can be any more important than another; to the trained ear, each sound is distinct and pleasurable. Nor is the melodic line any more beautiful than the harmony and rhythm that support it. The lifetime achievements of each player are as nothing if the whole entity does not create an experience for the listener that is intense, focused, and charged with electricity. At the same time, the ultimate product is a testimony to the genius of the individual. If one tone is flat, the entire enterprise suffers.

## Silence

You may be surprised to find silence listed as a musical element, for how can the absence of sound be considered a component of the art of music? Yet silence—when you think about it—*is* the unpublicized "ingredient" that makes music possible in the same way that the empty space around a sculpture makes the sculpture possible, or the judicious use of wall space can make or break an art exhibit. Just imagine 25 original van Goghs crammed together: "Where is *Starry Night*? Oh, there it is. We almost missed it. Funny, but somehow it's just not as exciting as I thought it would be."

Ever hear a symphony on tape at accelerated speed? The sound is ludicrous, definitely unmusical, but not just because the tones are not being played at the proper cadence. The acceleration has erased the silences, which are as significant as the tones themselves. *Music is the shaped sound between silences.*

If we would deepen our appreciation of music, we must learn to hear and to enjoy silence itself. The pauses in the second movement, the "Funeral March," of Beethoven's Third Symphony are as famous as the themes that precede and follow them. The effect is like that of someone trying valiantly to hold back tears. The main theme of the movement, a dirgelike melody appropriate for a funeral procession, comes in a halting, irregular rhythm, the silences between the tones enlarged. Think of the last time you were in the presence of someone struggling for self-control while obviously overcome by a powerful surge of emotion. Were not the silences full of meaning? Great composers handle silences in the same way that great artists since Leonardo have known how to handle shadows. Great stage actors owe something of their greatness to the mastery they have achieved over the words in a play that they do *not* speak.

The hush that comes either before or after the great moments in the arts is often responsible for those moments' greatness, though people are not always aware of the fact. Perhaps the most famous solo theme for French horn occurs soon after the opening of the fourth movement of Brahms's First Symphony. The moment is heralded by a tympani roll and then a pause, which dramatically intensifies the significance of what follows. No one could listen to the sequence without experiencing a sudden heightened awareness. The French horn enters like an actor making at long last an appearance for which the audience has been eagerly waiting.

Perhaps the best-known moment in all of theater history comes when Hamlet, believing himself to be alone on stage, begins the most celebrated soliloquy ever written. It has become traditional for the performer to pause, *not* to launch at once into "To be or not to be . . .", or else to allow a long pause between phrases: "To be . . . or not to be."

What ultimately distinguishes one aspiring musician from another in a music conservatory is not the ability to play the notes as written and at the proper tempo, but the musical *intuition* that manifests itself. One way in which the professional ear can detect the presence of this intuition (or this "feeling for the music" as it is sometimes called) is to listen to how the performer manipulates the silences that surround the tones. Three world-class pianists might record Beethoven's *Pathetique* Sonata, and though each plays exactly the same notes, giving proper attention to the pace and the mood indicated by the composer, the interpretation by each will have subtle touches unique to that musician. In almost every instance the telling factor is the handling of silence. Here a pause is elongated;

*. . . and she lay back, eyes already closed, no doubt, while the magnificent music rose in great waves toward that perfect moment at the end of every piece when there was silence.*
        Scott Turow
        The Burden of Proof

*Heard melodies are sweet, but those unheard/Are sweeter.*

        John Keats

*Ours is the age of the transistor, the Walkman, and the cordless headset. People run, exercise, and ride their bikes encased in a secret world of ear-splitting noise.*

there, foreshortened. As with the space surrounding a sculpture, silence in music helps to define, to single out, to create individuality.

In any group, the person who interests us, who seems to demand our careful attention, is the person with silences. Who is likely to warrant a second look? The one who calmly sits there with a faint smile, saying nothing? or the one who comes bursting into the room, breathlessly reeling off a torrent of words? Of course, the impression made by the silent person will be greater on a silent observer. People with silences appreciate each other.

Our age, however, is the age of the transistor, the Walkman, and the cordless headset. People run, exercise, and ride their bikes encased in a secret world of ear-splitting noise. One would think that particularly in urban areas, already noisy enough without electronic assistance, everyone would gladly seek moments of quiet, moments to breathe deeply, sort out one's thoughts and emotions. Is our addiction to noise an excuse *not* to look into ourselves for fear of what we might glimpse? The absence of silence in daily life as well as in music may be neither good nor bad, but it certainly is significant, affording us some insights into what we and our world have become. Perhaps we are a frightened generation, and loud noise is like the night light our parents used to leave on after they had tucked us in and left the room.

*If we would deepen our appreciation of music, we must learn to hear and to enjoy silence itself. The pauses in the second movement of Beethoven's Third Symphony are as famous as the themes that precede and follow them.*

## The Giants of Music

One would have to write a book several times this size to do justice to the multitude of musical geniuses who shine in the firmament of the humanities. There are so many styles, so many musical *genres* (opera, symphony, chamber music, jazz, folk song, and so on) that singling out a few is audacious indeed. We have, however, within the parameters we have set for ourselves, chosen three composers whose work readily illustrates what music can do for the artist and for us, whose work remains as vital as it was long ago and helps enormously to explain why the humanities are indispensable to a well-lived, happy life. The composers are Bach, Mozart, and Beethoven; we will focus on the musical genre with which the name of each man is almost synonymous.

*Music is the shaped sound between silences.*

### A Bach Fugue

Johann Sebastian Bach (1685-1750) was born in a Germany that did not consider music an art form; that did not recognize what music could do for humanity's spirit; that viewed music as court entertainment, composed and performed for upper-class amusement by hirelings paid to do a job, or else as an adjunct to religious services. The music with which Bach is associated, which indeed he came to epitomize, grew out of religion but went beyond religion in its impact and influence on the future of music as an art. It is the music we call *baroque*, belonging to a period in Western humanities ranging from the late sixteenth century to (for historians' convenience) the year in which Bach died.

The baroque period was characterized by architectural grandeur and an elaborate use of color and ornamentation. Civic buildings, such as those that still line the Ringstrasse in Vienna, were adorned with gilt, statuary, and other forms of embellishment, none of which was intended to be purely functional. Baroque buildings were to be enjoyed as objects of vision, not simply as places in which certain tasks were accomplished.

The baroque church offered perhaps the most characteristic architectural style of the period. In sharp contrast to the austere churches of the Protestant Reformation, which wanted to "purify" religion of its Catholic sensuousness, the baroque houses of worship reintroduced marble, brilliant colors, and statues, perhaps in an effort to reinvest religion with an appeal to both the spirit and the senses. Throughout Germany, Austria, and Poland there are churches, dating from the seventeenth century, with flying angels suspended from brightly painted ceilings and smiling gold cherubs peeking out from behind the tops of marble columns. These churches, many of which are Catholic, were for their time the last word in opulence, offering dramatic and esthetic appeal without apology.

*Confined both geographically and professionally, Bach found liberation in exploring the possibilities of musical knowledge.*

Catholicism found in baroque splendor one means of bringing defectors back to the fold. But the impetus toward elaborate ornamentation also touched many Protestants as well as secular artists. As the era progressed, composers, especially in Italy, sought to outdo one another in the intricacy of their compositions. A unique feature they used was *counterpoint*, playing one melodic line against another, both melodic lines being given equal value and dominance. *Harmony*, of course, was already standard in music, but counterpoint carried complexity a step further.

> It is a rediscovery of the world of which I have the joy of being a part. It fills me with awareness of the wonder of life, with a feeling of the incredible marvel of being a human being. The music is never the same for me, never! Each day it is something new, fantastic and unbelievable. That is Bach, like nature, a miracle!
>
> Pablo Casals

Baroque counterpoint at first sounded strange to the ears of Bach's congregation in Arnstadt, where he was employed as church organist, an artisan who happened to compose his own pieces and whose appetite for experimenting with organ sound was insatiable. Seeking to expand his musical horizons, Bach went to Sweden in 1705 to study with the famous organist Buxtehude; he returned to Arnstadt with new works of such intricacy and virtuosity that the church choir often could not sing them. Bach achieved some fame throughout Germany as word spread of the new music. Eventually he became musical director and choir director at St. Thomas's Church in Leipzig, where he remained for the better part of his productive life, scarcely traveling more than a few miles in any direction. His reputation began to fade as he grew older, though the complexity of his work deepened. He became known as an eccentric; though music itself in Germany was attaining stature as an art form, the great repertoire of Bach—the cantatas, the oratorios, and the magnificent displays of counterpoint known as fugues—were considered dated even before they were ever really discovered. Bach's music would have to wait a full century before it would take its place among the acknowledged masterworks of humankind.

Confined both geographically and professionally, Bach found liberation in exploring the possibilities of musical language. The baroque style called for long, highly fluid melodies and countermelodies, but also for *improvisation*—a spon-

*Johann Sebastian Bach (1685–1750) (Culver Pictures)*

taneous variation or set of variations on a given theme. Through improvisation Bach could take wings and soar into the endless skies of inner space.

Bach lived in an era when music's only purpose was to be an adjunct to something else, such as a public or a religious ceremony. Few would have understood if a composer had stated unequivocally a belief that music should express the composer's own personality or inner feelings. While Bach's music is frequently labeled "intellectual" and is today preferred by many mathematicians to that of all other composers, surely there is an emotional side to mathematics. Listening intently to Bach's great Toccata and Fugue in D Minor, we are drawn into a vortex of sensations that are all but indescribable. The ear discerns the many melodic strands that play against each other, and the inner eye translates the sounds into patterns of light and lines that crisscross, engulf each other, and continually change into shapes never before seen or imagined.

A *toccata* is a freestyle musical form designed to allow the performer of Bach's day to display virtuosity and is frequently, as in the case of the D Minor work, followed by a *fugue*, which is more strictly controlled by established musical laws. In a toccata the composer or performer may improvise on the stated themes, taking them in virtually any direction. This practice has definite counterparts in jazz. It is no coincidence that jazz players often acknowledge a strong debt to Bach, particularly for his genius at improvisation, and often include variations on Bach melodies in their repertoire. The fugue allows for the simultaneous hearing of different melodies played or sung; it is a usually rapid form, which is stabi-

*It is no coincidence that jazz players often acknowledge a strong debt to Bach, particularly for his genius at improvisation.*

lized by the laws of counterpoint. That is, the melodic lines heard simultaneously must complement, not conflict, with each other.

You need only listen to the D Minor work to be astounded that one pair of hands could engage in so difficult a task. The idea behind the fugue is to demonstrate that what should not be a coordinated effort (that is, what for the average person would be an impossibility) is indeed well within the capabilities of the performer. Thus the Bach fugue in particular satisfies (harmonizes) two of our needs that at first seem to be in conflict—the need for total freedom (or the lack of coordination) and the need for some principle of control. It offers an experience continually on the brink of getting beyond control, but which always stays within its form.

*In baroque music we experience the complexities little by little, note by note.*

The music of Bach also parallels in sound the richness of the entire baroque period. We sometimes suspect that music, rather than art or architecture, serves as the ideal expression of baroque taste, because its linear (sequential) form allows us to experience its complexities little by little, note by note, rather than have them overwhelm the vision as many baroque interiors do.

## A Mozart Opera

We pointed out in a preceding section that opera had its beginnings in the court entertainments of the Renaissance. By the seventeenth century it had established itself as an important genre. In Italy, the land of its birth and early development, opera became the rage. Composers who could skillfully blend voices, text, and orchestra were desperately sought, and those who won favor with the courts were assured of lifetime success. Eventually the new genre became so popular that everyone, not just the privileged few, demanded access to it, and the great opera houses were built. Every major city required one: Rome, Florence, Venice, Milan, Bologna. Soon all of Europe had heard about the glories of Italian opera: the singers (including the *castrati*, who sang the women's roles and some of whom became rich and famous); the ballet dancers; the glorious arias, which were to opera what Shakespeare's soliloquies were to drama; the scenery, because new technology, such as cutting slits into the stage floor, now made it possible to slide sets on and off the stage easily; and, above all, the magnificent opera houses themselves, with their tier upon tier of boxes for aristocrats and their great chandeliers supporting huge candelabras to light the stages.

By the eighteenth century even small cities had their own versions of the opera house, which began to rival the town church as the focal point of community pride and activity. The entire population, not just the upper class and the aristocrats, could attend. There were no questions asked in those days about why all of the dialogue had to be sung or why the story was so hard to follow! Sung drama was simply a given, as basic to the culture as its favorite foods or the paintings and sculptures that everybody took for granted as the collective heritage.

Into this almost exclusively Italian cultural context arrived a young musician from Salzburg, Austria, a city that also boasted a great musical environment. He was Wolfgang Amadeus Mozart (1756–1791), who at the age of 13 had already been made concertmaster for the Archbishop of Salzburg and had then been decorated in Milan by the Pope himself. Having been a composer from the age of 6, when he created five pieces for the piano, he was probably not unduly surprised when at the advanced age of 14, he was asked to write an opera for the Milanese audiences. Mozart not only composed but directed *Mithridates, King of Pontus*, accomplishing everything by his sixteenth birthday. For the next nine years, without the patronage of Emperor Franz Josef of Austria, he struggled for financial security; nevertheless, he gave expression to perhaps the most prodigious outpouring of music the world has ever received from one human being in so brief a time. Opera intrigued him—the challenge of combining so many elements into one unified work. Having mastered the complexities of orchestration and developed a distinctive style—which was at once personal and characteristic of his cultural heritage and the strong influence of his predecessor Franz Josef Haydn (1732-1809)—he composed his first major opera, *Idomeneo*, with, of course, an Italian text. This was followed by *The Abduction from the Seraglio*, a delightfully complicated comic opera that has become famous for two reasons aside from its share of lilting and graceful music. It introduced the truly Mozartean operatic style: melodious arias alternating with dialogue that is sometimes spoken and sometimes intoned with musical background. The latter, called *recitative*, allowed Mozart to move the plot quickly along and to save his great melodies for the important moments. Boldly—and shockingly to many operagoers of the time—the libretto was in German, rather than in the standard Italian. This was assuredly as revolutionary in 1782 as opera in English still seems to be today. Mozart's contemporaries, like our own, must have thought opera was defined as a stageful of people singing in another language. Today the opera houses of most English-speaking cities flash translations above the proscenium arch, a practice that seems to annoy as many people as it pleases. (Apparently opera *should* be impossible to understand!) Similarly, new works by British and American composers have a difficult time getting produced. In addition to the unfamiliar modernity of the music in these new works, the dialogue actually makes sense—something Mozart desired a great deal.

Nonetheless, in 1786 he met up with a clerical poet and dramatist named Lorenzo da Ponte, and thus three of the four great Mozart operas—*The Marriage of Figaro* (1786), *Don Giovanni* (1787), and *Cosi fan tutte* (1790)—are set to

*Mozart struggled for financial security but gave expression to perhaps the most prodigious outpouring of music the world has ever received from one human being in so brief a time.*

*Wolfgang Amadeus Mozart (1756–1791) (Culver Pictures)*

Italian libretti, while only the fourth—*Die Zauberflöte, or The Magic Flute*—is in German. The language hardly made a difference, however; the operas were only partially successful in Mozart's lifetime. He died at the age of 35, having been poor for much of his life, and rests in an unknown grave somewhere in Vienna.

One of the bitter ironies in Mozart's life—and indeed in the entire history of the humanities—is the reputation that *Figaro* has achieved over the years as perhaps the greatest of all operas (surpassed, in the opinion of some, only by Mozart's own *Don Giovanni*). Lovers of Verdi, Wagner, and Puccini might easily advance convincing arguments for their favorite, but surely no one denies that *Figaro* continues to maintain a firm hold on the world of opera. Why then was the work at first a complete triumph only in Prague?

Some music historians believe Germany and Austria were still very much under Italian influence when the opera was first performed. Even though the text was in Italian, the composer was an Austrian by birth. With the wide popularity of Peter Schaffer's play (and film) *Amadeus*, almost everyone knows by now that the official composer of the Emperor's court in Austria was an Italian named Antonio Salieri. Though the fictional plot would have us believe that Salieri was obsessively envious of Mozart, the facts appear to tell a different story. In Mozart's lifetime Salieri was far better known and praised in the highest musical circles.

Yet *The Marriage of Figaro* has been seen by an incalculable number of audiences since its first, cool reception in Vienna. What charm does it possess? The music, to be sure, first and foremost. The opera contains aria upon aria that falls enchantingly upon the ear. One marvels that any human being could have poured forth so many melodies at one time, melodies the listener does not mind hearing again and again, melodies at once subtle and simple, allowing each of us to make private associations quite apart from their place in the story.

*Announcement for the first performance (May 1, 1786) of* The Marriage of Figaro, *perhaps the greatest of all operas. (The Granger Collection, New York)*

In *Figaro* Mozart perfected the technique of *singspiel*, opera that contains much dialogue that is half-spoken, half-sung, opera that is partly aria and partly rec- itative. The lover of Mozart has no difficulty with the question "Why do they sing everything in between the arias?" The answer is that Mozart has "merely" idealized human interaction. If Shakespeare's characters can talk to each other in verse, why should Mozart's not in music? The realism of the current cinema is, after all, *not* real. Explosions are carefully staged; so are prison riots. A mobster shoot-out leaves no one dead. Yet we allow ourselves to believe; we make a contract with the performers that, if they entertain us, we will not say we see through their tricks. Mozart's recitatives are also part of the make-believe world of entertainment.

In *Figaro* da Ponte and Mozart were working from a standard kind of French farce, a genre that had long proved itself stageworthy, using a typical cast of characters. A middle-aged Count has grown tired of his Countess and seeks fresh young conquests. These are not hard to come by, since he is rich and employs a large staff. According to custom, he has *le droit du seigneur* ("the privilege of the master" to enjoy the sexual favors of any servant he chooses). The young lady he desires is a beautiful maid who is engaged to marry Figaro, another servant. The two, in league with the Countess herself, weary of her husband's philandering, cleverly outwit the *seigneur*, who denounces the folly of his ways in time for a rousing finale in which the sun shines happily on both couples. So far, fairly stock material, wouldn't you say?

Mozart was nothing if not an innovator. With his boundless gift for mel- ody, his genius for orchestration, and, especially, his adoration of the female voice, he took this standard French farce and gave it a depth and a universal, enduring relevance that lift *The Marriage of Figaro* above possibly all operas, that place it among the most wondrous achievements in the humanities.

The usual treatment of the wife whose husband is unfaithful to her is to make her a comic figure. In the male-dominated traditions of the past, the phi- landerer tends to be a sympathetic character, while the wife is a nagging shrew, or at best a stock character who lacks the dimensions of a real person. In *Figaro*, however, the Countess becomes the prototype of all betrayed wives, left to stare into a mirror and face the pain of rejection and loneliness. Mozart wrote two of his greatest arias for the Countess. In the first, "Porgi, amor," she asks Love itself, which had once filled her life with joy, for one final favor: restore her husband's affections or help her to find peace in death. In the second, "Dove sono," she asks a question that people have been asking for centuries: where have the golden mo- ments fled? Why do happiness and love and youth slip through our fingers before we even realize what we are holding?

Finally, the opera of *Figaro* greatly expands and deepens the political theme touched upon in the French original. The servants outwit their master. The *droit du seigneur* is challenged—condemned, in fact, if contemporaries chose to see it that way. In Mozart, the condemnation is hard to mistake, since the two ser- vants are the leads, and we experience the action through their eyes. The rights of the common person are another of the opera's great themes; this may be another reason the work was not an overwhelming triumph in Vienna, a city accustomed to having an Emperor in the Royal Palace. We must remember that the French Rev- olution took place just three years after the first performance of *Figaro*, a revolu- tion that seemed inevitable and that attracted the sympathies of liberal minds throughout the world. For a young composer struggling to eke out a living from his music, writing the work involved a tremendous risk. While Mozart can by no

*The rights of the common person are among the themes of* The Marriage of Figaro. *The opera was not a triumph in Vienna, a city accustomed to having an Emperor in the Royal Palace.*

*A recent production of* The Marriage of Figaro *at Northwestern University. (Courtesy Northwestern University School of Music)*

means be considered as consistently revolutionary in his sentiments as Beethoven, *The Marriage of Figaro* and its glorious music will always remind humanity that everyone deserves equal attention—servants as well as neglected wives.

## A Beethoven Symphony

*Nobody has proposed that Beethoven leads all the rest solely because of his rhythm, or his melody, or his harmony. It's the combination.*

*Leonard Bernstein*

In the baroque musical tradition, which Bach epitomized, composers worked in a limited range of musical forms to find their own way through the music. Bach achieved greatness by making the forms accommodate his tremendous musical intellect and his need to explore inner space. Ludwig van Beethoven (1770-1827) may well have outdone Bach—in fact, every other composer—by exploring his own needs and inventing new musical forms to fulfill them. In so doing, Beethoven earned his place as the greatest composer. Music would never be the same again.

Whereas Bach was primarily a church composer/performer, Beethoven composed for churches, concert halls, small salons, private performances, royal chambers, but, above all else, for himself. When he completely lost his hearing during the peak of his musical career, Beethoven turned inward, and out of his complex and anguished soul came sounds no one had yet heard. Even today, more than a century and a half after the composer's death, when every note written by him has been played and interpreted by thousands upon thousands of musicians and heard by millions, new listeners can find in the music some as yet undisclosed aspect of Beethoven's personality as well as some unexplored region of their own inner space.

Of course, Beethoven did not emerge from a vacuum. He was building upon the new expansive tradition in German music established before him by

Haydn and Mozart. This tradition combined secular, religious, and nationalistic trends into one. It declared that the music of northern Europe was every bit the equal of Italian music—indeed would become supreme in all the world.

One can trace the evolution of the symphony, that major musical form, in the work of these three composers. Haydn wrote 104 symphonies, Mozart 41, and Beethoven "just" 9. (Later, Johannes Brahms, intimidated by the majestic symphonic creations of Beethoven, would spend 20 years working on his first symphony and would leave the world "just" 4!)

In 1804, Beethoven, after having given the world two symphonies in the tradition of Mozart, who had already stretched the limits of the form beyond anything yet known, came forth with his Third, or E-flat Major, Symphony, later to be called the *Eroica*. The premiere proved to be an occasion for which the music world was not completely prepared. Mozart's Forty-first, and last, Symphony, the titanic *Jupiter*, was massive in its conception and was thought to have said the last word as far as symphonic works were concerned. After all, a symphony was originally intended to be a 15- or 20-minute concert diversion, consisting of four movements: the first moderately paced, the second slow and lyrical, the third rapid and light-hearted, and the fourth rousing and climactic. The four movements were related only in terms of the composer's characteristic style, but taken together, they were not expected to make a unified statement of any kind. The *Jupiter* changed all that and by all rights should have remained the symphonic achievement of the centuries.

Then emerged the *Eroica*—twice the length of Mozart's masterpiece—a work so huge in conception, so complex in execution, and so overwhelming to experience that by all rights it should have invited immediate comparison with Michelangelo's *David* or the Sistine Chapel ceiling. Unfortunately, many of the first listeners could not accommodate themselves to the work's heroic dimensions or to its daring innovations, particularly Beethoven's heavy use of seventh chords, up to that time a musical taboo, considered barbarically dissonant, unfit for civilized ears.

In the opinion of music historians, the most astonishing aspect of the *Eroica* is that it is not the work of a musical adventurer, creating bigness for its own sake. One critic sums up the matter:

> We are used to the scale of the *Eroica*, but what is forever new is a musical substance which requires every second of the vast time expanse which Beethoven organized to contain it. In its size it is wholly efficient, as fine an example of economy of structure as any four-minute Bach fugue.[1]

We have a great work of art when the magnitude of the artist's message so fits the vehicle that carries it that we never lose sight of it, never let go of the communication. In contrast, Tchaikovsky's *1812 Overture*, with its thousand musicians and its exploding cannons, is too big for its own good and, like a huge rocket that has cleared the tower, soon leaves the onlooker far below.

In the *Eroica*, the four movements not only constitute a unity, but each succeeding movement sounds like a perfect complement to the one before it. It is clear that Beethoven did not finish one movement and then tack on another as though the preceding one had not existed. The first movement of the *Eroica* is on as grand a scale as Western music has ever reached. The story is that Beethoven

*Beethoven's* Eroica—*a work so huge in conception, so complex in execution, and so overwhelming to experience that it should have invited immediate comparison with Michelangelo's* David *or the Sistine Chapel ceiling.*

*Ludwig van Beethoven
(1770–1827) (Culver Pictures)*

had been inspired by the heroic image of Napoleon and created in this opening movement a music that paralleled his feelings. The work was originally dedicated to the man Beethoven perceived as the savior of the free world. When word reached the composer that his hero had demanded to be crowned Emperor, Beethoven rescinded the dedication.

One is tempted to hear in the second movement a musical parallel to Beethoven's profound disillusionment. Profound sorrow is certainly there, as indicated by the tempo notation: *marcia funebre* (funeral march). It is the slowest of all slow movements, dirgelike and heartbroken. We have already spoken of it in the section on silence as a musical element. Whether Napoleon was the direct cause of the sorrow or whether Beethoven, having exhausted the range of noble emotions, found himself exploring the depths of sadness, we cannot know; but we *can* say that the first two movements of the *Eroica* strongly suggest an experience common to nearly everyone: the passage from heroic, idealistic youth to tragic maturity.

The third movement, by contrast, almost shocks us with its galloping pace and precise horns, all of it sounding like nothing so much as a hunting party. Out of place? Surely not. If you listen carefully to every note of the funeral march, you'll find there is only so much emotional "wrenching" you can take. Life must go on. The depressed spirit must pull itself up from despair.

The finale begins with a graceful, dancelike melody suggestive of polite society: civilization restored, so to speak. This leads through an intricate development back into the same heroic mood that opened the symphony. We have passed from romantic illusion to the depths of tragedy and, through struggle, upward again to a more mature, sober, and deliberate affirmation. The *Eroica* is Beethoven's *Divine Comedy* and *Paradise Lost*—one of the very few times an artist has captured the human soul in full range. It would not mark Beethoven's last glimpse of paradise.

Beethoven's Ninth, and final, Symphony was composed around 1818, when he had become totally deaf. It is easily four times the length of a late Mozart symphony, and double that of the *Eroica*. Not the journey of a young man's soul coping with the sobering realities of life, the Ninth Symphony is rather the final statement of a gigantic mentality that has struggled for years with both physical and creative suffering—of a person who has labored to find and capture it all, as Michelangelo, two centuries earlier, had sought perfection in marble, and as Einstein, a century later, would seek the ultimate equation for unifying all interactions among all parts of the universe.

During the first three movements of the Ninth, Beethoven gives us one haunting melody after another, complex rhythms, intricate harmonies, and shattering dissonance. He seems to be striving for nothing more or less than to find a musical equivalent to every feeling that can be experienced. By the fourth movement he appears to have concluded that the orchestra alone was not enough to express the sounds he must have heard in the far recesses of his silent world. Other composers before him had written large choral works: Bach's *Passion According to St. Matthew*, Haydn's *Creation*, and Mozart's *Requiem*, to name three supreme examples. But Beethoven pushes the human voice farther than many believed—and many *still* believe—possible.

There remains considerable controversy about the final movement of the Ninth. Some critics have said it takes us as close to the gates of heaven as we can get in this earthly lifetime. Some have called it a musical embarrassment, totally unsingable. One soprano, after attempting it, vehemently declared that Beethoven had no respect whatever for the female voice. Anyone hearing the movement for the first time is likely to be swept away by its incredible momentum and may be hearing not human voices at all, but dazzling combinations of sounds there is no time to identify. In an interview with the authors, a tenor described what being in the huge chorus is like:

> I keep my mouth open and manage to hit about every third or fourth note. The pace is frantic and the notes, the conclusion of the work, are beyond my reach. I think they are really beyond the reach of most voices. Nonetheless, a curious exuberance is created which compensates for the straining of vocal chords. The singers' struggles are concealed by the crashing of the orchestra, and the entire work, perilously close to disaster, miraculously escapes and achieves a glory most people experience only a few times in their lives, if they are lucky enough to do even that.

The poet Theodore Spencer, in calling Shakespeare's *King Lear* "the greatest single work of mankind," hastily added that Beethoven's Ninth is its closest rival for the honor.

By far, the majority opinion about the work is that it transcends its own "unsingability" and any breach of musical taste it may commit. Something so vast is its own awesome self—like a colossus that stands framed against the horizon, dwarfing the surrounding earth with its unearthly size. Asking whether one "likes it" or not seems beside the point. One can only feel humbled by its majesty. Listening to Beethoven's Ninth Symphony is discovering what human creativity *really* means.

*At the moment when the theme of joy appears for the first time [in Beethoven's Ninth Symphony] the orchestra stops abruptly, thus giving a sudden unexpected character to the entrance of the song. And this is a true touch; the theme is rightly divine. Joy descends from heaven enveloped in a supernatural calm.*

*Romain Rolland*

*Beethoven's Ninth Symphony—something so vast is its own awesome self, like a colossus that stands framed against the horizon, dwarfing the surrounding earth with its own unearthly size.*

# Popular Musical Forms

Bach, Mozart, and Beethoven still hold out their hands to us, and one may easily accommodate their music while having a keen ear for the musical sounds of one's own time and place. Allowing the past and the present to live side by side, allowing each to enhance the quality of our lives, is indeed a goal of the humanities. The greater the variety in our musical taste, the greater the knowledge of our total selves, for the sounds we long to hear are the sounds that represent us, that *mean* us amid the clanging hodgepodge of noise that is the random audio environment. Thus we do ourselves a disservice when, having discovered the glories of the musical past, we shut ourselves off from other musical experiences.

## The Song

For many of you, our readers, your earliest musical experience will have been a song, a musical form that, like the sonnet in literature, is usually restricted in length. The standard pop "tune" is comprised of 32 measures (a *measure* is the basic musical unit). The standard rhythm is what we call quarter time, or 4/4 time. This means that a measure contains four rhythmic beats. If each tone in a measure is equally stressed, then the measure will contain four notes, called quarter notes. If there are eight tones (eight notes) in the measure, then the eight counts have to be accomplished in the length of time it takes to beat out four quarter notes. You undoubtedly know that 1-2-3-4 repeated over and over constitutes the rhythmic underpinning of a great many songs and dances. You will not find many songs with 32 measures each containing just four notes, but the typical song has a total of 128 beats.

We are certain the Greeks had songs, but assuredly those songs were not limited to 32 measures. We do not even know that the Greeks had any units such as the measure. Very probably there were minstrels who sang the heroic poems like *The Iliad* and *The Odyssey*. In the Greek plays the action was interrupted by odes sung and danced to by a chorus. As we have said, the earliest Western music may well have been sung words. Such a phenomenon would not have been surprising for the Greeks, who venerated rational discourse above all else. The musical accompaniment was perhaps intended to heighten the effect of the words, not to be a source of enjoyment in and of itself.

Lyrics to songs (except for the rock tunes of our noise-dominated age, whose words are not always meant to be clear) are as important as the melodies. There are the nursery songs that constitute our first musical experiences; the popular songs of our adolescent years, many of which we forever associate with the happy times before responsibility set in and which preserve our memories of first loves and faraway friends; and songs that remain in our minds to mark the milestones of our existence. "What were they playing the night I fell in love? the night our first child was born? the day our family moved into our new house?"

But whether we're talking about a personal repertoire of meaningful songs or a song recital or a musical comedy we attended, there are *always* lyrics to draw from us a response: "That's *exactly* how I felt when I became aware that I had met just the right someone!" or "when I knew for certain that the right someone was all wrong!"

A great many song lyrics seem immune to time and change. Elizabethan composers set to music the plaintive words of lovesick swains whose sensibilities were probably similar to those of young people today. When Madame Butterfly, blind to the obvious implications of her American husband's departure from her and their unborn child, sings with a smile that "one fine day" he will return, we are listening to a grand-opera version of the very same emotions we can find in popular songs of this century, expressing the illusions we all need for survival. Don José's final condemnation of the faithless Carmen is different in style, not in feeling, from countless lyrics that tell of the love-filled hatred of the betrayed.

Why do we listen over and over to lyrics that tell us nothing we do not already know? When the great French entertainer Edith Piaf stood in a solitary spotlight, her huge eyes moist with tears, and sang of "La Vie en Rose"—sang that life *must* be seen through rose-colored glasses—she was not conveying any startling new insights to her audience.

The power of song—often the simpler, the better—lies in the enormous importance to human beings of *network*—a reaching out of hands and hearts, a touching of souls. Just knowing that others feel what we feel brings a reassurance that is one of life's comforts. The songs we collect as our personal treasures—from the most soaring of arias to the earthiest of blues—make us feel part of a warm circle of human beings whose lives have very much in common. Without songs to bind us together, each of us would feel more loneliness than we might be able to bear.

Song is an established musical form and thus can be evaluated esthetically, even as a new symphony or opera must be. Unfortunately, today's standard for popular songs is the Top 40. A song that fails to sell is considered a flop. By this yardstick just about every song written by Franz Schubert would have had to be placed in the reject file.

At its most effective, a song is a unified blend of music and words that makes a simple restatement of a very universal experience (as in Leonard Bernstein's "Lonely Town"); that finds a new way to express an old feeling (as in Stephen Sondheim's remarkable "Send in the Clowns," whose very title says much about the absurdity of a love relationship); or that suddenly opens a new door and reveals something about ourselves we hadn't thought about or at least hadn't expected to find in a song (as in Don McLean's "Vincent," which reminds us of how often we fail to listen and how little we see). What distinguishes a song from other experiences in life is the fact that the experience—the insight, the feeling—is there every time the song is heard. A great song is thus one that has been around for quite a while, or that we are sure *will* be.

*Without songs to bind us together, each of us would feel more loneliness than we might be able to bear.*

## Folk Music

Folk songs are likely to be exceptions to the esthetic "rules" we have mentioned. A wry lecturer on the college circuit once observed that the reason folk music is so bad is that it is written by the folks. One presumes the speaker was not able to take folk songs seriously as a significant form of human expression. Often the dedicated concertgoer considers folk music altogether too haphazard in its origins and careless in its execution to warrant serious consideration. But folk songs do indeed fulfill a major requirement of art: *They have endured.*

Folk music is not intended as a concert experience. It is a participant's art. It has strong sociological functions. It is an external anchor not so much for one's personal self, but for one's group or ethnic identity.

Folk music can tell a story or else have no real point. The popular tune of a few years back "I'm Looking over a Four-Leaf Clover" was no doubt jeered at by musical purists. Yet if only one person in a group starts to sing it, most assuredly everyone will join in. Or let a fiddler introduce the first few notes of "Turkey in the Straw" and almost immediately people are clapping their hands or dancing. Something has to be said for music that can so dramatically alter group behavior.

The history of folk music includes *commemorative songs*, which derive from times before people had written records of important events. During the Middle Ages, for example, troubadours kept people informed of battles and skirmishes. Maritime lore abounds with songs commemorating events that took place at sea, such as atrocities committed by a pirate captain or the sinking of a ship to its lonely, watery grave.

Of particular interest is that the narrators of commemorative songs seldom if ever identify themselves. The song's opening words are likely to be something like: "My name is nothing extra / So that I will not tell." One song winds up in this self-effacing manner: "Now to conclude and finish, too far my lines have run." The focus is clearly the event itself, and the obscurity of the balladeers makes possible an easy transfer to the group. It is always *our* song, never *their* song.

The *work song* is highly durable, for it is hard to imagine a time when work will not be central to most people's lives. In some cases the work song reflects great hardship and a state of tension between management and labor. Often, however, the music is jolly and the words are full of bounce and nonsense:

> *I've been workin' on the railroad*
> *All the livelong day;*
> *I've been workin' on the railroad*
> *Just to pass the time away.*

The nineteenth-century folk ballad "John Henry" reflects the conflict between worker and machine at a time when the steam drill was about to replace hammers swung by human arms. John Henry became a folk hero, the prototype of the superhuman individual who is stronger and smarter than a machine.

The *accumulation song* is deliberately never-ending. Songs like "The Twelve Days of Christmas" and "Old MacDonald" start off with one detail (one gift, one animal) and then add more, always repeating the list from the very beginning. Accumulation songs exist to keep the group together and prolong the high spirits of the gathering.

The *scoundrel song* celebrates the Dionysian personality—the perennial favorite of our hidden selves—the lawless, irresponsible, but endlessly charming rogue you couldn't trust or marry or put in charge of an important operation but who is always fun. An Irish favorite is "The Moonshiner," which upholds a life of drinking, carousing, gambling, and avoiding work. The hero proudly announces that if you don't like him, you can "leave me alone." Who can argue with that premise? He intends to

> *. . . eat when I'm hungry and drink when I'm dry,*
> *And if moonshine don't kill me,*
> *I'll live till I die.*

To be sure, society would perish if it depended upon wild rovers, but at the same

*Types of folk songs: commemorative, work, accumulation, scoundrel, spiritual.*

time, nobody ever composed a folk song about a law-abiding accountant or a pious minister or a faithful husband.

During the 1960s, a period of wholesale fragmentation and alienation in the United States, a significant revival of folk music took place. Young people, often far from home, got together for the night around a campfire and became instant—if temporary—friends through the common bond of singing.

Sophisticated performers like Bob Dylan, Joan Baez, and Judy Collins revived old songs like "Amazing Grace" and soon had as many as 10,000 voices joining in, often with hands interlocked in a show of togetherness. They sang songs like "We Shall Overcome," destined to become part of the folk tradition, and they wrote new folk songs, using the familiar structures of the past, to make statements against war, pollution, and the corrupt establishment. Bob Dylan's "Hard Rain's Gonna Fall" and John Lennon's "Give Peace a Chance" are two of the folk songs written and sung in protest against the war in Vietnam; they will endure until the sun rises upon a world of peace and equality.

*A significant revival of folk music took place in the 1960s. Young people, far from home, got together around a campfire and became friends through the common bond of singing.*

Folk music has inspired composers of all nationalities and in all periods. Aaron Copland (1900-1990) consistently used folk themes as the basis of major works like *Billy the Kid, Appalachian Spring*, and *El Salon Mexico*. In a unique reversal of the usual process whereby a well-known folk theme helps to popularize a new concert work, in *Appalachian Spring* Copland resurrected an old Shaker hymn called "Simple Gifts," which has become a standard in the repertoire of folk singers because of the great popularity of Copland's piece.

This renaissance of the folk song brought back into our national consciousness forms like the *spiritual*, which had had its special beginnings in the black need for a cosmic identity. Taken—stolen—away from their homeland, blacks in the United States of the last century, with no future except slavery, pain, and death, concentrated on their relationship with God and an ultimate reward in a

*Aaron Copland consistently used folk themes as the basis of major symphonic works. (Culver Pictures)*

paradise where everyone was free. The socially aware generation of the 1960s recognized that such pain was not a thing of the past, that the need behind the songs was still, tragically, there.

In spirituals there is much emphasis on God's personal concern for each person, however obscure that person may be in the eyes of other mortals. For instance:

> *I sing because I'm happy,*
> *I sing because I'm free,*
> *For His eye is on the sparrow,*
> *And I know He watches me.*

*Folk songs do indeed fulfill a major requirement of art: they have endured.*

If all music does not have to express or appeal to the emotions, the spiritual is one kind that exists to make emotional release possible. We cannot imagine what life would have been like for slaves, or what it would be like today in the impoverished sections of inner cities, without this profound music of earthly sorrow and religious hope. That such music came into being hardly excuses those responsible for the suffering, nor is the music ample compensation for the conditions that produced it. We can only be in awe of the power of its simple message.

## Jazz: An American Musical Form

*Jazz evolved from the everyday life of the people—far from music conservatories, institutions of higher culture, or the great tradition of the concert repertoire.*

Jazz is so popular throughout the world that one might suppose every country claims to have been its originator. But jazz is American in the way that a folk song like "John Henry" is American. Jazz has much to do with the *insistence upon freedom*. It evolved, as much American art has evolved, from the everyday life of the people—far from music conservatories, institutions of higher culture, or the great tradition of the concert repertoire.

It evolved from many strains of folk and popular music, arising out of churches and fields, brothels and bars—all of these, but mainly out of the brothels, the houses of prostitution where, in the early years of this century, black musicians could get work and were free to weave whatever musical spells suited them so long as the paying customers stayed happy.

Accounts of how jazz got started sometimes give the impression that the performers were all untrained musicians who just "happened" to come up with something that had style and grace. In truth, we don't know much about the pioneers, but as the decades of the twentieth century rolled by, the form did attract a range of musical geniuses, some who taught themselves, some who had been classically trained. They had—and continue to have—one thing in common: They know how to maintain a balance between control and the need for soaring release.

As we pointed out, jazz instrumentalists and composers admire Bach because he more or less invented improvisation, the art of taking flight from a set theme. A typical jazz piece follows a disciplined pattern. The group, or the soloist backed by the group, will play the main theme once through, sometimes a well-known song, sometimes an original tune composed for the group. Then one instrument after another performs a variation of the theme. Original jazz works have deliberately offbeat titles, like "Take the A Train," "One O'Clock Jump," and "Stompin' at the Savoy." The philosophy behind such titles is that jazz must be its own thing. Jazz shapes and defines the "cool scene"—a late-night coming together of sophisticated people too mellow to be concerned about affairs of the day.

*Charlie Parker often improvised for 10 or 15 minutes before returning to a theme. (UPI/ Bettmann)*

In the early decades of this century, great jazz soloists like Charlie Parker and Louis Armstrong became famous for going off on lengthy variations, often improvising for 10 or 15 minutes before returning to the theme. The literary novel *Young Man with a Horn* was inspired by the tragically interrupted life of Bix Beiderbecke, a cornet player known for his extraordinary improvisatory flights. The book deals with a musician's unsuccessful quest for a perfect note, beyond the known range of his instrument. Fortunately we can still listen to the recorded improvisations of Beiderbecke as he strained his cornet to the limit—and further.

Musical histories that deal with jazz as a serious and major art form give preeminence to Edward Kennedy—known universally as Duke—Ellington (1899-1974), the person who did the most to bridge the gap between the concert hall and the cabaret. A bandleader who had Manhattan society driving to the Cotton Club in Harlem during the late 1920s, Ellington sought to expand the range of jazz through continual experimentation

> with what he called his "jungle effects." When the sounds of "growling" trumpets and trombones, sinuous clarinets and eerie percussion were recorded, the originality of the orchestration was immediately grasped internationally by music critics and record buyers. . . . As a jazz arranger his great gift was in balancing orchestration and improvisation.[2]

Ellington brought jazz to Carnegie Hall, where it could be played and evaluated "up there" with the great names in music. In so doing, he wrote out elaborate and

*Duke Ellington bridged the gap between the concert hall and the cabaret. (Culver Pictures)*

complex orchestrations—something no one had done before him. He did leave room for solo flights (or else it would not have been jazz), but his own compositions and his arrangements display a classic sense of discipline and musicianship.

Another major American composer brought jazz to Carnegie Hall in the early years, and that was George Gershwin (1898-1937), who started his career as a Tin Pan Alley songwriter, then moved on to compose the scores for Broadway revues of the 1920s. Yet Gershwin, who had been classically trained and could

*Ella Fitzgerald, a major jazz vocalist of this century. (UPI/ Bettmann)*

*George Gershwin put an American art form—jazz—on the international musical map. (Culver Pictures)*

have been a world-class concert pianist had he chosen that path, was hungry for greater things. In 1924 he found his chance. Paul Whiteman, a bandleader also hungry for "serious" recognition, commissioned him to write a concert jazz piece. The result was *Rhapsody in Blue*, which combined the textures of romantic works for piano and symphony orchestras with the pulsations, dissonance, and syncopated rhythms found in jazz. Gershwin had put an American art form on the international musical map. The *Rhapsody* became an overnight success and would sell over a million recordings. It remains a part of the standard symphonic repertoire.

*With* Rhapsody in Blue *Gershwin put an American art form on the international music map.*

## Epilogue

We cannot deal in a single chapter with all possible musical experiences. We have explored some; that is the important thing. The more we listen, the more variety we will develop in our musical tastes and the stronger will become our identity with sound. To limit ourselves to only one form of music is to know only part of our personality.

There are hundreds of composers today no longer satisfied with what Beethoven did, seeking to expand the limits of musical form and musical sound in ways that are meaningful to *them*. There are composers working with electronic instruments and composers who say that anything (even a washboard) can be a musical instrument. You can hear sounds today that would have scandalized Beethoven himself, who in turn had shocked his own generation with dissonance that some critics said ought never to have been inflicted upon the human ear.

As Beethoven won his case and set new standards, so will many of today's new composers eventually have their day and win acceptance. The smart listener is the one who takes chances, is open to new sounds, is among the first to applaud. If you are that person—and even if time proves you wrong—what have you lost except time spent on an unusual experience? Where is the art of being human except in seeking out experience, being aware of it, savoring it, pondering it, wondering at it? But first, of course, take the time to listen, really listen, to the sounds that have already graced the audio environment, to the important sounds we have identified in this chapter. Then spend part of a day with your silences.

*To limit ourselves to only one form of music is to know only part of our personality.*

# Glossary

*dissonance:* A principle in music whereby two or more uncongenial notes are sounded or sung at the same time, producing an unfamiliar and usually unpleasant effect. The effect is almost always deliberate; the reasons for it, quite varied. Often, however, the composer or arranger is attempting to avoid overused harmonic patterns that fall pleasantly but unexcitingly on the ear.

*fugue:* A musical composition, or a section within a larger composition, in which two or more melodic lines play against each other. The form, popular during the baroque period, was given its most memorable embodiment by J. S. Bach.

*harmony:* A principle in music whereby two or more notes, congenial or otherwise, are sounded or sung at the same time. Harmony includes both dissonant and nondissonant effects.

*improvisation:* A spontaneous variation, or a set of variations, on a stated musical theme.

*melody:* Either any arrangement of notes in a flowing sequence, or a significant sequence of musical notes that form a unity and are usually meant to be distinguished from what comes before and what follows.

*minimalists:* Contemporary composers who reject the idea that music ought to be the expression of inner emotional states or that it exists to produce such states in the listener.

*monochord:* An early instrument used by the Greeks, made of a wooden box with an opening on top and a single string tightly stretched across the opening.

*plainsong:* The major musical form of the late Middle Ages; a continuously flowing melodic line, intended to be sung, without harmony, by an indeterminate number of voices so that the effect is as of one person singing.

*rhythm:* The alternation of stress and unstress in music, usually created by a percussion instrument. Its effect is to unify the sounds. When rhythm is very pronounced, one is almost compelled to move the body, as in dancing. So basic is the "rhythmic urge" that a reasonable argument could be made for the possibility that all music began as pure rhythm for human rites.

*symphony:* The major orchestral musical form from the late eighteenth century to the present, consisting of separate movements of contrasting tempi. Originally no unity of style or feeling was intended, but as the form developed, composers increasingly insisted upon such unity. In symphonies from the latter half of the nineteenth century to the present, one will even hear the same themes recurring in different movements.

*toccata:* A more or less unstructured musical form, popular in Bach's time, usually composed for organ or harpsichord and allowing for an overpowering display of musical virtuosity by the performer.

*tone:* A single sound produced either by a human voice or an instrument. In the basic scale there are seven different full tones. When tones are written down, they are called *notes*.

*variations:* Melodic sequences based on previously heard themes, similar enough to them to evoke associations but changed sufficiently to allow the listener to move ahead to new experiences.

# Notes

1. Abraham Veinus, Syracuse University (quoted on the jacket to the Vanguard recording).
2. Alan Bullock and R. B. Woodings, eds., *20th-Century Culture* (New York: Harper & Row, 1983), 212.

## Suggested Listening

Bach, Johann Sebastian. Toccata and Fugue in D Minor and *The Passion According to St. Matthew.*

Beethoven, Ludwig van. Symphony no. 3, Symphony no. 6, and Symphony no. 9.

Brahms, Johannes. Symphony no. 1.

Copland, Aaron. *Billy the Kid* and *El Salon Mexico.*

Ellington, Duke. *Take the A Train, Mood Indigo, Satin Doll,* and *Sophisticated Lady.*

Gershwin, George. *An American in Paris* and *Rhapsody in Blue.*

Grofé, Ferde. *Grand Canyon* Suite.

Haydn, Joseph. String Quartet in C, Op. 76, no. 3.

Mozart, Wolfgang Amadeus. *The Marriage of Figaro, Don Giovanni, The Magic Flute,* and *Cosi fan tutte.*

Stravinsky, Igor. *The Rite of Spring.*

Tchaikovsky, Peter Ilyich. Piano Concerto no. 1 and *Romeo and Juliet* Overture.

Thomson, Virgil. *The Plough That Broke the Plains.*

Verdi, Giuseppe. *Aida* and *La Traviata.*

*Oskar Kokoschka, Kokoschka, Drama-Komoedie (1907) (Lithograph, 46-1/2 x 30. Collection, The Museum of Modern Art, New York. Purchase Fund)*

# 4

# Theater: Two Masks

## Overview

Greek amphitheaters were so vast that stage makeup—even if the Greeks had such—would not have sufficed. Instead, actors wore large masks with greatly exaggerated expressions. The actors could not very well change masks every time their characters changed emotion. So the sorrowful mask of tragedy was worn for that kind of play in which the outcome was catastrophic, and the grinning mask of comedy was worn for lighthearted plays with happy endings. Thus began the separation between the tragic and the comic.

Life, however, is neither wholly tragic nor wholly comic; instead, it is made up of events we interpret as happy or sad—or as somewhere in between—to the extent that they conform or fail to conform to our individual hopes. Pure tragedy and pure comedy exist only in the art of theater, and not always even there.

Theater art has come to recognize that a subtle blending of the tragic and the comic brings the drama closer to reality, even though classic and contemporary works in which the clear separation is maintained are still produced. In this chapter we shall examine differences between the "two masks," similarities between them, and, finally, ways in which both tragedy and comedy can serve as resources for living.

## The Experience of Tragedy

Traditionally, dramatists aspire to create important tragedies, partly out of respect for this earliest of dramatic forms and partly out of the desire to move people as profoundly as theater has the power to do, through important, universal conflicts. Tragedy combines feeling and thought. It was the art form analyzed by the world's first drama critic, Aristotle, and his *Poetics* remains a significant discussion of the elements that make tragic theater effective. This section will examine some of the elements of classical tragedy as they have been found in the early period in Athens, will trace some of the changes brought about by Shakespeare, and will attempt to explain the concept of tragedy in our own time.

### The Importance of Plot in Tragedy

*Aeschylus made possible the vital dramatic element of conflict by introducing the two-character scene.*

According to Aristotle, drama began as a religious ritual in which a chorus of worshippers chanted praise to the god Dionysus. They were clothed in goatskins in an effort to appear like satyrs, the half-goat, half-human followers of Dionysus. There was a leader of this chorus, and later, the first actual character appeared, played by the world's first actor, Thespis. Although we don't know what the actor said to the leader or how the chorus responded, we can surmise that they were involved in a story of some kind, though it must have been short on plot as we know it. With the addition of a second actor by the fifth-century-B.C. dramatist Aeschylus, a vital theatrical element appeared: *conflict*. One actor could now want what the other actor did not want him to have, and in their reenactments of great legends about Prometheus, Agamemnon, and other legendary heroes, these conflicts could be shown to audiences assembled at a festival in the spring, the only time of year when plays were presented. Still, the chorus remained predominant, representing the common people and commenting on the terrible dilemmas of the tragically doomed characters, who were generally aristocrats, persons of power. When Sophocles introduced yet a third actor, the plots became *really* interesting, because it was now possible for this new character to take sides with one actor in opposition to another. The scenes and dialogue became more important than the comments by the chorus. Modern readers or viewers of Greek plays, accustomed as they are to conflict as the essence of drama, tend to concentrate on what *happens*— on *plot*—rather than on how the chorus comments on and interprets these events.

*Justice might be shown to win out or to be nonexistent.*

The conflicts arose from a variety of causes: a curse on a family, hatred within a family, a duel between believers in two kinds of power, emotions run wild, gods versus people. No orthodox religious position was necessary for any of the playwrights who won the right to show their plays to the public, numbering as many as 20,000 people, during the three-day festival. Playwrights could tell stories showing the human beings as too proud or too weak. The very existence of the gods could be doubted. Justice might be shown to win out in the long run, or justice might be shown to be nonexistent. All that was necessary was to tell a familiar story, to emphasize whatever theme was desired, and to relate the story in such an impressive way that the audiences would respond with strong feelings.

By the fourth century when Aristotle wrote his *Poetics*, the age of the great tragedians was over; nevertheless, Aristotle was able to observe the effects of their plays on audiences moved to tears. As a critic and a scientist, he was interested in analyzing events, always wondering how things worked. How could these vicarious experiences be so strong? Aristotle decided that *empathy*, the identification of audience members with the actors, allowed them almost to experience the same pain being suffered before them. But why were some plays more effective than others? He decided that the most effective plays had the strongest plots, but he was also interested in character and thought.

It isn't hard to see why plot should come first. There is, after all, something riveting about a well-told story with a definite beginning, middle, and end. In real life, our "plots" just keep going until we, the principal characters, are no longer here. Our stories are filled with significant moments, but we lack the artist's ability to underscore, to heighten these moments. We speak in prose, not poetry, and our speech itself is filled with pauses, repetition, and late responses that make us wish some artist could have provided the right word for the right moment. We have no clear-cut, single purpose moving toward a definite climax and finale. Our lives just keep rolling along, filled with missed moments—the late arrival, the word not spoken, the anticlimax.

*In real life, our "plots" just keep going until we are no longer here.*

Aristotle's famous definition of tragedy indirectly explains why the philosopher considered plot its principal component. Tragedy, he advises,

> is the imitation of an action that is serious, complete, and of a certain magnitude; in language embellished with each kind of artistic ornament . . . ; in the form of action, not narrative; with incidents arousing pity and fear so as to bring about the proper purgation of these emotions.

Historians of theater development stress the phrase "proper purgation" and believe that for Aristotle the aim of tragic drama was for the audience to undergo a release of emotion—or a *catharsis*. The inventor of logic must assuredly have favored an approach to living that was characterized by the calm of reason, not the turbulence of emotion. What better source of emotional release than in a theater, where one could become deeply involved in the make-believe pain of actors? Presumably, one would then be prepared to handle real-life crises without confusion.

*For Aristotle the aim of tragic drama was for the audience to undergo a release of emotion—a catharsis.*

Now, what brings the audience to the catharsis of emotions is often the manner in which the dramatist arranges the events of the play. Plot is thus not the story in itself, but rather the way in which the sequence of actions is structured. The most promising story can fail to involve the audience if the plot is carelessly constructed. Central to the success of plot structure is a significant conflict that emerges. Sometimes the conflict generates such strong emotions in the audience that perfect plotting is less important.

*Plot is not the story itself, but the way in which the sequence of actions is structured.*

## Two Classical Tragedies

Two of the great tragic works from the classical period are the *Antigone* of Sophocles (496-406 B.C.) and the *Medea* of Euripides (480-406 B.C.). The first is representative of the kind of play that Aristotle greatly admired: almost flawlessly structured, with each scene leading the protagonist toward his inevitable doom, concluding with a speech of recognition in which he accepts the moral rightness of his suffering.

The second is less complete than the first. There is no sense of moral rightness about its catastrophe. It is the work of a psychological dramatist who seemed to understand a great deal about the human soul in turmoil and who may have thought this turmoil was what drama was all about.

*Antigone* is the story of a strong-willed young woman, daughter of the doomed Oedipus, whose tragic tale Sophocles later told in *Oedipus the King*. She is in conflict with the ruler of her country, a powerful man named Creon, who has decreed that the body of Antigone's slain brother shall remain unburied as a warning to others against leading rebel forces against their king. Antigone chooses to follow her conscience and the customs of her religion by burying the young man's body and ensuring his passage into the next life. Arrested and brought before Creon, the defiant woman denounces the king's laws as well as Creon's audacity in believing a mortal has the right to place himself above the gods.

Creon, not Antigone, is the tragic protagonist of the play. For Aristotle "proper purgation" of the emotions came about as the audience identified with the downfall of a human being of noble and virtuous qualities, except for one glaring weakness, a flaw that suffocated all of the goodness. Aristotle observed that in the great tragedies he had seen the flaw was always the same, and it was called *hubris*, mortal pride, a blindness to one's mortal limitations, the misguided assumption that worldly power placed one on the level of the gods.

> *For Aristotle tragedy was about the downfall of a human being of noble and virtuous qualities, except for one weakness:* hubris, *the misguided assumption that worldly power placed one on the level of the gods.*

*Katharine Cornell as Antigone. (Culver Pictures)*

Creon is caught in the midst of two terrible dilemmas. One is to persist in enforcing his own laws, even if it means putting to death a woman who acted out of widely respected religious motives *and* who is engaged to marry his own son! The second dilemma is what brings him the greater suffering. If he carries out the death sentence, he will prove his strength as king; he will show his subjects that he is worthy of their unquestioning obedience. He will also prove that personal obligations or love for his family do not sway him. If he frees Antigone, he earns the everlasting love of his son, but at the cost of his kingly integrity.

In choosing to put Antigone to death, Creon sets into motion a series of events that make his total downfall inevitable. He rejects his son's pleas, rejects the warnings of a holy prophet, and does indeed behave as if he has become a god. In the agonizing climax to the play, Creon discovers that his son has secretly entered the cave in which Antigone was sealed and, finding her already dead, has taken his own life. This disaster is quickly followed by news that the queen has also committed suicide.

Like many of the great tragic protagonists, Creon delivers a heartbroken speech in which he recognizes fully what his arrogance has caused and in which he bears full responsibility for the tragedy:

> Lead me away, I have been rash and foolish. I have killed my son and my wife. I look for comfort; my comfort lies here dead. Whatever my hands have touched has come to nothing. Fate has brought all my pride to a thought of dust.

In his definition Aristotle said that tragedy imitated events that were "serious, complete, and of a certain magnitude." By "complete" one may assume the philosopher meant that the catastrophe was fully comprehensible in terms of the protagonist's flaw of character. There is a certain moral rightness about the catastrophe, even though the character has suffered mightily, as have those deeply affected by the flaw.

Aristotle was not insisting that all tragedies had to conclude with a speech of recognition by the protagonist, giving a sense of completion to the work. In fact, in the *Poetics* he singles out the work of Sophocles' contemporary Euripides as being the most tragic of all, despite having reservations about the younger dramatist's lack of tight plot structures.

One of the most popular Greek tragedies with modern audiences is the *Medea* of Euripides, which *is* tighter than most of the dramatist's other works. This play is driven by the terrifying inevitability of a jealous wife's murder of her children as an act of vengeance against her husband. Many critics have even proclaimed Euripides as the first modern playwright, more interested in the emotional and psychological turbulence of his characters than in bringing his work to a satisfying completeness.

Medea is married to Jason, a man she helped to escape from peril. She has left her own country, destroyed her family, and used her powers of witchcraft to help Jason find the Golden Fleece. In addition, she is now living in a country that shows little regard for foreigners or for women.

When Jason comes to tell her that he has made plans to marry another woman, the princess of the country where they are living, Medea pretends to be pleased. Their sons, she is told, will have the advantages of living in the same household with royalty, and their future will be assured because they will be half-brothers to any offspring of Jason and the princess.

*Zoe Caldwell as Medea.
(Courtesy WQED/Pittsburgh
and* Kennedy Center Tonight.
*Photo: Ken Love)*

Medea sends a wedding gift to the princess, a toxic robe that sticks to her body and kills her. This murder is not enough, however. Medea gets revenge on Jason by taking her sons into the house and stabbing them to death.

When the heartbroken Jason arrives to see his sons, he is not even allowed to touch their dead bodies. Medea has succeeded in destroying his prospects by killing the sons she loves. Bitterly she tells Jason, "I loathed you more than I loved them." Then she rides off to a refuge provided for her by the king of a nearby country.

*Medea* was shown during the spring festivals honoring the gods, but the story scarcely sounds religious. Where are the gods in all this? Why doesn't somebody stop this killer? Did justice triumph? Are there any laws? The answers are ambiguous, but it would be fair to say that the playwright has doubts about the power of the gods and doubts about whether they exist at all, or if they do, whether they take any interest in human affairs. As for "justice," the play suggests that maybe human emotions are more important. There is indeed sympathy for the injured foreign woman, but the playwright is not claiming that her lowly status is in any way linked to the "rightness" of her actions. Instead, audiences still come away from this powerful, well-told story and perhaps ask some of the preceding questions.

## Shakespearean Tragedy

Not only tragedy but the theater itself disappeared for many centuries following the demise of the classical world and the later spread of Catholicism. When the dramatic impulse once again asserted itself, the products were not tragedies, but short plays about events in the lives of Christ and the saints. Tragedy was not possible in a Christian world, because a sinner who made a bad choice could yet be saved through repentance, and therefore heaven prevented the permanence of his or her fall. If no salvation were sought, then the protagonist would not have been worth the audience's time.

William Shakespeare (1564-1616) wrote during the English Renaissance, a period whose strength was in the *word*. The English language, still developing, was bulging at the seams with new words taken from Latin, French, Scandinavian, and Germanic tongues. Shakespeare himself, though apparently limited to a grammar school education, is said to have possessed a vocabulary in excess of fifty thousand words. Even the uneducated masses who watched his plays while standing in the "pit" at floor level were enthralled with language. The elements of character and thought, both expressed through an ornamented language that would have dazzled Aristotle, were better suited for the word-happy Elizabethan playhouses than were carefully constructed classical plots.

*In Shakespeare's playhouse, character and thought were better suited to word-happy audiences than carefully constructed classical plots.*

When Aristotle spoke of "action," he meant a conflict of ideas springing from a moral dilemma. For Shakespeare and his theatrical contemporaries, action also meant *physical* excitement: armies attacking each other, multiple stabbings, and dashing swordplay. Words themselves provide action. At its best Shakespeare's language soars or moves us to tears, as when King Lear, realizing that his beloved daughter Cordelia is dead and will never come again, speaks the same word five times: "Never, never, never / Never, never. . . ."

Whether Shakespeare knew the works of Aristotle we cannot be sure, but we *are* certain that he was not writing to imitate a classical model. He borrowed most of his plots from other sources and was not always faithful to the probabilities of human experience. *Romeo and Juliet* (1594), everyone's favorite love story, depends on a coincidence in order to have its sad ending in which the lovers die together. More important, their tragedy is not brought about by a bad choice for which they are entirely responsible. In the Aristotelian sense the play is not complete.

*In classical tragedy action is a conflict of ideas. In Shakespeare action is armies attacking each other, multiple stabbings, and dashing swordplay.*

In his greatest tragedies, however, we find character and thought without equal in the entire realm of drama. Educated in the formal sense or not, Shakespeare must have been an avid reader and clearly had a lifetime love affair with ideas. His major characters do not say only what is appropriate to the circumstances of the story. They go from the particular to the general, finding broad moral principles that offer profound insight into the meaning of our lives.

Insight in Shakespeare often accompanies the downfall of the protagonist. Thus does Macbeth, whose usurped kingdom lies in ruins and whose enemies are closing in on him, respond to news of his wife's death:

> *She should have died hereafter;*
> *There would have been a time for such a word.*
> *To-morrow, and to-morrow, and to-morrow,*
> *Creeps in this petty pace from day to day*
> *To the last syllable of recorded time,*
> *And all our yesterdays have lighted fools*
> *The way to dusty death. Out, out, brief candle!*
> *Life's but a walking shadow, a poor player*
> *That struts and frets his hour upon the stage*
> *And then is heard no more: it is a tale*
> *Told by an idiot, full of sound and fury,*
> *Signifying nothing.*[1]

If Shakespeare's universe is lacking in a forgiving God, it is not lacking in a moral order. Bad intentions motivate evil consequences, which eventually destroy the perpetrator. In this sense, the feuding parents of Romeo and Juliet violate the moral order by keeping the lovers apart, and they probably would have been the main characters had the same play been written by the mature Shakespeare.

Most of Shakespeare's major tragic protagonists, like Oedipus and Creon before them, recognize their responsibility for the disaster. Hamlet is the major exception. It is not clear that the prince of Denmark reaches his doom because he has violated a moral order, though some believe his flaw is procrastination. Had he killed the king, the murderer of his father, right after his promise to his father's ghost that he would do so, he would not have died through the king's treachery. On the other hand, when murder is the required deed, procrastination might not be a violation of the moral order. *Hamlet* works on the stage for reasons that are not necessarily clear, except that it offers us perhaps the most complex and fascinating hero in all of drama and gives him speech after speech with ideas and words of incredible subtlety. If it is not the clearest specimen of tragedy, *Hamlet* is surely one of the most profound inquiries into the meaning of life ever penned.

The work is also the first of the great tragedies. In *Macbeth, King Lear, Othello,* and *Antony and Cleopatra,* Shakespeare gave full expression to what became his major tragic themes: power destroying itself by its own excesses, overriding ambition that does not know when to stop, ego fattened beyond all reasonable bounds so that it loses contact with reality.

In *Othello* (1604) Shakespeare gives us a protagonist who is both a Moorish prince and a general of the Venetian army, a man of high integrity and intellect, eminently suited to lead others—a man with everything going for him, married to a woman he deeply loves, the highborn and beautiful Desdemona. At the opening of *Othello*, everything is perfectly in place within the moral order established by the playwright.

*In many of Shakespeare's tragedies the protagonist violates the moral order of the universe and is eventually destroyed.*

*Paul Robeson as Othello and Uta Hagen as Desdemona. (Culver Pictures)*

Of course, when one human being has it all, circumstances immediately create the opportunity for making bad choices. Others become envious and start plotting. The morally perfect individual must steer an unwavering course through perilous seas. Working for Othello is an ensign named Iago, who harbors a profound hatred for his superior. The clearest reason is that Othello has promoted Cassio, another ensign, to lieutenant's station instead of Iago. A hinted-at reason is Iago's racism. Othello is black and is married to a most desirable white woman, one whom Iago possibly loves as well.

Iago is no mere stereotypical villain such as we find in melodramas that simplistically divide two-dimensional stick figures into good and bad characters. The evil inside him arises from a profound cynicism, a philosophical distrust of all people who do not think as he does. This cynicism makes him arrogantly indifferent to others, to the point that he can contemplate murder. With a frightening precision he plots to destroy the Moor by exploiting the one weakness he has somehow spotted in the otherwise perfect moral armor of Othello: jealousy.

*The evil in Iago is a hinted-at racism as well as a philosophical distrust of all people who do not think as he does.*

In his one seamless plot, so tightly constructed that Aristotle might have praised it, Shakespeare drove his action relentlessly forward. Iago convinces Othello that Desdemona has betrayed him with Cassio, working on his jealousy with a ruthless thoroughness that brings the once-glorious general to the brink of madness and to an irreversible obsession to kill his wife.

In one of drama's most chilling moments Othello, dressed all in white, which for him represents a sign of the sacrificial priest, enters Desdemona's chamber and, despite her pitiful pleas for mercy, smothers her to death. Note that it is not Iago who *does* this terrible deed. Othello's jealousy is irrational, much of it based on the flimsiest of evidence: a handkerchief accidentally dropped by Desdemona and planted in Cassio's room by Iago. A perfect leader must be able to act rationally in such circumstances. A perfect leader must not be ruled by emotion. We know that Othello is capable of far better things. He should see through Iago, should at least give his wife the chance to answer the charges. Yet for some complex reason, which every actor who plays the role must determine for himself, there is that one flaw, that flaw that ultimately negates all of the man's noble qualities and brings him to his doom.

After the disaster and after he has discovered too late the truth about Iago, Othello does two things that put the major Shakespearean protagonists on a plane unreached by those of any other dramatist before or after. First, he makes a passionate speech of recognition, taking full responsibility for what he has done. Second, he reminds his listeners of his former greatness. In some plays, such as *Julius Caesar*, Shakespeare gives the "reminder" speech to another character, as when Mark Antony calls Brutus the "noblest Roman of them all," despite the fact that he helped to assassinate Caesar. In *Othello* both elements—the recognition and the reminder—are handled by the doomed protagonist in the same speech:

*Soft you; a word or two before you go.*
*I have done the state some service and they know't.*
*No more of that. I pray you, in your letters,*
*When you shall these unlucky deeds relate,*
*Speak of me as I am; nothing extenuate,*
*Nor set down aught in malice. Then must you speak*
*Of one that lov'd not wisely but too well;*

*Of one not easily jealous, but being wrought,*
*Perplex'd in the extreme; of one whose hand,*
*Like the base Indian, threw a pearl away*
*Richer than all his tribe; of one whose subdu'd eyes,*
*Albeit unused to the melting mood,*
*Drop tears as fast as the Arabian trees*
*Their medicinal gum. Set you down this.*
*And say besides, that in Aleppo once,*
*Where a malignant and a turban'd Turk*
*Beat a Venetian and traduced the state,*
*I took by the throat the circumcised dog,*
*And smote him, thus.*

(He produces a concealed weapon and stabs himself, falling beside the body of Desdemona.)

*I kiss'd thee ere I kill'd thee: no way but this,*
*Killing myself, to die upon a kiss.*

(Falls on the bed, and dies.)[2]

Thus the moral order in Shakespeare's universe is always reaffirmed. The audience has been emotionally devastated, but both the state and the cosmos are set to rights and function once again as they are supposed to. The tragic protagonist is like diseased tissue that *must* be removed so that the body may regain its health. Macbeth may call life "a tale / Told by an idiot," but the typical Shakespearean restoration of order gives the lie to that assessment. A tragic protagonist on the way down cannot be expected to appreciate the beauty of life when the world works as it should.

## Neoclassical Tragedy

*Rather than* show *emotion, neoclassical characters talk about it, analyze it in often very subtle ways.*

Neoclassical drama and literature deal principally with the importance of reason's control over emotion. Seventeenth-century upper-class society prized restrained and civil behavior in real life as well as on the stage. Plays were performed only for this audience. No longer did the common people stand in the "pit." Theaters offered elegant evening entertainment because indoor lighting from glittering chandeliers was possible. Audiences no longer approved of the searing passions of the Shakespearean tragedy. Rather than *show* emotion, neoclassical characters talk about it, analyze it in often very subtle ways. A major theme in neoclassical drama is the conflict between the rational sense of what is acceptable and the irrational deeds that emotion causes.

Playwrights of the period rewrote many Greek plays for audiences already familiar with the plots and characters. Greek conventions had made emotionalism and violent action on stage all but impossible, though they had been cornerstones of Shakespearean theater. The major neoclassical tragedian was Jean Racine (1639-1699), whose play *Phaedra* clearly illustrates the difference between the neoclassical and Shakespearean periods in theater development.

Having developed a hopeless desire for her husband's son Hippolytus, Phaedra learns that the young man prefers a woman his own age and that he is repelled by his stepmother's advances. In revenge, the queen tells her husband,

Theseus, that Hippolytus made advances to *her*. In a rage (another irrational emotion) Theseus does not question his son. Instead, he prays to Poseidon to destroy Hippolytus, and the young man is killed by strong waves that overwhelm him along the shore.

After the disaster, Racine creates the neoclassical version of the recognition scene. Theseus must learn what he has done, and Phaedra must suffer the consequences of her terrible crime. She confesses:

> *I must break an unjust silence; to your son*
> *Restore his innocence. He was not guilty. . . .*
> *Hear me, Theseus. It was I myself*
> *Who cast upon your chaste and modest son*
> *Unholy and incestuous eyes. . . .*[3]

Before she dies, Theseus acknowledges his own error:

> *Of my own error now*
> *Only too well enlightened, let us go*
> *To mix the blood of my unhappy son*
> *With tears; to embrace the little that remains*
> *Of that dear son, and expiate the madness*
> *Of my detested prayer. . . .*[4]

Perhaps reminder speeches were thought unnecessary for the audience. Note that even in ruin, these tragic figures display proper behavior and remain role models of decorum. They remain socially acceptable.

Most important, audiences could leave a Racine play impressed by the eloquent lines spoken by gifted actors and actresses and by the certainty that the social order (as opposed to the moral order) had been restored once the destructiveness brought on by passion had been transcended.

## The Tragedy of "Ordinary" People

For centuries tragic theater was dominated by both the Greek and the Shakespearean image of what a tragic protagonist was supposed to be. Though the conventions of these two enormous dramatic forces were very different, they shared at least one major component of tragedy: *the nobility of the protagonist*. Aristotle was quite clear about the matter. The downfall of an ordinary person was just not "big" enough to lead the audience to an emotional catharsis. For Shakespeare the emphasis was not the same, but the results were. Shakespeare apparently viewed power as a curse, something that inevitably corrupts and leads to ruin. Since ordinary people had no power, they could not be brought to disaster on a grand scale.

During the last part of the nineteenth century a new kind of theater evolved, not necessarily demanded by its audience, but definitely reflective of their problems. Western society on both sides of the Atlantic found itself in the throes of monumental changes. The Industrial Revolution had expanded the job possibilities for millions who would once have been the "lower" classes, doomed to a lifetime of servitude and need. In this new kind of society driven by economics they were lawyers, doctors, bankers, even steel magnates and oil barons. A new type of protagonist could thus fall from economic if not royal power. In addition, there were innumerable dramatic possibilities in the disastrous consequences awaiting those who dared to challenge the demanding social code of the moneyed (as opposed to the hereditary) aristocracy.

Advances in theater technology also played their part in the new drama. More sophisticated indoor gas lighting—eventually replaced by electricity—supported dramatists' interest in writing plays about people who were caught up in the dilemmas of the new society. The theatrical movement known as *realism* was inevitable. Audiences were finally won over by the excitement of seeing characters who were familiar to them, who in fact *were them*, living and suffering in surroundings that looked exactly like their own homes.

The major figure in late nineteenth-century realistic theater was Norwegian Henrik Ibsen (1828-1906), in whose later, mature work we find the growth of the tragedy of ordinary (that is, nontitled) people. Perhaps his most famous single piece remains *A Doll's House* (1879), often hailed as the first work to espouse women's liberation. Ibsen presents a grim if not tragic portrait of the plight of the housewife in a middle-class Victorian-type household. Ibsen's heroine is victimized by the expectations of a rigid social code but manages to break free by leaving her husband and children, regardless of how she may suffer for her actions.

In the 1885 *Ghosts*, Ibsen came upon a legitimately tragic theme within the real context of middle-class society as he knew it. Violating past traditions of tragedy, the protagonist again is a woman (even as Euripides had violated the traditions of his time by writing *Medea* and making his protagonist tragic without being either noble or a man). Mrs. Alving is an affluent widow whose husband had been well respected and socially prominent—to all appearances, a model of the virtuous family man and community leader. In reality, the deceased husband, like many real-life models Ibsen knew, was a morally bankrupt hypocrite who failed to practice any of the virtues to which he gave lip service. Unfaithful on a grand scale, Alving contracted syphilis, which was in Ibsen's time an absolutely unmentionable disease. (Even though Ibsen does not in fact use the word, one critic at the time still denounced the play as "an open garbage can.")

For this morally sensitive society, allowing one's body to be so infected was the nineteenth-century equivalent of the horrendous crimes committed in the doomed families of Greek mythology—like the incest of Oedipus, for example. As in the Greek tradition, moreover, Alving's son is cursed by this sin. Oswald Alving is born with his father's affliction. Once this fact is revealed, *Ghosts* proceeds with all the inevitability of a Sophoclean tragedy.

Mrs. Alving is a respectable woman, more concerned with social reputation than with facing the reality of her marriage. Instead of coming to grips with her own feelings and trying to seek a new life for herself, she has devoted her widowhood to covering up the traces of her husband's hypocrisy: pretending her marriage had been ideal; pretending her husband had been an admirable man up to the last; pretending she had been a happy and fulfilled woman. The social code, not her own needs, has ruled her behavior.

In a scene of riveting irony, Oswald confesses to his mother that he is so debilitated by the disease that all he can look forward to is a gradual destruction of his brain, madness, and death. He pleads with her to show him mercy and, at the first sign of brain deterioration, to give him the poison capsules he carries around with him. Being placed in so terrifying a position would be cause enough for any dramatic character to be overwhelmed by Euripidean emotions, but Mrs. Alving has another horror in store. Because she has hidden the truth of her husband's

*In* Ghosts *Ibsen found a middle-class tragic theme: the downfall of a woman trapped by social mores, for whom reputation is more important than reality.*

*But* Ghosts *is tragedy on a small scale. Mrs. Alving's flaw does not devastate an entire kingdom.*

*Jane Fonda as Nora in* A Doll's House. *(The Museum of Modern Art/Film Stills Archive)*

moral depravity, her son believes the disease is the consequence of his own sins. Unable to give him at least moral peace of mind by telling the truth for once in her life, she stands by and watches her son slip into a mental fog from which no release will ever be possible. All she has left is to make a decision that is both within her power and impossible: the decision to kill her own son or to spend the rest of her life taking care of a creature bereft of all awareness, all intelligence. Oswald sits in his growing madness, babbling, a frightening embodiment of the monstrosity that Ibsen saw as "polite" society.

Contemporary as was his theme and realistic as were his conventions, Ibsen in *Ghosts* wrote a modern Greek tragedy, with the exception of its nonroyal protagonist and its relatively small scale. (Mrs. Alving's tragic flaw does not devastate an entire kingdom.) Playwrights of the twentieth century who seek to create tragedy draw their characters on an even smaller scale, a scale even more remote from the ancient roots of tragedy. Theirs is a theater of moments, of small insights into the pain of obscure people who are often illiterate and unable to express their feelings in words.

A most ambitious attempt at modern tragedy is Arthur Miller's *Death of a Salesman* (1949), in which even the title encourages us to accept the ennoblement of a common man. Willy Loman—a "low man," not a king or a prince—has reached the age at which he is no longer successful at selling and has been reduced to the humiliating position of having to beg for even an office job that will guarantee him $60 a week. There is no question about audience identification in our understanding of Willy's total acceptance of the American Dream, a success that has escaped him all his life.

Now that he is old and must accept charity from the boss, he refuses to see how he has given up his whole life in the pursuit of something never within his grasp. Instead, he does what so many do in Willy's situation: He transfers the dream to his children. He looks upon his son Biff, once a football hero and now a "buck-an-hour" drifter, as a prince who will yet bring importance to the family.

*. . . the play has taken on the status of an American document, an earnest, painful work close to the heart of our common experience.*

*Richard Gilman*

*Lee J. Cobb as Willy and Mildred Dunnock as Linda in* Death of a Salesman. *(Culver Pictures)*

*In* Death of a Salesman *the tragic protagonist is a victim of a business society, not a royal personage whose flaw destroys him and others.*

Willy's flaw is similar to that of Oedipus: blindness to reality. The man's ardent belief that his son "is going to be magnificent" leads him to a suicidal death in a traffic accident so that Biff will have the insurance money to make a new start in life.

Warnings by his wife, Linda, that Willy is contemplating suicide do indeed introduce a decided note of Sophoclean irony into the play. Doom, symbolized by the towering landscape of New York City that dwarfs Willy's little house, stares at us from the curtain rise until the final "requiem" scene at Willy's grave, in which Linda whispers to her dead husband the news that the house is finally paid for and "we're free!"

There is no recognition speech, a convention lacking, for one reason or other, in every modern tragedy. In *Salesman,* the American dream of success, which has motivated the entire plot, is not the same as the moral order of ancient times. Willy does not violate the dream—quite the contrary. Miller, a decidedly political writer in the decade of the 1940s, wished to show that the dream is a fundamental evil in a business society that destroys everyone in its path. To that extent Willy Loman is a victim, as Oedipus and Othello are not. Whether the victimized "low man" can ever attain the stature of the great tragic heroes is still being debated.

*Some critics say that modern life prevents us from developing a character important enough to be tragic.*

A reason often given for the absence of recognition speeches is modern psychology, which has shown that true self-knowledge is rare. If writers are to strive for realism, they know that people driven to the depths of despair, whether by a tragic flaw or by an economic system over which they have no control, are not rational enough to recognize what is happening to them.

Yet, if we lack the stirring recognition speeches of old, we have impressive substitutes, such as the final scene of Tennessee Williams's *A Streetcar Named Desire* (1947), in which the protagonist Blanche DuBois, driven to madness by a brutal sexual assault, timidly greets the people who have come to take her to an institution. She puts herself in their hands with the pitiable statement that she has always depended on "the kindness of strangers."

Both Williams and Miller seem to be asking: Is this the best we can do for human beings? In theater the very best we can do may well be to create shattering plays about ordinary losers, not kings. After all, if we remove the mask of nobility or the old belief in a moral order that governs the universe, what we have left may be the losers. Perhaps life at its most tragic *is* a slow and agonizing process of losing.

Losers are ultimately shown not to be responsible for their fate. We would thus say that the American Dream, not Willy's tragic flaw, causes his tragedy, and Blanche's deeply neurotic loss of touch with her personal identity causes hers. It appears that the old myth of nobility gave to people like Oedipus and Othello the aura of being entitled to better things because of their innate dignity and rationality. Our tragedies *at their best* offer terrifying glimpses into the disordered lives of people destroyed by *the flaws of existence itself*. If this is the case, then we may say that Willy and Blanche *never* could have led happier, more fulfilled lives.

It has been said that tragedy at its greatest appalls us with the waste of human potential. Perhaps it is this sense of waste that is most conspicuously lacking in present-day theater. But we cannot blame the dramatists. The price of democracy may be that no one person is considered indispensable, so in what respect is the destruction of any life a waste? The price of psychological insight may be that disaster and rationality are seldom believed to go hand in hand; we cannot expect to have tragic protagonists who really know what is happening to them. Pity may be the strongest emotion our theater can evoke.

On the other hand, Aristotle, long ago, said that a tragedy pulls from us the emotions of pity and fear. Whatever has led to their tragic downfall, we pity those who suffer, and we fear that the same thing could happen to us. Democratic tragedy, after all, may not be too far from Aristotle's concept of tragedy in this all-important, this *human* respect.

*Masterpieces of the past are good for the past: they are not good for us. We have the right to say what has been said and even what has not been said in a way that belongs to us.*

*Antonin Artaud*

*Marlon Brando as Stanley, Jessica Tandy as Blanche, and Kim Hunter as Stella in* A Streetcar Named Desire. *(Culver Pictures)*

# Laughing Matters

The Greeks invented the art of stage comedy because they wanted to send their audiences home in a happy state of mind after they had sat through three (count them—THREE!) full-length tragedies in the course of a single day. The apparent theory behind comedy was that it helped confirm the audience's notion of what was normal and rational by displaying abnormal and irrational behavior that could be laughed at. The Greeks discovered that laughter was a healthy release of tensions, especially when thousands of people were engaging in it all at the same time. We know that laughing alone is seldom as satisfying as laughing with the rest of an audience.

Comedy can be divided into three basic types. The first emphasizes situation and two-dimensional characters and is called *farce*; the second deals with more well-rounded characters, and we designate it as the *comedy of character*; and the third, intended to make us think, has two subcategories: *satire* and *the comedy of ideas*.

## Farce: Its Character Types and Situations

In a *farce*, characters are deliberately two-dimensional, easily described in a word or two. Once the character types have been identified through costume, speech, and mannerisms, little more will be revealed than what appears at first glance. At the end of the play, no one will have changed much. There will be no greater understanding, no earth-shaking revelations. Because the characters are deliberately superficial, audiences are not expected to identify with anyone or to dig beneath the surface. Surface is all there is. Comic types are like dolls, and indeed some of them were once puppet characters in traveling shows. As a result they are very close to not being people at all, and when they are abused physically or emotionally there are no lasting effects. They are like the animals in modern-day cartoons who reappear whole in a scene after they have exploded or have been kicked off a cliff. Consider a few examples:

*Three basic types of comedy:*
*farce*
*comedy of character*
*comedy of ideas*

> the stingy old man who sees everything in terms of money
> the sex kitten
> the bragging coward
> the health nut
> the clumsy, unpolished social climber
> the spoiled, destructive brat
> the totally self-absorbed actor (or beauty queen)
> the dumb athlete
> the fast-talking wise guy
> the shrill, overbearing, unsympathetic wife
> the innocent fellow from the country

You can probably add to this list of comic characters. Audiences who laugh at their antics tend not to feel cruel, although some of these types, if presented in a "close-up" rather than in the usual mechanical way, might make good candidates for the psychiatrist's couch and our compassion. We need never worry that someone will probe motives and say, for instance, "Tell me, Mr. Miser, when did money begin to be so important to you? How has the love of money interfered

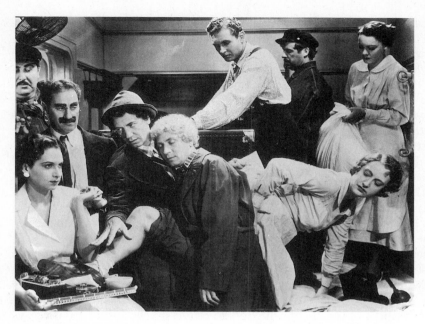

*Still from* A Night at the Opera: *No one expects plausibility in this kind of comedy.*
*(The Museum of Modern Art/Film Stills Archive)*

with other pleasures in life? Do you want to change?" Such questions would spoil
our fun. The comic type is ridiculous, and audiences can enjoy ridicule without
feeling cruel, for the comic type is not a total human being.

Once the character types have been selected, the playwright must put
them into combinations that will make up the scenes of a play. For instance, what
if . . . a very proper social dowager enormously concerned with etiquette were
to be wooed by a crude fortune hunter? Make the setting a very formal one, such as
opening night at the opera, with the lady a prominent benefactor; have the fortune
hunter sitting at her side in a box. His silk hat falls, is handed to him by one of the
operagoers in a nearby seat. He tips the man a quarter. Meanwhile, his uncouth
companions in ill-fitting clothes are selling peanuts and popcorn while the orchestra turns the pages of the overture to *Il Trovatore* and plays the score of "Take Me
Out to the Ballgame," which the clowns have stuck to the musicians' pages with
chewing gum . . . and so on.

It took the inventiveness of the Marx Brothers and the authors of the 1935
film *A Night at the Opera* to make the preceding formula work well, but farce always includes the interplay of unlike types. Later in that same scene, the villainous
tenor (we know he's a villain because he loses his temper at the innocent Harpo,
will sing only for money, and makes insulting remarks about the purity of the heroine, Rosa) tries to sing while the scenery behind him keeps changing. Harpo is
running around backstage, climbing the ropes and pulling one backdrop down
and another up. The tenor continues singing his Italian aria, first in front of a battleship, then before a fruit stand, then at a railroad station—one inappropriate
backdrop after another.

The tenor is exhibiting one of the prime attributes of comedy, *single-
mindedness*—a comic flaw leading to the undoing of its possessor. Nothing will
stop the tenor's pretentious ambition, and, of course, the orchestra goes along,

*Farce emphasizes physical
action, comic types, and an
ending filled with wild
coincidences.*

playing as if nothing were wrong. The audience goes along, too, enjoying the mechanical behavior of both. No one expects plausibility in this kind of comedy—called *farce* because it emphasizes physical action, comic types, and an ending filled with wild coincidences.

The writer of another sort of comedy begins with the following question: What if a fanatically neat man were to share an apartment with a complete slob? The answer is found in Neil Simon's hilarious *The Odd Couple* (1966). An enduring question of ancient comedies is, What if twin brothers separated from birth are both in the same town but neither knows the other is there? In addition, the notion of mistaken identity has fascinated writers going all the way back to classical Greece and Rome. Shakespeare adapted these old plots for *A Comedy of Errors* (1591), *Twelfth Night* (1600), and *Two Gentlemen of Verona* (1592). The confusion potential in the phenomenon of twins delights audiences, perhaps because personal identity is so important in our culture and the mixing up of that identity, normally a reason for serious concern, we laugh at willingly. The universal constant in laughter is its reaffirmation of normalcy, when chaotic misunderstandings are not supposed to happen.

While the comedies of the Greeks and Romans exerted tremendous influence on later theater, of equal impact was the *commedia dell'arte*, an Italian theater movement originating in the middle of the sixteenth century. Given its name because its performers were highly skilled professionals rather than amateur actors, the *commedia* was equally at home in a royal court or in the streets, attracting huge crowds and dispensing the healing medicine of laughter wherever it played. Many of the stock character types still found, especially in television comedy, derive from *commedia* traditions.

The "plays" had scenarios that were little more than rough outlines of the action, which always concerned the interaction of two young lovers trying to get together, the miserly father of one lover, a pedantic old bore who thinks himself a

*The universal constant in laughter is the reaffirmation of normalcy.*

*The remains of the theater at Epidaurus, still functioning.*

*Many of the stock character types found in television comedy today derive from the* commedia *traditions.* ( *Giraudon/Art Resource* )

suitable mate for the girl, and a bragging soldier who is exposed as a coward. All the actors wore exaggerated masks except the young lovers, who were never considered funny and served only to give the plot some direction. The *commedia* comic types are the ancestors of the buffoons and clowns of subsequent periods, winning our laughter from the physical abuse and pratfalls they continually suffer. The Marx Brothers, Laurel and Hardy, the Three Stooges, Jerry Lewis, and Lucille Ball—all great performers adept at bodily contortions—are benefactors of the Italian legacy. Above all, the comedies of Molière (discussed on pages 131-132) would not have been possible without it.

Television situation comedies and parodies have their share of two-dimensional types, notably Ethel and Fred Mertz, the nagging wife and tightfisted husband of *I Love Lucy*; the man-hungry Major Margaret Houlihan of *M·A·S·H*, who conceals her desires behind an obsession for maintaining military discipline; and the continually frustrated and lazy Peg Bundy, married to the clumsy Al of *Married with Children*.

Like the *commedia* masks, farcical names are usually a tip-off to the particular kind of absurdity the actor represents. For instance, Dudley Do-Right and Snively Whiplash were the obvious—too obvious—hero and villain of the cartoon *Rocky and Bullwinkle Show*. Playwrights of the seventeenth and eighteenth centuries specialized in the identification of the comic trait through names. Without knowing anything about the plays in which they are found, consider what you can already guess about characters called Sneerwell, Waitwell, Fidget, Quack, Squeamish, Lady Wishfort, Sir Fopling Flutter, and a scoundrel named Horner. In those days, if you held up two fingers behind the head of an unsuspecting husband, people would know what you meant: The unfortunate man had been the victim of *cuckoldry* (infidelity by his wife and a lover). The two fingers symbolized horns, and horns became the symbol of a deceived husband. Audiences of the day, looking at the cast of characters in the program, knew at once the sort of rogue whose trickery would be celebrated in the play, and they looked forward to it immensely.

*The Marx Brothers, Laurel and Hardy, the Three Stooges, Jerry Lewis, and Lucille Ball derive from the Italian legacy of* commedia dell'arte.

## The Rogue Hero

The knave, or rogue, is not funny in the way the pedantic bore of the *commedia dell'arte* is funny. He is not derided by the audience for single-mindedness or clumsiness. Instead, he is witty and clever, and if he resorts to less than honest (or moral) means of getting what he wants, he is usually seen as less blameworthy than the corrupt or stupid people he deceives. The rogue hero has been popular for centuries and still is very much with us. He does the underhanded things we all fantasize doing, and thus he provides a useful escape from the tensions created by our conformity.

Rogue heroes are con men, making false claims for shoddy merchandise—like the Pardoner in Chaucer's *Canterbury Tales* (1387-1400) pretending to have supernatural powers; like the hero of Richard Nash's *The Rainmaker* (1953), who deludes an entire drought-ridden town into believing he can cause rain, for a price; or like the stranger in Meredith Willson's *The Music Man* (1958), who sells band uniforms to another gullible town, on the promise that he has a miraculous method for teaching music overnight. Rogue heroes have charm and far more personality than most of the people we deal with in everyday life—people who walk the straight and narrow but nevertheless are *dull*.

During the seventeenth century, in both England and France, moral codes became more liberal than they had been, but behind closed doors. On the surface, aristocratic society was bound by rigid codes of behavior, and the rogue hero flourished on the stages of London and Paris. Even a final-act exposure of the culprit was never intended to be taken very seriously or to cloud the memory of the hero's magnificent naughtiness.

One of the most notable such creations is the very same Mr. Horner mentioned in the preceding section. The central character of William Wycherley's *The Country Wife*, a scandalous success of 1675, Horner has deliberately spread the false rumor that he is sexually impotent and that therefore London husbands are safe in allowing their wives to see him. Among his willing "victims" is Lady Fidget, delighted to be unfaithful to her marriage vows so long as she can maintain the illusion of social respectability. In the famous "china scene," Horner has been locked in a back room with Lady Fidget, ostensibly helping her choose a piece of china from his valuable china collection. After a long time, Lady Fidget returns to the front room, where her husband and friends have been waiting. The scene is full of *double entendre*, or double meaning, a favorite source of humor, especially when the second, or "hidden," meaning is unacceptable to polite society. Here's the dialogue:

| | |
|---|---|
| *Lady Fidget:* | And I have been toiling and moiling for the prettiest piece of china, my dear. |
| *Horner:* | Nay, she has been too hard for me, do what I could. |
| *Mrs. Squeamish:* | O Lord, I'll have some china, too. Good Mr. Horner, don't think to give other people china and me none; come in with me, too. |
| *Horner:* | Upon my honor, I have none left now. |
| *Mrs. Squeamish:* | Nay, nay, I have known you deny your china before now, but you shan't put me off so. Come. |
| *Horner:* | This lady had the last there. |
| *Lady Fidget:* | Yes, indeed, madam, to my certain knowledge, he has no more left. |

| | |
|---|---|
| *Mrs. Squeamish:* | Oh, but it may be he may have some you could not find. |
| *Lady Fidget:* | What, d'ye think if he had had any left, I would not have had it too? for we women of quality never think we have china enough. |

London upper-class audiences were delighted by the clever Mr. Horner, his lustful female companions, and their foolish husbands. The hero might have been a pleasant fantasy for women trapped in an unexciting marriage and men who secretly recognized their lack of sexual aggressiveness.

On the other side of the English Channel, one of the greatest playwrights of all time, Jean-Baptiste Poquelin, who called himself Molière (1622–1673), filled the stage with comically blind, incessantly self-deluded creatures and, in one glorious instance, with one of the greatest rogues of all time: the title character of *Tartuffe* (1664), who claims to be more pious than anyone else. Tartuffe has gained the confidence of a wealthy man and has been invited to move in with the family. Though the other characters talk of him from the beginning, he doesn't actually appear until almost halfway through the piece, when he calls to his manservant: "Hang up my hair-shirt, put my scourge in place." He then whips out a handkerchief and demands that the maid cover her bosom with it, an action he is willing to perform himself. Before long he has attempted to seduce Elmire, the wife of his benefactor ("I may be pious, but I'm human too"), and has promised to keep their affair a secret if she will agree to let him worship her beauty in an intimate way. While directing his lust toward the attractive Elmire, he directs his greed toward the fortune of her husband, and nearly succeeds in escaping with all of it.

The rogue hero, perhaps more than any other comic tradition, has an enduring record of popularity. He has never gone out of style, though he flourishes more richly in certain periods than in others. It's a good bet he is more appealing in times of tighter social mores than in times of rampant permissiveness. Earlier in this century, when Victorian morality was dominant, we had W. C. Fields and his rogues' gallery of delightful con artists, forever cheating at cards, forever making wry antiestablishment comments out of the sides of their mouths. We had Groucho

*Famous rogue heroes: Mr. Horner, Tartuffe, Mack the Knife, Hawkeye Pierce.*

*The rogue hero does the underhanded things we think about doing in our fantasy life, and he is thus a useful escape from the tensions created by our conformity.*

*W. C. Fields, a delightful antiestablishment con artist during a time of Victorian morality. (Culver Pictures)*

Marx, with the ever-present grin and the long cigar, flicking his ashes on the carpets of polite society. We had Mae West, flaunting her sexuality at the prim and proper, wiggling her hips and finding no reason to believe immorality does not pay. "Goodness!" cries a middle-class housewife, staring at Mae West's expensive mink. The reply: "Goodness had nothin' to do with it."

The German music-drama *The Threepenny Opera* (1928) has a totally amoral hero, Mack the Knife, who bribes the police, cuts throats, lies to women— and gets away with his crimes thanks to a thoroughly implausible pardon from Queen Victoria at the end of the play. The rogue hero's outwitting of the system constitutes a cynical attack on the idiocy and corruption of a society in which such a person can flourish.

The 1960s would seem to have been a period when the rogue hero was replaced by the rebellious loner, a character openly flouting the establishment rather than cleverly pretending to be part of it and undermining it from within. The "hippie hero" or "hippie heroine" was not meant to be a comic figure, nor did he or she reflect mainstream values, which were still basically conservative. The term *Moral Majority* was gladly applied by the mainstream to itself. Its disapproval of activists and draft-dodgers intensified the more the resistance movement grew. Yet the Moral Majority was bound to elicit a comic response, and it came in 1970 in the person of Hawkeye Pierce, rogue hero of the film and later of the classic television series *M·A·S·H.*

Hawkeye is a brilliant surgeon, drafted into the army and sent to the front lines in Korea to serve in the 4077 Mobile Army Surgical Hospital, where he and his weary colleagues toil, sometimes for 20 hours straight and in primitive facilities, to sew a glimmer of life back into terrified soldiers so they can be sent back into action to face death once more. Hawkeye is not like rogue heroes of the past, however. His underhanded attempts to thwart a rigid military establishment are carried on in the name of rationality and human decency, *not* out of self-interest. Hawkeye totally disregards Army rank, is almost never in uniform (preferring to wear Hawaiian shirts, much to the annoyance of visiting brass), steals when he

*Alan Alda as Hawkeye Pierce in* M·A·S·H *(Gary Burghoff as Radar at left). (Kobal Collection/SuperStock)*

thinks human need warrants it, always looks out for the underdog, and is especially helpful to Army misfits (with whom he easily identifies). He became a spokesperson for all those who deplored the Vietnam War, and the continued popularity of *M*·*A*·*S*·*H* in reruns strongly suggests that he remains the spokesperson for those millions who work in some way against militarism.

More recently, the rigid, rule-bound police establishment has helped make a star of Eddie Murphy, who specializes in rogue heroes. In *Beverly Hills Cop* (1984) Murphy's character easily outwits the system. Replacing the seventeenth-century wit and elegance of Horner with street-smart "cool," he nonetheless makes himself at home in formal society, which is never a match for him. Like Hawkeye, Murphy's character will break the laws if necessary, but both characters have their hearts in the right place. Unlike earlier rogues, *they* break the law in a higher cause. The idea behind these characters is a simple one: Society is a shambles, and *somebody* has to save it!

*The rogue hero's outwitting of the system is a cynical attack on the idiocy and corruption of a society in which such a person can flourish.*

## The Comic Fool

As we observed, the rogue hero is not someone we laugh at, but someone we laugh *with*. He is so much smarter than the society around him that we cannot help siding with him, no matter how unethical his tactics may be. The main body of comedy, however, is made up of fools, characters we willingly laugh at, characters who, like the comic types in farce, are single-mindedly obsessed with something and evoke almost merciless laughter from us. Often they are duped by the rogues, but their stupidity (often coupled with arrogance) prevents us from feeling pity toward them. We know they deserve what they get.

Some philosophical analyses of comedy call comic fools antisocial and potentially dangerous persons. Their single-mindedness is a rigid barrier against growth and change, and society cannot function unless the majority of its members are rational and willing to alter their behavior when they realize it is harmful to the well-being of others. Fools are interested only in their own petty problems and never see what is done to others. Laughter is society's revenge. Laughing at fools helps us confirm our own sanity.

Almost every comedy with a rogue hero has a fool he can deceive. In the case of Tartuffe, the fool is Orgon, a man single-mindedly driven by his desire for holiness. In becoming the slave of the hypocritical Tartuffe, Orgon believes he is living a good life. As usual in a Molière play, the fool is also blind to his family's real needs and tries to force his daughter to marry a man she despises, in this case Tartuffe himself. The old man never hears the daughter when she entreats him to spare her. Even when he hears the very words of an indecent proposal made by Tartuffe to Orgon's wife, he denies the evidence and instead believes Tartuffe's absurd explanation.

*The comic fool's single-mindedness is a rigid barrier against growth and change.*

Molière specialized in fools. He remains the master of comedy as Shakespeare is the master of tragedy, because his fools include universally and timelessly antisocial types. There is never a danger that an audience will find them unfunny. His roster of fools includes

      a man overly concerned with his health, who wants his daughter to marry a doctor

      a man overly concerned with social status, who wants his daughter to marry a man with a title

a man overly concerned with money, who wants his daughter to marry any man who will take her without a dowry

a man overly concerned with the innocence of his bride, to the extent that he whisks his chosen one away from the temptations of Paris to be properly supervised in an isolated country house

Molière's contributions to the art of comedy are so rich and varied that we must never believe he limited himself to one single-minded fool or one rogue hero in any given play. *The Would-Be Gentleman*, for example, has for its central character the man, just listed, who expects his daughter to marry the titled aristocrat of his, not her, choosing. But the play generously offers other fools as well. Monsieur Jourdain, who has no intelligence, grace, or social charm, hires tutors in music, dancing, fencing, and philosophy. Not only are his own pitiful efforts deliciously funny, but the tutors themselves are single-minded mockeries of what their professions should represent. Each tutor is so immersed in his own specialty that he refuses to acknowledge the importance of the others'. Without *his*, the world could not exist. The dance "master" claims, for example, that studying dance brings about a world of peace, for, after all, "war begins with a false step." The philosopher, calmly explaining to the others that philosophy teaches moderation, suddenly bursts into irrational violence when his opinion is challenged.

## The Comedy of Character

What would happen if poor bumbling Monsieur Jourdain, the would-be gentleman, were allowed by his creator to exhibit a degree of sensitivity? What if he recognized, even only a little, that his tutors were laughing at the hopelessness of turning him into an aristocrat? Or if he were the victim of a cruel and inhuman joke—as indeed he is in the final act—but suspected that others were taking advantage of his stupidity? The answer to these questions is that we would soon find him less funny. As the art of comedy developed and became more and more sophisticated, dramatists took more chances, tried new kinds of plots, often veering away from the traditional comic types, especially the bumbling fools, replacing them with characters who begin to approach true human beings. In real life people are not as single-minded, as blind to their own inadequacies, as the comic fools. *In real life, nobody is continually funny.*

The comedy of character, which is what we call the sort of play in which people who are funny also acquire more complex human characteristics, existed well before Molière carried fools and rogues to new heights of comic greatness. Shakespeare has also given us well-rounded comic as well as tragic figures, but none more comic than Sir John Falstaff, the heavy-set, hard-drinking, roguish companion to young Prince Hal in *Henry IV*, Parts 1 and 2 (1597 and 1598).

Since these were history plays intended to be serious chronicles of the early years of the British empire, Shakespeare—practical man of the theater that he was—probably introduced Falstaff and the prince's other barroom cronies to add a bit of variety and to give the plays a welcome change of pace. As so often happens, the comic relief steals the show.

Falstaff, who is far more than either a rogue or a single-minded fool, is the great philosopher of fun and corruption. Nothing is sacred, nothing is to be taken too seriously in this all-too-brief existence. Knowing that Hal will one day become Henry V and assume the awful responsibilities of the monarchy, heavy burdens that will eventually wear him down, Falstaff encourages the prince to eat, drink, and be

---

*Molière is the master of comedy as Shakespeare is the master of tragedy, because his fools include universally and timelessly antisocial types.*

*As a voter I never take anyone seriously who takes himself seriously. I have to believe most people are like that. They trust people with a sense of humor because that's what humor is— truth—with a little exaggeration and self-effacement thrown in to make it palatable.*

*Erma Bombeck*

*Orson Welles as Falstaff, the great philosopher of fun and corruption. (Springer/Bettmann Film Archive)*

merry, and in so doing, he becomes the world's spokesperson for the carefree, irresponsible life.

Falstaff is a consummate rogue. Faced with the task of arming a group of men for war, he spends the allotment on himself instead of on uniforms. He is also a consummate—and unashamed—coward. Faced with the chance to meet a member of the opposing force in hand-to-hand combat and possibly cover himself with glory, he rolls over and plays dead, after first delivering a speech on the dubious value of honor:

> Can honour set to a leg? No. Or an arm? No. Or take away the grief of a wound? Honour hath no skill in surgery, then? No. What is honour? Air; a trim reckoning! Who hath it? He that died o' Wednesday. Doth he feel it? No. Doth he hear it? No. 'Tis insensible, then. Yea, to the dead. But will it not live with the living? No. Why? Detraction will not suffer it.[5]

Falstaff amuses us because what he stands for is not what we are taught to admire, but we *like* him in a way that we cannot really like Molière's Monsieur Jourdain. What is the difference? Falstaff is honest, and Jourdain is not. Falstaff knows who he is and what his limitations are; Jourdain does not. There are things about Falstaff that are scandalously admirable.

In *Henry IV*, Part 2, there occurs a scene in which Hal rejects Falstaff, and the laughter stops. We can never be sure of every Shakespearean dramaturgical motive, but in this case we can safely conjecture that, when it came to the moment of Prince Hal's coronation as Henry V (who, by the way, was to defeat the French at the Battle of Agincourt and thus become the most revered of all English monarchs before Queen Elizabeth I), the dramatist could not afford to offend the queen by having it believed that her ancestor kept a ne'er-do-well as a lifelong friend. Even in *Henry IV*, Part 1, Hal delivers a soliloquy in which he tells the audience that he is only acting the role of a playboy, but when the proper time comes, he will step forth in the shining light of his true royal self.

Outside Westminster Abbey, Falstaff and his drinking buddies await the arrival of the man, now king, whom they believe to be one of their own. The overjoyed Falstaff attempts to approach, calling the king "my sweet boy!" Outraged, King Henry pushes him aside:

*I know thee not, old man: fall to thy prayers;*
*How ill white hairs become a fool and jester!*
*So surfeit-swell'd, so old and so profane;*
*But, being awaked, I do despise my dream.*
*Make less thy body hence, and more thy grade;*
*Leave gormandizing; know the grave doth gape*
*For thee thrice wide than for other men.*[6]

In Shakespeare's defense for what readers and viewers have often regarded as an unforgivable crime against their favorite character, King Henry *does* add that should Falstaff reform his roustabout ways, he will be taken care of for life. On the other hand, most of us secretly hope the old man will not take the bribe. In our fantasies we still see him in the tavern at Eastcheap, pinching a buxom waitress and pleading for one last pint.

Whatever the queen's private feelings about the image of her ancestor may have been, we know that Falstaff was far from horrifying to her. In fact, so enamored did she become of this glittering creation that she asked Shakespeare to do another play in which the same scoundrel would be the central character and his amorous adventures the central theme. The result was *The Merry Wives of Windsor* (1600). Today Falstaff is still very much around; he appears on the label of a popular beer named for him as well as in performances at New York's Metropolitan Opera House as the hero of the great Verdi comic opera named for him.

Like any great character in drama, Falstaff transcends all the circumstances of all the plots in which he has been involved. He has become a prototype by which we can evaluate people in real life whose behavior (and also the excuses for it) reminds us of his.

## Sentiment and Psychology

The coming of the so-called common man movement in the eighteenth and nineteenth centuries brought about a change in the way some characters were treated on the stage. We must remember that Shakespeare's audiences, accustomed to the right of monarchs to show no feelings toward a person, would not have blamed the king for the rejection of Falstaff. In fact, throughout the seventeenth century, which was also the period of Molière, audiences would have considered a playwright's display of emotion toward his characters extremely vulgar. Well-bred people simply did not publicly show or express their feelings. For this reason, Monsieur Jourdain and Molière's other fools could have expected no mercy either.

*The common man movement of the eighteenth and nineteenth centuries brought about a change in comedy. It was considered heartless to laugh at simple, untutored people.*

After the revolutions on both sides of the Atlantic, however, the adventures of ordinary people became fit subjects for literature and drama. The great English comic novel *Tom Jones* by Henry Fielding (1749) exemplifies the new trend. It has its share of farcical types left over from the previous century: self-deceiving tutors, sexually frustrated, aggressive women who hypocritically maintain an aristocratic air of detachment, and so on. Its hero, Tom, a foundling, should by all rights be classified as a comic country bumpkin with no urban finesse whatever. Tom can be amusing, yes, in his sexual naiveté and in his innocence, which allows him to be used and deceived by a good many cleverer people. But Tom has feelings, and these are respected by the author. Indeed, why else would a bumpkin be made the hero and not just a figure in a comic subplot? Fielding may have been infected with an early dose of an emerging philosophy called *primitivism*, which held that the natural wisdom and goodness of simple, untutored people was worth more than the learned traditions of past intellectual greats. Primitivism held that feelings were healthy and good, and one should not be ashamed of having them. Nor should one laugh at others because they might lack social graces.

As a matter of fact, by the late eighteenth century important new comedies were absent from the theater. Between Richard Brinsley Sheridan, the outstanding comic dramatist of the 1770s, and the emergence of Oscar Wilde and George Bernard Shaw in the late 1800s, the English theater could boast of no major writer of *any* kind. The reason appears to be the enduring popularity of sentimental, or "feeling," plays at which audiences were allowed to weep copiously but to neither laugh nor think. (The emphasis on excessive feeling also led, as we would expect, to sheer melodrama, or what Hollywood used to call the *tearjerker*. The plots for nearly all Italian operas came out of this kind of theater, and if you have read a synopsis of any opera plot, you know what real melodrama can be like. Farcical types—those unbelievable buffoons from the past—were replaced by tragic types—not funny, of course, yet no more believable.) *One cannot have major comedy in times that do not allow for intelligent audiences to laugh at human folly. One cannot have major comedy in times that do not encourage the belief that rationality is more important than indiscriminate emotionalism.*

What is the case in our time? Is important comedy being written today? Already-mentioned contemporary works like *M*A*S*H* indicate that it is. Is *M*A*S*H* closer in spirit to, say, the work of Molière or to that of novelist Henry Fielding, with his mixture of humor and sentiment? The answer is a very complex one.

Hawkeye Pierce, as we stated, is a rogue hero, but not in the sense that Tartuffe is. He is well-rounded, sensitive, humanized. He has feelings for others, and we feel for *him*. Like Falstaff many centuries before him, he transcends his material and becomes a real person for us.

We are not living in a period of neoprimitivism or neosentimentalism. The "common man" movement is supposedly a thing of the past, to be taken for granted by now. But there *is* something central to our time, something that was not there in the late eighteenth century when the comedy of character was replacing the theater of rogues and fools, and that something is psychology. How can one laugh at, let alone judge, anyone whom one understands? Understanding replaces the indiscriminate feelings of the earlier period. Indiscriminate laughter seems cruel as one draws close enough to sense hurt feelings, shyness, embarrassment. The clumsy boob of an earlier time would now seem to be someone who wants to be graceful and doesn't know how, *but who should not be ridiculed for it*.

Whom then do we laugh at? People we *don't* understand? How does one pick and choose? Or do we laugh at people who should be understanding but are not? People whose educational background and social advantages should make them well-rounded, caring human beings but who are so absorbed in their own ambitions they blind themselves to the reality about them? Such people are still fair game. In *M*A*S*H*, whom does Hawkeye try to outwit? Pompous army brass. Hypocrites with rank but no human feeling. People he considers stupid but who, considering their advantages, have no right to be stupid.

Nowadays we also have the barbed wit of the political satirist Mark Russell, especially poisonous during presidential election years. Are politicians fair game in this era of "understanding"? The answer again is yes. The premise appears to be that those who aspire to be the world's major leaders should not have the ordinary human weaknesses we can excuse in others. Or, if they do, these weaknesses need to be exposed, not graciously ignored.

*One cannot have major comedy in times that do not encourage the belief that rationality is more important than indiscriminate emotionalism.*

Psychology has helped spawn a kind of comedy that is peculiar to our time: the art (and often we are generous in using such a label) of the stand-up comic. Often using scandalously obscene language, comics remind us that perhaps all of us think these things but are afraid to say them aloud. Their alleged purpose is to help us shed our outer covering of social convention and to be comfortable being who we are. The problem is that not all of us may be who these comics say we are supposed to be. True stand-up artists like Robin Williams specialize in the right to be themselves, however we may or may not identify with them, and serve as role models for off-center personalities, an encouragement to the rest of us to honor, not be ashamed of, our own differences.

Also peculiar to our time is the comedy of self-criticism. Comics like Woody Allen and the early Joan Rivers allow us to laugh at the merciless exposure of their own weaknesses, hang-ups, hidden fears, and guilt complexes. They help us understand the universality of the neurotic personality by directing the laughter at themselves and away from us, and in so doing they invite us to face ourselves without defense mechanisms.

That so much of contemporary comedy is of the performance rather than the literary variety has much to do with the decline of language. Wit and double entendre flourished on seventeenth-century comic stages, when audiences not only tolerated but eagerly sought intellectual exercise by straining to catch verbal subtleties. About all we have left nowadays are outrageous one-liners like those Hawkeye tosses off from the side of his mouth.

## Satire and the Comedy of Ideas

Every comedy, except, of course, for the wildest kind of pie-in-the-face burlesque, has a dominant idea, a rational point of departure in terms of which what we are seeing is supposed to amuse us. Some comedies, on the other hand, put the idea first, not the laughter. Their intention is to have some effect on the thinking of the audience. *Satire* is perhaps more urgent. It wants action, usually social or political reforms. The works of George Bernard Shaw (discussed later in this section) are true *comedies of ideas*. They can be called comedies only in the broadest definition of the word. They contain wit and humor; they have some characters whose outrageous behavior evokes chuckles. But mainly, the viewer's critical intellect smiles inwardly as it recognizes Shaw's subtle ironies.

Earlier in this chapter we pointed out that the Greeks invented the art of comedy as a means of ending their all-day festival of tragedy on an "up" note. The final piece of the day was called the *satyr* play, because that mythological creature, which was half man and half goat and traditionally a central figure in very off-color folk tales, was its star attraction. We have only hints of what satyr plays were like from scattered historical records, but we do know that each dramatist who entered the competition for best work of the festival was required to present three tragedies on a related theme and one comic afterpiece. Presumably, the satyr play poked fun at the tragedies the audience had just witnessed. Since each tragedy consisted of a few main actors and a unified chorus of some kind—citizens of Thebes or women of Troy, say—which commented on the action, the comic afterpiece used a chorus of satyrs, which must in itself have been howlingly funny. From the satyr play, then, derived the word *satire*, which is the art of poking fun.

Aristophanes (445-385 B.C.) is, to our knowledge, the world's first entirely satiric playwright, writing no tragedies at all. Since this is the case, we should not be surprised that he developed the art, used a varied assortment of choruses—frogs and birds, for example—and made fun not only of tragedies but of existing wrongs in the city-state of Athens. Aristophanes is thus the first known dramatist to use the stage as a forum for ideas he hoped would lead to change. He was an angry young man, aware that the noble experiment in democracy, shaped earlier in the fifth century by Pericles, was beginning to come apart.

For years, young Athenians had been sent off to die in extremely unpopular wars, first against Persia, then against Sparta (a war Athens finally lost). The culture of Athens had very definitely been peace oriented. After the victory over Persia—a wholly unexpected one—Athens became complacent, refused to maintain a standing army, thought itself invincible, and finally became a sitting duck for the disciplined and militaristic Spartans. During the time of uneasy peace, the state became riddled with corrupt government officials. There was moral decay in society and esthetic deterioration of the arts, including the theater itself. The time, in short, was just right for the emergence of Aristophanic satire.

The art of satire is a devastating weapon, causing us to laugh even at things we normally respect. It does this by taking something that is true to some extent and then exaggerating it until it becomes so ludicrous we can never quite respect it again. The television series *M\*A\*S\*H*, which has been given much praise in this chapter, belongs to the Aristophanic tradition of satire. Despite much to praise in the way our military operates, *M\*A\*S\*H* made us far more aware of the absurdities of bureaucracy, petty egos, and false priorities.

Thousands of years ago, the very idea of war as a means of solving human problems struck Aristophanes also as absurd. In *Lysistrata*, perhaps his most enduring work, he created a plot in which women of both Athens and Sparta call a sex strike, refusing to consort with husbands or lovers until all hostilities ceased. Like any great satire, *Lysistrata* hits at more than one target. Not only is war a target of ridicule, but so is human weakness, as some of the strikers find abstinence a high price to pay.

War has probably been the most common satiric theme over the centuries. Stanley Kubrick's film *Dr. Strangelove: Or, How I Learned to Stop Worrying and Love the Bomb*, a 1963 work we shall mention again in Chapter 14, concerns the dropping of a nuclear bomb on the Soviet Union and the Soviet retaliation in the form of a Doomsday Machine designed to rid the planet of all life for the next 99 years. As politicians and military strategists on both sides prepare to take shelter deep underground, they look forward to the time when their descendants will be able to continue the hostilities, once the earth has breathable air again.

Another popular target for the satirist is an idea or a philosophy that is popular with a great many people but, in the satirist's opinion, does not deserve to be. The philosophy is ridiculed in a way that would make it difficult for any rational person ever again to take it seriously. A classic example is *Candide* (1759), by the glitteringly cynical French novelist, philosopher, and social critic François Marie Arouet, who wrote under the more familiar pen name of Voltaire (1694-1778). In this novel Voltaire attacks a popular optimistic philosophy of the day, associated with a German thinker named Leibniz, that this is the best of all possible worlds. Looking at the world around him, which a benevolent God had supposedly created, Voltaire decided somebody must be crazy, but it was not he.

The hero of *Candide*, whose name reflects his innocence, is raised by a tutor, Dr. Pangloss, and taught the philosophy of Leibniz. Candide, his lady fair, Cunegonde, and Pangloss are then separated by a series of catastrophes, including the Lisbon earthquake. They are captured by all manner of barbarians, sold into

*Aristophanes is the first known dramatist to use the stage as a forum for ideas he hoped would lead to change.*

*War has been the most common satiric theme over the centuries: from* Lysistrata *to* Dr. Strangelove *to* M\*A\*S\*H.

*Satire he used as a weapon to "mend the world," to lash ignorance and corruption, in the belief that men were open to correction, not irretrievably lost.*

*Harold Williams on Swift*

slavery, beaten almost to the point of death, and sentenced to hang. All the while, Candide continues to believe that everything must be happening for the best in this best of all possible worlds. Following the earthquake, while Candide is repeating the maxim (which is bringing less and less comfort to him), he is overheard by a high-ranking official of the *Inquisition* (an austere Catholic court of no appeal that tried and sentenced—often to the stake—those found guilty of heresy against established Church doctrine). The official is appalled and charges Candide on the spot with heresy on the grounds that if everything happens for the best, it must happen according to a predetermined plan, thus ruling out the possibility of free will, thus challenging official Church dogma. In an absolute mockery of the Inquisition hearings, Voltaire shows us how the Grand Inquisitor hands out sentences according to the whim of the moment and with no relation to the seriousness of the charge: a hanging here, a burning there, and, in the case of Candide, a "ritual flogging" for the crime of "listening to a philosopher."

After much suffering the now-broken hero is willing to say that "if this is the best of all possible worlds, I would hate to see the others." He and the once-fair but now ugly Cunegonde are finally reunited—somehow—and decide they will spend the rest of their lives tending to their own garden and expecting nothing from God or from other people.

One of the bitterest of all satiric works had already appeared in 1729, exactly 30 years before the publication of *Candide*, and that was a relatively brief pamphlet called "A Modest Proposal for Preventing the Children of the Poor People in Ireland from Being a Burthen to Their Parents or Country, and for Making Them Beneficial to the Public." The author was Jonathan Swift (1667-1745), an Irish-born Anglican priest who became Dean of St. Patrick's Cathedral in Dublin but never once sacrificed his brilliant and deadly satiric pen for his religious duties.

*Swiftian irony: a technique whereby the satirist pretends to be the very sort of person he is denouncing and to espouse the very cause he finds despicable.*

Swift believed the Irish did not deserve the cruel and inhuman treatment inflicted upon them by their close neighbors across the Irish Sea. His heart ached when he thought of the filth and disease in which the children of the Irish poor were raised while English aristocrats stuffed themselves in their country manors. He gave vent to his anger in "A Modest Proposal," and in so doing, invented a new satiric technique we still call *Swiftian irony*, by which technique the satirist pretends to be the very sort of person he is denouncing and to espouse the very cause he finds despicable. Writing in a matter-of-fact, rational way, Swift proposes the breeding of Irish babies as potential gourmet entrées for London dinner parties:

> I have been assured by a very knowing American of my acquaintance in London, that a young healthy child well nursed is at a year old a most delicious, nourishing, and wholesome food, whether stewed, roasted, baked, or boiled, and I make no doubt that it will equally serve in a fricassee or a ragout.

Swift was in such control of his prose that his horrible suggestion sounds increasingly plausible as he continues. He goes into elaborate detail about the fees to be paid the mother, the best method of breeding this "livestock," the delivery procedures, and the appeal of this novelty menu item to bored hostesses.

To the obvious question, "But how can you suggest such a barbaric thing?" the satirist could have responded, "Why in the world not?" "Because," you retort, "it's not what you do to human beings!" "True," says the satirist. "But what do you call what the English are doing to the Irish?"

Satire *must* have a point. The satirist must know what is wrong and what ought to be done to fix it. For instance, in 1965 Tony Richardson's film *The Loved One*, based on Evelyn Waugh's novel of the same name, went beyond its source in making savage fun of the funeral business in the United States and the generally unrealistic attitude toward death held by many Americans. The setting of the film is a Disneyland kind of mortuary-cemetery in Hollywood, which instantly reminds us of Forest Lawn, the real-life, expensive Los Angeles resting place of many former stars. In the film, the mortuary is filled with garish, often nude statues of angels and other heavenly creatures, has canned music blaring over loudspeakers day and night, and includes segregated areas where "like-minded" corpses and their loved ones lie together in plush, moisture-proof, silk-lined caskets. The film makes fun of hysterically grieving but hypocritical survivors, motivated by greed, and money-grubbing funeral directors out to seize their share of "the take." It offended many people, and it intended to do just that. The film also led to an investigation of the price structures of many funeral institutions.

The nonsatiric, fundamentally *serious* comedy of ideas, as we pointed out, is easily associated with the towering figure of George Bernard Shaw (1856-1950), who began writing for the theater during the late nineteenth century. Shaw, a great supporter of Ibsen, whose works were having a difficult time finding audiences, also believed the time had come for the theater to do more than casually entertain. Shaw, however, was not plodding and heavy-handed, but used a scintillating wit and an ability of Shakespearean proportions to create fully rounded human beings in order to drive his ideas home. His plays deal with the impoverishment of British education, foolish romanticism, war profiteering, hypocrisy, capitalism—almost any subject a serious dramatist might treat.

The moving force behind Shaw's work is what has been called *Shavian irony*. Shaw's ironic technique was to present a given situation or a set of relationships toward which we are encouraged to develop a particular attitude, and then at the end to pull the rug out from under us by showing that the opposite attitude is really the more intelligent of the two. A good example is *Major Barbara* (1905), a play that remarkably anticipates the so-called generation-gap idea of the 1960s and the rebellion of idealistic young people against their establishment parents. Barbara is the daughter of Undershaft, a munitions manufacturer. She has been raised in luxury but then denounces her background, becomes a street marcher (and Major) in the Salvation Army, and engages in idealistic debates with her father over his profession. The audience is at first totally on her side. But Undershaft

*I learned from reading George Bernard Shaw years ago that you can get away with murder as long as you make people laugh.*

*Saul Bellow*

*Wendy Hiller as Major Barbara.
(Culver Pictures)*

makes a deal: He will visit the Salvation Army headquarters and observe the "good" that Barbara claims is being done there if she in turn will agree to visit his munitions plant. The girl willingly agrees, certain that there will be no contest.

The visit to the Salvation Army is not what we expect. The well-meaning volunteers, who are all from genteel backgrounds, cannot cope with the angry street people, for whom a piece of bread and a badly sung hymn are scant recompense for a lifetime of poverty and governmental neglect. The munitions plant, on the other hand, is modern, well equipped, clean, disciplined, and peopled by happy, well-fed, well-paid workers. To Barbara's objection that their salaries are possible because somebody plans to blow up society, Undershaft responds that every so often society *has* to be blown up! Barbara's idealism is shattered, and the audience leaves with a very different idea from the one originally entertained.

A socialist, Shaw believed England could not survive in monarchy and with rigid class barriers. While he made that point quite clearly in *Major Barbara*, his greatness lies in the fact that he did not belabor the same point in every other play. Each work of Shaw's tackles a complex new idea with subtlety and with the author's piercing intellect. No other playwright in history has been able to make intellectual dialogue, the exchange of truly intricate thoughts, so engaging and absorbing. Shaw lifted comedy to heights it may never reach again. He is to comedy what Shakespeare is to its counterpart, tragedy.

*Shaw's comedies of ideas deal with the impoverishment of British education, foolish romanticism, war profiteering, hypocrisy, capitalism—almost any subject a serious dramatist might treat.*

# Glossary

*catharsis:* The release, or purgation, of the emotions that ideally takes place at the conclusion of a powerful tragedy. Aristotle, the first known critic of the drama, held catharsis to be the purpose of the art form, because, having undergone emotional purgation, the viewer is able to reestablish a rational balance without which, Aristotle believed, the proper conduct of life was impossible.

*comedy:* A form of drama that displays some violation of the audience's rational expectations regarding human behavior and human relationships. The gap between the norm and the situation creates an inner tension that is eased through laughter. Thus it is said that a sense of humor is an invaluable asset to the restoration of sanity.

*commedia dell'arte:* Originally, an Italian theater movement of the mid-sixteenth century; an improvisatory theater in which highly skilled professionals created comedies on the spot, using stock characters, such as the foolish old man pursuing a very young girl.

*double entendre:* A comic device, popular for centuries, in which lines have a double meaning, the second of which is usually unacceptable to polite society.

*farce:* A highly exaggerated comic play using two-dimensional stock characters, unbelievable situations, and improbable resolutions.

*hubris:* A Greek term for "pride"—the usual failing of character that drives the protagonist in Greek (and other) tragedy to his or her doom.

*melodrama:* A form of theater that often resembles but is not legitimate tragedy; it deals with the conflicts between two-dimensional characters, who are usually very good or very bad.

Poetics: An enduringly influential work of dramatic criticism by Aristotle, of which only his essay on tragedy remains.

*primitivism:* An eighteenth-century philosophy which holds that people living the simple life, close to nature, are nobler than their educated, city-bred counterparts.

*satire:* A form of literature that greatly exaggerates a situation the humorist finds intolerable. By inducing others to laugh at the situation, the humorist hopes to bring about a change for the better. Satire is the most moral of the comic arts.

*satyr play:* The comic afterpiece to a three-part tragedy performed in ancient Greece, probably to make fun of what had gone before and send the audience home in a brighter frame of mind. Origin of our word *satire*.

*Shavian irony:* A technique used frequently by

playwright George Bernard Shaw whereby a play turns out to mean something quite different from what we at first thought.

*single-mindedness:* The most universal flaw in comic characters—an irrational tendency to respond to whatever happens in terms of one overriding passion.

*Swiftian irony:* A satiric method, named after Jonathan Swift and in which this creator of *Gulliver's Travels* excelled, whereby the humorist pre-tends to espouse the very thing he or she is against (though in an exaggerated and distorted version) in order to point up its outrageous failings. Swift's "A Modest Proposal" contains one of the purest examples of this technique.

*tragedy:* A form of drama in which the audience is carried to a purgation of the emotions through an intense involvement with the downfall of a sympathetic protagonist, generally one who deserves a better fate.

## Notes

1. *Macbeth*, V.v.17-18.
2. *Othello*, V.ii.330-360.
3. *Phaedra*, V.vi.
4. *Phaedra*, ibid.
5. *Henry IV*, Pt. 1, V.i.12-21.
6. *Henry IV*, Pt. 2, V.v.51-58.

## Suggested Reading

Aristophanes. *The Clouds*. A satire that pokes fun at intellectuals and their endeavors.

———. *Lysistrata*. A classic satire on the war between nations and the war between the sexes.

Aristotle. *The Poetics*. The first major piece of literary criticism, this work contains a complete essay on tragedy, with the famous definition and discussion of the tragic hero, and the first (and only surviving) sentence of an essay on comedy, which is "Tragedy is life seen close at hand; comedy is life seen from a distance."

Barnet, Sylvan, Morton Berman, and William Burto. *Eight Great Tragedies*. New York: New American Library, 1985. From Aeschylus to O'Neill, this perennial best-seller provides the humanities student with an opportunity to view the whole span of development in the tragic theater.

Bergson, Henri. "Laughter." In *Comedy*, ed. Wylie Sypher. Garden City, N.Y.: Doubleday, 1956 (and in other editions and translations). The respected metaphysician deals with laughter as humanity's way of restoring equilibrium in the presence of the irrational, the incongruous, and the outrageous.

Brooks, Cleanth, John G. Burser, and Robert Penn Warren. *An Approach to Literature*. Englewood Cliffs, N.J.: Prentice-Hall, 1976. An anthology with some very good introductions that explain and analyze elements of drama.

Davis, Tracy C. *Actresses as Working Women: Their Social Identity in Victorian Culture*. New York: Routledge, Chapman, and Hall, 1991. This book discusses the fact that for centuries the theater was considered an unfit profession for women of good background. This fascinating book also studies the struggles of actresses to win social acceptance and a sense of personal dignity during a time when women's rights were almost nonexistent.

Kitto, H. D. F. *Greek Tragedy*. 3d ed. New York: Routledge, Chapman, and Hall, 1966. This has long been the definitive study of the origins, performing conditions, and meanings of the art of tragedy in what many consider its first and most golden age.

Miller, Arthur. *Death of a Salesman*. (1949). The prototype of contemporary ordinary-people tragedy.

Molière. *The Miser*. Tr. H. Baker and J. Miller. London: Dent, 1962. A wonderful translation, if it can be found, of what is often considered the comic genius's masterpiece. It certainly demonstrates that single-mindedness is humanity's major comic flaw.

Reinert, Otto, and Peter Arnott, eds. *Twenty-three Plays*. Boston: Little, Brown, 1978. About as comprehensive a collection of great plays of the past and present as there is in print, from Sophocles to Amiri Baraka's savage modern play about race relations, *Dutchman*.

Shakespeare, William. *Complete Works*. Exists in innumerable editions and can be purchased for a variety of prices. Every humanities student should own a copy.

*Vivien Leigh as Scarlett O'Hara in* Gone with the Wind. *(The Museum of Modern Art/Film Stills Archive)*

# The Motion Picture:
# Art and Industry

## Overview

The motion picture is indeed a vehicle of creative expression, and no study of the humanities is complete without considering it. Some of its practitioners have been and are touched by genius. But of all the outlets for human creativity since the very first esthetic impulse breathed through our remote ancestors, film (along with its companion medium, television) has proved to be the most profitable. It has become a mega-industry. A study of film cannot ignore the industry's potential for making people rich very quickly. Sometimes art is created using the very formulas that guarantee wealth. Sometimes one has to choose between art and commercial considerations.

A clue to the art-versus-commerce problem was present right at the outset of moviemaking. No other medium ever progressed so far so fast. There is a span of only 26 years from the first official motion picture, in 1889 (which lasted a matter

*Before the advent of cinema, it took the best of poetry, prose, and drama—the combined effort of literature through centuries of time—to make clear to us that when we discover the balance, the fusion of mind and spirit we view as order and civilization, which causes human life to become productive and livable, that life, that order will always express the highest aspiration of our poets, our philosophers, our prophets, and through them our hopes for mankind.*

*So do the screenplay and cinema at their best.*

*Sam Thomas*

of seconds), to the appearance in 1915 of the first motion picture epic, *The Birth of a Nation* (which lasted nearly 3 hours!). What are 26 years compared to the length of time humanity has had to develop the visual arts, music, drama, and philosophy? Think of the stir the movies created in the early days. On both sides of the Atlantic the infant art was like a new technological toy, and entrepreneurs were quick indeed to realize and exploit the financial possibilities.

An artist's need to create and the human desire for wealth are not necessarily warring opposites. True, some creators have shown little concern for anything *except* their work. But the majority of the people whose achievements we celebrate throughout this book were not averse to the good things money can buy. Discovering that one's art can bring financial rewards need not lead to creative impotence.

Nonetheless, the film industry was and continues to be dominated by people who seek to do far more than break even. Sometimes legitimate works of motion picture art manage to get themselves born, though no one is aiming specifically at art. With *Casablanca*, for example, art developed quite unexpectedly from an *entirely* commercial enterprise. With *Citizen Kane*, genius insisted upon being served whether the mass public was ready for it or not and no matter what the producers thought.

In this chapter we shall look very briefly at milestone events in the relatively brief history of the motion picture. We shall single out a few notable achievements that illustrate the peculiar strengths of this art, indicating along the way some artists of film who are likely to take their place in the history of the humanities. We shall focus on those motion pictures that have held their critical reputations over a span of years and that may justifiably be regarded as classics.

## Early Milestones

Some say the motion picture got its start as far back as 1824, when a seemingly minor event occurred that would have a direct bearing on the development of a new kind of art. In that year, in France, Peter Mark Roget, creator of the popular *Thesaurus*, formulated a theory that he labeled "The Persistence of Vision with Regard to Moving Objects." Roget gave some thought to something we all do thousands of times every day, yet never consciously: *blinking our eyes*. When we blink our eyes, should not our vision be continually interrupted by intervals of blackness, however brief? In fact, we see as if we never blink at all. The reason, according to Roget's theory, is the eye's ability to retain an image for a split second after the stimulus is removed, that is, during the time it takes for the eyelid to close and reopen (like a camera shutter). Though our eyes keep blinking, the images retained keep overlapping each other, producing the *illusion* of continuous vision.

*The origin of motion pictures can be traced to the theory of Roget—the* Thesaurus *man—that the eye retains an image for a split second after the stimulus is removed.*

An early proof came with the discovery of a "trick" that is well known to all of us: A series of drawings was made of a figure in successive stages of motion, then stacked up and held firm so that a person could easily flip through it with his or her thumb. The result, as you can predict, is that the figure actually appeared to move! We know, of course, that it was the papers that moved, not the figure, just as we know it is celluloid film inside a projector that is moving, not our favorite actors up there on the screen. It is Roget's theory that explains the trick. If our eyes could not retain the images for those split seconds, we would "catch" the still photographs as they were being projected onto the screen.

During the mid-nineteenth century people were charmed by this "trick" and tried to exploit it by any means possible. The development of photography gave further impetus, for pictures of actual people could replace drawings. Animation thus came first, quickly to be followed by "real" (photographed) subjects. Inventors on both sides of the Atlantic went to work to develop mechanisms to move the pictures faster and create an ever-better illusion of actual motion. One mechanism was a circular drum with slits through which the eye peered. Inside the drum one could fasten still images, and when the contraption spun around, the eye saw fluid motion.

Thomas Edison, who is usually given credit for having invented the motion picture camera and projector, certainly knew about the excitement moving pictures were creating. He was, however, more concerned with trying to invent the phonograph. But his faithful assistant William Dickson took up the challenge. On October 6, 1889, Dickson gave his employer a private premiere of a movie. Running about ten seconds, the movie starred Dickson himself, who both moved and spoke.

*Thomas Edison, given credit for inventing the movie camera and projector, was more interested in working on the phonograph. His assistant made a ten-second movie in 1889.*

Image technology was, however, far in advance of sound technology. The race was on to see who could build a better projector. Aided, of course, by electricity, inventors were obsessed with the goal of providing large enough pictures for a group of people to watch at the same time, pictures that could replace the peep shows, which could accommodate only one person at a time. Think of how much more profit could be made! By 1896, people were going to the movies to watch extremely brief films, each of which presented one unified action, such as a person swimming or running or even going through the agonizing phases of a sneeze.

Despite these rapid advances, films were not big business at first. While audiences were delighted by them, movies were at best only a few minutes long, shown at neighborhood vaudeville houses as novelty "acts." The peep show, which was Edison's personal contribution, proved to be a bigger financial boom at the turn of the century. The peep show machines, simple ones requiring little maintenance, were turned out by the thousands as the penny arcade industry catered to the great demand. The peep show was the video game of its time.

*By 1896, people were going to the movies to watch extremely brief films presenting one unified action, such as a person swimming, running, or sneezing.*

## D. W. Griffith

In 1915, the year in which the elegant and huge Strand Theatre opened on Broadway, D. W. Griffith gave *The Birth of a Nation*—all three hours of it—to an adoring and dazzled public. This was the same year in which Metro Pictures Corporation, with Louis B. Mayer at the helm, came into being. In that brief span from 1889 to 1915, movies had indeed arrived as a mature form of entertainment, crafted by skilled artists, like Griffith.

*The Birth of a Nation* is epic in scope, following the course of the Civil War and the period of Reconstruction in the South. It was the film that unquestionably established the movies as a mass medium. Alternately praised as art and denounced as backlash racist propaganda, inciting audiences both to cheers and indignant taunts, the film had everyone talking in a way that had probably never happened before. The more intense the controversy, the longer the lines at the movie houses.

*The Birth of a Nation* is treated with appropriate respect because it was the first film to exhibit a definite directing *style*, one that Griffith did not happen upon by accident but that seems to have been carefully planned. There are distinct

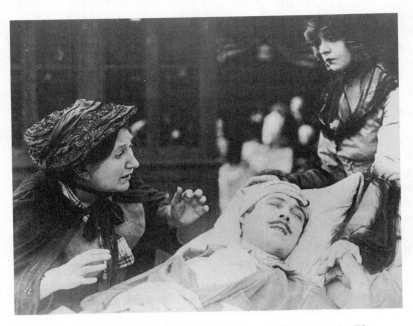

The Birth of a Nation, *the first film to introduce a definite directing style. (The Museum of Modern Art/Film Stills Archive)*

*Contributions of D. W. Griffith to Cinema Art*
*Directing style*
*Rhythm*
*Lingering take*

ways in which Griffith's camera moves in for a close-up at a climactic moment, then cuts to a scene that moves at a very different tempo. Griffith's work was the first to be labeled *rhythmic*, because of the manner in which editing is used not simply to tell a story, but to control the pace at which the story is experienced by the audience.

Extraordinarily ahead of its time was the *lingering take*, which Griffith employed—sparsely, it is true, but always unexpectedly and therefore effectively. A lingering take is a shot that remains on the screen for a longer time than mere plot demands require. Directors since Griffith, especially those making mystery or horror films, have put this technique to abundant use. Who has not seen a film in which a handful of characters, having engaged in a conversation of some sort, all make their exit, leaving behind an empty room? Instead of cutting to an exterior scene to follow the characters' further progress, the camera remains behind, brooding mysteriously on the emptiness and raising tantalizing questions: Is there some unseen presence in this room? Will something tragic happen here later? Is there some clue staring us in the face?

During one famous moment in *The Birth of a Nation* a young Confederate soldier, rushing across a battlefield, stops at the sight of a corpse lying on the ground. It is that of a Union counterpart who, it turns out, was the boy's close friend before the war. The soldier's grief is short-lived, for he is suddenly pierced by a bullet and falls across his friend's body. Griffith did not cut to the next scene but allowed his camera to hold the moment silently. There they are: two close friends, both dead in a cause neither is old enough to comprehend. If the film were being made today, one cannot imagine a director's improving on what Griffith did.

## Silent Comedy

Filmgoers of today sometimes think of the era of silent films as "prehistoric," with silent movies being what people had to endure because they were unfortunate enough to be living at a time before sound in the movies. This attitude stems from the uninformed arrogance of those who view time as a carefully developed, ever-improving sequence. Nonetheless, as some literary critic once put the matter, the ancients never knew they were ancient.

Audiences who waited in line to see *The Birth of a Nation* or who roared with laughter at Charlie Chaplin as they tried to forget the grim reality of war in 1917 included college professors, other actors and actresses, famous writers, and political figures. These were not silly, naive people who "didn't know any better"; they had discriminating taste and knew that some movies were better than others. The very best films were those that were totally visual, communicating through imagery, the proper language of the screen. The less successful were those that had to stop every few seconds and insert a word card so the audience could tell what the actors were saying. The imagery of the screen was especially suited for comedy.

The silent films brought into preeminence two major comic artists: Mack Sennett (1884-1960) and Charlie Chaplin (1889-1977). Sennett's name is associated with movie slapstick—a brand of rapid and violent farce in which people lose their human dignity completely, get struck in the face with pies, crash their cars into each other, and wind up getting doused with water. Sennett's world is

*Charlie Chaplin, the most famous and popular figure the screen world has ever had. (Harry Ransom Humanities Research Center, Hoblitzelle Theatre Arts Library, The University of Texas at Austin, Austin, Texas)*

*The Keystone Cops, a band of idiotic, incompetent, bungling law officers. (Culver Pictures)*

one of total chaos, kept in disorder by a band of idiotic, incompetent, bungling lawmen known as the Keystone Cops.

From our lofty, all-knowing historical perspective, we tend to think that the speeded-up, jerky movements of the Sennett films were the results of inferior technology. Nothing could be further from the truth! Sennett became obsessed with the "sight gag" and with the potentially unlimited resources of film to provide it. One obvious thing a director could do was control the speed at which motion was viewed on the screen. Sennett photographed action at an average of 10 frames per second, but ran the film through the projector at an average of 18 frames per second—almost twice as fast as it really happened. The effect was to dehumanize all of his characters so that the violent catastrophes—his stock-in-trade—could not be taken seriously.

*The speeded-up, jerky movements in silent films were sometimes deliberately employed for comic effect.*

While working for Sennett, Charlie Chaplin happened to put together a comic costume for himself for a crowd scene in which a certain amount of improvisation was allowed. In baggy trousers and shoes much too big for him Chaplin became a tramp, a social misfit, but this persona was lost amid the usual Sennett confusion.

Chaplin's developing interest in using character, not sight gags, as the principal source of comedy led him to leave Sennett and strike out on his own. The result: Charlie Chaplin became the most famous and popular figure the screen world has ever had, the first truly big and international *star*. His comic creation, the Little Tramp, waddling ducklike through an incredible number of films, remains one of the great artistic achievements of motion pictures. The Little Tramp's characteristic appearance is beautifully summarized by film critic Bosley Crowther:

> At first glance, the Little Tramp looks foolish, a callow and nondescript grotesque, too ludicrously put together to be anything more than a caricature. His large head set on narrow shoulders and topped by an antique bowler hat that requires frantic clutching to prevent it spinning off into space; his diminutive, pencil-thin body packed into a

too tight coat, usually an old-fashioned jacket buttoned up to a bat-wing collar and tie; his oversized, baggy trousers; his obviously much too big shoes; his moustache; his bamboo cane—they shape up into an image that is outlandish and absurd.[1]

What are the characteristics that made this persona such an endearing figure for the audience? First and most obvious, the Little Tramp is an *incongruity*—a being that is always out of place wherever he is—and people can laugh at incongruities. Second, while laughable, he is not so ridiculous that he ceases to have humanity, as Sennett's outrageous Cops do. What humanizes the Little Tramp is the attempt at dignity, implicit in both the costume and the face; people can identify with someone who refuses to see himself as a loser. Third, the Tramp *is* a survivor. The world is harsh and cruel, but he manages to summon up the know-how to get by, even if this means an occasional lapse into cheating or stealing. Fourth, though the Tramp is thin and weak-looking, the villains and bullies who threaten him are always naive and trappable. The ongoing myth in Chaplin films is the eternal triumph of the underdog, which is funny because we know what the world is *really* like and that underdogs do *not* succeed as much as we might like. This myth is also uplifting to the spirit.

*Charlie Chaplin's Little Tramp, one of the great comic creations of all time, is laughable but never ceases to have humanity.*

Among Chaplin's silent masterpieces is *The Gold Rush* (1925). Like many major comedies, its plot contains elements of tragedy. The Little Tramp comes to Alaska with hundreds of others, lured by the dream of sudden riches. But in this struggle for survival, he is no match for the cruel environment or the continual threats from physically stronger bullies. Like Don Quixote he is an idealist and falls in Platonic love with a woman who seems to him the embodiment of the most wholesome beauty. She, however—a streetwise dance-hall hostess—finds him absurd and rejects him.

In this film Chaplin reached the summit of his creative powers. There are laughs galore: The Little Tramp gets desperately hungry, so he cooks his shoes and eats the laces like spaghetti. His tiny cabin is blown to the edge of a cliff during a blizzard, and he unknowingly exits through the door—nearly to his doom.

But we become deeply involved, even through the laughter, because of the Tramp's human fragility. We care even as we laugh, an extraordinary feat that no other film artist has ever been able precisely to duplicate. Suddenly we realize why it is that this unique blending of the serious and the comic *works* so well. Chaplin's Tramp is so likable, so in need of our protection, that without the softening edge of comedy we would be unable to tolerate the disasters that befall him. Thus it is that the film gives us the kind of happy ending for which Hollywood has become famous: Charlie strikes gold, becomes wildly rich, and does indeed marry his heart's desire.

There is little doubt that Chaplin was knowingly perpetuating a myth. He was far too wise to think life works out for the best, and perhaps his happy endings also have a bit of the funny and sad intertwined. Many of his films end with the Tramp waddling away down the street, twirling his cane confidently as he becomes smaller and smaller in the distance. Wherever the plot has taken him, he will, we know, remain the outsider.

## Eisenstein

Some people think movies started in New York, then moved to California. In truth, *American* movies did just that. But other countries had audiences just as eager to be entertained by the new art. For instance, motion pictures were especially welcomed in Russia, where Soviet directors, fresh from the Bolshevik Revolution of 1917, seized upon this obviously mass medium as a golden means to the true purpose of all art: the celebration of the working class. No less an imposing figure than Lenin himself made the comment that of all the arts, the cinema was the most important.

*Film editing became serious art in Russia, most notably in the work of Sergei Eisenstein.*

In the early years following the Revolution the Russians had to rely mainly on imported films, but they quickly evolved skills of film editing in order to make sure these films had the correct message for the Russian people. In fact, they became so enthralled with the craft of snipping and pasting to achieve a desired effect that they were really the first to devise an elaborate theory of the medium. They were the first "intellectuals" of the new art. Their editing was clever enough to make acting almost superfluous.

The Russian director who first looked through the camera with the eyes of an editor was Sergei Eisenstein (1898-1948), as great an artist in his own right as Griffith or Chaplin. His *Potemkin*, released in 1925, the same year as *The Gold Rush*, is still required viewing in all film schools; it contains one scene in particular that has set the standard for editing techniques ever since: the depiction of a massacre by cossack troops on a long flight of steps in the city of Odessa.

*The massacre on the Odessa steps in Eisenstein's* Potemkin *set the standard for editing techniques ever since.*

Before the making of *Potemkin* Eisenstein had immersed himself in the study of films, and the study rapidly became an obsession. Even more than Griffith he was concerned with the rhythm or flow of a film, and he coined the term *montage*, meaning the way the director arranges the shots so as to assault the emotions of the viewer. Though Eisenstein was a loyal party member and was committed to the Soviet doctrine of art as anticapitalist instruction for the masses, he was also artistic and used film in an innovative way that went beyond mere propaganda.

The most famous innovation for which Eisenstein is credited might be called the *elongated moment*. If, Eisenstein reasoned, the wonder of film is that

*Eisenstein coined the term* montage *to describe the way the director arranges the shots so as to assault the emotions of the viewer, as he did in* Potemkin. *(The Museum of Modern Art/Film Stills Archive)*

the director is not limited to the fixed perspective of the theater and is thus able to cut from place to place and time to time, why not take similar liberties for a given location and a given time?

Let us suppose that the action of a film covers a number of years, during which time the main characters, through artfully applied makeup, age from 20 to 50. The audience will accept this convention, though they have been sitting in the theater for under two hours. By the same token they will accept the fact that an action that in real life could take place in a minute or two requires a longer period of time in this film. Eisenstein was the first director to dissect time and show it in its complexity, revealing what would normally be missed.

*Potemkin* is indeed a memorial to a bloody period in Soviet history, one that in 1925 was still fresh in the people's memory: the attempted uprising against the Czar that took place in 1905. (Recent evidence, however, has shown that Eisenstein's famous scene of the Odessa steps massacre was a fabrication.) The sailors on the battleship *Potemkin* have mutinied, causing the dockworkers in the port of Odessa to stage a sympathy strike. The strike in turn brings on a thunderous assault by mounted cossack troops, riding through the town and killing citizens indiscriminately. Eisenstein was apparently driven by the need to reinvent the facts to make a powerful statement.

The scene endures as one of the mightiest ever filmed. Like Griffith before him, Eisenstein decided to shoot on location, to create the illusion of absolute authenticity. He found the long flight of steps on which the massacre had supposedly occurred. His directing instincts seized the opportunity, and the result was a six-and-three-fourths-minute sequence depicting a minute or at the most two minutes of real time and requiring in all the splicing of 157 different shots. The result: a microcosm of inhumanity.

The sequence begins with 57 separate shots that show an assortment of happy and unconcerned Odessa townspeople on the steps just before the massacre. Carefully, Eisenstein introduces key figures to whom he will return again and again while the atrocities are being committed. But most significant of all, the director chooses to show us a young mother wheeling her baby in a carriage—the very symbol of innocence about to be destroyed.

Then the troops come thundering to the top of the steps, splattering carnage as they ride. Eisenstein cuts from one of his key figures to another for six and three-fourths minutes of unrelieved terror. The massacre is experienced by the audience over and over. Now it is a little boy separated from his mother and crushed to death in the stampede. Now it is the mother, having found her son's body, lifting him up as an appeal to the soldiers, who respond by gunning her down. Back to the baby carriage sequence. We see the mother being mangled by cossack sabers. Now a close-up of the abandoned carriage rocking back and forth dangerously at the edge of the steps, pushed ironically over the brink as the mother, bleeding to death, falls against it for support. A close-up of the innocent child inside the careening vehicle, which is hurtling down the steps over and around hundreds of corpses.

Another character whom Eisenstein involves is an apparently cultured woman wearing fragile reading glasses. From the moment we first see her, we can tell she has never been subjected to any cruelty. We feel protective toward her, as we do toward the baby. Throughout the massacre the director returns to her, and each time she is more splattered with blood. Finally we see a cossack rider slashing out at something out of our view, followed by a rapid cut to the woman's face.

*Film is strongest when it makes greatest use of what is peculiarly its own—the ability to record time and space, slice them up into fragments, and glue them together in a new relationship.*

*John Bigby*

She has been mortally struck in the eye. As one noted film editor says of this moment:

> It never occurs to us that we did not actually see the saber strike her. (Any more than we are aware, while watching Alfred Hitchcock's terrifying adaptation of this technique in *Psycho*, of the absence of direct knife hits during the shower sequence.)[2]

We are living at a time when filmmakers are like guests at a buffet table filled with a wide array of special screen effects. Their appetite for blood and violence is especially insatiable. One would think they would realize by now that true terror—a very legitimate emotion for motion pictures to make their audiences feel—has never been accomplished through direct graphic means. Audiences have always shuddered at the dark hallway, not the ghost itself.

We might say that Eisenstein was led to art through necessity. Using the cinema for the purpose of stirring up antiroyalist sentiments in the Soviet audience, he found the most effective means of doing just that. He did not overstate his case. The artist within him prevailed.

Others in the new filmmaking industry were not as scrupulous as Eisenstein. At about the same time that Eisenstein was planning his directing strategies for *Potemkin*, a film version appeared of Thomas Hardy's tragic novel *Tess of the d'Urbervilles*. Louis B. Mayer, the producer and one of Hollywood's legendary titans, objected to Hardy's ending, in which the heroine, having killed the man who seduced and deserted her, is sent to the gallows without mercy. Though this denouement is a bitter pill for the reader to swallow, literary critics have always recognized that it is consistent with Hardy's pessimistic view of human existence. Mayer decreed the film be given a happy ending in which Tess's basic virtue is ultimately rewarded. In England, Thomas Hardy—unhappy at what Hollywood had done to his work—sadly observed, "I am an old man and have no defense against this sort of thing."[3]

This would not be the only time that Hollywood would use the cinema to uphold popular moral attitudes and reaffirm the myths that people seemed to need in order to live.

## An Artistic Eruption

No one knows exactly why, but the history of human art abounds with certain spectacular eras in which hosts of geniuses appear all at the same time. The movies had been a going concern for about half a century when the audience for art was forced to admit that a new form had indeed arrived and had to be taken as seriously as music or painting or drama.

Certainly the signposts for an artistic eruption were there almost from the outset. Chaplin and Eisenstein were not only "pioneers," they were significant artists in their own right. Each took the silent film about as far as the medium would allow. But by the late 1930s and the 1940s, cinema artists were putting all of the current components together: the cut, the lingering take, the elongated moment, the montage, color as well as artful advances in black-and-white cinematography, and ever more realistic sound as well as its significant opposite, silence.

Sound, introduced in 1927 for the Al Jolson musical drama *The Jazz Singer*, had originally been nothing more than a novelty aimed at bringing more

*Contributions of Sergei Eisenstein to Cinema Art*
*Montage*
*Elongated moment*
*Use of film editing to convey a message*

*I am an old man and have no defense against this sort of thing.*

*Thomas Hardy on Hollywood*

money to the box office. People paid to see anything that made noise. But an artist like Chaplin disdained the new technology until well into the 1930s. Since films could talk all they wanted, early sound movies were often imitations of talky stage plays. For a time, stilted dialogue replaced action and the sophisticated editing techniques à la Eisenstein.

Yet, again in an astonishingly short period of time, artistic advances came about in the use of sound. Not only did the technology itself improve drastically, but so did the quality of the dialogue. The 1930s, in fact, saw the heyday of a genre that the motion pictures both invented and perfected: the screwball comedy.

## Screwball Comedy

The screwball comedy was named for the well-known baseball pitch that doesn't come straight at the batter but takes an erratic course. The plots of these films did just that, using short scenes, frequent cuts, and fast-moving, witty dialogue to lift audiences on a magic-carpet ride through an escapist world of rich, sophisticated, but thoroughly disorganized people: the perfect antidote for a Depression-weary country headed for another war. The characters—usually a husband and a wife who basically love each other—become enmeshed in a ridiculous disarray of circumstances that very nearly but not quite terminates the marriage. One or the other meets someone else. Infidelity is suspected. People hide in closets or under beds. Husband and wife hurl abuses at each other in clever dialogue, as neither takes the time to listen to the facts.

In many of these films women, who often had been the drooping violets of the silent film, attained a somewhat elevated status. Stars like Claudette Colbert, Myrna Loy, Katharine Hepburn, and Irene Dunne brought intelligence, glamour, and elegance to the screen. They played wives who refused to accept the traditionally subservient roles society had ordained for them. In the popular *Thin Man* series—which includes sterling examples of the detective movie genre—Myrna Loy and William Powell played a married investigative team for whom the solving of murders was almost incidental to the verbal banter they exchanged. Naturally it was she who apprehended the killer, not through the logical methods employed by her husband but through a mysterious kind of intuition that clearly only a woman could possess.

On the whole, the screwball comedy did not consciously strive to be screen art. Its formula required that it take place amid affluent surroundings and that its plot revolve around the doings of upper-class, hence educated, people. Therefore its stress was on the witty interchange between civilized men and women. But, as frequently happens with movies, art develops when least expected.

Frank Capra's *It Happened One Night* (1934) stands quite apart from all other screwball comedies. It belongs to the genre mainly because of its rapidly moving plot line, but it is a film that is at once witty, entertaining, believable, and truthful.

Claudette Colbert, a major star of the screwball comedy, plays Ellie, a rich, bored, and, on the surface, brainless young woman engaged to marry an equally wealthy and brainless, but also arrogant and instantly unlikable, man named King Westley. Unable to bear the thought, she runs away from home, determined to make it on her own with no idea of what she is doing (so far, very formula screwball). With very little money, she takes a bus, on which there is riding a young, handsome, and more than slightly sexist reporter played by Clark Gable. Discover-

*Screen writers had to invent dialogue that was at once rich and colorful, pungent and amusing, but also stripped of inessentials. They had to learn not only what to say, but also how much could be left unsaid—how much could be left to the camera and the actor and the director to put on the screen through action and gesture or by implication.*

*Arthur Knight*

*The screwball comedy genre produced at least one work of genuine screen art:* It Happened One Night. *It is at once witty, entertaining, believable, and truthful.*

*The final message of* It Happened One Night *is typical of screwball comedy: Love is more important than money. (The Museum of Modern Art/Film Stills Archive)*

ing who she is, Gable pretends to be interested in her, hoping to write the exclusive story on the runaway heiress and strike it big in the newspaper world.

What Capra does with the formula is to humanize it. The reporter is the culturally acceptable macho hero, who changes as a result of a real connection with the young woman. Ellie, in turn, is a dizzy and irresponsible "rich girl" because her upbringing has demanded that she play this role in life. But experiences on the road bring to the surface a toughness, an instinct for survival, lurking inside. In the beginning she doesn't even know how to dunk doughnuts. Soon she is able to steal fruit and vegetables from a farm and to hitchhike by showing her leg to a passing motorist—something her macho companion is unable to do! When at length she returns to her wealthy home and her waiting groom, she stuns the wedding guests by refusing to say "I do" and jilting the brainless suitor at the altar.

The final message is typical of the screwball genre: love is more important than money. But the difference here is that the choice is a real one, made by a three-dimensional human being. Ellie has actually given up a fortune—something that never happens in the other comedies, in which rich characters talk about the priority they will give to love, while remaining rich at the same time. Moreover, the chemistry between the two main characters goes beyond the witty interchanges audiences came to expect. It develops out of the adventures they have shared, becoming integral to both of them. Each changes in ways that are consistent with their experiences: she becoming a high-spirited, strong-willed, independent woman with a very definite idea of the man she wants; he becoming less chauvinistic and attracted in the end to an assertive woman who neither needs nor wants to be sheltered.

*The screwball comedy has all but disappeared from the Hollywood repertoire because the cinema, like the stage, seems to be afraid that people will not listen to language.*

The screwball comedy has all but disappeared from the Hollywood repertoire, not because movies have downgraded women but because the cinema, like the stage, seems to be afraid that people will not listen to language. As cinema technology has grown during the past three decades, stunning visual effects and wraparound stereophonic sound batter our senses. There is very little time for wit and very little likelihood that anyone could note it if it were there.

There is a distinct possibility that the reason motion pictures erupted as a major art form during the late 1930s and into the 1940s is the existence of *just enough*—but not too much—technology.

## *Gone with the Wind* (1939)

The novel *Gone with the Wind*, which was published in 1936, was the work of an unknown Southern writer named Margaret Mitchell, who had researched the Civil War and then told the story from the Southern point of view. She created an enormous panorama of antebellum Georgia, the war itself, and the chaotic Reconstruction period that followed. The book, running more than one thousand pages, caused a national sensation.

The novel seemed to be just what escape-oriented Americans needed in 1936. The detailed recreation of the homes, landscapes, and battles of the period enthralled the readers. But most of all, Margaret Mitchell had created a hero and a heroine so real that people everywhere discussed their stormy relationship as if it had actually happened. Scarlett O'Hara and Rhett Butler are, in fact, still alive today in the imaginations of millions, because they were born at a time when screen art was waiting to embody them.

The movie of *Gone with the Wind*, partially the work of director Victor Fleming, who died before completing the film, announced to the world the real potential of films, for its stars Vivien Leigh and Clark Gable were full artistic collaborators with the author of the novel. Clark Gable *was* Rhett Butler, somehow jumping into the author's typewriter and entering her world. With *Gone with the Wind* the cinema played an unprecedented role in turning a myth into reality, giving to the characters a lasting presence far more immediate than we can find in the pages of the novel. Not necessarily *better*, but definitely more accessible.

*Gone with the Wind* spares audiences nothing. In the chaos of war, the good as well as the wicked suffer. Neither side is idealized. The genteel Southerners, though idealistic, are not really fit for battle. The North wins, but follows up the victory by allowing a ruthless exploitation of the South by carpetbaggers. Out of the wreckage the titanic figures of Scarlett and Rhett survive and marry, as befits a myth, for there is no one else the equal of either one. But they do not live happily ever after. Their child, who was to save their marriage, is thrown from a horse and killed. Scarlett, with the blood of fictional rebels like Huck Finn in her veins, shares with them the curse of restlessness. Rhett Butler is wealthy, yet despite Scarlett's possessing every material comfort she ever thought she wanted, she is still in love with Ashley Wilkes, the romantic idol of her youth. Scarlett will always be in love with people not available to her, and she will always cast her eyes on the distant horizon. Such is the burden of being an American heroine.

The typical happy ending upon which audiences are supposed to thrive does not materialize. Rhett Butler, fed up with Scarlett's instability, decides his own future is more important than hers, and so he packs his bags. As he stands at the door, listening to her repertoire of "defenseless female" tricks, audiences wait with hearts loudly beating to hear whether the movie will allow Rhett to give the novel's final answer to Scarlett's final question, "If you leave me, where will I go? What will I do?" As everyone gasps, he *does!* "Frankly, my dear, I don't *give* a damn."

*During the screening there is no time for critical reflection. Each new image and sequence stimulates immediate emotional responses. Unless the projector breaks down, you can't call time out.*

*John M. Culkin*

Down on her luck once again as she was when, after the fall of Atlanta, she had returned to Tara, her home, to find the place in ruins, Scarlett has to pick up the pieces and begin again. Just as the great American novels *Huckleberry Finn* and *Moby-Dick* "end" with their respective heroes starting life over after a series of disasters, both the novel and the film conclude with Scarlett's renewed surge of optimism: "Tomorrow is another day."

*Gone with the Wind*, for all its excessive length, is a masterwork of screen art, not only because it retains the integrity of the novel, but because it finds an eloquent screen language of its own. Color, for example, was still very new to Hollywood in 1939. Instead of the sharp and vibrant hues we are accustomed to, audiences of the 1930s saw lighter, more delicate color, often resembling the pale pastels of the French impressionist painters. Some of the visual images in *Gone with the Wind*, such as the famous shot of Scarlett and her father standing under a tree, silhouetted against a Georgia sunset, have museum-worthy artistry.

Building on the innovative camera techniques of people like Griffith, the film pushed available technology as far as it could go. The burning of Atlanta remains one of the most awesome sequences in film history. No trickery was involved. Atlanta was not a small-scale model, set ablaze with a cigarette lighter and photographed at close range. The director actually burned down old studio sets. This meant the shooting had to be perfect the first time around, and *that* meant weeks of planning. Hundreds of shots were to be used.

As in Eisenstein's Odessa steps sequence, cameras elongate the time span by cutting from burning buildings to fleeing people to frightened horses stampeding. In the center of this carefully designed confusion are Rhett and Scarlett driving a rig out of the doomed town as screaming people try to climb on. The horse, blindfolded to keep him from panicking, nearly trampled hundreds of extras to death. The effect comes close to matching Eisenstein's powerful sequence.

*One cannot think of a passage in literature in which words express the horrors of war with more eloquence than the railway station scene in* Gone with the Wind.

Then there is the famous scene at the railway station. Scarlett's close friend Melanie is in labor with her first child. Scarlett rushes wildly into the street to find the family doctor, who is desperately trying to save lives at the train depot, now become not a hospital but a cemetery of unburied corpses. Blundering onto the scene and, in her dazed condition, unaware at first of where she is, Scarlett slowly perceives she is in the midst of death on an unbelievable scale. The camera very gradually backs away from her horrified face as the scene "opens" for us wider and wider as if it were never going to stop. One cannot think of a passage in literature in which words express the horrors of war with more eloquence than does this scene from *Gone with the Wind*. In the final analysis the true measure of screen art is the same as that of a great poem: One must be convinced that there is no other way of expressing something.

## *Citizen Kane* (1941)

*Citizen Kane* *was not a box-office sensation; its techniques were too unfamiliar for too many viewers.*

Two years later, in 1941, appeared *Citizen Kane*, a film produced, directed, and coauthored by an amazing 26-year-old named Orson Welles. Several years before, he had done a radio adaptation of H. G. Wells's *The War of the Worlds*, about a Martian invasion of the earth, performed as a news bulletin "alert" and executed so realistically that people tuning in after the opening credits believed the invasion was really happening. After the national panic and subsequent notoriety for Welles, Hollywood came clamoring, seeing in this exciting talent a potentially bankable star. *Citizen Kane* was not a box-office sensation; its techniques were too unfamiliar for too many viewers. But its reputation as screen art has grown steadily with

*Citizen Kane reveals the hollowness of the American Dream and the tragedy of those whose only concerns are money and power. (The Museum of Modern Art/Film Stills Archive)*

each passing decade. Orson Welles acquired a deep respect from many who normally denounced movies as being not art but a business interested only in profit. From 1941 until his death in 1984 Orson Welles was known as Hollywood's most fiercely individual artist/director, a man who did what his taste compelled him to do, whether it made money or not.

In *Citizen Kane* the myth is the American Dream, which is, of course, as much a part of our folklore as Scarlett's survival instinct. The film is based on the actual success story of William Randolph Hearst, who in the early years of our century rose from obscurity to become owner and ruler of a newspaper empire. But Welles had no intention of romanticizing the truth. His film ultimately reveals the hollowness behind the dream and the tragedy of those whose only concerns are money and power.

Audiences were startled by the use that theater-trained Welles made of lighting. His sets—enormous ones to embody the bigness of the theme—are perpetually underlighted. Whether we are in Kane's mansion, Xanadu, or in the vaults of the public library, everywhere we look are corners hidden in deep shadow, as if Welles were searching for a visual equivalent to the shadowy regions of Kane's mind.

Despite the man's wealth there is a melancholy deep inside him that we do not at first understand. In fact, the entire movie represents a young reporter's search for a clue to the tragedy that has haunted the great man up until his death. The famous opening sequence, in which the camera travels from the imposing fortresslike gates of Xanadu through corridors filled with the costly and useless trappings of success into the huge bedroom where Kane lies dying, culminates with a shot, taken at floor level, of Kane's face. On his lips, as the very last breath escapes them, is a single word: "Rosebud!"

*In* Citizen Kane *Orson Welles did not romanticize the American Dream. His film ultimately reveals the hollowness behind the dream and the tragedy of those whose only concerns are money and power.*

Unlike *Gone with the Wind, Citizen Kane* was written directly *for* the screen, in screen language—the language of external imagery. Knowing that the camera cannot photograph what is inside a human being and that in reality we can only guess at what lies hidden in each of us, Welles makes the investigating reporter the central character. The camera becomes his (and our) eyes. Together we must try to solve the mystery of "Rosebud," a seemingly trivial thing in comparison with the might of Kane's fortune.

Welles works indirectly, moving always *around* his subject, as his camera moves around and under objects, seldom shooting a scene head-on. The reporter interviews everyone who knew Kane and also goes into the cavernous vaults of the public library in an attempt to recreate every incident of a life that begins for us with Kane as a little boy playing happily in the snow just before he is told that he has inherited a great deal of money and must leave home to claim his fortune. As the reporter begins to piece together the fragments, we follow the success of Kane's first newspaper venture, the opening of his chain of papers, his increasingly gaudy lifestyle, his developing megalomania—the total self-absorption of someone who seems to have everything but is never satisfied. Kane wants to be governor, then perhaps president, to be a world figure with a firm place in history. America is a democracy, but with enough money and power one can become *royal*.

In one famous sequence Welles demonstrates not only Kane's power-madness but the blindness it creates. He also demonstrates that film can do in a very brief time what novelists do—and perhaps less memorably—in many words. We find ourselves onstage at a great opera house, where Kane's second wife is making her debut. He has literally bought her way into the company. She is dull-witted, with almost no singing ability, but Kane believes he can accomplish any feat with money. As the lady drones on and on in uninspired cadences, the camera slowly ascends from stage level, up through the massive riggings that raise and lower the backdrops, finally coming to rest on a grid-walk that seems to be hundreds of feet from the appalling desecration below being witnessed by a formally attired crowd of first-nighters and critics. On this walk are two stagehands, old-timers who, we know, have heard many legendary voices. As one stagehand looks on in amusement, the other pinches his nose with two fingers to signify that the great debut is giving off a distinct odor. What words could have the same effect?

Similarly, words could never carry the impact of the scene in which Kane and his socially prominent first wife are shown breakfasting at either end of a very long table. He has married her for the prestige she will give him; she has married him for his wealth. There has been little communication between them ever; both are reading newspapers. From the smile on Kane's face we assume he is reading one of his own papers, but the camera reveals that Mrs. Kane is absorbed in a rival paper. It would take many, many prose paragraphs to give us the details of a failed marriage. It took Orson Welles just a minute.

In the very final sequence, all of the deceased millionaire's expensive but meaningless art treasures are shown boxed and labeled in the tomblike cellar underneath Xanadu. The scene opens with the epic image of thousands upon thousands of boxes, reminding us of the thousands of dying soldiers lying outside the Atlanta railway station in *Gone with the Wind*. Only, Welles *reverses* Victor Fleming's technique. If you recall, the Fleming sequence begins with a close-up of Scarlett's anguished face, then opens up wider and wider until the full horror of the scene is revealed. Welles's camera allows us to see the full might of Kane's material empire, then slowly begins to move in toward a flickering light seen in the dis-

Citizen Kane *was written directly for the screen, in screen language that presents in brief visual images what would require many pages in a novel.*

*The final scene of* Citizen Kane *reverses the technique used in the Atlanta railroad station scene in* Gone with the Wind. *The camera starts wide, without focus, then zooms in on a trivial object—Kane's childhood sled.*

tance. As we draw close, we see that it comes from a furnace into which a workman is tossing the "junk" nobody wants. At length, this motion picture of incredible scope reaches its final shot in a relatively confined space: the interior of this furnace, where, about to be consumed in flames, is the sled which, we remember, the young Kane was playing with in the snow just before he was taken away from his simple and, we suppose, happy childhood existence. Was this insignificant object the thing that has haunted him all his life? Is it a symbol of the ordinary pleasures money cannot buy? The film raises more questions than it answers, but the rich imagery gives us much to think about long after the film has ended.

Often throughout his career Orson Welles remained on the fringe of Hollywood—recognized as a cinematic genius, but gaining a definite reputation as a high box-office risk. He never compromised. Though not every venture was the artistic equal of *Citizen Kane*, he always allowed himself to be governed by his taste as an artist, not his ambition as a producer.

## *Casablanca* (1942)

*Casablanca* illustrates how film art can suddenly appear in the midst of commercial considerations. The producer, who understood the Hollywood success formula, made sure he had all the right ingredients for a slick adventure film. For director he chose Michael Curtiz, who had gained a reputation for making fast-moving action movies, a man who knew how to get the most from a script, knew about pacing, how to build suspense, and how to pare dialogue down to its bare essentials. For leading lady he chose Ingrid Bergman, an actress recently imported from Sweden in a Hollywood attempt to capitalize on the respect critics were beginning to give foreign actors. But by far the major coup—*how* major they could not have predicted—was to cast Humphrey Bogart as the leading man.

In *Casablanca* we have perhaps the finest example of screen art achieved through a *persona* adopted by a particular star. In the context of motion pictures, the term *persona* refers to a character type that suits the abilities of a given star. What generally happens is that an actor or actress plays a certain role so well, is so believable to the public, that producers begin looking around for other scripts that involve a similar character or that can be rewritten to include one. If the actor or actress succeeds a second time, he or she finds that material is being tailor-made for the persona. After a time the public so identifies the star with his or her persona that it becomes all but impossible for him or her to create any other kind of character. Gary Cooper, for example, was such a "specialty" performer. Whether playing a sheriff or a homeless drifter, he was always a man of few but wise words, quiet intensity, impeccable integrity, and unflinching bravery. The public naturally assumed that Cooper in real life was exactly the same person as Cooper on the screen.

At its best, the tradition of the screen persona has the powerful effect of true art. The characters are so real to us that if their value system is impressive and admirable, then they have contributed a standard by which we can measure our own actions, our own values. Sometimes a persona is so convincingly cruel and callous as to be the very definition of evil—another sort of standard by which we tend to get our bearings. The psychologist/philosopher Carl Jung (see Chapter 11) speaks of the *archetypes*—the heroes, villains, themes, and symbols—found in the world's major myths, which help to shape our belief systems and our visions of reality. The great screen personae are examples of mythic archetypes.

*The Bogart Archetype*
*Kills when he has to.*
*Is antisocial but not psychotic, because he is always a superrealist.*
*Often operates on the wrong side of the law but is never lacking in ethics or integrity.*

*With* Casablanca, *a work of film art emerges from all the right ingredients for a slick adventure film. (Springer/Bettmann Film Archive)*

The Bogart persona had not yet been fully realized prior to *Casablanca*. Somehow there occurred an almost miraculous blending of the plot circumstances and the actor's own growing awareness of the persona he was becoming. The character overwhelmed the public, and the studio front office, traditionally conservative, obliged by bringing him back again and again, but never with the same impact.

Who is this character? And why has he held his reality for nearly half a century? To comprehend the phenomenon, we need to see how he evolved. Bogart made his stage debut in 1930 in a drawing-room comedy as a spoiled, pleasure-loving young man of leisure who actually spoke the famous line "Tennis anyone?" He was genteel and thoroughly innocuous, but when he got to Hollywood, somebody thought he could play a gangster.

Throughout the 1930s Bogart developed a specialized approach to the gangster persona, and the persona of *Casablanca* would use some of those traits. The persona is ruthless, to be sure, but not in the totally unfeeling, sometimes sadistic manner of others. Without question he is menacing, because you always know he will shoot to kill *when he has to*. He is a gangster because the times require it, not because the profession is necessarily his number one choice. He is not shown as the victim of a bad environment, hence he is not an underdog. The Bogart gangster is a superrealist whose code is, "It's either you or me, and it sure isn't going to be me!" Such a character is dangerous but not illogical, antisocial but not psychotic. Such a character has a peculiar kind of integrity that fascinates audiences.

In 1941 John Huston, an artistic and perceptive director, found a script in which both he and Bogart could explore and deepen the character. Instead of portraying a gangster, the actor would play a "private eye," for the novelist Dashiell Hammett had in *The Maltese Falcon* created a seemingly coldhearted realist of a detective that exactly suited Bogart's screen style and personality. True, he would be on *this* side of the law, but just barely.

Sam Spade, the private investigator, lives and works in San Francisco, a meeting place for the cleverest, most sophisticated of international crooks. His partner has been murdered, and, though tracking the killer should be the work of the police, Sam the realist knows that, if he wants results, he must take the law into his own hands. "When your partner is killed," he comments without emotion, "you're supposed to do something about it." The dictates of reality are the constant Bogart guidelines.

As Bogart and Huston worked on the film and the persona evolved, the character of Sam Spade deepened. The superrealist with the tough exterior developed vulnerability. In fact, he falls in love with a woman who turns out to have been his partner's killer. Spade hides his feelings of both love and disillusionment. In a world like this, Spade seems to say, you cannot afford to take a false step, cannot afford to let emotion cloud your vision. He turns the woman over to the police, commenting soberly that if she escapes hanging, he'll be waiting for her. If not, "I'll always remember you." The Bogart persona had become the tough, unflinching man of steel with a susceptible heart and an uncanny ability to survive both danger and heartbreak.

In *Casablanca*, Sam is now Rick Blaine, operator of a cafe that is also an illegal gambling casino. Casablanca, the capital of French Morocco, is theoretically neutral territory, and to it come hundreds of desperate people trying to escape the Nazis and get to the free world. But freedom really means having enough money to buy an exit visa from the corrupt French police. In an effort to raise the needed money, these people gamble at Rick's place. As we would expect, Bogart's Rick is an unemotional realist, at heart concerned about these people, but seldom willing to become involved in their lives. He cannot afford to. He needs the blessing of the French chief of police in order to keep his place running.

Despite the general state of the world in this time between the fall of Paris in 1940 and the American invasion of Normandy in 1944, despite the dangerous intrigue that surrounds him, Rick is peculiarly content in his well-ordered, unemotional life. But all of this changes abruptly and his role as the detached observer is put to a severe test when the Laszlos come into the cafe.

Victor Laszlo is the world's number-one Nazi-fighter and therefore the

*Humphrey Bogart (left) as Sam Spade in* The Maltese Falcon, *with Peter Lorre, Mary Astor, and Sidney Greenstreet. (The Museum of Modern Art/Film Stills Archive)*

Nazis' number-one target for extermination. He has come to Casablanca to buy his way to freedom. The problem for Rick, however, is that Laszlo's wife (Ingrid Bergman) had been Rick's lover in Paris but had disappeared with no explanation after promising to run away with him. Now he understands the reason—her earlier marriage. Still, the chemistry between them is there. Hidden beneath the hard exterior are the tenderness and vulnerability Bogart showed in *The Maltese Falcon*. He agrees to aid the Laszlos in their dangerous mission, knowing that, to be successful, he must outfox the French chief of police. The plot reaches its crisis when, having obtained not only visas but two tickets on the Lisbon plane, Rick must decide whether to use them for himself and Laszlo's wife—an outcome she seems to want very much—or to allow Laszlo to escape with her.

The final scene has become famous in film history. Pursued to the airport by a frenzied Nazi official, Rick is forced to kill the man. But presumably Rick is now someone who will do anything for love. With Mrs. Laszlo waiting for him outside the plane, whose engines are throbbing in the fog-engulfed night, Rick tells her that Laszlo is already on the plane and she must go with him. She seems not to comprehend his reasons, nor perhaps does he completely; it is here that the full complexity of the Bogart persona is glimpsed.

*Is* the hard-shelled realist what the chief of police accuses him of being: a sentimentalist at heart? Is he someone who, for all his apparent amorality, cannot desecrate the sanctity of a marriage, especially when the wronged husband is a noble individual? Or is he perhaps thinking that their love would probably not last? After all, what does? Or is the whole truth an irreducible combination of motives? The realist survives, however, even as the sentimentalist takes one last look at the woman's beautiful face and, knowing that beautiful moments are inevitably pushed aside by the onward surge of time, says simply, "Here's looking at you, kid."

To seem real and three-dimensional and to be lasting, a character need not, *should* not, be transparent and easily understood. The fact that audiences continue to watch *Casablanca* and wonder why Rick did not board the plane is ample evidence of the character's durability. Characters whose motivations are transparent soon become uninteresting to us. In real life we seldom "know" each other any better than we "know" ourselves.

*Casablanca* is legitimate screen art like *Citizen Kane* and for the same primary reasons. Both films employ dialogue sparingly. Neither central character reveals his personality and his motives through words. Both films use the screen medium to create a complex reality that we must interpret, even as we do in real life. Neither one makes a direct, easily phrased statement about people or existence. The great works never do!

Yet *Casablanca* and *Citizen Kane* each achieved their status as art through very different means. *Citizen Kane* was consciously designed to be a quality film from the very beginning. The youthful director had no ties with Hollywood and was more or less allowed to go his own brooding way. In short, the studio took a chance on him and hoped for the best. *Casablanca* grew to be what it is in what can only be described as hit-or-miss fashion. Paying Bogart and Bergman very high salaries, the producers had to make sure they would get their money back and therefore kept tinkering with the film. The chaos surrounding the making of the film is now legendary. Bergman reported in an interview that she was convinced the movie would be a disaster. How Bogart was able to maintain the integrity of Rick Blaine is an unanswerable question; scenes were shot, reshot, and often replaced as the plot line sputtered, came to a halt, and then—somehow—chugged itself back to life. The cast did not know about the final scene until the day of filming. Cast and crew eased their tensions by making fun of the whole enterprise. Art, one must assume, is continually creating itself by some means not always known even to the artist.

A final note of some interest: Several years back, during a revival of *Casablanca* at the Harvard Square Theatre in Cambridge, the sound track broke down for a few minutes. Not at all disconcerted, the audience chanted the missing dialogue until the spoken words were restored.

*When the sound track broke down during a revival of* Casablanca, *the audience chanted the missing dialogue until the spoken words were restored.*

## Auteurism

When the Pulitzer Prize for best play is announced, the respective authors receive the credit. When the Oscar is given for best picture, the *producer* is the person who climbs onto the stage, not the director and not the author of the screenplay. Nonetheless, a gifted director can have a more profound influence on a film than any other individual.

Occasionally a director attracts critical attention for a significant body of work, films that share a common style of camera angles, lighting, pace, and even subject matter. The top directors have tended to select material that they truly believe in and that embodies a certain view of reality that they hold. Usually they collaborate with the screenwriter on at least the final draft of the script, heavily influencing the direction and outcome of the plot and the fate of the characters.

The dominance of a powerful director over the story and the actors has caused the great French filmmaker Jean-Luc Godard (b. 1930) to apply the word *auteur* (author) to such a director and to coin the term *auteurism* as a label for the detailed critical examination and appreciation of a significant body of film work. Auteurism as a film study is parallel to literary criticism that focuses on a certain important writer, a movement (such as romanticism, discussed in Chapter 15), or a given period in literary history. Godard's terminology has been borrowed by a number of film critics, who often apply the *auteur* label to Godard himself, as well as to a few others. One assumes that film auteurs will be given a prominent place in the history of twentieth-century humanities.

*In film criticism an* auteur *is a director who attains worldwide prominence by developing definite stylistic traits which often transcend the script itself. Some film auteurs, consciously or not, inject their own philosophy into what they do, so that all of their work appears to express them—as if they were indeed authors.*

## Ingmar Bergman

Other countries also have film histories and traditions. Sweden, in particular, is rich in screen art and could easily have been the focus of this chapter. During the 1940s, Swedish director Ingmar Bergman (b. 1918) began to practice his craft and did it so well that he has become one of the great auteurs of this century. Bergman did not come to the movies because of their glamour and the promise of quick wealth and stardom. Like Orson Welles he was a serious theater director very much intent on creating art, and he saw in films a challenging medium that could afford him a greater freedom than the stage to explore his subjects. For a decade he studied the technique of cinema, and then by the mid-1950s he had made Sweden very nearly the film art capital of the world.

In the span of two years, 1956-1957, Bergman gave the world two masterworks, *The Seventh Seal* and *Wild Strawberries*, indicative of a creative intensity probably no other director will ever match. Bergman was, and is, a philosopher/filmmaker, and in the 1950s he was wrestling with ultimate questions about the

*Ingmar Bergman, the existentialist as film director, was forced to reach some conclusions in order to provide an ending for* The Seventh Seal. *(The Museum of Modern Art/Film Stills Archive)*

*The films of Ingmar Bergman ask why we create rigid norms of civilized behavior and impossibly high intellectual standards that imprison the multi-dimensional human being within each of us.*

human place in existence. We are fortunate that the artisan and the philosopher came together at just the right moment.

In the years following the end of World War II, Sweden, like much of Europe, was caught up in a philosophical movement known as *existentialism*. (For a fuller discussion, see Chapter 7.) The central assertion behind this movement is that we can be certain only of the *fact* of our existence; that is, ideas about the *purpose* and *destiny* of humanity all rest on assumptions that we derive from religions, other philosophers, and mythology. How do we know that we are made in the image of a divine nature? How do we know that there *is* a divine nature? Since we are human, how can we even comprehend such a thing? All philosophies must begin with the simple fact of existence and work from there.

Yet many people can go no further. Without a sense of God, without the belief that they are in this world for some reason, they feel themselves alienated, cut off, mere meaningless entities walking around on the earth for a few years then vanishing into an endless night. We shouldn't be surprised that such was the mood of a devastated Europe during the 1940s.

*The Seventh Seal* is a medieval fable about a young knight who has just returned from the Crusades and ironically finds Death awaiting him, though he has up to now escaped the grasp of this black-robed figure carrying a scythe. Feeling he has nothing to lose, he challenges Death to a game of chess, the contract being that he can stay alive until Death holds him in check. The knight's purpose is to delay the inevitable until he is satisfied that his life has had some meaning. So, while the fantasy game is proceeding, the knight is also journeying about the countryside in search of something—a person, a cause, a religion—that will convince him existence has not been an absurd waste of time. The plot is ideal for the existentialist as film director, for it forces Bergman to reach some conclusions about life in order to provide an ending for the film. (Bergman also wrote or collaborated on all of his screenplays.)

In the great tradition of the mythic journey, the knight has many adventures and interacts with many people along the way. The least satisfying encounters are with the Church. Organized religion gives humanity a sense of sin and guilt, but does not make existence seem valuable. The knight discovers that life is rich and full only when he meets a young married couple (named Joseph and Mary) and their child. Only in the loving warmth of the family circle, where people support and nurture each other, does life seem to make sense. Not to have lived is not to have known love and joy. Bergman's message is simple but not simplistic. He finds it only after struggling with utter *nihilism* (the belief that all comes to nothing in the end). With the knight's help the young family escapes Death. Though the *knight* will die, his is a joyous vision, and the film ends with a dance led by the figure of Death, with a parade of people all celebrating the bliss of simply *being*.

But, of course, *The Seventh Seal* is set in the Middle Ages. Bergman was not ready to shape an identical vision in contemporary terms. *Wild Strawberries* is the story of a 78-year-old doctor facing death, not in allegorical terms, but in very real, biological terms. As in *The Seventh Seal*, Bergman finds an ingenious and simple situation and uses a journey as his plot structure. The old man must travel to a great university in order to receive an award for distinguished life achievement. The journey gives him an opportunity to look closely at his life and ask himself whether it has *really* amounted to something.

*The Seventh Seal* mixes fantasy and reality. *Wild Strawberries* blends reality, dreams, and memories of the past with such sophisticated editing techniques that one cannot believe it was made decades ago. Using the storytelling economy that film makes possible, Bergman shows us the present state of the doctor's relationships with his mother, his wife, his son, and his daughter-in-law. All are strained and lacking in either warmth or spontaneity. Clearly, neither they nor he derive any value from the fact that they are members of the same family.

Picking up some hitchhikers, including two young men and a girl who are casually dressed, unconventional, and utterly lacking in the awe that the university and the award ought to inspire, the old man finds that it is still possible for him to enjoy the company of people just because they are human. He has no intellectual rapport with them, but they help to free him from the emotional repression that has destroyed his family relationships. Gradually he slips into daydreams of summers in the country when he was a free-spirited boy, long before he became a victim of the codified adult, university world—a time when he could be as spontaneous as he feels when he stops with the hitchhikers to pick and eat wild strawberries by the roadside.

Again Bergman's message is simple. If this present existence is all we know for certain, why then do we ruin it for ourselves? Why do we create rigid norms of civilized behavior and impossibly high intellectual standards that imprison the multidimensional human being within each of us? *Wild Strawberries* is an ageless and poetic plea for humanity to hold fast to youth, to love, to caring.

## Other Auteurs

We have barely scratched the surface of screen art, nor have we exhausted the subject of auteurism by looking at the work of one notable director. Our intention in the last section was to illustrate the reason one film artist, Ingmar Bergman, reached the level of auteur. Other artists could as readily have been the choice for that discussion.

One such auteur is the Italian Federico Fellini (b. 1920), who began his career, significantly and not uniquely, as a screenwriter before taking his stance behind the camera. His first major success was *La Strada* (1955), a simple and touching tale of a slow-witted girl and a restless scoundrel who takes advantage of her devotion. Working within the conventions of postwar Italian screen realism (using actual locations and supporting actors hired literally off the streets), Fellini moved into heavy symbolism with *La Dolce Vita*, a sensuously filmed study of the decadent lifestyle of midcentury Roman affluence. In *8½* his focus became himself as a director trying to find meaning amid the bewildering images and sensations that overpower the central character. Fellini has achieved auteur status less for his confused quest for meaning than for the lush images, visual symbols, and startling, often grotesque characters that have become his trademarks. Often these combine to produce a sardonically humorous effect. If Fellini confronts a meaningless void, he never fails to smile.

*Federico Fellini has achieved auteur status for the lush images, visual symbols, and grotesque characters that have become his trademark.*

In the United States there is the auteur Frank Capra (1897-1991), already mentioned as the director of *It Happened One Night*, perhaps the greatest of the screwball comedies. Capra has achieved critical acclaim, however, mainly for his socially conscious Depression-era "message" films, such as *Mr. Deeds Goes to Town* (1936), in which a playboy with inherited wealth undergoes a profound awakening through contact with the unemployed and the homeless; *Meet John Doe* (1941), in which a newspaper exploits a man down on his luck just for his story, without humane interest in the man himself; and most of all, for the 1939 classic *Mr. Smith Goes to Washington*, in which an idealistic young man is elected to Congress with the help of an unscrupulous political machine that tries, unsuccessfully, to control him. Often accused of excessive sentimentality, as in his perennially popular *It's a Wonderful Life* (1947), Capra is nonetheless admired for the unmistakable honesty of his views and his sincere, almost poetic faith in the innate goodness of the ordinary citizen.

*Frank Capra's auteur status derives from the unmistakable honesty of his views and his sincere, almost poetic faith in the innate goodness of the ordinary citizen.*

Stanley Kubrick (b. 1928) is another director who may be deserving of

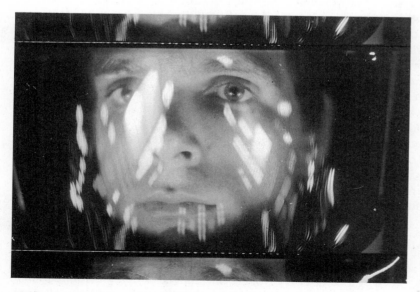

In *2001: A Space Odyssey, Stanley Kubrick used extraordinary visual effects that Einstein would have understood and applauded. (Kobal Collection/SuperStock)*

*Woody Allen and Diane Keaton in* Annie Hall. *(Culver Pictures)*

auteur status, particularly because of stylistic innovations. His *2001: A Space Odyssey* (1968) has extraordinary visual effects that Einstein himself would have understood and applauded, effects not used simply for shock value. Kubrick is also known for his inventive use of sound, as when he underscored the first appearance of the space station in *2001* with a symphonic orchestra playing *By the Beautiful Blue Danube*. In *A Clockwork Orange* (1971) Kubrick juxtaposed Rossini's *The Thieving Magpie* with a speeded-up sequence of a murderous encounter between gangs. Throughout the movie he used the "Ode to Joy" from the final movement of Beethoven's Symphony no. 9 in ironic contrast to the brutal actions of his central character (who in fact loves Beethoven almost as much as he does violence).

Still to be reckoned with in this rarefied category is Woody Allen (b. 1935), once a stand-up comic, now a writer/director/actor with deep insight into and compassion for lonely, unfulfilled, sensitive people. Allen the actor has immortalized the persona of the pallid, underweight, neurotic Jewish kid, plagued by feelings of guilt and sexual inadequacy. Allen the writer has captured both tragic and comic portraits of people struggling to survive in the big city, especially Manhattan, a city Allen both adores and fears. Allen the director has learned from Bergman, his idol, how to use black-and-white cinematography to suggest and evoke associations, to engage the mind of the viewer through indirection and subtle symbolism. *Annie Hall* (1977) is, however, considered Allen's masterpiece at present; it is a film in color and *without* symbolism, in which he revels in his favorite theme—the contrast between two problem-ridden cultures, the traditionally morose New York Jewish milieu and the complacent, materialistic middle-class Anglo-Saxon heritage. What makes *Annie Hall* so unforgettable is that the two lovers, who embody their respective and doomed cultures, manage through the power of their unlikely, often comic love affair to rise above the madness of their backgrounds.

*Woody Allen, once a stand-up comic, now a writer/ director/actor with deep insight into and compassion for lonely, unfulfilled, sensitive people.*

# Today at the Movies

Major works of film art like *Gone with the Wind, Citizen Kane*, and *Casablanca* appeared close together in time during the early years of film history. We do not mean to imply that nothing significant is being achieved in film anymore. Yet there is an important point that must be made: In 1939, the year of *Gone with the Wind*, audiences had to choose only between two electronic media: going to the movies or listening to the radio. The two media were vastly different. The visual excitement offered by movies won out more often than not.

*The film industry today must compete with television and the video-rental store; and for these markets it must produce horror films, animated cartoons, and action-adventure stories.*

Today, however, potential ticket-buyers have their television sets, some of them half the size of the living room wall; their video games; and, above all, their neighborhood video-rental outlet. The average wait between the time a new movie appears in a first-run movie theater and a video store is less than a year. With the disappearance of the drive-in movie and the chance to bring a carload of family members for a night's entertainment at nominal fees, families now tend to opt for the weekend rental of several films. Filmmakers realize that to meet the demands of the rental market, they must produce certain types of movies: horror films, animated cartoons (though some of these, like *Beauty and the Beast* [1991], aspire to the level of art), and that trustiest of all film genres—the action-adventure story.

What is more, with the soaring union wages, the huge production and distribution costs, not to mention the enormous salaries commanded by top stars, producers are understandably wary of venturing very far into unexplored territory. One wonders whether the 26-year-old Orson Welles would have been able to do *Citizen Kane* today.

Nonetheless, art will out, and the past decades have produced a number of artistically significant works. In 1972 Francis Ford Coppola scored a major hit with *The Godfather*, the saga of a Mafia family with all the sweep and scope of a modern-day Homeric epic. The major characters are mobsters, but Hollywood had in the 1930s idealized the figure of the gangster along with that of the cowboy.

*Marlon Brando as* The Godfather. *(Courtesy of Paramount Pictures Corporation)*

*American soldiers burn a Vietnamese village in Oliver Stone's* Platoon. *(Kobal Collection/SuperStock)*

Coppola's gangsters are cut from the same heroic mold, but raised to larger-than-life proportions. Their peculiar ethics (honor among thieves; the kiss of death before the execution) are neither sanctioned nor condemned. Coppola endows the characters with humanity and lets them live and die as they will.

In 1978 Michael Cimino gave us *The Deer Hunter*, the first major film epic to try putting the Vietnam War into perspective. The work is very long, allowing for the subtle development of character and increasing audience involvement in the tangled relationships.

That unpopular war has inspired much notable work, especially from younger directors, some of whom were in Vietnam and experienced the destruction firsthand. Among these is Oliver Stone, whose growing reputation suggests he may soon be included among the important auteurs of our time. In 1986 his offering was *Platoon*, one of the greatest antiwar statements ever made on film. Among the memorable scenes is one that rivals the impact of the burning of Atlanta in *Gone with the Wind* or the massacre on the Odessa steps in *Potemkin*. In the scene, American soldiers set fire to a Vietnamese village, with women and children running wildly in all directions to escape the attack of the invading force. Instead of the usual deafening sound track, Stone has a symphony orchestra quietly playing Samuel Barber's Adagio for Strings.

Unfortunately, too many modern directors seem to like noisy sound tracks more than the eloquent silences that set apart many of the great moments in drama and film. In addition, they especially love to employ the special-effects department. Often, all we have to remember from our night out at the movies are spectacular car chases and supernatural beings of all shapes and dimensions tearing away layer after layer of their victims' flesh.

The industry aspect of filmmaking may have the upper hand for the moment, as it fights for its economic survival. But art is still very much alive, if not always under the emblem of the big studios. Some very impressive work is being done by young independents, who are proving that an important theme and significant characters can still stir an audience, without one car having to burst into flames.

*Gus Van Sant's* My Own Private Idaho *shows that the opportunity is still there for those willing to set their sights on the mesmerizing things that film can do. (Kobal Collection/SuperStock)*

There are film festivals in major cities on both sides of the Atlantic—most notably Cannes and New York—which give important time to new works from independents. In Utah there is the annual Sundance Festival, devoted exclusively to showcasing the achievements of young cinema artists, like Gus Van Sant, whose *My Own Private Idaho* (1991) uses haunting music, surrealistic backgrounds, and poetic cinematography to tell a mournful story of a street wanderer who sells his body to other men for money and longs for a tender, understanding relationship.

Apparently the opportunity is still there for those willing to set their sights on the mesmerizing things that film—and no other medium—can do, rather than on the distant promise of huge fortunes.

## Glossary

*archetype:* A term used by philosopher/psychologist Carl Jung to denote characters, themes, and symbols found in the world's major myths and other works that aspire to myth status and that help to shape our interpretations and expectations of reality. Classic archetypes are heroes and villains, the good guys and the bad guys. Hollywood has been a rich source of contemporary archetypes, including the famous Bogart persona discussed in this chapter.

*auteur:* A French term for "author"; used in this chapter to refer to certain film directors who develop a reputation as artists, whose imprint is to be found in every film they make, and who have recognizable camera styles, rhythms, themes, and symbols. Ingmar Bergman, the Swedish director, is a consummate example of the film auteur.

*cut:* A cinematic technique whereby the flow of a scene is interrupted and the audience finds itself in another scene or looking at the same one from a different point of view.

*elongated moment:* A technique invented by Sergei Eisenstein and imitated by many directors, in which an action is broken down into many component parts shown in linear succession so the entire scene takes far longer than it would in reality.

*existentialism:* A modern philosophical movement, popular in Europe following World War II, which holds that we can be sure of nothing except the basic fact that we exist. We do not know for certain why we exist—or whether we even have the right to ask such a question. But we *are* indeed free to define our existence, provided we take the responsibility for what we make of ourselves.

*genre:* A French term meaning "type" or "category"; used mainly in literary or film analysis as a convenient means of communicating some general characteristics of a work without having to go into a lot of detail. For example, if we know that a movie is a detective story, we already know quite a bit about it.

*incongruity:* Two usually unrelated items found together, making us laugh; for example, someone in a formal dress and sneakers.

*persona:* In this chapter, a characterization used by a screen star in more than one film, and one that becomes closely associated with him or her, often to the point that the public comes to believe the star is very much like the character.

*screwball comedy:* A special genre of film comedy usually involving at least one upper-class character (an heiress, for instance) doing improbable and not very dignified things, accompanied by witty dialogue. The name comes from the way a baseball can be thrown in an erratic, rather than a straight, way to confuse a batter. Screwball comedy was popular escapist fare during the Depression era.

*slapstick:* Originally a stick constructed to make a noise when it hit a clown. Now the term refers to wild, farcical action with a lot of physical movement.

## Notes

1. *The Great Films* (New York: Putnam's, 1967), 49.
2. Ralph Rosenblum and Robert Karen, *When the Shooting Stops . . . the Cutting Begins* (New York: Viking Press, 1979), 55. Rosenblum, incidentally, has been the favorite editor of Woody Allen for a number of years.
3. Bosley Crowther, *The Lion's Share* (New York: Dutton, 1957), 87.

## Suggested Reading

Crowther, Bosley. *The Great Films*. New York: Putnam's, 1967. A wonderfully illustrated analysis of 50 great films, selected by the former dean of American film critics, who reviewed for the *New York Times*.

———. *The Lion's Share*. New York: Dutton, 1967. Probably no longer in print, this book is nonetheless worth the search. It offers a historical panorama of the early days of film, centering on the development of the Metro-Goldwyn-Mayer empire.

Everson, William K. *American Silent Film*. Fair Lawn, N.J.: Oxford University Press, 1978. A comprehensive history of the growth of a genre, from early peep shows to the art of Griffith and Chaplin.

Knight, Arthur. *The Liveliest Art*. New York: Mentor Books, 1957. One of this century's leading film scholars traces in depth the pioneer years of filmmaking.

Krutnik, Frank. *In a Lonely Street: Film Noir, Genre, Masculinity*. New York: Routledge, Chapman, & Hall, 1991. Though the chapter does not use the phrase *film noir*, it does contain a discussion of the Humphrey Bogart persona in the classic *The Maltese Falcon*, generally regarded as a masterpiece in the *film noir* genre. The phrase literally means "black film" and refers to a species of detective movies, popular in the 1940s and 1950s, with a wisecracking, fast-talking private eye hero whose clashes with evildoers have left him cynical about human nature. This new study ties the genre to the American male's search for the affirmation of his manhood, while having to suppress feelings of warmth and tenderness.

Mast, Gerald. *A Short History of the Film*. New York: Pegasus, 1971. A readable account of milestones in midcentury film history.

Rosenblum, Ralph, and Robert Karen. *When the Shooting Stops . . . the Cutting Begins*. New York: Viking Press, 1979. A good introduction to the art and contributions of the film editor, which should greatly interest those with a developing need to learn more and more about how films are made.

*Louise Nevelson,* An American Tribute to the British People (Gold Wall) *(1960–65)*
*(The Tate Gallery, London. Photo: Art Resource)*

# 6

# *Western Philosophy*

## *Overview*

Philosophers do not attract much popular attention. They write, if indeed at all, quite a bit less than do authors of best-sellers, whose readers number in the millions. Since the invention of printing in the late fifteenth century, Plato's *Republic*, held by many to be the single greatest philosophical work ever penned, has sold fewer copies than recent paperbacks dealing with the revelations of a reformed drug user or a ruthless tycoon unable to find true love. Countless people go through life and do quite well for themselves, thank you, never having heard of Descartes, Hume, Kant, Schopenhauer, James, Kierkegaard, Russell, or Dewey. Philosophy courses usually enroll fewer students than do courses on practical subjects, like accounting and physical fitness.

The philosopher is just not very visible, gliding phantomlike through the commerce of everyday life, appreciated by perhaps a few friends who listen. Extraordinary fame almost never comes to a philosopher. Socrates, the West's first major philosopher (as far as we know), did achieve a measure of renown for his teaching and his supposedly anarchistic pronouncements. But what he got for his fame was a trial, conviction, and execution—not a very appealing model to attract the uninitiated.

*Most philosophers never become famous. Socrates did, and what he got for his fame was a trial, conviction, and execution.*

Philosophers are people who become disturbed by either of two conditions: (1) widespread acceptance of an invalid belief held by other reputable intellectuals, or (2) persistent, unanswered questions. When philosophers think the existence of a belief has been accepted as valid by too many others of respectable intellectual stature, they try to set things right, to clear the air, to make a strong rational case for an opposing view. Possibly the most famous example of this philosophical "repair service" occurred several thousand years ago, in the fifth century B.C.

Protagoras, a dominant personality in Athens at the time, led a professional sect called the *Sophists*. Together they operated what amounted to the world's first law school. That is, for a specified fee they would teach the rhetorical and dramatic skills needed to win a case in court. Their business irritated Socrates no end, primarily because it was predicated on the assumption that no such thing as absolute justice existed. If a Sophist-trained person won, justice apparently triumphed. If this person lost, justice miscarried. Looking deeper into their philosophy, Socrates discovered they were cynics who believed in no absolute truths whatever.

Though Socrates himself wrote no works—at least none that have survived—his best student, Plato, *did*, giving the world, among other great books, the *Republic*, in which the cynical idea of justice propounded by the Sophists is to Plato's satisfaction corrected once and for all. Written as a series of dialogues with Socrates as the principal character, the *Republic* sets out to prove it an error of thought to maintain that justice can be one thing here and another thing there. A character in the *Republic* who frequently challenges Socrates is Thrasymachus, and he is made to sound exactly like a Sophist. At one point Thrasymachus defines justice as whatever is in the best interest of the ruling party: in short, might makes right. Socrates quickly pounces on this, asking Thrasymachus whether in his opinion it would ever be possible for the ruling party to make a mistake—to pass a bad law that would *not* turn out to be in its best interest. Of course it would, replies the unsuspecting Sophist, who is then forced to confront the embarrassing implication that the ruling party could theoretically be in the position of requiring obedience to a law that is *not* in its best interest. If this is so, then, according to Socrates, the definition given by Thrasymachus cannot be valid. The ruling party would be forced to admit an *in*justice was being done by demanding obedience. For Socrates both justice and injustice were equally and universally recognizable, and were therefore the same for everyone.

*Philosophers love to show us the intellectual traps into which humanity is likely to fall and, if possible, to rescue us from them.*

Socrates thought the relativism of the Sophists was dangerous indeed. To contend that the truth is "whatever works," as the Sophist approach to law implied, to say there are no universal values, is to throw the civilized world into chaos. The contribution of Socrates' philosophy to the human enterprise is here impressively demonstrated.

The other condition that can disturb the philosopher, even as it does the scientist, is the persistence of unanswered questions. The difference between these two kinds of people is that the scientist is always willing to address questions that can be answered with experiments and observations, while the philosopher tends to deal with questions that can be answered through reason or intuition, but that lie, at least for the time being, outside the domain of science.

Much early thought, which we now regard as pioneer philosophy, was considered scientific at the time. Later in this chapter we shall meet Thales of Miletus, a sixth-century (B.C.) astronomer who thought reality must be something other than it appears to be. Particle physicists of today, searching for the most minute form of matter (or energy, whichever comes first), would understand Thales' quest. The reason he is now classified as a philosopher is that he had to "resort" to speculative thought alone. He had no particle accelerator—a huge tunnel several miles long in which atoms and molecules can be made to travel at unimaginable speeds so that they crash into each other, releasing even smaller particles. Reason alone told Thales there must be a common principle underneath the world we see. Scientists are still looking for this principle. Insofar as they venture an opinion—with no immediate means of proving it—they are talking the talk of philosophy. When Einstein, working at the Princeton Institute for Advanced Study, suggested that the amount of regularity that exists in the universe might indicate the presence of a God-force, he probably should have been considered a guest in the Princeton Department of Philosophy.

Philosophers have for centuries been fascinated by the question of whether God—or *a* god—can exist. If God does exist, what is the divine nature, and what is human responsibility toward a deity that may not be aware of humanity at all? These remain high on the list of unanswered questions in the sense that no one can be certain that any answers advanced are right or whether there can *be* any right answers. Even though the prospect of not knowing *for sure* may loom as a virtual certainty, the philosopher is likely to go on thinking anyway. Using, developing, and strengthening the rational powers inherent to human beings is irresistible, in fact is *habit forming* once you get started.

Reading the ideas of ancient minds can be exhilarating, even though we know much more about the world than they did. As someone wryly pointed out, any schoolchild today is smarter than Aristotle. But wiser? More rational? When we consider the very limited extent of human knowledge in Aristotle's day, we may well be astonished at the sheer volume of the man's thoughts and the range of subjects that his insatiable curiosity explored.

Most significant, however, is the number of unanswered and unanswerable questions entertained by that vast mind, questions that continue to fascinate thinkers because they are worth asking again and again, because they *must* be asked. One of his major works, *The Nichomachean Ethics*, covers the entire range of human behavior and moral responsibilities—matters we still wonder about, even if the particulars today are things Aristotle would not recognize. Becoming philosophical, we might ask ourselves whether it is all right for an athlete to use steroids. Or all right for a town council to ban the sale of a record somebody thinks is filled with obscene messages. Should adult movie houses and bookstores be closed down even if attendance is a matter of personal choice? These are unanswered, and perhaps unanswerable, questions.

*Two conditions tend to disturb the philosopher: the widespread acceptance of an invalid belief and the persistence of unanswered questions.*

Right and wrong may be moral opposites, but are they always defined in the same way? Is it possible to imagine a society in which definitions are reversed? Decades ago the anthropologist Margaret Mead shocked a good many readers by publishing *Coming of Age in Samoa*, in which she asserted that sexual mores in that remote South Pacific paradise required young women to yield up their virginity at a very early age. Historians often cite this work as having exerted a strong influence on the sexual permissiveness of late 1920s. More recently other anthropologists have called Mead's studies into question. Comprehensive data seem to show that Samoans are, and always have been, sexually conservative. Observing the entire controversy, a philosopher might ask, Did Margaret Mead do a bad thing? Is sexual conservatism more desirable than permissiveness? For whom? For everyone, or just for the person who thinks the answer is yes?

One need not be a professional philosopher to realize such questions are intriguing and worth the time to think about or discuss or hotly debate. Why? Answers to *that* question are also intriguing—and also in the domain of philosophy, which is, as we can see, a place we all visit from time to time. Those who find thought addictive are likely to stay there; they write books, which in turn inspire in us the habit of thinking *when it is not absolutely necessary to think*. Some of them contribute big ideas that stay around for a long while to tantalize other minds.

In this chapter we shall focus on three areas of thought that have always engaged the philosophical mind. The first happens to deal with mind itself. What can be known for sure? What is it that does the knowing? What exactly *is* mind? Are we born with something we can call a mind? Or do we develop it as we go along? What is reason? Is it a skill or a capacity? Is reason inborn or developed from experience? If it is not inborn, how do we *learn* anything? How do we know what it is we are experiencing?

The second area is vast, and we won't pretend to do it full justice. This area considers reality. What is reality? The familiar world "out there" that we see every day of our lives and take for granted as certainly existing? Or is reality something else altogether, something we can't see? Whatever reality ultimately *is*, how did it get here? When did it come into being? Out of what?

Asking such questions inevitably brings the philosophical mind into contact with a third—and much, much vaster—area of thought. This area addresses ultimate reality. Is God that ultimate reality? What reasons have we for thinking so—or not thinking so? Have these reasons changed through the centuries?

Those who are content with their lives and believe none of the preceding questions are worth asking are missing out on the opportunity to observe how adventurous minds have always thought boldly, have taken risks, have refused to accept traditional ideas without probing into them. If we do not learn how to imitate them, we may one day discover that someone else has been doing our thinking *for* us!

*Philosophy inspires in us the habit of thinking when it is not absolutely necessary to think.*

*If we do not learn how to think for ourselves, we may one day discover that someone else has been doing our thinking for us.*

## Mind

> What is mind? No matter. What is matter? Never mind.
>
> *Bertrand Russell*

In the above lines the modern philosopher Bertrand Russell is passing along to us one of philosophy's perennial and favorite jokes. As in the best witticisms, however, there is an extremely serious subtext. Philosophers have argued the issue for centuries, but the final words have yet to be said or written on the subject of *mind*.

No one doubts that human beings *have* such a thing as a mind. It has a legal identity, if not a definite philosophical one. Murderers have escaped severe punishment on the grounds that they were legally insane, or not in their "right mind." We speak about mind all the time as if it were a thing in its own right, despite the fact that no one has ever seen it. Sometimes it appears to be a place, as when we say we have "ransacked our minds" or "gone over every inch of our minds" in an effort to remember something.

*Joan Miro,* Painting *( 1933): We speak about mind as if it were a thing in its own right. ( Oil on canvas, 68-1/2" x 6'5-1/4." Collection, The Museum of Modern Art, New York. Loula D. Lasker Bequest, by exchange )*

Since, whatever it is, mind *appears* to be immaterial—at least *not* the sum of material parts (blood, cells, nerves, and so on)—some people have claimed that mind is not part of our bodily makeup. Thus it never could have been "born" when we were, and, consequently, cannot "die" when we do. Many cling steadfastly to a belief in life after death on these, rather than religious, grounds.

The classical view of mind ( that is, the one held by the ancient Greeks and Romans ) sees the mind as a nonmaterial entity, one that distinguishes humanity from the animal species. Classical humanism is predicated on the assumption that humanity is superior to everything else on this planet by virtue of its possession of mind.

So accustomed are we to using the term *mind* that we usually fail to remind ourselves that it has *yet* to be defined for universal applicability. The argument goes on. At the heart of the argument is the question of whether we know because we have experienced and have thus learned from what we have experienced, or whether we can learn because we *know how to know*. If mind is part of our body and develops after birth like organs and muscles, how does mind develop unless there is something we might call intellect present from the beginning to "make sure" we learn? What we learn is not necessarily the same thing as the process of learning!

But if mind is something that precedes our experiences, is it with us from birth? Where is it located? Where did it come from? Why are not all minds the same? Or do they merely fail to develop equally their potential? If the latter is the case, what after all *is* such potential?

*At the heart of the argument about mind is the question of whether we learn from experience alone or learn because we are born with a mind and therefore know how to learn.*

## Plato's Theory of the Forms

Plato thought about the preceding questions, but if he encountered some difficulties along the way, his ultimate contribution to the issue was quite certain and unwavering. The inquiry led him to one of the truly giant conceptualizations ever to come from our species: the theory of the Forms. If few believe the theory implicitly today, few also will deny the impact it has had over the centuries or the issues it can still raise. The foremost value that Plato's theory of the Forms has had for generations of thinkers is probably its beauty as a myth that, if accepted, explains almost anything that might puzzle us about mind. Plato's theory establishes the ghostly presence of mind inside each of us—an invisible organ without which none of us could function.

Many centuries after Plato, other philosophers would come along and try their hand at thinking through the problem of how to define and explain mind, and many of them would contend that mind is nothing but the sum total of ideas we derive from experience. Each would wind up in a maze of complexities, because none could satisfactorily explain how we learn from experience without having something that does the learning for us.

For Plato, mind is in us from birth. It contains the knowledge of what he called the *Forms*, or what we might call *universally understood abstractions*. Among these, one presumes to say, are the generic abstractions without the knowledge of which we should have a difficult time functioning in this world. If we did not know what an "ideal" tree was, for example, how could we understand that four vastly different entities—such as a weeping willow, a date palm, a cypress, and a monkey-puzzle tree—belong to the same generic family? Of great importance to Plato, however, were the intangible, the nonmaterial, and, he believed, the universal and unchanging Forms.

At the top of the list were the Good, the True, and the Beautiful. Simply put, we are born with the capacity to recognize the goodness of a deed, the truth of a statement, and the beauty of a face or a work of art. Beauty is *not* in the eye of the beholder, but inherent in an object. Nor are good and bad or true and false relative to individual perception.

So accustomed are we to accepting the relativity of abstractions that we might be easily tempted to dismiss the theory of the Forms as just another ancient myth that cannot possibly mean anything to us. Still, it is worth pausing a moment to consider an interesting point: Perhaps arguments about whether a statue is beautiful are valid, but if we had not experienced a good deal of previous agreement among people about what constitutes beauty, we could not understand what we were arguing about. Even Plato might agree, in other words, that a difference of opinion is possible; but he would go on to say that the debaters in question are working from a common comprehension of the Beautiful, differing only in the matter of whether the *specific* statue being discussed actually belongs to the universal category.

Take another example: the Good. In the familiar ethical dilemma of Heins, the devoted husband whose wife is dying from a terminal illness and who cannot afford the inflated prices being charged by the local pharmacist for a pain-easing drug, the issue is whether Heins should steal the drug or whether stealing at any time and for any reason is bad. The issue is *not* what is meant by good and bad, whatever the course of action. The specific case in question offers room for argument. If Heins steals the drug, is his deed a good one or not? No one can decide, Plato would insist, without an ability to *recognize* the Good. If you think back to our discussion of the debate between Socrates and Thrasymachus, you will remember that Socrates makes the same point—good and bad are universally recognizable.

The contention that we recognize goodness because we are *taught* what it is may not solve the problem. What does this contention imply? That our elders have in the past pointed out certain actions as good ones? "Good girl! You put your toys away neatly." "Good boy! You saved all those pennies to buy Mommy this lovely perfume for her birthday." Imagine that two such "good" people have met,

*For Plato, mind is in us at birth. It contains the knowledge of what he called the* Forms, *or universally understood abstractions.*

married, and continued their frugal, intensely disciplined lives, working so hard without a vacation that both are on the brink of a nervous breakdown. One day they phone in sick, rush to the bank, remove their savings, and fly to Acapulco for three months, returning home poor but rested and happy. A good action? Not according to the "elders" who taught them to be frugal, but maybe according to others. Once again, goodness can only be determined by how we choose to apply our knowledge of the *universal* Good. Plato would tell us that values are "relative" only in that we do not always discern the Good in the same way.

If abstractions—or Forms—are with us from the beginning (since we could have "gotten" them no other way), we are naturally curious to know where they come from. Plato's answer is that minds—like what Christians were centuries later to call souls—are immaterial entities that can neither come into or pass out of existence. They move—or migrate—from body to body. Mind therefore has nothing to do with your particular personality, your characteristics as this person rather than that one, your idiosyncrasies. All minds are equal in the sense that one cannot say one abstraction is different from (clearer than, *truer* than) another. Thus Plato's theory requires us to accept the conclusion that abstractions like justice and virtue are also the same for everyone.

While one is easily tempted at first to smile condescendingly at the notion that all abstractions are the same to everyone, Plato's defense of it is quite powerful indeed. It occurs in *Meno*, the dialogue named for its principal character, a wealthy nobleman of Thessaly who challenges Socrates (Plato's spokesperson, and the central figure in all of his dialogues) to explain how the abstraction of virtue can be taught to anyone who has not experienced many deeds that have been called virtuous and thus developed a general knowledge of virtue in the process. Socrates makes an analogy with the general knowledge of color. We understand when we are told the specific color of a certain object because we already possess the general concept of color. If we did not, what we are told would not make any sense to us whatever. Then Socrates makes the famous declaration that "learning is remembering." Meno, unconvinced, demands to see an example of such "remembering" at work. He challenges Socrates to produce universal knowledge from an untutored subject, and invites one of the slaves in the household to join them. Supremely confident, Socrates asks the boy to explain some complicated axioms of geometry. At first confused, the boy—seemingly mesmerized by the gentle prodding of the master—begins to display an accurate grasp of mathematical principles. Where did the boy come by such wisdom? Did someone teach him? "You are sure to know that," Socrates smiles at Meno, "since he was born and brought up in your house."

Education, then, is the activity by which young people are patiently guided not forward but *backward*—back to the knowledge they already have. When a teacher, recognizing that a certain point has been understood, cries out in undeserved triumph, "You've got it!", the actuality is that the pupil has remembered, even as one might recall a song title. The pupil has threaded his or her way through a morass of sense impressions, which are not the source of knowledge, and has come at last to a truth. Both teacher and student know when this has happened, for both possess the same truth.

If all minds are the same, what accounts for obvious differences in what we call intelligence? What accounts for what passes widely in the educational profession as a "learning disability"? Can anyone really be stupid? Can anyone be forever barred from "scaling the heights of intelligence"? Or is "it" all there, just

*In the dialogue* Meno *there is the famous incident in which Socrates, by asking the right questions, shows that a slave boy possesses an inborn understanding of geometry.*

waiting for a patient Socrates-like teacher to come along? Despite the widespread criticism of Plato's theory, we should not be so quick to label anyone stupid. There are too many absolutely astonishing success stories on record: people diagnosed as retarded who suddenly display acute insights into complicated subjects like trigonometry; people who escape a predicted future on public aid and become genuine leaders.

Those in the academic world know that Plato's theory is still quite viable, is in fact at the very heart of a current educational controversy over whether values should be and *can* be taught. If justice, truth, honesty, right, and wrong are indeed universals, as Plato believed, then they are the same for everybody, and "teaching" them means only reminding students of what they ought to know. Those who oppose values-education do so, of course, on the arguable grounds that values are relative to time, place, and culture. For them Plato is in error.

An apparently defensible position is one that accepts Plato's belief that abstractions are universal without having to say also that they are born with us. The contemporary philosopher Mortimer J. Adler (b. 1902), for example, agrees with Plato that there are some objects in the mind that are purely sensible (particular dogs, trees, cows, and so on) and some that he calls "purely intelligible." Among these he lists liberty, infinity, and God—abstractions that are public by nature, not private, even though they are not objects that we can see in the material world. They are public because two people can have a conversation about them without confusion. One person can say he does not believe in God, and the other that she indeed does, without either of them misunderstanding the issue. Adler believes not in mind (a ghostly entity in us from birth) but in intellect, a process peculiar to the human species, which enables us to abstract classifications of things and general principles from experience with particulars.

Adler has won fame for keeping alive not only the spirit of the philosophical giants but the enduring validity of their ideas as well. That he should even have *wanted* to take on so awesome an intellectual task is a strong sign that our philosophical heritage is not for dust-covered shelves alone, but that it still lights the way for those who find nothing so worthwhile as thought.

## "I Think, Therefore I Am"

The statement in this section's title is perhaps the most famous contribution given by philosophy to human vocabulary. It represents at once a milestone achievement in thought, however simplistic it may at first sound, and the beginning of a philosophical nightmare that Descartes, its author, did not intend.

René Descartes (1596-1650), alternately called the first major modern philosopher and the man who nearly killed philosophy altogether, was a fervent Catholic who had been taught to accept the teachings of the Church on faith alone. He was also caught up in the wave of scientific fervor that was sweeping Europe during the emergence of scientific methodology, fueled by such things as Galileo's development of the telescope and the audacious announcement by Polish astronomer Copernicus a century earlier that the Church had been wrong in teaching about an earth-centered universe.

Descartes had no intention of upsetting the centuries-old traditions of Christian thought in which he was thoroughly trained. But he was a man of his times, and he thought it was possible for the human mind, utilizing the scientific method, to achieve certainty in all matters. He even used philosophy to "prove" the existence of God, though the Church had so often and so vigorously denied that such proof was necessary. His idea was to make the certainty of God's existence compatible with science. There was a God, no matter whether a person came to this conclusion through faith *or* through science. Unfortunately, his intellectual adventures did not have quite the results he anticipated.

Following the scientific method, Descartes made an initial assumption: One cannot assume the truth of things to be already present in the mind, as Plato had long ago maintained. In fact, one cannot assume *anything*. One starts out, in short, as though one knew nothing whatever. Then, to make sure he was in the proper state of "mindlessness," Descartes proposed to doubt everything he thought he knew, and to keep on doubting until he arrived (if indeed he *could* arrive) at a position, a certainty, that defied further doubt. Not only did he doubt the familiar truths that were supposedly his human heritage—the Platonic abstractions of virtue, love, justice, liberty, and so on—but he also doubted the evidence of his senses:

> Accordingly, seeing that our senses sometimes deceive us, I was willing to suppose that there existed nothing really such as they lead us to imagine. . . . [W]hen I considered that the very same thoughts which we have when awake may also come when we are asleep, while there is at that time not one of them true, I supposed that all the objects that had ever entered my mind when awake, had in them no more truth than the illusions of my dreams.[1]

When you doubt that there is any world at all "out there" and that the image of yourself you think you see in the mirror is actual, you would seem to be at an impasse. Everything can be doubted, and thus there can be no certainty *anywhere*. Right? Descartes's answer was a very stirring "Wrong!"

Pretend you are experimenting with the method of doubt, absolutely committed to doubting everything you can. You doubt there is a world at all. You doubt there is a you in that world that isn't there to begin with. In a passing jest you wonder why—if there is nothing—you *imagine* that you see and hear things. Then you even toy with the idea that instead of God there is a Grand Deceiver somewhere up there who thoroughly enjoys weaving illusions for us. Then you are forced to doubt even *that*. Then you ask yourself (pretending there is a you, of course) whether you can even doubt that you are doubting. Why not? You've successfully doubted everything else. Is it possible to go on doubting to infinity? To doubt that you doubt that you doubt that you doubt . . . ?

Now comes that little point of truth that Descartes was seeking, one of those ingenious, incredible flashes of insight that seem so absurdly simple—that, in fact, *are* absurdly simple yet have the distinction of being solely and completely one's own, in this case Descartes's. He said, *I cannot doubt that I doubt.* If I were to do this, if I were to go on doubting into infinity, I would still be confirming something, namely, that I am doubting. If one doubts that one doubts, one must admit one is doubting; otherwise the act could not be accomplished. Or, if one adopts the opposite view—not to doubt that one is doubting—one is affirming the act all the same. Either way, one is doubting!

For Descartes, confirming the doubt also meant confirming his own existence, for there could be no doubt without a *doubter*—someone who engaged in the doubting process, which is also a thinking process. Thus was he led to declare,

*Descartes said, I cannot doubt that I doubt. If I were to do this, if I were to go on doubting into infinity, I would still be confirming something: namely, that I am doubting.*

"*Cogito ergo sum*" (I think, therefore I am). Presumably Descartes could as easily have said, "I doubt, therefore I am."

> I observed that I could suppose that I had no body, and that there was no world nor any place in which I might be; but that I could not therefore suppose that I was not; and that, on the contrary, from the very circumstance that I thought to doubt of the truth of other things, it most clearly and certainly followed that I was.[2]

His existence assured, Descartes could define himself only as a "thing that thinks." He could as easily have said, "I am a mind." Only the mind can doubt, and only of doubt had he reached a certainty. Of course, he recognized it would be foolish to leave the matter there. His behavior surely was based on the assumption that his body as well as the entire material world of things and other people did in fact exist. But could he turn this assumption into a rational truth?

To do so, Descartes created a *hypothesis*, a tentative proposition that both scientists and philosophers use. A scientist will say that a certain observation may or must be the case because no other observation makes sense. There is, however, no way to prove it without experimental data upon which the world of science can agree. A hypothesis is, in other words, a theory. The observation by Copernicus that the earth and the other planets must revolve around the sun drew hostile responses from all sides, especially from the Church, which had been teaching for centuries that God created the earth and placed it, stationary, in the exact middle of the universe. The world of science, however, tended to agree with Copernicus. Certainly by the seventeenth century, the age of Descartes (often hailed as the period that gave birth to modern science), the hypothesis of Copernicus was treated by a good many as if it were a *law*. Yet in fact the theory was not actually proved until the nineteenth century, when a telescope was invented powerful enough to measure the different angles of nearby stars with respect to positions on the earth.

In philosophy a hypothesis *never* becomes a fact or a law because it cannot be scientifically validated, but depends on reason. How acceptable a hypothesis is to other philosophers will depend upon the thinking method used to arrive at it. Let us see how Descartes "proved" that not just mind but the material world truly existed.

While the philosopher was working through his method of doubt to reach the famous "*Cogito ergo sum*" (sometimes referred to only as "the Cogito"), he allowed himself, you recall, to suppose that everything grasped by the senses, including the existence of his own body, was merely an illusion as insubstantial as a dream. He reasoned that even though he might never be able to go beyond that point, he could not deny that he *was* in fact experiencing illusions.

He had already proved to his satisfaction that his mind existed, and so was it not reasonable to conclude that these illusions—if that was what they were—had to be experienced by the mind? True, he nodded, but all he had shown so far is that everything we think is real in the world only exists in the mind.

Now, however, he discovered that there was something else besides mind. *Imagination!* Had he not been using imagination all along as part of his method of doubt? His imagination was confirmed as soon as he confirmed his doubt. That is, if he could doubt that a chair in his room was there, he must have been imagining that he saw it.

Then he realized that when he had compared objects in the world to ob-

*Descartes started out as a scientist, seeking to prove philosophical truths using the skeptical methods of the scientist, but his fame rests largely on his confirmation of reason, not observation, as the road to truth.*

jects in a dream, he had made a mistake. He could, for example, imagine that someone was sitting in the chair in his room one minute and that the figure was gone the next minute. But he could *not* will that the chair itself could disappear! In other words, some things were clearly in his imagination alone, and some things, such as the chair, were obviously independent of his imagination. Descartes concluded that his body must also certainly exist independent of his imagination, for, while it is possible to look at one's outstretched arm and wonder whether it is real or not, one cannot will it not to be there at all.

We have called Descartes's reasoning process the method of doubt. The phrase most used by philosophers to identify the act of reaching conclusions by mind alone is *a priori reasoning*. The term *a priori* in Latin literally means "from before"—that is, thoughts arrived at outside of (or before) experience. When people say they "just know" something—such as the existence of God—they are saying that direct experience of it is not necessary. They have *prior* knowledge in the sense that the certainty they know they have is not the same certainty as they experience when they suddenly come upon a burning building and "know" there is a fire. With the coming of science in the seventeenth century the existence of a priori knowledge was very much in doubt. Descartes started out as a scientist, seeking to prove philosophical truths using the skeptical methods of the scientist, but his fame rests largely on his confirmation of reason, not observation, as the road to truth.

## Empiricism

Because of his a priori method, a designation for the philosophy of Descartes is *rationalism*. Its opposite is *empiricism*, which holds that we can know only what we can experience through the senses. On the whole, science is empirical in its approach, relying on observation and experimentation, not reason alone.

After Descartes, extreme forms of empiricism developed in philosophy, often in direct reaction to his work. This trend was particularly true in England, possibly because of the pervasive influence of Francis Bacon (1561-1626), founder of the modern scientific method, and the philosophy of John Locke (1632-1704), who rejected Plato's theory of the Forms. Locke believed that at birth each of us is a *tabula rasa*, or "blank tablet," upon which our senses leave their impressions. All ideas come from these impressions. In other words, we are not born with minds; we develop minds through experience.

George Berkeley (1685-1753) went to extremes with these views and contributed *radical empiricism*, which holds that we can know nothing except what we are directly experiencing with our senses. Further, all we know about what we are experiencing is that it is an idea in our mind. By "idea" Berkeley meant "sense impression."

The Scottish philosopher David Hume (1711-1776) was also an empiricist; while he agreed that sense experience (and the memory of it) was the beginning of knowledge, he also realized that mind somehow existed and that it was more than the sum total of sense impressions. Like most empiricists, Hume probably did not *want* to reach this conclusion, because the whole point of the empirical revolution in thought had been to come to a scientific understanding of the process of learning. Plato's belief that learning was remembering what you really knew from birth was an absurdity with no place in the empiricist's camp. Yet there remained for Hume many nagging doubts about pure empiricism. He realized

Rationalism: *a philosophical method which holds that truth can be arrived at through reason alone*

Empiricism: *a philosophical method which holds that truth can be arrived at only through experience*

there are things that we know—and that are therefore part of our knowledge—without our having perceived them.

In *A Treatise of Human Nature* (1735) Hume presents a scenario that questions some empirical assumptions:

> Suppose, therefore, a person to have enjoyed his sight for thirty years, and to have become perfectly well acquainted with colors of all kinds, excepting one particular shade of blue, for instance, which it has never been his fortune to meet with. Let all three different shades of that colour except that single one be placed before him, descending gradually from the deepest to the lightest. . . . Now, I ask, whether it is possible for him, from his own imagination, to supply this deficiency, and raise up to himself the idea of that particular shade, though it had never been conveyed to him by his senses? I believe . . . that he can.[3]

What did Hume mean by "imagination" in this context if not "reason"? Hume is suggesting that reason, which has learned from past experience, will supply the missing shade of blue.

It is not, in other words, sense impressions *by themselves* that constitute knowledge but an inborn capacity we have to do something with them and eventually to function without them when necessary. How else can we explain a sudden flash of insight reached by *one* member of a scientific group *all* working on the same experiment? The reasoning capacity was sharper in one person, though all had absorbed the same impressions!

It may well be that what we call mind is a combination of reasoning capacity *and* experience. How else to explain the phenomenon of Helen Keller (1880-

*Hume believed that we learn from experience because we have an inborn capacity—reason—that allows us to do so.*

*Theodore Rousseau,* Under the Birches, Evening *(1842–43): All ideas come from the impressions of the senses. (The Toledo Museum of Art. Gift of Arthur J. Secor)*

1968), deaf and blind from infancy, yet able to become a celebrated author and a major intellectual force? Apparently the rational capacity was there all the time, inside her, waiting for the impressions to come. All she needed was for someone—in her case, her patient teacher, Annie Sullivan—to find a way to let her know that tactile sensations, odors, and tastes *were* impressions. Helen Keller's extraordinary achievements appear to indicate strongly that impressions alone without understanding will never lead to knowledge.

In the world of philosophy the debate over whether mind exists before or as a result of experience has been going on for many centuries. Helen Keller was not a contemporary of Descartes; otherwise the debate might have ended right there, so strong was his belief that the mind could exist without experience. Of all our contemporary thinkers, only Susanne Langer (1895-1985) has taken much notice of the evolution of Keller's intelligence from what experts had considered a hopeless void. According to Langer, Keller's mind began to manifest itself at the moment when she first recognized what a symbol was—that the peculiar tapping patterns that Annie Sullivan made on the palm of one hand *meant* the cool water she felt pouring over the other hand. Langer believed Keller was responding to the mind's inborn need for meaning, the need to combine experience with understanding. It was the discovery that the tapping meant the water that liberated her mind. Langer says we need meaning for its own sake, just as we need food. Or, we can put the matter this way: we need food *and* meaning for survival. Meaning is the food of the mind.

Apparently, however, not everyone recognizes this need. The body is nourished—often—while the mind sometimes starves. How wonderful it is that the miracle of Helen Keller's discovery of meaning is indeed available to anyone who can feel the hunger for it.

## What Is Reality—Really?

We talk about "reality" about as much as we talk about "mind." If, as we have seen, there has been no end of discussion about what mind is and where it comes from, just think how much disagreement exists whenever the subject of reality arises!

Let us say you have a mind. Let us say it contains ideas. But are they *real*, or are they just figments? Berkeley's radical empiricism, which we touched upon in the preceding section, led some philosophers to conclude that since nothing exists except what you perceive, you must have power over all existence. Maybe that means *you alone are real*. If you enjoy collecting terms—especially the -isms, -ologies, and -ics—you can add *solipsism* to your collection. It is the position, actually contemplated by some, that only the individual self exists.

An alternative to this rather lonely view is often called the *common sense* approach. How absurd to suppose only oneself is truly here! Besides, isn't there widespread agreement among people about things "out there"? Don't most of us see and respond to the same world—often referred to in this connection as the *familiar world*? What is all the fuss about anyway? The familiar world is what we mean by reality, and that is that.

Yet there are thousands who have pondered the question of reality, and to the above statement their response might be, "Not so fast!" Plato, remember, believed that only the Forms were real, because the Forms, being universal abstractions and never having had material substance, could therefore never change. Plato believed things that changed—the familiar world as well as the people in it—

*Rene Magritte,* The Treason of Images: *Just think how much disagreement arises when the subject of reality arises! (Los Angeles County Museum of Art. Purchased with funds provided by the Mr. and Mrs. William Preston Harrison Collection)*

could not possess reality, because if they did, we would have to say that real things could come into and pass out of existence. How can they be real one minute and not real the next?

Of course, we might argue, "Here we go again splitting hairs. Didn't Plato sit down, consume food, walk along a street? Was he not real? What difference does it make *what* we call real?"

If Susanne Langer is right when she tells us the mind needs to think, needs to understand meanings and draw conclusions about the world, then the attempt to define what constitutes reality needs no justification. Yet there is more at stake than philosophical pastimes. Science itself is joining forces with philosophy and is vitally concerned with the ultimate definition of "reality." When the United States dropped the first atomic bombs to end World War II, when explanations of nuclear fission became commonplace reading, everyone thought that atomic energy was the ultimately real. The most minute reality in all the universe was not the atom after all; it was the energy that science had learned how to liberate. We now know that we have yet to define the smallest particle of reality, if indeed such a thing exists. When or if we locate the very heart of reality, what will we do with the discovery? Shall we learn how everything works? Shall we restore dying eco-cycles? Regenerate the ozone layer? Shall we take part in our own evolutionary process? Shall we become the creative forces that control the destiny of this planet and everything on it?

*Science and philosophy have joined forces in a search for what is ultimately real, and it still hasn't been found.*

## The First Substance: Early Answers

Talking about what is ultimately real often means talking about something we call the first substance. What was here before there was anything else? Did this substance cause everything that followed? Or did *it* have a cause? If it did, what was this cause, and is *that* the first? . . . and so on.

In philosophy the term *substance* has a specialized meaning: that which exists independent of the will, that which exists independent of the knowledge of it. Of course, one might ask, "If I have no knowledge of some substance, how do I say it is there?" The answer is that in both religious and philosophical circles, a substance—or a one and only substance—can be said to exist because reason or faith requires it to exist, though human beings have no direct awareness of it. No one has actually "seen" God. Or, at least, for everyone who claims to have seen God, you will find many more who refuse to believe it. By the same token, in modern theoretical physics there are infinitesimal particles at the subatomic level that many say *must* exist in order to explain certain observable data. Some scientists accept these hypotheses, while others scoff.

The earliest philosophers on record lived around the sixth century B.C. in cities bordering the Aegean Sea, which separates the peninsula we now call Greece from what used to be called Asia Minor and is now Turkey. This area produced some minds that were quite advanced for their particular time. Many of them thought about substance. They asked what the familiar world was made of, and so in a sense they were seeking to define a first substance—not necessarily the cause of the familiar world they saw around them, but that which was behind it.

What is of special interest is their rejection of the very ancient idea that the universe was composed of four elements: *earth, air, fire*, and *water*. They seemed to believe that one of these elements, or else an unknown substance altogether, was there first, all alone. In our Western tradition of thought one rather than many has proved a more appealing concept.

*In 585 B.C. the astronomer Thales predicted an eclipse of the sun, a feat which may have led to the idea that the world was understandable.*

In Miletus, on the west coast of Asia Minor, in the year 585 B.C., an astronomer and mathematician named Thales predicted an eclipse of the sun, and, according to all historical records, he was quite accurate. Perhaps his success helped induce the conviction that the world was understandable, that things about nature were discoverable, that with its intellect humanity possessed the power to know it all.

Thales eventually asked the question we hold to be the first known philosophical inquiry: What is the world made of? He probably was not aware that he was dabbling in philosophy. If the choice had been his to make, he would probably have called himself a scientist. He was a seeker of truth, a claim made by philosophers and scientists alike. But Thales lacked technology. He could not *prove* his answer, and so philosophy rightfully claims him as a distant pioneer. Lacking instruments, Thales had to seek an answer through his reason. What he came up with is recorded for us in Aristotle's *Metaphysics*, which credits Thales with having been the discoverer of "first principles." The work states that Thales believed that *water* was

> the original source of all existing things, perhaps taking this supposition from seeing the nurture of all things to be moist, and the warm itself coming-to-be from this and living by this (that from which they came-to-be being the principle of all things)—taking the supposition both from this and from the seeds of all things having a moist nature, water being the natural principle of moist things.[4]

Thales does not come right out and say that water is the *cause* of the familiar world, but by calling it, in Aristotle's words, the "original source of all existing things," he came very close to the Big question that one day would lead many to sleepless nights: what is the first cause of all things?

Thales had no idea of the controversy he was about to create. He was being, he believed, eminently logical. But, of course, he sidestepped the whole question of whether, if water was indeed the "natural principle" of things, it was also the prior reality that existed before anything else.

Anaximander, a pupil of Thales and 14 years his junior, noting that there

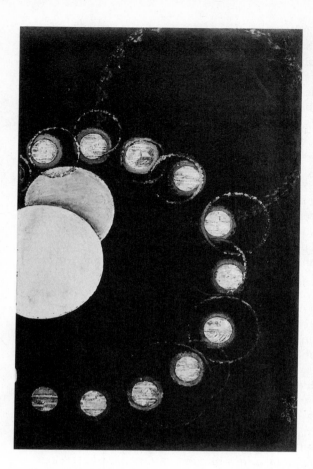

*Frontisek Kupka,* The First Step *(1909): Philosophers ask the question, What is the world made of? (Oil on canvas, 32-3/4 x 51". Collection, The Museum of Modern Art, New York. Hillman Periodicals Fund)*

*The early philosophers all reached the conclusion that, whatever reality ultimately was, it was one thing rather than a number of separate things.*

were four basic elements—earth, air, fire, and water—saw no reason to single out water, or indeed any of the others, as the first substance. Instead he set forth the theory that all four derived from something he called the *apeiron,* the "indefinite." Glimpsing the cause-and-effect problem—and perhaps wishing to sidestep it—he said the indefinite, being also infinite, was *by definition* something that had always been here; it contained the seeds of the four elements. (Notably, the big bang theory, which many now accept as an explanation for the origins of our universe, also holds that the "seeds" of everything had to have been right there inside whatever it was that went *Bang!* )

The philosopher Heraclitus, born around 540 B.C. in Ephesus, also on the western coast of Asia Minor but somewhat to the north of Miletus, made his contribution to the controversy by wondering why there had to be a substance other than the separate things we see around us. Since these things are forever changing, perhaps we could say that *change itself was reality.* "You cannot," he once said, "step twice into the same river."

Yet even this "commonsense" approach has its difficulties. Heraclitus, knowing that the notion that whatever is out there is what's real could not tell the whole story, said reality was the *principle* by which all things change. But even if we argue that the principle is "bound up" in material things and need not be considered apart from them, we still have to show where it came from. Can a principle by itself be the one and only reality? At any rate, these early philosophers had quite convinced each other of one all-important requirement: *the ultimately real was one thing*. Even if the changing things that Heraclitus spoke of each had their own identity, the parent of them all was a principle—one principle—the principle of change.

Parmenides, from the city of Elea in what is now southern Italy, most emphatically denied that the principle of change could be the ultimate reality. He proved—at least to his satisfaction—that change could not even exist at all, that nothing really *can* change. For a thing—or a person—to change implies that it becomes something else, something other than it was before. But how can *becoming* be real? Reason requires that there be either being *or* becoming, not both. If something is, it is. We cannot speak of what it shall become, because that has no existence. If this is true, then how does "what it shall become" ever have an existence? What is true always is that something *is*. Certainly we can say that things, that people, *appear* to change, but for Parmenides change was only an illusion. The secondary qualities that things and people acquired in this world were what could change, and therefore they were not real.

*Parmenides believed that ultimate reality was the principle of being itself, a condition that required that there be something rather than nothing.*

What, then, is unchangeable? It is being itself—the fact that anything exists, the fact that everything *must* exist. Or we might say, *worldly goods and those we love come into and pass out of existence, but being does not, Cannot!* There will always be *being*, but this will take different forms. Scant consolation for our losses, but Parmenides as a philosopher was interested in the truth.

As we shall see in the next chapter, the medieval philosopher St. Thomas Aquinas restated the Parmenidean theory as one of his proofs of God's existence. If there were not a necessary principle of being, Aquinas claimed, something inherent in the universe that requires it to be at all, why then, there would be nothing. We can plainly see that there is something. Aquinas, however, insisted that only God could create a necessary principle of being. Parmenides had said that a necessary principle of being *by definition* was simply there and had always been there. Nothing or no one was responsible for it, otherwise it would not be *necessary*.

The debate between Heraclitus and Parmenides is by no means confined to the ancient world. There are still legal problems, for example, that hinge on whether we accept the principle of change or the principle of necessary being.

Say that a man commits a felony, steals $300 while in an impoverished state. He can find no work and becomes desperate to provide food for his family. He eludes capture, moves to another town, and eventually becomes a successful businessman as well as one of the most influential members of his community. Then the law catches up with him. He is charged with the theft and admits it openly. His defense is that circumstances have greatly altered him and he is no longer a person who could ever steal, no matter how desperate he was. Should the man be sent to prison?

If change is real, then people must be expected to change without necessarily becoming blameless for actions committed at a time when they were *other* people. Thus the man should be punished. If only being is real, then, presumably, people are accountable only for what they are at the given moment. Hence the felon that the man was has passed out of existence and cannot be charged with a crime.

In the fifth century B.C., Democritus and Leucippus decided there was no good reason for believing that a first substance was not material, for what evidence was there that anything except the material world really existed? They invented the philosophy of *materialism* and said that reality was ultimately reducible to little bits of matter they called *atoms*, which in Greek means "things that cannot be cut or divided." They were convinced there was an underlying world people could not see, and that the world that seemed to be "out there" was made up of these elementary building blocks. Further, they believed atoms always existed and were therefore exempt from the law of cause and effect.

Duly impressed by this first atomic theory, the Roman poet Lucretius, in the first century B.C., drew a picture of what the world was like eons ago, before there were oceans and trees and mountains and people. At that primeval time there was nothing but a *rain of atoms*—little particles just falling endlessly through a great void—until something caused them to start knocking into each other. The cosmic collisions led to mounds of atoms, some of which solidified to become the familiar world around us.

With the advent of Christianity and its hold on the thinking of much of the world, materialism took a back seat to the accepted belief that there were two kinds of substance—God and matter—and that matter was brought into being by God and was whatever He wanted it to be. There was no need to ask how God came to be. Insignificant humanity was never meant to comprehend such things.

*Democritus and Leucippus invented the first atomic theory, saying that reality was little particles of matter that could not be divided.*

## The Old Questions Continue

For many centuries in that part of the world dominated by the Judeo-Christian vision of creation, the issue of the first cause was considered a nonissue. But with the dawning of the seventeenth century and what would become the unstoppable rise of modern science, there were new meanings to the word *cause*. Newton's discovery of the laws of motion and the force of gravity paved the way for a cause-and-effect view of the world. The Newtonian theory guarantees that for every action, there is a reaction. If this is the case, what then was the antecedent to the "reaction" that we call the universe? Newton was a churchgoing man and surely gave no thought to the future implications his scientific investigations would have for religion.

Darwin's theory of evolution, first presented in *On the Origin of Species* (1859), dealt perhaps the most devastating blow to established religious truths. How could it be said that material substance was what religion had taught that it was when the behavior of that substance was beginning to be shown in a very different light? How could God have created the world out of nothing in six days when evolutionary theory claimed the process to have been extremely gradual?

*Impact of Darwin on religion: How could God have created the world in six days when evolutionary theory indicated the process had been extremely gradual?*

In some quarters, believers tried to reconcile evolution and biblical teaching. Soon after the new science of geology had become a legitimate arm of university research, a book dealing with the age of the earth appeared. The first three words of its extremely long title tell the whole story of what it attempted to do: *Vestiges of Creation*. Here was proclaimed a new way to show that God truly existed: make a scientific study of how the divine plan for the world had shown itself. Other reconcilers tried to prove that evolution itself was God's method of creating humanity. Some said that because the Hebrew word for "day" also means "age," the Bible really meant six *ages* when it spoke of the six days of creation. Early in the twentieth century, religious philosopher Teilhard de Chardin (1881-1955) applied evolution to divine substance itself, postulating that the divine was in the process of becoming. Eventually the Super Christ, as he called it, would make an appearance in the world.

These efforts to reconcile religion with evolution are interesting details in the much larger picture of how modern science is influencing modern thought. First there was Einstein's redefinition of both time and space as events relative to varying circumstances, rather than as philosophical absolutes. Then there was the introduction of particle physics: the hunt for the ultimate substance, or the most minute form of matter, on subatomic levels undreamed of even fifty years ago. No one yet can say how many more times we can divide reality before we find its "core," if indeed such a thing exists—or ever *could* exist.

At the moment the scientists' speculations about ultimate reality are running far ahead of the technology for conducting experimental research. It used to be thought that atom-smashing machines were all we would ever need to give us a glimpse of the world as it really is deep down. But now we have particle accelerators, tunnels that extend for miles and in which collisions of particles take place at unimaginable speeds, releasing infinitesimal particles that are being given names like *quarks* and that may very well be gigantic in size compared to the even smaller particles no one has yet found!

While science continues its relentless pursuit of tiny particles, which may be the thinnest kind of cosmic "strings" that vibrated and brought the material world into existence, some modern philosophers may be waiting for big answers before deciding where to go next. In addition to the question of "Is there an end to the number and kinds of particles or strings underlying matter?" there is still the question of a first cause. The questions are definitely related, as indeed they always have been. "What was the first type of matter?" is inevitably followed by "Where did it come from?"

Through much of the twentieth century scientific speculation about first causes has tended in the direction of black holes and the big bang. Black holes do exist; that much is certain. They are made up of densely packed matter that has collapsed from the force of gravity and compressed so tightly that nothing, not even light waves, can escape. Hence the term *black hole.* They are in fact invisible, yet we know they are there from the terrific gravitational force they exert.

But was there an original black hole from which the known universe emerged? Enter the big bang theory. It has been and still is widely believed that the universe is the result of a tremendous explosion, that it is actually the debris from the blast, debris that is still flying outwards in space. All of us mortals live on a speck of cosmic dirt, part of a vast expansion that may someday (billions of years from now) reverse itself and send time hurtling backwards as the debris is propelled by the force of gravity once more into whatever it once was—perhaps the original hole of densely packed matter.

This possibility brings us back to that old question of first cause. If it were an original black hole that blew up, was it always there waiting to explode? What put it there? Perhaps the latter question comes to mind because of the thousands of years people have been asking, What started the universe? Maybe we shall have to be content even with the idea that the explosion came from nothing or that there was no explosion at all, but only matter stretching into infinity.

Another possibility is that we may have to revise our old thinking about what nothing is. Absence of matter, of activity of any kind, may not mean that a void has to remain forever in the same condition. For nothing to lack the power to bring something forth, it would have to be stable, that is, absolutely and dependably nothing. But what if it were *un*stable?

*In November 1989 a satellite known as COBE was placed in orbit "to study the cosmic background radiation, that faint microwave glow that's everywhere in the sky. It is radiation that no star nor any other known object could have produced. This radiation came directly from the act of creation itself—the Big Bang."*

*Donald Goldsmith*

*If it were an original black hole that blew up in the big bang, was it always there waiting to explode?*

> Just as there is a tiny chance that virtual particles will pop into existence in the midst of subatomic space, so there may have been a tiny chance that the nothingness would suddenly be convulsed by the presence of a something.
>
> This something was an inconceivably small, inconceivably violent explosion, hotter than the hottest supernova and smaller than the smallest quark, which contained the stuff of everything we see around us. The Universe consisted of only one type of particle—maybe only one particle—that interacted with itself in that tiny, terrifying space. Detonating outward, it may have doubled in size every 10-14 seconds or so, taking but an instant to reach literally cosmic proportions.[5]

Could it be that ultimate reality in our world is an unstable void that "shook" a little bit and lost its identity as a void? A void that became a single particle and, in less time than it takes your eyes to blink, expanded to become "our" universe?

Or is ultimate reality in our world time itself, which began in the big bang and set in motion cause-and-effect processes that may not exist in other universes that did not start with an explosion and that operate—if that is the word—by principles entirely unknown to us?

All of our questions may be answered someday. The big questions, however, may remain unanswered. Philosophers born into this age, which has grown unaccustomed to taking daring leaps of thought, have their work cut out for them; who would begrudge them the excitement this work will bring both to them and to us, if we would stay in touch?

## God in Philosophy

*The Song of Bernadette*, a 1940s film about a peasant girl's visions of the Virgin Mary and the miracles that followed, opened with this comment to the audience: "For those who believe in God, no explanation is necessary; for those who do not believe in God, no explanation is possible."

*For the most part, the existence of God has been either an intellectual necessity or an intellectual impossibility.*

Yet explanations for and about God have been advanced in philosophy, both inside and outside religious circles. For the most part, the existence of God has been either an intellectual necessity or an intellectual impossibility. In our own big bang/black hole era, when questions about initial causes are once again being raised, God remains the key explanation for many.

### God as Intellectual Necessity

Socrates speaks of God in the singular in a time and place—fifth-century Athens—dominated by polytheism. The population of Mount Olympus, where the gods dwelled, was fairly extensive. Perhaps an apparent monotheism was a reason the state accused Socrates of teaching atheism to his students. On the other hand, Socrates is speaking words written by Plato. Centuries afterward, many Christian thinkers believed Plato must have been visited by their God. Or perhaps Plato, who created the theory of the Forms, believed God was the original mind that contained the Forms.

To our knowledge Aristotle, however, was the first philosopher to use a

*Katsushika Hokusai,* The Wave: *Could God have had any purpose in creating the world? (Clarence Buckingham Collection. The Art Institute of Chicago, All Rights Reserved)*

God concept boldly—as a rational explanation for a problem that would otherwise be unsolved. In his *Metaphysics* (from the Greek "beyond nature"), Aristotle was led by reason to postulate the necessary existence of a being responsible for setting all things in motion.

The cosmic view he advanced was that of a cold, unmoving universe, waiting for motion to set it working. Lacking the modern mathematical complexities, this view is similar to that of present-day thinkers who believe the big bang caused time and everything else to begin. Aristotle's God is not a conscious, human-oriented being, but a force, or maybe a principle, with a basic need to create motion without itself having to move. He termed it the unmoved mover—a philosophical concept that establishes the necessary existence of something that is exempt from a characteristic (motion) shared by everything else, yet is responsible for it. This concept strongly resembles the God figure in both Judaism and Christianity, except that it lacks a personality or human qualities.

The God of Judaism comes to us through the glory of the Biblical writings. He is a patriarch, a father who cares for his children in addition to being the causer of all things. He demands, as in the Book of Job, unquestioning obedience. He is not reasoned into existence. His existence has been revealed to the prophets and must be accepted without question. Nor does Christianity reach its view of Christ as son and Messiah through logical analysis, but through the Gospels, which were held to be historical truths set forth by eyewitnesses to the events and therefore binding on all believers.

Nonetheless, Christianity did produce some philosophers in the first few centuries after the death of Christ. (The ghosts of Plato and Aristotle were still around, after all, and they had an effect on Christian thought.) These first Christian philosophers found themselves confronting some puzzling questions, for the traditional qualities of God as loving patriarch, promising a reward in paradise to those who held fast to their faith, did not always seem compatible with what occurred to reason. Here are some examples of the questions these philosophers asked.

*Can this world be the extent of God's creation?* If the ability to create matter *ex nihilo* (from nothing) is intrinsic to God, then why must we believe that creation stopped with this one achievement? At the same time, the thought that God might go on endlessly creating worlds staggers the mind.

*Could God have had any purpose in creating the world?* Revealed religion maintains that God created this world for humanity, and this fact alone requires worship and adoration of God in return. Yet how may an all-powerful God be so limited as to have had a purpose? Purpose implies an existing need. How could a God be all-powerful who had a need?

*Does God think?* Human beings engage in the act of thought in order to know something that was not known before. What can an all-knowing as well as all-powerful God have to think about?

*If God does not think, how can God then respond to human need?* What is the use of praying to a God who does not think and therefore cannot be concerned about us? Is it not futile to believe that God will intervene in human affairs or that God's mind, once made up, can be changed?

As the centuries rolled on, the concepts "all-powerful" and "all-knowing" became at once impossibilities for human thought and intellectual necessities within that thought. The first of the great Christian philosophers, who was ultimately to say that philosophy cannot take Christians where they need to go, was Saint Augustine (A.D. 354–430). Before he came to this conclusion, he wrestled with some other agonizing questions.

## How to Explain Evil

If God is good—an assumption as necessary for believers as the assumption that God is all-knowing—how do we account for the terrible things that happen in this world? How do we account for both natural and human evil? for devastating storms and earthquakes that wipe away millions of innocent people? for ruthless dictators who give orders to maim and kill and often seem to flourish anyway? These questions are with us now, as they always have been.

Like Paul, who preceded him by several centuries, Augustine became a convert during his adulthood. In his case the catalyst was a Christian mother who had despaired over his wanton ways and kept urging him to reform and to devote the rest of his life to God's work. Though Augustine eventually renounced his life of sin and entered the Christian fold, he did not do so easily.

Augustine's *Confessions*, one of the most personal and candid works ever written by a philosopher, deals with the intellectual difficulties facing him upon his conversion. One of his first concerns was intellect itself: Why was he given such a thing by God when it was inadequate to comprehend the divine scheme? The *creatio ex nihilo*, the necessary belief that God, the divine substance, both preceded material substance and created it from nothing, was at first repugnant to his reason, as shown by the following excerpt:

> Nor in the whole world didst Thou make the whole world; because there was no place where to make it before it was made, that it might be. Nor didst Thou hold anything in Thy hand, whereof to make heaven and earth. For whence shouldest Thou have this, which Thou

*Faith—an illogical belief in the occurrence of the improbable.*

*H. L. Mencken*

*At first Augustine had to wrestle with many Christian truths that seemed repugnant to reason, among them the idea that God created the world from nothing.*

hadst not made, thereof to make anything? For what is, but because Thou art? Therefore Thou spakest, and they were made, and in Thy Word Thou madest them. But how didst Thou speak?

Augustine considered the existence of evil—or the *apparent* existence of evil—both physical and moral, to be an even graver problem. If God created the world, it follows that the world must be an ideal order. How might a perfect God make a mistake and bring into being something less than perfect? Yet it is clear that things are far from ideal. From physical disasters to moral depravity, the human race is continually plagued by monstrous deviations from perfection. How do we reconcile the existence of evil with the belief that God, being perfect, is all-good?

Evil, Augustine concluded, cannot be a "thing," cannot exist in the way that material substance exists, for if it were a material substance, would evil not be—as is all matter—the creation of God? The problem posed by Augustine stipulated that nothing made by God can be evil, but yet evil exists. Or does it? Augustine answered the problem by defining evil as *the absence of good*, comparing it to a disease that temporarily attacks the body:

> In the bodies of animals, disease and wounds mean nothing but the absence of health; for when a cure is effected, that does not mean that the evils which were present . . . go away from the body and dwell elsewhere: they altogether cease to exist; for the wound or disease is not a substance, but a defect in the fleshy substance—the flesh itself being a substance, and therefore something good.

Augustine's analogy raises many questions—more indeed, many critics have said, than it answers. First, is disease necessarily evil? One may believe that material substance is by its very nature subject to decay and ultimately to death. Why raise the question of evil at all? But not raising the question in one connection does not mean it should not be raised in another. Is moral evil the absence of good? If so, where did the good *go*? Can goodness appear and disappear? If it can, does not God, being all-powerful, control its behavior?

This last question was not ignored by Augustine. It is, after all, the question at the very heart of Christianity: the question of *sin*. Let us ignore for now the problem of where goodness goes when it is absent. We have been told often enough that moral evil is the result of human sinfulness, of *human beings deliberately disobeying the will of God*. Should not this explanation be the end of the problem? It creates, however, another altogether *awesome* problem.

If humanity can sin, as the Church teaches, humanity is then answerable to God. Such accountability implies the option of choosing between right and wrong. But an all-knowing God must be aware *in advance* of what choices will be made. If such is the case, we must conclude that human destiny is already mapped out. Before one is even born, God must know whether one's actions will be good or evil. Is one then responsible for them? The answer is yes, even though reason cannot comprehend why.

Augustine finally accepted the idea of *predestination*, for nothing else was compatible with the necessary idea of God's perfection. Predestination and human responsibility appeared to cancel each other out, yet one could not be a Christian without accepting them both. The answer had to be that human reason, being a quality of material substance, cannot understand divine substance; otherwise it

*Augustine's problem: To an all-knowing God the future has already happened. He knows who is going to sin. Are they then responsible for sins they had no choice but to commit?*

*Augustine at length concluded that God has given us the gift of faith, which allows us to accept many things that seem to violate reason.*

would be equal to it. It is thus not necessary or possible for us to reach all conclusions through reason.

In his infinite mercy, said Augustine, God has given us *faith*, which is the faculty of believing without understanding. What seems paradoxical to the human mind must not be so for God. And if God understands, we know *the issue is understandable!* Why does it have to be understood by *us?*

## Faith Is Not Enough

*The university movement, called* Scholasticism, *created a new approach to religion that attempted to reconcile faith and reason.*

The certainty that transcended human analytical thinking began to lose its hold on Christian intellectuals at about the time that the great universities of Europe were being founded. The University of Oxford, the University of Paris, and the University of Bologna, to name a few, opened their doors to young men studying for holy orders. But the growing need for disciplined training of the mind as well as the spirit set in motion an inevitable intellectual movement. A university by its very nature brings together students and teachers engaged in the common purpose of learning and teaching a body of doctrine, and exchanges of and debates about ideas surely must take place. Little by little the university movement, also called *Scholasticism*, created a new approach to religion, one that attempted to reconcile faith and reason.

*Aquinas attempted to prove logically what Augustine had accepted through faith alone.*

The most ambitious effort to prove God's existence through analytical means came from Saint Thomas Aquinas (1225-1274), who many believe epitomizes the Scholastic movement. Educated originally by Benedictine monks, he then entered the University of Naples, became a Dominican, and later moved to Paris, which was already a major intellectual center. Here Aquinas came into contact with the analytical method of Aristotle and achieved his major fame as a philosopher by applying logic to every phase of Christian doctrine. More than any other person, Aquinas was responsible for making the philosophical approach to religion both fashionable and acceptable after many centuries dominated by mysticism and faith. Even today, students in Catholic seminaries are thoroughly trained in Thomism, the name given to Saint Thomas Aquinas's logical method of teaching Christian doctrine.

Aquinas developed the famous five proofs of God's existence, which can be briefly summarized as follows:

### Argument from Motion

Some things in the universe are in motion. It is clear that what is in motion must be set in motion by something else. But it is impossible to trace motion back infinitely. There has to be a first mover, which is itself unmoved. Only God can be the first mover.

### Argument from Causation

There is no known case of something's having been the cause of itself. Everything is caused by something before it. But as with motion, it is impossible to trace causation back infinitely. There has to be a first cause, which is itself uncaused, and this can only be God.

### Argument from Being

Though we have only to look around to see that things are, it is indeed possible to imagine that they should not be. That is, the possibility of there never having been existence can and does occur to reason. On the other hand, though it is possible for nothing to be, it is clear that there is existence. Hence there must be a necessary being from which all other being derives, and this can only be God.

### Argument from Gradation

Wherever we look we see greater or lesser amounts and qualities. We do not conceive of "better" unless it is also possible to imagine "best." Everything we know of points to the existence of an ultimate—a best in everything—and this can only be God.

### Argument from Design

Since there is evidence of order and design in the universe, there must exist a designer, a superintelligence responsible for this order, and this can only be God.

Probably the best example of proving God by definition is the argument advanced by Descartes, who in the Thomist tradition tried to prove God's existence through reason. He put his proof this way:

God is a perfect being.
Nonexistence is not a characteristic of a perfect being.
God cannot possess nonexistence.

A large blow against Thomism was struck by Immanuel Kant (1724-1804), who was not irreligious himself, but who philosophically asserted that logical proofs for God's existence were foolish and trivial, since they were true only by definition. According to Kant, Descartes defines God in such a manner that his conclusion is inevitable. Aquinas, in the same way, defines God as the only possible unmoved mover. Kant simply asked, What if the unmoved mover were a force of some sort, not God? (Could it be a force like the one that many modern-day scientists say may have caused the big bang?)

Thomism survives, though it is not the only way to reach God through philosophical means. The American philosopher William James (1842-1910) said belief in God could be a viable option for people who find no good reason to disbelieve. In other words, God can be a psychological reality, existing for some, but not for others.

*Absence of evidence is not evidence of absence.*

*Carl Sagan*

Reason has also been employed to prove there *cannot* be a God. Atheism is a philosophy deserving our attention. Its favorite line of thought is the *reductio ad absurdum*, by which is meant that a particular statement—for example, God does not exist—is held to be true because its exact opposite—God does exist—is an absurdity. The atheist argues that any positive statement about God's being or qualities has no legitimate function in philosophy, since the idea of God's existence is absurd. On the other hand, we can readily accept the truth of the proposition "Two and two are four," since it is absurd to say that two and two are *not* four.

In such a spirit did the philosopher Nietzsche utter the famous words "God is dead." He did not, of course, mean this literally. Rather, he was declaring that all philosophical attempts to establish God's existence had failed.

## Epilogue

The arguments presented in this chapter are clearly far from being the last word on the subject of God's existence, even as the big bang theory may not be the final solution to the problem of how the universe began. None of what we have presented in this chapter is intended to represent the way you *should* think. The most exciting aspect of the humanities is the variety of options we find in our study of what others have thought.

Whatever understandings, whatever solutions you may reach, you must make the journey by yourself. All we ask is that you take that first step.

## Glossary

*atheism:* A philosophy that seeks to prove by logical means that God cannot possibly exist, that a belief in God is an absurdity.

*big bang:* A theory, held by some, disputed by others, that the known universe had its beginnings in a vast explosion.

*black hole:* A mass in space, caused by a collapsed star, that is so densely packed from the weight of its own gravitational force that nothing can escape it, not even light waves.

*faith:* A technical term in Christian thought, used by Saint Augustine to refer to God's gift to humanity of the ability to accept without question many things that appear to violate the laws of human reason (such as *creatio ex nihilo*).

*Forms:* In the specialized use of the word associated with Plato, this word refers to universal ideas—such as beauty, honor, and justice—which exist independent of the individual and can never change. Plato's theory is still very much with us and is still cited by those who insist that fundamental human values are universal and not subject to individual interpretation.

*mind:* The subject of much philosophical debate: Is it material, like blood, cells, and nerves? Or is it an immaterial substance? (There is disagreement over just what that means.) Is it born with the body? Or is it separate from the brain? Does it exist at all? Plato believed mind is separate from sense experience and that it exists eternally in one body or another.

*reality:* A complex philosophical term, which can mean the first cause of existence (e.g., God); or the ultimate stuff the universe is made of, such as the atom; or the tiniest particles of matter; or cosmic strings; or cosmic energy; and so on.

*reductio ad absurdum:* A technique used by some logicians by which a proposition is proved true by showing that its opposite is absurd.

*Sophists:* A group of Athenian philosophers, contemporary with Socrates, who would teach, for a fee, rhetorical devices to assist in winning an argument on any side of an issue.

*substance:* In ancient philosophy, that which exists objectively, independent of the will or of private awareness. A major issue has been whether there is one substance, divine or material, or two substances, divine *and* material, totally distinct from each other. Christian and Jewish thought has traditionally held the latter view.

*Thomism:* The logical system of thought devised by Aquinas to prove the truths of religion. Almost interchangeable with the term *Scholasticism.*

*unmoved mover:* According to Aristotle, a causeless causer, the force that set everything else in motion but that is itself exempt from all known laws and is responsible for the beginnings of the universe. This force is not the same as the Biblical God, for it makes no rules for humanity and has no interest in human affairs.

# Notes

1. In *The Age of Reason*, ed. Stuart Hampshire (New York: New American Library, 1956), 68.
2. Ibid., 68–69.
3. In *The Age of Enlightenment*, ed. Isaiah Berlin (New York: New American Library, 1956), 171.

4. G. S. Kirk and J. E. Raven, *The Pre-Socratic Philosophers* (New York: Cambridge University Press, 1963), 87.
5. Robert P. Crease and Charles C. Mano, *The Second Creation* (New York: Macmillan, 1986), 405.

# Suggested Reading

Adler, Mortimer J. *Ten Philosophical Mistakes*. New York: Macmillan, 1985. The author, sometimes considered the greatest living philosopher, presents his views on basic errors in modern thought and how they can be corrected.

Anderson, Maxwell. *Barefoot in Athens*. New York: Dramatists Play Service, 1952. A highly entertaining play about Socrates and his wife, Xanthippe, and their debates over the usefulness of a life devoted to rational thought exclusively.

Calder, Nigel. *Einstein's Universe*. New York: Viking Press, 1979. An easy-to-read summary of the special and general theories of relativity, upon which much contemporary philosophical and scientific thought is based.

Campbell, Jeremy. *Grammatical Man: Information, Entropy, Language, and Life*. New York: Simon & Schuster, 1982. An explanation of what many believe to be the law of universal *entropy*, that is, the belief that the direction of all natural things is toward disorganization and decay—all except perhaps the human mind, which may be the only thing that improves with age.

Crease, Robert P., and Charles C. Mann. *The Second Creation*. New York: Macmillan, 1986. An extraordinary work that goes deeply into the thought processes of contemporary physicists as they search for the most minute particles and as they speculate about the big bang, black holes, and other possibilities of first causes.

Ferris, Timothy. *Coming of Age in the Milky Way*. New York: William Morrow, 1988. A major

scientific writer traces the history of human understanding of the cosmos and brings us up to date on present theories, reaching the conclusion that nature will probably never be fully comprehended.

Gleick, James. *Chaos: Making a New Science*. New York: Viking, 1987. A fascinating study of the science that studies chaos—not as the total breakdown of everything, but as the way complex systems really work. While most scientists seek simplicity in new discoveries, the "chaos group" tackles complexities and irregularities. Perhaps nature's ultimate law is *not* to have laws.

Hawking, Stephen W. *A Brief History of Time*. New York: Bantam, 1988. A widely read physicist of our time shares his speculations on the beginnings of the universe and questions whether there were indeed beginnings.

Stone, I. F. *The Trial of Socrates*. New York: Doubleday, 1988. The author questions the traditional depiction of Socrates as a martyr in the cause of truth.

Stove, David. *The Plato Cult and Other Philosophical Follies*. Oxford, U.K.: Basil Blackwell, 1991. A whimsical book by a whimsical philosopher that punches holes in a lot of revered philosophical traditions, particularly the thought of Plato, whom he accuses of having led the world away from reality.

*Rembrandt,* Sacrifice of Isaac *(The Hermitage, Leningrad. Bildarchiv Foto Marburg/Art Resource)*

# 7

# *The Moral Issue*

## *Overview*

The term *morality* means different things in popular as opposed to philosophical usage. In popular usage, it is often spoken of as a corrective to such problems as inappropriate clothing, low productivity, or teenage pregnancy. These are seen as moral issues because underneath are assumptions about what people *should* be wearing to look decent, how hard they *should* be working to compete, and what they should *not* be doing in their search for love. Moralists who disapprove of certain practices are often accused of limiting the freedom of others, of being hypocrites by not practicing what they preach, and even of being inconsistent and unable to agree among themselves. Moralists respond to such accusations by pointing out that rules are all that protect civilization from base human nature. The accusations fly, and the talk goes on. Every time people call something "unfair," they are talking about morality, at least vaguely so.

Talk without thought, however, is a random exchange of passionate opinion, heat without light. Philosophers move beyond opinion to attempt to associate morality with its broadest implications: the search for the good life through a clear examination of the nature of right and wrong. This examination includes fundamental human concerns: whether or not humankind is free; whether or not there are universals like justice and virtue; whether ideals ever take precedence over self-interest; how we can know the source of right behavior; how right behavior can be enforced; and how (or if) we can apply general rules to particular problems, large and small.

One major source of such rules has been human reason. Philosophers who ponder the nature of the good life maintain that there must be a rational way to describe how people *should* behave toward each other. What would make sense? What would provide the best social and political environment? How may human beings avoid the obvious evils of war and other forms of cruelty? Philosophers with a belief in reason seek universal rules, principles that they say must surely be apparent to anyone willing to think about the best way to live.

Religious representatives are still likely to argue that moral principles need not be rationally defended, since they are, after all, the teachings of God. The so-called Golden Rule is perhaps the best known of such principles, but it can also be cited by nonreligious thinkers as the most sensible way to order a society. Doesn't it make sense, they ask, to keep a promise? Would you want to live in a society in which you could not depend on other people's promises? It logically follows therefore that we should require of ourselves what we require of others.

*The psychologist often replaces both the philosopher and the theologian as moral guardian. Psychology avoids* shoulds *and* should nots.

In recent years the psychologist has often replaced both the theologian and the philosopher. The psychologist, who explores human nature as a kind of social science, avoids *shoulds* and *should nots* in favor of descriptive (rather than prescriptive) terms. Certain activities encourage "mental health." Others are clinically "antisocial." Human beings have different needs, based on parental training and societal taboos. What appears to be individual choice can also be traced to either genetic or external influences. In any case, they say, all moral choices are based on the individual desire for pleasure and contentment. People who transgress social codes are to be understood, not censured.

Once pleasure becomes a measurement, so worry some philosophers, there is a less firm basis for inhibiting certain behavior, such as stealing. Without either divine commandments or a belief in reason, one might agree with Ernest Hemingway that "What is moral is what you feel good after." Other, more popular, sayings emphasize individual pleasure: "Do your own thing"; "Look out for number one." Neither statement takes into account the feelings of others. Even the seemingly benign recommendation "Live and let live," with its unlimited tolerance, offers no suggestion of what this really means. The rule then becomes "There are no rules," except that in return for your neighbor's expecting nothing of you, you supposedly expect nothing of him or her.

We can only outline the extent of the problem. This chapter will examine how a number of prominent philosophies examine specific cases involving moral choice, whether based on principle or consequences. It will span the centuries and include a variety of opinions drawn from a variety of regions, political structures, and philosophical climates. It will refer, where appropriate, to the moral observations of literary figures and economists as well as to the more traditional philosophers and to a sampling of contemporary beliefs about moral behavior. It is hoped that the wisdom of these varied and provocative thinkers will start you on a lifelong search for answers to some of our most vital questions.

# The Sources of Moral Values

Any debate over moral values invariably deals with human nature, with whether people are naturally able to reason, to govern themselves, to seek justice as an end in itself. Debates begun two thousand years ago continue today, for these concerns may hold not only the future of the human species but the fate of the planet itself.

Moral philosophers agree on one point: namely, that freedom is basic to moral decision. Without freedom—if destiny has planned every significant event in our lives—we cannot be held responsible for our actions. We begin therefore with the assumption that there is free choice, whether the issue is large or small, and therefore that moral issues are meaningful.

*We begin with the assumption that there is free choice, whether the issue is large or small, and therefore that moral issues are meaningful.*

## Self-Interest: Glaucon

In a debate with Socrates, as recorded in Plato's *Republic*, one of several young men argues that people are virtuous because the laws require them to be so and because they fear possible punishments for breaking these laws. Doing wrong, Glaucon maintains, is basic to human nature; it is pleasant. But because punishment is so unpleasant, the person with the power to do wrong is held in check by these laws. If, however, all restrictions were suddenly removed, virtue too would disappear.

To illustrate this point Glaucon tells the story of two men who possessed magic rings. Whoever wore the rings had the power to become invisible. One man, Gyges, a shepherd, was totally ruthless. He used his power to take whatever he wanted without fear of being caught. He stole, raped, murdered—all with impunity. Despite his actions, his invisibility protected his reputation in the community.

The other man was as virtuous as Gyges was ruthless. Still, Glaucon argues, even the virtuous man would, having the same power to become invisible, behave in the same way. He too would "go to the marketplace and fearlessly help himself to anything he wanted, enter houses and sleep with any woman he chose, set prisoners free and kill men at his pleasure."

Glaucon believes that this behavior, when both men were sure of not being caught, is "strong proof that men do right only under compulsion; no individual thinks of it as good for him personally, since he does wrong whenever he finds he has the power." He argues that the virtuous man is driven by the same motive as the ruthless man, namely his good name in the community. His scorn for crime is allegedly out of his respect for virtue, but if everything except virtue were taken away from him, he would find little satisfaction in his virtue. If he were thrown into prison for crimes he did not commit, his innocence would not comfort him.

*In Plato's "Ring of Gyges" dialogue Glaucon maintains that people avoid committing wrong for fear of what others will think of them.*

If the opposite were true, if a ruthless man had the reputation for being virtuous, he would be able to enjoy all the benefits of society: "With his reputation of virtue, he will hold offices of state, ally himself by marriage to any family he may choose, become a partner in any business, and having no scruples about being dishonest, turn all these advantages to profit."

Society, concludes Glaucon, expects virtue to be only an appearance. Morality is the result of pressure brought to bear upon each of us, not of the human capacity for reason.

It is the capacity for reason that Socrates relies on in his debate with Glaucon. As quoted by Plato, Socrates maintains that moral values are universal and unchanging and that when faced with a moral choice, people select the rational action rather than the one that promotes their own interest. Socrates argues that the virtuous man values the virtuous act for its own sake. The rational man, he maintains, would live according to the law, even if the law in a particular case were harmful to him.

In a sense, Socrates paid with his life for his trust in reason. The law was against him in a particular case—his trial on the charge of corrupting the youth of Athens. He was found guilty, jailed, and eventually executed by poison. He had an opportunity to bargain for a lighter sentence, life in exile rather than death. He even had the opportunity to escape from prison by bribing a jailer. He refused both, preferring to die according to the principle of law; after all, he had taught his followers that Glaucon was wrong in insisting that self-interest was the only moral guide. Of course, we know the jury that convicted Socrates was not guided by reason alone. If it had been, Socrates would have been acknowledged as a virtuous and honorable man, and would have been acquitted. But there were political factors involved—Socrates' teachings sometimes challenged the state—and so the self-interest of the state triumphed.

In *The Republic* Plato ultimately admits that the majority of the people *will* always be governed by self-interest and that the ideal state needs to be governed by the most enlightened human being who can be found: a philosopher/king. Other, less wise citizens would be assigned tasks not requiring intricate thought or decision making. Since no one has ever put the idea into practice, we cannot know how well Plato's plan would actually work.

In the meantime, it is probably easier to find people who agree with Glaucon on the importance of appearance and reputation over reason and individual integrity. Do we call Glaucon's followers cynics? Realists? Pragmatists?

## Self-Interest: Machiavelli, Smith, Bentham

During the more than two thousand years since Socrates lived, great works of fiction and philosophy have dealt with the issues of good and evil, reward and punishment, and the temptations of power. One of the most famous arguments for self-interest based on distrust and practicality was advanced by an Italian of the Renaissance, the Florentine political writer Niccolò Machiavelli (1469-1527). In *The Prince*, Machiavelli argues that the best rulers—the Princes—must assume that their subjects are guided by self-interest. Effective leaders cannot make laws that assume that people will ever seek a justice inconvenient to themselves. He therefore urges leaders to demand respect and obedience through fear rather than love. Leaders should dress well and be surrounded by the trappings of power. (In his day, these would have included magnificent carriages rather than limousines and private planes.) Leaders should appear in public with a large retinue of friends, security personnel, and local politicians seeking to be seen with a great person.

*Machiavelli viewed humanity as selfish and prone to corruption, and therefore he maintained that the ruler is justified in using strong measures to maintain order in society.*

Today the term *Machiavellian* may actually imply approval for a clever leader who has managed to deceive and outwit his rivals and even his followers. The Machiavellian, through concentration on the human desire for self-interest (including his or her own), will never be deceived by a naive trust in the inborn goodness of anyone. There are many who applaud this view, which they regard as realistic.

In writing *The Prince*, Machiavelli was at least admitting that self-interest was adequate motivation for the leader. By ostentatiously parading power and setting aside all notions of honest affection or humility, the Prince was an ideal

Renaissance leader, unencumbered by the restraints of a Christlike existence demanded in the Middle Ages. Machiavellianism is enlightened self-interest for the privileged few who can benefit by exploiting the self-interest of the general population.

In the eighteenth century, the economist Adam Smith (1723-1790) said that self-interest worked for the benefit of everyone. The businessperson is the indirect benefactor whose enterprise provides jobs for everyone else. Naturally the businessperson desires a profit, but in choosing a product to manufacture, market, and distribute, he or she is providing employment for all those who help. No one needs to think in terms other than personal profit. What holds an entire society together therefore is *mutual benefit*. Certainly it is not in anyone's interest to continue to make a product that does not sell.

Smith believed in the free-market system—allowing all people to do what is best for themselves without interference from government. Smith's doctrine, which he called *laissez-faire*—meaning, literally, "allow to do"—remains the classic basis for capitalism. With perfect trust in the workings of the free market, each person can be part of a system working for the benefit of everyone. This market is self-correcting. The entrepreneur who becomes too greedy, seeks too much profit, according to Smith, is automatically priced out of business.

Smith's theory—that business is at the heart of society—gave a sense of dignity to the merchant, long a subject of ridicule by writers like Molière (see Chapter 4), who wrote for those made wealthy by birth, not by their own initiative.

How realistic was Smith's theory? Has capitalism turned out to be the system that best accords with Smith's view of human nature? Smith believed the free market would always correct itself according to the law of supply and demand, but reality has not been equivalent to his vision. Producers of goods will often cut production when they are dissatisfied with the price structure. Competitors can also get together to "fix" prices.

What of Smith's certainty that it is right and good for each of us to try to fare better than anyone else, that competitiveness is healthy and aggressiveness the law of life? That self-interest underlies *many* of our actions would seem undeniable, but that it is the only way to understand humanity is open to serious debate. Does the "law" of self-interest automatically ensure that people really want what they think they want? Or are we sometimes pressured into wanting things we don't need? To pay for our so-called self-interest, many of us work at jobs that deaden the mind and seem to remove from life all of the pleasure, which is what self-interest is supposed to promote to begin with. In the long run, the free market does not always seem to care about hazards to health and the environment or about the quality of human life.

In the beginning of the nineteenth century Jeremy Bentham expounded the moral philosophy of *utilitarianism*. Like Machiavelli, Bentham believed that people were selfish and pleasure-loving, but he did not turn to cynicism or despair. Instead, he formulated a scheme called a *hedonic calculus*, which was designed to make moral judgment numerical through an accounting system that gave a specific value (plus or minus) to actions relative to the pleasure or pain caused by each. Assuming that the search for pleasure was the universal motivation therefore determined numerically that the most moral action was that which promoted the "greatest good for the greatest number."

For the individual, the hedonic calculus, according to Bentham, would be the guide in all decisions about marriage, travel, care for family members, even

*Adam Smith's theory of* laissez-faire, *which is the eighteenth-century basis of capitalism, maintains that the key to a sound economy is to allow each person the freedom to advance his or her own interest, for in this way everyone profits.*

*Utilitarians also viewed humanity as being driven by self-interest.*

leisure time. In public life, decisions made by officeholders and the electorate would take into account the plusses and minuses of a new tax, a zoning ordinance, or a law limiting the rights of one group of citizens against the rights of another. All is done by numbers, and the majority rules.

Some philosophical implications arise out of utilitarianism. In practice it may be difficult to administer, since there will always be disagreement about the number of minus points assigned to those made unhappy by a given choice; there may well be a temptation to adjust the computations to coincide with a decision arrived at by other than mathematical means. In addition, there is the question of whether, even in a society in which all people may be *politically* equal, their pleasures are also equal. What is the effect of having majority rule in matters of public taste? Doesn't easy, cheap, distasteful literature largely drive out that which can be enjoyed by the relatively few who have been educated to respect the more demanding? Another effect of majority rule can easily be seen by a glance at television ratings. But more than the arts is involved here. What of the moral impact of some practice enjoyed by the many but still harmful to the few? A startling example is provided by Robert Paul Wolff in a discussion of utilitarianism:

> Suppose that the Americans, like the ancient Romans, positively enjoyed watching people being tortured. . . . Now Bentham will obviously believe that torture is an evil to the person who suffers it, for torture is painful and pain is evil. But the pleasure that a group of sadists get from watching the torture is good, for pleasure, says Bentham, is good. So for a utilitarian, torture can be justified when the total pleasure produced outweighs the total pain produced. . . . We shall therefore institute a new TV show called "Torture of the Week." This is a live show in which real victims really do get tortured. . . . According to utilitarians, if there are enough viewers who are ecstatic at the sight of this torture, then their pleasure might outweigh the pain suffered by the victim. And if no other show on television has anything resembling its high ratings, then we can assume that putting on the torture show is not only justified, but positively morally obligatory.[1]

The self-interest of Bentham is one source of moral values, based on the assumption (for Bentham, the *fact*) that human beings are selfish, pleasure-loving animals and that the only way to guarantee that everyone gets as much pleasure as possible is to pass legislation providing a good life for the greatest number of people. Yet not every philosopher has held or now holds the view that the good is what *feels* good.

## The Universal Sense of Ought

Immanuel Kant (1724-1804) believed, with Socrates, that people do right because they know what right is. Kant postulated that the pursuit of moral good is a built-in capacity. Like the laws of mathematics, which are consistent throughout time and space, there are universal laws governing moral behavior, and each of us understands them, in a sense, *instinctively*.

In fact, we understand anything that we do understand because we are born with *categories*, mental pigeonholes, of built-in knowledge. Even today we

*Joan Miro,* Carnival of Harlequin *(1924–25): Without categories of knowledge, said
Kant, the world is a series of bewildering fragments of disconnected events. (Albright-
Knox Art Gallery, Buffalo, New York. Room of Contemporary Art Fund, 1940)*

speak of knowing something *categorically*. Or else we *categorically* deny that
something is true. We understand time, space, and causality, for example, not
because someone taught them to us; rather, we are able to learn what they are
because of various categories of knowledge. Without them, says Kant, the world is
"unknown and unknowable"—a bewildering series of disconnected events.

One of the categories he called the *categorical imperative*, or the universal
sense of *ought*. While rewards and punishments mold our earliest relationship to
yes and no, they do not give us much insight into what is universally right or
wrong. As we grow in the ability to reason, our insight into morality deepens,
because our awareness of the categorical imperative grows stronger.

Kant suggested that a person contemplating an action should will that it
be universally required, since each of us knows intuitively what is universally right.
If we planned to commit robbery, for example, we should say, "It is right and just
that all people steal." If as potential thieves we could *not* do this—and the categorical imperative, Kant was convinced, would prevent us from doing so—we would
then have to regard ourselves as the single exception to a universal law. Everyone
would agree on the absurdity of such a position. To put the matter a different way:
Wrongdoers understand and accept the moral decency of most people. In fact,
they *count* on it; otherwise they could never surprise their victims. Hence they are
indirectly affirming the universality of the good and just.

Another universal law, according to Kant, had to do with human dignity:
Treat people as an end in themselves rather than as a means to an end. That is, no
one was to be cultivated as a friend in order to achieve future profit. (In today's
world, this would prohibit us from making lists of "prospects" or business "con-
tacts" from which an eventual sale or signing of a contract is our actual goal, while

a pretended friendship is our means of achieving it.) People were not to be degraded. The logical argument might go this way:

*Major Premise:*    All persons have dignity and are worthy of respect.
*Minor Premise:*    *X* is a person.
*Conclusion:*       Therefore, *X* has dignity and is worthy of respect.

When we recognize that Kant died before the abolition of slavery and the widespread adoption of legislation to control the abuse of workers, we can see how revolutionary were his ideas of universal laws for the treatment of people as people rather than as objects for personal gain.

Kant was also concerned with the motive behind a good action. Not satisfied with just the end result, he insisted that actions should be based on principle. To give reluctantly or because an act of charity would increase one's reputation, for example, was to destroy the goodness in the act of giving.

*Many view Kant as the last major thinker to bring to philosophy a vision of universal rational and moral order.*

Many historians of ideas view Kant as the last major thinker to bring to philosophy a vision of universal rational and moral order. In the century following Kant, philosophy often became a poetic declamation about the glory of the individual or a vigorous defense of human rights and the cause of freedom. Ego was often deemed more important than a universal morality, because a system of thought like that of Kant required individuals to subordinate themselves to higher principles.

In this century philosophy has often become the art of minutely analyzing questions without providing answers. In the opinion of many so-called analytical philosophers, moral issues do not exist, since the terminology used to formulate them has no clear meaning.

## Religious Authority

In addition to being a philosopher who used reason to reach conclusions, Kant was a religious man. However, he did not provide us with a category by which God is known. Instead, he postulated that the truth of God's existence is arrived at through means other than rational understanding, means he called "practical" philosophy. That is, God is understood as a matter of common sense. We ask ourselves, How can this world exist without a God to have created it? Then we answer, it cannot. If one is convinced of the rightness of the question and the obviousness of the answer, then who is to argue with this position?

*For both Jews and Christians the Bible offers indisputable truth that there is an omniscient God who can read the thought and motivation of each person. This God has forged in the human heart a conscience that knows right from wrong.*

For Kant moral values were understood and validated through *categorical knowledge*. For billions of people, however, the phrase *moral law* is appropriate. Moral law comes directly from God or a divinely inspired prophet. It is a central component of many major religions: Judaism, Christianity, Islam, and Buddhism, among others. Taken together, their followers constitute an overwhelming majority of the world's population, and moral law for each believer is binding and unconditional.

For both Jews and Christians the Bible offers indisputable truth that there is an omniscient God who can read the thought and motivation of each person. This God has forged in the human heart a conscience that knows what is right and wrong.

In Psalm 139 we find this passage:

*O Lord, You have examined me and know me*
*When I sit down or stand up you know it;*
*You discern my thoughts from afar*
*You observe my walking and reclining, and*
*are familiar with all my ways*
*There is not a word on my tongue*
*but that You, O Lord, know it well* . . .

There is no place to hide. God's awareness is all-pervasive.

The Hebrew Bible (often called the Old Testament, or the Hebrew Scriptures) sets forth commandments governing property, sacrifice, charity, punishment of crimes, treatment of strangers, behavior toward servants, and preservation of customs. Many have seen in the Hebrew Bible the cornerstone of much civilized behavior. The Ten Commandments, said to have been received by Moses directly from God on Mount Sinai, prohibit, among other things, murder, theft, adultery, the dishonoring of parents, and the worshiping of other gods whose laws might be less demanding. Biblical law preserves the good conduct of the individual and holds together the tribe, the city, and the nation, but it is not a social contract that can be broken if the people vote to do so, nor is it legislation that can be repealed. Commoner and king have the ability to sin against the law, but both risk punishment by God, a more powerful deterrent for many than the punishment of society. Religious spokespersons believe that fear of God's anger, not fear of imprisonment or even of the death penalty, is what truly controls the passionate outbursts that lead people to acts of violence.

*Michelangelo,* Moses: *Biblical law preserves the good conduct of the individual. (Alinari/Art Resource)*

The Ascension of Mohammed:
*Mohammed being rewarded
with heavenly bliss. (British
Museum, London)*

*The Islamic holy book is the
Koran, in which are
collected the teachings of
Mohammed, who on a
lonely mountain near Mecca
experienced a mystic vision
in which an angel appeared
to him and set forth the
word of Allah, much as
Moses received the Ten
Commandments on Mount
Sinai.*

The Islamic holy book is the Koran, in which are collected the teachings of
the prophet Mohammed (571-632), whose early life was spent as a shepherd, then
as a camel driver. At the age of 40 he experienced a mystic vision on a lonely moun-
tainside near the city of Mecca, which continues to be the center of Islamic worship.
In this vision an angel appeared to him and set forth the word of Allah, much as
Moses received the Ten Commandments on Mount Sinai. (*Islam* is an Arabic term
meaning "submission"—that is, submission to God's will and God's law.)

Islamic moral law stresses good conduct in social relationships, particularly
those between the sexes. Chastity outside of marriage is insisted upon. Men are
forbidden to take paramours or to desire even chaste women not of the faith.

The Koran calls for justice in all dealings. Humanity is to fear God's wrath.
Islamic moral law is socially oriented, made up of strong regulations necessary for
the original Muslims, a nomadic people in an area and a climate that were often
harsh and unfriendly. Wild and uncontrollable behavior within the group, or leaving
the group altogether to seek a different life under a different god, would have
helped to destroy the nation.

In both Judaism and Islam the moral law is pragmatic. The Hebrew Bible
and the Koran do speak of a "next life," but their moral governance is clearly of
this world. Their promised rewards to those who observe their laws are mainly
related to this life.

Buddhism is also centered on earthly conduct; here there is no god figure at all. Instead of an afterlife, there is *nirvana* (explained more fully in the following chapter), which is a state of total bliss in which one is free from all pain and sorrow. Nirvana, however, does not exist in a particular place. Buddhist moral law stresses the good actions that will lead one to nirvana. It is thus a guide to moral living, stemming not from God's commandments but from *enlightenment*, the wisdom that came to one man, Gautama Buddha, during a long period of meditation. Though the origin of Buddhist moral law is not a god, it is absolute and binding on the billions of people who have practiced and are practicing a Buddhist way of life. Despite the lack of a god figure, Buddhism is a religion, with the Buddha, who was mortal, a god*like* person to his followers.

What is called the New Testament (or the Christian Scriptures) contains the four Gospels, which are somewhat differing versions of the life of Jesus Christ as reportedly given by four of his disciples: Matthew, Mark, Luke, and John. The most succinct delivery of Christian moral law is found in Matthew 5: the Sermon on the Mount. Here Jesus accepts the earlier Hebrew laws, but he adds a new admonition, as in this example from Matthew 5:21-22:

*The most succinct delivery of Christian moral law is found in Matthew 5: the Sermon on the Mount.*

> Ye have heard that it was said by them of old time: Thou shalt not kill; and whosoever shall kill shall be in danger of the judgment. But I say unto you, That whosoever is angry with his brother without a cause shall be in danger of the judgment.

God's awareness, says Jesus, thus extends to both the inner and the outer human being. There are sins of rage as well as sins of bad intent. To wish someone dead is as bad as to slay the person in actuality.

Christian moral law includes the charge *Judge not, or you will be judged*. Its more popular form is the Golden Rule. Also stressed is forgiveness of one's enemies, presumably a replacement for the "eye for an eye" code found in both Judaic and Islamic moral law. Like Buddhism, Christian moral law insists that nonaggression is the way of the godlike person, and it urges Christians to follow in the footsteps of Jesus by "turning the other cheek" when attacked by another.

In Judaism, *judgment* appears to be understood as the earthly consequences of God's wrath: the flood that destroyed all the world, sparing only Noah and his family, for example. As the influence of Christianity spread throughout what became the Western world, interpreters of Christ's teachings turned this judgment into the meting out of rewards or punishment in the next world. The popular conception of the afterlife became that of an actual place, originally owing much to the description given in *The Divine Comedy* of Dante Alighieri (1265-1321). The medieval poet depicts hell—called *Inferno*—as a deep pit containing seven ledges on which condemned souls suffer torment for eternity. He also describes *Purgatorio*, a seven-tiered mountain on which "lesser" sins are punished, but not forever. Souls purified on the mountain, as well as those who died sinless, are allowed to pass into the nine heavenly spheres of *Paradiso*, where they live in everlasting bliss.

*It is Dante's vision of the afterlife that has helped make the concept of heaven and hell real to generations of people.*

Much of the poem is actually political in nature, since Dante placed his enemies (who were still living!) in the deepest, most painful areas of hell. Yet it is Dante's vision of the afterlife that has helped make the concept of heaven and hell real to generations of people. Even for the vaguely religious, images of heaven and hell can be lifelong incentives to consider the moral consequences of one's actions.

Many who could not accept traditional religious teachings have nonetheless

*George Grosz,* Punishment *(1934): The popular conception of the afterlife became that of an actual place. (Watercolor on paper, 27-1/2 x 20-1/2". Collection, The Museum of Modern Art, New York. Gift of Mr. and Mrs. Erich Cohn)*

been profoundly influenced by the idea of heaven and hell and the inevitable price that must be paid for misdeeds. Fyodor Dostoevsky (1821-1881) dramatized a personal, inner hell in his novel *Crime and Punishment*, in which an individual's guilty conscience takes the place of God's awareness. The Persian poet Omar Khayyam, author of *The Rubaiyat*, a series of hedonistic poems recommending an "eat, drink, and be merry" philosophy, recognizes that even for the atheistic pleasure-seeker there comes a time of searing inner guilt: "I Myself am Heav'n and Hell."

## "Of Course"

An awareness of right and wrong begins for most of us in childhood, with the acclaim or disapproval of the parents who observe our actions. In the earliest years, comments directed toward a child are almost always moral, are matters of yes and no. There is praise for learning to drink from a cup or climbing stairs without help and anger for touching hot stoves or crossing the street without looking. At first, childhood morality centers on survival. Later on it branches out and becomes part of the socialization process. Being required to kiss grandparents, whether one wants to or not, teaches family attitudes toward the elderly and puts a restraint on preoccupation with self.

Among the rules learned are some not directly pointed out. Children observe and listen to adults fighting with and praising each other as well as discussing the behavior of other people. From these observations come many of the automatic assumptions of later life, assumptions that become rules of courtesy, order, or concern for the opinion of others. Children who often hear, "What will the neighbors say?" may for the rest of their lives have difficulty getting over the feeling that someone is watching them and that this someone's opinion is important.

Parental moral authority is sharp, direct, and to the point. Often a sudden blow is the stinging reminder that the authority is over five feet tall and has very powerful eyes—and hands. In school, the teacher and to some extent the other students also exert an authority that helps to form the unexamined assumptions of later life. People sometimes go through their entire life thinking that such learned behavior is "natural," to be taken for granted. Unexamined assumptions underlie statements prefaced by "Of course."

Subtle, pervasive, and hard to pin down, the authoritarianism of the "Of course" moral code grows in intensity as we approach adulthood and often stays with us for a long time, if not forever:

"Of course there is no excuse for being late."
"Of course you may not stay out until midnight."
"Of course you may not date someone of a different religion."
"Of course you must take required subjects. Why else would they be required?"
"This is your very first year to vote, darling. Of course you will vote for the family's party."

The family circle has swift and direct ways of dealing with violations, ranging from corporal punishment in the early years to the steady application of guilt in adolescence. Passing into adulthood does not guarantee safety from family justice. Who does not know of close kin who haven't spoken to each other in 40 years because of some now-forgotten breach of family ethics?

School is even swifter in inculcating morality. Posted signs everywhere inform children of what will "of course" be done and who may do it. Report cards and honors assemblies reinforce, reward, or depress. Less obvious is classroom structure, with a standing leader watching the suspect children while a favored group is approvingly called upon to read or go to the chalkboard to demonstrate expertise before the disgraced and the envious. Children know, without being directly told, who are expected to achieve. At an early age they learn to admire or envy achievement, to size themselves up on the achievement scale: *Hey, what did you get?* Often they carry into life these initial attitudes toward themselves as worthy or unworthy beings. The sense that the world is ready to approve or disapprove—or that we at last no longer care about approval—underlies many of our moral choices in later life.

Fortunate are those whose early and later years are so much the same that they never have to adjust. Even more fortunate are those who in later life recognize all the early, unquestioned assumptions and are then able to discard or retain them in the light of mature reflection.

*The family circle has swift and direct ways of dealing with violations, ranging from corporal punishment in the early years to the steady application of guilt in adolescence.*

## Popular Slogans

When moral philosophy is taught, sloganism is seldom mentioned as an important source of values. Yet the *moral aphorism*—a concisely phrased, eminently quotable axiom—is so much a part of our daily lives that we can ill afford not to give it consideration. Professional philosophers probably assume they themselves are beyond the influence of slogans. But the rest of us need to be reminded of how deeply rooted are the ramifications of the homespun ethics we sometimes turn to when a situation involving moral choice arises.

Still with us—but of declining impact—are some basic slogans deriving from the Calvinist beginnings of our country. There are aphorisms that extol not only the dignity but the Christian reputability of hard work: *Idle hands are the devil's workshop*. Others, including *A stitch in time saves nine*, discourage laziness and advocate careful planning. Likewise, in the days before rampant inflation, we had *A penny saved is a penny earned*.

If, as the sociologist Max Weber (1864 - 1920) believed, there is a documentable relationship between the Protestant work ethic and the rise of capitalism, then the numerous slogans encouraging self-interest as an acceptable motive for actions are also legacies of our Puritan past, even as they seem especially applicable to present society.

*Looking out for number one* is a modernized version of a fundamental capitalist tenet, which holds that it is not only acceptable but right and just that people act so as to advance their own cause. The father of capitalism, Adam Smith (discussed earlier), indicated that, in serving themselves, people really benefited all of society. This attitude has never met serious challenge from the vast majority.

*Charity begins at home* has been around for centuries and is still going strong, especially in these days of reaction against continual pleas from nonprofit organizations for contributions. This time-tested aphorism is always appropriate to justify turning a deaf ear to sometimes desperate appeals for support.

The idea that if we find money or some other valuable possession we are not obliged to return it or even to undertake a reasonable search for the owner is adequately covered by the enduringly popular *Finders keepers, losers weepers*. This axiom also has rhyme, hence literary tradition, going for it.

As either the rate of inflation or the unemployment figures rise, we note a corresponding rise in overt cynicism about the importance of altruism. In a game of economic musical chairs, when some must wind up on the floor, there are whimsical-seeming but deadly earnest perversions of axioms that once advocated concern for others. Thus the Golden Rule becomes *Do unto others before they do unto you*.

Should we doubt for a moment the morality of self-interest, there are aphorisms to justify a life dedicated to hedonistic or materialistic pursuits, such as the ever-present *Eat, drink, and be merry, for tomorrow we die* and the insistent *Nothing succeeds like success*. In our society we cannot readily abandon the quest for fame and fortune without experiencing pangs of guilt.

Human-growth-and-development specialists, appalled that people dislike examining their actions too closely, causing them to resist change, offer substitutes for what they consider dangerous slogans such as *I like you just the way you are*. In recent years they have given us *This is the first day of the rest of your life*, an aphorism immediately countered by *If this is the first day of the rest of my life, I'm in trouble*. Rather than support the idea of change and growth, popular morality prefers *Hang in there!*, not to mention the classic denial of growth, *The more things change, the more they remain the same*.

Finally, despite the consciousness-raising efforts of those who herald a new dawn of sexual equality, the slogans continue to support chauvinism, and women who object haven't gotten new ones into the public consciousness yet. Perhaps we hear less of *It's a wise father who knows his own child*, but there seems no let-up from *Isn't that just like a woman?* or the more subtle, but no less sexist, *Leave it to a woman!* This slogan extols the virtue of intuition, without directly confronting the notion of the "supremacy" of male rationalism. We can only hope that the future will bring new slogans that do not rely on old stereotypes. But none of us may live to hear that *A man's place is in the home.*

## Work

Preoccupation with work is so central to our culture that it crops up everywhere. We hear of businesspersons who don't know how to relax and who fall victim to stress, for example, and we have denigrating terms for those who don't work: lazy, bum, loafer. Work is certainly crucial to an understanding of contemporary morality.

   One of the most poignant reminders of work's fierce hold on us is contained in this passage from a novel by Isabel Allende, *Of Love and Shadows* (1987). Looking at the body of his brother Javier, Francisco, the hero, tries to understand what would have led the man to kill himself. Javier has been unable to find work after the military authorities blacklisted him. Then Francisco finds a connection between the family work ethic and his brother's sense of worth:

> He remembered his father's lesson: work as a source of pride.
> Idleness was foreign to the family. In the Leal household, holidays and
> even vacations were spent in some worthwhile undertaking. The
> family had had its difficult moments, but they had never dreamed of
> accepting charity, even from those they had previously helped.[2]

Javier, a biologist, tries to find any kind of work, but the authorities block his efforts. Hours of waiting and rejection result in humiliation and sleeplessness:

> Without a job, he gradually lost his identity. He would have accepted
> any offers, however mean the pay, because he desperately needed to
> feel useful. As a man without employment, he was an outsider,
> anonymous, ignored by all because he was no longer productive, and
> that was the measure of a man in the world he lived in. . . . The day
> his youngest son put on the kitchen table the few coins he had
> earned walking rich men's dogs, Javier cringed like a cornered animal.
> Since that moment he never looked anyone in the eyes; he sank into
> total despair.[3]

   One need not be as desperate as Javier to sense the importance of work. It affects our attitudes toward time, ambition, respectability, appearance, marriage, and satisfaction with ourselves. Even retired people boast of being exhausted from their many activities, as if leisure time must be "spent" as actively as paid employment. Time must not be "wasted," as it would be if one were to sit around "just" thinking. The worker who is satisfied with a job may be questioned about the future—"Where do you go from here?"—as if one must continue to climb. Parents boast of children's occupations with high earning potential and worry about an announced intention to do something fulfilling in other ways. Many never examine even the *benefit* of the work they do, whether it is making cigarettes or assisting in an operating room; work, no matter what kind, is often done for the paycheck rather than the consequences.

Literature is full of scenes recording the importance of work, ambition, and the appearance of success. In Shakespeare's *Hamlet*, Polonius tells his son Laertes to dress well, to look good: "Costly thy habit as thy purse can bear./But not expressed in fancy—rich, not gaudy./For the apparel oft proclaims the man" (I.iii. 70-73). Polonius was not meant to be one of Shakespeare's heroes. Throughout the play he is presented as a windy fellow, and it is clear that Shakespeare had other measurements besides clothing for judging the worth of a man. But today, national magazines urge that we not only have the qualities of a good worker, but that we "dress for success."

*Schulberg's* What Makes Sammy Run? *was written in 1941 to show readers how awful is a life devoted solely to material success, but now college students congratulate the author for having given them a role model.*

In 1941 Budd Schulberg wrote *What Makes Sammy Run?*, a satiric portrait of a hustling little man with more nerve than creativity who was able to make a fortune by exploiting his friends, lying his way to the top, and winning everything but true affection. The author thought at the time that he was writing a morality tale by showing readers what an awful life his main character was living. Now when Schulberg meets college seniors, he says, they *thank* him for providing them with a role model for success!

In our democratic society we do not yet introduce people by their (or their husband's) title, as some cultures do. At the same time, one's work is apt to be mentioned soon after one's name, and today that work is often elevated to a *profession*, once a title granted only after years of study and dedication. Today, we hear about the "profession of realtor" or "professional hairdressers," with the term

*Honore Daumier,* The Third-Class Carriage *(1862): Many never examine even the benefit of the work they do. (The Metropolitan Museum of Art)*

*professional* meaning "dedicated to something besides just making money." We hold professionals to a higher standard than the clock-watching clerks. We would like professionals to be morally upstanding and we are therefore far more outraged when a lawyer dips into a trust fund or a professor claims credit for another scholar's effort than we are when we read about a holdup in a local store.

People may also be disappointed at their own jobs. Somehow, despite all the importance society places on work, they may find themselves to be replaceable parts in a large machine, their names barely recognized by the receptionist, even after they have put in years of service. The gulf often widens between the workers and the managers. Both sides accuse each other of immoral behavior: hints of managers plotting to reduce costs in a way that will adversely affect the product or service, workers retaliating by using up sick leave, taking longer coffee breaks, and failing to work hard unless directly supervised.

A reason often cited for this job dissatisfaction and attendant behavior is the growing separation of workers from the products of their labor. Can the assembly-line worker who fastens engine bolts into place all day long ever point to a particular automobile and think, "I have a share in that beauty"? Computer experts may take pride in having figured out a way to save the company millions of dollars, but there is no actual thing standing there to represent their creativity— nothing except the computer itself, which somebody else, or some corporation, has created. We are fast becoming a nation specializing in services, not products. The tangible product of our labors is often nothing more than a monthly bank statement.

## The Public Moral Conscience

Truly devout believers perceiving a daily struggle with Satan often take it as their responsibility to assist others along the path of "righteousness." Early Puritan church leaders rudely awakened those who slept during long church services. Even the Salem witch trials ostensibly had salvation as the underlying justification for persecuting and then hanging those found guilty of traffic with Satan.

The Puritans lived in tight communities. Everyone knew everyone else's business. Puritan morality instantly became the community morality. During the witch hunts, the Puritans were linking themselves to an ancient tradition, stretching back long before the Judeo-Christian era—a tradition in which the community possessed one mind when it came to right and wrong. Evildoers had to be driven out, or else the entire community would suffer the vengeance of some deity.

*. . . advice-givers serve as guardians of the dominant, mainstream morality.*

In modern communities some of the same tradition survives. Certainly we note lingering reminders of the Puritan public moral conscience in the advice people give to others on how to live their lives or how to raise their children. Whether conscious of it or not, the advice-givers serve as guardians of the dominant, mainstream morality, which has had both religious and communal sanctions for so long that no one dreams of questioning it. Instant guilt often accrues to the parent who is told by a neighbor, "Far be it from me to tell you what to do about your own children, but if that were my daughter, I'd want to know who she's with until all hours of the night."

If such moral advice is acceptable to those who receive it, if it does indeed lead to a positive change in behavior, then the public conscience is not necessarily a bad thing or an invasion of privacy. Some parents probably do not know what to do with their children. Often the children themselves sense the confusion of their parents and look to other sources to exert strong moral authority over them. The public conscience, which exists in every community in the world, acts as a check upon flagrantly antisocial behavior.

On the other hand, the public conscience is notoriously conservative, updates itself very slowly, and can leave untold damage in its wake. A magazine article printed in the *Victorian England* of a hundred years ago had this comment: "Poverty and misery, be it remembered, are more generally the results of vice, laziness, and improvidence, than of misfortune." A century later one would not be surprised to find many people staunchly agreeing that welfare recipients are lazy good-for-nothings and that if the unemployed really wanted to work, there would be no unemployment.

People often believe in what is convenient, and it is often highly convenient to use the public moral conscience as a mask for self-interest, as a reinforcement for the way we have chosen to view things.

Morality is all too frequently what other people do wrong, and becoming a member of a disapproving mob is a means whereby an individual may find safety in numbers. During the nineteenth century the great libertarian philosopher John Stuart Mill wrote a famous essay called "The Tyranny of the Majority" in which he said that the

> object of this essay is to assert one very simple principle, as entitled to govern absolutely the dealings of society with the individual in the way of compulsion and control, whether the means used be physical force in the form of legal penalties, or the moral coercion of public opinion. That principle is, that the sole end for which mankind are warranted, individually or collectively, in interfering with the liberty of action of any of their number, is self-protection. That is, the only purpose for which power can be rightfully exercised over any member of a civilized community, against his will, is to prevent harm to others. His own good, either physical or moral, is not a sufficient warrant. . . .

Though Mill's intentions are clear enough, many sensitive questions still arise: Who decides what constitutes or truly threatens the "self-protection" of the majority? And what constitutes "harm to others"? Are people who abuse their bodies through alcohol or narcotics really harming only themselves? If so, are these people entitled to the support of family and public institutions, such as county hospitals? If "self-protection" does warrant interfering with someone's liberty, then who decides what methods of protection are justified? For some, even violence against the transgressor would be nothing more than the efforts of a "civilized community" to preserve its standards.

A psychiatrist, Dr. Thomas Szasz, carries Mill's idea of fundamental liberties one step farther, urging upholders of public morality to stop interfering with the rights of individuals to do whatever they like to themselves, including suicide. No one, according to Szasz, has the right to label as "insane" or "undesirable" behavior that happens to be *different*.

## Zealotry

The flip side of the public moral conscience is zealotry. Zealots are crusaders who detach themselves from the crowd because they perceive that something in society is amiss. They can think of little else. They rally supporters around their cause, make television appearances, write passionate letters to the editor. Sometimes they run for office, always driving home the same message. They are so convinced of a particular moral truth, religious or secular, that they continually seek converts.

Religious zealots have a long history. During the Restoration Jeremy Collier, a seventeenth-century Anglican priest, tried single-handedly to shut down the thriving English stage on the grounds that it was immoral and a menace to the spiritual well-being of society. Before Collier, a monk named Girolamo Savonarola (1452-1498) had taken on the emerging Renaissance in art and politics. He had tried to convince people that the naked bodies on canvas or in marble, the rich and sensuous colors in which artists depicted worldly scenes, and the new secular-oriented politics (which were attempting to do away with the absolutism of church law) were all the work of Satan.

We still have religious zealots, denouncing the moral corruption of our time from pulpits and from television screens. Many can attract crowds as large as those for a rock concert. Now and then one such zealot is exposed as a fraud, perhaps for soliciting money for personal profit rather than for the moral crusade, but another zealot soon stands on the same platform. Scandalous headlines seldom stop the force of zealousness, for the message, once delivered, has a life of its own and can influence the moral beliefs of many for years.

The secular zealot is just as powerful an influence on popular thinking and is often as fiery an orator as the religious zealot. Today he or she is apt to be pointing out the dangers of smoking or eating meat; campaigning against political corruption or inequitable laws; pleading with us to care about the homeless, the unemployed, or the conditions under which migrant workers are forced to live; or begging us to love and care for this earth, which is our only and our often-abused home.

When evaluating a zealot, the critical thinker must decide whether the zealot's goals are indeed admirable and whether all of the tactics used to achieve the goals are necessary. Sometimes one is concerned that the zealot, however admirable, is sacrificing too much, even all hope of personal happiness. Yet often such sacrifice is necessary to bring about a better world. In such instances zealousness becomes a role model of behavior that most of us could never hope to emulate.

The inspired zealousness of a Martin Luther King, Jr., or a Mohandas Gandhi can change the course of human history and dramatically reinforce the one moral law that perhaps most dignifies the human potential: *the elimination of hatred and aggression*. King delivered his memorable "I Have Been to the Mountain" speech shortly before his assassination in 1968, apparently in full awareness of what would inevitably happen, yet stating for all time that the cause of equality is worth any price.

The cause of nonviolent resistance to prejudice, war, and other inhumani-

*The one moral law that perhaps most dignifies the human potential:* the elimination of hatred and aggression.

ties was put simply, yet no less zealously, by Gandhi in answering a letter from a young child:

> I was delighted to have your sweet notes with funny drawings made by you. . . . Yes, it is little children like you who will stop all war. This means that you never quarrel with other boys and girls or among yourselves. You cannot stop big wars if you carry on little wars yourselves. . . .[4]

## Two Contemporary Moral Philosophies

When we discussed the moral influences of popular slogans, we failed to mention one phase that has been around for a long time: *Handsome is as handsome does*. This slogan is very much American in its emphasis on judging people in terms of what they do. In modern times there have emerged two dominant moral philosophies in which the deed and its consequences are the crucial factors, not traditional moral laws or popular sources of morality, such as slogans or "Of course" statements. These two modern philosophies attempt to define right and wrong in terms of the effect on others of what we do.

### Situational Morality

Even people who have never read the moral philosophers have occasion to comment on wrongdoing, sometimes in reaction to a news account of a horrible crime, sometimes by serving on a jury. In almost every case, there will be the need to examine the circumstances, the motivations, and the number of people who were affected. Such an approach to morality is called *situational*, and it underlies such comments as "They never had a chance," "It wasn't a fair fight," and "She was only a child!"

*Situational morality examines the circumstances, the motivations, and the number of people who were affected.*

Say a hunter goes into the woods to shoot an animal. The moral absolutist—one who believes hunting is wrong no matter what the situation—condemns the very intention. The hunter spots the prey, takes aim, and fires, wounding but not killing the animal. A situationalist might ask, "Did the hunter take the necessary steps to find the prey and finish the job? Or was the animal left to die a painful death or to live on in agony?" The absolutist would condemn *any* outcome, but the situationalist, upon discovering that the hunter put the wounded animal out of its misery, might well decide the act was not an immoral one.

The situationalist believes that moral choice has to be examined in relation to circumstances, motivations, and consequences. For example, motive doesn't matter if no one is harmed. Likewise, inflicting pain, even causing death, can escape condemnation if the circumstances make violent actions appear justifiable.

There is a famous legal case involving the aftermath of the sinking of a great ocean liner. A high-ranking ship's officer found himself on a lifeboat that could accommodate no more than 25 persons. Amid the panic and desperation many more than 25 people attempted to climb on board. The officer instructed several crew members to throw the "extras" into the sea to ensure the survival of those already on the lifeboat. In a few instances those who resisted were shot.

Later the officer was tried for murder, found guilty, but subsequently pardoned. The case attracted widespread attention. Some observers pointed out that the issue was not whether the murders were justified, but whether the method of selecting those who remained on the lifeboat was fair. The officer, as a matter of fact, had tried to restrict the deaths to men only, but the suggestion was made that straws should have been drawn for the "honor" of leaving the lifeboat.

In another famous case, two men and a young boy were marooned at sea on a life raft. Recognizing that the child was clearly weakened and near death, the men decided to end his life so that he could be eaten and thus ensure *their* survival. They too were found guilty but were pardoned.

The situationalist is fond of citing such cases, for they are the stuff of which real life is made. Can we say that murder is always wrong? Or that cannibalism is never justified under any circumstances? Does the need to survive take precedence over any other need?

The situationalist knows that answering these questions is not easy. To say that murder in one instance is not the same as murder in another gives the judge an awesome responsibility. Yet to argue the reverse—that murder is never justified and is never to be condoned—can lead to miscarriages of justice.

The advantage of situationalism, say its advocates, is that each problem is examined on its own merits and not in terms of an abstract moral code devised long ago to fit a very different world. The disadvantages, say its critics, are that situations can be interpreted to someone's private advantage and that unfortunate precedents are always being created. For example, if it was morally permissible for the two men on the raft to kill the young boy, what would prevent some future survivors on a raft from taking a person's life long before it was evident that that person's life was nearly over?

*Advocates of situationalism contend that each problem is examined on its own merits and not in terms of an abstract moral code devised long ago to fit a very different world.*

## Existentialist Morality

As we have seen, morality can be, among other things, a matter of law, supported by the authority of God; a product of unexamined assumptions from our early years; a result of society's attitudes; an attempt to follow a slogan derived from a variety of sources; an effort to calculate pleasure and pain mathematically; or a rational conclusion about what constitutes universal righteous behavior. Some philosophers have insisted that human beings are naturally inclined to do the right thing, while others have claimed that humans are naturally selfish, even ruthless, unless carefully watched.

We now come to the contemporary moral philosophy that builds on the assertion that there is no such thing as human nature and that a person cannot be described in terms of purpose in the way that we can define, say, a paper cutter. Without a nature and without any apparent reason for existing, human beings cannot be expected to perform actions "appropriate" to the species. Instead, each action is performed on the basis of a conviction, clear or confused, at the moment of choice. No book or person can give advice on particular instances. At the moment of choice each of us is alone.

During the last century a Danish philosopher named Søren Kierkegaard (1813-1855) acquired the distinction of being the founder of this new school of thought. Called by him *existentialism*, the new philosophy was really not a philosophy in the traditional sense of the word, for it held that existence could be comprehended only through the concrete realities of living, not in terms of abstract intellectual concepts. It held that human reason was incapable of discovering, with absolute certainty, a vast cosmic scheme and that consequently reality must always be a subjective matter.

Kierkegaard began as a pious Christian, went through phases of agonizing doubt and feelings of abandonment, and finally reaffirmed his Christianity on radically new grounds. To Kierkegaard, religion was a psychological need, not a philosophical truth, and had to be dealt with on that level. When one reached the point of absolute despair and felt ready to turn to God, one could take a "leap of faith." One chose the path of faith because one was compelled to, not because the choice could be justified in terms of an intellectual system.

In that leap, however, lay undeniable anxieties. The leap had to be made over many counterarguments, especially scientific evidence that seriously questioned religious beliefs. On one's knees in the darkness of a church, one might feel one's prayers soaring heavenwards and have an almost mystic sense of union with God, but one could not know for sure that God was listening—or was even there at all. To have faith in the existential (that is, to have faith in the concrete existence of something, even something cosmic, such as God) meant exactly that; it did not mean to know. It meant to *believe without knowing*.

To dramatize the existential plight of the believer, Kierkegaard recounted the Biblical tale of Abraham and Isaac in his book *Fear and Trembling*. An angel appears to Abraham and tells him God demands the sacrifice of his son Isaac. Abraham is no doubt appalled, but what can he do? If God wants the sacrifice and if he is God's servant, he must obey. But in that leap of faith, in that raising of the knife, must not Abraham experience unutterable anguish? Suppose the angel was not really from God—what then? This anguish of Abraham represented for Kierkegaard the very heart of the existential dilemma of humankind.

Contemporary existentialism has developed since World War II. The tradition begun by Kierkegaard is usually referred to as Christian existentialism, and it has its supporters. But the most influential strain of existential thought is undoubtedly that associated with the French philosophers Jean-Paul Sartre, Albert Camus, and Simone de Beauvoir, all of whom represent an atheistic approach. Existence, they say, is absurd in that it cannot be shown to serve any purpose. Species simply are whatever they are, *including* humanity. Since God cannot be shown to exist, there can be no such thing as a divine plan for humanity, no such thing as humanity's basic "nature." If humankind has no purpose, the brutal fact must be faced that each of us is alone in an absurd situation.

Who can go on living with such a knowledge? Yet once we recognize the fundamental absurdity of our existence, we also recognize the basic premise of existentialism: People are completely free to define themselves as they wish, free to create their own reason for being:

> If man, as the existentialist conceives him, is indefinable, it is because at first he is nothing. Only afterward will he be something, and he himself will have made what he will be. Thus, there is no human nature, since there is no God to conceive it. Not only is man what he conceives himself to be, but he is also what he wills himself to be after this thrust toward existence.[5]

*For Kierkegaard . . . when one reached the point of absolute despair and felt ready to turn to God, one could take a "leap of faith."*

A person, says Sartre (1905-1980), has two and only two choices. He or she may accept the existential challenge, defining his or her own nature, creating his or her own identity, and taking responsibility for it; or else he or she may decline the challenge, remaining undefined, uncreated, unauthentic, and hence irresponsible. A person may remain a thing, instead of becoming a fully human being. In other words, to be human is to be authentic, to announce to all the world who and what we are and to be consistent with the identity we have developed. It must be added that as Sartre grew older, he became increasingly pessimistic about the willingness of the average person to accept the challenge. People, he believed, do not want to define their own natures because they do not want responsibility.

If we do attempt to become authentic, however, we run into the same problem as Kierkegaard's Christian existentialist; that is, we can never be completely sure of choosing rightly, or of choosing well. It is one thing to be free and responsible; it is another thing to have choices proven wise. But to become human, we must act from the full integrity of our defined being and then hope for the best.

For this reason, existential choice is filled with anguish for the chooser. An existentialist ship's officer, faced with the awful decision of having to kill people or risk sinking the lifeboat (see the preceding section), might decide to shoot certain people in cold blood. But he would not be able to argue later that he had been a victim of circumstances. He would have to admit responsibility for his actions.

*As Sartre grew older, he became pessimistic about the willingness of the average person to accept the challenge. People, he believed, do not want to define their own natures because they do not want the responsibility.*

## Existentialism Revisited

Existentialism swept over the philosophical world in the 1940s like a cyclone. It had been around since Kierkegaard in the nineteenth century, and possibly long before that. Some have even claimed Socrates was the first existentialist, arguing that the Greek philosopher was, after all, talking about personal integrity and bearing responsibility for one's actions—the same message Sartre was delivering to the World War II generation. The European philosophical world was, however, ready in the 1940s for a system of thought that was rooted in the self—something almost buried in the debris of bombed-out cities—and in the idea of freedom—something Europe had nearly lost. Both sides of the Atlantic were ready for a system of thought that seemed to promise that people of vision and integrity could, if they chose, create a new and brighter future.

Moral philosophers, however, have tended to be wary of existentialism, though a new, solid basis for morality was exactly what the philosophy promised. One person may say, "You reneged on a verbal agreement. That's wrong." The other may say, "Not according to *my* set of values."

In the world of human relationships, existentialism seems to fail. Sartre himself was hardly a model individual. His biographies show us a man who could use people rather ruthlessly, who permitted no criticism of himself or his work, and who often rushed into print information about other people without carefully checking his facts. Yet, say his critics, a profound moral philosophy is supposed to assist one in handling relationships with integrity, with *authenticity*.

Sartre does talk a great deal about the "other"—the non-me with a different set of values—and the difficulties these "others" create. His critics ask how we

*Can one who creates his own values do anything at all that is morally wrong?*

   *Dagfinn Follesdal*

can possibly have a world of "others" in which everyone is both free and responsible. In Sartre's most famous play, *No Exit* (1944), occurs the ringing line "Hell is other people." This line recognizes the agony of trying to keep oneself pure and whole in the midst of conflicting egos. But must one thus retreat to a desert island and have no relationships of any kind?

Sartre believed that the shame and guilt each of us experienced from having treated someone else badly would act as a check against the danger of unbridled freedom. This resembles the Judeo-Christian idea of conscience, with one important difference: In Sartre there is no God to take note of what we have done. It is up to the individual to decide whether his or her actions have truly hurt another, and so one can always decide that the hurt did not really take place. Dagfinn Follesdal, a Norwegian philosopher and a critic of Sartre, puts the matter in this way: "Can one who creates his own values do anything at all that is morally wrong?"[6]

> *If we're all free, why can't we handle our relationships better than Sartre says we can?*
>
> *Carlin Romano*

## Epilogue: On Making Moral Judgments

Looking back, one might well come to the conclusion that the morality issue is hopelessly complex, that unless one is driven by a fervent belief in the moral law of a strong religion or by the uncompromising zeal to crusade for a better world, one is left with personal moral choices among a bewildering variety of options. If so, why bother looking at moral philosophies at all? Why bother *having* a set of moral values if one cannot be sure that others are living by the same rules?

There is no simple answer. One possible reason is that we are going to make moral judgments *anyway*, and many of these are going to motivate actions towards others. The rational path would seem to be that of maintaining one's integrity, that is, adopting a moral code that is meaningful and then standing by it in all instances. No small task! Day-to-day living involves us in moral perplexities at every turn. Avoiding hypocrisy is like sailing through iceberg-packed waters.

For example, what happens when individuals of moral integrity perceive something very wrong in the workplace? In calling attention to it, they become *whistle-blowers*, a species often despised in bureaucracies. They put their jobs on the line and risk the scorn (or worse, the pity) of fellow employees. Thus such individuals often remain silent or are ignored—with disastrous results.

Following the Challenger space shuttle disaster in 1986, NASA revealed that they had had early warnings that the spacecraft might not be safe. The effect of unusually cold weather on the shuttle's O-rings (which led to the disaster) was either known about and overlooked or dismissed as the nervous objections of unnecessarily worried maintenance personnel and administrators. The decision was made not to delay blast-off any longer for fear of losing public interest, vital to the funding of government projects.

Another recent case involved the manager of a company who would, from time to time, set aside a certain amount of food for donation to his favorite charity. The assistant manager reported him to company superiors. There was an investigation, and the manager was discharged. His replacement heard the story, and, within a short time after taking over, discharged the whistle-blower himself. "I know what you did to the other manager," he said, "and it's not going to happen to me." A lawsuit resulted, as the former assistant manager tried to get his job back. One of the charges against him had been that he acted out of self-interest rather than for the good of the company when he had reported his original manager. It alleged that he had wanted the manager out of the way so that *he* would eventually be promoted to the job. (Apparently the belief in self-interest as the only source of action can be so strong that even an apparently moral act becomes suspect.) The case is pending. Whether or not the assistant manager is ever reinstated, his case illustrates the trouble that whistle-blowers bring on themselves in their efforts to do "good." Even the term *do-gooder* is often mentioned with cynical derision.

Those who deride the whistle-blowers on the grounds that such practices are not in anyone's best interest are, whether they know it or not, saying that moral values are entirely subjective. In such a view, moral values need not be the basis for an action, and in fact they are not worth having at all, since no one is going to live by them.

In *The Closing of the American Mind*, the American thinker Allan Bloom claims that the source of our moral confusion is the state of education today. It has become so permissive that students leave school believing that all values are "up to the individual"—a theme that became popular in the nonfiction of the 1970s. By now, Bloom says, a kind of arrogant stupidity has spread like cancer throughout this nation.

The philosopher Hannah Arendt (1906-1975) was an interpreter of the moral tragedy known as the *holocaust*. She attributes this horrible event to an extreme moral relativism that became institutionalized and then militarized when the Nazis tried to see that their standards would prevail. Yet is this not what happens when any group takes a gun to society on the grounds that they are victim of the wrong moral code, which must be avenged in terms of *theirs*?

We are certainly not suggesting a return to a condition of moral absolutism, for then there arises the question of *whose* absolutes to return to and how are they to be enforced. An underlying premise of this book is the right of the individual to make personal choices among significant options, based on critical thought. Perhaps the risk of running afoul of someone else's different moral code, enforced by bully tactics, is simply a part of the human condition. Even so, the risk does not necessarily justify the abandonment of integrity. If we do that, we shall have lost far more than we can gain; we shall have lost the human tradition.

## Glossary

*absolute:* An eternal, unchanging truth or value that supposedly holds for all people in all cultures and in all periods of time.

*categorical imperative:* An inborn condition of the mind that Kant believed determined everyone's knowledge of right and wrong.

*existentialism:* A philosophy that stresses both the necessity and the anguish of choice as well as the need to assume full responsibility for the consequences of choice. The freedom to choose is both the glory and the burden of the human race.

*hedonic calculus:* Jeremy Bentham's application of strict mathematical values to actions giving either pleasure or pain. By using it, the state, he believed, could determine "the greatest good for the greatest number."

*moral:* A word referring to a choice among

significant options, the outcome of which will either benefit or harm others. Thus, a moral *problem* precedes a significant choice, and a moral *dilemma* occurs when one is caught between equally desirable (or undesirable) alternatives.

*morality:* A set of values (whether derived from reason, religion, family, peer group, education, state, or some other source) that serves as the philosophical basis for making important choices.

*situationalist:* One who believes that all actions are to be evaluated in relation to motivation and consequences and that the validity of choice in one situation may not apply in another.

*utilitarianism:* A nineteenth-century school of philosophy that holds that the pursuit of pleasure is the natural goal of human life. Since no one can have unlimited pleasure without interfering with the rights of others, however, some system of curbs is absolutely necessary. Utilitarians were early proponents of civil rights in their belief that no government should interfere with a person's promotion of legal means to achieve a good life.

## Notes

1. Robert Paul Wolff, *About Philosophy*, 3d ed. (Englewood Cliffs, N.J.: Prentice-Hall, 1986), 66–67.
2. Isabel Allende, *Of Love and Shadows*, tr. Margaret Sayers Peden (New York: Knopf, 1987), 115.
3. Ibid., 116.
4. Entry for August 24, 1932, in Mahadev Desai, *The Diary of Mahadev Desai*, 308–309, included in *The Essential Gandhi*, ed. Louis Fischer (New York: Random House, 1962).

5. Jean-Paul Sartre, *Existentialism and Human Emotions*, tr. Bernard Frechtman (New York: Philosophical Library, 1947), 15.
6. Dagfinn Follesdal, "Sartre Imitates Life," *The Village Voice Literary Supplement*, November 1987, 15.

## Suggested Reading

Arendt, Hannah. *The Recovery of the Public World*, ed. Melvyn A. Hill. New York: St. Martin's Press, 1979. A series of essays on aspects of Arendt's work, including her assessment of the Nazi war criminal Adolf Eichmann during the time he was on trial in Jerusalem.

Bloom, Allan. *The Closing of the American Mind*. New York: Simon & Schuster, 1987. The work that caused a storm of controversy by indicting the American educational system for feeding students platitudes about the relativism of all values.

Camus, Albert. *The Myth of Sisyphus and Other Essays*. New York: Modern Library, 1948. A lucid presentation of existential thought by one of its most cogent proponents.

_____. *The Plague*. New York: Alfred A. Knopf, 1955. A story of the ethical positions an atheistic physician assumes as he battles a fearsome epidemic.

Coles, Robert. *Privileged Ones: The Well-Off and the Rich in America*. Boston: Little, Brown, 1977. Dr. Coles, a noted modern thinker, investigates the source of moral values in affluent children.

Kierkegaard, Søren. *Fear and Trembling* and *Sickness unto Death*. Garden City, N.Y.: Doubleday & Co., 1954. The first of these two essays contains the author's famous treatise about Abraham's moral dilemma.

Plato. *The Republic*, tr. Francis MacDonald Cornford. London: Oxford University Press, 1945. This famous dialogue appears in various editions, but this translation is recommended. Chapter 5 of Part II is of special interest because it contains "The Ring of Gyges."

Watts, Harold H. *The Modern Reader's Guide to the Bible*. New York: Harper & Brothers, 1959. This guide contains scholarship that deals with the Bible as a work of literature evolving over a period of time.

*Sesshu Toyo,* Landscape *(1495) (Tokyo National Museum)*

# 8

# *Western Territory,*
# *Eastern Space*

## Overview

In the preceding two chapters we examined the role of the philosopher and looked at some key philosophical questions, particularly those that involve the moral life. Since the discussion moved about a good deal in time, we assume that by now you recognize the importance of historical context. In other words, while some of the issues we have dealt with have remained viable over many centuries, their focus and the conclusions about them differ from one historical period to another.

Beliefs and issues must be placed in *geographical* as well as historical contexts, especially the two major geographical contexts of "East" and "West." The ideas, assumptions, and value systems with which we have been thus far concerned can be called "Western," if only because they belong to philosophical traditions that can be traced from major centers in the United States and Europe back to their origins in the Greek and Roman worlds.

*Some Typically "Western" Beliefs*

*The importance of the individual*

*The reality of ideas*

*The desirability of owning things*

Despite the changes in emphasis that historical context discloses, there are several assumptions that run through time in the West. One is the importance of the *individual*, a word that often means in philosophy the soul, the self, the mind, the intellect. Even the generic term *reason* is usually rooted in an individual's rational processes used to reach some conclusions. We also think about the personal soul, self, mind, or intellect as a definite entity inside us with the same tangible reality as, say, the heart or the lungs. Psychoanalysis, for example, is a distinctly Western invention. The psychoanalyst diagnoses the ills of an individual's *psyche* (Greek for "soul"), as the physician diagnoses the ailments of the body.

A second and intricately related assumption in the West is that since the mind is a solid entity, its products, which we may call thoughts, ideas, concepts, principles, and so on, also have a certain kind of solidity. In short, *ideas are real*.

Despite the centuries-old tradition of Judeo-Christian thought focused on God, the fact remains that Western values are generally rooted in the material world and in the importance of understanding, shaping, and owning that world. After all, if we have no part in divine substance, how can we be *realistically* concerned about it?

Central to the lives of most Westerners is the importance of possessing material objects—farms, animals, other people, coins, jewels, machines, etc.—and, by inevitable association, the reputation that goes along with having things. The possessors are admired and respected, not merely for the power they display, but for the things their success makes possible.

None of what we have just said is meant to imply that people in the East do not care about possessions or that they do not believe in the self or the reality of thoughts. We live, as Marshall McLuhan informed us several decades ago, in a "global village," that is, on a planet where distances keep shrinking and where people can interact in a matter of milliseconds.

Does the fact of our living in a global village therefore obliterate the importance of geographical context? The answer is no. Do "East" and "West" still have meaning as points of reference? The answer is decidedly yes. We can see the differences in so simple and straightforward an example as an automobile factory in Japan, where so-called quality control is maintained by making the ultimate product more important than the worker's "self." The product, further, is admired for its overall excellence and esthetic beauty, though it is also created to be exported to the West in order to satisfy someone's need for ownership.

Fortunately, the reduction in our world's size gives us options in the ways we can live our lives. Tokyo has made so much money from Western obsessions that it is beginning to look more like New York, and Western popular music and fashions are almost obsessions there. Conversely, if you have the money, you can find an architect to design a house with teakwood furniture, rice-paper sliding doors, and a lily pond. In some areas of the United States—notably northern California and Colorado—serious interest in Oriental religions, customs, and values is growing. In particular, interest in Buddhism has grown.

## Buddhism: Religion or Philosophy?

Chapter 6, "Western Philosophy," often dealt with religious writers and religious viewpoints. Augustine and Thomas Aquinas are important philosophers in the history of Western thought, and they are also saints in the Catholic religious tradition. Their ideas and their reasoning processes were brought to bear on philosophical problems arising from their religion. Augustine, for example, wrestled with the question "If God is all good, why is there evil in the world?" Aquinas said faith is not enough; we should be able to prove that God exists through logic. Thomism, the name given to his philosophy and its logical methods, is not a religion, though it has led and will continue to lead many *to* religion.

Buddhism is often referred to as the dominant religion of the Far East. In our country Buddhist temples are generally looked upon as churches and their members are accorded the same right of separation from the state given to churches and worshippers of Western religions.

Buddhism *is* a religion to the extent that it often involves certain rituals practiced in places appropriately designated and held sacred, and it has an ancient tradition of belief that unifies those people born into it or choosing to follow its principles. Buddhism also has a system of moral values binding on all its practitioners. (For example, it encourages a vegetarian diet because of its respect for all life.) Its doctrine of egolessness manifests itself in a helping network within each Buddhist community—or *sangha*—quite similar to the charity groups at work within most religious sects.

It has monasteries as well as priests and nuns, who were often persecuted during the Communist conquests earlier in this century. In Marxist fashion, Asian Communists regarded Buddhism as a religion and therefore dangerous to the social state. During the conquests both priests and nuns frequently martyred themselves (usually by burning themselves to death) to protest the closing of the temples and the monasteries and the outlawing of public rituals.

Yet Buddhism is *not* a religion like Islam, Judaism, and Christianity, because it has no principle of godhead. Its dominant ritual—meditation, or the act of sitting quietly without any particular object—resembles prayer, but is not prayer. Buddhist meditation is a technique for gaining an intense awareness of the subtleties of the present moment; for understanding the pattern of inner sensations, thoughts, and emotions that separate us from the reality of human experience; and for cultivating a wakeful state in which one is in direct contact with that reality. There is no transcendent god with whom to communicate.

Buddhist meditation helps to detach one from a sense of self. If one acquires the discipline of sitting for long enough stretches of time, one gradually loses the sense of being a solid, separate, isolated individual. To the Buddhist, self is an illusion. We are sensations, thoughts, and feelings that drift in and out of consciousness. There is no bounded entity inside each of us, except one that we pretend is there if we accept the myth of the self.

Of course, there might be nothing wrong with believing that each of us has a personal identity that is clearly distinct and more important than all others *if* such a belief made us happy and responsible. Fundamental to Buddhism is the conviction that the myth of self is responsible for most of our suffering and for our unethical behavior.

In this chapter we are concerned with Buddhism as a dominant mode of Eastern thought, for all of the behavior we recognize as Buddhist rises from a philosophy. That philosophy offers a view of reality, of the mind, of the "self," and of what constitutes the best way to live. Above all, that philosophy is very different from the characteristically Western belief in the predominant importance of the individual self and its actualization as well as the Western tendency to place a high premium on individual achievement and the tangible rewards it brings.

*Buddhism is a religion to the extent that it involves certain rituals and has priests and nuns. It is not a religion like Islam, Judaism, and Christianity, because it has no principle of godhead.*

*Buddhism believes that no one is a solid, separate, isolated individual, but the myth of the self is responsible for most of our suffering.*

Seated Buddha: *A typical statue of Buddha. (Seattle Art Museum, Eugene Fuller Memorial Collection)*

## The Buddha

For most Westerners unfamiliar with Buddhist lore, Buddha (without the article *the*) appears to be a god. They know that throughout the Orient one finds temples with many statues of "Buddha," who is often depicted as a very fat man sitting in the lotus position with his eyes closed and an expression of great peace on his face. Documentaries about Eastern religion often show thousands of people engaged in what looks like prayer in front of an altar or shrine.

Meditation practiced in a temple before a shrine that contains a statue or painting of *the* Buddha is, in fact, a centuries-old ritual. It is intended to free the self as well as to pay homage to the timeless wisdom (or enlightenment) that, it is believed, was attained by a prince named Siddhartha Gautama, who lived in India around 500 B.C., roughly a hundred years before the death of Socrates. Reaching enlightenment made Siddhartha worthy of the title of "the Buddha," which in Sanskrit means "the one who is awake."

According to many historians, Siddhartha was a prince of the Brahmin caste, the very highest social class in the Hindu system of rigidly separated castes. He had immeasurable wealth, a beautiful wife, a handsome son, and many servants who cared for the family in a resplendent palace. He was the epitome of what we in the West regard as a successful man.

Siddhartha was educated in the tradition of Hindu thought, but there was one Hindu belief that gradually came to make less and less sense to him: reincarnation. According to that doctrine, when people passed from this present life, their accumulated *karma*, or moral debts, made it necessary for them to be reborn in a different body. In the new body they would have the opportunity to pay off those debts—in short, to live a better, more ethical life. If one's karma were excessive, one would be reborn into a lower social class. If one's moral debts were light, one would move up the ladder. The lowest social class was inhabited by the diseased, wretched, homeless people known as "the untouchables." The highest caste belonged to the Brahmins, the aristocratic order of people who were considered holy because they were closest to enlightenment. If one died a morally pure Brahmin, one was then eligible to enter the state known as *nirvana*, which was not a heaven (though many Hindus probably did and still do regard it as such) but a condition of eternal oneness with the soul of the universe, free of all pain and unfulfilled desires. One never had to be reborn again.

What troubled Siddhartha was the paradox of his own life. If he were a Brahmin and presumably one step away from nirvana, why was he so unhappy? Why did his pleasure-filled existence seem such a waste of time? How could he have lived before in a *worse* state than he was in now? And if a prince with unlimited wealth and a beautiful wife was restless and bored, who indeed was happy? What was bliss, after all? Should he not be able to have at least a glimpse of what was in store for him?

Perhaps his discontent, Siddhartha thought, indicated that he was not yet ready to take the next step. If so, he might have to be reborn into a lower class and thus prolong his dreary, unhappy lot. He was familiar with the belief that some people take thousands of years to attain nirvana. The only ray of hope—and it was a slim one—was the Hindu scriptural prophecy of the Buddha: Every eon—or roughly twenty-five thousand years—there would be born a perfect individual who would reach nirvana after only one lifetime. This was the Buddha: He who is awake, who fully and profoundly realizes the full potential of being human.

Unable to find peace and happiness at home, Siddhartha left his wife and son and embarked on a long search, without knowing what he was looking for or what he might find. At first, he tried the life of a hermit, eating, so legend has it, one sesame seed a day, spending his hours in intense thought. All he found was further confusion. He grew thin, emaciated, and weak.

At length he resolved to seek a middle way between the two extremes of total materialism, his former life, and total asceticism, his present life. After restoring himself to health, he continued his wandering, still sick at heart. The explanation given by Buddhists for Siddhartha's unhappy state at this time is that the prince was experiencing the profound despair of having been caught up in *samsara*, Sanskrit for the general futility of a life lived for the satisfaction of momentary desires. But where was another kind of life? And how could one find it?

One day, so the story goes, Siddhartha sat to rest under a rose apple, or Bodhi, tree. After a while he became increasingly and vividly conscious of his surroundings. Little by little the torment he was feeling inside began to slip away. As his ego awareness vanished, his awareness of reality—*everything exactly as it was*—became sharper and a deep peace came over him. Some say he sat there, totally wakeful, for 40 days and nights.

Hindu tradition taught that the coming of the Buddha—a totally enlightened human being—had been foretold for thousands of years, in the same way, for example, that the Old Testament foretold the coming of a messiah. Siddhartha had been destined for his transformation from birth, though he became aware of it only during his meditation under the Bodhi tree. While he sat there, wondrous things supposedly took place:

*Siddhartha was caught up in* samsara, *which means the general futility of a life lived for the satisfaction of momentary desires.*

*The coming of the Buddha was prophesied in Hindu scripture: he would be a human being able to attain nirvana in one lifetime.*

Mandarava flowers and lotus blossoms, and also water lilies made of gold and beryl, fell from the sky onto the ground near the Shakya sage,[1] so that it looked like a place in the world of the gods. At that moment no one anywhere was angry, ill, or sad; no one was evil, none was proud; the world became quite quiet, as though it had reached full perfection.[2]

The reference to "the gods" is wrapped up in Buddhist folklore; the gods are a throwback to Hindu mythology. *Buddhism*, the philosophy that grew out of the teachings of Siddhartha, has no central god figure, but it does have symbolic deities that symbolize states of mind. The anonymous author of the preceding passage knew no other way to describe the phenomenon of the enlightenment.

Other stories indicate that evil demons attempted to distract the Buddha during the long sitting, to prevent the enlightenment from taking place. In any event, it *did* happen. Thoroughly immersed in the world as it really was, he realized that self and separateness were illusions. Without the barrier of inner thoughts and emotions, he became part of all he saw around him. He experienced the unity of all being. He had, in short, attained nirvana, and as the prophesied Buddha, he had accomplished this feat in one lifetime.

When Siddhartha finally arose from his long meditation, he did so because he had decided not to remain in nirvana, which he could have claimed as his right, but to go out into the world to share with others what he had discovered: the path to enlightenment. And so began Buddhism, the philosophy of the path. The very first way in which it was to differ from Hinduism was in its teaching that the nearly endless cycle of death and reincarnation was not essential, that one could, like Siddhartha, find peace at virtually any time. Above all, it taught that Buddhahood was not a condition reserved for only one special person every twenty-five thousand years.

*According to legend, the Buddha could have entered the blissful state of nirvana and stayed there forever. But he chose not to; he chose to go among the people and show them the path to bliss.*

## The Dharma

The Buddha went among the people and taught them how to live. What he told them constitutes the *dharma*, or the way. Central to his teachings is the denial of an absolute self or personhood.

*Egolessness*, as Buddhists call the condition of being nonseparate, is neither self-sacrifice nor loving one's neighbor as oneself. It is the belief that nobody is a "me" enduring through time as an unchanging central core. A contemporary Buddhist philosopher explains:

A man does not have a core or a soul which he can consider to be his true self. A man exists, but he cannot grasp his real being—he cannot discover his own core, because the existence of a man is nothing but an "existence depending on a series of causations." Everything that exists is there because of causations; it will disappear when the effects of the causations cease.

The waves on the water's surface certainly exist, but can it be said that a wave has its own self? Waves exist only while there is wind or current. Each wave has its own characteristics according to the combination of causations—the intensity of the winds and currents and their directions, etc. But when the effects of the causations cease,

> the waves are no more. Similarly, there cannot be a self which exists
> independent of causations.
>
> As long as a man is an existent depending on a series of causations, it
> is unreasonable for him to try to hold on to himself and to regard all
> things around him from the self-centered point of view.[3]

The Buddha recognized that what is usually called the "inner self" is made
up solely of thoughts and feelings that come and go. Take away the causation, and
the self disappears. By extending this logic, we see that if we are not chained to
causations, we will not be chained to an idea of self. The self can be known only
when these thought processes—these reactions to causations—are happening.
But if the thoughts themselves become transparent, so does the self.

One of our thoughts concerns this very impermanence. Fundamentally we
recognize how fleeting and how unstable the self can be. It is discontinuous, and
in the gaps "we" disappear. To resist such discontinuousness, the illusion known
as ego is created. It too is a thought, an idea; it is a reaction to a causation, namely,
the fear of nonexistence. To sustain the illusion, thoughts keep generating themselves. Buddhists call this "mind chatter." We are afraid to let it stop, for then the
sense of self fades.

To most of us in the West the very idea of letting go of the sense of self is
unthinkable, even insane. If we think of the pain and torment we experience

*Utagawa Kuniyoshi*, River Between High Banks in the Rain *(19th c.): A wave has no
self. It exists only when there is wind or current. (The Metropolitan Museum of Art,
Rogers Fund, 1936)*

when, say, an all-consuming love has fizzled out, we say that pain is happening to an "us." The Buddhist would say, however, that the "us" is the very *reason* for the pain to begin with!

Pain, resulting from the myth of ego, became for the Buddha the fundamental roadblock to nirvana. Thus did he teach what he called the *four noble truths*:

Life is filled with pain.
Pain is caused by the need to possess.
There is a way out of pain.
The way to nirvana is the eightfold path.

The *eightfold path* is the middle way the Buddha had sought for so long a time. It is divided into the fundamental segments of each person's life, which need to be approached without ego. These segments are

| | |
|---|---|
| Right views | Right livelihood |
| Right intentions | Right effort |
| Right speech | Right mindfulness |
| Right conduct | Right concentration |

If one were able to sit (or meditate) continuously, there would be no need for the eightfold path, or indeed for the four noble truths. The problem of pain begins when one rises from the Bodhi tree, so to speak, and becomes immersed once more in the commerce of everyday life, the world of samsara. Then does the cycle of cause and effect start all over. One reinvents the myth of ego and becomes defensive, aggressive, and covetous.

One cannot avoid samsara. One can, however, carry the sitting attitude into the cycle of human affairs. That is the meaning of the eightfold path. *Right* means "intelligent"—doing all things with the understanding that the self is not a sacred, indivisible entity. The last component of the path is concentration, which refers to the sitting attitude, and is by far the most important element. To retain the sitting attitude is to be not a self existing continuously, but an impersonal intelligence operating appropriately.

Because of the illusion of ego, say the Buddhists, we face the world with illusory expectations. Most of the time the events we experience are not what we want to happen according to the false picture of the world we nourish inside. Instead of allowing impersonal intelligence to observe what is actually the case, we attempt to manipulate reality so that it agrees with our false picture.

Intelligence sees that ego always acts out of self-interest. It decries such actions, for since the self is an illusion, there can be no such thing as self-interest. It is insane to behave out of illusory motives. No sane result can take place. This, the Buddhists tell us, explains why the world is always in a state of chaos. *There are simply too many conflicting illusions serving as the basis for what people do.*

According to *Buddha-dharma* (or the way of the awakened), seeing through the illusions of ego will reveal compassion as a fundamental fact of existence. This does not mean feeling sorry for others. Pity is very often a subtle action of ego; it bolsters our illusion of a positive self to believe that others are going to pieces. The nature of *compassion* is described by one American Buddhist practitioner as follows:

*The present world atmosphere is not healthy. Things are decided by force, guns and money.*

*The Dalai Lama*

*We have been convinced that we are free and independent agents and yet, the very agent referred to is actually a social role that is defined by other people and has no real freedom to act at all.*

*R. H. Blyth*

It's not really a question of the need for compassion, but in fact when there's no demand, only then can real compassion take place. Actual compassion is based on a person's ability first of all to be clear about what's going on in a situation: what's going on with his own energy, his own desires, his own uncertainties as well as those of other people. When he sees those things clearly, then spontaneously he does what is appropriate to the situation. This is the real meaning of compassion.[4]

As we meditate and understand the patterns of the mind, we become more and more even-handed about not only our own processes but about those of other people as well. We recognize with ever-deepening insight what drives others to say or do certain things. It is not a matter of forgiving and forgetting, nor of turning the other cheek. We merely withhold judgment and respond intelligently.

*The world is always in a state of chaos because there are too many conflicting illusions serving as the basis for what people do.*

The foregoing represents an interpretation of Buddha-dharma by many contemporary practitioners of Buddhism, particularly those psychologists who believe Siddhartha Gautama, the Buddha, was able to reach a state of total mental health resulting from a total contact with reality, unobstructed by the barrier of the self.

The eightfold path leads not to riches, happiness, or personal satisfaction. In the contemporary psychological view of Buddhism, these goals cause continual frustration. When we move toward total contact with reality, we are also moving beyond personal goals. Buddhists do not believe that life is *supposed* to yield dividends. Life is simply what it is—to be taken as it unfolds.

If, however, we insist upon a reward, we could say that in overcoming self-preoccupation, we are spared the suffering caused by the conflict between reality and the desires of self. But contemporary Buddhists caution us not to suppose that theirs is a dry retreat from the world. They insist that what is gained is a continual delight in experiencing the dance of life.

## Tibetan and Zen Buddhism

Since its founding twenty-five centuries ago, Buddhism has split into many sects. They all share a fundamental acceptance of the eightfold path, but they differ with respect to ritual and practice. Two of the most prominent sects in the United States are Tibetan Buddhism and Zen Buddhism.

*In Buddhism a sense of delight accompanies the experience of life.*

### The Tibetan Tradition

Tibetan Buddhism has emphasized the Buddha's decision not to enter nirvana but to remain in the world to guide others. It is based on the concept of the living, ongoing Buddha-mind, as opposed to a centralized homage to the historical Buddha. Siddhartha Gautama was, we might say, a role model of the totally aware human being. In this respect, the Tibetan school appears most congenial to the concerns of psychology.

This school also places great importance on and devoutly honors the transmission of wisdom from one generation to another through the lineage of enlightened beings. In Tibetan Buddhism one seeks a teacher who either belongs to this lineage or who has been trained by someone who does; the teacher becomes a lifelong friend and confidant. One identifies with the mind of the teacher and is perpetually guided by it along the path of life.

*Buddhism is not a dry retreat from the world.*

Tibetan Buddhism can be considered somewhat more democratic than the mainstream Buddhism of Asia, in which homage to the historical founder gives to the practice features in common with other world religions, such as Judaism, Islam, and Christianity. Mainstream Buddhism may well have lost sight of the promise in ancient Hindu scriptures that at the end of each eon a new Buddha will appear. Siddhartha Gautama was, in this sense, the "most recent" Buddha.

In the view of Tibetan Buddhism there will continue to be more Buddhas, just as there are now on earth many *bodhisattvas* (those who are destined for enlightenment). Each generation, as a matter of fact, produces a hierarchy of bodhisattvas, beginning with the recognized Dalai Lama. The term *Dalai* means "the sea—measureless and profound." (A *lama* is a teacher of Tibetan Buddhism.)

The Dalai Lama's position is not inherited. It is not passed down from generation to generation in the same family. The incarnation of the Dalai Lama for each age must be discovered by means of an elaborate ritual:

> The first step is to find out from the State Oracle the locality in which the Dalai Lama has reincarnated. As soon as this important fact is known, search parties, which have been selected by lot or by the State Oracle, are sent out. On the basis of their reports the government draws up a list of possible candidates. In the meantime, the Regent of Tibet visits the sacred lake believed to be the abode of the Goddess Kali—for she appeared to the first Dalai Lama and solemnly vowed to watch over all his successors—and there he sees in the depths of the lake a vision indicating the location of the Dalai Lama's new birthplace.[5]

But the Dalai Lama is not the only bodhisattva in each age. In Tibetan belief there can be a number of others, some totally unrecognized, living in humble circumstances and dedicating their lives to guiding others along the spiritual path to enlightenment.

The bodhisattvas are regarded as potential Buddhas at the middle stage of the way to enlightenment. But even having reached a middle stage in the progress toward spiritual perfection is awe-inspiring; thus the bodhisattvas earn the highest possible praise and respect from their followers.

Implicit in Tibetan Buddhism is a hierarchy of persons, arranged according to their proximity to the ultimate goal, which is the full incarnation of Buddhahood. A lama is a bodhisattva and also a *guru*, or holy teacher. There are many gurus, and not all of them become lamas. But even so, the guru is a very special, very fundamental unit in Tibetan Buddhism.

The Tibetan tradition stresses the *sangha*, or community (though all Buddhist strains recognize the importance of the fellowship of meditators). Without the community, meditators run the risk of being overwhelmed by space long before coming close to their goal.

## The Legendary Origins of Zen

Zen Buddhism is that strain of the parent philosophy that has come to be most closely associated with Japan. It originated in India at the same time as Buddhism itself. In the beginning it was that aspect of Buddhism intensively concerned with meditation and the techniques one must acquire to master it. Its name stems from the Chinese word for meditation: *Ch'an*.

The founding of the Zen tradition as a specific school of Buddhism with its own rituals, methods of sitting, and folklore is attributed to an Indian monk named Bodhidharma. A thousand years after the enlightenment, Bodhidharma traveled to China with the missionary zeal to win converts to the Buddha's teachings, described in the following passage. Zen legend sometimes adds the awesome story of how Bodhidharma sat so still for a full nine years that his legs fell off, thus demonstrating in somewhat hyperbolic terms the tremendous importance of the sitting practice in the Zen tradition.

*Zen meditation is very long and sometimes very painful. In a very real sense Zen intelligence begins in the buttocks and works its way slowly upwards.*

> Obeying the instruction of Prajnatara, his teacher, Bodhidharma started for the East and arrived in China in 520 A.D. The Emperor Wu-ti invited him to Nanking for an audience. The Emperor said: "Since my enthronement, I have built many monasteries, copied many holy writings and invested many priests and nuns. How great is the merit due to me?" "No merit at all," was the answer. "What is the Noble Truth in its highest sense?" "It is empty, no nobility whatever." "Who is it then that is facing me?" "I do not know, Sire." The Emperor could not understand him.[6]

This anecdote demonstrates the traditional Zen delight in indirection, whimsy, and cryptic utterances. Of all the schools in Buddhism, Zen has become the most systematically devoted to the transcendence of not only ego but of the rational process as well. It views pure intelligence as something greater than rational knowledge. This intelligence is arrived at through the intuition that comes only after years and years of steadfast, disciplined meditation. In a very real sense Zen intelligence begins in the buttocks and works its way slowly upwards.

## Zen Today

Complex historical currents carried the Zen school from China to Japan, where it eventually found a lasting home. To explain how and why this happened would require a detailed analysis of the Japanese character and way of life, both of which have found in Zen a most congenial practice. We do not have space for such an analysis here, but we can make a few points.

For example, the Japanese have traditionally exhibited a strong feeling for the beautiful, especially the delicately, exquisitely beautiful. Graceful movement and hand gestures in drama, dance, and puppetry are prime examples of the Japanese esthetic bent. The Japanese delight in taking that which can be clumsy and graceless and making it fluid and rhythmic. They delight in fine craftwork—in the tiny brush strokes of the painter's art or the intricacies of the carver's art. In short, the Japanese prize all artistic expression that can be achieved only after long years of often painful discipline. Discipline and form are quintessential to the Japanese, and of all the schools of Buddhism, Zen is probably the most formal and the most disciplined.

*The traditional Japanese sense of the beautiful as well as the profound silences of Zen meditation must now compete with the modern Japan of automobiles, electronics, and the most crowded mass transportation system in the world.*

Of course, the traditional Japanese sense of the beautiful as well as the profound silences of Zen meditation must now compete with the modern Japan of automobiles, electronics, and the fastest-moving, most crowded mass transportation

*Tea ceremony water jar (late 16th c.): The Japanese delight in fine craftwork. (Hatakeyama Memorial Museum, Tokyo)*

system in the world. Amid these hectic surroundings, ancient Japanese customs sometimes gasp for air.

Still, the centuries-old influence of Zen has not totally disappeared. There are the martial arts: judo, karate, and aikido, for example. They teach one—through long and painful discipline—to protect the body when necessary but not to be aggressive. Like all forms of life, the body is sacred; the ego is not. Not surprisingly, martial arts are becoming popular in the United States, which has seized upon their competitive possibilities. The original meaning of *karate* is, however, "open palm," a meaning consistent with the open position of the hands during meditation and one that can suggest nonaggressiveness.

Family honor remains central in Japanese thinking. This sense of honor sometimes motivates such acts as suicide, resorted to by many who fail to be accepted to a prestigious university or who fall short in the business world. Suicide has long been accepted by Japanese society as the dignified way to save a family the embarrassment of having a failure in its midst.

This stress on the family gives evidence that ego and personal reputation are generally not as important to the Japanese as they are to Americans. Indeed, one cannot imagine a less gratifying prospect to the ego than the admission of failure and the willingness to do the expected thing for the sake *not* of oneself but of others. In this sense, family honor is analogous to the handed-down wisdom— the lineage—in Buddhist traditions. The Japanese regard for family is also similar to the Tibetan Buddhist regard for sangha, or community. In all cases, the personal self is dwarfed by much larger considerations.

The full and devoted practice of Zen is, however, accomplished by the individual, who, whether in solitude or in community, must learn through long months and years of sitting to become detached from the foolishness of the everyday world. The practitioner also becomes detached from the self. Zen masters are the sternest of all gurus, believing that other Buddhist sects are too free with the word *enlightenment*. Sitting for as long as 12 hours at a time without stretching the legs or taking in sustenance of any kind is not an uncommon practice in a Zen monastery or in the *zendo*, a community of persons voluntarily living under the same roof, practicing meditation, and sharing chores.

*Zen masters can be very rough indeed. An overseer who catches someone beginning to doze during meditation may take a long stick and strike the nodder soundly on the shoulders.*

Zen masters can be very rough indeed. There is always an overseer to the *zazen*, or sitting period; an overseer who catches someone beginning to doze may take a long stick and strike the nodder soundly on the shoulders.

The position of the Zen master is that the battle against ego is hard won, if at all, and that too many persons deceive themselves into supposing they are well on the way to nirvana when in fact they are proud as peacocks over their accomplishments. Such persons have come, in reality, not one step along the way.

Sitting in Zen is not intended to be exhilarating or relaxing or a positive spiritual experience of any kind, though many beginners, both here and in the Orient, probably hope it will be just that. The point of sitting for hours at a time is not to transcend the pain and the boredom until a state of euphoria is reached, but to confront that pain and boredom directly—to discover the void that underlies all existence. Zen masters know that beginners entertain themselves with mind chatter and so must keep sitting until they grow weary of entertaining themselves and are able to see the void for what it is. Only then have they begun to understand and free themselves from ego:

> The Zen tradition in Japan creates a definite style of boredom in its monasteries. Sit, cook, eat. Sit zazen and do your walking meditation and so on. . . . The black cushion is supposed to suggest no color, complete boredom.[7]

While Zen has become popular in certain parts of the United States, especially California, one of the most difficult tasks facing Americans who submit themselves to this rigorous discipline is the attainment of a passive willingness to do anything required, no matter how lowly and demeaning. In Zen, all tasks must be absolutely the same to the practitioner, whether he or she is asked to sweep the floor or carve a statue. Zen people cannot say, "But that's not my job" or "Do you know who I am?" An oft-repeated Zen maxim is "Wash your rice bowl," given as a terse reply to any objection based on self-interest.

Because of the emphasis on the destruction of ego, Zen masters can be biting and satiric, seizing every opportunity to deride, revile, and humiliate. They enjoy making students aware of their mind confusions, especially the absurdities and nonsequiturs in their conversation. On one occasion a group of American filmmakers visited a Zen master for the purpose of filming an interview. Tea and cakes were being served. One of the visitors bit into his cake and commented, "It doesn't have any sugar in it." The statement hung there in the room with nowhere to go, but a colleague came to the rescue: "Mine doesn't have any sugar either." The master, with a twinkle in his eye, bit into his own cake and said that it too was free of sugar, adding, "Why don't we go around the room and find out if anybody has a cake *with* sugar?" Nobody said anything. Nobody dared!

Zen has been called antirational, but this is not the case at all. It works against the chaos that passes for logical discourse. It seeks to empty the mind and allow the light of pure intellect to take over, intellect devoid of personal concerns.

Zen does not value language. It views language as a barrier between the intellect and reality. What really *is*, simply *is*—it has no name. Zen teachings are full of paradoxes and riddles, all of which stress the fact that the real truth is always staring people in the face but that they are too caught up in their own mind chatter to see it. For instance,

> Kassan had a monk who went round all the Zen temples but found nothing to suit him anywhere. The name of Kassan, however, was often mentioned to him from far and near as a great master, so he

*A monk said to Seppo, "I have shaved my head, put on black clothes, received the vows—why am I not to be considered a Buddha?" Seppo said, "There is nothing better than an absence of goodness."*

*A Zen master*

*Zen teaching often takes the form of riddles and paradoxes. Its point is to empty the mind of false and limiting logic and allow the light of pure intellect to take over.*

came back and interviewed Kassan, and said, "You have an especial understanding of Zen. How is it you didn't reveal this to me?" Kassan said, "When you boiled rice, didn't I light the fire? When you passed around the food, didn't I offer my bowl to you? When did I betray your expectations?" The monk was enlightened.[8]

But what is the truth? The Zen answer, typically cryptic, is, *If you have to ask, you will never understand it.* And yet the "truth that has no name" is also absurdly simple, perhaps best summed up in this simple line by the old Chinese sage Lao-Tzu: "Everything is what it is." There is just what happens—the flow of things—nothing more. It is to be observed with neither joy nor sorrow, without judgment, without analysis.

## The East in the West

To many Westerners the East probably remains remote and mysterious, a place unlikely to be visited, populated by beings difficult to comprehend. They may have acquired a few bits of information, but, likely as not, they cannot imagine themselves in any way involved in Eastern issues. As far as they are concerned, human existence begins and ends in their own backyard.

For others, however, Eastern modes of living hold genuine options. The Buddhist East is beginning to effect a radical change in the way some Americans live. There are American Buddhists—people born in Kansas as well as New York or California—gainfully employed and eminently functional in American society, commuting to work just like everybody else. In their homes, however, they have meditation rooms, lit by candlelight, where they sit in the lotus position for long periods and confront the stillness of things as they are. American Buddhists take strong issue with some Western values they find no longer acceptable.

### Success and Failure

Prominent among these values is the polarization of success and failure. This either/or proposition has blighted many worthy lives for a long time. For all too many, the perception of their worth can take place only within the parameters preordained by society. Evaluating oneself as being close to or far from "success" becomes ultimately a lifelong obsession.

What is worse, the definition of "success" keeps changing as we advance even closer to "the goal." One must keep getting ahead, moving always upwards from one plateau to another. It is difficult, therefore, to be egoless when one must always worry about one's standing in the imaginary hierarchy of successful people.

Buddhism, on the other hand, is opposed to the evaluation *at all* of events, people, or achievements. Things happen; things change; people come and go. Life is a continual flow, an unending *moving on.* It is not a ladder. Success and failure are imaginary opposites, distorting the perception of events as they really happen. Say a man loses his job after 20 years. He cannot find another job. In a short time he has exhausted all his funds. As he walks along the cold and windy streets, he looks at the city as a cruel, heartless place and upon himself as a total failure.

In Buddhist philosophy the feelings you have about yourself are *only* feelings. You may harbor them if you wish. You may project them out into the world, as our jobless man did, and imagine that the world is an embodiment of them: You are a failure; the windy day *looks* like failure.

*Western*

*You have lost your job; you walk along the cold and windy streets of a big city, which you regard as a cruel and heartless place, and you see yourself as a total failure.*

*Eastern*

*The feelings you have about yourself are only feelings; you may project them out into the world if you wish, but feelings have no objective existence.*

*Western*

*Territory is everything—your possessions, your thoughts and feelings, your supposedly continuous identity.*

In Buddhism everything you feel about yourself is entirely up to you. Feelings have no objective existence. Nor do evaluations. "Successful" people may speak of themselves as such and manipulate you into believing them, but you have the option of believing nothing whatever about them. The recognition that success and failure are of one's own making has proved for some Americans a welcome antidote to the poison gushing forth from a wounded ego.

*Eastern*
*Forget self, forget possessions, develop an expansive, panoramic sense of total reality.*

## Territory and Space

Siddhartha finally understood that the need to possess things and people was a sickness of the soul. This became the second of his noble truths. One can never possess enough; therefore one is forever dissatisfied. Or else one fears that one cannot *keep* what one has accumulated. For the possessive and the covetous, life is an endless succession of worries, paranoid obsessions, even guilt-shattered sleep, for if they have indeed amassed a goodly number of possessions, perhaps they secretly feel that they have not earned them.

People, says Robert Ardrey in *The Territorial Imperative*, are property oriented, sharing this characteristic with all other animals. The instinct to find, protect, and preserve a nesting place is basic to all animals. Behavioral psychologists, however, say human beings do *not* have instincts, claiming that all their tendencies and actions are the result of conditioning.

Buddhism agrees in this instance with the behaviorists. The obsession to accumulate territory is bred into us by the culture in which we live. For example, in the early years of this century young American boys were encouraged to read the books of Horatio Alger, all of which were variations on one plot line: the inexorable rise in the business world of a virtuous, hard-working young man of respectable parents and a Christian upbringing. The relationship between the accumulation of wealth and Christianity has been noted by intellectual historians, including Max Weber, whose principal work is *The Protestant Ethic and the Spirit of Capitalism* (1930). According to Weber, the Protestant belief that success in business ventures is a sure sign of God's favor has permeated our cultural unconscious to the point that even nonbelievers generally accept the notion that success at work should be their number-one priority.

*According to Weber, the Protestant belief that success in business ventures is a sure sign of God's favor has permeated our cultural consciousness to the point that even nonbelievers generally accept the notion that success at work should be their number-one priority.*

According to an earlier observer, Thorstein Veblen, an economist whose study of Western consumerism *The Theory of the Leisure Class* appeared in 1901, we are less interested in the work ethic that leads to success than we are in the conspicuous display of money and possessions. In fact, conspicuous consumption, as he calls it, is our total obsession: *One must be perceived as owning many things.* In today's vortex of plastic credit cards we could add that our obsession is to be thought to own things even if they are not paid for.

Buddhism, on the other hand, believes that since such "territorialism" is cultural rather than instinctive, we have the option of rejecting the urge to own. Most of the songs and stories that arose from the attempted cultural revolution of the 1960s focused on the jobs of the open road, communal living, and dropping out of the so-called establishment. Not to have a permanent home or job—to own nothing, in fact, except the backpack one carried—was regarded as the highest good. This is very definitely an Eastern value, and, not surprisingly, American interest in Eastern modes of living and thinking quickened during the 1960s.

In America, Buddhism is not evangelical, though it likes to share its vision of ultimate happiness with those who are seeking an alternative to conditions that do not satisfy them. It has no illusion that it will ever bring peace to a well-fed population with every possible convenience. Rather, it believes the secret to be that joy and territory are irreconcilable opposites.

More subtle perhaps but no less dominant in the Western scheme of things is the need for *inner* territory, what the Buddhists call the myth of ego. In Western circles, it is meaningful to say that someone has behaved in a most "uncharacteristic" manner. If one departs too radically from society's perception of allowable behavior, one is labeled mentally ill. Buddhism, as we have seen, does not believe that we exist continuously and therefore always in a characteristic way. Buddhism believes the law of life is that of continual change. How can there be an unchanging inner self?

Buddhists in America know that sitting in meditation discourages clinging to thoughts and the sense of self. Instead, it encourages the individual to be open to what Chögyam Trungpa has called the "fluid intelligent quality of space":

> The fear of the absence of self, of the egoless state, is a constant threat to us. "Suppose it is true, what then? I am afraid to look." We want to maintain some solidity but the only material available with which to work is space, the absence of ego, so we try to solidify or freeze that experience of space.[9]

Thus there is a Western fear of physical space—that is, being without territorial possessions—as well as a Western fear of inner space—that is, having outer-directed consciousness without a solid inner orientation. The Western intellectual life, in particular, has had as its goal the achievement of a focused rational mind inside each of us that accurately views and processes events as they take place. The vast uncharted land of inner space has traditionally been regarded in the West as a place of hazard, far too dangerous to wander in. The underlying premise of psychoanalysis is that one must bring all of one's thoughts and feelings under the conscious control of the ego. To operate spontaneously from the unconscious is to be neurotic, perhaps psychotic.

Buddhism in America does not blind itself to the reality of mental illness caused by a fragmentation of consciousness, a person's being driven by drives and impulses of which she or he is unaware. Indeed, it sees mental illness as one of the gravest problems in our society, and it attributes its prevalence to our immersion in samsara, the continual round of acting and reacting without ever detaching ourselves from the process. Buddhism advocates sitting meditation as an alternative to both the illness itself and to the hours of therapy often required to heal it. If one would sit, say the Buddhists, mind chatter would begin to fade away; one would see one's behavior from the detached vantage point of an uninvolved observer.

Instead of the conscious, controlling ego of Western therapists, Buddhism speaks of wisdom or enlightenment, both of which are terms for the perception of all things exactly as they are. This perception has nothing to do with individual personality. One person is not wiser or "smarter" than another. One has either opened oneself to enlightenment or one has not. There is no in-between.

In a very real sense, the Western tradition of philosophy began on a note that was much closer in spirit to the East than we are now. Plato and Aristotle, when dealing with what they called reason, were indeed talking about something eternal and possessed by all. In Plato's dialogue *Meno*, mentioned in Chapter 6, Socrates contends that if given proper time and attention, a slave boy would be

*Many Americans hold important jobs and then go home to practice meditation at night. East and West do not offer incompatible ways of living.*

able to handle exceedingly complex mathematical problems. Why? Because all persons are born with identical wisdom. They differ, as Aristotle was later to make clear, in terms of *the degree to which they actualize their potential.*

In Aristotelian language we could say that the guru, the bodhisattva, and the Buddha all represent a hierarchy of actualization. Each is closer to the condition of total wisdom. Plato shows actualization taking place not through sitting meditation but through stimulating interchange with a teacher—in his case, Socrates. But the way Socrates prods and challenges his students, recorded for us in *The Republic* as well as in other dialogues, is similar to what happens between the Zen master and the Zen novice, except that the latter relationship is often filled with derision and even physical punishment designed to sharpen the awareness.

Since the Renaissance, however, the West has undeniably shifted toward the idea of great individual minds who, because of their special insights, are able to bring about significant changes in the world. There is no scientific and technological tradition in the East to match what has been called "Western progress," spurred by individual initiative. True, the East, particularly Japan, is catching up. In electronic and computer technology there is frequently no contest anymore, with Western businesses regularly importing Japanese know-how. Could we not say that this state of affairs represents the West moving into the East, even as meditation centers in the West represent an opposite trend?

Buddhism is not, however, an alternative to progress or to creative endeavors. Many American Buddhists attend or have graduated from the most prestigious universities in America. Many no doubt hold key positions in top U.S. companies of all kinds. Buddhism believes that long years of sitting meditation can so enlarge one's perspective that one is both enlightened and able to deal with complex problems that would defeat someone else whose life is fragmented by concerns. Buddhism thus believes that the enlightened practitioner is more valuable in the world of commerce than the neurotic "go-getter."

Some American Buddhists have done very well in business but have given up lucrative jobs and the promise of financial security in order to join a sangha and devote most of their time to sitting. A 9-to-5 job does not give them this time. They do not believe they are wasting their lives because they are not "making a name for themselves." They want no part of what they regard as a vicious circle of challenge and response that leaves them confused, exhausted, and always unfulfilled.

Critics of Buddhism in America argue that the sitting practice is less effective in our upwardly directed society and more effective in less-developed countries, where individualism is a weaker force than in the United States. It works best, they say, for people whose lives tend to be without hope and are so monotonous that the boredom of continual meditation is easily accepted. Americans, on the other hand, are raised to be continually active. The passiveness of sitting is foreign to their nature.

For their part, American Buddhists are not likely to be swayed by criticism, even that lodged by families who despair over a son's or a daughter's lack of initiative or "unproductive" way of life. The decision is often painful, however. What will happen to the family business if the heir or heiress prefers a zendo to an executive office? But then, we need not suppose Siddhartha failed to experience the pain of remorse as he waved goodbye to his wife and son.

The art of being human is the art of recognizing options. There is always a price to pay for each choice. If the marketplace has taught us anything, it is surely that we need to weigh the price against the joy we may receive from a choice.

*In a sense, Plato and Aristotle were closer in spirit to the East than to the West when they spoke of reason as something eternal and unconnected to individual personalities.*

# Glossary

bodhisattva: In ancient Hindu belief, the name given to the incarnation in each lifetime of the next Buddha—the "Buddha on the way," so to speak. In Tibetan Buddhism, a bodhisattva is one who is recognized as being on the road to full enlightenment and whose teachings are therefore worth heeding. There can be more than one bodhisattva alive in any period.

compassion: In Buddhism, the capacity for recognizing the motivations and goals of others. Through meditation one becomes detached from one's own inner processes, in the sense that one sees them objectively. When this happens, one begins to observe the processes of others from the same detached viewpoint. (Note, however, that "detached" in Buddhism does not mean "unconcerned," but rather "without emotional confusion.")

dharma: In Buddhism, the structure of moral and social obligations underlying all existence. Unlike the moral law of Judeo-Christian belief, the dharma was not imposed by a deity, but is implicit in the nature of existence.

egolessness: According to Buddhism, the fundamental condition in which we live. The conscious awareness at any given moment is an intersection of cause and effect. That is, either one is reacting to a previous cause or one's action is about to have an effect. There is no such thing as a constant, unwavering self that endures through successive instants in time. There is, however, an illusion of such a thing, and we call it ego.

Gautama: The legendary founder of Buddhism, who maintained that contrary to Hindu scripture, anyone could achieve nirvana within the space of a single lifetime.

Hinduism: The most ancient of the world's major religions. It is still practiced today in India and elsewhere by millions of people, who believe as their ancestors did that one must live through many cycles of birth and rebirth before one is blessed with the gift of nirvana. In Hindu scriptures the Buddha is the one exception to this cycle of lifetimes, a being who, having actualized his Buddha nature, attains nirvana without ever having to be reborn. In Buddhism, however, anyone who follows the Buddha's path may attain nirvana in a single lifetime, though the way is admittedly difficult.

karma: A Sanskrit term, of central importance in Hindu religion, meaning the moral debt each of us accumulates in a lifetime that must be paid off during the next lifetime.

meditation: A central practice in Tibetan and Zen Buddhism, which consists of sitting in the lotus position, spine erect, for a length of time sufficient to enable one to achieve a totally wakeful state and to see the reality of the immediate moment exactly as it is without the barriers of thought or emotion. In many Buddhist sects meditation is accomplished through chanting and the repetition of a particular word.

nirvana: In Hinduism, the final emancipation from the pain of birth and rebirth, and ultimate reunion with Brahman, the universal soul; in Buddhism, a release from suffering brought about through intense meditation and the renunciation of ego.

samsara: A Sanskrit term, found in both Buddhism and Hinduism, meaning the seemingly endless round of give and take in which we become involved when we plunge into the daily business of life without the detachment and separation from ego necessary to achieve inner peace.

Tibetan Buddhism: A strongly democratic strain of Buddhism centering on the belief that more than one Buddha is possible in any given era.

Zen: Originally the most austere and monastic form of Buddhism, it means today the highly disciplined practice of meditation and egolessness in which one aspires to nearly total detachment from worldly concerns. It is also a systematic method of transcending the rational activity of the mind, which Buddhists believe prevents us from seeing things as they are.

# Notes

1. Some say Gautama was born a member of the Shakyas, a warrior tribe living near the foothills of the Himalayas. He is thus referred to as the Buddha Shakyamuni (or "Sage of the Shakyas").
2. *Buddhist Scriptures*, tr. Edward Conze (London: Penguin, 1959), 51.
3. Junjiro Takakusu, *The Essentials of Buddhist Philosophy* (Delhi: Motilal Banarsidass, 1975), 17.
4. From an interview with David Rome, executive secretary of Vajradhatu, the central administration of the Tibetan Buddhist meditation centers in North America, conducted July 21, 1977, in Boulder, Colorado.
5. Lobsang Phuntsok Lhalungpa, "Buddhism in Tibet," in *The Path of the Buddha*, ed. Kenneth W. Morgan (New York: Ronald Press, 1956), 231.
6. Takakusu, *The Essentials of Buddhist Philosophy*, 167.
7. Chögyam Trungpa, *The Myth of Freedom* (Boulder, Colo.: Shambhala Publications, 1976), 25.
8. R. H. Blyth, *Zen and Zen Classics*, vols. 1-5 (Tokyo: Hokuseido Press, 1960-1970).
9. Trungpa, *The Myth of Freedom*, 21.

# Suggested Reading

*The Bhagavad Gita*. An epic Hindu poem containing the dialogues of a warrior and his charioteer Krishna, an incarnation of the god Vishnu. The work contains the essentials of Hindu morality, which is similar to that of Buddhism.

Conze, Edward. *Buddhist Scriptures*. Baltimore: Penguin Books, 1959. An accurate, poetic, and highly readable translation of Buddhist sacred writings, containing a picturesque account of the Buddha's enlightenment.

Fields, Rick. *How the Swans Came to the Lake*. Boulder, Colo.: Shambhala, 1981. A well-researched history of the coming of Buddhist influences to America through the opening of the East during the nineteenth century.

Hesse, Hermann. *Siddhartha*. Tr. Hilda Rusner. New York: New Directions, 1951. A story, not of the historic Buddha, but of a wealthy young Brahmin who seeks spiritual fulfillment, meets the Buddha only to be disillusioned by him, and eventually becomes aware that the Buddha nature can be found only in himself.

Lao-Tzu. *The Way of Life*. A series of exquisite poems, each of which conveys a simple yet complex insight into an aspect of life or death. The work is like the Bible to the Taoist religion, born in China in the same ancient era as Buddhism.

Rohe, Fred. *The Zen of Running*. New York: Random House, 1975. A simple and beautiful book about running as a form of Zen meditation, allowing one to achieve a state of mindlessness and a panoramic sense of one's surroundings. It has many photographs of the runner in nature.

Suzuki, D. T. *Essays in Zen Buddhism*. New York: Grove Press, 1961. Highly readable essays on various aspects of the philosophy and practice of Zen, directed at the Western consciousness. Of particular interest is the relationship between Zen master and student, discussed at length in the book.

Trungpa, Chögyam. *The Myth of Freedom*. Boulder, Colo.: Shambhala, 1976. A compilation of Buddhist teachings addressed to American sensibilities by a foremost Tibetan guru.

Watts, Alan. *Nature, Man, and Woman*. New York: Pantheon, 1958. Once the foremost Western spokesperson for Zen Buddhism, the philosopher contrasts Eastern and Western beliefs and values in the matter of sexual identity and relationships.

*Alberto Giacometti,* The Palace at 4 a.m. *(1932–33) (Construction in wood, glass, wire, and string, 25 x 28-1/4 x 15-3/4". Collection, The Museum of Modern Art, New York, Purchase)*

# On Being a
# Critical Thinker

## Overview

Toward the end of William Wharton's novel *Dad*, the main character, en route to his father's funeral, gets a glimpse of his own aging and eventual death:

> I'll become a bore to others, a drag in conversation, repeat myself, be slow at comprehension, quick at misunderstanding, have lapses in conceptual sequence. All this will probably be invisible to me. I won't even be aware of my own decline.[1]

What he fears is the loss of a highly treasured human trait, the power of thought. He is clearly a man who has enjoyed the use of his critical faculties, and while they may eventually fail him, his life will have been richer because of their use. He is only one of many who have paid tribute to—and feared the loss of—that unique human skill, the ability to think critically.

Of all the creatures on earth, from the smallest to the largest, apparently only human beings can understand concepts. Other creatures have instincts. They seek food and shelter and cleverly achieve these ends; they have families and nurture their young; they fight, run, and even play. But they don't plan or read or make word jokes or find similarities in apparently unlike objects. They lack the power to contemplate, to speculate, to make valid inferences, and to laugh at foolish inconsistencies. So do computers—those amazingly quick, astonishing storehouses of memories. Computers, however, possess skills that are dependent on the creative imaginations of those who manage their circuits and prepare their software. Human beings are thus the only creatures capable of the joy of thinking.

The man who said he feared the loss of comprehension has at least been able thus far in his life to enjoy thorough use of his brain. What can be said of those who refuse to take advantage of what they have? What would make people reluctant to use that frequently unused human faculty, the mind? Why do some people think only during school examinations and then escape to leisure-time activities that require as little thinking as possible? And why does that special form of thinking called "critical" have such a bad reputation?

*Criticism is not limited to finding faults.*

We will begin by rejecting one definition of critical thinking. A critic is not necessarily a person who enjoys finding fault, who tears down rather than builds up. Criticism may involve praise of the highest order or the withholding of judgment until more information is available. Criticism is analysis leading to an evaluation. It is the state of mind that should precede choices and actions. Though capable of both spontaneity and intuition, the critical thinker depends less on them than on careful observations and reasoned conclusions.

*Critical thinking is the ongoing process of criticism. It is the disposition of the mind to define, describe, and analyze as accurately as possible. It is a lifelong commitment.*

*Criticism*, then, is an activity of the mind that carefully defines, describes, and analyzes something—a movie, an event, a presidential decision, a daughter's desire to move into her own apartment. It probably should be, but often is not, the mental activity that people enjoy engaging in more than any other. The following things are opposed to critical thinking: constant complaining; the suspicion that the troubles of the world derive from plots and conspiracies; the habit of claiming to be right at all times; the tendency to form conclusions at once, refusing to be led astray by facts; and the tendency to fall immediately into line with another person's viewpoint.

Critical thinking is also the ongoing process of criticism. It is the disposition of the mind to behave in a certain way, that is, to define, describe, and analyze as accurately, as fairly, and as dispassionately as possible. It is a lifelong commitment.

Critical thinkers quickly become known, become identified as people whose opinions can be trusted. Many times over they have demonstrated a knack for assessing a matter reasonably and making a memorable pronouncement on the subject.

*Signs of Noncritical Thinking*
*constant complaining*
*conspiracy theories*
*claiming to be always right*
*jumping to conclusions*
*always agreeing with*
    *opinions of others*

It is not at all difficult to distinguish critical from noncritical thinkers. The latter take things literally and fail to move on quickly to the next step. They have a hard time figuring out why people say what they say. They are not aware of what we might call the shape of experience. The morning after a party, noncritical thinkers cannot put the event into perspective. Critical thinkers, on the other hand, will tell you concisely what happened and what it felt like to be there.

Critical thinking is not an exact science, but it has identifiable characteristics. It has goals. There are certain ways of achieving it. The purpose of this chapter is to systematize these ways as much as possible.

# Thinking About Thinking

The first step in becoming a critical thinker is to develop some idea of what is meant by thinking. For centuries, speculations about the mind belonged exclusively to philosophy. It was believed by many that the mind was a spiritual, or at least a nonmaterial, entity, floating somehow within but not connected to the body. Today psychologists believe that all functions of the mind, from dreams to the most complex series of interwoven ideas, are localized in the brain. Take away the brain, and the mind disappears. For all practical purposes, the brain *is* the mind.

## Old Brains, New Brains

By making plaster casts of primitive brains on indentations found inside ancient skulls, California anthropologist Ralph Holloway has constructed a theory that the brain has gradually grown larger. Carl Sagan (in *The Dragons of Eden*) describes a three-part division of the brain, the bottom and middle sections being the survivors of millions of years of evolution. These are the "old" brains. The topmost section is most advanced in *Homo sapiens*—humanity in its present form.

*Characteristics and Concerns of the Reptilian Brain*
*aggression*
*territory*
*chain of command*
*ritual*
*resistance to change*

The oldest, or *reptilian*, brain once belonged to early inhabitants of planet Earth. These creatures needed a brain to process information delivered by the sense of sight as they foraged about for food and shelter. They also needed to be alert to danger. Hence this brain developed survival techniques, including aggression ("Get them before they get you"); what Robert Ardrey has called the "territorial imperative" ("This area is mine, so keep off!"); and an insistence upon and respect for hierarchy ("You'd better take orders from me, or I'll kill you").

*Characteristics and Concerns of the Mammalian Brain*
*insights*
*intuitions*
*shelter*
*family*

As time went on and mammals began to evolve, a new kind of brain was needed to process information passed on from the sense of hearing, developed out of the necessity for recognizing threatening sounds from a considerable distance. The mammals, traveling at night when the reptiles were sleeping, developed a brain with insights and intuitions of both danger and safety. This brain came to value all those things associated with shelter, including the family instinct, love, charity, and self-sacrifice. As leadership of Earth passed into the keeping of the mammals, brains, not brawn, assumed priority. The reptiles that remained became smaller, and the mammals grew larger. Today whales and especially dolphins exhibit versions of this middle brain. Examples of their intelligence as well as their "tender" qualities have been documented.

The topmost brain in Sagan's theory is, of course, "ours." Courses in the humanities are likely to tell you that by virtue of being *born* human, we have a glorious heritage. The brilliant achievements of our species are proof that to be human is automatically a reason to marvel at oneself. But potentiality is not actuality. Aristotle pointed that out twenty-five hundred years ago, though he stressed that the potential for achievement is always there.

It is clear that we don't always belong to the tradition of human achievement. Consider what humanity is doing to its own environment and to its prospects for survival on this planet. Have we not been told that the present generation is the first to wonder whether it will be the last? Make a list of our present inhumanities and one of our humanities. Which is longer?

As our understanding of the human mind increases, old ideas about the brain's span of usefulness are changing. Traditional notions about aging are being

---

### *Bottom-Brain Thoughts*

---

What shall we have for supper tonight?
Can we afford to pay the rent?
I was here first.
I'll get to the top if it takes me ten years.
How much does he earn?
Who does she think she is?
Who's in charge here?
Now that I'm the manager, I'll need a larger house.

### *Middle-Brain Thoughts*

---

Be home by ten.
Don't go out with him; he's not for you.
Married ten years and only one child?
She's old and helpless; we have to take her in.
I'll get a job if you promise to stay in college.

---

*Tests indicate that those who spend their lives in nonmental pursuits display brainpower loss at an age when their mentally agile contemporaries are still engaged in productive intellectual labors.*

put aside. Loss of the rational faculties and loss of short-term memory (senility), for example, are less and less thought to be inevitable by-products of age. Recent intelligence testing of people as they grow older is revealing that those who continually use their brains can grow *more*, not less, intelligent with age. In his early nineties, Bertrand Russell was still writing, lecturing, and working on complex philosophical puzzles that would have baffled much younger people. George Bernard Shaw lived to be almost a hundred, showing little if any diminution of his mental powers, especially his legendary wit. And George Abbott, to celebrate his own centennial year, opened a play on Broadway. On the other hand, tests indicate that those who spend their lives in nonmental pursuits display brainpower loss at an age when their mentally agile contemporaries are still engaged in productive intellectual labors.

It is important to recognize that the brain needs exercise just as much as do legs and arms. An exercised brain will reward you even more than other parts of the body. Physical well-being is gratifying, but the exhilaration that comes from having completed a taxing bit of mental work—reading a difficult book, writing a complicated paper, solving a tricky puzzle, say—is incomparable.

If some continue to exercise their minds while others do not, the future of humanity—assuming we can keep from blowing one another up—could be one in which brain levels can be placed in a large hierarchy. At the top will be those who have powers of analysis and synthesis far beyond anything known today. But how many of these "superbrains" will there be? How many others, with less brainpower, will be placed at the bottom? And, more important and more frightening, will the superbrains limit the freedom of those with less developed minds?

## Behind Closed Doors

The false but dangerous belief that critical thinking is confined to a small part of the populace is shared by those who have such abilities and by those who don't.

Those who think critically may hold this belief in order to retain the skill that sets them apart from others and thus maintain their superiority. If the ability to think is not teachable, then well-paid and prestigious work remains out of reach for the majority, even those willing to work hard. If this is the case, critical thinking is something you have to be born with, like an aristocratic title. Education that serves only to develop the intellectual capacity one already has would have value for only a few. With such reasoning, critical thinkers can justify inequitable education systems.

In his satirical anti-utopian novel *Brave New World*, Aldous Huxley created a well-run society in which the brainy people are the ones in power. The Alphas make all the decisions because they have literally been *bred* in test tubes to have the intelligence required for governing the rest. Other groups, conditioned to be pleased with their own special, but lower, qualities, do not expect to improve their ability to think. In the real world, critical thinking is often considered beyond the range of all but a small segment of the people. Corporate bureaucracy is based on the assumption that managing directors and chief executive officers have to make the tough, intricate decisions, or the company will fall into chaos. Power thus remains behind closed doors for the relatively few.

But those with power are not the only ones who claim that critical thought is a special gift. People with poor self-concepts (sometimes the result of parental reinforcement) tend to agree. Sure that they won't be able to do the job, they give up without really trying. Each penalty for poor performance leads them to the certainty that the next failure is preordained. After a time, it is.

## The Feeling Level

Those who work outside the closed doors of the critical decision makers often maintain that people who *feel* more than they think are somehow more trustworthy and charitable than their highly paid, less emotional "superiors." The ability to express emotion—even uncontrolled anger—is valued in our thought-suspicious times. "Feeling" people tend to attract our sympathies. They sometimes see themselves as martyrs, perennial victims of injustice at the hands of the callous and calculating. Conversely, those "unable to feel" are often urged to let themselves go and be "human." But there is no reason to equate humanness with feeling, or lack of humanness with critical thinking. The emotional approach to life can be a whole lot easier and a whole lot less effective than trying to analyze what is really happening and coming up with a workable solution to genuine problems.

Thus a lack of perceived compassion for the weakness of others is deplored, while illogical thinking either goes undetected altogether or is dismissed as insignificant. Even when there is little evidence to indicate that nonthinkers are automatically warm and tender, they are often thought to be. Since many people avoid what they believe will be the "pain of thought," they display an easy tolerance for mental lapses in everyone else. The "difficult" subjects in school are always those requiring the closest reading and the most intense concentration; low grades in such subjects tend to be laughed off by many.

Each of us is able to operate on different levels of consciousness. The first we might call "casual." In everyday conversations with friends and family or in just letting the mind ramble on in its usual, undisciplined way, we are hit-or-miss in our thinking. Sometimes some of us carry a thought process in a direct line for a minute or more. Mostly we can't. The level of critical thinking—which is the third

*The ability to express emotion—even uncontrolled anger—is valued in our thought-suspicious times.*

level of consciousness and involves sustained, careful maneuvers of the mind through the shoals of irrelevance—requires time, solitude, and silence. It seldom competes successfully with the second, or feeling, level, which is even less difficult, at least for some, than casual conversation. Frustration, anger, and resentment, or concern, warmth, and passion . . . all can be summoned front and center without needing our concentration.

> We allow our ideas to take their own course, and this course is determined by our hopes and fears, our spontaneous desires, their fulfillment or frustration; by our likes and dislikes, our loves and hates and resentments. There is nothing else anything like so interesting to ourselves as ourselves.
>
> James Harvey Robinson

The time has come to seek a balance among the three levels of consciousness. We want sometimes to chit-chat with our friends (or ourselves), to let our mind amble along at its own pace and go wherever it will. If we have tenderness or anger to communicate, we want the right to do so. But without the critical level, we run the risk of becoming permanently displaced in a world of never seeing very clearly what we and others are about. We risk not being able to transcend events, observing issues and principles at work.

## Exercising the Critical Faculties

If we believe there is an immediate survival reason for every human skill developed since our species first evolved, we could argue in favor of letting the brain work only when necessary. If we are not trapped in a burning building, lost in a dense forest, adrift in a remote sea, or struggling to remember an obscure date on an important examination, we may safely ease out of the girdle of tight thought and "let our minds go." We may also conclude that if we have no present need of muscle power—for instance, if our car has a flat tire and we need to use the jack— the body may safely be allowed to flop into an easy chair directly after dinner. But not exercising the body could mean not having what it takes to accomplish a physical task when the need arrives. By the same token, when the brain is left to flounder and grow flabby from nonuse, the capacity for sustained logical discourse may just not be there when the need arises.

*When the brain is left to flounder and grow flabby from nonuse, the capacity for sustained logical discourse may not be there when the need arises.*

In this section we look at a few examples of how the critical faculties can be exercised on a daily basis. After all, even great dancers still report to the studio each morning for their barre exercises.

### Beyond Chit-Chat

As pointed out in the preceding section, we spend a great deal of time on casual thinking, which is not sustained and nearly always lacks transitions from point to point, and on casual conversation, which is even less organized. Long, rambling conversation seems harmless enough, in the same way that junk food, with its heavy concentration of starch, sugar, and salt, seems safe enough "now and then"— that is, for lunch every day but never for dinner. But chit-chat's cumulative effect on the mind can be every bit as dangerous as the cumulative effect of sweet soft drinks.

Social conversation can be turned into an exercise in critical thought. Avid fans of a sport can spend highly enjoyable time in serious analysis of the coach's strategy. Monday-morning quarterbacks can play their own critical game of "If . . . then . . . and that would have provided the opportunity to . . ." Between games there is talk of player contracts and front-office decisions. When talk is knowledgeable, not merely the recitation of statistics or preferences, it is *critical* talk.

There need be no immediate outcome of critical conversation, of course. Someone remarks, for instance, "I suppose I should root for one of the teams in the playoff." A friend answers, "It makes it more interesting. But I can't find any reason to care about the teams that are left. Neither is from a city I've ever lived in, and there's no one player I care about." Another says, "I usually wait till one team has lost two games in a three-out-of-five series, and then root for the underdog." Yet another pipes in, "Or the team with a lot of older players. It's their last chance to make it." The environmentalist adds, "Or from the standpoint of fuel conservation, teams that are close to each other . . ." Infuriating to a passionate fan, this type of conversation is critical in that it rises above—or outside of—unexamined "rooting" and makes tentative remarks about the reasons behind a choice. People are making statements and noting their reasons for doing so. At least some kind of thinking is taking place as they talk.

If we always make choices without analyzing them, then we will fail to develop the capacity for making crucial choices when we *really* must. We may "naturally"—for reasons obscure to ourselves—root for *any* underdog, but this basis for choice may not be appropriate or make sense if we think about it.

*Long, rambling conversations are like concentrations of junk food.*

*If we always make choices without analyzing them, we will fail to develop the capacity for making crucial choices when we* really *must.*

## Solving Problems

The problems of everyday life offer the most obvious chance for most of us to tune the critical faculties. For example, a family member who always needs help of some sort is a problem for almost everyone.

The typical solution, which is to ignore the problem and hope it will go away forever, is not the critical approach. The attitude of "It's easier to help than to have the hassle" may well avoid a painful thought, but not a painful scene further down the line.

The first step in solving a problem is to determine whether there is one at all. Whether to place an aging relative in a nursing home or provide home care yourself may not be a problem if no legitimate choice exists. Should money not be an issue, one obvious question suggests itself: "Do I want to assume the responsibility of caring for my grandmother?" If the answer is no, then the "problem" disappears, unless the original question can be replaced by yet another: "Will I be able to handle the guilt I may feel after I've signed the papers?" However, guilt versus responsibility may be an unbalanced set of alternatives. Is nursing-facility care better suited to your grandmother? Or is she still well enough and alert enough to experience a harmful feeling of rejection? In the first instance, the logic of choosing the nursing home should make guilt unnecessary. In the second, the alternatives seem equally compelling: no, for the good of your relative; yes, for your own good. So you may conclude that you definitely have a problem.

The second step is usually to determine who owns the problem, or, in the

*The first step in solving a problem is to determine whether there is one at all. Whether to place an aging relative in a nursing home or provide home care yourself may not be a problem if no choice exists.*

case of the nursing-home dilemma, whether you are the sole owner. Are there others in the family who could share the need to choose? Often we make ourselves miserable by supposing that we are not, or ought not to be, sole owners. "Why me?" is a frequent, if rhetorical, question people ask. If there is no answer, then the question is foolish but psychologically damaging. It's necessary to be hard-nosed— that is, brutally realistic—about deciding the question of ownership. To be so saves time and emotional wear and tear.

Recognizing that we seldom receive rewards for good deeds puts us well on the way to not expecting any. The business of living can be much easier without fantasies.

## Challenging Assumptions

A good exercise for the critical faculties is to pay close attention to what people say and, just for fun, to freeze the action and examine the statement. If the cost of hurting people's feelings by reporting your "findings" aloud is too high a price, then examining assumptions in the privacy of one's thoughts is free.

Suppose, for example, you hear someone say, after reading a front-page story: "They shouldn't let those people out of mental hospitals and turn them loose to hurt innocent people." Immediately you might list a number of assumptions being made:

1. Everyone in a mental hospital deserves to be there.
2. All people admitted to mental hospitals are both incurable and violent.
3. Those in charge of mental hospitals are in no position to make accurate judgments about the future behavior of any patient released.
4. Confinement to a mental hospital should be permanent.

Having listed the assumptions, you are now in a position to question them.

---

The word "criminal" is not only on a much higher level of abstraction than "the man who spent three years in the penitentiary," but it is . . . a judgment, with the implication "He has committed a crime in the past and will probably commit more crimes in the future." The result is that when John Doe applies for a job and is forced to state that he has spent three years in the penitentiary, prospective employers . . . may say to him, "You can't expect me to give jobs to criminals!"[2]

S. I. Hayakawa

---

*A good exercise for the critical faculties is to pay close attention to what people say and, just for fun, to freeze the action and examine the statement.*

The noncritical person in a debate is likely to be unable to stay with the subject and will become personal as well as shrill. For instance: "You never come up with any good ideas . . . just like your brother. I once knew someone who was in a mental hospital . . . at least I think so. Anyway, all psychiatrists are crooks." Assumptions, such as the latter statement, come to the surface suddenly, then dive below just as rapidly. Personal fears, old prejudices, and unresolved guilt mix with illogical thinking to produce a pandemonium of wild talk that can absolutely stagger you once you set about to really listen.

The highly emotional assumption maker may be too far gone to benefit from your relatively calm analysis of the assumer's argument. But where rational confrontation is possible, you, the critical thinker, advance your own cause and that of the assumer by assisting in the process of recognition. The challenge should, however, be gentle, never officious or self-righteous, for to be such is to throw around a few untested assumptions of your own.

## Taking School Examinations

Educators may disagree on principles and strategies, but there is general agreement on the value of critical thinking in school. In order for students to answer critically, they must go beyond the recall level, which consists of factual answers to factual questions. The authorship of *Don Quixote*, the temperature at which water boils, the nationality of Kierkegaard, and the definition of Manifest Destiny are facts worth a few points on objective tests.

The best essay questions are valuable critical exercises, though even straight recall helps tune the brain. If the lecturer has described the court of King Louis XIV and the Palace of Versailles and has then played music of the mid-seventeenth century, the student who can recall what the lecturer said about the history of the time and the way the arts reflect that history is still on the level of recall. An essay question about the relationship between the music and the formal gardens of Versailles forces the student to make a connection on her or his own. Making responsible connections is at the heart of critical thinking.

Or, having given an overview lecture on the neoclassical age with Versailles as a prime example, the instructor may ask the student to provide her or his own overview about an entirely different period. The essay question then might read, "In what way did the arts of the Renaissance indicate a belief in the greatness of humankind?" A wealth of "evidence" could be used by the student—Michelangelo's statue of David, the paintings of Leonardo, the great heroes of Shakespeare, and so on. The essay would require the student to match concrete examples with general principles about the Renaissance as a whole, showing ways in which implicit belief is exemplified in art.

Here are some other critical topics:

1. Explore the possible audience of a local radio station by listening to the vocabulary of the announcers and making inferences about the prospective users of the products advertised. What part of the population seems to be the target? How do you know?
2. Examine the "signals" being transmitted by the people and surroundings in two different parts of the city. Observe carefully the manner of dress, the types of stores, and the lettering on signs that alert visitors would notice. What types of neighborhoods are these areas?
3. Read or see a play that has been called tragedy. Without resorting to quotes from authorities, tell how you think it does or does not match classical principles of tragedy.
4. Describe an incident you have experienced or observed that offers a clear moral choice. Demonstrate your knowledge of two ethical ideas by describing two courses of action and the implications of each.
5. Using all the information you have about a historical event (the French Revolution, for example), tell under what circumstances it might have been avoided.

Note that some of these suggested assignments combine recall information with other kinds of knowledge. The critical thinker knows the basic definition (of tragedy, for example) and is familiar with the plot of the play, but is not willing to be content with mere summary. It is in the matching of plot with definition that the higher order of thinking occurs.

*The question "Did you like it?" is basically not a critical one at all.*

Not included in the exercise on tragedy are the questions "Did you like it?" or "Is it great?" The former question is subjective, often valid, but not basically critical; the latter is evaluative, requiring the ability to describe and compare before the pronouncement that a work of art may be called "great" has any meaning beyond empty words.

For national examinations such as the Scholastic Aptitude Test and the Graduate Record Examination as well as for tests to determine eligibility for law school, critical thinking is apt to be required. Because there is so much variation in the curricula of school systems throughout the country, the test questions must seek evidence of critical thinking rather than the memorization of specific information. A law school candidate may be asked, for example, to match a general principle with a specific situation which involves the ability to recognize the difference between bribery, extortion, and theft. Instead of writing definitions, however, the would-be lawyer must be able to relate the proper charge to the real issue. Doing this requires practice in careful, systematic thinking.

Or one may be asked questions about the meaning of particular lines or words of a poem. In "Loveliest of Trees" by A. E. Housman, for example, there appears the line "Now, of my threescore years and ten, twenty will not come again." The examination asks, "How old is he?" The distracted or impatient test taker translates "three score years and ten" and gives "seventy" as the answer. The more careful test taker answers correctly, "Twenty."

At the end of that same poem are the following lines:

> And since to look at things in bloom
> Fifty springs are little room,
> About the woodlands I will go
> To see the cherry hung with snow.[3]

The critical reader, noticing "in bloom," knows at once that the season mentioned is spring. Asked to identify an image in the poem, the critical reader remembers that a poetic image is indirect, figurative, and allusive and answers that "snow" is an image referring to the blossoms rather than to a phenomenon of winter.

How does one develop the critical skills required to score well on essay examinations? The absolutely wrong approach is to use the chit-chat model, whereby you begin writing without the slightest awareness of what will come forth. Instead, you should survey the situation, gain a perspective on the question, formulate precisely in your mind what is being asked, then determine the best available strategy for answering. The skillful essay is clearly introduced and summarized, not long and rambling with no center of gravity.

## Looking for Principles

In listening to the statements of others, we sometimes fail to hear principles—or the ones that are *actually* there. A principle is a particular kind of assumption, a moral or ethical judgment that is held to be universally applicable. The confusion of principles is one of our commonest errors.

According to the philosopher Kant (as discussed in Chapter 7), to test the moral validity of a proposed act we should will that it be universally binding. For example, the thief who justifies robbing a grocery store must agree that everyone who has been unfairly treated by society should steal from others. The "others" would, of course, have to include the thief. But a thief who is robbed on the way home from committing a robbery is unlikely to approve the action of the second thief. Therefore the thief's "thinking" prior to the stealing has to be revised: "Robbery is not acceptable, except when I do it."

*A thief who is robbed on the way home from committing a robbery is unlikely to approve the action.*

You are waiting for a bus, and you hear a bystander remark, "Mother's Day came and went, without even a lousy card from my son." As a critical thinker, you entertain yourself by seeking out the principle from which the remark springs. How about starting with "Evidence of love is a greeting card arriving by a certain day." You can push the analysis further: the woman's "even" suggests that a card is minimally acceptable, that an expensive gift would be a stronger sign of love. Turning the assumption into a principle, you have: "Children ought to show their love for their parents by giving them expensive presents by a particular deadline." A moment's reflection should tell us that this is a very dubious universal principle.

Here is a statement reported in a newspaper account of a trial in which a former professional football player was charged with selling drugs: The athlete's attorney quipped, "So this is the thanks he gets for all the pleasure he has given the public!" To turn that remark into a universal principle, try starting out with "People who play football professionally . . ." or "As long as someone is engaged in an activity that entertains the public, that person may . . ." Or try this: "In such cases, the public's duty is to . . ." At the very least the attorney was saying, "Outstanding athletes should be judged by different standards from other people." Having "straightened out" the statement, we are now in a position to analyze it. We may well begin by questioning the phrase "has given the public." Since the man was a highly paid player, "given" seems inappropriate. In light of the hero worship of young fans, we may be tempted to ask why an outstanding athlete should not be held to an even higher standard of behavior than those not in a position to become role models.

Here's another statement, also reported in a newspaper: "It is just as dangerous to allow poisoned literature into the school library as to allow poisoned food into the school cafeteria." The principle seems clear: "We may safely base moral judgments on analogies." But is a valid comparison really being made here? The critical thinker notes differences. The logic of the analogy centers on the equal applicability of "dangerous" in both school areas. Laboratory analysis can tell us what is poison in food and what is not. But what device will detect poison in literature as objectively?

All of us, surely, would like to believe that we operate according to clear and approved principles. Some of us, however, become very confused when we attempt to match a concrete example or detail with an appropriate principle.

## Literalists and Figuratists

Because people do not easily fall into categories, it is not fair to insist upon hard-and-fast distinctions. Critical thinkers are not always critical. They are capable of being impulsive, overemotional, and childish. They are inconsistent, too, being hurt on some days by remarks that on other days they would have overlooked or laughed at. Sometimes they become discouraged by the inability to solve a problem, when the brain seems to let them down.

But people who make up their minds to adopt the critical approach to living do acquire certain definite characteristics, and so do those who choose not to. In this section we are concerned with the way in which critical thinkers respond to and talk about experience. Critical thinkers tend to be figurative rather than always literal in their speech and their understanding of things.

## On Being Literal

The literal person, or literalist, avoids or does not see general principles but concentrates on specific details. For example, suppose you are making a general complaint about ingratitude. "My brother," you remark, "is so selfish he expects to take, take, take and never give anything in return. After all the times he and his family have come to my house for holiday meals, he never entertains. I've helped him out with money when he needed it, let him use my car, even though he never filled the tank—and now, when I told him I'd appreciate it if he'd take care of our cat for three days while we go to Chicago, he said he wouldn't." There are any number of possible responses your listener could make—a sympathetic nod, a similar story about ungrateful relatives, or even an offer to help with the cat.

The literalist has not really been listening and, in concentrating on self, remarks, "I've never been to Chicago."

Anyone who has ever listened to the question period following a lecture by a guest speaker will recognize the presence of literalists. No matter how stimulating the subject, the literalist will insist on inquiring of the speaker something totally off the point, like "What do you think of our city?" or "Are you related to . . . ?"

Here is another example of the literalist in action:

> *A:* I wish life would provide experts. I'd love to have someone whom I could ask important questions: where to live, whether to change jobs, what school is best, what suntan lotion to use.
>
> *B:* My dermatologist gave me the name of a good suntan lotion. Just a minute. I have the name written down.

A is making a rueful observation that there is no certainty, that in a philosophical sense we are all alone. This is the general principle behind the observation. B hears only the examples, but not the random nature of them. B, who is not accustomed to hearing or discussing principles, is unaware that A is uninterested in suntan lotion no matter what his or her actual words may have been.

Consider still another imaginary conversation:

> *Mother:* I find the only safe topic with my teenage son is something noncontroversial. I can't talk about his car, expenses, girlfriends, or his plans for school and a career. I know he's interested in baseball, so this morning I mentioned how well the Dodgers are doing. I told him they were six games ahead, and he corrected me. Ten games! It gave him a chance to explain something to me,

Friend A:    and it worked. At least we didn't fight this morning.
Friend A:    I know. The only safe topic in our house these days is the new television lineup.
Friend B:    The Dodgers are actually twelve games ahead.

Which friend is the literalist? More important, by what process did either reply come to be what it is? Friend A listened to what was being said by Mother. Friend A heard the general principle: Since it is difficult to communicate with the younger generation on our own terms, we must find terms that will work. Knowing the point of the observations, Friend A replied in kind. Friend B, on the other hand, is probably not in the habit of listening very carefully to begin with.

Literalists see object by object, hear sound by sound, but are unaware of wholes. Their conversation tends to be tedious, except perhaps to other literalists, because they themselves do not speak to significant issues or principles. The literalist back from a trip can give endless details about gas mileage, every morsel of food eaten at each stop, and the cost of items purchased or passed up. Even a pause now and then to sum up—"It wasn't worth it!" or "Travel is a pain, but you have to get away sometimes"—would break the total concentration on pointless detail.

*Literalists are unaware of wholes. They give endless, pointless details.*

Literalism also stems from self-preoccupation. Literalists are too busy waiting for their turn to speak, too busy thinking of what they might say to hear what others are saying. Even a transition like "I have nothing to contribute to this discussion. May we turn to another?" gives evidence of a critical mind at work and is easier to deal with.

Literalists seldom seek a perspective on world events. They are likely to have some interest in national problems, more in state issues, much more in matters relating to the city, and above all, the neighborhood. Characteristic of literalists, once again, is self-centeredness. The closer the problem comes to home, the greater the involvement.

*Thought would destroy their paradise.*
*No more; where ignorance is bliss,*
*'Tis folly to be wise.*

*Thomas Gray*

During a conversation, uncritical thinkers will be thinking ahead to what they will say when it is their turn to speak. Perhaps a joke they have just heard the day before will occur to them, which they are anxious to tell to others. They may impose the joke on the group whether the moment is appropriate or not. They are forever changing the subject, not having followed the thread of the conversation to begin with. They are so immersed in their own problems or so anxious to impress others with some good fortune that has befallen them that often their sole concern is to talk as frequently and as long as possible.

The compulsive need to talk and not listen, however, does not always erupt into overt speech. A noncritical person can be shy and introverted, so fearful of being rejected by others that he or she does not dare say much of anything. But reticence does not mean the person is listening. He or she may be carrying on an internal dialogue.

*Literalists are usually so wrapped up in personal concerns that they never listen to what others are really saying.*

It is surely ironic that unassertive, unassuming people often give the impression of needing to have their egos built up, while the cool and confident critical thinker is often identified as an egotist. This is precisely what the critical thinker is *not*. People who are unsure of themselves, who are defensive, must always personalize whatever happens, whether they do so openly or not. You cannot become a critical thinker until you learn that impulsive, self-centered responses are not the only ones that can be made. A rule of thumb is to delay reacting.

Personalizing what happens and what others say is usually a cover-up for a lack of perception. We may have become so accustomed to leaping without looking or listening that we are easily confused by events. We manipulate them inside our own brains so that they are not confusing: "Oh, I see what that's all about" or "Nobody can fool me on that one." Another ploy is to force someone else to support our manipulations: "Am I right? Wouldn't you have done the same thing? Sure you would have!" Other people, perhaps involved in their own personalizations, may offer positive support just to avoid having to figure out the situation for themselves.

For most of us, the roots of imperception lie buried in our childhood. Think back to dinner table talk. Was it full of silly little details, such as "Who spilled the salt?" or "Finish every mouthful of that meat, or you'll get no ice cream"? Or were real subjects discussed?

---

One must become able to transcend the narrow confines of a self-centered existence and believe that one will make a significant contribution to life—if not right now, then at some future time.

Bruno Bettelheim

---

Literalism is not always a sign of a nonthinking person. Some very bright people have proved incapable of moving from immediate details in any conversation. One reason may very well be a humorless approach to life, a belief that mind play is childish and that all thought and discussion not directly related to action or the making of money should be avoided. Such people are used to working with the concrete realities of each moment and adjust their responsiveness to experience accordingly. Life is detail after detail. They are often not so much blind to general principles as impatient over wasting time. Sometimes they enjoy discrediting those who are not dedicated to "important" matters but spend their time idly chatting about books or world affairs that obviously have nothing to do with making a living.

## Recognizing Contexts

No one goes through life completely isolated. We cannot live on an island, never making contact with others. Therefore, everything we say or do occurs in a context—a framework of circumstances and relationships. The *figuratist* perceives context; the literalist seldom does.

The experience of living is divided into contexts. Home is a fundamental context. There is always some unfinished business or ongoing problem at home. The nature of this context changes constantly, so we must keep tuned in. The literalist easily ignores this context, forgetting the other family members and believing that the peculiar nature of the family circle provides exemption from having to view family matters objectively.

Visiting a new place provides another context. For the figuratist, the first day at college offers many clues about the new environment: messages on bulletin boards; football memorabilia for sale; petitions for either radical or orthodox causes. The figuratist places all these details into a single context to understand the general atmosphere of the new place, perhaps saving herself or himself from the embarrassment of appearing out of place. The literalist only notes the details.

Some contexts happen without warning, and the literalist is caught napping. A nervous twitch, an ironic reply, the exchange of glances between two other people—and a context is set up. Anthropologist Gregory Bateson laments that too many people live in terms of "pieces," but "the pieces of . . . patterns are not the patterns."

Contexts exist whether recognized or not. Almost any remark contains assumptions that provide a hidden context. For instance, if someone giving a party remarks, "Let's invite Laura for Albert," there is the assumption that couples are better off at parties than individuals; that Albert can't find his own date; that matchmaking is an honorable enterprise; and even that an "unattached" man or woman would somehow be an intrusion for others at the party.

What is the context of the following remarks?

"You'll appreciate your college education more if you find a part-time job."

"When you were in India, what did you learn about the country and the people? No, more importantly, what did you learn about yourself?"

"If God had intended women to be men's equals, he would have made them so."

"You come to my house for dinner this time. I went to your house last time."

Literalists make and hear context-ridden statements without knowing they are doing so. Do you think any of the above remarks were made by figuratists? Can you justify your answer?

## Linguistic Tip-offs

Figuratists are so called because their language gives them away. It is colorful and imaginative, not literal. Their language declares their independence of the details. Instead of telling you everything that happened, the figuratist sums it all up in a few bold strokes.

---

Don't look back. Something may be gaining on you.

Satchel Paige

The law, in its majestic equality, forbids the rich as well as the poor to sleep under bridges.

Anatole France

The difficult we do right away. The impossible takes a little longer.

Business sign

---

Literalists frequently mix their metaphors. The literalist says, "People walk all over me, but I'm putting my foot down!" (Whose foot is down?) The figuratist is likely to reply, "If people walk all over you, make sure you have a good strong mattress." And the literalist may add, "I buy almost everything at Sears."

The secret of figuratism is knowing what is appropriate to think and say about a given phenomenon. When the state representative reports to a group of his constituents, all teachers, that his bill for a higher educational budget was defeated because "the conservatives literally emasculated me," the figuratist lifts an eyebrow. How well is he handling his job up there in the capital?

> *Parent:*     You're foolish to go to the dog races so much. Don't you
>               know you win one night and lose it all back the next?
> *Offspring:*  Okay, I'll go every other night.

When it is appropriate—and it is not always appropriate—figuratists operate from general principles rather than from a long string of specific instances. It strikes the figuratist as a waste of time to bore friends with a blow-by-blow description of all the incompetents met during the course of a single day, and the figuratist would rather ignore the matter altogether—on the grounds that everyone is familiar with the existence of incompetence at every turn. The observation "I also did some shopping today and was pleased to see that standards of incompetence are being met in every store" ends the subject.

*In this world there are only two tragedies. One is not getting what one wants, and the other is getting it.*

                    *Oscar Wilde*

> *Lady Bracknell:*  Do you smoke?
> *Jack Worthing:*   Well, yes, I must admit I smoke.
> *Lady Bracknell:*  I am glad to hear it. A man should always have an
>                    occupation of some sort.

Literalists relive their days over and over because they never stray very far beyond their own egos. If they do discover a general principle, it is usually that people and events are conspiring against them. They are fearful of being objective, of seeing things as they are, for if they ever do they might not find their way back to their own version of reality.

Figuratists, on the other hand, are free spirits, not easily threatened by situations, not easily cowed by other people. They do not have to talk about themselves all the time, because they are not insecure about their own worth. At the same time, they save themselves from arrogance by the very fact that they do attempt to be objective about all things, including themselves. They make mistakes like anyone else, but do not hide guiltily from them. They may even joke about them. Nobody can be a critical thinker all the time. There are times when only the hard details matter:

*Put all your eggs in one basket and—WATCH THAT BASKET.*

                    *Mark Twain*

*"Business is business."*
*"Family is family."*
*"Boys will be boys."*

> *Mechanic:*   The distributor cap is cracked, the points are worn, and
>               the rotor needs replacing. As a matter of fact, the points
>               should be gapped with a gauge; the dwell should be
>               checked with a tach, and the timing needs resetting.
>               The gap should be set at 35, the rpm at 750, and the
>               timing at 6 degrees before top dead center.
> *Bewildered:* Why doesn't the car run?

| Situation | Impulsive Noncritical | Delayed Critical |
|---|---|---|
| People are talking about a book you have not read. | "I hope they don't ask me to give an opinion." | "What is the book basically about?" |
| You discover your brother in the kitchen bleeding profusely. | "I told you to be more careful with a sharp knife!" | "We need to get to the emergency room right away." |
| You read that two small third world countries control much of the Earth's supply of energy. | "What's that got to do with me?" | "How can we develop new energy sources?" |

Parents often make the mistake of supposing that children are immature and can thus be dealt with in any way that suggests itself at the moment. Many parents do not bother to prepare their children to act like responsible, critical adults. If the family watches a television show together, is it talked about afterwards? Or does the following happen? "Turn off the set and march right up to bed." If a bedtime story is read, does the parent show an obvious desire to turn out the light and leave the room, or is the story discussed? It is a sad fact of human experience that little of general, impersonal concern is mentioned within the family circle.

Most of us grow up, as Paul Goodman put it, "absurd." Most of us grow up any way we can. There is very little we can do about how we grew up. But we can decide it is high time to start thinking, to start examining our remarks and our thoughts for the amount of personalizing and the lack of general awareness we will find. The very best way to start is in silence and with a determination to hear and notice more.

## The Critical Thinker as Critic

In its more formal aspects, criticism is associated with literature and the arts. A professional critic is someone paid to read, view, or listen and then present an informed opinion. Society absolutely needs such people. Critics are to plays and concerts what medical specialists are to designated parts of the body. Professional critics must discern and evaluate with cool detachment.

> Once there were two performers—one a literalist, one a figuratist—opening in new plays on the same night. After the performances both entertained friends and fans in their dressing room.
> One performer asked, "How was I?"
> The other performer asked, "How was it?"

But the general public, too, can increase its enjoyment of the arts by practicing some of the skills of the professional critic. Since no one begins with those skills, we achieve competence gradually. With growing experience and with attentive listening or reading or watching, we begin to discern the various elements of the music or the play; to compare the work with different interpretations in previous performances; and to see what the composer or author is driving at. Each new experience is added to the old. At this stage we require more knowledge: information about the musical or the literary genre, the compositional technique, the sounds of various instruments, and the methods of acting.

Reviews, program notes, and art catalogs for museum exhibits produced by professional critics are often helpful. Professionals have the trained eyes and ears; they are the guides until we are ready to pick our *own* way along unfamiliar trails. Since the artist is frequently ahead of—or at least traveling in a different direction from—the public's taste, we, the critical thinker as critic, should withhold judgment until a work has been thought about for a time. It would be totally unacceptable to make up our minds in advance, pretending to like something because the experts do, or ridiculing it because it is unfamiliar. The opportunity to be a critic does not depend entirely on visits to concert halls or museums. There is always television, which we may approach with an equally dispassionate and analytical mind. When a news event is considered important enough to be carried simultaneously by major television networks, the critical viewer thinks, "Is this really that important?" And if the news report deals with a government-sponsored program, further questions occur: "What should the state encourage? pay for? withdraw support from?"

---

A well-known entertainer, on in years but still popular, died suddenly and unexpectedly of a heart attack while in Europe. Two of his friends, also famous entertainers, were asked for comments.

One was very personal: "I feel crushed, abandoned. I idolized him. I used him as a model. I would never have become successful had it not been for his encouragement. Life for me will never be the same without him."

The other recognized a larger context: "He changed the entire history of popular songs. He introduced a style of singing that countless have imitated. He was the first performer to use the microphone instead of merely standing behind it. He created a sound that will probably never be forgotten."

---

After a while, critical thinking becomes an enjoyable part of being a spectator, though there will always be the uncritical friend who insists, "I'd rather not think about what I see. I'd rather enjoy myself." And there's no way to convince that friend it is possible to do both.

# Glossary

*context:* The environment, the background, the special circumstance that affects understanding.

*critical:* An adjective referring to one who makes a habit of standing back and surveying a situation as a whole before reaching a conclusion about it.

*criticism:* Analysis leading to evaluation (*not* used

here in the narrower sense of "the act of finding fault with").

*figuratist:* One who knows what is appropriate to think and say about a given phenomenon; who engages in "mind play" rather than passively existing; who has acquired the good habit of noticing and listening instead of being preoccupied with self; whose language is full of fancy and good humor; and who, above all, practices the art of critical thinking.

*literalist:* One who sees specific instances rather than general principles; who moves from point *A* to point *B* in a thought sequence without grasping the essential point of a discussion; who seldom identifies contexts, is generally self-centered, and speaks in plodding clichés.

## Notes

1. William Wharton, *Dad* (New York: Avon, 1981), 419–420.
2. S. I. Hayakawa, *Language in Thought and Action* (New York: Harcourt Brace Jovanovich, 1978), 191.
3. From "Loveliest of trees, the cherry now" from *The Collected Poems of A. E. Housman* by A. E. Housman. Copyright 1939, 1940, ©1965 by Holt, Rinehart and Winston. Copyright ©1967, 1968 by Robert E. Symons. Reprinted by permission of Henry Holt and Company, Inc.

## Suggested Reading

Brustein, Robert. *Seasons of Discontent.* New York: Simon & Schuster, 1965. A classic statement from a major twentieth-century critic, defending critical elitism and reaffirming the classical view of the critic as guardian of public taste. A highly provocative work that may enlighten or infuriate.

Ferris, Timothy. *The Mind's Sky: Human Intelligence in a Cosmic Context.* New York: Bantam, 1992. The author of *Coming of Age in the Milky Way* discusses whether the human mind is really capable of interpreting the universe or whether intelligence may not be central to the scheme of the universe.

Gardner, Howard. *Frames of Mind: The Theory of Multiple Intelligences.* New York: Basic Books, 1983. The author presents a widely researched theory from what he calls a "psychobiological" perspective, showing how human intelligence evolved into not just one capacity but many different capacities as humanity learned to adapt to a variety of conditions. This is a must-read for those who mistrust intelligence tests.

Gregory, Richard L., ed. *The Oxford Companion to the Mind.* Oxford, U.K.: Oxford University Press, 1987. A compendium of everything you ever wanted to know (and more) about the mind: its relationship to the body, especially the brain; the workings of thoughts and emotions; and short bios of every scientist and philosopher who has delved into this still-mysterious realm.

Morrison, Philip and Phylis. *The Ring of Truth: An Inquiry into How We Know What We Know.* New York: Random House, 1987. The subtitle says it all. The book represents an attempt to account for human intelligence from a purely scientific point of view, demonstrating how we see, how we transfer what we see into internal imagery, how we abstract, and how we think.

Sagan, Carl. *The Dragons of Eden: Speculations on the Evolution of Human Intelligence.* New York: Ballantine Books, 1977. The famous physicist and stargazer turns his mind and brilliant wit to a consideration of human thought and finds that the brain does not change completely as it evolves but carries with it the entire evolutionary past of the species.

# Themes of the Humanities

If we were to explore every subject, every issue, every concern, every emotion that finds expression in the humanities, we would need a volume many times the size of this one.

Sometimes, as in philosophy, the expression is direct and rationally structured: arguments that follow each other to a carefully articulated conclusion. Sometimes, as in a work of music, the expression is to be felt, "intuited." If you stare long enough at an abstract painting, you may begin to hear its silent voice. Two people viewing may hear two different voices, and both can be right.

In the second part of this book, we have chosen several of the major themes that many readers, listeners, and viewers have discovered over and over in great and important works from the past and present: how society treats the artistic personality; how myths have influenced and continue to influence the way human beings view themselves and the universe; the many faces of love; the divergent roads to happiness; why we fear or do not fear to die; how people have loved and mistreated the natural environment; and what it means to be free.

Looking at themes of the humanities does not constitute a means of appreciating important works in their totality. We doubt that any text can—or should—attempt to inform you about Everything that is to be seen, understood, or felt in the presence of the great works. Rather, we entertain the more modest hope that our approach will serve to bring you a little closer to achievements that might otherwise seem distant, awesome, or unconnected to your personal interests. Our secret belief is that once the "human" concerns of the humanities are glimpsed, you will want and need to make further discoveries on your own.

The first discovery is sure to be the realization that the makers of the humanities speak our thoughts, feel our emotions, and dream our dreams.

*Auguste Rodin*, Burghers of Calais *(Musée Rodin, Paris)*

Auguste Rodin
1840—
1917

Strong emotion

Look up

Video

H77A
#24

Sculp. Mean
Thru The
Body
Form

# 10

# Society Versus
the Humanities

## Overview

The humanities are sometimes the private expressions of artists who have no other outlet for their thoughts and feelings. Sometimes they are the work of those who master the challenges of their media, whose main concern is to bring something of beauty into existence. The humanities also include the rational arguments of those whose main concern is to discover and articulate truth as well as the glorious labors of those who work to please us with their performances or their writings. In all of these cases, society would seem to be the winner, profiting from the insights, the music, the poetry, the beautiful objects, and the magical sounds of great artists. Without them, our lives would be very poor indeed.

Yet the tragic fact is that society does not always recognize the riches it stands to receive. Sometimes it is outright hostile. Sometimes it rejects what is created because the language is too raw, the sound is too unfamiliar, the ideas are too radical, or the figures on the wall are too provocative. Sometimes the artist is

271

told in advance what will be funded, and a crucial decision has to be made: integrity or money, conformity or the end of a career.

*Artists who seek funding must sometimes choose between integrity and money.*

Artists usually know what is expected of them. If they deliver something else, the reason is usually that public acclaim is less important than the distant drumbeat to which they are marching.

Holding out against society, however, is no guarantee of greatness. Nor is creating a work for a mass audience an indication that the product will be lacking in power or beauty. Some of the great orations in history were composed for special occasions by speakers who knew how to move a crowd. Bach was hired to play the organ and compose hymns and other music befitting religious services. Much of what he composed is a good deal more, but some of it is Bach simply doing his job. Shakespeare was very popular in his day, but wanting to please his audience did not stop him from writing plays that were often far better than they had to be.

Often the artist creates for a particular occasion, hoping that the work will be pleasing, and is surprised to discover otherwise. One such occasion was the premiere of a ballet called *The Rite of Spring* at the Théâtre des Champs-Elysées, Paris, in May of 1913. The music was by the modernist Igor Stravinsky and the choreography by Vaslav Nijinsky, both of whom had already achieved recognition as artists who were giving exciting new directions to their art forms. The event was an important one, both socially and esthetically, and there is no reason to suppose either man was deliberately trying to be revolutionary.

Nonetheless, the orchestra had scarcely played more than a few opening notes before the whistling and booing started. In seconds audience disapproval grew so loud that the orchestra was altogether drowned out. Fights broke out between protesters and defenders, though neither the conductor nor the dancers could have known there were any supporters at all. One critic the next day reported that the score sounded like "a barnyard come to life."

Stravinsky was to outlive the scandal and learn that his score had changed the course of modern music, but Nijinsky's mental health began to deteriorate in 1917. Though he lived until 1950, one doubts that the celebrated dancer ever really knew he had been part of a historic moment in the history of the humanities.

*Artists often face obstacles in the form of government oppression, religious condemnation, racism, sexism, bad timing, and a sudden change in public taste.*

New art does not always create an uproar. Van Gogh's paintings were simply ignored, and the artist ended his own life believing that he had failed. Others have had to face oppression and rejection from their governments and from powerful religious leaders. Further obstacles include racism, sexism, bad timing, and a sudden change in public taste. Distrust between artists and society is manifest. One often wonders why artists still try to communicate.

In this chapter we shall examine a few key examples of the struggle between society and those who create the humanities. Understanding this conflict as an ongoing condition is as important as viewing, listening to, or reading what the humanities have provided for us. *We*, after all, are part of society; each of us may become involved in a decision with enormous consequences for both the artist and that society. Who knows how many great artists have remained unknown because they lived at a time or in a place that did not encourage them? Doubtless there is a whole tradition of humanities forever hidden in shadow.

*Doubtless there is a whole tradition of humanities forever hidden in shadow.*

## The Artist and the Moral Code

All societies have moral codes: written or unwritten rules governing human behavior. These rules determine what is or is not acceptable to society, to God, to small groups wielding power, or to governments, which often avail themselves of the right to turn moral restrictions into laws with severe penalties for violators.

It is infrequently within the artist's (or the philosopher's) nature to become a spokesperson for the moral system of the group or the established majority. Plato was a moral absolutist, but not because religion or the government asked him to be or because he wanted to be an apologist for them. Far from it! Socrates, his mentor, also believed in an absolute morality, but his open and inquiring mind challenged Athenian society; he was executed because he was considered danger-ous. Plato wrote an account of the trial and execution, and it stands as the classic story of artistic integrity threatened and ultimately engulfed by a hostile society.

*Plato's account of the trial and execution of Socrates stands as the classic story of artistic integrity engulfed by a hostile society.*

Dramatists in particular have experienced punishment when they violated a prevailing code. After all, when the essence of your art is to present your vision of life to an audience, you must sometimes expect swift feedback. So it came to John Millington Synge, the Irish playwright who opened his *Playboy of the Western World* in 1907 at Dublin's Abbey Theatre. The audience appeared to be barely but nonetheless politely tolerating the story of a group of people in a rural Irish pub who not only protect but make a hero out of a man who claims to have savagely murdered his father. But when the hero spoke the word "shift" (a woman's undergarment), the opening-night audience started to hiss and continued to do so until the final curtain. During the second performance, despite the presence of police, the hissing turned into an uproar that caused the dialogue to become inaudible. The point here is not that the moral lynching of a playwright by the audience caused a change in his style, but that incidents of this kind, which are fairly common, have had a profound effect on the arts. Who can say how many potentially great works have been changed or have gone unfinished because some-one feared the audience might hiss?

*Who can say how many potentially great works have been changed or have gone unfinished because somebody feared the audience might hiss?*

## Moral Censorship

Visual art, theater, and films have been the targets of moral censorship over the centuries, especially in societies that have subjected human behavior itself to close scrutiny. Michelangelo's *The Last Judgment*, painted for the Sistine Chapel at the Pope's request, dismayed a good many among public and clergy alike because of its realistic nudes. The artist, however, had established such an awesome reputation that nothing could be done about the painting until after his death, when little pieces of cloth were attached appropriately to each figure. A lesser known artist might have fared quite differently.

As recently as the 1930s and 1940s, the city of Boston had the municipally supported Watch and Ward Society, which had the authority to ban plays, books, and films before they reached the public. The historical novel *Forever Amber*, which recounted the affairs of a courtesan (a highly paid mistress) in the court of Charles II, was banned; on the day the film version of the novel opened, a high-ranking member of the clergy rode a white charger in front of the theater urging people to boycott the movie. The novel *Strange Fruit*, about an interracial romance, was also banned, as were dozens of others, often at the whim of just one persuasive council member.

The moralistic critic is still with us, though perhaps in a less open stance. He or she can be recognized from certain underlying assumptions about art, the principal one being that art cannot simply mirror reality. The artist *must* have a message. That message may no longer have to be the triumph of virtue and the foiling of vice, but the critic must approve of the message to recommend the film.

*[handwritten margin notes:]*
*Whitman—homosexuality*
*D.H. Lawrence*
*Sons & Lovers*
*The Awakening*
*Kate Chopin*

*Auguste Rodin,* The Kiss *( 1886): Rodin's statue appalled many moralistic critics. (Musée Rodin, Paris)*

One New York critic, for example, praised Francis Ford Coppola's 1972 film *The Godfather* because he believed the director's intention was to draw a parallel between the operations of the Mafia and those of American business. Another New York critic panned the film because she believed the director's intention was to glorify the Mafia bosses. An academic critic, writing for a scholarly journal, praised the film because of its supposed updating of the mythical struggle between Dionysian energies and Apollonian restraint. In all of these cases the critic had definite ideas about what was or was not praiseworthy about the film. Not one of them dealt with the director's handling of the film medium. The art form itself was clearly subordinated to the art *message*.

On the other hand, in our time we have a new art form, that of the stand-up comic, whose intentions are both to entertain an audience and to deliver social criticism through laughter. Often "profanity," which nowadays means "swear words," is an integral part of the routine. Surely one reason is to jolt us out of any complacent or rigid attitudes we might have. Eddie Murphy, George Carlin, Robin Williams, and the late Lenny Bruce have established themselves as masters of the form; all have been subjected to eyebrow-raised criticism from those who cannot tolerate the language, the irreverent comments, or both. (Often these critics are the very targets of the comics' satire.) Lenny Bruce was accustomed to having police officers in his audience, waiting for an excuse to cart him off to prison.

Everyone is familiar with the rating system of motion pictures: G, PG, PG-13, R, and X. Who establishes these labels? What are the criteria? Rational or otherwise, corrupt or not, the system is one of continuing moral censorship that has nothing to do with the art of film. Studios can be controlled by the system. For fear of getting an R rating—or the once-deadly X—studio bosses have had scenes and

*Lenny Bruce was accustomed to having police officers in his audience, waiting for an excuse to cart him off to prison.*

entire films edited beyond recognition. The probabilities of human behavior often have been discarded in favor of having characters say and do what the mysterious raters will approve.

Before the rating system there had been an organization called the Motion Picture Producers and Distributors of America, a unique union comprised of representatives from each of the Hollywood studios whose job it was to screen each film before it was released. Its first chief was Will H. Hays, a man with a politically conservative and religiously respectable background. In 1922, when the organization was established, Hollywood had unlimited freedom. Hays was told to save the film industry from being buried under an avalanche of protest lodged by an aroused citizenry.

The Hays office drew up the Motion Picture Production Code, which was modified in 1956 and continues to influence those responsible for the rating system of today. The three general principles of the code are

1. No picture shall be produced that will lower the moral standards of those who see it. The sympathy of the audience shall never be thrown to the side of crime, wrongdoing, evil, or sin.
2. Correct standards of life, subject only to the requirements of drama and entertainment, shall be presented.
3. Law—divine, natural, or human—shall not be ridiculed, nor shall sympathy be created for its violation.

This code cannot be blatantly disregarded, but, as you have probably already realized, the second principle constitutes a gigantic loophole; the "requirements of drama and entertainment" phrase is open to a huge number of interpretations. The issue in question, however, is not how filmmakers "get around" the code, but the control that this code exerts over an art form. Note that film censorship began with an organization of producers and distributors, not writers or directors.

Over the years the code has demanded the deletion of numerous "objectionable" items, including the birth of a buffalo (in a Disney film); the words *rape* and even *censorship* itself; the word *virgin*; an open discussion of pregnancy, birth control, and illegitimacy; the bare flesh showing above a woman's blouse; a long and passionate kiss; and, on one occasion, the graphic descriptions of venereal disease in a film warning against it. A film version of *Carmen* was condemned in certain quarters because the girls in the cigarette factory were shown smoking cigarettes.

The problem of moral censorship is far from simple. Should we suggest that *no one* be concerned about the effects that the arts can have? Yet if someone is appointed to "oversee" what is shown to the public, who should that person be? Who would ever be satisfied that the right decision had been made in every case?

Complaints are raised on every side today about the moral degeneration of society. Very often the arts are blamed for behavior that no one knows how to control. One doubts there exists a documented case in which a social ill was "cured" by the suppression of a film or novel or by the mere expunging of obscene language or graphic sexual acts. One doubts that censorship is ever the answer. Raising our esthetic sensibilities, demanding art that deals honestly with truth and that exercises restraint, which is far more exciting than a profusion of noise, blood, and four-letter words . . . maybe *these* goals come closer to addressing some of society's problems.

*One doubts there exists a documented case in which a social ill was "cured" by the suppression of a film or novel.*

## Lifestyles of the Rich and Infamous

Artists and performers who lead scandalous lives, especially those who have achieved stature enough to make tongue-wagging worthwhile, have always shocked (and indeed continue to shock) the moral establishment. When they break the law, public censure can be quick and decisive. Many years ago a prominent film actor, who often portrayed private investigators on the trail of hardened criminals, was arrested for marijuana possession. This happened before drug abuse was considered the country's most serious problem; people arrested for the same offense were usually given suspended sentences or asked to do some hours of community service. The judge who sentenced the actor to a year in prison said he was doing so *because* the man was a star and must therefore be a role model.

During the romantic period (see Chapter 15), extending from the latter half of the eighteenth to about the middle of the nineteenth century, the reputation (or perhaps the myth) of the "bohemian" artist was born. People came to expect artistic personalities to be eccentric and amoral. Often public fascination with their eccentricities worked to their advantage. The poetry of Lord Byron, for example, may have attracted public interest because of the flamboyant exploits of the poet himself, including an incestuous romance with his half sister. Some of the romantics became famous for flouting middle-class conventions with their divorces, mistresses, unpaid debts, ceaseless travels, hot tempers, and bizarre clothing. The French novelist George Sand was a woman who dressed like a man and was celebrated for going from lover to lover, including the poet Alfred de Musset and the composer Frederic Chopin.

All the while, however, the Puritan substratum of middle-class society was emphasizing hard work, thrift, sobriety, and the sacredness of the family. It may

*Eugene Delacroix,* Portrait of George Sand *(1838). (Culver Pictures)*

have been fascinated by the artist in secret, but it also viewed unconventional behavior as a threat to all the most worthwhile virtues.

The romantic period gradually gave way to a period increasingly dominated by unbending middle-class morality. Throughout the last half of the nineteenth century the middle class was becoming richer and richer as merchants, managers, lawyers, physicians, and accountants. The Puritan focus on hard work and thrift finally paid off. The reward for hard work and a steadfast loyalty to virtue was lots of money. Artists who made money but did not observe the moral code were prime targets for moral criticism, even if it sometimes contained a little hidden jealousy.

The classic example of the artist with a highly divergent lifestyle who became a victim of a morally repressive society is Oscar Wilde (1854–1900). The relative shortness of his life can be directly attributed to the devastating effects of a two-year prison term at hard labor. The tragic irony is that the novelist and playwright had reached the zenith of his career on both sides of the Atlantic when he became the central figure in a moral scandal of unprecedented notoriety.

The action that ruined his career and would indirectly end his life was his involvement with a young aristocrat, Lord Alfred Douglas, whose father was the Marquess of Queensberry. The latter, a skillful hunter and the author of the famous rules of boxing that still bear his name, was no doubt disappointed that his son had not followed in his own manly footsteps and enraged beyond reason that Alfred was the talk of London. On the opening night of Wilde's greatest success, *The Importance of Being Earnest* (February 14, 1895), Queensberry, who had planned a disruptive demonstration inside the theater, decided instead on sending a note to Wilde at his private club. It was addressed "To Oscar Wilde posing Somdomite"— a misspelled repetition of the charge that the Marquess had made on a public street. Against the advice of close associates, Wilde sued the man for libel and was placed in the difficult position of having to prove in court that Queensberry was lying. The Marquess, for his part, having used the word "posing," had only to prove that Wilde's behavior was decidedly unmasculine.

Queensberry, as it turned out, had an easy time, because Wilde proved to be his own undoing before the jury, which must have forgotten after a time that the Marquess was the defendant, not Wilde. The playwright, known for his wit both in the theater and in public, alienated the jury with his apparent self-confidence and cavalier remarks. Convinced that Queensberry had every reason to attack the man responsible for corrupting his son, the jury found for the defendant. A few days later Wilde was arrested and soon was tried for the crime of sodomy. The case against him, including the reading of a damaging letter written to Alfred and a philosophical defense made by Wilde of "the Love that dare not speak its name," mounted quickly.

Also going against him was Wilde's art-for-art's-sake philosophy, his total commitment to the esthetic life. He was arrogant in his steadfast references to himself as an artist. When, for example, the incriminating letter was read, Wilde replied that it was intended as a poem and indeed later became one. The prosecution then asked, "Suppose a man who was not an artist had written this letter, would you say it was a proper letter?" Wilde's answer could not have won much favor with the jury: "A man who was not an artist could not have written that letter, because nobody but an artist could write it."

Convicted—after a jury deliberation of only a few hours—Wilde was sent to prison for two years of hard labor. His wife divorced him and changed her

*Wilde's total commitment to the esthetic life probably helped turn the jury against him.*

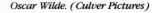

name. His children were alienated from him. Lord Alfred Douglas denounced him and, after his release, refused to see him. Wilde died almost penniless, convinced that his name would rust in oblivion.

Ironically, on February 15, the day after the opening of *Earnest*, the *New York Times* had given this review: "Oscar Wilde may be said to have at last, and by a single stroke, put his enemies under his feet."

## Government Power and Free Speech

No study of the humanities can ignore the ongoing conflict between powerful governments—or factions within those governments—and the burning need for freedom of expression. Those who wield the pen have been targets of suspicion and sometimes persecution because of the ever-present "danger" that through direct attacks or indirect satire, they may arouse the populace.

Even a philosopher like Plato recognized that freedom of expression was not always desirable. In his blueprint for the ideal society, outlined in *The Republic*, he found no place for artists, who were likely to lead the public astray through the distortion of reality. He considered poets to be afflicted with a "divine madness," which, however tinged with genius, was an enemy to rational thought. The arts were not concerned with truth and were therefore dangerous.

Over the centuries the definition and recognition of "truth" in the arts have always been clouded. Artists have never thought of themselves as communicators of falsehood, but repressive agencies and governments have often accused them of lying. (No government has ever said boldly that the truth was punishable by imprisonment or death.) Plato's mentor, Socrates, was in fact put to death by the government of Athens for a number of probable reasons, including his close friendship with Alcibiades, considered a traitor to the city, and the general paranoia often experienced by governments that have in their midst a prominent figure known for speaking his or her mind. The legal charges, however, were the teaching of atheism and in general corrupting the youth of Athens. The assumption, of course, was that atheism (which Socrates did *not* teach) was a falsehood.

*No government has ever said that the truth was punishable by imprisonment or death. Instead, dangerous artists have been accused of lying.*

## Pioneer Freedom Fighters

Champions of freedom have usually argued that there is more danger in the suppression of speech, even of falsehood, than in the wide distribution of any ideas, including the mockery of those in power. One of the most famous defenses of absolute liberty is John Milton's *Areopagitica*, which contains the ringing words "Give me liberty to know, to utter, and to argue freely according to conscience, above all liberties." Though Milton was a Puritan, and Puritans were known for intolerance and the repression of all ideologies that ran counter to theirs, he was ideologically a liberal. In fact, there has always been a suspicion among certain critics and historians of literature that Lucifer is really the hero of the great epic poem *Paradise Lost* (1667). After being banished from heaven because he has led the rebellion of the angels, Lucifer becomes king of hell and delivers one of numerous ringing lines: "Better to reign in Hell, than serve in Heav'n."

Milton's un-Puritanic ideas, including a belief in divorce (expressed in an essay written during his honeymoon), did not run the risk of government reprisals because the Puritan government was toppled in 1661. Others were not so fortunate with other authorities. Daniel Defoe (1659-1731), author of *Robinson Crusoe*, was sentenced to a year in jail for writing a satire on religious intolerance. John Wilkes was committed to the Tower of London for writing that the king (George) had not told the truth. Benjamin Harris was pilloried, fined, and then imprisoned for openly criticizing the king, and James Franklin was publicly censured and jailed for the same offense.

The cause of free speech was greatly advanced in a milestone legal decision delivered in 1735 in the American colonies. John Peter Zenger (1697-1746), a German immigrant who became a New York journalist, was sued and tried for having said in his newspaper that the people of New York were in jeopardy because of the administration of Governor William Cosby. (Zenger was also known for having printed mock advertisements of strayed animals with the features of recognizable politicians.) The specific charge was "printing and publishing a certain false, malicious, and scandalous libel." The pivotal issue of the trial was the use of the word "false." Apparently without realizing what it was doing, the prosecution walked into a trap. Until that time, British law had held that defamatory remarks (especially against a government official) were never justified, even if they were true. Nor did the reputation of the defamed party matter. But because the charge included the word "false," the prosecution had to prove that the people of New York were not in jeopardy, that, in fact, Zenger was lying. If truth is hard to prove, falsehood is too; a case requiring such proof is immediately on shaky ground. The jury found Zenger not guilty, and he was set free. Benjamin Franklin hailed the decision, but it was fifty years before British law again allowed truth or falsehood to be a factor in libel suits.

## The "Art" of Propaganda

Powerful governments can, of course, do whatever they want. Though they can suppress artists if they choose, they can also promote their own versions of art without fear of censorship or imprisonment. Theirs is the quintessential state of "free speech." A long-standing tradition exists of government involvement in the popular arts, especially the mass media. Recently the primary Russian newspaper *Pravda* removed the Communist party logo from its front page, an indication that Communist authority was weakening. Yet for decades the paper had been the means by which the party communicated what it wished to be known. When the Soviet Union was a totalitarian country, it carefully controlled television and motion pictures as well so that the stories and images in these media would carry a pro-Soviet message.

A famous example of government propaganda is the film *Olympia*, a documentary account of the 1936 games held in Berlin. The work, directed by Leni Riefenstahl, is generally admired for its esthetic qualities, especially the camera work, which was highly sophisticated for the time. One sequence depicts the diving competition, but abstracts the human body as an object of beauty in itself, unrelated to the purpose of the games.

The director, however, does not allow us to forget that purpose. In that year the Olympic games were supposed to be a showcase for the skill, beauty, and majesty of the Nazi athlete. Thus Riefenstahl intercuts from close-ups of the divers to shots of admiring faces looking upward, an approving Adolf Hitler, swastika flags, and Nazi salutes. As we approach the end of the diving sequence, the director imposes a series of deliberately artificial shots seldom found in a documentary. The divers no longer hit the water; they soar, suspended in air, all of them immune

*The diving sequence from Riefenstahl's* Olympia. *( The Museum of Modern Art/Film Stills Archive)*

to gravity. The viewer cannot help being stirred by the awesome power of these athletes. They indeed become the *übermenschen* (supermen) of Nazi mythology.

Because of the film's evident propaganda objectives, the Anti-Nazi League in the United States tried to prevent its release in this country. Leni Riefenstahl herself came to the United States in an effort to win the American market. Not once was she able to separate esthetics from politics, however. After a visit to a black theater in New York, she was heard commenting on the "breathtaking jungle ability" of the performers, but unfortunately they had "no brains and no inspiration." She also warned that blacks and Jews "working together would bring Bolshevism to America." Apparently there were many who could not detect the propaganda mission. Riefenstahl was a celebrity and was feted by such notables as Henry Ford and Walt Disney. Pop journalist Walter Winchell called her "pretty as a swastika." Her blatant Nazism even disturbed the German consul, who urged her to leave the United States. Before she did, the infamous *Kristallnacht* occurred in November of 1938, during which synagogues and Jewish-owned stores were burned and vast numbers of Jews were beaten, murdered, or thrown into concentration camps. The impact of these atrocities was not, however, able to offset the ballyhoo of the director's visit.

At the same time, the German government was working to suppress films they deemed unsympathetic to Nazism. When a sequel to the film version of Erich Maria Remarque's *All Quiet on the Western Front* (1929) was in production, the studio executives received letters warning them that this and any other film like it would never be distributed in German-controlled territories. The boycott would extend to any film "detrimental to German prestige in tendency or effect in spite of the warnings issued by the competent German authorities." Though the film was being made on American soil, the threats worked. The ending of the film was changed. Romantic scenes were added, and political ones, removed. The studio shipped a copy of the film to the German ambassador for his approval. A joke circulating around Hollywood at the time was that the German consul in Los Angeles should have been listed in the credits as *film editor*.

*Anti-German sentiments in an American film were ordered deleted by studio executives, who feared the loss of the German market.*

Though the cinema artistry of Leni Riefenstahl is still recognized as well as studied in film schools, the outstanding European film director of the 1920s and 1930s was probably Sergei Eisenstein (see Chapter 5), whose *Potemkin* (1925) won international acclaim for its extraordinary techniques. Only in retrospect have we discovered the extent of the propaganda content, though the discovery in no way diminishes the film's power. The most famous episode in the picture shows a massacre of innocent civilians on the Odessa steps by cossack warriors loyal to the czar. Historians now assure us this event never took place. The film also indicates that the people of the city sent food to the mutinous sailors on board the *Potemkin*—a sign that the sailors were joining the people's struggle. No such widespread uprising occurred, however, nor did the other ships in the harbor join in. The purpose of the film is clearly to glorify the early heroes of communism. Eisenstein was in high favor with the Communist party, enjoying privileges accorded to only a few.

The artistic integrity of the director, however, maintained for a time a delicate balance with the demands of the party. Eisenstein was driven by the need to experiment, to see how he could improve upon his own screen art. *Ivan the Terrible* (1944) was hailed internationally for its spectacle, its sweeping scenes of violence and bloodshed, and its moments of sheer poetry. The Kremlin was apparently pleased by the depiction of an infamous czar, but the planned sequel to the film was not pleasing. The work was canceled by order of the Soviet leader, Joseph Stalin. As time went on, Eisenstein, like many other artists caught up in a political vortex, gradually surrendered much of his artistic integrity. But the contemporary cinematographer Nestor Almendros, himself a refugee from a Communist society, writes: "Don't be fooled. Eisenstein was Stalin's man." There is no indication that Eisenstein was unhappy with his lot. He reported that as an artist he always felt an "exhilarating" sense of being alive at a momentous time in history. His place in the humanities is secure. He is judged by his contributions to screen, not propaganda, art. Many other artists have been less fortunate.

*Eisenstein, like many other artists caught up in a political vortex, gradually surrendered much of his artistic integrity.*

## A Witch-Hunt

Ever since the 1692 witchcraft trials in Salem, Massachusetts, which led to the execution of some twenty innocent people, the word *witch-hunt* has been a part of our vocabulary. It refers to an outbreak of panic among people in a government or a powerful group over the suspected presence of individuals who are unacceptable because of religious, philosophical, political, or lifestyle differences.

In 1947, just after the end of World War II, the House of Representatives convened a Committee on Un-American Activities; its prime mission was to ferret out Communist sympathizers and party members working in positions of authority. Though the Soviet Union had been our ally during the war, the fear now became widespread that the Communist world was the new enemy and a devastating confrontation was inevitable.

The House committee (or HUAC) amassed incredible powers. Using propaganda techniques of its own—bold statements in newspapers, appearances on radio panels, and carefully manipulated newsreel stories—it soon had government officials and millions of citizens convinced that war with the Soviet Union was inevitable and that the country was crawling with once-loyal Americans spying for the enemy. Since public media were the primary vehicles for propaganda—often for the government itself—the HUAC felt it knew exactly where to look for enemy propagandists. Newspaper and magazine articles, short stories, novels, radio and stage plays, and above all *motion pictures* would be the most likely "fronts" for dangerous ideas.

*In 1947 the House Un-American Activities Committee (HUAC) was organized and convinced millions that the country was crawling with once-loyal Americans spying for the Soviet Union.*

The HUAC summoned to its hearings writers, actors, directors, technicians, costumers, makeup specialists—anyone about whom there was the slightest suspicion. They had to answer under oath the now-famous question, "Are you now or have you ever been a member of the Communist party?" Many of those questioned had had party affiliations in the 1930s before the party was outlawed; they admitted as much but added that they were no longer members. They were not forgiven. Many reputations were destroyed. The dreaded blacklist was circulated around Hollywood, and studios dared not hire anyone whose name was on it. Sometimes the HUAC offered a "deal": give us the names of associates known to be party members, and you will be exonerated. A number of celebrities did indeed testify against close friends in order to protect their livelihoods, but many did not and spent years in obscurity.

Folksinger Pete Seeger (b. 1919) became an outspoken critic of the HUAC. Looking back at the witch-hunting period in *The Incompleat Folksinger*, he writes with bitter irony:

> It is a fact well known to old-timers that the U.S. folk song revival was spearheaded in the Dirty Thirties by New Dealers and leftwingers.

(Leadbelly sang for $10 at house parties raising money for Loyalist Spain when no one else would hire him.) This fact has seemed very confusing to young people who came along in a rush of enthusiasm for this favorite new music of theirs and then heard it accused of being subtle Communist propaganda.[1]

Seeger was summoned to appear before the HUAC in 1955. He refused to answer any questions, but he also declined to use the Fifth Amendment, as many others had done. The amendment protects people from self-incrimination. Anyone testifying under oath has the right to say, "I refuse to answer on the grounds that I may incriminate myself." To both juries and the general public, taking the Fifth Amendment is often a clear indication of guilt, and it is likely that Seeger, a passionate defender of human rights, was really protesting against the whole witch-hunting process. Instead of answering the committee's questions, he described the various places in which he had sung: "in hobo jungles" and "for the Rockefellers" as well as for pacifists and soldiers alike. As a result of his refusal to answer, he was cited for contempt, eventually indicted, and tried. The jury found him guilty of not answering ten questions. Though he had never been charged with being a Communist, the judge nonetheless asked him if he *was* one. Seeger cited the First Amendment and said that it "prevented *any* official from probing, under pressure, an American's private beliefs." He was given a sentence, but he appealed, and the judge's decision was eventually reversed.

The HUAC hearings, led by Senator Joseph McCarthy, proved to be a media circus. Many sessions were shown in their entirety on television, which was still the country's new toy and was desperate for "entertainment" to fill its programming hours. Seeger's case received so much negative publicity that his career suffered at least momentary setbacks. School officials denied him the right to sing on school property, for example; there were a number of petitions to prevent him from appearing in concert halls built with taxpayers' money. Seeger was actually glad to have controversy following him, so that he could more passionately defend his belief in total equality and total freedom of thought and speech.

A number of this century's most prominent playwrights were among those questioned by the HUAC. Lillian Hellman (1905–1984), author of some highly successful Broadway hits, such as *The Little Foxes*, was more interested in constructing well-made plays than in using the stage for propaganda. Nevertheless, she was summoned before the committee and asked about her own political affiliations and those of her close friends. Hellman remained bitter about the HUAC until the end of her life.

In 1953 Arthur Miller, whose *Death of a Salesman* is discussed in Chapter 4, wrote a new play called *The Crucible*, which is in fact *about* the original Salem witch-hunts. There is no question in anybody's mind that the dramatist was reacting directly to the HUAC hearings. He was particularly concerned about what he considered the outrageous bypassing of due process of the law. Since none of those summoned had been charged with a crime, they were not given the customary legal protection. For example, they could not hire lawyers to speak on their behalf or to question their questioners. All of this reminded Miller of the Salem witch trials, in which innocent people were hauled into court on the hysterical testimony of a few children. The children, it was later discovered, pretended they had seen the accused dancing with the devil or making dolls associated with witchcraft to protect themselves from punishment. The only way the defendants could avoid being found guilty and then being imprisoned or executed, however, was to

*Lillian Hellman and Arthur Miller were among the prominent theater people summoned before the HUAC hearings.*

confess their alliance with Satan. Refusing to confess was taken as an admission of guilt.

To Miller, taking the First or Fifth Amendment before the HUAC was an act of integrity and the right of every citizen of a free society. That careers were being destroyed because the action was widely accepted as evidence of guilt infuriated him; as he researched the incidents in Salem, he kept seeing unmistakable analogies. But before drawing this direct parallel, he in 1950 did an adaptation of Ibsen's *An Enemy of the People*, updating it so that its story clearly applied to the HUAC hearings. In the play, a town council persecutes a doctor who has discovered and intends to publicize the fact that the mineral baths for which the town is famous have become polluted. In its original production, the play made some audience members nervous. They considered it an attack on conservative public opinion—an attack on what is today sometimes referred to as the "moral majority." Ibsen was thought to be saying that truth is on the side of the minority.

*To the HUAC Arthur Miller might have been a great playwright, but he was also dangerous.*

Miller might well have argued that he was "only" refurbishing an honored classic of the stage, but the HUAC was suspicious of anything he said or wrote. Had he not questioned American capitalism—the American Dream—in *Death of a Salesman*? With the appearance of *The Crucible* all doubts were removed. Arthur Miller might be a great playwright, but his was a dangerous voice.

His hero is John Proctor, a historical figure who was indeed persecuted and eventually hanged, not for witchcraft, but for a passionate denunciation of the irrational and cruel procedures in the Salem court. Lines like "you know in all your black hearts that this be fraud" could not have endeared the author to the committee. When the time seemed right—it was in 1956—Miller himself was finally summoned and asked about his own membership in the party (which he denied) and whether any of his friends and colleagues carried Communist party cards.

The irony is that the Miller hearings were in a sense reenactments of the final scene in his play. Just before sunrise the prosecutor visits Proctor in his cell and offers him one last chance to save his life. He must sign a confession that he has seen the accused women consorting with the devil. Though he nearly relents and though he wants very much to live, he cannot sign his name to such a document:

> Because it is my name! Because I cannot have another in my life! Because I lie and sign myself to lies! Because I am not worth the dust on the feet of them that hang! How may I live without my name?[2]

Appearing before the committee, Miller, like Proctor, refused to name names. Though others had similarly refused, the HUAC had a giant in Miller and wanted to make a public example of him. He was cited for contempt of Congress and summoned to appear before the entire House. He was found guilty of the contempt charges by an overwhelming majority. He had to pay a $500 fine and received a one-month suspended sentence. But Miller, like Proctor, was a fighter. He went all the way to the Supreme Court and, a year later, had the decision reversed.

*The McCarthy hearings remain a dark episode in the history of the humanities in America.*

Arthur Miller survived, his good name untarnished. A number of others, however, remained on the blacklist and either continue to live or have died in relative obscurity. Ultimately Senator McCarthy himself was discredited, and the committee was dissolved. But the hearings remain a dark episode in the history of the humanities in America.

# Stereotyping: A Form of Repression

Who has not heard the old "joke" which says that everyone in America is equal, but "some are more equal than others"? In Gilbert and Sullivan's comic operetta *HMS Pinafore*, the arrogant Sir Joseph Porter, lord of the Queen's Navy, deludes himself into thinking he is warmly democratic in his outlook. At one point he announces that a "British tar is any man's equal"; there is a pause, and then he adds, "excepting mine." Laughter aside, there probably never has been nor ever will be a society in which the concept of total equality is ingrained in the heart of every citizen. Stratification occurs no matter where we go: *some* form of class system— even among members of a given group that collectively combats the suppression of human rights.

While the philosophical basis of our society was clear before the ink was dry on the *Declaration of Independence*, the implementation of that document has been inconsistent. Millions of people have come to these shores expecting to be handed their natural rights as soon as they landed, expecting the freedom to pursue their dreams and to amass the unlimited wealth that now seems in retrospect to be *the* American myth.

Those who were able to consolidate their power first, make their fortunes, and establish their communities have been called *the establishment*. This group is primarily white, middle-class, and driven by the Puritan work ethic, which says that honest labor and thrift will inevitably be rewarded. While they may support the doctrine of natural rights *in theory*, their actions are often quite different in practice. One of the earliest indications of the split between the establishment and the other groups is *stereotyping*, a specialized form of bigotry in which minority groups are depicted in the narrowest terms, with a few highly exaggerated characteristics. Bigotry is a vicious cycle, continually feeding upon itself. The popular arts reflect popular misconceptions in the mass mind, which in turn is influenced by what it sees in the popular arts.

The situation is less pronounced than in the past, but that it has "improved," as some would have us believe, is highly questionable. For example, the phenomenally successful sitcom *All in the Family*, which dominated television during the 1970s, was allegedly a satire on bigotry. Its hero was Archie Bunker, a crude, uneducated dock foreman and part-time taxi driver, who characterized every ethnic minority with the most offensive slang term possible. His vocabulary would never have been permitted on television except that the program was presumably making fun of him and his attitudes. Yet, if you watch any of the reruns carefully and listen to the laughter of the studio audience, you will note that what most delighted the audience was the outrageous language. Did the supposed "moral" go along with the language? Or was the success of the show attributable to the fact that Archie Bunker was saying what the popular audience *would* say if it dared?

*Was the success of* All in the Family *attributable to the fact that Archie Bunker used bigoted words the audience would say if it dared?*

## A Capsule View of Stereotyping

Anytime we try to find a neat explanation for how something works in society or in the mind, we are bound to run into innumerable exceptions. Our "capsule view" presented here by no means describes the thoughts and feelings of every member of the so-called establishment, but it can be taken as a reasonable generalization. At any rate, there is enough truth in it to make us look more critically at our own tendencies, should we consider ourselves part of the establishment, or at those of close associates who are.

Women must be regarded as a minority group for the current purpose, even though women born or married into establishment households may share certain assumptions about other minorities held by males, without quite realizing their own subordinate status.

We can see four broad stages in attitudes toward minority stereotyping. First, there is the *early stereotyping* stage, when the establishment is so firmly rooted in traditional opinions about minorities that no secret guilt exists. Establishment people don't even know, in fact, what stereotyping *means*. They think, "That's the way things are. Such-and-such people are lazy, while those over there are sneaky and not to be trusted, while we on the other hand . . ." During this stage, establishment people almost never form close associations with minorities, that is, "close" in the sense of insightful, caring, and sensitive. If, for example, the wife in a household is in fact an invisible, or "closet," minority, the husband's relationship to her is definitely not close.

In this stage, any utterance is allowed concerning minorities. A group may be called names that it privately considers demeaning, but which the establishment considers realistic. Not too long ago establishment husbands in the company of their peers spoke of "the little woman" or "the missus" or, more subtly discriminatory because it wasn't meant seriously, "my better half." (Note the unconscious use of the possessive *my*.) Women other than wives fared much worse and were referred to as "broads" or "chicks."

Also in this period, minorities are given qualities—for example, stupidity—that make them seem barely human. They are made the butt of jokes with punch lines that depend on commonly accepted distortions and a lack of awareness of how greatly individuals differ from each other. Who has not heard, "How many [fill in the minority] does it take to change a lightbulb"?

The joked-about minorities in defense may tell jokes to each other and turn the establishment into fair game. Or members of a particular minority group may call each other by the insulting names invented by the establishment. These are ways of divesting the language of its power to hurt and erecting an invisible wall around the group.

During the second stage, stereotyping begins to be seen for what it is. People who still use it may stop and titter or wink at each other as though to say, "We shouldn't be doing this, but anyway, have you heard the story about the . . ." We may call this the *gentler but still separate* stage. Minorities no longer seem to be a threat but are often viewed as "lovable" or "childlike"—almost acceptable. On stage or in films they can be depicted as being friendly with a member of the dominant group. They are beginning to "fit in," so long as they continue to know their place.

The third is the *near-assimilation* stage. The now-classic sitcom *I Love Lucy*, which dominated television during the 1950s and into the 1960s, offers a prime example of what happens to a minority figure during this stage. First, there was Lucy herself, as portrayed by Lucille Ball—an actress who knew exactly what the public at that time would accept and even adore. In the early phases of the series (which began in 1952), Lucy, a housewife married to Ricky Ricardo, a Cuban bandleader, is the lovable and childlike—and essentially stupid—woman-as-minority of stage two. She is disorganized, devoid of talent, but forever trying to sneak into show business and make her husband proud. On his part, Ricky loves

*Four stages in minority stereotyping:*

*early (unquestioning)*
*gentler but still separate*
*near-assimilation (but not quite)*
*multicultural (difference with pride)*

*The Book says we're all dead level in the eyes of God. Our Forefathers claimed everybody's created equal (of course, by the time you get delivered nine months later, seems like social class, skin color, looks, and health have pretty much knocked the pins out from under Conception's fair shake).*

*Allan Gurganus*
Oldest Living Confederate
Widow Tells All

*Edouard Manet,* Le Dejeuner sur l'Herbe: *Establishment husbands in the company of their peers spoke of "the little woman" or "the missus." (Musée du Jeu de Paume, Paris)*

her *because* she is childlike and stupid, and so is forever thwarting her schemes to be a performer.

When the series entered the 1960s, however, and the sexual revolution was closely followed by a radical redefinition of sexual roles, Lucy was shown as a much cleverer manipulator of her husband, someone who *pretended* to be stupid but was in actuality the true boss of the household. True, her schemes always failed, as usual, but her incessant determination to be something other than what society had demanded of housewives sent subtextual messages to women fighting for liberation. By the mid-1960s *I Love Lucy* could no longer survive. Women could no longer be given ambiguous characters. Lucille Ball went from show to show, trying to regain star stature, but the manipulative woman willing to play the submissive role did not belong in the 1970s and 1980s. The new audiences could accept strong-willed women capable of making important political and executive decisions.

Black characters have also undergone significant changes. Early on, blacks on stage and in films were clearly second-class human beings. D. W. Griffith's 1915 epic film *The Birth of a Nation* (see Chapter 5 for a fuller discussion) was a movie version of a novel, *The Klansman*, which depicted the Ku Klux Klan as a vigilante group that guarded the rights of the dominant white culture and was necessary to intimidate the freed blacks during Reconstruction.

During the 1920s and 1930s blacks were "acceptable" as paid entertainers, especially if they were jazz musicians. Motion pictures, which grew in a popularity that seemed unstoppable, offered blacks a lot of work, provided they played loyal servants or let themselves be targets of laughter. Magazine advertisements showed

*Lucille Ball's Lucy was disorganized and stupid during the 1950s, but a clever manipulator of her husband in the 1960s.*

*Early films gave blacks lots of work, provided they played loyal servants or let themselves be targets of laughter.*

a smiling mammy on a box of pancake mix. She wears a bandana and seems pleased to be providing a hearty breakfast for her "family." A breakthrough came in 1939 with the film version of *Gone with the Wind* (see Chapter 5), for the mammy in this film (actually named Mammy) was no longer a generic, stereotypical character. She was a strong-willed person in her own right, as played by Hattie McDaniel (who, by the way, became the first black actress to win an Oscar). She was not a slave, and she was clearly the person responsible for raising the O'Hara children. Easily a match for the strident Scarlett, who respected her more than she did all other living souls, Mammy was a tough survivor, uneducated but with an inborn wisdom the film's heroine only gradually acquires, largely because of Mammy herself.

*The radio sitcom Amos 'n' Andy in the 1930s offered blatant racial stereotyping and two white actors playing the leads.*

Hattie McDaniel's marvelous performance in 1939 did not, however, mean that blacks were as a group welcomed to stage three. The early stereotypes were still very much in evidence. Throughout the 1930s *Amos 'n' Andy* was a popular radio sitcom, offering us no better example of blatant stereotyping than in the fact that the parts were played by two white actors. They spoke in stereotypical dialect, "I'se regusted" and "Ain't dat sumpthin" being familiar trademarks. They interacted with other characters given stereotypically quaint names like "Kingfish" and "Sapphire," who were close to the unpleasant caricatures of the old minstrel shows of the nineteenth century, in which white performers with black makeup would shuffle around, hitting themselves with tambourines.

As early as 1931 there had been efforts to take the show off the radio, but little could be done when even Roy Wilkins of the NAACP gave it an endorsement, saying that it had "all the pathos, humor, vanity, glory, problems and solutions that beset ordinary mortals, and therein lies its universal appeal." Twenty years later, when the show had moved to the new medium, television, Wilkins changed his mind. Black actors played the parts now and somehow seemed more offensive than they had been as voices coming out of the radio. The black community seems to have been more upset by seeing than by hearing African-American comic stereotypes.

In stage three, minorities begin to win (sometimes grudging) acceptance because they are starting to distinguish themselves in fields they are allowed to enter, such as acting. But this acceptance is still very much under the control of the dominant group. World War II, which required people of all groups to serve in the armed forces, did much to close the gap, but it was still there nonetheless. Women, for example, were shown on the screen performing heroic acts, such as in one film in which the heroine blows up an enemy camp with herself in it (but perhaps this deed, in a male-written screenplay, can be interpreted as merely an extension of a woman's mythic role of self-sacrificing earth mother).

Attempts at real equalization are often shot down in stage three: "Yes, I accept you as a human being, but don't move next door" or "I love you and care for you as my wife, but never forget that I make the final decisions."

A good example is white protest against the character of Rochester on the Jack Benny Show in both its radio and television heyday. As black servant to the tight-fisted Benny, he delighted audiences with his wisecracks about the boss's stinginess. White studio executives were worried, however, that the character, played by Eddie Anderson, might be observed as being "too familiar" and that his put-downs of the boss might be "inappropriate."

Some more adventurous artists tried to confront racial issues with some degree of realism, but were in the 1950s generally unsuccessful. In 1959 Hollywood decided to do a remake of a 1934 "racial" film ambitiously titled *Imitation of Life*.

It concerns a mulatto's efforts to "pass for" white, bringing great grief to her old-fashioned mother, who believes in the separation of the races. In the film's most famous scene the daughter, having been accepted by white society, refuses to acknowledge her mother when they meet. Eventually the mother dies broken-hearted, while the daughter realizes too late what she has done. The alleged moral: segregation breeds tragedy. The (perhaps) *real* moral: attempted integration breeds tragedy.

Any time films or television broached the subject of prejudice, the story was required to end with reconciliation and peace between groups, or at the very least an uplifting sense that the future will definitely be better. In 1947 both the novel and the film *Gentlemen's Agreement* were widely praised for what was considered a bold assault on the hidden anti-Semitism existing within the dominant white culture. The subject was indeed appropriate, for despite Jewish achievements in all areas of endeavor, in many quarters those who had come as immigrants or were the descendants of immigrants were still regarded as outsiders.

The novel and film touched upon the "closet" jealousy and the lack of Christian understanding on the part of those who called themselves Christian. They showed that the non-Semitic heroine, who was thought to be beyond prejudice, was able to find a great deal of it in her own heart.

What often escaped notice was the fact that the hero was a reporter *pretending* to be Jewish in order to do a story on discrimination. At the conclusion, the lovers, earlier separated because of latent prejudice, are joyously reunited, the heroine having learned the error of her ways and resolving never to be prejudiced again. The moral: equality is indeed possible so long as people only pretend to be minorities.

*In* Imitation of Life *the alleged moral is that segregation breeds tragedy; but perhaps the real moral is that attempted integration breeds tragedy.*

Gentlemen's Agreement *was widely praised for its bold assault on the hidden anti-Semitism in the dominant white culture. (Culver Pictures)*

*An early treatment of race relations in* Guess Who's Coming to Dinner. *(Culver Pictures)*

In the 1960s, when the young attempted to break down all racial, sexual, and class barriers, the popular arts tried to follow suit but could not risk completely alienating the older generation. Some risks were nonetheless taken. In 1967 the Oscar for best picture went to *In the Heat of the Night*, a story of racial tension in a small Southern town. But in the same year Katharine Hepburn won the Oscar for playing an affluent housewife who "bravely" comes to terms with her daughter's decision to marry a black. The title of the film, *Guess Who's Coming to Dinner*, was supposed to make the white audience painfully self-conscious of its stereotyping. The film studio, however, felt compelled to make the minority character an almost perfect human being. The daughter's fiancé is a brilliant, supereducated scientist played by Sidney Poitier, easily the most popular black actor of the day. Critic Judith Crist, reviewing the film on television, correctly pointed out the implication of this character: "The real question this film asks is: Would you want your daughter to marry Sidney Poitier? My answer is no. *I* would want to marry him myself."

## Are We There Yet?

Not having exhausted by any means the complexities of stage three and realizing that all of the first three stages are regrettably still with us in some form, let us look at stage four. At this *multicultural*, or *difference with pride*, stage, ethnic origins, gender, and stereotypes begin to vanish; people are viewed as human beings and evaluated by each other in terms of individual circumstances. This stage is, of course, the goal of a free society. Even with the problems of urban life in our time, there are hopeful signs that new generations may be less encumbered by prejudices than has been the case.

*The fourth stage—difference with pride—is, of course, the goal of a free society.*

We note great changes in the handling of minority characters in the popular arts. Compare, for example, reruns of *The Mary Tyler Moore Show* of the 1970s with contemporary sitcoms like *Love and War, Murphy Brown*, and *Design-*

*ing Women.* In the former, the focus is on the problems of a single woman struggling to hold her own in what is still a man's world, but by and large the basis for the weekly plots is the heroine's need for and great difficulties in finding suitable male companionship. The assumption is still that a woman's life revolves around the presence or absence of a man.

*In* The Mary Tyler Moore Show *of the 1970s, the heroine struggles to hold her own in what is still a man's world. Today we have heroines who are as strong as their male counterparts and deal with issues not related to romance.*

Of late, however, we have heroines who are just as strong as their male counterparts—sometimes stronger—or who, significantly, deal with issues that are *not* related to romance. A pivotal series of the 1980s and 1990s has been *The Golden Girls,* with three heroines, all in their fifties (it goes without saying that senior citizens form another minority group). Their problems arise from a variety of sources, certainly not limited to either age or the need for love. The dynamics among three people (plus one woman's mother) trying to share a house are central to the series.

Black sitcoms find willing producers and sponsors, but, as with any television entertainment, the stars must be what inside the trade is called *bankable.* We have not reached the point at which a stark truth is reason enough for production, but that has been the case with TV shows about *any* group. Fancy a weekly series about homeless people.

In the 1960s some brave pioneer took a chance with a sitcom about an impoverished black family, deriving its humor not from artificial plots with laugh-track accompaniments, but from the characters' fierce will to survive. Called *The Sugar Hill Family,* it lasted only a few months. Audiences wanted no part of a story in which how to scrape together the rent money is more important than whether the teenage children can use the car for their big dates.

*But fancy a weekly series about homeless people.*

In the 1980s *The Bill Cosby Show* enjoyed top ranking in the powerful Nielsen ratings, which continue to determine which shows will continue or be cancelled. The series is a reasonably truthful account of daily life in the home of an affluent black physician, with few problems stemming from discrimination. It has been widely praised, not for showing the current state of race relations, but for showing what it someday *may* be.

Less benign than Bill Cosby's loving father are Eddie Murphy and Richard Pryor, stand-up comics who talk of crime, drugs, poverty, and bigotry in their acts. But it needs to be pointed out that such truth telling was acceptable only after these performers had become famous.

In addition, black directors are making their mark in films. (Twenty years ago, black subjects had to be products of white filmmakers, or funding would not be available.) Hollywood now is even willing to gamble on stories of racial conflicts that do *not* end with a forced, improbable reconciliation. For example, the locale of Spike Lee's 1989 film *Do the Right Thing* is New York City, where, as in most major cities, racial tensions have not been resolved. A frustrated pizza deliverer destroys his employer's business as the film ends. *Jungle Fever* (1991) by the same director deals with an interracial love affair that does not receive the blessings of either society and that, more importantly, creates tensions between the lovers themselves. We are thus beginning to see something new in projects dealing with minorities: character rather than stereotypes.

Stage four is visionary. The signers of the *Declaration* may have dreamed of a totally free society, but they could not have foreseen the extent of future cultural pluralism and the struggle for supremacy among the various groups. Only rarely—if ever—has the entire population rallied behind the single identification of "American."

*A contemporary treatment of race relations in Spike Lee's* Do the Right Thing. *(The Museum of Modern Art/Film Stills Archive)*

*Revivalism: allowing those weary of the crushing problems of today to take refuge in a past that never really existed.*

One factor that operates to retard the progress of stage four is an almost automatic "revivalism"—a return to popularity of songs and styles from bygone periods, which can reawaken old stereotypes or at least a nostalgia for a status quo that is no longer defensible. Thus we have a chain of diners in a major American city, built in the art deco style of the 1930s, featuring a red, white, and blue color scheme and a prominent slogan that invites the customer to reexperience the way "things used to be." The clothes and dance trends of 25 years ago are currently making a comeback. Cable television has both a Nostalgia and an American Movie Classics channel, so that those weary of the crushing problems of today can take refuge in a past that never really existed. We are also seeing a surge of *Our Town* revivals by academic and community theaters. The Thornton Wilder hit from 1940 brings us back to a time when a playwright could present Grover's Corners, New Hampshire, with its homogeneous white population as a microcosm of American society.

A second factor that emerges in stage four, when some minorities begin to have a definite say in the direction of society, is pressure from within the minority group itself. The group begins to monitor its own image, instead of standing by while others determine that image. There are sufficient numbers of minorities in the entertainment industry today to help make certain that the elimination of old stereotypes does not result in the creation of new ones.

Homosexuality, for example, once a taboo subject for any group, can generally be portrayed today so long as it is shown as a problem of the established culture. Minorities are less likely to be enthusiastic about having to share the problem. For example, documentaries on AIDS can freely show the danger to the black community from causes other than gay sex, but they must be careful to show that homosexuality is practiced among *all* groups. A recent film made for television by a black director who is himself HIV-positive—intended as a passionate warning to all people—was rejected by a Public Television official who feared indignant protest from the black community, which, understandably enough, does not want other issues to interfere with the ongoing struggle for equal rights.

Meanwhile, the gay community, comprising representatives from all walks of life, has become another minority with stereotypical images in the popular arts.

If an upstanding member of the establishment is shown to have a secretly gay side, the treatment of the subject must be tragic. Recent critically praised films like *Longtime Companion* (1990) and *Paris Is Burning* (1991) attracted "crossover" audiences, largely because the characters were pitiable in their suffering.

The answer to the question "Are we there yet?" is certainly a resounding No! We may never get "there." The old idea of the melting pot is probably a myth. It is not self-evident that divergent cultures coming en masse to a new land will or even should shed their cultural identity and blend into whatever is waiting for them.

How sad to think, now that we have at least glimpsed the terrain of stage four, that we cannot pat ourselves on the back for the progress we have made. But getting rid of some stereotypes is only the barest beginning. We need a profound revision in the way we think about our society and the people who inhabit it.

*The answer to the question "Are we there yet?" is certainly a resounding No! We may never get "there."*

## The Shaping Influence of Television

A subtler, potentially more dangerous, form of stereotyping reaches vast numbers through television. What was welcomed as leisure-time entertainment in the 1950s has become an evolutionary milestone: an alteration in the way we receive and process information.

Images from the TV screen hit the eye, the ear, and the mind simultaneously. The brain can relax, no longer having to sort out the meaning of scattered impressions from the surroundings, for TV impressions come prepackaged and preprocessed. Characters who look and sound "real" generally embody unambiguous and stereotypical characteristics. Commentators and anchorpersons have authoritative, hypnotic voices, so that for many viewers the difference between fact and opinion altogether vanishes.

We inhabit a world with two planes of reality side by side, but we have become so accustomed to staring at "the tube" that we see—really see—less and less of the living room and the people in it. The eyes and ears of the human race are functioning differently as a result. Perhaps future generations will be born "cable-ready." If so, the humanities may become an endangered species.

*Perhaps future generations will be born "cable-ready."*

**Priorities.**    "I saw it on TV" has become the definitive way to affirm the reality of an event. If something is not caught by the video camera, maybe it never really happened, no matter what the newspaper says. As we know, television news departments have planned schedules. The *Six O'Clock News* is of premier importance. Anything occurring after six o'clock had better be major enough to warrant an interruption of a regular network show; otherwise it makes the late and less significant news at eleven.

Finding ourselves at a public event with cameras present, we often glance toward the red light to learn what the camera operator thought worthy of note. The dull speech we are hearing suddenly acquires stature. We know it will be replayed on TV. Television puts a frame around experience.

**Blurring of Age Differences.**    Because television reaches so many children, sophistication comes earlier than ever; as a social historian recently pointed out, there is a sharp switch from infancy to adolescence, rather than the prolonged period of childhood studied and carefully catalogued by childhood specialists like Jean Piaget. There is no longer need to send young children out of the room while adults talk. Children see it all: the ads, the grown-up problems, marital infidelity, illegitimate offspring, the escape into drugs. Nothing is "beyond" anyone's years anymore. Children enter the adult world without having to be invited.

**Control over Time and Space.**    Since the world has shrunk to the size of your TV screen and time is experienced in terms of when a soap opera comes on or when the football game starts, the increasing numbers of viewers who own videocassette players may now control both time and space in ways that a nineteenth-century physicist would envy. By pressing a few buttons, we can command our favorite show to be there at *our* convenience. We can rewind and rerun sights and sounds at will. If something is not pleasing, we can speed up time with another button. Moments of artistic beauty, once believed all the more touching because of their brevity, can be frozen or relived as often as we wish. No one has yet come up with an equally powerful way to approach reality and our expectations from it. Significant, perhaps, is the current expression "tune out," used for uninteresting activities and people.

**Impatience with the Untelevised.**    For the average child reared on television, a merely human teacher may well be an anticlimax. Compared to cartoon figures, human beings just stand there, remaining the same size and shape, with no camera zoom or other trick cinematography to add interest to their appearance. Similarly, a mere book, with or without pictures, cannot compete for attention with the colorful and active images on the screen—images transmitted immediately, without the viewer's having to learn how to recognize and decode letter shapes. *Sesame Street* may be "brought to you by the letter *A*," but the letter *A*, all by itself, would not fare nearly so well in the ratings.

**Expectation of Repetition.**    Television viewers expect information to be broadcast more than once. Commercials repeat the name of the product several times in 30 seconds. Summer brings reruns of favorite shows. During sporting events announcers replay significant moments instantly, often from different angles. Not needing either to watch or listen the first time around has an impact on many, who come to expect repetition in nontelevised events, such as a doctor's crucial list of do's and don'ts or a teacher's last-minute checklist of points to be studied before next Monday's test.

**The Disrepute of the Ordinary.**    "Just plain folks" and "salt of the earth" were once phrases no one was ashamed of. With the coming of motion pictures and television, an attractive face is a basic requirement for nearly anyone who hopes to succeed. Makeup and lighting techniques can readily compensate for some flaws of nature, and even the aging process can be slowed by the placing of gauze over camera lenses. As a result, real-life looks may appear highly unsatisfactory by comparison. Close self-scrutiny in the morning mirror is never advisable for the late-night television habitué.

*With the coming of motion pictures and television, an attractive face is a basic requirement for nearly anyone who hopes to succeed.*

## The Impact of Television on Storytelling

Storytelling was once a leisurely medium of communication. Folk tales were spoken and sung to audiences who were in no particular hurry to leave. Audiences responded with repetition of phrases, nods, claps, and a chorus of praise or blame for the characters in the narrative. Long epics of Africa and Europe were told in this way.

Printing allowed any reader to possess a mass-produced book. Eventually it was common for novels to be in several volumes, and for continuing stories in magazines to run for months—a leisurely process indeed.

In his eighteenth-century novel *Tom Jones*, Henry Fielding is so leisurely he even takes time out of his story to address the reader with philosophical essays. He labels each chapter with a hint of what is to come, as if to say that his main purpose is not suspense. He and the reader will instead share in discovery: "Containing as much of the birth of the foundling as is necessary or proper to acquaint the reader with in the beginning of this history" begins Book I.

Storytelling on television frequently includes a "teaser," a glimpse of the climactic moment to come later. Viewers who have been sufficiently intrigued may wait through the opening commercial and expository scenes. There will not be sustained narrative of any length, for television depends on the break every few minutes for a commercial or public service announcement. Even when time has not been sold, the breaks come anyway, to make it convenient for announcements should there be eventual reruns.

The viewer thus accepts a rhythm of narration broken by these interruptions, often at a suspenseful moment. Long years of such viewing condition viewers to brief attention spans, so that when longer attention is needed (to a sermon or class lesson, for instance) we must make a real effort to keep from squirming. It is said that children in kindergarten and first grade have grown so accustomed to television, even the "good" educational content of *Sesame Street*, that they find it difficult to visualize stories read aloud by the teacher—or to concentrate on any one activity for longer than the interval between commercials.

## Women in the Arts

It is one thing for an artist or a would-be artist to create stereotypes because of social attitudes, but quite another for an artist to be denied the very *right* to create because she or he is viewed in a stereotypical way. In an important essay entitled "Why There Are No Great Women Artists," art historian Linda Nochlin points out that the paucity of feminine names in art history courses has nothing to do with hormones (as was often believed) and everything to do with social institutions and customs. The primary institution hindering female artists has been a limited educational system, and the primary custom, a woman's traditional role as nurturer to the family.

In Greek and Roman society, women were either slaves or homemakers responsible for maintaining the "gracious" arts of civilized living. These arts did not include fashioning statues out of heavy stone or carving the façades of public buildings. In the Middle Ages the closest a woman could get to education was learning the duties and prayers of sisterhood or, again, the gracious arts supervised by the lady of the castle. The latter might include embroidery or tapestry weaving, but never installing a stained-glass window or painting a triptych on a church altar.

During the nineteenth century, when a number of significant women novelists and poets *did* emerge (though often with masculine names), when education beyond home economics was no longer unheard of for a woman, training for a career in visual arts remained unthinkable. Women were not allowed to look upon nude models of either sex. Since education in the most fundamental exercises in art was forbidden, women were denied access to art studios and thus to the tutelage of master teachers—something all artists need as they mature. At the very most, women produced pleasant watercolors of flowers and bowls of fruit, similar to the playing of a harp or piano for the amusement of after-dinner guests.

An interesting exception was Edmonia Lewis (1844-?), who for a time overcame the obstacles of being both black and female in the white-male-dominated nineteenth-century American art scene. Perhaps because of her minority status and a ferocious will not only to survive but to succeed, she was able to avoid the traditional forms of a "genteel" feminine education and take painting and drawing classes at Oberlin College. While there, she ran into a mountain of hostility. Accused of nearly killing two of her friends with a poisoned drink, dragged off by an angry mob, brutally beaten and left to die, she was forced to halt her academic studies. Instead she moved to Boston, determined to vindicate herself by achieving fame in an arena that had been shut tight against minorities. She quickly found she had a genuine talent for realistic sculpture, scoring a mild sensation with a bust of Robert Gould Shaw, an eminent Bostonian and Civil War hero. Soon she had earned enough money from her work to follow in the footsteps of many other American artists: moving to Europe and becoming an expatriate. She opened a studio in Rome, which for a time became the fashionable place for visiting Americans who desired to commission expensive busts of themselves and their family.

What is most significant, perhaps, is that despite her success, Lewis has not been able to secure a firm place in the history of American art. People who do family portraits for money seldom are given much respect. Lewis is beginning to

*Edmonia Lewis,* Hagar *(1875): Despite her success, Lewis has not been able to secure a firm place in the history of American art. (Courtesy of the National Museum of American Art, Smithsonian Institution. Transfer from the National Museum of African Art. Gift of Delta Sigma Theta Sorority, Inc.)*

receive some belated recognition for pieces such as *The Marriage of Hiawatha*, based on themes and incidents from Longfellow's poem *The Song of Hiawatha*, and *Hagar*, a statue of the Biblical woman chosen by Abraham to be the mother of his children and then cast out after Sarah, Abraham's wife, became fertile. In the first work, Lewis as a minority identified with native Americans; in the other, with an alienated, abandoned, homeless woman, much like the blacks only just freed from slavery. In other words, recognition for Lewis had to wait until her "underground" themes became understood for what they were.

Belated recognition has also come to the Mexican artist Frida Kahlo (1907–1954)—that is to say, recognition as an artist in her own right. (In fact, she has even risen above the subcategory of "Women Artists" that one finds in some art books or museums.) Announcements of her early exhibitions always indicated that the work was by "Frida Kahlo (Mrs. Diego Rivera)." We note no similar announcements of works by, for example, "Max Ernst (husband of Peggy Guggenheim)." In another marriage of two extraordinarily gifted artists, Georgia O'Keeffe and Alfred Stieglitz (discussed in Chapter 2), recognition came late for the wife because the husband's reputation at the time of the wedding was already established and because he tended to insist that his work (photography) must come first. Their summers were spent at his family retreat in the company of his relatives, a situation that seriously intruded on her "alone" time.

Males in the humanities have seldom encountered the problem of finding a private place where they could have solitude in which to create, unless, of course, the problem was strictly economic. Women, however, have had to worry

*Frido Kahlo,* Self-Portrait on the Borderline Between Mexico and the United States *(1932): Announcements of Frida Kahlo's early exhibitions indicated that the work was by Mrs. Diego Rivera. (Private Collection/Photo: Christie's, New York)*

about not only their husband's relatives but the daily needs of their own children. Fancy reading the following about van Gogh:

> Although he wanted to paint in the south of France, he was prevented from making the trip by the demands on his time of his wife and children.

Virginia Woolf's famous essay "A Room of One's Own" contrasted facilities offered to male and female students at Oxford University. She was denied admission to a library reserved for male students. Women were almost never allowed the privilege of living in a private room. Many aspiring young male talents attracted outside sponsors who paid their rent, an investment rarely made for a woman, even if she were equally talented.

At one point Woolf imagines what might have happened if Shakespeare had had a sister as creatively endowed as he. Had she followed her brother to London to carve out a career as a writer and an actress, she would have fallen prey to a seducer taking advantage of an unaccompanied woman. The disgrace of giving birth out of wedlock would have followed, along with the responsibilities of motherhood and the need to eke out a living while somehow making a home. One doubts that, with all her genius, she would have written one line.

*If Shakespeare had had a genius for a sister, she would probably not have had the time or opportunity to write one line.*

Women have had to live down the stereotypical images of themselves that arose in the world of the humanities. For example, it was once said that women could not think logically or concentrate for any length of time and were given to incapacitating illnesses caused by "nerves." In addition, they have had to free themselves from the stereotypical notion that their role in life is to go from adoration of the father to adoration of the husband.

The history of the humanities records one unusual case in which a woman, born Alma Schindler (1879-1964), struggled under two overwhelming burdens: her own considerable talents, which needed expression, and her skills as a nurturing mother figure, which attracted insecure male artists. In the latter role, she exerted so much influence that she deserves a place in any study of the arts.

She began her "nurturing" career without realizing it when, at the age of 17, she proved an inspiration to Gustav Klimt, an established artist 20 years her senior. Klimt had been a husband and a father for a number of years and had grown weary of his uncreative domesticity. Without informing Alma of his legal entanglements, he became engaged to her. Needless to say, the relationship was not a stable one, and it did not last long.

Besides, Alma's passion was really music. Before she finally met and married her first husband, she had already inspired a fellow music student, Arnold Schönberg. One of his students, Alban Berg, also became a close friend, so close indeed that he dedicated the score of his opera *Wozzeck* to her.

Then she met the composer Gustav Mahler, whose reputation in Europe was already on the rise. Whether she loved him for himself or for their mutual interest in music, we shall never know; she did believe they would nurture each other's careers. Mahler, however, had very different ideas. When she compared their marriage to that of Clara and Robert Schumann, he laughed and said it had been a "ridiculous" relationship. Then he demanded that Alma give up composing. She was expected to live for his music alone. He was now a recognized genius who answered to no one but the emperor.

*Alma Mahler was told by her husband that she must give up composing and live for his music alone.*

Mahler—coincidentally, another man 20 years older than Alma—was now director of the Vienna Opera. He was the first director to demand that lights be dimmed during the performance to aid audience concentration and that latecomers not be seated until an appropriate time. With similar autocracy he told Alma that she must nurse the children, create a quiet home with well-prepared meals, and copy all of his manuscripts. At one point, in despair she wrote:

> I realize that the man who had to spread his peacock train in public wants to relax at home. That after all is woman's fate. But it isn't mine![3]

Still, she could not escape the magnetic hold of his genius (and his far greater accomplishments). "I often feel as though my wings had been clipped," she said. "I feel so often how little I have in comparison with his immeasurable riches."[4]

Alma's quiet suffering, the price of giving up her own career, was not entirely lost on Mahler. Troubled, the composer even spent an afternoon with Sigmund Freud and, with the psychoanalyst's help, reached some understanding of his wife's artistic needs. Afterwards he returned home, began to play her songs, and finally cried, "What have I done? These songs are good. You have got to go on working. They must immediately be published."[5]

Whether Mahler would have followed through on his promised support of a revived career for his wife we cannot know, because the composer soon fell gravely ill. The very least we can say, however, is that he came to a full realization of Alma's sacrifice before the end: "Nobody knows and can ever know with what absolute selflessness she subordinated her life to me and my work."[6]

Alma Mahler had a passion for the arts—all of them. Her life would include more close relationships with artists: with Walter Gropius, the architect, her second husband; Otto Kokoschka, an artist and her lover; and her third husband, Franz Werfel, author of *The Forty Days of Musa Dagh* and *The Song of Bernadette*.

In the company of many other famous artists she and Werfel endured a three-year flight from Hitler-dominated Europe. We can be sure she held her own in this august company, which included Thomas Mann, one of the greatest novelists of the twentieth century; Max Reinhardt, a renowned German director; Arnold Schönberg, a major composer in the early twentieth-century avant-garde movement in music; and Bertolt Brecht, one of the most influential of all modern playwrights.

Alma Mahler was not obscure in her lifetime. The artists with whom she freely associated recognized two things about her: one, that she might have become a full-fledged artist in her own right had she chosen that course, and two, that inspiration and encouragement on her level of insight are really arts in themselves and belong to humanities studies.

She lived to be 84. Near the end of her life she was able to rejoice, "God gave me to know the works of genius in our time before they left the hands of their creators."[7] Here was surely a woman who overcame the prejudices and stereotypical thinking about her sex, surviving in a unique and memorable fashion.

## Epilogue

What should we hope to have accomplished with this chapter? The end of all stereotyping? The end of moral censorship? of government repression? The guarantee of free speech and equality for everyone in the world? These are noble ambitions, but not yet practical. Having said that, do we throw up our hands and decide that a far wiser policy is to go about our business and forget about the unattainable?

The humanities have many side effects, implications beyond the immediate pleasure we derive from reading a great book, seeing a great play, listening to a major symphony. Understanding the struggle artists have undergone within their different societies can serve to enlighten us and to liberate us from stiff, unbending thought systems. One asks oneself: *what do I do that inhibits or advances the cause of building a society without the barriers that have been and still are being erected against those who have so much to give?* The smallest step in the right direction is better than inaction. The failure to act can encourage the builders of obstacles.

The humanities, as we have said many times, are more than just the history of art, music, philosophy, and so on. They are also a way of life. They are the process by which we practice, not merely study, the art of being human. The growing recognition of what artists need from *us* is a sign that we are walking with them.

## Glossary

*double entendre:* A statement that can be taken two ways—one quite innocent, the other richly suggestive; widely used in comic plays and films.

*establishment:* A reference to the dominant culture, usually made by those who do not wish to be considered part of it.

*esthetic:* In this chapter, a term describing a way of life attributed to certain artists, like Oscar

Wilde, in which an attempt is made to have every moment filled with beauty and a variety of intense sensations.

*witch-hunts:* A phrase borrowed from the old Salem witch trials of the seventeenth century and applied to the House Un-American Activities Committee hearings of the 1950s.

## Notes

1. Pete Seeger, *The Incompleat Folk Singer* (New York: Simon & Schuster, 1972), 466.
2. From *The Crucible* by Arthur Miller. Copyright 1952, 1953, 1954, renewed © 1980 by Arthur Miller. Reprinted by permission of Viking Penguin, a division of Penguin Books USA Inc.

3. Walter Sorell, *Three Women: Lives of Sex and Genius* (Indianapolis: Bobbs-Merrill, 1975), 15.
4. Ibid., 16-17.
5. Ibid., 27.
6. Ibid.
7. Ibid., 69.

## Suggested Reading

Clurman, Harold. *The Fervent Years*. New York: Harcourt Brace Jovanovich, 1975. A classic on modern theater, this work by one of the founders of the Group Theatre in New York analyzes the dramatic esthetic that led to the creation of the first American company dedicated to developing the Stanislavsky system on native soil. This esthetic eventually became the well-known school of Method acting. The book also chronicles the conflict between members of the Group, including playwright Clifford Odets, and the House Un-American Activities Committee.

Ellmann, Richard. *Oscar Wilde*. New York: Knopf, 1988. Probably the most comprehensive biography of Wilde and his tragic undoing. Long and minutely documented, the book suggests that Wilde was secretly hoping to be caught, perhaps because of deep-rooted guilt.

Ely, Melvin Patrick. *The Adventures of Amos 'n' Andy: A Social History of an American Phenomenon*. New York: The Free Press, 1991. Probably the best, most in-depth study of stereotyping in black entertainment.

Evans, Faith, ed. *Clamorous Voices: Shakespeare's Women Today*. New York: Routledge, A Theatre Arts Book, 1989. Feminist interpretations of great monologues in Shakespeare by top actresses of the Royal Shakespeare Company, including Carol Rutter, Sinead Cusack, Fiona Shaw, and Juliet Stevenson.

Hellman, Lillian. *Three: An Unfinished Woman, Pentimento, Scoundrel Time*. Boston: Little, Brown, 1979. Taken together, these three works constitute the playwright's memories of the moral issues of her time. She talks about the struggle to establish herself and her moral integrity despite segregation, the Nazis, the HUAC hearings, Watergate, and prejudice in every area of life. Particularly poignant are the memories of how she and Dashiell Hammett, the novelist, suffered through the McCarthy era and the disillusionment with their "friends" who named names to avoid being blacklisted themselves. A real-life version of Miller's *The Crucible*.

Miller, Arthur. *After the Fall*. New York: Bantam, 1964. A long, painful play by America's great tragic dramatist, recounting his love affair and marriage to Marilyn Monroe and the anguish he suffered during the McCarthy hearings.

———. *The Crucible*. New York: Bantam, 1959. The classic tragedy dealing pointedly with McCarthyism, disguised as the Salem witch-hunts.

Smith, Wendy. *Real-Life Drama: The Group Theatre and America, 1931–1940*. New York: Knopf, 1990. Covers the same ground as Clurman's book, but it is the work of a theater scholar, well researched and well illustrated. Those who read both books will be thoroughly grounded in a knowledge of a critical period in the history of American humanities.

*Oskar Kokoschka,* The Tempest *(Kunstmuseum Basel/Photo: Hans Hinz)*

# 11

# *Myths*

## *Overview*

This chapter is not about lies people tend to accept without question. Yet when the word *myth* is introduced, people almost immediately think of "untruth." Unfortunately, the word *myth* can be used in a number of conflicting ways.

In popular usage, myth is something erroneous, yet widely believed—something to be exposed. Look at any library bookshelf, and you will see titles like *The Myth of Self; Napoleon—the Man and the Myth; The Myth of Mental Illness;* and so on. The sensationalistic advertisement screams MYTH OF CALORIES EXPOSED! EAT ALL YOU WANT AND GET THIN! If we are to limit ourselves to this one definition, we should be convinced that wisdom can be attained as soon as we recognize and then exorcise all of our useless myths.

Yet when we talk about *mythology*, we are dealing not with stories that represent erroneous views of life but with an entire discipline within the humani-

*The mythmaking process reveals much about how humanity copes with the puzzle of being alive.*

ties, a discipline that has had as profound an influence on human development as religion, philosophy, or any of the arts. The major myths of the world—and they exist in every culture—were created because they had to be. They helped people explain the world and their existence. They helped people give vent to their longings or their innermost fears. Myths come in all literary forms and with varying degrees of "truth." But they are all important, whether or not they are still "true," because the mythmaking process reveals much about how humanity copes with the puzzle of being alive.

Mythology is not ancient history. Even in our enlightened age, people are nervous, frightened, and in need of heroes. Heroes come from the collective mythology of the human race. So do villains and mysterious strangers who come out of the fog and solve our problems before disappearing once more.

*Three categories:*
  *Myths of childhood*
  *Myths as explanation*
  *Archetypal myths*

We shall discuss three categories of myth. The first we will call *myths of childhood*. Sometimes named *fairy tales*, these are stories found in many cultures with similar ingredients, such as witches, demons, elves, and strange, often terrifying, landscapes. On the surface, they are obviously ways of teaching children the moral code of their society, one that is similar throughout the world. These stories, however, have many disturbing elements, such as violence, death, and amoral occurrences. The effect of these elements upon children is controversial, but there is no doubt the myths of childhood do much more than present a simplified version of reality that children are able to comprehend. They have loose ends that children probably do *not* understand.

A second category is *myths as explanation*. Many of these arose in what are sometimes called "prescientific" times, centuries before there was anything like urban civilization. They seem clearly to have been fanciful explanations of natural events that had to be understood: storms, volcanic eruptions, eclipses, thunder, lightning, and other natural phenomena against which our ancestors must often have felt helpless. Imagine living at a time when nobody knew why the sun rose and set or what the stars were. Imagine, also, the genius of our ancestors, who were *not content with ignorance*! Perhaps this discontent is the true heart of being human, the indissoluble atom of humanness that causes our species to constantly change the destiny of the earth.

Explanatory myths address more than just natural phenomena. A significant portion of them are focused on a subject that must have haunted our curious ancestors: *the origins of trouble*. They knew that hardships were a part of living, but one suspects it was not their nature to sit back passively and accept disaster without wondering what caused it. Many of their answers will strike the modern reader as having a masculine bias, since woman is often cited as the source from which human troubles emanate. Myths are not "true" in a scientific sense, but no one can deny their impact as psychological truth, forming a core of centuries-old assumptions. Indeed, if such were not the case, the feminist movement might have had much less work to do.

The third category is regarded by many mythologists (scholars who study myths and try to discern what motivated them and what they have in common) as the most important; it is *archetypal myths*. These are found the world over. One cannot imagine a culture that did not invent, tell, and pass along stories in which certain characters (like heroes) and certain recurrent themes (like magic numbers) have influenced the way people understand their existence.

An *archetype* is a model by which other characters, events, or ideas resembling it can be identified. The hero is an outstanding example. As we shall see, the hero—a person who stands out from the crowd because of very special characteristics—is a universal mythological phenomenon, indicating to us that people have always needed and continue to need a belief in the amazing powers of a rare few, born to lead: men and women of insight and courage who are able to take on challenges and obstacles that would defeat ordinary mortals.

Archetypes need not be people. They can be beliefs that are found in myth after myth and that underlie many of our assumptions about life. One such belief is that good deeds will be rewarded and bad deeds punished, or *What goes around, comes around*.

The Roman poet Ovid tells an old story in which the gods Jupiter and Mercury, wishing to entertain themselves, come down to earth disguised as poor wanderers to see whether anyone will show them hospitality. Door after door is slammed in their faces until an elderly couple—Baucis, the wife, and Philemon, the husband—who are as poor as they are old, take them in and share what little they have. Finding out that the neighbors have persecuted the couple for many years and have scorned them in their poverty, the gods send a devastating flood that wipes out the entire neighborhood, leaving a very happy—and much richer— Baucis and Philemon behind.

The assumption that a good deed has to be rewarded (even that the reward can be the *purpose* of the deed) is an archetypal idea that is handed down from generation to generation in many cultures of the world. People born into deprivation and who spend their lives in poverty may have little use for it, but they probably value archetypes of charity, sharing, and surviving.

## Myths of Childhood

Our earliest encounter with mythology is often our first encounter with literature and the humanities. Only recently has this childhood literature, the literature of fairy tales, been taken seriously. Perhaps many of us hated to admit how much our lives were molded and conditioned by these "silly" stories. Still fewer like to admit that fairy tales are still in our blood, subtly influencing our expectations.

### What We Learn from Fairy Tales

Children would be disoriented and bewildered were it not for what their parents tell them about the world; much of this talk has its roots in fairy tale. Much of what parents say is moralistic—usually warnings about the dire consequences of disobedience. "The Three Little Pigs," for example, advises children how to plan sensibly for the future, tells them that hard work and diligence, not fun and frivolity, are what pay off in the long run. Little Red Riding-Hood is explicitly warned by her mother not to talk to strangers. Similarly, the mother goat in "The Wolf and the Seven Kids" goes off, leaving her children home alone with the admonition not to open the door to anyone. Like Red Riding-Hood, the seven little goats pay for their disobedience by being eaten whole, but, of course, as often happens in fairy-tale land, they are rescued, none the worse for their ordeal.

The teaching function of the fairy tale is nowhere better illustrated than in Hans Christian Andersen's "The Emperor's New Clothes." Perhaps a bit sophisticated for the youngest of children, the tale stays in the back of our minds until we are ready to apply its message that our fear of power and authority blinds us to the reality of the people we bow to.

Modern interpreters of fairy tales, especially psychiatrists, point to early misconceptions and warped expectations that children derive from fairy tales. The hunter will come and take care of the wicked wolf. The Prince will kiss Sleeping Beauty and awaken her from her century-long slumber. Prince Charming will discover that the wretchedly dirty girl in the corner has the only foot capable of fitting the glass slipper. And so, they contend, we grow up believing that true love will find a way and that bad people always get what's coming to them.

Closely related to these tinsel expectations from life are the stereotyped thinking, the class distinctions, and the sexism that some critics see in fairy tales. Characters are seldom named, and, when they are, their names often represent broad characteristics (Prince Charming, Sleeping Beauty, Snow White, the Beast) instead of unique individuals. Rumpelstiltskin, with his eccentric, distinctive name, is an ugly little fellow with a devilish sense of humor.

*Would the prince look twice at someone who was only virtuous and a good worker?*

Physical good looks are stressed as important. Cinderella's stepsisters are not only nasty, they are ugly as well, which is made to seem as bad. Underneath all the grime Cinderella is breathtakingly beautiful; she must be, for would the prince look twice at someone who was only virtuous and a hard worker? Older characters almost never fare well in fairy tales, and critics point to this fact to explain why children often shy away from close contact with the elderly and the wrinkled, who resemble the fairy-tale witches.

Fairy tales take place in magic kingdoms dominated by rigid class systems, for, after all, they originated in a time when it was believed, as the folk saying goes, "class will tell." The heroine of "The Princess and the Pea" is so innately sensitive—so much a member of the upper class—that she spends a sleepless night because of one pea that has been slipped under several mattresses. Likewise, the Biblical story of Joseph and his brothers can be seen as a fairy tale of true worth lying hidden beneath humble rags.

*Sleeping Beauty can only wait for the kiss of life, as women in general were expected to wait for a fertile male to arrive and give meaning to their life.*

Feminists today are not happy about the depiction of women in these old stories. Women are expected to be pretty, refined, and docile. As the weaker sex they must be taken care of as a matter of course. Sleeping Beauty can only wait for the kiss of life, as women in general were expected to simply wait for a fertile male to arrive and give meaning to their life. Dynamic, aggressive women, like Snow White's stepmother, are bound to be scheming and wicked.

## What Children Don't See in Fairy Tales

In *The Uses of Enchantment* (1976) Bruno Bettelheim, a Freudian psychiatrist, sees in fairy tales more than simple fables teaching simple morals. He views fairy tales as myths that do not tell "the whole story."

Mythology proper tells truths about life that are handed down from generation to generation and passed from culture to culture. Much of it tends to be tragic, for early people, learning how to experience the joy of living, must have been hard-pressed to justify death. Often they could not.

Bettelheim sees "terrible truths" embedded in the fairy tales, but not discernible to the child, who probably absorbs them unconsciously. Fairy tales take place in magic kingdoms, true; but there are dark forests, wicked witches, goblins, bats, skulls, and other reminders of evil, death, and decay. There are devastating storms, shipwrecks, and as much violence as you find in today's goriest films. What does the child do with these images?

For Bettelheim the fairy tale is crucial to normal psychological develop-

*Gustave Doré,* Little Red Riding Hood and the Wolf: *Terrible truths not discernible to the child. (From* Les Contes des Perrault, *Paris, J. Hetzel, 1862)*

ment. At heart, he says, fairy tales are completely amoral stories that evoke multiple responses and work on many different levels.

Let us look at "Snow White." On one level we have the stereotypical figure of the beautiful innocent preyed on by evil forces but emerging triumphant at the end. We have the "happily ever after" motif, shared by nearly all fairy tales. Death, or near-death, does occur—Snow White is even placed in a glass coffin. But "resurrection" soon follows, and Snow White is rewarded for her passive virtue.

Bettelheim's research has shown him that children find much more in the story than the stereotypes we have noted, but on a "pre-conscious level." When the evil queen is in the spotlight, the child may identify with *her*; she has power, and small children often identify with power figures, like their parents. Children know when power is being wielded, and they know when someone is defenseless against that power. There is, according to this view, no reason for the child to identify *exclusively* with the powerless.

Parents have repeatedly told children how naughty they are, so it may be difficult for them to identify with the purity of Snow White. There may well be far more of a secret alliance between children and the ruthless queen than adults ever dream. But this alliance does not last.

As the queen's powers become focused on destroying the beautiful inno-cent, the child's involvement changes. A familiar structure is now recognized: the parent is on the way *with punishment*, namely, the poisoned apple. In the guise of the ugly old woman, the queen probably becomes increasingly remote; she comes to represent the entire adult world bearing down on that of the child. It is now that the necessity for thwarting the queen's power becomes critical, and children once again identify with the innocent.

*Bettelheim believes parents should not interpret all fairy tales but allow children to experience the stories as they must.*

Some parents seek to overdo the moral function of a tale by eliminating all threatening motifs, and sometimes the results can confuse the child. One parent, worried about frightening her daughter, was careful to change the popular ending of "Little Red Riding-Hood," in which the grandmother is devoured by the wolf. She chose instead the alternate ending in which the hunter comes to the rescue, kills the wolf, slits open his stomach, and finds the grandmother whole and happy. The storyteller looked up and found her audience in tears, grieving over the wolf's horrible death. Finally, in desperation, the woman told her daughter a mistake had been made in the details of the story: "Actually, the grandmother went to her sewing basket, found a needle and thread, and sewed the wolf up again. The wolf was so grateful that he ran back into the forest and was never wicked again."

This anecdote is not in Bettelheim's book, but he does admonish adults to let fairy tale mythology work upon children as it will:

> As to fairy tales, one might say that the child who is not exposed to this literature is as badly off as the girl who is anxious to discharge her inner pressures through horseback riding or taking care of horses, but is deprived of her innocent enjoyment. A child who is made aware of what the figures in fairy tales stand for in his own psychology will be robbed of a much-needed outlet, and devastated by having to realize the desires, anxieties, and vengeful feelings that are ravaging him. Like the horse, fairy tales can and do serve children well, can even make an unbearable life seem worth living, as long as the child doesn't know what they mean to him psychologically.[1]

In other words, children need fairy tales to recognize and accept the intense emotions, both "good" and "bad," that they feel but are not yet old enough to confront. Without such stories as a buffer, the world and their own feelings could be too much for them.

There is a story about a scientific father who wanted his son to be armed with the toughness required to face a harsh world. He decided the fantasy of Santa Claus was nonsense, and on his son's fifth Christmas, he forced the boy to stay awake all night to observe the source of his presents. The child, rubbing his eyes, watched as his parents assembled the gifts under the tree. At dawn he pleaded to be allowed to sleep. His father, however, insisted that he have breakfast and then play with his toys. Before he was allowed to eat, the boy was required to finish the sentence "There is no  . . ." When the boy kept meeting the command with silence, the father became angry and threatened to beat the child if he did not comply.

Wearily, the little boy looked up and said: "There is no father."

## Myths as Explanation

For early people there were two major aspects of being alive that must surely have baffled them. One was *natural phenomena*, which they had few means to investigate. To be sure, this obstacle did not always stop human genius, as the extraordinary stone circle at Stonehenge clearly indicates. Of uncertain age but definitely ancient, the stones appear to have been a way of following the course of the sun throughout the year—a way of forecasting seasonal changes. Yet as scientific as this circle was for its time, those who constructed it probably believed also that a good harvest meant that the gods were happy, and a bad one, that the group must have done something displeasing. Mythical explanation was thus a human necessity.

The other baffling aspect of living must have been *how to account for all the trouble that seemed to come with life*. No arrangement of stones could have predicted human tragedies, but stories could account for them or at least help take away the fear that life was innately evil.

## The Natural World

Many early myths were designed to explain nature, and many early rituals were efforts to control it. In Scandinavian communities, for example, the fertility deity was Freyr, who was thought to bring rich harvests to the earth. He did so by wooing a maiden, symbolizing the union of earth and sky. Rituals that honored Freyr and the abundance he gave were essential for survival. In almost all early cultures help from the gods was needed if crops should fail or were insufficient, for then the mortals had to turn to the sea, where food could be found only if the storm god could be placated.

According to an Aztec myth, before the universe was formed there were gods. A fight developed over who would create which part of the world. Eventually a snake divided in half; one half to create the upper part, the other half to create the lower part. The one who created the earth felt that she was less important and began to quarrel with the one who did the heavens. As compensation for her inferior position the gods added to her importance by allowing different parts of her body to be the source of important elements—the rivers and streams coming from her eyes, for instance.

One cannot think of a culture in which the origin of the natural world is not attributed to a divinity that preceded its existence. Judaism, Christianity, and Islam share a common belief that the world was brought into existence by an all-powerful God who controls everything that happens in it and can destroy it at will. The Christian poet John Milton (1608-1674) wrote his epic poem *Paradise Lost* as a way of explaining God's plan for the world and the people in it; he gives us this image of what was here before the creation:

> *First there was Chaos, the vast immeasurable abyss,*
> *Outrageous as a sea, dark, wasteful, wild.*
>                 [7.211-212]

In Greek mythology, "pre-creation" is depicted in a similar fashion. It is called the "formless confusion of Chaos," existing only in darkness. Chaos in some mysterious way gave birth to two children: Night and Erebus, or Death. Night placed an egg in the depths of Erebus, and from it was born Love. Love's first act was to create Light and Day.

Interestingly enough, the Greek gods came after the creation, but this is not surprising when we consider that in the Greek myths the power of Fate appears to be greater than that of the gods. While the account of creation is as mystical as it is beautiful, we may perhaps say that for the Greeks the power of Fate always existed, was responsible for the coming of Night and Death, and must therefore be reckoned as a divine force.[2]

*Easter Island stone figures: One cannot think of a culture in which the origin of the natural world is not attributed to a divinity that preceded its existence. (Art Resource)*

One of the most famous of all the early explanations of the seasons comes, once again, from Greece. According to the story, the goddess of the earth, Demeter, had a beautiful daughter named Persephone, whom she adored. The abundance provided by the earth was explained in terms of Demeter's joy at the very thought of Persephone. But one day the girl wandered away from her playmates and became lost. Pluto, the lord of the underworld, eyed the beautiful creature, mounted his chariot, and stole her away to be his bride. The mother was so overcome with sorrow and grief that the earth's abundance withered away and the land was covered by snow and ice.

This was how winter came to be; if Zeus, the king of the gods on Mount Olympus, had not intervened, all human life would have ceased. But Zeus was so touched when he saw the extent of Demeter's grief that he sent this message to her: Persephone would be allowed to live with her mother for all but three months out of the year; those she owed to her husband, the king of darkness. Demeter had no choice but to accept the terms, and so it came about that, each year when Persephone went back to her husband, the earth froze over and nothing grew. When, three months later, Persephone returned once more, the mother's renewed happiness caused the green abundance of the earth to bloom.[3]

The Greeks explained the alternation of winter and spring in another myth. The god Dionysus was the male deity who governed the abundance of earth, and in his story winter came about because he died. Not only did he die, but in the underworld he was torn to pieces and eaten. Since the old storytellers knew that the earth renewed itself in the spring, those who retold the myth of Dionysus had to tell their listeners that "somehow" the god was resurrected and became whole every year, only to meet his terrible fate again and again.

## Human Sacrifice

In a sense the fates of Persephone and Dionysus can be regarded as sacrifices that ensured rebirth. Very early, then, was the idea that without sorrow or death there can be no springtime joy. In the midst of devastation there is always the promise of better things to come. As Percy Bysshe Shelley says in his "Ode to the West Wind":

> *O Wind,*
> *If Winter comes, can Spring be far behind?*

*In very early mythology was the idea that without sorrow or death there can be no springtime joy.*

We know that Greek tragic theater sprang from annual spring festivals honoring Dionysus. Some believe an ancient practice in these festivals was human sacrifice to make sure Dionysus would keep returning. The thought is not far-fetched when one considers all the evidence that early people the world over performed this rite.

From what is now Ghana in West Africa comes a story of how the country flourished because the people sacrificed a beautiful girl each year to a giant serpent, which was the source of their prosperity. One year, however, the victim turned out to be an especially beautiful girl, dressed in the best clothing and jewels. They led her to the pit where the serpent waited, tied her there, begged her forgiveness, and left her to die. Rescue came in the form of a brave young man engaged to marry the girl. He stood by while the serpent twice appeared and spat venom on the girl, because he knew the secret: only on the third appearance could the reptile be destroyed. At the appropriate moment, the young man beheaded the serpent, only to find that it kept growing new heads—seven in all. The girl was saved, but the serpent nonetheless had its revenge. As the last head was cut off, it flew away, saying, "For seven years, seven months, and seven days, Ghana will receive neither rains of water nor rains of gold." A drought ensued, destroying the populace and a once-great empire. In this tragic myth we do not find the cycle motif, but only an unhappy explanation for a catastrophe that must actually have taken place, at least in some form. Interesting also is the fact that the element of rebirth is found only in the horror of the reappearing heads.[4]

In North American Indian mythology, human sacrifice was needed in order to make the heavens work properly. After four worlds that had not worked (the final disaster including a devastating flood), a fifth world was revealed, but it was discovered that the sun and moon could be set in their courses only by the death of a Navajo each day and the death of another each night. Later, when human beings claimed credit for the prosperity of the world, they were punished by plagues and monsters.

In Scandinavian myth, it was a giant whose sacrifice was necessary. Ymir, who was nourished by a cow, was the giant responsible for forming men and women (from his left armpit); eventually he was killed and his body "used by the slayers to form the world—his flesh providing the soil, his bones the mountains and rocks, his blood the sea and his hair the vegetation of the earth."[5]

In the modern world we still find sacrifices being made as part of certain observances, generally involving the giving up of material possessions or some form of pleasure. During the season of Lent (an archaic term for "spring"), Catholics are asked to do without something that is particularly enjoyable to commemorate Christ's sacrifice on the cross. On Yom Kippur, the Day of Atonement, Jews are expected to fast in order to expiate their sins. In Brazil there is an annual holiday in honor of Jemanja, goddess of the sea, who once was believed to protect fishermen and keep lost sailors from drowning. She could also be responsible for many deaths by making the sea furious. On her day, Brazilians gather by the water and place gifts for Jemanja in small boats that the tide carries out to sea, where presumably the goddess waits to receive them.

## The Command Not Kept

*The myth of the golden age celebrates an idyllic time before some misdeed caused humanity to be afflicted with mortality and suffering.*

The need to explain how death and evil came into the world is as old as the need to explain nature. In ancient myths, the explanation for human troubles is often that God, or some god, was at some point offended by human sinfulness. Such myths often begin with a "golden age," an idyllic time before sin and death were in the world. But then some misdeed causes humanity to be afflicted with mortality and suffering.

One Greek myth explains disaster through the tale of a girl named Pandora, into whose keeping the gods placed a wondrous box containing all harmful things. She was commanded never to open this box, or terrible consequences would follow. Pandora was unbearably curious, however, and could not resist taking a peek. When she did so, out flew death, sorrow, plagues, war, and every imaginable calamity that has ever been visited upon mortals. Realizing what she had done, Pandora slammed the box shut and resolved never to open it again. What she did not know was that something good—the *only* good—was left trapped inside the box: hope.

*In much mythology woman is seen as the cause of human ills.*

In three other versions of the origin of death and evil, the sin of a woman is also to blame. In the Judeo-Christian tradition there is the story of Adam and Eve and the commandment not to eat the forbidden fruit (traditionally depicted as an apple, though not specified as such in Genesis because apples were surely unknown in the Middle East). The fruit was growing on the Tree of Life, and it contained the knowledge of good and evil, a knowledge Adam and Eve in their innocence presumably did not need. Yet Eve could not keep away from the tree. She ate the fruit, and Adam did the same.

Note that Genesis does not say Eve prevailed upon Adam to follow her into sin, though later versions have turned the story into a myth of woman's weakness. In Milton's *Paradise Lost*, mentioned earlier in this chapter, God judges Adam more harshly than he does Eve, on the grounds that even though Eve sinned first, Adam's sin was greater since he was a man and therefore should have known better.

In some African myths a woman is also the cause of everything bad. The Burundi tell an old story of a time when Death used to be chased away by divine dogs and was thus unable to touch human beings. One day Death approached a woman and promised he would give her and her family special protection. When the woman opened her mouth to speak, Death jumped in. Questioned by God, the woman lied and said she had not seen Death, but God knew what had happened. Ever since, human beings have shared the same awful fate.

In another tribal tale, the first man, Kintu, and his heavenly wife, Nambi, were hurrying to leave the land of the sky in order to escape from Death. Nambi, however, decided to go back to ask for grain, and so Death followed her as she sought to rejoin her husband. The result was the punishment of death for all future

*Albrecht Dürer,* Adam and Eve: *Later versions have turned the Adam and Eve story into a myth of woman's weakness. (Museum of Fine Arts, Boston. Centennial Gift of Landon Clay)*

generations, because Kintu had been warned and should not have allowed Nambi to go after the grain.

In a tale from Zambia, the chief of men was a nomad, but he decided he wanted to become a farmer and asked God for help. God replied by sending messengers with small bundles of seed, which were not to be opened. The curious messengers untied the forbidden bundles, and Death appeared. One assumes, however, that in this instance the messengers were not women.

There are two famous stories that do not account for all evil, but coming from very different cultures, they do illustrate what may be a universal belief that *some things are better left unknown.* A Greek story tells of Orpheus, whose songs could melt the heart of a confirmed cynic. Orpheus loved the beautiful Eurydice, lost her to death, and followed her down into the land of darkness. There he worked his musical magic upon the king of the underworld and was given the opportunity to return to life with his beloved. The condition: Orpheus must walk straight up the path to the world of the living, without once turning his head to see whether Eurydice was following. The pact was almost kept, but at the very last moment, the hero, unable to bear the suspense, turned around for the barest glimpse of the maiden. The command broken, Eurydice was reclaimed forever by the powers of darkness.

The Biblical story of Lot's wife contains similar circumstances. Allowed to escape the destruction of Sodom and Gomorrah, Lot and his family were given one condition—that they not turn around to see what was happening. Lot's wife (in this case the woman, we note) could not resist the temptation, did indeed look at the dying cities, and was immediately turned into a pillar of salt.

The broken command as an explanation for human misery—as an alternative to the suggestion that humankind is innately corrupt—has proved widely useful, especially for generations of men able to point to Pandora or Eve as the source of their troubles. But the myth has had less blatantly sexist uses as well—in fact, uses that are not tragic at all. If Eden has been lost, the garden (or age) of innocence is still there, waiting for the pure in heart to find it. Where else did the idea for Oz, Shangri-La, or Bali Ha'i come from?

## Family Ties

A dominant myth for the Greeks was that of the family—or, specifically, the family that was doomed because of an ancient sin. No matter what the descendants did, they were born to suffer a wretched life and often a miserable death because of an ancestor's unspeakable crime. No one knows exactly why the Greeks were prone to such unhappy tales, but perhaps the reason has something to do with their overwhelming sense of fate—the idea that your destiny is already determined before you even have a chance to decide what to do with your life. We include the family myth not because we want to focus on Greek mythology, but because in all societies with tight family units, family background is often blamed for the failures that sons and daughters experience. Maybe a widespread human trait is to avoid taking full responsibility for one's life. Logically, those who do so ought not to take full credit for success, but somehow we find a great many who are willing to do *that*!

In fairy tales an older family member is often downright rotten and represents the evil that must be escaped before a son or a daughter can be free. We are familiar with the way the stepmother tried to get rid of Hansel and Gretel, the treatment Cinderella received at the hands of *her* stepmother, and the assault on Snow White by yet another terrible guardian. (Incidentally, both myths and fairy tales contain numerous missing "true" parents, who are generally good and kind people.)

Bruno Bettelheim, the psychiatrist whose interpretations of fairy tales we have discussed, says we can flip this family theme over and find another version. Here the children are the problem—at least for the older family members who hide from reality. In the story of Snow White, for example, the queen, a once-beautiful woman, becomes angry when she realizes that she will no longer be judged "the fairest of them all" with a younger beautiful girl growing up in the same house.

Two major family myths are those of the house of Atreus and the house of Cadmus. In the first story, descendants are cursed because of the fact that Atreus killed his brother Thyestes' two children and served them to their father as food. The atrocity is committed as an act of vengeance against Thyestes, who at one time had made love to Atreus's wife. Nonetheless, the gods—or fate—did not believe Atreus had been justified and so doomed his family.

The two sons of Atreus are Menelaus and Agamemnon. The former is married to the beautiful Helen, who runs off to Troy with Paris, thus precipitating the ten-year Trojan War. Agamemnon, who fought on his brother's side during the war, returns home, only to meet death at the hands of his wife and the lover she has taken during her husband's long absence.

The two adulterers are murdered by Agamemnon's son Orestes at the urging of his sister Electra. Because he has committed matricide, Orestes is pursued by the Furies, demonic women who scream and taunt him night and day—and seem to be an early Greek version of conscience. Tried in a heavenly court presided over by Athena, goddess of wisdom, the young man is finally exonerated, and the family curse comes to an end. The reason for his acquittal will be of interest to modern readers: The court decides that the dead wife's crime was a greater one *since she has killed a man*!

The house of Cadmus is the family of Oedipus, the unfortunate king who kills his father and marries his mother without knowing it. Cadmus, however, committed no atrocity like that of Atreus. Instead, he was a happy and prosperous man, the founder of Thebes; presumably the gods—or fate—became jealous of his prosperity and doomed his family accordingly.

Laius, son of Cadmus and king of Thebes, takes Jocasta as his queen. At the birth of their son a prophecy is delivered that the son will one day slay his father and then wed his mother. Wishing to avoid the terrible destiny, they order a servant to take the child away, bind his ankles together, and leave him to die on Mount Cithaeron. The servant, feeling pity for the child, gives him to a shepherd in the neighboring kingdom of Corinth. Knowing that the king and queen of Corinth are childless, he makes them a present of the boy, who grows up believing himself to be prince of Corinth. In young adulthood Oedipus (which means "swollen foot," the name given him because of his bound ankles) hears the same prophecy his parents heard: that he will kill his father and marry his mother. Trying to escape his fate, the prince leaves Corinth, and on the road does battle with his true father in an argument over who has the right of way. Oedipus kills the old man. He then arrives in Thebes, which is now kingless and in a state of chaos because of a dreadful creature called the Sphinx, half-woman and half-bird, who will stop her attacks only when somebody is able to guess her riddle: "What creature walks on four legs in the morning, two in the afternoon, and three at night, and moves most slowly when it has the most feet?" Oedipus correctly responds, "Man," recognizing the human progression from crawling (when we move most slowly) to walking to using a cane. In so doing, he wins what appears to be a prize: to rule over Thebes and to wed the queen. Thus is his terrible fate finally complete.

*The terrible fate that befalls Oedipus and his whole family is attributed to the gods' jealousy of his grandfather's prosperity.*

Three of Oedipus's four children by his own mother fare no better. The two sons kill each other in battle; one daughter is Antigone, about whom Sophocles wrote the great tragedy we discussed in Chapter 4. Her destiny, you may remember, is to hang herself after being sentenced to death for defying an order that allowed proper burial for one brother, loyal to Thebes, and denied it to the other, leader of a rebel force. Only Ismene, sister to Antigone, avoids a disastrous fate; she lives out her life in lonely isolation, however.

The myth of the doomed family has influenced literature for thousands of years. The American playwright Eugene O'Neill (1888-1953) retold the story of the house of Atreus in *Mourning Becomes Electra* (1931), except that doom comes not from the gods or fate but from uncontrollable sexual passion and unconscious drives. Ezra Mannon (instead of Agamemnon) is a Civil War hero whose wife has committed adultery in his absence. Returning from the war, he is murdered like his Greek predecessor. Meanwhile, his son Orin (instead of Orestes) is goaded on by his sister Lavinia (instead of Electra, though the mythical character's name is in the title) to kill his mother. O'Neill is not a Greek tragedian, however, but a twentieth-century playwright influenced by Freud and his theory that much of our behavior can be explained in terms of the suppression of forbidden sexual drives. Freud used Oedipus for the name for his famous Oedipus complex, according to which the young male child harbors secret desires for his mother. Orin, attracted to his mother, is naturally reluctant to carry out his sister's wishes. She, one suspects,

*In updating the tragic tale of the house of Atreus, Eugene O'Neill substitutes Freudian sexual drives for Greek fate as the force that dooms the family.*

*In* Mourning Becomes Electra, *doom comes not from the gods or fate but from unconscious drives. (The Museum of Modern Art/Film Stills Archive)*

is suffering from the female equivalent of the Oedipus complex, named, appropriately enough, the *Electra* complex, according to which the young female harbors secret desires for her father. Orin carries out his sister's wishes, only to be tormented by guilt and his unresolved longings for his mother. O'Neill further complicates his play by subtly suggesting that brother and sister have incestuous feelings for each other. We are thus not surprised by Orin's suicide and are left with the desolate image of Lavinia, who will live the rest of her life in mourning.

We have dwelt at some length on the myth of the doomed family because it is a strange and powerful theme of the humanities. It has inspired some of the world's greatest dramatists, from the great tragedians of Greece to America's Eugene O'Neill and Norway's Henrik Ibsen, especially in his play *Ghosts*, also discussed in Chapter 4. It provides a major instance in which the humanities have had an impact on psychology. The need and often the inability to free a disturbed personality from bondage to a destructive family background is as viable an issue today as it was for the ancient Greeks.

## Myths and Archetypes

The psychologist/philosopher Carl Jung (1875 - 1961) maintained that all persons are born with an instinctive knowledge of certain archetypes, the models by which we comprehend our experience and cope with the enormous and often baffling task of being human. Jung believed these models are shared by societies all over the world, though they may take different forms. The archetypes are characters, symbols, and buried assumptions transmitted genetically from one generation to another through what Jung labeled the *collective unconscious*:

> From the unconscious there emanate determining influences which,
> independently of tradition, guarantee in every single individual a
> similarity and even a sameness of experience, and also of the way it is
> represented imaginatively. One of the main proofs of this is the almost
> universal parallelism between mythological motifs.[6]

Jung's theory is not accepted by all psychologists or scholars of myth. But
without it or another theory as strong, we have a difficult time accounting for the
continued appearance of certain myths: the tales of a terrible flood and the salvation
of one good man; the stories about dangerous journeys into the land of death and
darkness; and, above all, the tales about the major stages in the life of a singular,
partly human, partly divine being known as the hero. There are, however, some
alternative explanations.

*Archetypes are characters, symbols, and assumptions that are somehow transmitted from one generation to another. Jung believed they were inborn—part of the "collective unconscious."*

One is the *external* theory, the most scientific of the possibilities. According
to this theory, stories were spread along migratory routes. Myths originated in
specific places and then were transported as people warred, traded, and intermar-
ried with each other. In general, we find myth similarities among people whose
migrations we can trace.

An example of the migratory spread of old stories is the way the myths of
the African Yoruda tribe were transported to Cuba, where they were modified and
adopted by a whole new body of listeners. These stories gradually became sys-
tematized into both a religion and a philosophy known as *Santeria*, which offered
an explanation of universal origins that combined an African belief in multiple
deities with Catholic monotheism. Santeria continues to function in ritual practice,
albeit outside the law; it continues to involve animal sacrifices, with its followers
very outspoken about their right to freedom of religion. Their litany of heavenly
protectors offers a fascinating blend of African gods and Christian saints.

Yet another explanation for universal myths is the predictable one that
human beings share common basic insecurities, regardless of geography and level
of cultural sophistication, and thus certain elements found in all myths must play
their part in helping people to cope with the conditions in which they find
themselves. The very fact that the mythology familiar to those of us raised in a
Western tradition is still very much alive suggests that the need to cope has never
lost its urgency. We may assume that everyone experiences this need, so it follows
that mythological stories *should* be similar.

## The World Myth, or Monomyth

Called the world myth by some anthropologists and labeled the *monomyth* by the
Irish novelist James Joyce, the life and circumstances of the hero form Jung's
dominant archetype. As early as 1909, a disciple of Freud, Otto Rank, had discovered
the characteristics that many mythic heroes share:

> The hero is the son of parents of the highest station. His conception
> takes place under difficulty. There is a portent in a dream or oracle
> connected with the child's birth. The child is then sent away, or
> exposed to extreme danger. He is rescued by people of humble
> station, or by humble animals, and reared by them. When grown, he
> discovers his noble parentage after many adventures, and, overcoming
> all obstacles in his path, becomes at last recognized as the hero and
> attains fame and greatness.[7]

*THE MYTHIC HERO . . .*

*is born miraculously*

*has a strange destiny*

*is recognized through the performance of some extraordinary feat*

*reaches a pinnacle of fame through some youthful success*

*becomes a powerful ruler for a time.*

*THEN HIS FORTUNES GO DOWNHILL.*

Freud, a pioneer in the psychological interpretation of ancient mythology, maintained that the two families in the monomyth represented the child's parents as they appeared at different stages of the child's development. But Jung went beyond this interpretation, arguing that the components, or motifs, of this pervasive myth were primordial images, "or—as I have named them—archetypes."

Whatever the specific interpretations given, the world hero appears to represent humanity in an idealized form: nearly godlike, destined for better things, but beset by incredible obstacles. The world hero, unlike the wish-fulfillment figures of early-childhood mythology (like Superman), is not morally perfect and does not always triumph. The monomyth is an adult story and does not falsify life. Since it has been a primarily masculine myth, we will use the word *hero* and the masculine pronoun throughout this discussion.

From a synthesis of major scholars of world mythology, we can derive the following milestones in the life of the hero.

**Birth.**   In the monomyth the hero's birth occurs under wondrous circumstances: bowing trees; a shower of gold penetrating the ceiling of a room in which a young girl has been confined; the visit of a god in the guise of some other creature, animal or human; and mysterious prophecies. In most cases the hero is sired by a supernatural being or chooses to believe that he is. Among the Greek mythic heroes whose conception and birth were extraordinary we number Perseus, Hercules, Theseus, and Oedipus.

From the beginning of human awareness, the phenomenon of birth has preoccupied human curiosity. Eventually people came to know the causal sequence that led to reproduction. But even then, they must have marveled over that sequence, that such a miracle should be possible!

As a way of organizing human experience, the hero's story lives on in the private, more democratic mythology of us "ordinary" mortals. Each person who comes into the world through the miracle of birth is special in some way. The universe does not roll idly by, indifferent to each birth. The newborn child is a unique individual who matters, not just an entry in the Bureau of Vital Statistics, and the date of birth is not just another day on the calendar. One's birthday remains special for life.

As a human extension of the wondrous prophecy that attends the birth of the hero, the parents of the newborn child are given "best wishes," and the newly arrived hero or heroine is always thought destined for a wonderful future of love and success. In invoking these hopes, we are urging providence to take note of the hero or heroine.

Many grow into adulthood believing they have been earmarked for all good things; if the glorious future does not exactly materialize, they may consider themselves somehow "cursed by fate."

**Early Recognition.**   The hero must be recognized early in life as one who has been destined for greatness. Such recognition often comes about after the accomplishment of a spectacular physical deed—such as the young Arthur's removal of the sword Excalibur from the stone that had held it until the rightful owner should come along. Recognition of Theseus as a king's lost son came when he proved to be the only one capable of lifting a heavy stone that covered a golden sword and sandals. (One version of the myth credits him not so much with strength as with ingenuity in lifting the stone through devising a lever.) Sometimes recognition comes through the fulfillment of a prophecy, as when Jason arrives in the kingdom wearing only one sandal.

In displaying early recognition, myth identifies a universal need for acceptance. In the painful stages of early adolescence, we first ask, "Who am I?" and are fearful that the answer will be, "You're nobody." Children are so small in relation to the adults around them that it is no wonder they sometimes lack a sense of worth.

Many later admit that in early childhood they harbored fantasies of being "secret" princes or princesses stolen from their cradles by gypsies or given away by their true parents. This unknown identity allows the extraordinary child to live with such average people and to perform dreary domestic tasks unsuited for royal beings. One day, the child-turned-adolescent feels, the recognition of special status will surely arrive.

## The Great Deed.

The vital part of every monomyth is the hero's performance of a magnificent feat. This feat always occurs in young adulthood, at a time when the hero has left home, separating himself from his parents. It is a mythical version of the universal rite of passage: the attainment of adult status at puberty.

Almost every early culture has required the accomplishment of an arduous task to signify an end to childhood: enduring bitter cold, surviving the wilderness, conquering a predatory beast. Theseus destroyed the Minotaur of Crete, a creature with the head of a bull and the body of a man that had demanded the regular sacrifice of the finest Athenian youths and maidens. In order to kill the Minotaur—an extraordinary feat in itself—Theseus first had to find him by making his way through the labyrinth, an involved series of deceptive passages, which Freud-oriented myth commentators have viewed as the journey through the maze of childhood sexual stages. The ultimate discovery of the Minotaur becomes symbolic of the newly arrived adult male's sexual potency.

Many of the great deeds in world mythology are physical, but others are purely mental. Oedipus solving the riddle of the Sphinx is a good example. King Arthur's spectacular deeds included the drawing forth of Excalibur from the stone, but also the creation of a noble state governed by kindness and goodwill—a utopian world order that humanity has yet to see realized.

The empathic celebration of a hero's successful and wondrous feat is a need that stays with us long after our first exposure to myths. We mark the milestone achievements, and they are ways of structuring our personal calendars: Inauguration Day, the Academy Award ceremonies, the placing of a ribboned gold medal around the neck of an Olympic champion. The heroes of these achievements are unable to go anywhere as private citizens. Autograph seekers mob them; screaming fans press forward in an effort to touch them. They possess magic, which the fans think will rub off on them.

## The Loss of Power.

Myths as imaginative presentations of the human story do not end when their characters are on top. (Fairy tales do. When the Prince marries Cinderella, we never hear a word beyond "They lived happily ever after." Perhaps children are too young to hear complete stories.) In myth, the heroes inevitably fall from greatness.

Theseus, for example, soon runs into trouble at home. His wife persuades him that his son by a previous marriage has made improper advances toward her. In a rage, Theseus invokes Poseidon, the god of the sea, to destroy the young man.

*King Arthur's spectacular deeds included the drawing forth of Excalibur from the stone, but also the creation of a noble state governed by kindness and goodwill—a utopian world order that humanity has yet to see realized.*

*. . . Arthur was placed on the throne by destiny, compelled by his sense of justice and harmony to create the "civilized world" and the famous Round Table, to stimulate the Quest for the Holy Grail in an effort to keep man from killing man.*

*But a darker fate also dictated . . . the old king's downfall. Forgotten were his achievements for the Might of Right and for peace on earth.*

*T. H. White*

*When the best leader's work is done, the people say, "We did it ourselves."*

*Lao Tzu*

There is no miraculous rescue in the nick of time. Hippolytus, Theseus's son, is destroyed; only then does the wretched father discover that the advances were those of his wife, not the son. A tragic personal doom also awaits him, as he is treacherously pushed from a high precipice by a supposed friend of his father.

Nor is it enough that Oedipus finally learns the shocking truth of his parentage and incestuous marriage. Refusing to blame fate for his misfortune, the hero blinds himself and goes forth in shame to wander homelessly for the rest of his life. "I am the unclean one who has defiled this land" are his words to the citizens of Thebes. But why? A prophecy has apparently established all of the circumstances of the hero's entire life. What could be easier than to exonerate himself from all guilt? But in accepting full responsibility for the unmentionable crime of incest, Oedipus retains his noble status. In Sophocles' overwhelming dramatization of the myth, the doomed hero staggers forth from the city, but *he is not bowed*. The grieving citizens make a path for him. A vast presence is departing, and he will be mourned for many years to come.

The loss-of-power motif in the monomyth can be at once a courageous confrontation with the universal fact of failure and a strategy for coping with failure.

### The Fickleness of Society.

Not every mythic hero accepts responsibility for failure, nor is every version of the Oedipus myth exactly the same. What Sophocles did was utilize the subject in a way that suited him. But the potential was there in the myth.

Another strategy for coping with failure, also present in the monomyth, is attributing the loss of power to public rejection. The previously loyal subjects of

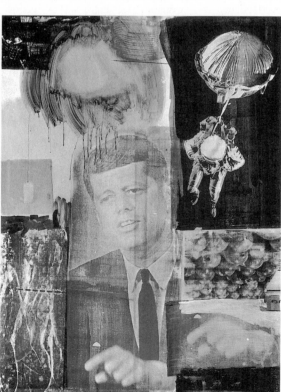

*Robert Rauschenberg, Retroactive I (1964): The history of Western civilization has recorded many instances of heroes rejected or highly controversial during their lifetime but revered after death. (Wadsworth Atheneum, Hartford. Gift of Mrs. Susan Morse Hilles)*

Theseus did not stand by him. Blaming him for the Spartan invasion of Athens at a time when Theseus was gone from the kingdom, the people drove out their ruler, forcing him to seek the hospitality of the king who eventually destroyed him. Significantly, however, the citizens later realize the mistake they have made and, remorseful over the hero's death, erect an enormous tomb to honor his memory. Thus failure is transformed into eternal reputation.

The human need for public recognition and lasting memory seems hardly limited to early mythology, though it may be predominantly Western in character. The history of Western civilization has recorded many instances of heroes rejected or highly controversial during their lifetime but revered after death: Joan of Arc, Galileo, John F. Kennedy, Martin Luther King, Jr., to name a few. The archetype of heroic failure incorporates the attainment of glory, giving all of us a resource with which to bear significant loss.

*In the monomyth the hero's failure is transformed into eternal reputation.*

## Other Archetypal Motifs

### The Belief in Magic

Magic is almost always present in myths—magic rings, magic weapons, magic monsters. One would *need* magic against some of the mythic opponents—a magic sword at least, or the assistance of a clever witch. One interpretation of this magic may be the human need to believe that the resources for coping with life are, like the magic sword, literally at hand. Another is that only *certain* people can do the big tasks. If you don't have the sword, don't take on the dragon! The magicians, like Merlin, reassure us that someone is there to do the impossible.

"Mystique" is probably a contemporary version of the magic archetype. While we all believed in magic as children, we grow up to discover that reality is not quite so wondrous after all—an awakening unforgettably captured in James Joyce's short story *Araby* (1926), in which a young boy returns to a bazaar after it has closed for the night and becomes disillusioned at seeing the two-dimensionality of all the marvelous exhibits. Although *we* gradually yield to the demands of realistic thinking, we exempt certain others, expecting magic from them: an idolized teacher; the dazzling uncle who lives far away and visits occasionally, always bringing a refreshing dose of good cheer; the new president, who has promised an end to hard times.

*We expect magic from certain others: an idolized teacher; the dazzling uncle who lives far away; the new president, who has promised an end to hard times.*

### The Power of Words

Language itself is a recurrent mythic symbol. "In the beginning was the Word," we are told, and also, "It is written." One interpretation of word significance is male jealousy over female reproductive powers. In early cultures, when birth was itself considered a magic act, men may well have sought ways to match or even surpass this phenomenon in which they seemed to play no part. So in myth, the power of the uttered word could be supreme. Men *could* talk!

The words "Open Sesame!" provided wonders for Ali Baba, even as *Sesame Street* serves as a modern archetype—the thoroughfare that takes children from ignorance to knowledge through the magic of letters and numbers and the fantasy creatures that attend them. In the fairy tale "Rumpelstiltskin," the young queen is in danger of losing her first child unless she can guess the name of the magical elf.

*One interpretation of word significance is male jealousy over female reproductive powers. In myth, the power of the uttered word could be supreme. Men* could *talk!*

Unless you are told "Simon says," you may *not* imitate the leader; unless you ask "May I?" you do *not* advance in the game Take a Giant Step.

For thousands of years the world of human (usually male) affairs has counted on the reliability of someone's word, as when a pact is made over a handshake and the inevitable "I give you my word." In this age of high technology we have yet to dismiss the crucial significance of giving one's word or to minimize the disappointment when people have broken their word. (*Break* is an interesting verb to use in conjunction with *word*, is it not? To break a word is tantamount to breaking a magic wand.)

## Mystic Numbers

Magic words in myths must often be repeated a specific number of times. Humanity soon discovered numerical units, as if numbers, like words, were basic to the design of the universe. In *The Divine Comedy*, Dante makes spectacular use of the number 3, in honor of the Trinity: 3 major parts; 33 cantos in each part (for Christ's age at his death); plus an extra canto to bring the total to what was considered the perfect number, 100.

People still have mystic feelings about numbers and sequences, expecting that news of two deaths will lead inevitably to news of another—often that of a famous person. A person doing 99 push-ups would probably do 1 more "to round it out." Tests tend not to have 14 or 19 questions, not just because scoring would be difficult but because the unusual numbers would hang inconclusively. Numbers help to provide the appearance of order. Nearly everyone has a "lucky" number that will guarantee winning the door prize; if the universe is orderly, it also contains magic, we seem to believe. Luck is archetypically incorporated within that order.

## The Circle

The circle as an ever-present geometric shape is frequently found in myth. It is found as a shield, a ring, a pendant, the sun, the moon, and the markings on cave walls or stones. Its importance to the mythmakers is paralleled by countless examples of circular structures throughout the world that have survived from early times: temples, stone circles, and, of course, that most intriguing of all round monuments to ancient humanity, Stonehenge.

The universal form of this myth symbol is the *mandala*, found in the art of almost any period. It is an enclosed circle, often with an intricate design representing the organization of the universe and the various deities that control it. The exact nature of the design is perhaps less significant than the implications of the circular shape. It tells us that the universe is an entity—*one* thing, as indeed our very word for it suggests. It tells us that if it could be viewed from an alternate universe, it would be a round object, something like a gigantic crystal ball, self-contained and distinguishable from anything else hovering in space.

*The circle, or mandala, told the mythmakers that the universe was manageable, within human comprehension.*

Eastern and Western minds apparently came to similar conclusions about the universe. Both decided on the circular, hence perfect, shape, which made the universe seem somehow *manageable*—that is, within the scope of human *comprehension*, if not control. Contemporary scientific theories, which imply that the universe is misnamed, believe it to be not one thing but an infinite series of galactic systems. Such scientific views push that dreamed-of comprehension of the universe so far into the future that it seems reasonable that we may never be able to understand it. Yet we also have Einstein's belief that space is both infinite and *curved*, curved because the principle of gravity is such that an object attempting to move in a straight line forever would be pushed by gravity into a circular orbit, making it eventually return to its place of origin.

Carl Jung saw in the mandala a universal symbol of not only cosmic but psychic organization. He believed that, just as humanity from the beginning appeared unwilling to exist within a shapeless, infinite universe, humanity resisted disorder in human existence by rejecting discontinuous sensations, made up of a hodgepodge of sensory reports, emotions, and thoughts. The circular shapes in myths, according to Jung, are projections of an inner need to identify a coherent *self*, a shaped self, one that can be thought about and discussed.

Just when human beings began to think self-consciously about themselves is hard to say. We do not find Plato or Aristotle talking about themselves in this way. The notion of an inner ego, or a self, seems absent from their work. One recent theory concludes that in Plato's time people still believed their inner thoughts were voices from the gods and that the self did not originate until people stopped believing in such supernatural phenomena. In any case, if Jung is right, the continual appearance of round objects in myths is an indication that early people were instinctively visualizing the human psyche as a shaped entity.

## The Journey

The journey is integral to the majority of myths—perhaps because human existence so obviously proceeds from one stage to another. Change is fundamental to existence, so why have stories in which people stay just as they are?

The journey of life is accomplished by the passing of one milestone after another—usually in the form of severe tests, such as the spectacular deeds we previously discussed. These deeds are mythic forms of the rite of passage, known to every anthropologist and social scientist. Today, they are often marked by ceremonies. Without the ceremony of commencement, would you really have graduated? Ceremonies remain important to us, as we continue to picture life as a passage. Society has taken the journey from early myths and transformed it into the means by which the course of anyone's life is defined and measured.

The mythical journey may be slowed by disastrous circumstances. Characters momentarily lose their way in dense forests. Magical potions force slumber and prevent motion. But sooner or later, the journey continues. Our expectations thus formed by myth, we look for progress in our own lives and in those of others. When the expectations are thwarted, we say, "He is behaving like an adolescent," or "She's still at the same old job!"

The mythical journey has a goal and is therefore a *quest*. The hero searches for his homeland, a buried treasure, the Holy Grail. The attainment of the goal gives shape and purpose to the linear journey, as though to say that, regardless of life's continual changes, it *does* come to something after all.

The twentieth-century philosopher Albert Camus once gave this capsule description of human life: "Man is born, suffers, then dies." In myth these things are also true, but there is more to the story. People are born with a significant destiny, they suffer because of their important quest, and they die only after they have accomplished something.

In myth, the circle and the journey ultimately intertwine. Recurrent motifs mark the course of the quest, and, when the goal is attained (even though death may soon follow), we can say that life has come "full circle." In myth the end is not

*Einstein's universe is circular: Space is at once infinite and curved.*

*For Jung, the circles in myths are projections of an inner need to identify a coherent self.*

*The journey is one of the secret influences of myth. It organizes our lives into goals, destinations, and milestones.*

*We are profoundly affected by two vast symbols, the circle and the journey. The incomplete life is unacceptable.*

thousands of miles from the beginning. In myth tomorrow is not just another day. It is eventually that long-awaited tomorrow that was foretold, that *must* happen, or else life is incomplete.

We are profoundly affected by these two vast symbols. The "incomplete" life is unacceptable—or tragic. "She died before her time" is a meaningful—and mythic—observation. So is "Here he is, 35 years old, and what does he have to show for it?" Myth keeps us from looking at life as simply "one thing after another."

## Shaping Our World

We do not want you to finish this chapter believing that (1) all mythology happened a long time ago, or (2) myths are curious phenomena people use when they don't know any better. Mythology is fundamental to the ongoing process of being human, and it is just as much alive today as it was for the ancient Greeks. Myths are not fanciful tales. They are psychological realities that help us shape our expectations and our way of interpreting the world. We absorb mythology in the act of growing up—from the culture surrounding us, from our family, from education and religion. All of these forces supply us with the symbols, themes, and archetypes that constitute what Carl Jung has called the collective unconscious. Without our myths we would not be the species we are.

### The Persistence of Myth

We have said that one form of myth is spawned by the need to explain nature. It is *pre*scientific rather than *non*scientific. For example, nobody believes anymore the old Greek explanation of lightning as being deadly spears hurled down upon the earth by Jove, king of the gods. At one time it was a legitimate myth because it gave sense to an occurrence that would otherwise have left people confused and frightened.

Prescientific beliefs are still around and contribute to the shaping of some people's ideas of the world. Astrology, for example, has fierce loyalty from believers. At a recent conference bringing together highly trained counselors, zodiac signs were used to divide participants into groups, on the professed assumption that those born under the same sign would automatically share common interests. The return of Halley's comet every 75 years is usually preceded by speculations about possible catastrophic or wondrous events that might occur. Mark Twain (1835-1910), it has been noted, was born in a year of Halley's appearance and died 75 years later with its reappearance. Many believed Twain's life was directly tied in with this celestial supershow.

In earlier decades, when alarms were being sounded over what industrial pollution and nuclear testing were doing to the atmosphere, Hollywood obliged by creating a superficial mythology of its own in which nature returned the favor by plaguing humanity with one disaster after another: devastating fires, killer earthquakes, volcanic eruptions, and radioactive insects and rodents grown to mammoth proportions. In some respects this mythology was not very far removed from Greek myths depicting the wrath of the goddess Nemesis, whose job it was to punish the sin of pride.

Even outside of environmental concerns, the myth of Nemesis stays with us. We cling to the fervent belief that those who live evil lives will not escape retribution—even when there are no religious grounds for such a belief. Retribution is somehow built into the scheme of things. When a speeding car cuts us off, nearly causing an accident, we hope to find it eventually apprehended and stopped on the side of the road. On the reverse side, we expect that a good deed will somehow be rewarded. Even scientists, people who otherwise maintain a detached, purely objective view of the world, may have such expectations.

Widespread also is the myth of science itself, the conviction that somehow Science—an Olympian god, rather than a vast, often disconnected series of hypotheses, experiments, and products— will solve what is now unsolvable. We speak of finding the cure for a certain disease as if the cure were an elusive forest elf jumping from one tree to another.

This myth can also be harmful. Thus one says to oneself, "I can keep on smoking, because by the time I'm old enough to be in danger, 'they' will have discovered the cure for lung cancer," or, "Of course, I occasionally think about the hole in the ozone layer that keeps growing every year, but after all, it's not my problem; somebody else is taking care of it."

Equipped with a vague and undefined phantom concept of science or impatient with its slowness to find a cure, many fall into the hands of certain practitioners who promise that people can control their own fates by, for example, thinking positively. We also seek cures through meditation, diet, and being touched by those with miraculous hands. Rightly or wrongly, this mythology underlies the expectations of a great many people and is often the cause of deep depression when expectations are not realized.

The myth of science also includes the complacent attitude of educated and sophisticated modern people who talk about mythology as the superstition of our ancestors, who couldn't possibly have known what we know now. Thus is the phantom science given a sibling name, "progress." This new mythology holds that each generation will be better off than the last, each new discovery will destroy a former scourge, and each new truth will obliterate a former falsehood—a steady, inevitable march toward the time when . . . when what?

The progress myth also has its opposite, which perhaps we can call the "downhill" myth: Time is running out. Each generation is worse off than the last. Our forebears never realized "how good they had it." Oh, why could I not have been born into a more innocent age, before automobiles, before computers, when people were genteel, civilized, caring; when crime was unknown?

## The Garden

A close kin to the downhill way of shaping experience is primitivism, an eighteenth-century but still surviving philosophy we discussed more fully in Chapter 4. *Primitivism* today is the belief in a reality we can call the "state of nature"—a condition in which one eats only the food of the earth (vegetables, fruits, nuts, grains) and lives in the simplest of habitats without "artificial" luxuries, like stoves, air-conditioning, and supermarkets. In such a state one is healthy, happy, and safe. No crime exists. There is no competition, for the earth, left to itself without human interference, will always produce enough for all.

The businesswoman, returning to her apartment after an exhausting day of intense, closed-door meetings, may well derive a fleeting bit of comfort in the dream of drifting in a tiny houseboat on a lazy river. All of us share this dream at one time or another. Suburbia itself is part of it. We must get out of the city, we tell ourselves. People in small towns are happier and nicer than people in the city. Let's go camping on our vacation.

In the eighteenth century, when places like London and New York were

*The return of Halley's comet every 75 years is usually preceded by speculations about possible catastrophic or wondrous events that might occur.*

*Widespread also is the myth of science itself, the conviction that somehow Science—an Olympian god, rather than a vast, often disconnected series of hypotheses, experiments, and products—will solve what is now unsolvable.*

becoming ugly, dirty, and overpopulated, the "unspoiled" countryside beckoned to everyone. The mythic figure of the noble, happy savage made a hugely popular appearance on the stage and in fiction. Primitivism gave birth to the story of Robinson Crusoe and his faithful Friday, a magnificent and benevolent savage who is what he is because civilization has never been close to him. The desert island, in fact, has never left the writer's or the world's stockpile of myth. Who does not have—tucked away in a remote corner of the semiconscious—the impressionist image of a secret retreat, a place where one cannot be reached, cannot answer the phone, cannot be held responsible for a single action?

Mark Twain—he of the comet birth—gave us Huck Finn and his wonderful raft, not to mention the eternal Mississippi River, a perpetual escape from civilization, its moral codes, its social demands, and its unhappy inhabitants. Sir James M. Barrie gave us Peter Pan, who eludes the aging process and lives an irresponsible boy's existence in never-never land. More recently, Steven Spielberg gave us E.T., the Extraterrestrial, an adorable, unspoiled being from outer space who manages to escape the clutches of humanity, which is—except for a tender and understanding little boy—unworthy of his purity. He waits somewhere "up there" for a true believer who can find a way out of the mess we humans have made of this once-beautiful earth.

Many scholars of myth believe that the archetype of the country (as opposed to the city) or the desert island (as opposed to civilization) is a variation of the original and powerful archetype of the Garden. The Bible is only one ancient source of the Garden symbol: the original, pure, natural place people enjoyed before something happened to change everything—and not for the better.

In the Bible there occurs, however, a countermyth with a countersymbol: Adam and Eve were expelled from the Garden of Eden for their sin, but there is the land of Canaan, promised to the descendants of Abraham. Though these descendants were originally understood to be the Hebrews alone, other cultures have developed their own versions of the Promised Land. In gospel songs and spirituals, blacks sing of crossing the Jordan and finding salvation. Hindus and Buddhists long for nirvana, which is not, philosophically speaking, a place, but which nonetheless holds out the promise of a better life. Native Americans thought about the happy hunting grounds.

The "discovery" of America in 1492 gave rise to a new version of the Garden archetype, the luster of which has never diminished: the idea of the New World. First came the explorers proudly planting their nations' flags on the "virgin" soil (often with the help of native Americans, of course). Then came fragile boatloads of pilgrims seeking a new start in life, seeking freedom. Then by the thousands came the immigrants seeking prosperity in streets "paved with gold." As the eastern half of the United States became densely populated and the dream of prosperity gave way to the reality of long hours of work and crowded tenements, the archetype of the Garden was transformed into the frontier, the wide-open West. Whatever disillusionment may have been suffered by however many millions, the symbol of the New World is still here as new dreamers arrive by the boatloads or as artists-on-tour defect from repressive governments.

When they come to the Promised Land, these modern immigrants bring with them a strong archetype, that of the family and the customs, traditions, beliefs, and rituals that hold the family together. They transplant these rituals to the new land. Sometimes they are received with enthusiasm by "the natives," and sometimes, regrettably, they are rejected. Often, members of the younger generation drift away, become part of the new culture. The elders sometimes intensify the

*The "discovery" of America in 1492 gave rise to a new version of the Garden archetype: the idea of the New World.*

traditional rituals, hold even more tightly to the Old World customs, close them-selves in for fear of losing their identity, self-respect, dignity. Disenchanted by the New World, they remember the "old country," where things were better, people were nicer, the streets were safer. Like Dorothy in the Land of Oz, they discover that maybe their original home wasn't so bad after all. The Garden seems always to be somewhere else. But if this archetype can cause disillusionment, it is also the source of much-needed hope.

*The Garden seems always to be somewhere else.*

## The Hero Today

We keep alive the archetype of the hero. We still have demigods and demigoddesses, if not as the literal result of the union between a deity and a mortal, as in ancient days, then in the form of celebrities whose exploits we follow in magazines, gossip columns, and television interviews. These new heroes and heroines set the trends in clothes, hairdos, language.

*We keep looking for the promised leader: that special someone who is not here yet, but should be, and could solve our problems for us.*

We revere the athletes who still perform Herculean tasks. We celebrate the record-breaking home run, the world's fastest mile, the first woman to walk the length of Tibet on foot. A few decades ago came the first astronauts to admire and marvel at. Our artists are less likely to be granted heroic stature, unless a few of them happen to strike it rich and become admired for their success. But the self-made person who climbs to the top of the corporate ladder and turns the business completely around—then writes a best-seller about the feat—is alive and well and very much in our thinking.

One reason intellectuals, teachers, and laboratory scientists almost never attain hero or heroine status may be not our celebrated lack of respect for intelli-gence, but our unconscious perpetuation of the rest of the hero myth: namely, the hero's downfall. We tend to care less about those who work steadily and diligently at their jobs than about those who will sooner or later topple from the heights. We secretly know the view from the bottom is ultimately safer than the view from the top. Nobody's up there forever. Eventually there will be a scandal we love to read about—public exposure, humiliation, loss of prestige, loss of riches. Like the Greek tragic chorus waiting for the king to tear out his eyes in atonement for his sins, we know our heroes and heroines will be joining us at ground level.

*We still worship heroes, but unconsciously await their downfall in a scandal we love to read about.*

On the other hand, we continue to look, as our ancestors looked, for the promised leader, that special someone who could solve all our problems for us. This archetype has been of particular importance in American mythology, perhaps because of the early dangers encountered in settling so vast a land and the demo-cratic structure of frontier societies in which leaders were not born into their roles but had to appear when they were needed. That they often failed to do so made the myths that much more valuable. A prime example of the "special some-one" myth can be found in George Stevens's film version of Max Brand's slickly commercial novel *Shane* (1952). The film—still widely available in video rental centers—features a mysterious stranger astride a white horse who rides out of the Wyoming hills to rescue a peaceful band of settlers from the evil cattlemen, shoots every bad guy in sight, and then rides back into the misty land of his origin. Today, we still long for that wonderful presidential candidate with precisely the right qualifications, honest down to the marrow, who will walk quietly into the Iowa caucuses and be instantly recognized as the new political messiah. On the other hand, we cannot seem to tolerate charismatic orators who announce their can-didacy, then are forced to withdraw when they are found to be error-prone like the rest of us.

We are living at a time when woman as heroine is no longer an impossibility, though she has some ground yet to make up. In the sci-fi movies we have had spacewomen who are allowed to exist on equal terms with men, who destroy monsters with the best of them. But the notion of "woman the mysterious" stays with us. If woman is no longer the root of all evil, as in many an ancient myth, she is still portrayed as holding forth the promise of forbidden fruit. In advertisements for luxury items, beautiful woman utter words like "tempting," "seductive," and "witchcraft." Models in perfume ads are made to look like descendants of the sirens who lured Odysseus. Some few honored and revered personalities—usually older actors—advertise stock brokerage firms or collections of popular light-classical music, but they are seldom women.

## Epilogue

*I've always preferred mythology to history. History is truth that becomes an illusion; mythology is an illusion that becomes reality.*

*Jean Cocteau*

Myth, originating in the depths of the unconscious and in the primordial prehistory of our species, can be an aid to clear thinking if we learn how to see which myths are shaping our experience and then sit back and select those we find beneficial and cast aside those that hinder critical thought. But myth tends to remain outside the critical realm. One cannot editorialize and suggest what myth ought to be or ought not to do.

Surely we know in our lucid moments that no myth contains the full truth. But perhaps this knowledge is less important than the mystery and magic at the root of our nature from which mythology springs. By studying myth objectively, we can see ourselves a little better, yet this does not mean we can change what we are—at least not entirely. Some mythology interferes with our judgment, and some is downright superstition. But then there are those haunting mazes and those magic rings and the wonderful stranger we keep expecting to arrive. We need a little mist in our gardens.

## Glossary

**archetype:** The model or original of something (e.g., the hero; our first parents) that, according to Jung, exists innately in the collective unconscious and can be found in mythology, and by means of which we organize our thinking about the universe and human life.

**hero:** Probably the most universal of all archetypes: The man or woman whose deeds and destiny automatically involve the listener, simply because he or she possesses the attributes most prized by the culture. We usually take heroes for granted, without analyzing what they mean to us.

**mandala:** A universal (archetypal) myth symbol: an enclosed circle often containing a design that represents the organization of the universe. The mandala is always circular, suggesting that in Western culture at least, the universe is one thing, as opposed to many unrelated things. The mandala also symbolizes the inner world, and in this function it suggests that many prefer to believe in a coherent self as opposed to an inner life comprised of a series of momentary sensations.

**monomyth:** Also known as the *world myth* and the *hero myth*. The universal tale, occurring from culture to culture and from age to age, with surprisingly similar characteristics. The story of Theseus is an example.

**myths:** Tales, transmitted from generation to generation, that project underlying psychological truths of the human race. There is a great deal of uniformity in mythic themes and symbols throughout all cultures and ethnic groups.

**primitivism:** An eighteenth-century philosophy which holds that people living the simple life, close to nature, are nobler than their educated, city-bred counterparts.

# Notes

1. Bruno Bettelheim, *The Uses of Enchantment: The Meaning and Significance of Fairy Tales* (New York: Knopf, 1967), 57.
2. Edith Hamilton, *Mythology* (New York: New American Library, 1969).
3. Ibid.
4. James Duffy, *Africa Speaks* (New York: Van Nostrand, 1961), 21.
5. Veronica Ions, *The World's Mythology in Colour* (London: Hamlyn, 1974), 224.
6. Cited in June Singer, *Boundaries of the Soul: The Practice of Jung's Psychology* (New York: Doubleday, 1972), 79.
7. Ibid.

# Suggested Reading

Berlin, Sir Isaiah. *The Crooked Timber of Humanity: Chapters in the History of Ideas*. Ed. Henry Hardy. New York: Knopf, 1991. A new edition of a famous work by a modern historian of ideas, tracing the impact of the pervasive myth that a long time ago there was an ideal state of existence, which was ended by a disaster (the form of which varies from culture to culture).

Bettelheim, Bruno. *The Uses of Enchantment: The Meaning and Importance of Fairy Tales*. New York: Knopf, 1976. The late psychologist looks into Freudian and other latent meanings in children's fairy tales.

Bulfinch, Thomas. *The Age of Fable*. New York: Crowell, 1970. This readable retelling of the myths in simple fictional form has introduced generations of readers to legendary heroes from different cultures. Ulysses, Beowulf, King Arthur, Cupid, and Robin Hood are among the characters to be found here.

Campbell, Joseph. *The Hero with a Thousand Faces*. New York: Bollingen Foundation, 1961. A scholarly and profoundly psychological study of the monomyth and its many revelations about us.

———. *The Power of Myth*. With Bill Moyers. New York: Doubleday, 1988. Shortly before his death, Campbell did a series of television interviews with Moyers about the origins and meanings of myths and religions. The book is a transcription of those interviews.

Capek, Karel. *Nine Fairy Tales*. Evanston, Ill.: Northwestern University Press, 1990. The playwright whose *R.U.R.* was an early attack on modern technology and the dehumanization of the race wrote a number of outrageous satires disguised as children's stories. A welcome reissue.

Hamilton, Edith. *Mythology*. Boston: Little, Brown, 1942. A comprehensive—and perhaps the best—collection of all the popular Greek, Roman, and Norse mythologies by the eminent classical scholar.

Le Guin, Ursula. *Tehanu: The Last Book of Earthsea*. New York: Atheneum, 1990. The author is a contemporary mythmaker, sometimes inaccurately categorized as a science fiction writer. This is apparently last in a series of novels about a mythical kingdom involved in assorted turmoils, with women as central figures.

*Mythologies*. Compiled by Yves Bonnefoy. Tr. under the direction of Wendy Doniger. 2 vols. Chicago: University of Chicago Press, 1991. This is an excellent companion to either Bulfinch or Hamilton, for the editor, a French poet, bypasses all the popular myths and includes mythology from Africa, Scandinavia, England, America, and the South Pacific.

Rackham, Arthur. *The Arthur Rackham Fairy Book*. New York: Weathervane Books, 1978. A funny—and also a little scary—updating of familiar fairy tales, with cynical twists. For example, Red Riding-Hood gets eaten—and not saved.

Walker, Barbara. *The Crone: Woman of Age, Wisdom, and Power*. San Francisco: Harper & Row, 1985. A feminist takes a new look at old mythology and finds it has been largely male-centered: conceived by males to explain the world of male anxiety. Negative events, like death, have been personified as women. Walker looks especially at the universal figure of the old crone, or hag, and finds that men have feared her because of her power to control, to work spells, and so on; this suggests the reason for such personifications must lie in woman's true (and hitherto suppressed) strength.

White, T. H. *The Once and Future King*. New York: G. P. Putnam's Sons, 1958. This wonderful retelling of the Arthurian legends was the inspiration for the musical *Camelot*.

*Titian,* Sacred and Profane Love *(Galleria Borghese, Rome. Alinari/Art Resource)*

# 12

## Love

### Overview

We can scarcely overestimate the importance of love to most of us. Even the successive marriages of the frequently divorced give evidence that people believe so strongly in love that they keep looking for it. Probably the search for love dominates the consciousness of people from early adolescence even up to advanced age, so that without love many believe their life has been wasted. The theme of many poems, novels, plays, operas, and works of visual art is love, in both its pleasurable and painful guises. Even if love cannot be described scientifically, has no objective existence (as some have insisted), and is solely the invention of human imagination, none of us could easily forge a life totally without it.

Not surprisingly, artists are often the most cynical in their denunciation of love or the most aggressive in labeling it a lie and a delusion. Perhaps the reason is that creative people want to believe in love so desperately and expect so much from it. But there are knowledgeable observers who view love as an authentic experience. The psychological theories of Erich Fromm and Eric Berne, for example, include the belief that love exists, however different it may be from its depiction in the arts.

This chapter does not pretend to offer a definitive resolution to the issue, only an analysis of ways in which through both art and life we are likely to be affected by the myth or the mystery of love. Recognizing this all-important obsession and its impact on our beliefs is crucial to the art of being human.

## Love in the Ancient World

Despite the sentiments in poems and songs that love is timeless, one is better off facing the truth that if it is to have any meaning as a major force in human life, love has to be considered in the context of history. *Love* has meant different things at different times and in particular places, and it is a safe bet that there are millions of people in the world today for whom the word is hollow and unrelated to the tough realities of their life.

The appealing use of the term—the idealization of a relationship between two or among more than two persons—comes to us very strongly from the humanities, as do so-called words of wisdom like "Love is blind" and "Love is the answer." We gain a definite and possibly helpful perspective by examining specific cases from art, literature, and philosophy of bygone days (which in our analysis is limited to Western humanities, though an investigation into the expression of love in other cultures would probably yield results that are just as interesting).

### The Classical Definition: Lust

It has been said that love is an invention rather than a natural instinct or need, and the fact that such societies as ancient Greece and Rome appear to have gotten along without it proves the contention. Of course, people had sexual relationships. People married and raised families. But the theory goes that they did so for practical reasons, not because they "fell in love." Some would go so far as to insist on calling lust a universal instinct, while love—when defined as something superior to lust— is a humanistic creation similar to the classical, unrealistic depiction of the human body. We know that the ancient Greeks and Romans also married for reasons of money and land—motivations that are still prevalent. But lust was the subject of their interest.

In Greek and Roman mythology we find much idealization of physical passion, together with a favorite theme: the sickness that comes from sexual desire. There is the Roman story of Venus and Adonis, for example, in which the goddess of Love is herself overcome after being wounded by an arrow shot by her mischievous son Cupid. As is the case whenever such wounding occurs, the victim desires the first man she looks upon; this time it happens to be Adonis, a young mortal. Noting that he enjoys hunting, she pleads with him not to go in search of dangerous game but to be "brave towards the timid." Such advice being distinctly anti-Roman, Adonis understandably ignores it and promptly is killed by a wild boar. To perpetuate his memory, Venus transforms his blood into a dark red flower called the anemone. But like passion itself, the anemone is short-lived, for "the wind blows the blossoms open, and afterwards blows the petals away."

*Love is . . .*

For Dante: *A macrocosmic force that moves the sun and other stars.*

For Samuel Johnson: *Of no great influence upon the sum of life.*

For H. L. Mencken: *A state of perpetual anesthesia.*

For Morton M. Hunt: *Any and every form of relationship between human beings when used in conjunction with the phrase "falling in love" or "being in love."*

*Men have died from time to time and worms have eaten them, but not for love.*

*Shakespeare*

*In classical mythology and literature, nothing good ever comes from love.*

*Robert Rauschenberg,* Monogram *( 1955–59): In classical literature, love is almost always depicted as a wrenching emotion that topples reason and renders a person unfulfilled. (Moderna Museet, Stockholm/Photo: Statens Konstmuseer)*

Though both Greeks and Romans enjoyed the pleasures of the flesh, their myths show these pleasures to be the source of both human and godly misery. In classical mythology and literature nothing good ever comes from love, which is almost always depicted as a wrenching emotion that topples reason and renders a person unproductive and unfulfilled. For the classical world, love was not an admirable goal of human existence.

## Plato's Definition: A Longing for the Ideal

In his dialogue *The Symposium*, Plato states that love is clearly the secret to living, but we must first understand that love exists on several levels. Fundamental to us all is the physical desire of one person for another. Since desire is a human instinct, it cannot be deprecated or regarded as a sickness. It is not a deterioration of the rational faculties but is its own separate and unique event in human consciousness.

In Plato's philosophy, however, physical union with another and the pleasures of the body can never be the highest possible good. He believes each of us is born with a soul, which is the rational capacity for comprehending all of the eternal truths, and that the soul soon recognizes it is imprisoned in a body. The body is subject to deterioration, pain, and death, whereas the soul is immortal. Upon the death of the body the soul finds a new home in a new body, and the same cycle is repeated. The constant longing of the soul is therefore to escape from the body.

A human being's attraction to another, even on the lowest, or physical, level, is at least a step in the right direction. It represents a preoccupation with something beyond the self. The goal of this attraction is reproduction, the generation of another life; generation is likewise closer to immortality than being trapped in the trivial, everyday "details of the self." It offers us a glimpse of the eternal, for we have substituted a new life for an older, decaying existence. In Plato's words:

*The beauties of the body are as nothing to the beauties of the soul, so that wherever one meets with spiritual loveliness, even in the husk of an unlovely body, he will find it beautiful enough to fall in love with and to cherish.*

*Plato*

> For here again, and on the same principle too, the mortal nature is seeking as far as possible to be everlasting and immortal: and this is only to be attained by generation, because generation always leaves a new existence in place of the old.[1]

One can only assume that Plato would cast a disapproving eye toward casual sex that seeks only momentary gratification of the senses. Physical love can be construed as a good only when it is an expression of the need for contact with what is not the self.

*Love has meant different things at different times and in particular places, and it is a safe bet that there are millions of people in the world today for whom the word is hollow and unrelated to the tough realities of their life.*

How does one know the difference? How does one know one's motives? The answer is that if we are truly on the right track, sooner or later we will glimpse the higher visions. We long for experiences that satisfy the soul itself, not just the senses. What is it the soul wants? To be at one with the world it leaves when it enters the prison of the body, the world of eternity in which resides the truth of all things. The soul desires the contemplation of this world—a condition of peace, serenity, and ultimate knowledge. In such a state one is free of the trivial details of self, free of the pain caused by bodily deterioration. Sometimes Plato calls this the state of contemplating *ideal beauty*. Ultimate knowledge and ideal beauty are the same thing. The attainment of full understanding has no end except itself and is thus an experience of the beautiful. There is nothing *to do* with beauty except to have it.

*A mathematician's love of a perfect equation is an example of Platonic love: a reaching out for the ideal.*

Think, if you will, of the mathematician's bliss when a complex and seemingly impossible problem has been solved. The answer is there in letters and symbols and has no reference whatever to the familiar world of everyday reality. The recognition that the solution "works" is a vision of perfection. The mathematician has reached a truth that will stand for all time. The equation is thus both true and beautiful; the mathematician feels love for it.

Thus, one can be in love—Platonically—with a person, a painting, a sculpture, a symphony, or any other phenomenon that is characterized by the approach to perfection of the parts, a perfection that exists only in the ideal world beyond the senses. It is such love for which the soul longs. This is the reason the physical desire for another person exists for Plato only at the bottom rung of a ladder that leads us past physical pleasure and upward toward experiences that cannot be expressed in words, but only felt by the soul:

> He who from these [bottom steps] ascending under the influence of true love, begins to perceive that beauty, is not far from the end. And the true order of going, or being led by another, to things of love, is to begin from the beauties of earth and mount upwards for the sake of other beauty, using these as steps only, and from one going on to two, and from two to all fair forms, and from fair forms to fair practices, and from fair practices to fair notions, until from fair notions he arrives at the notion of absolute beauty, and at last knows what the essence of beauty is.[2]

## Biblical Love

The French satirist and social reformer Voltaire (1694–1778) once defined the family as a "group of people who cannot stand the sight of each other but are forced to live under the same roof." The American poet Robert Frost (1875–1963), in his narrative poem *Death of the Hired Man*, has one character observe, " 'Home is the place where, when you have to go there,/They have to take you in.' "[3] Whether home and family prove burdensome depends upon one's maturity level, emotional stability, and willingness to work on the difficulties that arise from close relationships. Most would agree, however, that there are few households that glide serenely along on a perpetually even keel.

The majority of us are born into a family circle and take for granted having parents, siblings, cousins, and aunts. These close kin who sign letters and postcards "With love," hug and kiss us at family gatherings, and expect loyalties and favors from us—even as we expect such in return—without asking why; all these actions are performed under the rubric of the seldom-defined word *love*.

Nonetheless, even family love has roots in historical time and geographical location. Anthropologists studying the social structures of remote groups have found some in which tight family circles do *not* exist. One such group is the Ik, an isolated tribe in Africa in which children are nurtured by their mothers until the age of five and then are cast out to fend for themselves. In ancient Greece men ate separately from the women and children, sometimes even had separate living quarters. In *The Republic*, Plato suggests that in an ideal community, children should be taken from their parents and raised by the state.

The ancient Hebrews may possibly have given the world its first idea of the family as more than a convenient survival mechanism. In developing the father-children relationship between God and humanity, Judaism created a model for earthly existence. First came the tribe, the larger group comprised of interrelated families and governed by a patriarch, an older and presumably wiser man who exercised great powers of judgment over all members. Abraham and Moses are prominent Biblical patriarchs. One can easily see how such an arrangement was logically paralleled by the idea of God the father with the same power over human children.

Because of the harsh environment, the family circle inevitably became sanctified. It became imperative for the family to stay together, otherwise the larger unit, the tribe, would be endangered. Love for God, or Yahweh,[4] which included fear and respect, was also demanded for the father of the earthly family, who, like the tribal patriarch, had powers of life and death. Without obedience there was no order, and without fear there could be no obedience. Fear of God, fear of one's father—both were ways, the only ways, of showing love.

If Biblical historians are accurate, a group of Hebrew elders got together hundreds of years after the historical events we read about in the earliest portions of the Bible, gathered up all known written accounts of Hebrew history and cultural practices, and embarked upon the astonishing project of setting everything down in what they considered proper order. The Bible grew and flourished over many centuries, the work not of a few prophets, which tradition has associated with the books bearing their names, but of a number of poets, philosophers, and deeply religious people.

Many of the concepts belonging to ancient tribal customs are still in the Bible, but one also finds much that has come to belong to the entire human race. Hebrew scholars, in tracing their history back to the creation of the world, also revised and enlarged their vision of the deity. The God who created the heavens and the earth is clearly no longer the warlike Yahweh, concerned only with the Hebrew people. The God of creation is the omnipotent father of all people.

Even though the Biblical story of Abraham and the promise made to him by God is there as part of human history, the fact that others live in this world is not overlooked. Though the children of Abraham are God's Chosen, Biblical teachings are still heeded by all other religious denominations that accept the work as a valid history of the human race. Thus the Ten Commandments are perceived as binding on all, not merely on those in the lineage of Abraham and Moses. One of the Commandments—*Honor thy father and mother*—is a restatement and an enlargement of early tribal requirements. Both parents now are supreme authorities within the family circle. Fear of authority is not stressed so much as the gentler, more civilized "honor."

In fact, a close study of the Bible reveals radical changes occurring in the Hebrew vision of love. God does not remain simply a source of justice, punishing evildoers and demanding love in the form of fear. The famous Twenty-third Psalm, which begins, "The Lord is my shepherd," bears witness to a peaceful, mystical sense of union with a kind and caring God.

Many of the stories in the Hebrew Bible contain moral messages that do not differ very much from those of the parables in the so-called New Testament. The story of Susanna and the Elders, for example, has little to do with narrowly Hebrew concerns and everything to do with what is clearly a universal plea for honesty and charity toward others. Susanna, the beautiful wife of Joachim, is the secret object of the lust of two old men. The men also happen to hold positions of honor and respect in the tribe and serve as judges in legal matters. One day they demand physical favors from her, threatening that if she denies them, they will say they witnessed Susanna's committing adultery with a young man. Susanna calls their bluff, only to find herself on trial for her life. The tale would have ended

*Pablo Picasso,* The Lovers *(1923): A physical commitment—and something much more. (Courtesy of the National Gallery of Art, Chester Dale Collection)*

tragically but for the cleverness of the young defense lawyer, who asks each of the elders separately to name the tree under which Susanna and her alleged suitor were making love. Naturally the stories conflict, and so it is the elders, not Susanna, who are put to death.

In the books of the Prophets we also find a widening of the concepts of both God and love. In Jeremiah, for example, the message is that the suffering of the Hebrews is not the result of unfair treatment by enemies, but is the judgment of God upon them for their own wickedness. Jeremiah is more interested in teaching his people to behave ethically toward each other as well as toward those outside the tribe than he is in having them retain their tribal identity through the observance of certain laws and customs. In Isaiah, the prophet speaks of justice for all people, of a universal code of ethics, and of the idea of a universal family of humanity.

The New Testament, believed by Christians to be the history of the promised Messiah, offers in the teachings of Jesus a further articulation of the doctrine of universal love. Emphasis is placed on humility; on meekness; on loving one's neighbor more than oneself; on loving one's enemies because they are one's brothers and sisters; and on gentleness, tenderness, and mercy. All of these concepts can properly be said to have evolved throughout the long history of Biblical literature and philosophy. They have created a model of human behavior that is beautiful to contemplate, if not easy to achieve. The difficulty makes the vision no less precious, and the pursuit of this goal is more desperately needed now than ever before.

*The Biblical concepts of love have created a model of human behavior that is beautiful to contemplate, if not easy to achieve.*

## Romantic Love

Thus far our discussion of love has not dealt with the one subject that often comes to mind when the generic term *love* is mentioned, and that is *romance*. Despite the cynicism one encounters in many quarters about our present society's "myth of love" and its often casual attitudes toward relationships, the term *romance* has yet to disappear from our vocabulary. Romance novels constitute a billion-dollar industry, outselling most other types of so-called adult fiction.

Romance language includes phrases like "loving you until the end of time" and "madly in love." It suggests obsession that demands body and soul, and especially *heart*: "my heart's delight," "lost my heart," "a broken heart." To give your heart away to someone implies a physical commitment—and something much more.

Romantic love can be traced in Western society to the Middle Ages. (If it existed outside that society, it did so in forms and languages that are not familiar to those whose heritage is Western European.) *Romeo and Juliet* is probably the most beloved and enduring of romantic love stories, with values and assumptions that have their roots in the Middle Ages. Other cultures have surely been touched in some way by Shakespeare's tale of idealistic teenagers whose attraction to each other far transcends sexual longing (though it must be said that the passionate side of their devotion was ignored for centuries, wrongfully so). In short, *Romeo and Juliet* obviously belongs to the entire world now, and so does the tradition of romantic love, no matter how "realistic" people say they have become about love.

We may cite three sources for the growth and spread of the romantic ideal of love. One is the cult that grew up around the poets and artists who celebrated the glory of the Virgin Mary. Another is a sophisticated genre of literature *called* the romance. Central to these stories was a relationship between a young man and a young woman for whom a physical union was difficult if not impossible but who nonetheless pledged to each other their hearts.

*Three sources for the romantic ideal of love:*
  *the cult of the Virgin Mary*
  *the literary genre called the* romance
  *the code of chivalry*

Finally, there was the medieval code of *chivalry*, which existed in real life as well as in the romances, involving the relationship between a knight and his lady, to whose name he dedicated his glorious deeds of valor in jousting tournaments and on the battlefield. The idealism expressed in lines like "I would lay down my life for you" emanates from this code; for centuries afterward (maybe today, too, in some quarters) women have expected to be treated in a chivalrous fashion, treated like "ladies fair" who must be defended by a brave and handsome "knight."

The code of chivalry in turn gave rise to the tradition of *courtly love*, an early Renaissance version of romantic love, only more sophisticated than its medieval counterpart. It was a game played by cultivated aristocrats at a time when the status of women had risen considerably, so that the woman being wooed could make enormous demands upon the wooer and never, if she chose, "descend" to a physical level of love.

At any rate, all of these sources share the assumptions that

Women are deserving of the highest possible honor
Men must earn the devotion of women
Physical love is a means at best, never an end

We must not forget that the love of the Virgin is one of the strongest influences on the notion of ideal romantic love.

## Mariolatry

The Christianized world of western Europe evolved from feudal settlements— centering on castle-fortresses and the isolated lives of the land barons, their families, servants, and armies—into a collection of nations, principally France, Spain, and England. Each nation had urban centers, cathedrals, and highly cultivated monasteries containing libraries with carefully copied and illustrated manuscripts. By the "high" Middle Ages—the eleventh and twelfth centuries—the Christianized world of western Europe had given rise to the sophisticated philosophy known as Scholasticism, through which the revealed truths of religion were proved logically, and to an artistic tradition new to the world.

*Mary, who is not prominently mentioned in the New Testament, became a central figure in medieval Christianity.*

This new artistic tradition is sometimes given the name *Mariolatry*, a word meant to suggest idolatry of the Virgin Mary, mother of Jesus. In point of fact, the writings of the New Testament do not say very much about Mary; at least, the references are scarce when one considers the centrality of Mary in a good deal of Christian art and literature. After the account of the death of Jesus on the cross, there is almost no mention of his mother, except a passing reminder that on earth Jesus had been "born of woman." What happened to her is indeed a mystery, and certainly one might think it strange that a figure who has inspired countless artists, poets, and composers should have been given so little prominence in the New Testament.

Yet, like the idea of love itself, the idea of Mary is rooted in history. During the Middle Ages, as the Christian religion spread and the Christian artistic tradition grew, the subject of the mother became increasingly important and often charismatic. The simple words spoken by the angel Gabriel in the Gospel of Luke, telling the virgin girl that she would be visited by the Holy Ghost whose power would overshadow her, leaped forth from the pages of the Gospel into many creative minds. Thus was born the cult of Mary, whose members were impelled to canvas and poetry by the power of one supreme idea: the purity of this one woman honored among all others to be the mother of God's own son—an honor without human parallel. This honor was to elevate not only the idea of Mary, but—at least for a time—that of all women.

*Medieval creative minds were moved by the purity of Mary, honored among all others to be the mother of God's own son.*

A subject that was never exhausted in medieval and Renaissance paintings was the Madonna and Child. To complement these works came poem after poem extolling the glory of Mary as a holy and undefiled vessel, and, by natural association, the spiritual beauty of chaste women. References to placing women on a pedestal may well spring from the cult of Mary.

The idealization of women in Mariolatry was also found in popular literature. There the earthly love of a man for a woman was presented in spiritual terms, even if lust was involved as well. In this literature was born the ideal of romantic love, of serenading the fair lady under her balcony, of sending love poems tied around rosebuds; the ideal of a love in which spirit, not body, was the subject (at least the alleged subject) of desire. Platonic love would readily have been understood to be the pursuit of an ideal, pure, chaste, and true love, undefiled by lust— the love of man and woman that lasts through time and cannot be destroyed even in the grave.

## Romance and Chivalry

The word *romance* has never left our cultural vocabulary since its introduction in the very period we are discussing. In the beginning, however, it did not mean what we generally understand by the term: a courtship filled with thoughtful gifts and growing affection. During the eleventh and twelfth centuries the French word *roman*, meaning "long fictional narrative" (today, "novel"), was absorbed into English as the word *romance*, but with the same meaning as the French words.

*Romantic love is among the most enduring of ideals. Despite widespread cynicism about the younger generation, one suspects that our young people still look for tender love and considerate behavior from the "right" person.*

Since there was no printing press, stories circulated through recitation. One can imagine how popular the most exciting tales were—not to mention how many invitations the good storytellers must have received! The romances were not just about love. Some did not even contain plots concerning man-woman relationships; instead they were filled with breathtaking adventures. The Crusades were still within cultural memory. Enthralled listeners heard about distant, Eastern lands and the dangers lying in wait for noble Christian knights. Many of the best-loved romances were the stories about King Arthur, Camelot, and the Knights of the Round Table.

Out of the traditions of knighthood came the term *chivalry*. Stemming from the French *cheval*, meaning "horse," the word long ago referred to courageous feats performed by knights, who of course were often on horseback. Then the term acquired the specialized meaning of the particular qualities a knight was expected to possess. Respect for women was one such quality.

Many of the romances therefore *did* contain stories about the relationship of a brave knight with one particular lady in whose name he would perform valorous feats. The lady was not expected to reward her champion with anything except the honor of allowing him to do brave and daring things for her. In the jousting tournaments, for example, the lady would place her scarf around the knight's lance as a symbol of the honor she was bestowing. He would ride into actual battle holding his lady's scarf on high, prepared to die for her.

Relationships in the romances were nonphysical, even if the couple secretly (or openly) lusted for one another, because sex outside of marriage was sinful and few indeed would have allowed a storyteller to repeat a tale of lust and adultery. The "purity" of relationships in the romances is similar to the nonphysical relationships in the films of the 1930s and 1940s, when audiences never seemed to tire of the plot in which a woman must stand forever in the shadows because the man she loves is married, usually to a cruel and unfeeling wife who shouts gleefully that she will never give him a divorce. Or else the wife is an invalid, and the man is too noble to desert her.

*In medieval romances either the knight or the lady is married, and the love is doomed never to be consummated.*

Often in the romances either the knight or the lady *is* married, and the love is doomed never to be consummated. These were Christian times, however; Christianity considered human beings sinful, easily tempted creatures. Sometimes the lovers yield to temptation, and there is a tragic ending. Among the most enduring of the tragedies has been the story of Guinevere, Arthur's queen, and her love for Lancelot, which she tries so hard but unsuccessfully to resist. Another is the story of Eloise, a novice, and Abelard, a priest, who had fallen in love before either entered holy orders and who meet again when consummation is forbidden.

Why did the romances not give rise to stories of happy and unending love within the sacred bonds of marriage? Probably for the same reason that few people today want to read a book or see a film about happy people without problems. The romances were the escapist literature of the Middle Ages, counterparts of whatever escapist literature is currently in fashion, with the identical purpose of offering the listener or reader something quite different from daily life. Another reason is medieval marriage itself, which for the most part was a humdrum, businesslike venture joining two people for money and property. Love in what we have come to call the romantic sense of the term had little to do with the matter. It was there, if at all, strictly by accident. In reality, men and women probably longed in secret for other partners whom they could either never love in the flesh or do so sinfully, risking the pain of a guilty conscience. Neither option was a very happy one. Small wonder that the theme of tragic but pure love was dear to many hearts.

*The assumption was that love denied was nobler than marriage realized.*

Whether physical gratification ever took place or not, the assumption must always have been that the love denied was nobler than the marriage realized. Since the theme occurs in so many romances, we long ago took into the cultural vocabulary the term *romantic love*, which usually exists outside marriage, which may or may not have a physical side to it, but which is *always* comprised of genuine, tender emotions felt by two persons of honor and altruism who bear malice toward no one in the world and who, in our estimation, deserve only happiness.

*Despite modern cynicism, we have not lost the ability to be hurt by love.*

Despite the widespread cynicism about the younger generation and its supposed lack of strong values, romantic idealism remains very strong today and expectations continue to include tender love and considerate behavior from the "right" person. The remarriage-after-divorce plot is escapist fantasy, perhaps concealing our latent fears that the family unit, once thought to be the indestructible backbone of society, is crumbling. The root of the current problem of divorce may still be disenchantment, and the cause of disenchantment is very likely an ideal that refuses to die. We have not lost the ability to be hurt by love. What better indication that the myth—if that is what romantic love should be called—is one that continues to haunt our most sensitive selves?

# The Idealized Woman in Power

"How to handle a woman," muses King Arthur in the 1959 musical play *Camelot*. The hero decides after some analysis that the way to handle a woman is "to love her, love her, love her." The king had forgotten that his queen Guinevere is someone with whom he can discuss affairs of state and complex legal matters, but only up to a point. In any case, we are not to forget that she is obsessed with the need to be adored and that this obsession is a basic right belonging to her role.

The Arthurian times were mythical, but they reflect what was actually the case in the courts of England, France, and Spain in the late Middle Ages. In this era of romantic love, which, as we have seen, usually existed outside of marriage (and in which Guinevere herself was engaged without Arthur's knowledge), the man was expected to be chivalrous, brave, and always considerate of the woman, never, *never* forcing his attentions upon her or asking—let alone pleading—for more than she was prepared to give. The woman, on her part, could yield to his desire if she chose (as Guinevere ultimately did with Lancelot) or let him continue his attentions with never so much as a promise. In short, as romantic love became popular, it turned into a game with codified rules. It also, we might add, raised the status of women enormously, since they were given carte blanche to treat their would-be lovers in just about any manner they wanted, even if it were a momentary whim.

Readers may know Cervantes' epic satire *Don Quixote* (1605) or have seen the contemporary musical adaptation *Man of La Mancha* (1965). In both, the hero, an old man who lost his mind from devouring too many romances, believes himself to be a knight wandering forever in the service of the Lady Dulcinea, a lady he never expects to meet or to even thank him in any way. The code of *courtly love*—the game in which the male was supposed to endure any hardship for the lady—is nowhere better illustrated than in this letter from Don Quixote to his beloved:

> SOVEREIGN LADY,—The wounded by the point of absence, and the hurt by the darts of thy heart, sweetest Dulcinea of Toboso! doth send thee that health which he wanteth himself. If thy beauty disdain me, if thy valour turn not to my benefit, if thy disdains convert themselves to my harm, maugre all my patience, I shall be ill able to sustain this care; which, besides that it is violent, is also too durable. My good squire Sancho will give thee certain relation, O beautiful ingrate, and my dearest beloved enemy! of the state wherein I remain for thy sake. If thou please to favour me, I am thine; and if not, do what thou likest: for, by ending of my life, I shall both satisfy thy cruelty and my desires.—Thine until death,
>
> 'THE KNIGHT OF THE ILL-FAVORED FACE.'[5]

In his amusing and informative *The Natural History of Love* (1959), Morton M. Hunt suggests that the model for Cervantes' great work may have been a relatively obscure book of the thirteenth century called *Frauendienst* (The Service of Woman) by a real knight-errant, Ulrich von Lichtenstein. The book contains 30,000 lines of narrative verse, all claiming to be the autobiography of a man who literally sacrificed his entire existence for a princess who for years did not know he existed.

The book describes how Ulrich, when he was 12, knowing that if he were to become a knight he must adopt the role of the courtly lover, chose to serve the princess, became a page in her court, and forced himself to feel tenderly toward her. He secretly followed her everywhere:

> When he saw her hands touch the petals of flowers he had secretly placed where she would see them, he was all but in a faint. And when she washed her hands before dinner, young Ulrich would sometimes filch the basin, smuggle it off to his room, and there reverently drink the dirty water.[6]

After risking his life in tournament after tournament and developing a reputation as the strongest and bravest knight around, he at last made so bold as to send his niece to visit the princess and tell her of his all-consuming obsession. Scornfully, the princess sent back word that he was too ugly to be even a distant admirer, whereupon Ulrich underwent dangerous surgery to correct a harelip.

Even this failed to please the lady, though she went so far as to allow him to send notes to her. Her answers were usually filled with derision and heartless rebuffs. "But this," Hunt comments, "was exactly what was expected of her."[7] To show the extent of his devotion Ulrich then proceeded to cut off a finger and send it to her. Pleased at this sign of "her power over him," the princess sent back word that she would keep the finger if that would make him happy.

*A real knight, Ulrich von Lichtenstein, spent 15 years trying to please his lady, who rewarded his devotion with scorn and derision.*

After a number of years, the princess finally agreed to allow the lovesick and suffering man to visit her, but insisted he come as a leper in the company of other lepers. After spending a long, rainy night outside in a ditch, he was allowed into the lady's chamber, only to find a hundred candles burning and eight maids standing by the bedside. He entertained a fleeting hope that all of his suffering was but an elaborate prelude to a long-awaited night of joy. But true to her role as the cruel mistress, the lady told him to join the Crusades, earn a reputation for valor, and then maybe she would see him again. Fifteen years later Ulrich was still hoping for his reward, but all he can tell the reader, according to Hunt, is that she "wounded him in some fashion so cruel that he could not bring himself to name it."[8] Ulrich's book does contain some cynical observations about women—rare for the time, but understandable in his case. Nonetheless, he was undeterred from finding another object of adoration in whose service he spent the rest of his life, and with a somewhat happier outcome.

The term *courtly love* presumably derives from actual mock-court proceedings, held in the royal halls, in which women judges decided whether this or that suitor had acquitted himself according to the proper rules and should be granted the favors he so eagerly sought. Most of the time such favors were *not* allowed, an outcome that in no way was supposed to diminish the plaintiff's ardor. Hunt's research has led him to the conclusion that these courts of love had their origin in the twelfth century with Eleanor of Aquitaine, mother of Richard the Lion-Hearted.

Eventually the "rulings" in the courts of love were set down in writing as guides to the proper conduct of an "affair of the heart." The rules lasted for several centuries, well into the Renaissance, where we find them absorbed into a lively little book called *The Courtier* (1507) by Baldassare Castiglione, an Italian military hero and later ambassador.

In *The Courtier* we see the influence of Renaissance worldliness and sophistication. Nobody chops off fingers for love anymore, and ladies are no longer expected to be cruel and forever unreachable. Well-bred ladies are now allowed to have a degree of education, intended to give them wit and polish and to equip them for their role in life: to be a delightful, scintillating partner in the game of love.

Since among other things the Renaissance represented a new interest in classical art, literature, and philosophy, who should turn up in this updated version of courtly love but Plato himself? In *The Courtier*,

> the fundamental theme is that love is the source of all sweetness and moral virtue, since it leads men to concentrate on beauty, and beauty leads the mind toward the contemplation of divinity.[9]

This being the case, the lady could see and talk with the gentleman but was not expected to cheapen the relationship by allowing so much as a hint that she might be interested in a physical encounter.

## Love as a Game

By the later Renaissance the tradition of courtly love lost one of its major ingredients: the lovesick suitor prostrating himself at the feet of the scornful but adored object of his worship. Poets still used the theme of the cruel taskmistress and complained that they were near death because of her, but if you read between the lines, you can easily see that they are talking about unfulfilled lust.

Replacing the anguish and cruelty of courtly love was the idea of love as a delightful sport played by worldly-wise (and often world-weary) men and women, for whom sexual gratification was so readily available that it did not need to be their sole objective. Rather, the fun lay in the pretense that the lady was distant and unwilling while the suitor had to entice her with his verbal charms.

Shakespeare was fond of this theme. His *Much Ado About Nothing* (1599) contains the lovers Beatrice and Benedick, who play the game with stylish wit. Earlier, however, he had written *The Taming of the Shrew* (1592), in which Petruchio, in the name of suffering manhood, attempts to beat the strong-headed Kate into submission. Their game becomes violent at times, and there is every indication that they are both enjoying every minute of it. Feminists today decry the fact that the match does not end in a draw, but in a clear victory for the man: In her famous last speech Kate advises the women in the audience not to follow her example but to find happiness in surrendering to their husbands' will. Nonetheless, there have been productions in which Kate performs these lines with a decided wink, and as written, they lend themselves to such an interpretation.

During the latter half of the seventeenth century, the period known in England as that of the Restoration (beginning in 1661 when monarchy was restored to the English throne after 20 years of Puritan rule), sex roles reached an equality never before known. Charles II was famous for his amorous exploits and extravagant parties; his court was continually aglitter with banquets, dancing, and civilized conversation. Sexual mores changed considerably. Where the emphasis before had been on charming enticement without fulfillment, the lady was now permitted a wide range of options. Physical encounters outside of marriage were scandalous only if the cheating was blatant. The game of love became the game of seduction, and the rules became more rigorous than ever.

In this period women were expected to achieve a high degree of social and cultural grace. With the rise in status of the merchant class, people could be

*In* The Taming of the Shrew *the game of love becomes violent at times, but there is every indication that Kate and Petruchio enjoy every minute of it.*

ladies and gentlemen without necessarily having titles, and such liberalization helped the spread of the civilized arts now encompassed under the term *urbanity*.

The theater also underwent drastic changes. Women were allowed to become actresses as well as playwrights, and thus a more genuinely feminine viewpoint could be seen. Those who study the history of women's rights (or the lack of them) often point to the English Restoration as a period in which women took giant steps forward—before the nineteenth century was to set them back.

William Congreve's *The Way of the World* (1700), a giant among the plays of the time, sums up the rules of the game as played by two of the most civilized partners ever devised. Mirabell, the hero, is widely known for his attractiveness to women. Though the code of the time permits and in fact encourages faithlessness so long as one's social behavior remains carefully polished, he truly loves Millamant, also widely known for being the object of many men's desires. If the code were not so demanding, either one would probably forget the rules and declare their genuine feelings to the other. They cannot, however, and manage to conceal their true selves behind the surface banter of which the author definitely approves.

In the famous marriage contract scene in act 4, the would-be lovers meet to discuss their upcoming nuptials. Each lays down requirements for the other. First, Millamant demands that even after the wedding, he must respectfully *request* sexual favors from her, not considering them as rights automatically owed to the husband. She will also sleep as late as she wishes in the morning without obligation to administer to his every fancy. Nor will she permit him to call her names such as "wife, spouse, my dear, joy, jewel, love, sweetheart, and the rest of that nauseous cant." In fact, they are not even to exchange kisses in public, nor "visit together, nor go to a play together." She will carry on her own private correspondences without having to explain anything to him and insists she must

> have no obligation upon me to converse with wits that I don't like, because they are your acquaintance; or to be intimate with fools, because they may be your relations. Come to dinner when I please, dine in my dressing-room when I'm out of humour, without giving a reason. . . . And lastly, wherever I am, you shall always knock at the door before you come in. These articles subscribed, if I continue to endure you a little longer, I may by degrees dwindle into a wife.

Mirabell is agreeable to such "trivial" conditions, but adds a few of his own: She must like her own face as long as he does and "endeavour not to new-coin it." She must totally shun the use of cosmetics, and when she becomes pregnant ("Ah, name it not," she interrupts) she is not to squeeze her body into corsets and so pretend the blessed event is never going to happen. She and her friends may have their idle-minded feminine conversations at tea but may *not* sit around and drink in the fashion of men. "These *provisos* admitted," he concludes, "I may prove a tractable and complying husband." Her reply: "I hate your odious *provisos*." He answers with a smile, "Then we're agreed."

If Congreve's portrait of his society is accurate—and we have no reason to believe otherwise—gender roles were such that neither man nor woman could claim the upper hand. The marriage of Mirabell and Millamant thus promises to be as solid and as lasting a union as any writer has ever imagined.

*During the Restoration there occurred a move toward unprecedented sexual equality.*

*In 1700 Mirabell and Millamant of* The Way of the World *draw up a marriage contract, giving much freedom to both husband and wife, and probably will have as solid a marriage as any writer has ever imagined.*

# Love in the Modern World

By *modern world* in this context we mean the last two centuries—a rather large period of time to be considered "modern." But this period is not, after all, so great a span of time when you consider that Plato made his contribution to the philosophy of love twenty-five hundred years ago. The real reason for this generous definition of "modern," however, is the probability that many nineteenth-century ideas about love still influence our own ideas.

Romantic poets spoke of love in a variety of ways, including references to Plato's concept that the highest form of love is a reaching out to the beauty of another mind. Physical relationships may have existed in the background, but were seldom talked about directly. Instead, the poet Shelley speaks of a love for "all human kind" in his dedication to the cause of universal freedom. Even Lord Byron, not known for being reticent when it came to physical acts, wrote an epic poem about the world's most famous and frequent lover, *Don Juan*, using every kind of euphemism in order to *not* describe the hero's bedroom activities:

> *Haidee and Juan were not married, but*
>    *The fault was theirs, not mine; it is not fair*
> *Chaste reader, then, in any way to put*
>    *The blame on me, unless you wish they were;*
> *Then if you'd have them wedded, please to shut*
>    *The book which treats of this erroneous pair,*
> *Before the consequences grow too awful;*
> *'Tis dangerous to read of loves unlawful.*

The time of Byron, however euphemistic the language of love, was nonetheless apt to be more permissive about accepting sexuality in relationships not of the marital kind. The time that followed was quite different, however. Often labeled *Victorian* because it coincided with the reign of Queen Victoria in Britain (1837-1901), this period featured morally restrictive codes on both sides of the Atlantic and on the Continent. The Victorian era has had a strong impact on twentieth-century attitudes about love; its use of the word *love* as well as its carefully mapped-out guide to human behavior inside and outside the bedroom continues to affect millions.

*The definition of love in the Victorian era, with its morally restrictive codes and its carefully mapped-out guide to human behavior inside and outside the bedroom, continues to affect millions.*

## The Victorian Model

Descriptive phrases and labels are only a convenience, but they have their uses as a means of clarifying certain social tendencies and, especially, of pointing out how otherwise-differing societies have some things in common. In other words, we believe the label *Victorian* makes a great deal of sense in talking about some contemporary understandings of love as well as today's gender roles and the structure of some marriages. We use *Victorian model* in neither a pejorative nor an approving sense. You must surely be allowed the privilege of determining what works for you. We need to point out, however, that the humanities have for the most part viewed Victorianism negatively.

What *is* the Victorian model? Originating during the reign of Queen Victoria, it is a blueprint for courtship and marriage with several clear assumptions. It insisted that all relationships to which the term *love* is applicable must exist between men and women only. In Chapter 10 we discussed the tragic fate of Oscar Wilde, whose open homosexuality was not only socially condemned but earned for the author a prison term that indirectly killed him. Late-nineteenth-century Paris provided the sole exception and became a haven for many writers and artists whose sexual tendencies were not in accord with the prevailing moral code.

The Victorian model is centered on marriage, not courtship. It tends to be economically oriented. By the late nineteenth century the inherited wealth of the aristocracy was becoming a thing of the distant past. All during the Industrial Revolution, which brought prosperity to the merchant class and the entrepreneurs and which raised the living standards of the working class, the great families who once owned fortunes found themselves worth less and less. With more money in circulation, fixed incomes from inheritances were inadequate to meet the demands of the new society. Love increasingly acquired financial connotations. Fathers asked daughters, "Can your young man support you?" In evaluating the "kind of man we want for our child," parents usually meant someone with means and good connections. Consequently, marriages were often arranged without consulting or heeding the preferences of either bride or groom. Worse yet, when meeting an "eligible" partner, a man or a woman was likely to be favorably impressed by indications of wealth. Young men without family wealth were still able to marry attractive women from good backgrounds, however, provided they were viewed

*Toulouse-Lautrec,* Profile d'une Femme: *The groom had a "right" to a bride untouched by other men. (The Louvre, Paris)*

*Jean-Baptiste-Simeon Chardin,* Utensiles de Cuisine: *The wife's job was to run a good household. (The Louvre. © Photo R.M.N.)*

as having good prospects. The successful young business executive replaced the wealthy aristocrat as the ideal suitor.

In most cases the husband was the breadwinner. Even when the wife was the original source of income, the structure of the marriage was expected to be the one approved by society. Gender roles were clearly defined. The husband was the dominant figure in the household, making all the "big" decisions regarding where the family would live, what kind of education the children would receive, and when and whom they would marry. The wife's job was to run a good household, to deal with the servants, to determine the week's menus (always with an eye to pleasing her husband's palate), and, on appropriate occasions, to show off her husband's economic worth. The phrase *conspicuous consumption* was coined to describe the spending habits of this money-conscious age. The wife was expensively clothed at parties and at the theater, wearing as much jewelry as possible without the tacky excess attributed to lower-class people who had done well in business and were trying to buy their way into "high society."

The proper attire for a respectable woman was not only conspicuously expensive but usually uncomfortable and confining. High necklines and corsets were required and endured; husbands did not like to show off their wife's physical attributes, which could draw the envious stares of other husbands or of that particularly dangerous species, the bachelor.

A woman was expected to remain a virgin until her wedding night. The groom had a "right" to wed a bride untouched by other men, regardless of what escapades he himself may have enjoyed in the past. This double standard carried over into the marriage. A wife who committed adultery was ostracized forever from polite society, but a husband suspected of indulging in extramarital affairs usually incurred only mischievous winks from other men—wives were not allowed to mention the subject.

*The husband was the breadwinner, even when the wife was the original source of income. Gender roles were clearly defined.*

## Breaking the Code

The latter half of the nineteenth century was a period in which grand opera became the most fashionable as well as the most expensive artistic outing for respectable couples; most popular were the melodramatic Italian operas with their stories of doomed lovers. Guiseppe Verdi (1813-1901) was popular wherever an opera house was built. Audiences watched and listened over and over as the slave girl Aida and her royal lover paid for their socially unapproved love with death or as Violetta, the beautiful courtesan heroine of *La Traviata* (1853), joyously flies in the face of proper morality by singing "Sempre Libera" (Always Free), only to die consumptively, an outcast from all that is honorable.

Tragic grand opera was a Victorian escape. People could spend a few hours weeping over the beauty of "true" love (that enduring ideal from the Middle Ages) and go home satisfied that it was never rewarded if it was enjoyed outside the sanctity of the home—as it always was in the opera house. Who wanted to see an opera about real home life?

Though Violetta and her lover Alfredo have an affair outside of wedlock, they are portrayed as being truly and madly in love, older and more "experienced" than Romeo and Juliet but adoring each other with the same purity of devotion. Then, as always, the theatrical esthetic required that such love must not last forever. One thinks of Tony and Maria, the young lovers of Leonard Bernstein's *West Side Story* (1957), an updating of *Romeo and Juliet*. Like their Renaissance predecessors, the lovers fall romantically in love, only to lose everything in a bloody finale. The underlying reason for this mandatory tragic ending may be that audiences of the past and present could not bear to imagine ideal love having to move into a domestic setting, where, as we previously discussed, it would surely change. One could leave the theater, knowing secretly that somehow even in death the lovers were together and would always be young and beautiful and happy.

The literature and drama of the nineteenth century was inordinately devoted to tales of fallen women. We cannot be sure, but both husband and wife probably enjoyed these characters—for different reasons. Husbands may have found them more exciting than their respectable wives; the latter may have secretly envied their unrepressed sexuality. The humanities contain a gallery of these heroines.

*Fallen women were popular characters in the nineteenth century. Husbands found them more exciting than their respectable wives, while the latter envied their unrepressed sexuality.*

Two of them—the title characters of Emile Zola's *Nana* (1880) and Stephen Crane's *Maggie, A Girl of the Streets* (1896)—popularized the dark romance of the prostitute, whose shady lifestyle must have been an interesting contrast to the gaslit respectability of upper-middle-class households. In addition, they were shown as having no financial resources other than their body, adding a note of grim realism to the romance; indeed, women not able to marry well had few opportunities to succeed on their own.

In 1893 George Bernard Shaw (discussed at length in Chapter 4) offered the theater world a serious treatment of the subject in *Mrs. Warren's Profession*. In this play the heroine chooses prostitution for the usual economic reasons, finding that it is a lucrative business, far better than the sweatshops that were the sole alternative for poor, unattached women. Mrs. Warren has used her fortune to provide a respectable upbringing for her daughter Vinnie, who at first sympathizes with her mother's plight, then scornfully rejects her when she learns that Mrs. Warren operated a chain of brothels long after she stopped needing the money. This is not a tragic tale by any means. Vinnie may be one of the first liberated characters of the era. Profiting from the education her mother has given her, she rejects marriage to several conventional suitors and, as the play ends, is planning to make her own way in the world on her own terms, not society's. *Mrs. Warren's Profession* was denounced in Europe and America.

Probably the most famous of the fallen characters were the heroines of Gustave Flaubert's *Madame Bovary* (1857) and Leo Tolstoy's *Anna Karenina* (1877). Both of these characters are respectable women with good social standing, married to dull men and given to fantasies of forbidden worlds. Seeking escape from their misery, they stray from the rigid confines of their marriage, have adulterous relationships, and finally commit suicide.

A contemporary Japanese short story, "Sleep," by Haruki Murakami, indicates that the Victorian marriage structure is still with us and is not confined to Western society. The narrator is a 30-year-old housewife, married to a respectable but boring dentist. She suddenly finds that she has incurable insomnia but no longer requires any sleep. She embarks upon a secret life at night, beginning, significantly enough, by reading *Anna Karenina* three times. She does not seek an adulterous affair but simply drives aimlessly through dark, lonely streets and parks, where ultimately she meets a violent death—one she may have secretly engineered. This is an unresolved, cryptic, disturbing story, but one that suggests there are still many unsatisfied wives who for one reason or another do not seek liberation.

There were feminist attacks on the Victorian code even during the Victorian era. One came from the American poet Emily Dickinson (1830-1886), who chose not to marry but to remain a literary recluse—hence an oddity, an outsider. In one poem she describes marriage in this fashion:

> *She rose to His Requirement—dropt*
> *The Playthings of Her Life*
> *To take the honorable Work*
> *Of Woman, and of Wife*

Commenting on this poem, critic Paul J. Ferlazzo remarks:

> The husband . . . is here depicted not as lover, companion, or friend, but as a standardbearer of excellence. . . . Dickinson is clearly contemptuous of the enforced inferiority of women and of the fact that their value and individuality are recognized only in terms of the men they marry.[10]

Henrik Ibsen, discussed in Chapter 4 as a pioneer in stage realism, turned Western society on its ear with his revolutionary work *A Doll's House* (1879). This play is perhaps the strongest frontal attack ever made on a prevailing moral code.

Nora, the "doll" of the title, is shown to be living a lie, though she has a rich, responsible husband, Torvald, healthy children, and servants to help run the house. Her only role is to be a flirtatious and submissive plaything to her husband.

But Ibsen exposes the lie of the contented "doll." The plot is melodramatic, complete with a blackmailer who threatens to ruin the family's reputation if he doesn't get a position in the bank managed by Torvald. He holds a promissory note with her father's signature forged by Nora years before in a desperate attempt to borrow money to take her ill husband to Italy for the winter. Now that Torvald,

*Ibsen's* A Doll's House *is perhaps the strongest frontal attack ever made on a prevailing moral code.*

completely recovered, is in a position of power, the man holding the note prepares to strike. When she can conceal her deed no longer, Nora, the proper Victorian wife, tries the standard wifely method of communication of that time: tears, explanations, and promises, believing that her husband will assume *his* proper role, too: that of stern protector. Instead, he denounces her and orders her kept from their children; she is to be locked in her room, a prisoner in her—or rather his—house.

When at the eleventh hour the blackmailer returns the note and the threat is over, Torvald attempts to rediscover the happy past: "Nora, I'm saved." "I?" she replies. "I thought it was *we*." In a denunciation scene before walking out (scandalous for a drama in those days), Nora tells him that she must be first a human being before she can be a wife. She rejects his promise to change, hands him her wedding ring, and closes the door firmly on her way out. Nora was one of the first fictional women to awaken and reject her assigned role in life.

*A Doll's House* is often given credit for having altered the direction of the theater from a preoccupation with romantic melodrama to a direct confrontation of social issues. But though Ibsen was controversial and in some quarters scandalous, social codes did not change abruptly. Likewise, neither World War I, which brought to a violent end many Victorian traditions, nor the 1920s, in which striped blazers and flapper dresses challenged conventional values, could topple the conservative middle-class family from its secure position in the social hierarchy. Flappers smoking and drinking openly with men were exciting fantasies for the average housewife, but they were not to dictate her assigned role.

*Life with Father*, the Broadway hit play of the 1930s (which for a long time held the record for most successive performances on Broadway, running for around eight years), confirmed the validity of "old-fashioned" values. In it, playwright Clarence Day, Jr., fondly remembers his parents' marriage: Father Day is irascible, opinionated, and completely dominant—he thinks. But in one scene after another, Mother Day is shown getting her own way, never by direct statement or confrontation, but always by devious means. Sometimes she pretends not to understand, sometimes she plots with others, and sometimes she talks in such a disorganized manner that Father backs down after giving vent to one more roar of anger. Since the play is a comedy, nothing is a matter of life and death, but Mother does win the "right" to entertain visitors, spend more than her budget, and see to her husband's baptism, using what modern feminists would call "slave tactics." *Life with Father*, however, is a relatively modern piece and may be telling us a silent truth about the Victorian model that was kept secret by the repressed wives themselves: the Victorian wife is actually the boss of the house! Ibsen's Nora may have grown tired of using little coquettish tricks to please her husband, but by weeping and pretending to be defenseless, Mother Day succeeds in getting Father Day to relax his guard; she knows just how to take advantage when he does. This particular version of the Victorian model is still in favor with many women who denounce the liberation movement, preferring, by their own admission, to play the traditional role because it gives them more power than they could possibly have on their own.

*The conservative middle-class family was not shaken by* A Doll's House, *flappers drinking and smoking openly, or even World War I.*

*The version of the Victorian model, in which the supposedly defenseless wife really runs the house, is still in favor with many women who denounce the liberation movement.*

## Steps Toward Liberation

The terms *liberation* and especially *liberated woman* are so commonplace today that one often forgets to ask what they mean. To be liberated one must have felt at one time enslaved, or at least confined. Many young women of today call themselves, or are called by others, "*liberated*," because (1) they belong to the work force in positions of authority; (2) they are married but have kept their own names; (3) they have chosen to remain single, though they may have children; (4) they prefer a same-sex relationship and make no effort to conceal this fact; or (5) they embody any combination of the preceding. Yet some of these young women have never had to struggle to maintain the integrity of their views; they are children of parents—or a parent—who went through the struggle and won the battle. On the other hand, *liberated* can also refer to women who are not yet able to struggle, but who hold values that belong to a lifestyle they would practice if given the chance. They may be part of conservative families holding fast to old values, or they may be married to someone whose definition of the gender roles is essentially Victorian. *Love* and *liberation* have become complex, even confusing, terms in contemporary society.

Earlier in the twentieth century, however, *liberation* was a clearly defined cause, because both women and men still found themselves tied to the Victorian model. Some accepted, even continued to approve its value system. Others did not—and did something about it.

Before we continue, we need to explain why we are even discussing gender roles and the degree to which women in particular have been, still are, or refuse to be bound by these roles. The answer is that love can no longer be defined as an activity or a relationship apart from gender roles. In past times nobody knew about gender roles. Except for goddesses, women were the "weaker" sex and were prone to the consuming effects of sexual passion. Men were "stronger" both in body and mind and needed to exercise a guiding hand. Men were supposed to keep everything in perspective; this belief is the true foundation of the romantic love ideal. Men would make sure that love remained pure and untarnished by desires of the flesh.

Liberation from the manacles of defined gender roles may have begun with the upper-class woman's insistence on freedom of choice. Gwendolen Fairfax, heroine of Oscar Wilde's *The Importance of Being Earnest* (1895), does not rebel against her mother's decision not to allow her to marry the man she loves. She nonetheless has no intention of being governed by the Victorian code throughout her life. She informs her suitor of her plans:

> Whatever influence I ever had over mamma, I lost at the age of three. But although she may prevent us from becoming man and wife, and I may marry someone else, and marry often, nothing that she can possibly do can alter my eternal devotion to you.

Nowadays audiences simply laugh at the line about marrying often, but in 1895 more than a few eyebrows must have been raised. Women were not supposed to embark upon a *career* of profitable marriages. Gwendolen is as much as saying outright that if she cannot marry for romantic love (because that is impractical and *un*profitable) she will at least provide handsomely for herself. Gwendolen is "liberated" to the extent that she is bound by neither respect for her parents nor the requirements of romantic love. In medieval times the woman prevented from loving her heart's desire would have been miserable all her life. Gwendolen will be rich and happy—and will think fondly of her heart's desire every once in a while. Of course, the lovers are united at the final curtain, but only because Gwendolen's sweetheart turns out to be the lost heir of a prominent family. Realistic economic thinking was thus one step toward liberation.

The upper-class heroine of D. H. Lawrence's *Lady Chatterley's Lover*

*Love can no longer be defined as an activity or a relationship apart from gender roles.*

*Lady Chatterley's Lover was an early version of the "new" morality, in which the language is a tribute to the overwhelming beauty of pure sexuality, divorced from any connection with traditional ideas of love.*

(1928) won both notoriety and a censorship battle for her creator. The "lover" of the title is a gameskeeper working on the estate where a bored and unhappy Lady Chatterley lives with her crippled and impotent husband. The sexual coupling of the lady and the gameskeeper occurs almost without words, without ideals, without any effort to fight temptation, without even a conflict with the Victorian moral code—no agonizing, no analysis, no mention of the possibility that "it's wrong."

The words Lawrence uses to describe the relationship—metaphors drawn from the gameskeeper's outdoor life—are a tribute to the overwhelming beauty of sexuality. Lawrence objected to the oppressive morality of the Victorian period as "a denial of the purity of love," which was natural and basic to the species, and therefore good. For Lawrence, love was beyond the moral code.

In the British trial testing whether *Lady Chatterley's Lover* was either literature or pornography, one witness, a professor of literature, stated that the novel was well written, true to life, and deserving of a place on any library shelf. The judge pointed out that the book contained a number of "carnal acts of wanton intercourse" before either Lady Chatterley or her lover, Oliver Mellors, mentioned love; indeed, they hardly spoke. "Sometimes," replied the witness, "that's the way it is, my lord. . . ."

During the same decade Ernest Hemingway created still another upper-class lady who liberated herself from old ideals. Lady Brett Ashley of *The Sun Also Rises* (1926) pleases herself by moving from one sexual alliance to another. Sometimes one of her lovers protests when she is ready to move on, but she cannot help it if certain men attach undue importance to fidelity or to a lasting relationship. For Lady Brett love and sexual pleasure are the same phenomenon. She may not be happy, but Hemingway is not saying that she would be if she followed the proper moral code. Love is probably by its very nature something that does not, cannot ever last, so Lady Brett restlessly moves from lover to lover. We must find a way to be happy *despite* the fact that the fires of ardent passion inevitably die out.

The voice of liberation in the United States was Dorothy Parker (1893–1967), who satirized the remnants of the Victorian model, especially when it had become a game women played because they felt they must. In her short story "The Waltz" the heroine is forced to dance with a boorish and clumsy partner but nonetheless pretends she is having the time of her life. She has to; a woman cannot afford to throw away the slightest chance of marital security (as opposed to bliss). As a working intellectual, famous for her cynical poetry and acerbic theater reviews ("*The House Beautiful* is the play lousy"), she well understood what it meant for a woman to try to make a living in a "man's world." Successful or intelligent women might as well forget about a physical relationship with a man, or as Parker so dryly puts it:

> *Men seldom make passes*
> *At girls who wear glasses.*[11]

In one of her essays Parker describes how she resorted to trapping the opposite sex by placing a Men's Room sign on her office door.

In the late 1930s and 1940s Hollywood gave stardom to actresses like Rosalind Russell, Jean Arthur, Bette Davis, Claudette Colbert, Barbara Stanwyck, and, above all, Katharine Hepburn, all of whom specialized in playing strong, intelligent career women; underneath, however, they were seldom truly liberated.

Hollywood sized up the "paying customers" and realized they were by and large still governed by the Victorian code.

*Woman of the Year* (1942), with Hepburn and her long-standing costar Spencer Tracy, has long been considered a classic, though not by feminists of both sexes. The film illustrates how much Hollywood has done (and in many instances is still doing) to keep subtly alive the Victorian model. The heroine—rich, successful, brilliant, witty—finally renounces her husbandless life after discovering she is unable to cook breakfast—a skill she will learn as a wife.

In 1949 this great acting team followed with *Adam's Rib*, which promised to be stridently antisexist. This time Tracy and Hepburn played married attorneys on opposite sides in a case of attempted murder, ultimately won by the wife. The conflict of the trial has put such a strain on the marriage that divorce becomes inevitable. Just before the divorce decree is to be made final, the protagonists appear at an accountant's office to discuss tax deductions. Upon learning that the last payment has been made on their country house, the husband puts his head in his hands and cries. The wife, overcome by sympathy, changes her mind about the divorce, whereupon the hero reveals that women are not the only sex able to use tears to get what it wants. Thus the dominant male reasserts himself; the once-liberated female relents and accepts his dominance; and the sanctity of marriage, the Victorian fortress, is preserved.

Sometimes we find a liberationist message tensely undermined by a fear—conscious or otherwise—of abandoning the model that has "worked" for so long. Films like *Kramer vs. Kramer* (1979) have exploited the theme of liberation and changing gender roles with varying degrees of honesty, but seldom without confusion. *Kramer vs. Kramer* shows us a liberation-seeking mother walking out on her family—much like Ibsen's Nora—in order to establish her true identity, then returning to reclaim her son when she feels she is ready to be an honest mother. But in her absence the husband has assumed the mother's role and has performed it well. After a fierce legal battle the court decides the child belongs with the natural mother, but the latter, observing the close bond between father and child, heroically leaves again. *Kramer vs. Kramer* represents a reaffirmation of the family unit. The gender roles have not been redefined—merely reversed.

*Sometimes we find a liberationist message tensely undermined by a fear of abandoning the model that has "worked" for so long. In the film* Kramer vs. Kramer *gender roles are not redefined, merely reversed.*

## Theme and Variations

Today love need not be defined solely in terms of how close the participants are to "liberation." For many, liberation is no longer an issue; for others, it never *was*, because the Victorian model still works, either because they believe the man really *should* be the protective breadwinner or because the woman finds it easier to let him think so. For still others, the word *love* is beside the point. It is a mythological remnant from the dead past and has nothing to do with the economic, biological, and medical realities of life.

The views of love we find in the humanities may or may not have anything to do with the thoughts and feelings of readers, audiences, and gallery-frequenters—the so-called general public, who may, after all, read or view what is put in front of them while reserving their private opinions. Dramatic statistics about divorce, unwed parents, and AIDS need not imply the disappearance of love or the necessity for defining or redefining the term. If humanity has been called by anthropologists the "only species that loves all year round," one could then say that even science finds a use for the word.

By and large in the humanities, love is currently viewed in decidedly nontraditional ways. The *New Yorker* cartoon on this page illustrates the decision not to define it at all, or at least to acknowledge its indefinable existence. Both the man and the woman seem devoid of any real attraction to each other; nonetheless, they are enjoying a casual friendship, which may be all anyone has a right to expect. On the other hand, the cartoonist may be wishing that love had not lost its idealistic connotations.

In Wendy Wasserstein's Pulitzer Prize-winning play *The Heidi Chronicles* (1988), the heroine, Heidi Holland, who starts off in 1965 as an activist for women's rights, learns through experience and a determination to view it realistically that love is whatever it happens to be at a given moment. In any case, it need not be the pivotal event in anyone's life. For years Heidi has maintained a relationship with Scoop Rosenbaum, a self-proclaimed liberal, who turns out to be a political chameleon, espousing whatever view is fashionable or will advance his cause, which is himself. She also has a long-standing, nonsexual relationship with Peter Patrone, a pediatrician who happens to be gay, a fact that in no way interferes with the love Heidi has for him. At the end of the play Heidi has given birth out of wedlock to Scoop's child and fully intends to raise it as a single parent with no thought of ever being married. Wasserstein shows us a character who is not liberated (she has no bonds to break), but totally free—one who has had a sexual relationship, with a joyous result, and who continues to enjoy and hold dear a Platonic friendship, also with joyous results.

In *Love in the Time of Cholera* (1988) Gabriel García Márquez, the Colombian-born (1928) Nobel Prize winner, gives us a very clear definition of

*"I love you the way the French love Jerry Lewis."*

*(Drawing by Victoria Roberts; © 1992 The New Yorker Magazine, Inc.)*

*Georges Seurat,* Sunday Afternoon on the Island of La Grande Jatte *(1884–86): For many, the Victorian model still works. (Helen Birch Bartlett Memorial Collection. The Art Institute of Chicago, All Rights Reserved)*

love as a human need that survives every possible disaster and is *not* limited to sexual relationships. In the novel, the young Florentino Diaz, a rather unattractive and awkward sort of person, sees in Fermina Daza what Romeo saw in Juliet. Never has the romantic ideal been so apparent. The lady, however, marries a successful doctor, partially because she seems to find Florentino, her relentless suitor, peculiar, if not repulsive. Nonetheless the ardent admirer is loyal to her memory for over fifty years; when, at length, her husband dies, he renews his suit, though both are presumably well beyond the age at which there can be any question of sexual attraction. Fermina agrees to a marriage, perhaps out of weariness from the arduous task of repelling Florentino's advances. At first she has no intention of ever sharing her body with him, as they set sail on a long cruise in order to escape the cholera epidemic that is ravaging the country. One night, however, Fermina submits to his ceaseless demands in a wonderful—and by now classic—passage that both reaffirms and redefines the joy of love:

> Then he looked at her and saw her naked to the waist, just as he had imagined her. Her shoulders were wrinkled, her breasts sagged, her ribs were covered by a flabby skin as pale and cold as a frog's. She covered her chest with the blouse she had just taken off, and she turned out the light. Then he sat up and began to undress in the darkness, throwing everything at her that he took off, while she tossed it back, dying of laughter.[12]

So what is love in this instance? We cannot say the word is not appropriate, for it appears in García Márquez's title. We cannot say it has no sexual connotations, for this geriatric couple make love almost incessantly after their "wedding night."

We cannot say it is Platonic, for, having lost touch for over fifty years, they know almost nothing of each other's mind. Yet whatever they have together is clearly their salvation in this "time of cholera," and may well be the author's almost mystic answer to the world's many problems.

*Many of today's major love stories take place in the tragic shadow of AIDS, but AIDS may not threaten to obliterate love as much as it reinforces the idealization of it.*

Florentino and Fermina live and love in a period of great danger. Many of today's major love stories take place in the tragic shadow of AIDS. One cannot imagine a scene in drama more evocative of love than that in Larry Kramer's powerful *The Normal Heart* (1985) in which the nonafflicted partner comes home with a bag of groceries to find his dying lover shivering on the floor and in obvious pain. Bursting with passionate anger at the cruel fate to which this once exuberant young man is consigned, the roommate starts screaming at his lover to eat, to fatten himself up, to lead a normal life, all the while hurling the food at him in a rage. It could well be that the shadow of AIDS has not threatened to obliterate love so much as it has reinforced the idealization of it. Plays like *The Normal Heart* and films like Craig Lucas's *Longtime Companion* (1990) have resurrected a concept of "true love."

## Epilogue

Far from leaving us in a state of cynicism, the treatment of love in today's humanities offers cause for optimism, not in the sense that we may ignore unpleasant realities, but in terms of the many choices open to us. Fortunately we are not living in a period when strict guidelines are being imposed upon us.

We may, for example, enjoy a new kind of fairy tale, such as *Don't Bet on the Prince* (1986) by Jack Zipes. Here a wise and witty princess is introduced to a prince from a nearby kingdom. Sitting next to her at a royal banquet, he is swept away by her charm and beauty and falls instantly in love. Their families are delighted, and look forward to a wedding. When they both rise to dance, he is appalled to discover that she is taller than he; the next day, when he shows off on horseback and expects her admiration for jumping hedges and ditches, she smilingly reciprocates with a superior display of equestrianism. After the prince threatens to call off the wedding, she loses the use of her legs and takes to bed. Feeling superior to the princess once more, he condescends to visit her, but rejects her again when he discovers that she converses as skillfully as she rides. Forlorn, the princess loses her voice, and, now that she can neither move nor speak, she becomes an acceptable candidate for marriage. The story ends happily (at least for some readers) when the princess decides to reject the prince and accept a different suitor, one who is also shorter than she, but who admires her for her skills.

There is no question that today, fewer women are marrying, but a woman without a husband is more likely to be Heidi Holland than the modern equivalent of the Victorian maiden aunt whose task was to care for the sick elders. However the modern woman may choose to live, her taste in reading is not circumscribed. Enjoyment of a romantic novel, like *Wuthering Heights*, in which lovers torn apart by a Victorian class-conscious society are reunited in the next life, is still permissible. One may continue to be thrilled by nineteenth-century operas and the torments of lovers parted forever as the music reaches a crescendo. Doing so does not constitute an endorsement of attitudes one may no longer believe are realistic. To be enjoyable, art does not have to reflect what *we* believe.

On the other hand, romantic attitudes need not be confined to tragic stories on the stage or screen. We can hold them ourselves. There are still modern poets who tell us to trust our intuitions and to pay no attention to the researchers collecting new data on the demise of love in our time:

*Signature*

*If I sing because I must*
*being made of singing dust,*

*and I cry because of need*
*being born of watered seed,*

*and I grow like twisted tree*
*having neither symmetry*

*nor the structure to avert*
*the falling axe, the minor hurt,*

*yet of one thing I am sure*
*that this bears my signature,*

*that I knew love when it came*
*and I called it by its name.*[13]
                              *Hannah Kahn*

## Glossary

*courtly love:* An artificial and codified set of rules governing the behavior of the sexes that prevailed during the late Middle Ages and early Renaissance. Principal among these rules was the right of the lady to make any demands she wished to test the loyalty and devotion of her suitor.

*gender role:* A characterization of self grounded in traditional and social expectations of behavior appropriate for men and for women.

*Mariolatry:* The idealization of the Virgin Mary as practiced by a late medieval cult of poets and painters. Not only did it ennoble the life and characteristics of the mother of Jesus, but it tended to elevate the status of women as well.

*Platonic love:* Popularly considered to be any nonphysical relationship. In philosophy, however, it is a spiritual, intellectual relationship with others achieved after one has gone through lower (i.e., exclusively physical) kinds of attachment.

*romance:* A narrative tale popular during the Middle Ages, centering on the dashing adventures of a knightly hero and his idealized passion for a (usually) beautiful young lady.

*romantic love:* An idealized relationship (either vaguely physical or not physical at all) between two people. Full of tenderness, devotion, sensitivity, understanding, and altruism, it continues to thrive in movies, television, and popular fiction and to affect the expectations of people, probably more than most would admit.

*Victorian model:* The prototype of the male-female relationship borrowed from the Victorians and still very much with us. It includes definite gender roles, in which the male is the dominant breadwinning force in the home, and the female is the submissive bread maker, generally uninformed and requiring the protection of her husband. While the liberation movement has done much to undermine the Victorian model, one needs to be aware of the extent to which *both* sexes find little to quarrel with in its basic values.

# Notes

1. Plato, *The Symposium*, tr. Benjamin Jowett.
2. Ibid.
3. "The Death of the Hired Man," *The Poetry of Robert Frost*, ed. Edward Connery Lathem (New York: Holt, Rinehart & Winston, 1969).
4. The name *Yahweh* probably derives from *Yahu*, an old Canaanite thunder god.
5. Miguel de Cervantes, *The First Part of the Delightful History of the Most Ingenious Knight Don Quixote of the Mancha*, tr. Thomas Shelton (New York: Harvard Classics, P. F. Collier & Sons, 1937), 222.
6. Morton M. Hunt, *The Natural History of Love* (New York: Grove Press, A Black Cat Book, 1959), 134-135.
7. Ibid., 136.
8. Ibid., 139.
9. Ibid., 181.
10. Paul J. Ferlazzo, *Emily Dickinson*. (Boston: Twayne, 1976), 74.
11. Quoted in John Keats, *You Might As Well Live: The Life and Times of Dorothy Parker* (New York: Simon & Schuster, 1970), 102.
12. Gabriel García Márquez, *Love in the Time of Cholera* (New York: Knopf, 1988), 339.
13. From *Eve's Daughter,* by Hannah Kahn, 1962. Reprinted by permission.

# Suggested Reading

Bank, Mirra. *Anonymous Was a Woman*. New York: St. Martin's, 1979. A collection of letters and drawings by American women during more repressive times. Taken together, they reveal lives of bitter isolation and loneliness. The book also illustrates various male archetypes.

Beauvoir, Simone de. *The Second Sex*. New York: Knopf, 1953. One of the earliest examinations of role possibilities for modern women by the noted existentialist. The book that may be at least partly responsible for the feminist movement of today.

Clover, Carol J. *Men, Women, and Chainsaws: Gender in the Modern Horror Film*. Princeton, N.J.: Princeton University Press, 1992. A study of how women fare in the contemporary "slasher" films finds that women often are the force that conquers psychotic men.

Delumeau, Jean. *Sin and Fear: The Emergence of a Western Guilt Culture, 13th–18th Centuries*. Tr. Eric Nicholson. New York: St. Martin's, 1991. Since the author is French, his subject is the European development of the Christian hatred of the body and all worldly pleasure. His real interest, however, is to study the impact of this "guilt culture" on people ever since the eighteenth century.

French, Marilyn. *The Women's Room*. New York: Jove Publications, 1977. A popular novel of the 1970s, which chronicles the development of a female sensibility from traditional marriage and motherhood through divorce to a radical change in her self-image and attitude toward a woman's options in life. Of special interest is the heroine's relationship with a "liberated" man of feminist leanings, who turns out to be secretly playing a Victorian male gender role.

Fromm, Erich. *The Art of Loving*. New York: Harper, 1956. A detailed examination by a psychologist/philosopher of various kinds of relationships that can be called "love," with an emphasis on the author's recommended definition of love as mutual enhancement of two strong lives.

Hunt, Morton M. *The Natural History of Love*. New York: Minerva Press, 1959. A readable and witty but well-researched social history in which the author shows that there has been no universal view or practice of love throughout Western culture.

Kundera, Milan. *The Unbearable Lightness of Being*. Tr. Michael Henry Heim. New York: Harper and Row, 1984. A novel about conflicting meanings of love. One male character is driven by uncontrollable lust for many women but also by the need for a stable relationship with one particular woman. Another is a young man faithful to one partner, who loves him back, but not to the exclusion of other men. An inevitable story about what happens in permissive times.

Lieblich, Julia. *Sisters: Lives of Devotion and*

*Defiance*. New York: Ballantine Books, 1992. A study of modern nuns and what shapes their spirituality, especially as they seek equal rights.

Oppenheim, Janet. *"Shattered Nerves": Doctors, Patients, and Depression in Victorian England.* Fair Lawn, N.J.: Oxford University Press, 1991. A study by an eminent historian of medical malpractice and the effect of gender roles in Victorian England. One of the major points made is that many men, suffering from depression, never sought help because of the prevailing idea that the man was supposed to be invincible.

Tyler, Anne. *Breathing Lessons*. New York: Knopf, 1988. A rich and sensitive novel about a middle-aged woman numbed by the monotony of a conventional marriage in which the question of options for a woman never even arises. Tyler offers profound insights into how women cope.

Zipes, Jack. *Don't Bet on the Prince: Contemporary Feminist Fairy Tales in North America and England*. New York: Methuen, 1986. A delightful collection of modern fairy tales, which are actually satires on still-surviving sexist attitudes.

*Edouard Manet,* A Bar at the Folies-Bergère *(Courtauld Institute Galleries, London. Courtauld Collection)*

# *Happiness*

## *Overview*

Since this book is concerned primarily with themes of the humanities, an inquiry into the nature of happiness is inevitable. Consider how many novels and plays deal with unhappy people and either end sadly, all happiness denied, or somehow manage to conclude with a "happy ending." Think of how many poems express the intricacies of joy or despair. Some of the world's greatest art works capture human faces in moments made significant by the presence or absence of happiness.

Small wonder that a major branch of philosophy, ethics, devotes itself to exhaustive analysis of this apparently elusive state that most of us would say is more important than anything else. When we think of ethics, our natural inclination is to think of morality. And rightly so. But in its broadest sense, *ethics* is an inquiry into the nature of the good: not only what is good as distinct from bad or evil in human affairs, but what it is that makes *life* good. Inevitably the question arises of

*Happiness may be better experienced by its absence than any conscious state of present bliss.*

what constitutes happiness. Most people, if asked what they mean or understand by happiness, would offer a very wide range of answers.

One difficulty is that people often become acutely aware of happiness only when it appears to be absent from their lives. There is a sense of something missing, something lost, and then comes the desperate search for the correct definition, at least one that will *work*. People go to psychiatrists; they write or read any number of books on the subject of being happy. Bookstore cash registers jingle from the sale of hundreds of "how to make yourself happy" manuals. Those who dart from one author's prescription to another often wind up confused and frustrated.

This chapter does not necessarily have how-to implications. Instead, it pulls together some of the major viewpoints on happiness and then subjects each one to fair analysis and possible evaluations. Although the final answers will probably remain as obscure as most final answers are, *some* answers are available.

## Hedonism: Happiness as Pleasure

The Greek philosopher Aristippus (435-356 B.C.) declared happiness to be the *sum total of pleasures experienced during one's lifetime. Pleasure* he defined in purely physical terms: taste, sexual excitement, touch, and so on. People, he said, are selfish animals, concerned solely with their own comforts. The idea behind living is to seek out the most gratifying comforts, avoiding situations that yield few or none at all. Thus, if Aristippus is right, people prefer not to work, but they do so only because what they earn will provide them with pleasure. There is no satisfaction in work for its own sake. As a matter of fact, Aristippus believed there was no true satisfaction in the memory or anticipation of pleasure. Nothing counted except what could be experienced *at the moment. Hedonism* is the name given to this philosophy that happiness is pleasure.

Many people today are proud to call themselves hedonists. They openly boast of their income and possessions. They assert that with only one chance to live they should deny themselves nothing and try to "have it all." Other, more idealistic philosophies are disappointments to such contemporary hedonists, who maintain that only pleasure can be known with any certainty.

Others resist applying the term *hedonism* to themselves. While a good many admit that they seek comfort and avoid discomfort, they do not accept selfishness as their primary motive. High on their list of pleasures are giving and receiving love (in more than a physical sense), raising a family, finding a useful and satisfying occupation, having the chance to get ahead in the world, having security, pursuing intellectual stimulation, and expressing themselves creatively. Aristippus would contend that such persons are secret hedonists but are afraid to admit that they are and that they *ought* to be selfish. They seek pleasure, but deny themselves too much. They sacrifice everything for their children, only to be confronted later with a thankless "What did you ever do for me?" They live frugally so that their retirement years will be truly golden, and die just before their pension comes due.

### Hedonist Assumptions

Hedonists generally feel cheated. There never seem to be enough pleasurable moments in life. There seems to be so much undeserved pain. "Why me?" is a frequent question silently asked. "Did I deserve to be the sole support of my

*Diego Rodriguez de Silva y Velasquez,* Los Borrachos: *No amount of pleasure is ever too much for a hedonist. (The Prado. Alinari/Art Resource)*

parents when my brothers and sisters flatly refused to help? When am I going to get *my* chance to be happy?"

So assumption number one of the hedonist is that *everyone deserves as much pleasure as possible*. A variant of this assumption is that *people never really get as much pleasure as they deserve*. Other people always appear to have more. Other hedonists communicate (even exaggerate) their pleasures, especially unexpected bonuses, which point out how truly deserving they really are. To share unpleasant experiences is to advertise unworthiness, and nobody wants to do that. Hence the perpetuation of the myth that other people are "getting more from life."

A second assumption, vitally related to the first, is that *pleasure is automatically good*. During the Great Depression of the 1930s, when so many Americans were barely eating enough to get by, those who were able to eat anything they wanted were undoubtedly envied. Who thought to feel sorry for the affluent people who might overeat and overdrink?

Hedonists recognize that people cannot possibly have pleasure every moment of their life, but this does not stop them from thinking they should. A third assumption, therefore, is that *no amount of pleasure is ever too much*. There may be a submerged feeling of guilt about gorging oneself in an "All U Can Eat" restaurant or downing one drink after another at somebody else's open house, but the typical hedonist response is, "There will be time enough to cut down; don't bother me now." Besides, overindulgence in moments of plenty supposedly means "making up" for past disappointments.

A fourth hedonist assumption is that *the absence of pleasure is a misfortune for which compensation is due*. The son or daughter who sits with the baby four nights during the week is bound to claim the weekend as a right. Many who have been arrested while attempting robbery have believed they were only getting

*Hedonism in Oscar Wilde*
*I can resist everything except temptation.*

Lady Windermere's Fan

*How are you, my dear Ernest? What brings you up to town?*

*Oh, pleasure, pleasure. What else should bring one anywhere?*

The Importance
of Being Earnest

even with society. If you carry the hedonist viewpoint through life, you find yourself plotting continually: "Just wait until *I* have the upper hand!" Since moments without definite feelings of pleasure are an abomination, you entertain yourself by thinking of the moment when rightful pleasures are finally gained.

This particular mindset stems from the *big-earnings theory*. An earning is considered the pleasure owed to a deserving person. The oldest child in a large family, for example, may have gone to work to help out and to assure younger brothers and sisters of proper clothing, education, and so on. In the ledger many hedonists carry inside themselves, there is a strict accounting of pleasures owed them; eventually a vast number may accumulate. Unless something happens to change their philosophy of happiness, these hedonists may become obsessed with thinking about pleasures due. If they are paid off, life is good; if not, life is bad. Life is evaluated strictly in terms of total payments received. A supergood life is one in which no good deed is left unrewarded.

## Hedonism Reconsidered

Since it is one of the oldest-known theories of happiness, hedonism has been subjected to ongoing critical appraisal by philosophers and cultural historians alike. Hedonism seems to have inspired two major critical questions: first, whether this philosophy is based on an accurate view of human nature, and second, whether people are pleasure-loving at all times and in all places.

That we are living in a pleasure-oriented society is difficult to deny. Implicit in TV commercials is a general concern over what one is "getting out of life," and surely what people mean is pleasure. Hair must be shampooed to a silky sheen for the pleasurable touch. Both sexes must wear delicate fragrances to gratify the olfactory sense. Even the quasi-serious, somewhat intellectual magazines, directed toward "thinking" people, run page after page of liquor advertisements. In addition, nearly every popular song celebrates the glory of physical lovemaking. The casual talk of celebrities on interview programs often focuses on the high-class lifestyle their fame makes possible.

The Greek society in which Aristippus lived and wrote was hardly shy when it came to pleasures of the flesh. But it is one thing to justify hedonism on the grounds that we would rather do what the others are doing, and quite another to say that hedonism alone is in tune with human nature. Plato's famous analysis of the stages of love (see Chapter 12) does not discredit the pleasures of a physical relationship but recognizes and then elevates the nonphysical.

The crux of the argument may be how limited or unlimited is our definition of *pleasure*. Fundamental hedonism is clear: Pleasure is experienced through the five senses. People who spend time in thought—that is, on the mental plane— are denying themselves that much pleasure and, we assume, that much happiness. People who spend their lives working in a clinic a thousand miles from civilization, who expose themselves daily to the risk of disease and never achieve outside recognition for what the hedonist would surely call a "sacrifice," are supposedly doing without pleasure. But how can we assume that such people—and there are many of them—are deliberately perverting their own natures to follow a calling that requires them to labor in the interest of others?

Buddhist monks sitting alone in silent meditation for hours and days at a time lose contact with their "self" in ways that the hedonist could never understand. Are they robbing themselves of the pleasure that their natures crave? Are

*Hedonists become obsessed with thinking about pleasures due. If they are paid off, life is good; if not, life is bad.*

*Some Hedonistic Advertising Slogans*
*You deserve a break today.*

*If I have one life to live, let me live it as a blonde.*

*You only live once!*

*Gather ye rose-buds while ye may,*
*    Old time is still a flying:*
*And this same flower that smiles today,*
*    Tomorrow will be dying.*

*        Robert Herrick*

the analysts accurate when they tell us that the spirituality of the celibate Catholic priest is a "sublimation" of normal sexual passions? Or is human nature such that it cannot be narrowly defined? Might *sensory* pleasures be all-sufficing for some and less fulfilling to others? Are we to suggest that the social worker, the rabbi, the minister, and the hospital volunteer worker are wasting their time or denying themselves pleasure? Or perhaps is limiting the quantity and duration of personal pleasure for some the way happiness is attained?

If, as the existentialist maintains, no such thing as human nature exists at all and humanity is indeed a self-defining, self-determining species, then there is ample room for alternate ways of defining pleasure. In fact, if we choose we can relegate physical pleasure to a low position on our priority list.

Another argument against hedonist assumptions is based on a historical overview. The theory is sometimes advanced that the prevalence of hedonism indicates the *declining*, not the normal, stage of a civilization. In other words, human societies are seen as moving in cycles. During the disintegrating phase, when a civilization is falling apart at the seams, it becomes affluent, greedy, fat, pleasure oriented, and vulnerable. The cultural historian and sociologist Pitirim Sorokin (1889-1968) believed that growing societies experience three phases: a *religious* phase, in which concentration is non-self-centered; then a *political* phase, when they are oriented toward the development of great art and great institutions of learning and government; and then a *sensate* phase, when, overly secure after their power has been established, they gratify the senses and neglect their intellectual and spiritual needs. Sorokin, like Oswald Spengler (1880-1936) before him, saw Western civilization as being in the twilight of its greatness, mainly because of its selfish preoccupation with the senses.

Whether or not the cyclical view of history offers too neat an explanation, we can at least say that it presents us with choices. Sorokin's three phases *can* be applied to individuals and to societies, at least in part. Why should we be constrained by the need to single out only the last and say that *it* constitutes the norm? May not one possibility be that the sensate is the most immediate and therefore the quickest—but not necessarily the lasting—way to be happy?

## Epicureanism: Avoiding Pain

In a musical comedy some years back, the heroine, trying to explain to the audience in song why she loved the hero, compares her love to a number of familiar pleasures. She includes the smell of bread baking and the feeling she has when a tooth stops hurting. In the first instance, she is a hedonist, directly sensuous in her values. In the second, however, she turns to a different philosophy of happiness: *Epicureanism*. The sudden cessation of a toothache is not directly pleasurable in itself, but it *does* bring happiness, the happiness of not being in pain.

Epicureanism is named for the Greek thinker Epicurus, who first formulated its precepts. Aware of Aristippus and his beliefs, Epicurus was highly critical of a philosophy he believed weak in logic and, more than that, impossible to follow.

### Epicurean Assumptions

Epicurus indirectly accepted the initial premise of hedonism, that pleasure is a great good. But he refused to say with the hedonists that the more pleasure we have, the happier we shall be:

*Are we to suggest that the social worker, the rabbi, the minister, and the hospital volunteer worker are wasting their time or denying themselves pleasure?*

*The sudden cessation of a toothache is not directly pleasurable in itself, but it does bring happiness, the happiness of not being in pain.*

> And since pleasure is the first good and natural to us, for this very reason we do not choose every pleasure, but sometimes we pass over many pleasures, when greater discomfort accrues to us as a result of them.

Epicurus was particularly critical of recommending pleasures in excess, for these, he knew, would always be followed by both physical and moral pain:

> For from prudence are sprung all the other virtues, and it teaches us that it is not possible to live pleasantly without living prudently and honourably and justly.

For Epicurus, hedonism was a time-conscious, death-ridden philosophy. If happiness increased with the quantity of physical pleasures, then logically no life could ever be long enough. Death is never bearable, never coming at an acceptable time. But, surely, we are here for an uncertain amount of time, all of us subject to the gradual infirmities that come with age—if indeed we do not burn ourselves out before age ever becomes a problem. Therefore hedonists are fundamentally insecure and unhappy, unable to accept the inevitability of age and death, always worried about the loss of pleasure. So the major assumption of Epicureanism is that nothing lasts forever and we must thus accept this fact cheerfully.

Another Epicurean assumption is that no one can sustain pleasure over prolonged periods of time. How long can we gorge ourselves on delicious food? Indulge in sex? Stay drunk? Why, then, saddle ourselves with a philosophy of life that is so limiting from the very outset?

Unable to satisfy our pleasure-seeking instincts perpetually, we do the next best thing: seek material possessions or fame, both of which symbolize happiness without bringing happiness. Money and fame are constantly in the hedonist's thoughts. They are the compensations for what may be passing him or her by: the tangible embodiments of a successful hedonistic life. But Epicurus recognized that the pursuit of the wealth that often substitutes for physical pleasure was self-defeating, futile. The same is true of fame as a substitute. The wealthy or the famous person feels insecure and distrustful of others, certain that others are envious and scheming.

Why, asked Epicurus, burden ourselves with a philosophy with built-in disappointments, frustrations, and inevitable pain? Why not, rather, change the *requirements* for happiness? Epicurus was influenced by the materialistic philosophy that had been popularized by Democritus, a formulator of the first atomic theory (see Chapter 6). But Epicurus did not carry materialism as far as some would later do, that is, into a thoroughgoing determinism (see Chapter 15), which reduces human behavior to a matter of cause and effect and denies the role of human will. Epicurus assumed the person of reason had free will and could control his or her pleasures and therefore reduce the amount of pain to be endured. The Epicurean is highly selective.

Epicureanism is therefore not so much an all-out attack upon as a modification of hedonism. It assumes unpleasantness is part of life and plans strategies to ward it off as much as possible rather than march forward in the blind hope that things are going to be fine. The worst that can happen when you anticipate pain is that you will not be disappointed. But clearly, you have a good chance of doing something about much of life's pain before it occurs *if* you apply yourself conscientiously to the task.

The taste of exquisite food is high on the list of hedonists' priorities. So it is for the Epicureans. The difference is that the latter, anticipating the pain of overindulgence, stop themselves before reaching their limit. They will drink, but never to the point of drunkenness, and not at all if they are certain their health cannot stand it.

A character in one of Hemingway's short stories marries a beautiful but flirtatious woman considerably younger than he. He goes off to war, is injured, and during his stay at a rehabilitation center learns that his wife has run off with another man. His response is typically Epicurean: Instead of being angry or feeling sorry for himself, he admits to having made a mistake. A man, he comments, should never place himself in a position to lose so much.

The Epicureans pursue physical pleasures in moderation, realizing that any excess is likely to lead to pain. But they also seek out nonphysical pleasures. They are generally lovers of art, theater, books, and music. Intellectual and esthetic pleasures can be experienced in abundance without the fear of pain. Epicureans are, however, wary of becoming overly dependent upon such stimuli, for then they run the risk of being unable to compromise. You cannot spend all of your time reading or thinking; there are other necessary tasks that need to be done.

Epicureans tend to be highly disciplined. They are generally lean and trim, exercising their bodies to keep in the best possible shape. They are mentally agile and aware of the latest developments in many fields. They are good workers, and the one who finds a marital partner with a similar outlook is likely to build a reasonably happy home.

Pure hedonists, however, warn Epicureans that they sell themselves too short and may often settle for less than they have a right to expect from life. The hedonist maintains that unless you work aggressively at being happy, you will give up too easily, spending too much time planning for future pleasures.

## Epicureanism Reconsidered

While many people live as though pure hedonism were their creed, Epicureans have enjoyed considerably more prominence in philosophy through the centuries. Accepting a materialistic view of existence, not considering the possibility of a divine hand at work behind the universe, they continue to espouse a theory of happiness that is based on controlling one's attitudes and desires. "No one can make you happy but yourself," they say. The Epicurean alternative to the endless quest for pleasure is very tempting, and deserves a closer, critical scrutiny.

One objection that can be raised to Epicureanism is that it is as firmly rooted in self-interest as the philosophy from which it departs. We may question how profound or lasting would be the peace of mind that comes from the careful control of one's own life if such were achieved at the cost of worrying about the pain of others. Granted, classical theories of happiness focus on the individual, as though happiness *by definition* were a matter of how one's *own* life is faring. Social consciousness was not predominant in classical thinking. We could even argue that concern for the neighbor, stressed in Judaism and Christianity, is in contrast to the emphasis of Epicurus. Religious leaders have said that personal happiness is less important than caring for others, and not that the means to personal happiness is that very caring.

We cannot rule out the possibility that happiness can be and is often achieved only by working to combat pain wherever it is found, and sometimes the battle incurs personal suffering, which is accepted as the high price of success.

*One objection that can be raised to Epicureanism is that it is as firmly rooted in self-interest as the philosophy from which it departs.*

*Even with a hefty budget and an abundance of leisure, the Epicurean is likely to be a passive spectator rather than an actor in the drama of living.*

After all, there are people, seldom mentioned in history books, who voluntarily spend their shortened lives nursing the sick in leper colonies. What of the thousands who have forfeited the comforts of a good standard of living and gone off with the Peace Corps to remote villages, where adequate food and medical care are not available to them?

Now, social consciousness *might* be an extension of a principle stated by Epicurus: "The just man is most free from trouble." That is, happiness consists of an undisturbed conscience; if you want tranquillity, you must sometimes labor in the interest of others. After all, can you sit down to relish a gourmet meal with three ragged and starving children pressing their noses against the restaurant window? But it seems unfair to assume that all apparently selfless work is ultimately rooted in the effort to reach inner peace.

Another possible objection to the Epicurean way of life is purely economic. To pick and choose carefully among the available pleasures of life can be costly. The well-rounded Epicurean likes to read and listen to music, of course, but not all the time. Expensive food, drink, and travel are also desirable if one is to avoid the pain of unfulfilled longings.

Yet even with a hefty budget and an abundance of leisure, the Epicurean is likely to be a passive spectator and enjoyer rather than an actor in the drama of living. Epicurus stresses the suppression of want, deciding beforehand that the struggle to obtain something may well not be worth the pain of failing:

> He who has learned the limits of life knows that that which removes the pain due to want and makes the whole of life complete is easy to obtain; so that there is no need of actions which involve competition.

But the countersuggestion can be made that not risking much in a challenge means there is less chance for a significant victory.

## Stoicism: Strategies for Surviving

There is a famous poster showing a cat holding tightly to a knotted end of a rope and just hanging there in empty black space. The caption reads, *When You Come to the End of Your Rope, Tie a Knot and Hang On*. This, in capsule form, is the philosophy of *Stoicism*. It operates under even fewer illusions about life than does Epicureanism. It tells us neither to plan ahead for a lifetime of unlimited pleasure nor to expect to avoid pain through discipline and moderation. Stoicism asserts pain is intrinsic to living. Even the most dedicated Epicureans will feel a certain amount of frustration when their disciplined approach to living goes awry. The best possible course is to be prepared for the worst and to develop a technique for coping with it.

### Working On the Mind

Stoicism is still a popular philosophy of happiness despite the fact that it was born over two thousand years ago. Like hedonism and hedonism's modified offspring, Epicureanism, it is the product of Greek intellect; unlike the others, however, it lays heavy stress on human reason, on the belief that humankind is a superior form of animal life. Zeno, its first major advocate (?-264? B.C.), is therefore closer in spirit to Plato and Aristotle than to either Aristippus or Epicurus.

*The Epicurean*

*Moderate eating and drinking, the pursuit of intellectual pleasures,*

*and*

*an awareness of the impossibility of permanent pleasure.*

The name of the philosophy derives from the fact that the school founded by Zeno was located in a columned portico area called the *Stoa*. Central to Stoicism is that true happiness is not a matter of circumstance, of good fortune, or of what happens to us, but rather a matter of *how we respond to what happens*. Happiness, like sorrow, is an idea, not an object or an event. If no people exist to welcome the first day of spring, how can it be said that spring is a time of hope and joy? If in some remote civilization with peculiar customs and mores the birth of a child were considered a dreadful curse, then the inability to produce offspring might be regarded as a happy stroke of luck.

In other words, Stoicism teaches that to find the roots of unhappiness, one must look inward. Nothing is under our control except the way we think about things. Natural disasters, social upheavals, wars, revolutions, outbreaks of disease, rising crime rates—all happen as a result of either accidental or highly complicated causes. Our happiness should not depend upon their *not* taking place. We cannot alter external circumstances, but we *can* decide not to feel negatively toward them.

"How do you expect me to feel?" is a common response when we are asked why we are so glum about a certain outcome—say, not being promoted to a higher position. Stoics cite habit as the guilty culprit. That is, they contend people are conditioned by the values their society puts on what happens to or around them: This is acceptable; that is not. This is cause for joy; that is cause for tears. Reactions become automatic after a while. People come to *think* they are unhappy; hence they are unhappy. But typical responses can be altered. We can refuse to be affected in customary ways or as others tend to be affected.

*If you are told that such a one speaks ill of you, make no defense against what was said, but answer, He surely knew not my other faults, else he would not have mentioned these only!*

*Epictetus*

One of the best-known Stoic teachers was a Greek named Epictetus (A.D. 60?–120?), who became a Roman slave. His genius was finally recognized and he was allowed to conduct classes. But prior to that, Epictetus was tortured and oppressed in his captivity. On one occasion his leg was broken on a whim of his master's. During this period of extreme suffering, Epictetus was faced with the choice of surrendering to despair or finding some means of enduring. He chose the latter course, recognizing that nothing, not even torture, was unbearable unless one wished to find it so. After his "liberation," he dedicated his life to spreading the Stoic creed, which had preserved his spirit intact for so many years.

Stoicism found ready acceptance among the Romans and eventually became a sort of "official" state philosophy. Its emphasis on reason and the control of negative emotions accorded well with the Roman ideal of humanity. Besides, Rome was an empire-building civilization, requiring a superbly disciplined military machine to carry out its conquests. It therefore found a meaningful application of Stoic teachings: The rigors of military training as well as the hardships of war itself must never depress the human spirit. Good soldiers must have feelings so well under their command that they become indifferent to suffering.

*Live rationally, and part with life cheerfully.*

*Marcus Aurelius*

When Christianity began to spread through the Roman Empire, many of the converts had, naturally enough, already been exposed to Stoic beliefs. The by-then ancient and honorable philosophy accorded well with the outlook and needs of the Christians. After all, they had to face untold sufferings—continual persecution, torture, flight, starvation, separation from loved ones. The Stoic doctrine of inner control blended perfectly with the Christian belief that only the soul, not the body, mattered. One could endure all manner of pain and stay inwardly serene. Christians supposedly sang while waiting for the lions to devour them in the Circus Maximus.

*But I say to you, do not resist one who is evil. But if any one strikes you on the right cheek, turn to him the other also.*

*Matt. 5:38*

What more dramatic model of the Stoic being could there have been than

*Hieronymus Bosch,* The Bearing of the Cross *(c.1505): A dramatic model of the Stoic being. (Musée des Beaux Arts, Ghent)*

Christ himself? Had Christ not allowed himself to be mocked, taunted, whipped? Had he not carried his own cross to Calvary and then refused to come down from that same cross when the challenge was given? Had he not forgiven his tormentors?

Stoicism remains as pervasive as ever and offers to many a genuine alternative to hedonism. In a period of ever-accelerating change, of violence as a way of life, of depression in farm belts and neurosis in high-rent districts, it is small wonder that many are asking less for pleasure than for inner peace. While weekly pilgrimages to analysts continue, we wonder whether some principles of Stoicism are not at work here also. After all, self-knowledge is vital to psychoanalysis. It is the analysts' contention that, once people understand what is making them unhappy or ineffective, they will be able to transcend negative feelings. Happiness is really within our own power to create and preserve.

*God grant me the serenity to accept the things I cannot change, the strength to change the things I can, and the wisdom to know the difference.*

*Alcoholics Anonymous creed*

## Stoicism Reconsidered

Stoicism in modern dress is for many a viable theory of happiness. Its basic assumption remains much the same as always: Tranquillity is worth any price. Stoicism has something to offer the chronically poor and dispossessed, who also suffer from low self-esteem and cannot see that they deserve any better fate. Even the most zealous social worker might agree that in some cases a stoic attitude is better than false hope for a better tomorrow.

An obvious negative aspect of Stoicism is its convenience. If you're down and out, abandoned by family and friends, with no prospects that things will turn around for you, why not become a Stoic? Surely the distance is short from "Things are pretty bleak" to "There is no reason to believe things should be otherwise."

Suppose, however, that the ad hoc Stoic—the person who adopts this philosophy out of sheer desperation—suddenly experiences an unexpected reversal of fortune. Say he or she wins $5 million in the state lottery or, more modestly, a kindly social worker chances by and provides a paying job. Or suppose, as actually happened in the wake of a TV newscaster's human-interest documentary about the homeless in New York, a couple randomly singled out for an interview found themselves swamped with offers of money, jobs, shelter—even a film contract! What happens to Stoic doctrines then? Can a legitimate theory of happiness be Stoic one day and hedonistic the next?

If your answer to this question was "Why not?" let us analyze the response. If adversity can be endured because the rational control of emotion makes endurance possible, then dropping Stoicism when convenient negates the importance placed on reason to begin with. Indeed, that same reason that justified the initial adoption of the Stoic philosophy requires us to believe that good fortune is not likely to be permanent.

There is an old fable about a tyrannical king who, finding himself plagued by bad fortune, kept asking various wise men to give him grounds for hope. If they could not, their head was chopped off. Finally, one clever sage gave him a plaque to hang on his bedroom wall: *These Things Shall Pass*. The king, deriving much comfort from the plaque, rewarded the sage handsomely, until it came to pass that the king's fortunes took a turn for the better. The maxim, which had once buoyed up his spirits, now angered him, and he beheaded the once-favored philosopher.

Another frequently raised objection to Stoicism is that Stoics secretly want everyone else to be as miserable as they are. Adversity is more bearable when no one around you is having a run of good luck. Loving the company of the miserable may be a fundamental human trait. Enjoying nothing so much as the sad tales of other people's disasters may be as universal as secretly resenting the prosperity of others or supposing they must be lying about it. But sharing human characteristics is not the same as having a consistent theory of happiness.

But why should our idea of happiness have to be rational, or arrived at through logical means? The answer is, of course, that it doesn't have to be. We need not even entertain *any* belief about happiness. But Stoicism is based on the rational control of the emotions and so assumes the validity of the rational process. We could say, then, that yet another basis for criticizing Stoicism is that the Stoic is guided by something that appears to be reason, but actually is not.

Very often what passes for reason should really be called rationalizing, a process by which we find workable rather than logical reasons for believing something. The possibility exists that control for the Stoic actually means manipulating thoughts so that reality becomes bearable. When loved ones stop calling, do we endure the absence by admitting the possibility that they have transferred their affections or have ceased to be interested in us for this or that reason? Or do we more likely find acceptable reasons, such as a sudden trip out of town because of a relative's illness? The trip may well turn out to be the actual reason, but the point is that we pick and choose among comfortable versions of reality, bearing unpleasantness so long as it seems under our control. In this way, what masquerades as stoic resignation is secretly a way of gaining control over reality itself.

Classical Stoicism emerged from two cultures, the Greek and the Roman, which were fate oriented. The universe was run by all-powerful deities who could

*Suppose that the ad hoc Stoic—the person who adopts this philosophy out of sheer desperation—suddenly experiences a reversal of fortune.*

and did intervene in human affairs whenever they chose. The gods and goddesses were capricious, but human reason could counteract heavenly whimsy by expecting ill times before they occurred. In other words, the universe of the Greeks and Romans was predictably full of disaster. But perhaps the universe really does not make even that much sense. Perhaps disasters are no less certain than continual success. A very strong criticism of Stoicism is thus a recognition of the debilitating passivity that it can inspire. Expecting to fail has kept many a potential winner from even getting started.

*Expecting to fail has kept many a potential winner from even getting started.*

## Aristotle: Happiness Is Not Pleasure

For Aristotle (384-322 B.C.), Plato's famous pupil and founder of the Lyceum, an early version of the liberal arts college, happiness was a major concern. In fact, it was central to his curriculum—almost, we could say, the most important object of study. In analyzing this most complex of phenomena, Aristotle concluded that happiness is not a state to be experienced but a concept to be comprehended—a concept crucial to education, since it is the very goal for which we live.

### Pleasure, a Limited Goal; Happiness, a Complete Goal

Aristotle's great work on the conduct of living is called *The Nicomachean Ethics*. In analyzing the things that can be said to make life good, Aristotle was led to his famous theory of happiness. Since the pleasure creed was very much in the air, Aristotle gave it a fair share of reflection. He agreed that pleasure must be counted as something that makes life good. Obviously nobody hates having it. Nobody refuses to experience it when the occasion arises. But, he added, if pleasure is to be considered life's *highest* good, it must be our ultimate goal. It must be worth having for its own sake, and, once achieved, it cannot cause us to desire anything beyond it.

*If pleasure makes us happy, then it is a means, not an end.*

The hedonists, of course, claimed that there *was* no good greater than pleasure. As if to give them their due, Aristotle agreed that "any good thing . . . is made more desirable by the addition of pleasure." When you add pleasure to something good, the result is something even better. Can anyone deny this? We can imagine ancient hedonists shaking their head no. Then the master logician strikes!

In modern-day terms, let us suppose that a woman, popular with her office colleagues, is promoted to management. She likes her work and has traded family ties for a business career, at which she has been eminently successful. The promotion reinforces her view that both present and future are going her way. Under such circumstances, could anyone believe the promotion to be anything but a great good?

*Every good thing is sought in order that, by possessing it, one may become happy.*

*Aristotle*

To celebrate the happy occasion, the woman's colleagues invite her out for fellowship and several rounds of toasts. No one drinks to excess. There is simply the slow and mellow "attitude adjustment" that often accompanies so happy an occasion, one that even the most ardent cynic would have to admit deserves the label *pleasure*. In terms of Aristotle's analysis, "if pleasure combined with something else is better than pleasure alone, it follows that pleasure cannot in itself be the supreme good." That is, if we allow that the promotion is certainly a very high order of good, we can see how the pleasure of companionship and a few drinks, added to the promotion, creates something better than the promotion would be by itself. But—and here is the crux—the pleasure by itself is also not as great a good as the two things combined.

To carry the analysis further, let us isolate having a few drinks as a pleasure, as indeed it must be, since so many thousands seek it out. But indulging in a "happy hour" by oneself is for most people less desirable than having company in either joy or misery. Hence we see again that pleasure can be made more enjoyable by the addition of other goods.

Since logic tells us that pleasure cannot be the highest good, is it not then a means to an end, that end being happiness? People seek pleasure to be made happy by having it; otherwise there would be no point in it. By the same token, pleasure *can* lead to misery, as when we drink too much, or when the joy of being in love with another creates an overdependency that leads to the anguish of jealousy. At such times, many would agree, the pleasure did not produce what it should have: happiness!

What all of this meant for Aristotle was that in trying to determine the highest of all goods, we could easily imagine something better than pleasure. Could we not do the same for, say, health, which some people might suggest as the highest good? Indeed, yes. What could be better than health? The answer is, the thing for the sake of which we wish to be healthy—in other words, happiness. No one would wish for health if health brought misery. When we are healthy, we have a definite sense of well-being; when we don't have that sense of well-being, then we fail to be healthy to that extent. (Nowadays, healthiness includes mental as well as physical health.)

What of other possible contenders? Wealth, for example—or, in any event, "sufficient means"? Can we deny that the need to have financial security, for the poor especially, must rank close to the top in priority? But that person would have to be mentally ill indeed who became obsessed with the acquisition of wealth solely for itself. The American novelist Frank Norris used this obsession to characterize a dangerously sick woman in his novel *McTeague* (1899). The hero's wife, wanting not only to have money, but to possess it physically, keeps her money in gold coins:

> She would lock the door, open her trunk, and pile all her little hoard on her table. By now it was four hundred and seven dollars and fifty cents. Trina would play with this money by the hour, piling it and repiling it. . . . She polished the gold pieces with a mixture of soap and ashes until they shone. . . . Or again, she would draw the heap lovingly toward her and bury her face in it, delighted at the smell of it and the feel of the smooth, cool metal on her cheeks. She even put the smaller gold pieces in her mouth and jingled them there.[1]

For the average person, wealth, like health, can be separated from a greater good for the sake of which it is desirable: something, that is, *better* than wealth. This something is, again, happiness. Why have financial security if we are made miserable because of it?

Other goods we seek in order to be made happy include friendship, virtue, and wisdom. The last two Aristotle places in a special category because they are so close to happiness itself that they could *almost* be said to be equivalents. Once having attained an upstanding moral character and developed the mind to

*For Aristotle, the means to happiness are virtue, wisdom, health, sufficient means, and friendship, with the first two the most important.*

the fullest of its potential, we cannot fail to be happy. Surely these two goods never lead to anything *but* happiness. The perfectly virtuous and learned person may lack all of life's other goods without being one whit less happy. A high moral character guarantees that all relationships will be good ones, and reason controls any negativity that other wants could inspire.

The result of Aristotle's analysis is the recognition that happiness is indeed the highest good—and therefore the goal for which we live—because, having attained it, we can desire nothing else. Can we advance any reason for wishing to be happy? No, and we cannot even imagine having to do so. The question "Now that I'm perfectly happy, what is next?" cannot be made by the rational person. To no other good in life can we attribute total self-sufficiency.

While some twenty-five hundred years have rolled by since this theory was set forth, we must still regard it with awe and respect. People are *still* confusing happiness with the things they need to make them happy—and wondering why they are not yet satisfied. Obviously the new car in the driveway is not the goal itself. Aristotle's analysis also explains why the car may make us happy for a time, but not indefinitely. Only happiness in its pure essence endures through time. What we can say is that we change, but it doesn't. We glimpse it if we are lucky.

## How to Reevaluate Your Life in Aristotelian Terms

Revisiting the past in order to become familiar with a significant Greek philosophical achievement is more than paying tribute to lasting genius. Aristotle's theory continues to have many implications for us. One of the most striking, if unexpected, of these is the realization that *happiness in itself is not directly experienced*. We know we are happy by having in our hands the means to that end.

Another statement by Aristotle may help us to grasp this all-important point: Happiness is the quality of a life that has been made good by the presence of

*Edward Hopper,* Nighthawks *(1942): The temporary absence of happiness-bringing things. (Friends of American Art Collection. The Art Institute of Chicago, All Rights Reserved)*

good things. A life that in retrospect is seen to have included health, wealth, pleasure, friendship, and especially virtue and wisdom can be said to have been a happy one. But the things that carry us to that quality are what we experience along the way. By the same token, the temporary absence of some of those things deludes us into believing we are unhappy.

We can compare happiness to the ordinary air we breathe. Constantly around us, it becomes a factor when we cannot get enough of it, when, for example, a blockage of some sort exists in our windpipe. Hospital attendants then place a tube inside us, which permits air to pass into the lungs. We say we feel "relief," and are very likely to give thanks to the tube rather than to the air itself. We may even claim that the tube has saved our life. But that same tube, resting pointlessly on a hospital shelf, is not a life-saving instrument. Merely to hold the tube in our hands during times of normal breathing is not even sensible.

Unhappiness can be identified with the temporary absence of happiness-bringing things in the same way that patient discomfort can be identified with the temporary absence of an air-supplying tube. We can lack for air for a time without dying. Likewise, we can lack for health, wealth, and so on *without having to say that our life is an unhappy one*. Logic does not require that a happy life be defined as one in which the things that bring happiness are always present or present in equal amounts.

Consider this remarkable passage by Austrian psychiatrist Viktor Frankl, who was held prisoner at Auschwitz and, though continually in fear of imminent death, managed to be happy:

> The size of human suffering is absolutely relative. . . . It also follows that a very trifling thing can cause the greatest of joys. Take as an example something that happened on our journey from Auschwitz to the camp affiliated with Dachau. We had all been afraid that our transport was heading for the Mauthausen camp. We became more and more tense as we approached a certain bridge over the Danube which the train would have to cross in order to reach Mauthausen. . . . Those who have never seen anything similar cannot possibly imagine the dance of joy performed in the carriage by the prisoners when they saw that our transport was not crossing the bridge and was instead heading "only" for Dachau.[2]

In addition to the immediate realization that the prisoners were not going to the camp that meant certain death, Frankl, as we learn, retained his wisdom (including a life-saving sense of humor) and his moral character, which were for Aristotle the two major happiness-bringing conditions. Having these, Frankl would, in Aristotle's view, have possessed all he needed.

Many would argue—and not without some justification—that merely knowing your life will be assessed as a happy one after you have died is insufficient compensation for the lack of tangible evidence along the way. How about just a bit more wealth here and an occasional visit by a close friend there? How about the pleasure of having someone dear sitting next to you once in a while and holding your hand? Is this too much to ask?

Since virtue and wisdom are the closest of life's goods to actual happiness itself, we *can* experience the knowledge that ours is a happy life by deliberately improving our minds (using every means possible) and by always making choices that are in accord with rational codes of conduct among civilized people.

*How about the pleasure of having someone dear sitting next to you once in a while and holding your hand? Is this too much to ask?*

Having proceeded this far in his analysis, Aristotle knew that he had made a portentous discovery, not just about happiness, but about the very reason for which we live. Virtue and wisdom were the sentinels of happiness, the *bodyguards*, if you will. Nothing could provide more compelling justifications for existing than those states and the actions that manifested them. In other words, happiness was the complete goal of life, and those who displayed virtue and wisdom in their deeds gave clearest indication of having come close to it.

Aristotle went further. Having deduced the purpose of living as becoming happy, and practicing virtue and wisdom as the sure means of getting there, he wrote that human society and its institutions must exist for no reason other than to promote that end and those means. The political state could not logically exist to promote only the well-being of those in power, for, in so doing, it would be working against the well-being of everyone else.

But law and order in the well-regulated state are necessary to help people realize their ultimate purpose. People must be protected against their own baser natures so that their higher potential may be realized. State-supported education, we can say, exists in order that the mind can grow and the rational powers can become stronger. (How different from some modern assumptions about the direct and exclusive relationship between education and jobs!)

---

### How would Aristotle view these statements?

It is not enough to succeed. Others must fail.

Gore Vidal

Tragedy is if *I* cut my finger. Comedy is if *you* walk into an open sewer and die.

Mel Brooks

---

The reason Aristotle, like Plato before him, did not favor democracy is that he did not believe enough people had sufficiently developed rational powers to make decisions for their own good, let alone for that of others. He did not believe that the majority could be trusted to act in every instance with moral integrity. Hence rulers were necessary, but rulers could never forget that their job was to use their intellect to bring about the happiness of their people. Presumably our elected leaders understand the identical mandate.

*Aristotle did not favor democracy, because he did not believe the majority could be trusted to act in every instance with moral integrity.*

We assume that in the back of their minds, present-day leaders of state, both in the Western world and elsewhere, agree with Aristotle in principle. The only question we might raise is whether their view of happiness is always the same as the people's. More than likely, *both* can be confused about what happiness truly means and how it may be attained. Happiness is not a luxury; while, as Viktor Frankl demonstrates, it can be achieved despite appalling conditions, the state should guarantee that all reasonable measures are taken to remove the barriers that can make the practice of virtue and wisdom difficult indeed: barriers like hunger, illiteracy, and discrimination. What other reason can government have for existing?

## Possible Limitations of Aristotle's View

As often happens when we follow the impeccable, almost surgical, clarity of a great thinker like Aristotle, we nod, say, "Yes, how logical," then go back to the everyday world, which seems as confusing as ever. For example, a seldom-mentioned fringe benefit of the sheltered academic life is the scholar's ability to spend time in the company of great minds without their ever making the least bit of difference beyond the hallowed pages that preserve them. In the case of happiness, however, the appropriate definition ought to be one that *does* make a difference for all of us.

An alternative to the Aristotelian analysis of happiness is the personal example of people who have provided role models of the happy life and therefore deserve a place in the history of philosophy.

There are people to consider like Gandhi and Martin Luther King, Jr. Both of them advocated nonviolent resistance to oppression and, in so doing, triggered hostile reactions even among those they were trying to help. Both of them knew very well how dangerous it was to stand by uncompromising principles in the name of a cause higher than their own well-being. Both of them finally paid the supreme price for their cause. Can we say that Gandhi and King willingly sacrificed their happiness for a higher good? Or can we say that Gandhi and King were indeed happy men, even when most beset by danger?

*A possible limitation of Aristotle's theory is its assumption that the personal achievement of the good life is all that matters.*

A possible limitation of Aristotle's theory is its assumption that the personal achievement of the good life is all that matters. Take away the martyrdom of Gandhi and King—take away the universal significance of their deaths and the impact of their beliefs on millions of people they never met—and have you not lessened the degree to which their lives can be said to have been good? Now suppose that both men had preferred to practice virtue in a modest, everyday fashion, without martyrdom, and to allow a calm rationality to govern every decision. Surely their lives would still deserve to be called good, but perhaps not *as* good. Involvement in a cause that transcends one's personal happiness may bring *greater* happiness. In short, the Aristotelian analysis would seem not to discriminate among levels of good, though we could still argue that in Aristotle's time there existed no role model of humanitarianism. If we make allowances for social and cultural differences from one era to another, today's person of unimpeachable reason and virtue, unlike such a person in ancient Greece, would inevitably be led to the larger causes of injustice and deprivation.

*How much time he gains who does not look to see what his neighbor says or does or thinks, but only at what he does himself, to make it just and holy.*

*Marcus Aurelius*

But there is also the case of the many thousands who do not or cannot take the extreme steps of Gandhi or King, but who nonetheless care deeply about, say, the environment. These people find they cannot be personally happy in the midst of so much that is clearly wrong. They join the ranks of people who, though reasonably comfortable in their standard of living, think about hungry children in Asia or street people in New York—people for whom complete happiness requires a very different kind of world, particularly one in which responsible leaders do not even *think* about "winning" a nuclear war. The cynic might argue that those made chronically unhappy by the state of the world are secret hedonists who worry about their own loss of pleasure in these dangerous and corrupt times. But the chronically unhappy might argue right back that the cynics are taking the path of least resistance and finding quick and easy happiness regardless of the cost.

In any event, one good that Aristotle does not place near the top of his list is love, a fact that might strike some readers as surprising. That many prize love above all other goods tells us we cannot leave it out of consideration. On the other hand, Aristotle might well argue that unlike virtue and wisdom, love depends upon how others feel and what they do, that is, not on the exercise of a person's own rational powers and self-discipline. Making happiness equivalent to or dependent upon feelings of love might be to build extreme limitations before we even begin the quest.

The unhappiness brought about by the absence of love is, however, so universally recognized and shared that even the very hope of one day finding an ideal love is enough to reverse that condition for many people. Popular songs, magazine stories, and countless motion pictures have for years conveyed the same message: What good is having money, fame, even health, if one is unlucky in love? Here the myth—if indeed that's what ideal love can be called—is so powerful that the continual quest may itself be happiness. While many fall in love with love, they fall *out* of love with a particular partner. Lost love is certainly not a myth for millions of us, and thus the poets' and songmakers' expectation of finding the "new love" can also be very real. The glorification of the unending search for love indicates its importance to many of us.

As people grow older, they tend to substitute words like *companionship* and *understanding* for *love*. May we then say that the requirements for happiness can change with age? Some of the good things on Aristotle's list may indeed change with age. Those who are 65 and don't have *sufficient* means may well settle for barely getting by and not be unhappy. So too with health. You may reach an age at which you neither feel well continually nor expect to, but find happiness during times of relatively less infirmity. Or perhaps you can make a substitution for health altogether. Aristotle, of course, would contend that the two major requirements for happiness—virtue and wisdom—change with age only in the respect that they can and should shine more brightly.

Still, viewing the subject of happiness from the perspective of aging presents us with yet a final possibility: *work*. There are two senses in which we can understand the relationship between work and happiness. In the first, we achieve happiness by day-to-day activities that are meaningful, and we define *meaningful* in the way most appropriate for the circumstances of our life. The Manhattan executive, for whom a typical workday includes breathlessly catching a cab, holding 12 conferences, firing an employee, skipping lunch, and finally sinking into the leatherette peace of a stately hotel bar, may be less than satisfied by trading places with an Iowa farmer. The latter, on the other hand, might find the frenetic New York tempo absurd and pointless. Assembly-line workers who have never had a personal relationship with any final product may still miss their jobs after retirement and may *not* look back with sadness upon a life that Thoreau might have characterized as one of "quiet desperation." The author of a financially successful best-seller, envied by hundreds of unpublished garret dwellers, may secretly be ashamed of the "trash" he or she has written and ardently long for a burst of true inspiration.

In another sense, however, we achieve happiness only after doing work of universal meaningfulness, work that others recognize and applaud. Bertrand Russell, who lived into his nineties and stopped writing only at the very end, once said in an interview that nothing quite equals the satisfaction of having completed a really significant piece of work. For him this meant the publication of a provocative contribution to human thought that would be hailed by people of letters throughout the world. For the average person, "really significant" work is anything that requires the realization of an inner potential. Assembly-line workers may miss their job because they have never known anything else, but they still may be

*We achieve happiness after doing work of universal meaningfulness, work that others recognize and applaud.*

*Tsugouharu Foujita,* Cafe: The unhappiness brought about by the absence of love. *(Musée Nationale d'Art Moderne, Paris)*

vaguely aware of talents never developed and words of praise never heard. Socrates is famous for having told the court, "The unexamined life is not worth living." Perhaps we can add, "And the unaccomplished life is not worth having been lived."

On the other hand, what shall we say of those who walk with leaden steps through life, dissatisfaction written all over their face? Those who have not accomplished anything because they "know" they have potential but do not know what they can in reality *do*? While the poet Browning made himself famous by advising that "man's reach should exceed his grasp," he was not implying, as some no doubt believe, that no limits to achievement need ever exist. Perhaps the trick is to assess our resources fully, be stern and uncompromising with ourselves, and *then* create realistic expectations.

A clear-headed attitude toward the appropriateness of the work we choose to do is, therefore, a major consideration. Epictetus advised, "Desire that things be as they are." We can borrow that advice without necessarily becoming a complete Stoic, for Stoicism *can* make us relax a bit too soon, pull back with the finish line in sight, because "I probably wouldn't win anyway."

Literature is filled with admiration for the unrealistic striver. Cervantes created Don Quixote as a way of making fun of silly old romances, but appears instead to have given us the mad but wonderful gentleman who makes us weep as well as laugh when he undertakes the impossible task of restoring the golden age of chivalry. The apparently indestructible quixotism of the impossible dream is summed up in this poem by Stephen Crane:

> *I saw a man pursuing the horizon;*
> *Round and round they sped.*
> *I was disturbed at this;*
> *I accosted the man.*
> *"It is futile," I said,*

*. . . there must be a minimum of ignorance in order to perfect a life in happiness.*

Albert Camus

*Much madness is divinest sense—/To a discerning eye.*

Emily Dickinson

*"You can never—"*
*"You lie," he cried,*
*And ran on.*

In another corner sits the cynical but self-styled "realist," who advises us to become reconciled to boring routines on the grounds that nothing is worth trying anyway. In yet another corner, we have others espousing what amounts to the folk wisdom of our time and society: "Winning isn't everything; it's the *only* thing." While some tell us it's how we play the game that matters, Leo Durocher, the peppery manager of the old Brooklyn Dodgers, left his mark on our national consciousness with an incisive and curt "Nice guys finish last."

What work can mean and how "successful" we must be at it in order to make us happy has yet to be given definitive expression. Aristotle, as we have said, didn't mention it, perhaps because the nature and purpose of an individual's life did not in his time and place revolve around work, as they seem to do from *our* vantage point. The least that can be said is that a modern theory of happiness should include a vision of work and its relative importance to the totality of our lives.

## Glossary

*Epicureanism:* A philosophy of happiness developed and taught by Epicurus in third-century B.C. Athens. It takes exception to hedonism in particular, arguing that what makes life good is not the amount of pleasure experienced, but the absence of pain. It urges moderation in all things, for pain usually results from excess.

*hedonism:* A philosophy, advanced in fifth-century B.C. Athens by Aristippus and his followers, which holds that the happy life is one characterized by an abundance of physical pleasures. It is rooted in the assumption that human beings are selfish animals, dedicated—and rightly so—to their own enjoyments.

*Stoicism:* A philosophy, developed originally by Zeno, a Cypriot, in the third century B.C. and raised almost to the level of a national belief system by the Romans, which strongly influenced early Christian ideology. Its basic premise is that if one cannot control painful external events, one can control one's response to them and thus become relatively immune to pain.

## Notes

1. Frank Norris, *McTeague* (Cambridge, Mass.: Robert Bentley, 1971), 238.
2. Viktor Frankl, *Man's Search for Meaning: An Introduction to Logotherapy* (New York: Pocket Books, 1971), 70.

## Suggested Reading

Aristotle. *The Nichomachean Ethics.* There's no better way to delve into the still-viable Aristotelian theory of happiness than by reading the original.

Barrow, Robin. *Utilitarianism: A Contemporary Statement.* Brookfield, Vt.: Ashgate, 1991. The author comes to the defense of the utilitarian view of happiness. He says it is not completely hedonistic but places great value on beauty and moral integrity as sources of the good life.

Fisher, M. F. K. "Serve It Forth." In *The Art of Eating*. New York: Collier/Macmillan, 1991. A dedicated Epicurean expert on food and dining criticizes American "ham and cherry coke" culture for its insensitivity to the higher culinary arts.

Freud, Sophie. *My Three Mothers and Other Passions*. New York: New York University Press, 1988. The granddaughter of the famed psychoanalyst presents her views, many of them quite startling, about the nature of the fulfilled life. She displays an uncanny open-mindedness and broad tolerance for the lifestyles of dedicated people and has no inclination to advise others on how to live so long as their chosen way is not tearing them apart.

Merton, Thomas. *The Seven Storey Mountain*. New York: Harcourt, Brace, 1948. The classic autobiography of a very spiritual man who gave up many worldly advantages to become a Trappist monk.

Naranjo, Claudio. *How to Be: Meditation in Spirit and Practice*. Los Angeles: Tarcher, 1991. This book points out that meditation and medicine are closely related, each deriving from a Latin root word meaning "to care" as well as "to cure." The author believes the key to mental health is ancient meditative practices, which he explains in detail.

Simon, Neil. *The Prisoner of Second Avenue*. New York: Random House, 1972. We might call this play "early" Simon, but it is due for a revival soon. A dark comedy about the stressful New York existence of an upper-middle-class couple suddenly thrown smack into reality when the husband loses his job. Coping with existence in the indifferent and polluted city is not easy, and the author doesn't see much hope for the future. Simon didn't intend it, but the play can easily be viewed as a stinging critique of our hedonistic values, which leave us in a hopeless daze when disaster strikes.

Toffler, Alvin. *Future Shock*. New York: Random House, 1970. By now a classic, this work offers a detailed analysis of our present sense of alienation and bewilderment, which comes from the ever-accelerating rate at which change occurs. More than two decades after the book's publication, we can say with certainty that the rate of change has increased and that what Toffler predicted—especially the dizzying neuroses—has come to pass.

*Vincent van Gogh,* Hospital Corridor at Saint Remy *(1889)  (Gouache and watercolor, 24-1/8 x 18-5/8". Collection, The Museum of Modern Art, New York. Abby Aldrich Rockefeller Bequest)*

# 14

# *Coping with Death*

## *Overview*

For many, the fact of death is something to be ignored until it cannot be avoided. Such people believe that death is a "morbid" subject, and that only sick minds would dwell on it. To them the very word conjures up subliminal flashes of dark tombs, hollow corridors, skeletons, ghosts, solemn organ chords, gray caskets, cemeteries, the odor of flowers, tapered candles, a guest book on a fragile stand, whispers in a side room.

In one sense humanity has invented the very death it traditionally shuns. Throughout the history of the arts, people have painted this death, sung about it, spoken in trembling or resolute voice about that which no one knows for certain. Such images of death swirl around inside us, and small wonder that sometimes we want to close them off, push them into the subconscious—until the "proper" time, which is the hated time, the unfair time. Everything else about living—even the rough times—can be dealt with. But why must we die? How do we deal with *that*?

*And all our yesterdays have lighted fools
The way to dusty death.*

*Shakespeare*

383

The arts—especially what we sometimes call the popular arts—are perennial sources of negative death images. Ever since the middle of the eighteenth century, readers have gorged themselves on what used to be called "penny dreadfuls," set in haunted houses, dreary castles, remote inns—all with sliding panels, bodies hanging on closet hooks, distant shrieks of terror. Nowadays the penny dreadfuls cost twenty dollars or so and reward their authors with lucrative screen contracts. No celluloid image of gore can, apparently, be too horrible for us popcorn-eaters. Audiences are particularly fond of watching teenagers being slaughtered in all manner of clever ways during a summer vacation. Is it perhaps that we enjoy torturing ourselves with a superabundance of the very thing we hate to think about? Is it that we fear death less if we camp the subject? Or maybe we like to see others die in the popular arts because it takes our minds off what must in reality eventually happen to us.

*Maybe we like to see others die in the popular arts because it takes our minds off what must in reality eventually happen to us.*

All the same, the frightening images of death remain. No matter what our underlying purpose may be in reading or watching the dreadfuls, we haven't really faced the issue, have we? The phone ringing in the middle of the night is something we are never prepared to answer.

We have also looked to the popular arts for escape. There will always be the improbable happy ending: The diagnosis was wrong after all, or the real murderer confesses so that the hero doesn't go to the electric chair. The mythology of denial has always been around. No one is arguing that it doesn't help some of the time. Sooner or later, however, the intelligent move is to face up to reality. If we are to be strong and skillful in being human, we must not ignore death. As in the rest of the animal kingdom, death has its rightful place in the cycle of human things.

In looking at the subject directly, we find that—far from being successful in never thinking about death—many of us die a thousand times before we have to. Surely a crucial aspect of the art of being human is to find a sane and sensible way to live with the stable awareness that we do not go on forever.

## Attitudes Toward Death

The humanities are an abundant source of death attitudes, some mournful, others inspiring. Since many of our attitudes are directly influenced by what we read in books, hear in music, or see in paintings or on screens (both large and small), we clearly have a choice of which attitudes to be affected by.

The Greek slave Epictetus (discussed in the preceding chapter as a major exponent of the Stoic philosophy) observes, characteristically, that death in itself is not a terrible thing. The *attitude* that death must be terrible is what we really fear and what casts gloom over our last days. Rid yourself of this attitude, he advises, and the terror vanishes.

Death has been and continues to be depicted in a number of discernible ways: as an enemy, out to "get" us; as a natural event that is not horrible as long as one becomes used to the idea that life eventually ends; as a force that truly makes us all equal; as a glorious finale to the lives of the pious and the brave; and as a preordained end for which each of us is destined.

The problem death poses for many is, however, less a matter of choosing the attitude that "works" than of becoming trapped in a crisscross of contradictory attitudes. Tension about death is often a result of holding values that struggle against each other. One would *like* to believe the self is not central to the operation of the universe, but at the same time one somehow manages to reduce all concerns to self-interest. Or one might *say* an afterlife is definitely waiting, but nonetheless behave as though the pleasures of this life were all that matter. Viewed from this perspective, our death attitudes often constitute traumas that we could avoid with some insight into our beliefs.

## Death as Personal Enemy

Starting with the most pervasive image of death, we see "him" as the dark-robed phantom that either pursues us or waits in silence around the next corner. He pounces upon us without warning. Or with infinite cunning he leads us to an unjust and unexpected doom.

The idea that death is the final result of a struggle against odds that will fatally overwhelm us, however unfair the inevitable outcome, probably stems from the hero myth, a dominant myth of Western civilization (see Chapter 11) in which nearly superhuman heroes fight bravely against powerful foes. Sometimes the heroes win all battles and we hear no more about them—a version of the story that makes us all the more unprepared to accept the finality of death. Sometimes they win all battles but one. The greater these heroes are, the more irreplaceable they are shown to be and the more unacceptable is their death.

A cherished aspect of the hero myth depicts the realm of death as a mysterious place to which brave heroes go when they have accomplished all they can. Since we cannot bear to think they have physically died, we willingly believe they have sailed to Avalon, like King Arthur, or to the Grey Havens, like Frodo, hero of the popular trilogy *Lord of the Rings* (1955):

> And the ship went out into the High Sea and passed on into the West, until at last on a night of rain Frodo smelled a sweet fragrance on the air and heard the sound of singing that came over the water. . . . [A]nd he beheld white shores and beyond them a far green country under a swift sunrise.[1]

The Grey Havens is not, we must understand, a literary version of heaven, the Christian abode of the blessed after death. Neither Arthur nor Frodo is ever shown undergoing the physical act of dying. Never do they experience the cruel pain that Christ suffered on the cross or Joan of Arc at the stake. The pain-free death of Arthur and Frodo borrows from the Greek vision of the Elysian fields, a special land of immortality for warriors felled in battle who are whisked away before the stroke of death. Perhaps such myths are the source of our euphemism "pass away," which seems to circumvent the physical reality.

These stories, as well as the image of death as the Grim Reaper, indicate that the actual *moment* is deeply feared in our civilization, intensifying the belief in death as personal enemy. Perhaps for this reason we tend to be thankful when we hear that someone has indeed "passed away" during sleep. If the Grim Reaper *must* come, the least he can do is not let us know about it.

While the pain of death is naturally a source of great fear, there is also a strong correlation between fearing death and placing a huge and usually unquestioned value on the sheer act of *being*. We seldom put the word *die* in a sentence involving us. The furthest we want to go in talking about a future in which we are not around is perhaps to start a sentence with "If, God forbid, anything should

*What did it matter if he existed for two or for twenty years? Happiness was the fact that he existed.*

*Albert Camus*

*In the midst of the current technological emphasis on the success story of healing, the patient whose disease cannot be cured, the human being who is dying is inexorably perceived to be a failure to the health professions.*

*Elisabeth Kübler-Ross*

*Aubrey Beardsley,* The Pestilence: *The dark-robed phantom that waits in silence around the next corner.*

happen to me . . ." Even when we are businesslike and make out a will or purchase a cemetery plot well in advance, we have a difficult time thinking realistically about not being—in particular, not being *ourselves.*

The terror of ceasing to be ourselves will never stop tormenting us so long as our culture indulges in the worship of singularity. Unless one is born into a large rural family in which everyone has to work as soon as possible for the survival of the group and no one has time to lavish attention on a particular family member, one is usually raised to be self-centered. One is encouraged to aspire to great heights and to vicariously identify with those who succeed. In this context death is viewed as the great failure, hence a great injustice, for unless one dies at 95 having "lived to a ripe old age," one should always, of course, be alive and striving.

Believing in the injustice of the personal enemy is secretly an inward act of adoration. Well, you say, so be it. Is it not the nature of humankind to be self-centered? The answer is, perhaps not.

*In many a village in Mexico I have seen what happens when social security arrives. For a generation people continue in their traditional beliefs; they know how to deal with death, dying, and grief. The new nurse and the doctor . . . teach them about a Pantheon of evil clinical deaths, each one of which can be banned, at a price.*

*Ivan Illich*

## Death Without Self-Interest

It may come as a distinct surprise to some readers, but the slogan *Looking out for number one* is *not* as old as the hills. Nor is it universally accepted today. When an activity is more important than the person who acts, the myth of death as personal enemy is less influential as a molder of values. Think, if you will, of a research specialist who, having been told that she or he has a terminal illness, replies: "But the work will nonetheless proceed."

Socrates, the father of philosophy, must have had selfhood, but there is no evidence that he was preoccupied with self*ness.* In all the accounts of Socrates that Plato has given us, the mentor seems out of touch with himself in our sense of what *himself* means. Found guilty of alleged crimes against the state, Socrates was given a choice: death by poison, or a life in exile without the right to engage in free inquiry or philosophical discussion. Socrates chose death. Why? The answer, it seems, is that the activity of philosophy meant more to him than life. Without the activity there would be no point in living. The importance or the preservation of personal identity does not appear to have been the issue:

*Those of us who think that death is an evil are in error.*

*Plato*

> Someone will say: Yes, Socrates, but cannot you hold your tongue, and then you may go into a foreign city, and no one will interfere with you? Now I have great difficulty in making you understand my answer to this. For if I tell you . . . that I cannot hold my tongue, you will not believe that I am serious; and if I say again that daily to discourse about virtue, and of those other things about which you hear me examining myself and others, is the greatest good of man, and that the unexamined life is not worth living, you are still less likely to believe me.[2]

Assuming that Plato's portrait of Socrates is accurate—that Socrates was generally concerned with the mental act of reaching an understanding of certain absolutes like justice, virtue, and beauty—we do not detect any indication that Socrates was ever defensive or artificial. He always seems to have been genuinely interested in seeking wisdom and not at all interested in making people feel sorry for him or afraid of him. On his final day, when he drinks the poison, surrounded by the young intellectuals who adore him, Socrates shows a singular absence of self-consciousness. He sounds willing to let go of his hold on his own identity. He does not say, "Remember always what I have taught you" or "Promise to keep going what I have begun."

*To the question "If I should die, would you ever love anyone else?" the reply "Surely you would want me to find someone else" would not be understood, or there would not have been such a question to begin with.*

*Jacques Louis David,* The Death of Socrates *(1788): On his final day, Socrates shows a singular absence of self-consciousness. (The Metropolitan Museum of Art, Wolfe Fund, 1931. Catherine Lorillard Wolfe Collection. 31.45)*

Thus when Phaedo, one of the followers, observes that the master has drunk the poison "cheerfully," we have no reason to believe that Socrates was struggling to put on a brave act in front of his friends. And then there occurs a most telling statement:

> And hitherto most of us had been able to control our sorrow; but now when we saw him drinking, and saw too that he had finished the draught, we could no longer forbear, and in spite of myself my own tears were flowing fast; so that I covered my face and wept, not for him, but at the thought of my own calamity in having to part from such a friend.[3]

Phaedo's weeping for himself rather than for Socrates reminds us that the inability to cope with the death of another is more personal than we often realize. Is it perhaps a resentment that the personal enemy has struck rather too close to home? Is it an unwillingness to alter the daily course of one's own life to accommodate the disappearance of a component of that life?

Imagine two very dear friends who share pleasure in the same things. Perhaps they enjoy art, politics, sports, religion. They like to attend concerts, ball games, and the latest films. They enjoy trying new dishes at different restaurants. Neither suffers from an oversized ego or a neurotic inner sense of inferiority, so that neither one needs the other's self as complement or reinforcement to his or her own. Each enjoys the other as an important source of delight in a world of other delights, on the order of, but to a greater or lesser degree than, magnificent music. It is possible to suppose that the death of one can be accepted by the other without its having a shattering effect, without its leaving a void in a life that can never be filled. There is a certain rhythm to the existence of the mourner. There will be some grief—a normal and probably universal emotional response to death. But the stride will not break. Life will make the necessary adjustment—and move on. The reason is that the one who is still alive is strong enough not to need a reinforcement of identity. As with Socrates, the activities rather than the concentration on self have been central in life, and will continue to be.

Insecure lovers sometimes test each other with questions like "If I should die, would you ever get over it?" or "If I should die, would you ever love anyone else?" The expected answer is usually "No—I'd be miserable forever, if I didn't have you!" A reply like "Surely you would want me to find someone else" would not be understood, or there would not have been such a question to begin with.

*So, when our mortal frame
shall be disjoin'd,
The lifeless lump uncoupled
from the mind,
From sense of grief and
pain we shall be free;
We shall not feel, because
we shall not be.*

*Lucretius*

*Without death there would
scarcely have been poets on
earth.*

*Thomas Mann*

## Death the Leveler

We have said that death lends meaning to life, but sometimes it does so negatively. For some people the inevitable fact of death makes life mean precisely *nothing*. The fact of death causes a total reversal of the dominant life plan in our society: Grow up and become something; be successful at what you have become; surround yourself with the visible trappings of that success; and then think, as you age, of leaving behind a legacy for the future, some tangible embodiment of your having lived. Instead, some people decide in advance that the struggle makes no sense when they will not be around long enough to enjoy the spoils.

During the Renaissance the fact of death came to be viewed in a manner far different from the medieval Christian outlook. In the Middle Ages the true believer had no choice but to think of death as a happy exit from this vale of tears. Life was pain; death was release. Death was a passage to an eternal existence in paradise. This attitude can still be found in some parts of the Christian world; in Puerto Rico, for example, the death of an innocent young child is a cause for joyous celebration.

The Renaissance, of course, assigned a higher value to both human life and to the world in which it took place. People were less certain that there *was* a world beyond this one, or, if there were, that it was necessarily a better world. Renaissance poets sang the glories of love and other youthful sports that were here to be enjoyed, but as often as not they ended by brooding over the inevitable passing of youth. Yes, Renaissance art and architecture surrounded those who were alive with rich and sensuous color; Renaissance literature resounded with the clear tolling bells of passionate communication. But underneath the pomp and the glitter ran a deep vein of melancholy: We are born; some of us move on to greatness; the power of a signature can change the destiny of thousands; yet in the end all comes to nothing.

Shakespeare's works are obsessed with images of decomposition and a sometimes tragic, sometimes bitterly comic awareness of the final indignity that awaits us all. *Hamlet*, perhaps the greatest of all plays, is many things surely, one of them a vast and complex meditation on death. Hamlet says:

> What a piece of work is a man! how noble in reason! how infinite in faculty! in form and moving how express and admirable! in action how like an angel! in apprehension how like a god! the beauty of the world! the paragon of animals! And yet, to me, what is this quintessence of dust?[4]

The famous graveyard scene could almost be removed from the intricate context of the tragedy and played on its own as perhaps the most disquieting literary work on the futility of life ever penned. At the opening of the scene Hamlet comes upon two clowns digging a grave for what Hamlet does not yet know is the remains of Ophelia, the girl he has loved but who has gone mad and drowned herself. There is much joking between the gravediggers over the fact that the drowned woman is to be given a Christian burial, though they are certain this would not be the case had she been a commoner. Their irreverent banter sets the tone for the rest of the scene. Christian burial or not, commoners and noblepersons all wind up rotting in the earth.

Hamlet and his closest friend, Horatio, come upon the macabre proceedings. Fascinated by the place, Hamlet pokes about in the dirt and finds the skull of the late court jester, a man he remembers from his childhood as having been full of life and joy. Hamlet says:

> Alas, poor Yorick! I knew him, Horatio: a fellow of infinite jest, of most excellent fancy: he hath borne me on his back a thousand times; and now, how abhorred in my imagination it is! my gorge rises at it. Here hung those lips that I have kissed I know not how oft. Where be your gibes now? your gambols? your songs? your flashes of merriment that were wont to set the table on a roar? Not one now, to mock your own grinning? quite chap-fallen? Now get you to my lady's chamber, and tell her, let her paint an inch thick, to this favour she must come; make her laugh at that.[5]

So appalling is the fact of death, so powerful is this scene of decay that a mournful response is beside the point. All one can do—if one has any human feelings at all—is laugh. Then Hamlet decides (a few lines later in the same scene) that the greater the person, the more amusing death becomes: "To what base uses we may return, Horatio! Why may not imagination trace the noble dust of Alexander, till he find it stopping a bung-hole?"

Earlier in the play, Hamlet, continually obsessed with the idea of life's futility, has contemplated suicide—an option that is for many both sane and rational and that we shall discuss in a later section. But though "to be or not to be" is for Hamlet the only valid question, there is no simple answer. Death may be the common end, but who is to say what death is? If it were merely an endless sleep, an absence of consciousness, all well and good. But suppose it is something even worse than life? What then? Death is an "undiscover'd country from whose bourn/ No traveller returns." No one can tell us what may wait beyond the grave. The only course to follow is to play out the game of life until it is finally over.

If we do not know for certain what death is like, our artists generally have expressed, like Hamlet, the strong suspicion that it is nothing if not democratic. Thus does the poet Shelley in "Ozymandias" remind us of what worldly ambition amounts to:

*Looking upon death as an equalizer is not necessarily an unhealthy practice if it manages to buoy up one's sense of self-worth and impart the belief that one's goals are as valid as anybody else's.*

> *I met a traveler from an antique land*
> *Who said: Two vast and trunkless legs of stone*
> *Stand in the desert. Near them, on the sand,*
> *Half sunk, a shattered visage lies, whose frown,*
> *And wrinkled lip, and sneer of cold command,*
> *Tell that its sculptor well those passions read*
> *Which yet survive, stamped on these lifeless things,*
> *The hand that mocked them and the heart that fed;*
> *And on the pedestal these words appear:*
> *"My name is Ozymandias, king of kings:*
> *Look on my works, ye Mighty, and despair!"*
> *Nothing beside remains. Round the decay*
> *Of that colossal wreck, boundless and bare*
> *The lone and level sands stretch far away.*

Looking upon death as an equalizer is not necessarily an unhealthy practice if it manages to buoy up one's sense of self-worth and impart the belief that one's goals are as valid as anybody else's. Like many of his early-nineteenth-century contemporaries, Shelley was a champion of the poor and the oppressed, an opponent of unearned privilege, a believer in causes that contributed to the betterment of human life. This attitude says that everybody has to die and most of us may well be forgotten, but what matters is not to waste the energies and intellectual gifts one may possess. Life alone is real, and it is precious, though we must never lose sight of the destiny that unites us in brother- and sisterhood and makes despotic power unendurable.

This democratic view of death can therefore lead to either of two overall philosophies of living. One is Hamlet's: cynical, often wryly humorous, but so filled with shadows that endeavor seems hardly worth contemplating, much less pursuing. The other is life affirming.

A more recent example of Hamlet's view can be found in the writing of Ambrose Bierce (1842-1914), an American journalist whose obsession not only with death but with the belief that everything in life turns out as horribly as possible gave him the nickname "bitter Bierce." Collections of his cynical stories can be found under such engaging titles as *Cobwebs from an Empty Skull*. Though his most famous collection is *In the Midst of Life*, do not be tempted to believe the author is arguing for life affirmation; in fact, the title sentence concludes with the words *we are surrounded by death*. One of Bierce's best-known pieces is "Occurrence at Owl Creek Bridge," in which a Confederate prisoner of war who is waiting for the executioner to work imagines that he escapes and makes his way back to the arms of his beloved. So real is the fantasy that we find ourselves believing it, and the ending, in which the prisoner is suddenly hanged, seems doubly horrifying.

A contemporary of Bierce's was the poet Edwin Arlington Robinson (1869-1935), whose masterpiece "The Man Against the Sky" involves an analysis of possible approaches to living. Observing the silhouette of an unknown man walking along the crest of a hill, the poet finds himself wondering who the stranger might be and where he might be going. Of only one thing is he certain: Each of us is walking alone to a mysterious destination; each of us, alone, must determine whether the journey or the destination is meaningful.

Robinson's personal choice is an affirmation not only of life but of faith. If the end of life is veiled in mist, who is to say that what lies inside that mist is oblivion? Furthermore, if life is meaningless, why do we instinctively struggle each day, often against impossible odds, to achieve something?

> *Why pay we such a price, and one we give*
> *So clamoringly, for each racked empty day*
> *That leads one more last human hope away,*
> *As quiet friends would lead past our crazed eyes*
> *Our children to an unseen sacrifice?*
> *If all that we have lived and thought,*
> *All comes to Nought,—*
> *If there be nothing after Now,*
> *And we be nothing anyhow,*
> *And we know that,—why live?* [6]

There is still a timeliness about Robinson's essential question, Why bother, if nothing amounts to very much? The prospect of the death of civilization has been a strong concern for a number of generations now and has engendered within many not a justified cynicism but the need to engage in serious life-affirming activities that transcend a self-centered fear of extinction: activities like joining a worldwide humanitarian organization; taking part in demonstrations to protect the environment; or marshaling public support for a community need outside one's own group, such as senior citizens lobbying for school reform. The history of the humanities may well look back on our time and listen once more—and with admiration—to the songs of peace and world unity that abound despite the opportunity that is plainly here for thinking to oneself, Well, the planet is going to die soon enough, so why not have a good time?

## Death as Reward or Punishment: The Afterlife

Literature, religious sermons, music, and film often promote the prevalent idea that life continues beyond the grave. For some, the next life is literally that: A place where they will retain their earthly identities and will be reunited with loved ones, who still look and sound as they did. For others, immortality means living on in the memories of those who remain. For artists, it might mean achieving eternal life through the works they leave behind.

In Greek mythology the souls of the dead were rowed across the river Styx by Charon the ferryman. This service cost money, so the deceased was traditionally buried with a coin placed inside the mouth. At least a handful of dust had to be thrown across the body; otherwise, coin or no coin, Charon would refuse passage. Brave warriors slain in battle did not cross the Styx. Instead, they were spared the actual pain of physical death and were transported, body and soul, to a pleasant sunny land called the Elysian fields, which reminds us, in image at least, of the Christian heaven.

The latter has always been of a somewhat ambiguous nature. At times it is talked and written about as an actual place with a geography of its own, though this is not literally promised in the Christian Bible. Christ on the cross is reported to have told one of the thieves being crucified with him that he would be with him in paradise, and Christians believe that Christ, after rising from the grave, did indeed ascend bodily into heaven. Yet it is not clear that after death people continue to be themselves. Movies of the 1930s and 1940s frequently show lovers reunited in the next world, looking exactly as they did in this world except that their bodies are transparent and they will be presumably forever young.

Poets—especially nineteenth-century romantic and Victorian poets—often write of the dead as if they were still alive, living on as part of nature. Thus does Tennyson console himself after the passing of his close friend Arthur Henry Hallam:

> *Thy voice is on the rolling air;*
> *I hear thee where the waters run,*
> *Thou standest in the rising sun,*
> *And in the setting thou art fair.*
>
> .   .   .   .   .   .   .   .   .   .   .   .
>
> *Far off thou art, but ever nigh;*
> *I have thee still, and I rejoice;*
> *I prosper, circled with thy voice;*
> *I shall not lose thee though I die.*[7]

Here we have a mixture of romantic *pantheism* (the belief that nature is spiritual) and the literal belief that after death there is a continuation of human relationships.

Comforting words to the bereaved often promise that the departed is better off now that he or she is with God, though even the clergy are frequently reluctant to be too literal about what the next world really is like. What is usually stressed is the condition of eternal happiness, echoed in the Hindu concept of nirvana (see Chapter 8), which is not a geographical heaven but rather the condition of being eternally free of stress and anxiety. Indeed the last thing Hindu belief wants is an afterlife that is a perpetuation of painful earthly existence.

Despite "official" Christian ambiguity, some Christian sects do seem to

*Often the vision of an afterlife is accompanied by feelings of apprehension and fear, for a good many religions have focused on judgment after death.*

guarantee a literal afterlife. For example, one bumper sticker employs the langauge of real estate: *Heaven is a real place—have you reserved your spot?* During a tent revival meeting, a minister told the faithful that heaven is very much like earth. They would need a house when they got there, and that takes money. The money they placed in the basket, he told them, would be reserved for them in the "Bank of Heaven."

In Judaism the afterlife is the memory of a good person, who lives on in charitable works and the broad impact of a life well lived. The ancient Hebrews were a realistic people, and in their Bible the stress is on the hope of a better life *here*, free of persecution and despair. Canaan, the Promised Land of Abraham and the covenant, is a very real place, a highly desirable fertile area still coveted by millions who inhabit the region.

Often the vision of an afterlife is accompanied by feelings of apprehension and fear, for a good many religions have focused on judgment after death. The Christian Bible contains, in the Revelation of Saint John, vivid, sometimes frightening imagery of the world's end, the second coming of Christ, and the terrible suffering awaiting the sinner. The literature of hell is as prevalent as that of heaven. Most notable is "The Inferno," the first canticle of Dante's *Divine Comedy* (1302-1321), with its detailed description of each province, the kind of sinners consigned to it, and the agony especially designed for them. If the perpetuation of the body in heaven is often a vague concept, the actual physical torments of hell have long possessed a tenacious hold on the human imagination. The metaphors are so deeply ingrained that countless millions have feared and continue to fear death because of them.

A more recent view is that the dead go off to another plane of existence, retaining their identities for a short time only. In the third and final act of Thornton Wilder's 1940 classic *Our Town*, the dead of Grover's Corners are seated at one corner of the stage, sitting in straight-backed chairs symbolic of their cemetery graves. At the other side of the stage the funeral of Emily, the play's heroine, is in progress. When Emily joins the other dead, she is told that very soon she will begin to think less and less of her life on earth and that after a while she will become indifferent to it: "When you've been here longer you'll see that our life here is to forget all that, and think only of what's ahead, and be ready for what's ahead." Emily does not understand what these words mean, not at this point; nor do we. How can we? How can anyone? The playwright is *imagining* what it's like after death. The reader is free to decide whether the imagined and undefined "what's ahead" is more comforting than the view that at the very moment of death one passes into an endless void.

## Death as Predetermined End: Fatalism

Fatalism is both a serious philosophy and a popular death attitude. It was the foundation of Greek mythology and religious thought; without the concept, there would have been very little Greek drama. Though the artistic embodiment of fate was the three Fates—three women spinning, measuring off, then cutting the thread of human life—philosophically the idea went much deeper. Fate, as we saw in Chapter 11, was a mysterious, universal force that preceded the birth of the gods and the creation of the world. Greeks believed that in the short run, people were responsible for their actions; in the long run, however, whatever happened had been destined to happen. As you might suppose, these opposing beliefs were a source of considerable confusion.

Western religions are the source of much fatalistic thinking. They argue that if God is all-powerful and all-knowing, how can anything happen that God does not will? Even if one wishes to believe that God does not will atrocities like the Holocaust and the destruction at Hiroshima, God must have seen them coming. How can the future be unknown to an all-knowing God?

John Calvin (1509-1564), an extreme Protestant reformer upon whose views the Puritan religion of the first American settlers was founded, believed emphatically in predestination. Nothing else, for him, was compatible with God's omnipotence. A perfect being could not leave matters to chance and allow human beings to carve out their own destinies. The doctrine of predestination also extended to the afterlife. There was a heaven and there was a hell—everyone knew that. But only God knew the names of those destined for salvation and those destined for damnation. Calvin rejected the Catholic position—that humankind has free will to choose between right and wrong and thus has some control over reward or punishment in the next life. Historians of Puritanism sometimes wonder why any Puritan ever went to church at all, since according to their beliefs nothing anyone did in this life could alter one's eventual destiny.

The Hebrew Bible affords us many images of an all-controlling God who arranges and changes human destiny. Perhaps the classic statement of God's omnipotence and humanity's limitations is given to us in that extraordinary work, the Book of Job, which begins with an encounter between God and Satan. With some justifiable pride, God points to Job as a very model of the pious, humble, good man. With his characteristic cynicism, Satan reminds God that Job is good because God has showered him with a loving wife, with children, and with vast property holdings. Take it all away, Satan challenges, and see how pious Job will be. Accordingly, God allows Satan to inflict any sort of suffering on Job, short of killing him.

Suddenly the good man is visited by a series of disasters: His children are killed. He loses his livestock. His land becomes barren. Terrible boils break out on his body. Various friends come to offer him comfort, but all they can tell him is that he must in some way have offended God. His wife urges him to complain bitterly to God about the apparent injustice. But though he curses the conditions of his life, he maintains his famous patience for a long while. Just as Job can stand his existence no longer, just as his patience is about to crack, God's voice comes thundering out of the whirlwind. Job is told in no uncertain terms that it is not his, nor any person's, right to question the workings of God. Since human beings have no ultimate power, they must accept divine wisdom, no matter what happens to them. Though in one version of the story Job's possessions and his happiness are restored, that happy ending in no way alters the fatalism of the work. God gives and God takes away, and humanity must accept either action without complaint.

Art, music, drama, and literature abound with fatalistic themes and attitudes. The myriad of paintings depicting the figure of God show us heavenly power in control. Religious hymns, folk songs, and spirituals remind us that God is not only all-powerful but caring as well. He has "the whole world in his hands." His "amazing grace" saves even the most undeserving among us. We are advised to prepare for the Judgment Day, when this "Judge eternal, throned in splendor" will punish the evil and reward the good; nothing escapes the notice of God's all-seeing eyes. One suspects that the writers of such songs believed implicitly that they were destined for salvation. We know of no songs that celebrate the possibility of damnation, though the followers of Calvin, especially those in the ministry,

*All is, if I have grace to use it so,
As ever in my great Task-Master's eye.*

*John Milton*

*Then shall the dust return to the earth as it was:
And the spirit shall return unto God who gave it.*

*Ecclesiastes*

frequently said that the vast majority of human beings were born wicked and would face an eternity in hell's flames.

Thomas Hardy (1840-1928) is perhaps the best-known fatalist among literary figures of the last two centuries. Hardy was convinced that life holds nothing good for any of us. The characters in his novels do not just inevitably come to a tragic end. He implies and in fact *directly states* that there is something—or someone—in charge that simply does not like us or does not want us to be happy.

When Tess, the ill-fated heroine of the novel *Tess of the d'Urbervilles* (1891), mounts the gallows for having murdered the man who seduced and abandoned her, Hardy grimly comments that the "President of the Immortals had ended his sport with Tess." In this instance God is the actual embodiment of fate. In others, cruel fate is simply an indwelling force, the bleak condition in which existence occurs.

A major catastrophe in Hardy's lifetime was the 1912 sinking of the *HMS Titanic*, the "unsinkable" giant of the seas. Crowded with some of the world's richest and most successful people, the ship on its maiden voyage struck (or was struck by) an iceberg and sank in freezing waters, killing over a thousand people. Hardy was quick to respond, suggesting that God planned the disaster from the start:

### VI

*Well: while was fashioning*
*This creature of cleaving wing,*
*The Immanent Will that stirs and urges everything*

### VII

*Prepared a sinister mate*
*For her—so gaily great—*
*A Shape of Ice, for the time far and dissociate.*

### VIII

*And as the smart ship grew*
*In stature, grace, and hue,*
*In shadowy silent distance grew the Iceberg too.*

### IX

*Alien they seemed to be;*
*No mortal eye could see*
*The intimate welding of their later history.*

### X

*Or sign they were bent*
*By paths coincident*
*On being anon twin halves of one august event,*

### XI

*Till the Spinner of the Years*
*Said "Now!" And each one hears*
*And consummation comes, and jars two hemispheres.*[8]

There also exists a popular brand of fatalism with nebulous roots in religion. Many who believe they are religious and profess a faith in the doctrine of free will, not predestination, are also prone to fatalistic attitudes that come and go, as convenient. A person can, for example, be a fatalist and still refuse to take unnecessary risks, such as joining a parachute-jumping club or riding a roller coaster standing up. An individual might refuse to undergo a delicate operation with a fifty-fifty survival rate on the grounds that the odds are not favorable enough. But the same people who refuse risks for themselves can say of the death of another, "His time came," or use that unpleasant metaphor, "Her number was up."

Death is explained to children in fatalistic terms by people who may otherwise find fatalism confining: "God so loved your mother that he wanted her to be with him always, and so he took her up to heaven." How many adult anxieties have been caused by such a statement, which may seem comforting at the time, but which can lead to highly ambivalent feelings toward a God who could be so cruel?

## Self-Inflicted Death

A very different meaning is given to death by a vast number of people—probably far more than make themselves known—who believe that coping with *life*, not death, is the challenge. For them personal extinction—suicide—is a more attractive alternative than trying to come to terms with what is happening to them.

We really have no way of knowing exactly how many Egyptians, Mesopotamians, Greeks, Romans, Hebrews, and Christians of the past either contemplated or actually committed suicide. Studies *have* been made from historical records and religious writings, especially the literature of earlier societies. For example, Linnea Parsons, a Unitarian minister, in a provocative work called *Separate Paths*, finds that the Greeks and Romans generally condoned suicide for four reasons: "to show bereavement, to preserve honor, to avoid pain and shame, and for the benefit of the state."[9] Aristotle called suicide a "crime against the state," while Socrates, the spokesperson for Plato's philosophy in the dialogues, warned that human beings were the "property" of the gods and therefore not at liberty to dispose of their bodies as they willed.

From the beginning, Jewish law forbade suicide. But we find that early Christians, oppressed by hostile forces and made to suffer appallingly, frequently took their own lives. Christianity has since expressly forbidden the act, but Parsons raises the interesting question of whether martyrdom, accepted in certain instances by the Christian Church, should not be considered suicide. Does Christ's death on the cross belong in this category?

Within such parameters a case could also be made for regarding as suicides the deaths of Thomas à Becket, Joan of Arc, even Bernadette of Lourdes. In the case of Bernadette, failure to report that she was suffering from a terminal disease made medical intervention hopeless. And what of the thousands of soldiers who "gave" (as we prefer to say, rather than "took") their lives to save others?

Can we say, however, that martyrdom and heroic death are "special" kinds of suicide, while others are manifestations of mental illness or antisocial acts that are, strictly speaking, against the law? Sometimes those who fail at suicide find themselves strapped to a hospital bed under police guard. The assumption, in our society at least, is that the intent to kill oneself is an emergency for which "hot lines" exist. The assumption is that society has the right to place a value on your life even if you don't value it.

Philosophers have debated the question of life versus death. The French philosopher Albert Camus (1913-1960) reached the conclusion that life was essentially meaningless—absurd. He opens his essay "An Absurd Reasoning" (1942) with this ringing line: "There is but one truly serious philosophical problem, and that is suicide."[10] Yet the body of his thought can be considered a rational defense of staying alive, though he never discredits those who decide not to. Camus's argument against self-inflicted death hinges on a subtle turn of logic, not on an appeal to the emotions. Since reason, he argues, tells us life is absurd—without purpose or significance beyond what one wishes to impose upon it—it follows that there can be no absurdity without a human presence to be aware of it. Suicide, in other words, is illogical. The knowledge of absurdity is a truth, and this, paradoxically, gives life meaning after all.

Poets have also addressed—and contemplated—suicide. Two of the major women poets of the twentieth century took their own lives, and in both cases the decision appears to have been inevitable. Both were feminists. Both were married to intelligent, productive men who seemed to have understood their creative needs. Yet perhaps these needs were not after all compatible with the demands that even the most flexible of marriages still impose.

Sylvia Plath (1932-1963) had two small children and a writer husband (Ted Hughes) with his own requirements of creative time and solitude. In many such literary marriages there is tension, and Plath had a history of emotional breakdowns. As she neared her thirtieth birthday, her creative needs were not being met, and the inner tension brought her to the breaking point. The poet Robert Lowell once described her as being "a little like a racehorse, galloping relentlessly with risked outstretched neck, death hurdle after death hurdle topped."

The following lines, written when Plath was pregnant—and four years before her death—say a great deal about the frustrations of motherhood:

> *I'm a means, a stage, a cow in calf.*
> *I've eaten a bag of green apples,*
> *Boarded the train there's no getting off.*[11]

Anne Sexton (1928-1974) lived in a sophisticated eastern seaboard world of martinis, smart talk, broken marriages, abortions, and pills. A wife and mother like Sylvia Plath, she found she could not balance all of the conflicting strains of her life, and decided the rewards were not enough to offset the pain. Perhaps the opening line of a poem called "Live" gives us a clue to what she was feeling: "Live or die, but don't poison everything." Later in the same poem she adds:

> *I say* Live, Live *because of the sun,*
> *the dream, the excitable gift.*[12]

Apparently in the long run, these things were not enough.

The most notorious literary suicide of the century may have been that of Ernest Hemingway (1899-1961). Suffering from ill health and a dramatic loss of creativity, he ended his life with a violent blast from a shotgun. We mention this only because his novels and short stories deal with men who exist on the borders of violence and death and do so without fear. One cannot help thinking that when the decision was reached that his life was no longer of any use, Hemingway wanted to bow out in a heroic way—as if his readers would expect nothing less.

*In this country where people are killed every day because we will not enact effective gun control laws and where we do not provide adequate medical care to many who would seek it, it is hypocritical to shed our collective tears for those who have opted to commit suicide and immoral to condemn the compassionate people who help them.*

*Trude Hassberg*

As with Plath and Sexton, there are hints throughout Hemingway's work that the author is someone who would never allow the pain of living (or dying) to overwhelm him. In the short story "In Another Country" the central figure is an Italian officer recovering from wounds received in World War I. He speaks of his young and beautiful wife and then later learns that she has run away with someone else. He advises the young enlisted men that a man should never marry:

> He cannot marry. He cannot marry. . . . If he is to lose everything, he should not place himself in a position to lose that. He should not place himself in a position to lose. He should find things he cannot lose.[13]

Had the passage concluded with "in a position to lose that," we would have known the man was talking about his wife; the repetition of "lose," however, strongly suggests that more is at stake: a man must be able to win. If he cannot . . . well, there are alternatives.

In Europe there are suicide clinics, which offer sympathetic counsel to those who see no other way out. In England a group called "Exit" and here in America "The Hemlock Society" distribute pamphlets to their members, discussing the latest and most effective means to self-inflicted death. None of these groups—nor any of the writers we have discussed—recommend suicide as a solution for everyone. They do, however, hold out the option as a rational choice.

## Symbolic Forms of Death

The taking of one's own life may be a merciful end to unbearable physical or mental anguish. Regardless of how one feels about the matter, however, this much can be said: if "successful," a suicidal individual no longer has to face death; he or she can die only once.

Yet many of us forget that we owe life just one death. We "die" many times over, in many different ways. We often barely live because the shadow of symbolic death continually crosses our paths.

Feeling a sense of unworth, we kill ourselves in a number of ways. We hang back from taking growth-producing risks. We worry continually about what others are saying, though chances are they have more to do than gossip about us. We convince ourselves we shall fail before we ever make an attempt. Because of unresolved guilt in the past, we yield to failure because we secretly believe we deserve it. Growing older, we allow ourselves only certain acceptable forms of behavior, out of fear of not "acting our age."

*"I'm too old to do that."*

*"What will they think of me?"*

*"Nothing ever turns out right."*

Death attitudes can even influence our physiology. We can will ourselves into extinction. A recent case, which became celebrated among the medical faculty of a prominent university, involved a woman admitted to a hospital for treatment of what was thought to be a harmless leg infection. She remained there for six months, growing progressively weaker, losing 85 pounds though no signs of malignancy could be detected anywhere in her body. A psychiatric examination, administered while the woman was still relatively well, revealed a profound depression, induced by feelings of unworth. The depression became so massive that her entire system absorbed the message and succeeded in destroying itself.

True, we can say that this woman eventually found peace, but it cannot

*James Ensor,* Masks Confronting Death *(1888): We "die" many times over, in many different ways. (Oil on canvas, 32 x 39-1/2". Collection, The Museum of Modern Art, New York. Mrs. Simon Guggenheim Fund)*

have been on her own terms. The medical examiners probably believed she was better off; the irony is that even her actual death may not have been necessary had she not been symbolically dying all of her "life."

## Symbolic Suicide

On the symbolic level, suicide is far and away the leading cause of "death." Negative self-concepts decimate the energy not only of the victims but of others as well. Like the woman in the case just cited, symbolic suicides do not find peace in living. Some adopt survival strategies, which for a time appear to work, but which really leave little room for hope without a strong dose of realism.

*Negative self-concepts are the leading cause of "death" on a symbolic level.*

A celebrated literary example of symbolic suicide in action is James Thurber's "The Secret Life of Walter Mitty." The story originally appeared in 1942, and since then its hero's name has become synonymous with the inability to accept reality on its own terms. Walter simply disappears mentally and emotionally into a fantasy world. His trouble is rooted in his shrunken self-image, reinforced by a nagging wife who tells him how fast to drive, when to see a doctor, and even where to sit while waiting for her in a hotel lobby.

On one occasion Walter tries to rebel by announcing that he has forgotten some errand because "I was thinking." Mrs. Mitty responds, "I'm going to take your temperature when I get you home."

In his perpetual escapes from reality he lives as an airplane pilot making a perilous landing in a hurricane, a world-famous surgeon, a defendant in a murder trial, a war hero, and, in the saddest fantasy of all, as a man about to be executed:

> He took one last drag on his cigarette and snapped it away. Then, with that faint, fleeting smile playing about his lips, he faced the firing squad; erect and motionless, proud and disdainful, Walter Mitty the Undefeated, inscrutable to the last.[14]

Regrettably, the people who could be helped by seeing themselves in stories like "Walter Mitty," people who secretly know they have lost all control of their lives, are usually unwilling to confront the reality of their self-destructive behavior. These symbolic suicides thus limit their contributions to life and others to a level far below their capabilities.

In the opinion of psychologists, symbolic suicide—the desire to stifle the self—takes on many guises. Self-inflicted martyrdom is one: volunteering for any task that appears distasteful or time-consuming, spending long hours in conspicuous sacrifice so that others will say, "Oh, you poor thing!"

Compulsive gamblers are believed to be people who are not in desperate need of money, but who wager in the secret hope they will lose. Winning is a source of momentary joy, a sudden flash of self-worth. But after a win, most compulsive gamblers simply bet again, usually risking even more money. Like martyrs, they do not believe that they are worthy of respect or success. The only recourse is to try again—to lose. If they succeed in failing, they now have the opportunity for self-castigation: "Why did I bet so much? Why didn't I quit while I was ahead?" The symbolic beating administered to the self by the self is "just" treatment for such persons, who believe they will never amount to anything and deserve only scorn.

Other familiar symbolic suicides are the professional gloom-gatherers, who are followed by a private black cloud that rains only on them. The company of such individuals is depressing. They receive few invitations—a fact they secretly enjoy because it confirms their opinion of themselves. They tend to court rejection: "I didn't mean to call at this time of night, especially when I know you're in the middle of a party, but I just had to ask you about . . ." The flustered party host can either stammer out a few apologies about "mislaid" invitations or coolly ignore the hint. Either response is enough to constitute the insult that the gloom-gatherer is asking for.

## Symbolic Murder

We are surrounded by murders. At home, at school, or in the office we see people (or *are* people) whose way of dealing with buried feelings of unworth is to do harm to others, particularly those who appear to be self-confident, successful, and admired.

*Gossip is the most universal form of symbolic murder.*

Gossip is the most universal form of symbolic murder. Literature, especially drama, offers innumerable characters with nothing to do in life except to discover (or invent) and spread rumors about "friends." Richard Brinsley Sheridan's classic comedy *The School for Scandal* (1775) is the definitive work about people whose sole concern in life is what others are doing wrong. Mrs. Candour has become the prototype of the symbolic murderer, a woman who pretends to decry idle gossip but cannot wait to pass along any rumor that she has "from very good authority." She insists she does not believe any of the vicious lies she helps spread.

> I confess, Mr. Surface, I cannot bear to hear people attacked behind their backs; and when ugly circumstances come out against our

acquaintance I own I always love to think the best. By-the-by, I hope 'tis not true that your brother is absolutely ruined?

One suspects that as long as our species is around, "bad-mouthing" will be a favorite sport. Letters signed "From a friend" are sent to appropriately inappropriate parties. In the work setting, twisted remarks are made to a boss or a supervisor about someone in line for the promotion one hopes to receive: "Not that I want to say anything, but  . . ."

Often, symbolic murder takes place without any knowledge of it on the "killer's" part. Envy can be so deeply rooted that we become oblivious to the extent of the actual hatred we harbor for another, usually convincing ourselves that we are totally supportive of that person's achievements. This kind of relationship is found in some of the theater's strongest works, because dramatists thrive on creating characters with conflicting intentions, especially members of the same family.

In 1955 Carlotta Monterey O'Neill, wife of the man many consider the greatest playwright America has yet produced, Eugene O'Neill (1888-1953), secured the copyright to an unpublished and unproduced work by her husband, which he had titled *Long Day's Journey into Night*. The play had been written as early as 1941 but kept a dark secret—"this play," he wrote in the dedication of the original manuscript to his wife, "of old sorrow, written in tears and blood," was written because "your love and tenderness  . . . gave me the faith in love that enabled me to face my dead at last  . . ."[15]

Perhaps O'Neill's masterpiece, the work is about love *and* hate—about the love/hate complex of emotions that can be felt only by people close enough to do sometimes irreparable harm to each other.

The "day" of the title happened long ago in the playwright's painful memory, when, as a youth spending the summer at the family's New England summer home, he kept trying to communicate to his father, mother, and older brother that he was dangerously ill and in need of immediate treatment.

Nobody wants to hear Edmund, the name O'Neill gives to his self-characterization. The mother, Mary Tyrone, is hopelessly addicted to morphine after a physician has prescribed it for her various ailments; the father, James, is a once-famous Shakespearean actor, now over the hill, escaping through alcohol from a realistic assessment of himself; and the brother, Jamie, is a self-designated failed actor who runs from himself through drinking and carousing in the town's brothel.

In one of the play's (and American theater's) most hauntingly affecting moments, Jamie staggers into the house and confronts Edmund, who has also sought comfort in alcohol and self-pity. Jamie's intention is to show his brother at last how deeply he loves him, but instead he attempts symbolic murder by blurting out (in garbled speech) the truth of his hatred of Edmund, born out of hitherto unexpressed jealousy of his younger brother's obvious genius:

> Never wanted you succeed and make me look even worse by comparison. Wanted you to fail. Always jealous of you. Mama's baby, Papa's pet!
>
> *He stares at Edmund with increasing enmity.*
>
> And it was your being born that started Mama on dope. I know that's

*The love/hate complex of emotions can be felt only by people close enough to do irreparable harm to each other.*

not your fault, but all the same, God damn you, I can't help hating
your guts—! . . .

. . . But don't get wrong idea, Kid. I love you more than I hate you.
My saying what I'm telling you now proves it. I run the risk you'll hate
me—and you're all I've got left. But I didn't mean to tell you that last
stuff—go that far back. Don't know what made me. What I wanted to
say is, I'd like to see you become the greatest success in the world.
But you'd better be on your guard. Because I'll do my damndest to
make you fail. Can't help it. I hate myself. Got to take revenge. On
everyone else. Especially you.[16]

*The victims of symbolic
murderers may suffer less
than their killers, if they
realize what is motivating
the attacks.*

In Jamie Tyrone, O'Neill has created the prototype of the symbolic murderer. Watching him, we realize that in relationships with such people, the victims
in the long run may suffer far less than their killers. The victims, if they are
observant, can emerge the stronger, having realized what is motivating the attacks.
The murderers, acting out of feelings of unworth, are not and may never be in
control of their life.

We need to catch ourselves in the act of slipping in the symbolic dagger—
and then laugh inwardly at our own absurdity. If we cannot do this—if we always
see a problem as the result of another person's failures and misfortunes and
stupidity, never as the result of *our* envy and *our* insecurity—then we can cause
the symbolic deaths of ourselves and others without knowing it.

## Fear of Aging

*In view of the utmost
relevance of death, the
avoidance and denial of the
problems related to this area
are truly astounding. Aging,
fatal disease, and dying are
not seen as a part of the life
process but as the ultimate
defeat and a painful
reminder of the limits of our
ability to master nature.*

*Stanislav Grof*

Our society is in the throes of the greatest antiaging campaign in human history.
Fitness is not only a fad but a multibillion-dollar industry. Almost any new diet
makes the best-seller list. Cosmeticians and plastic surgeons charge unbelievable
fees. Television commercials exhibit product after product guaranteeing that the
user will retain the appearance of youth. Older people are shown, if at all, playing
golf or, looking trim and fit, doing high kicks at the clubhouse in rehearsal for a
musical event. No one ever advertises the "quieter" pleasures of age. No one ever
says that the lovely retirement village contains an extraordinary library. We are
conditioned to believe that to resist age, not to accept the biological and sociological changes that age inevitably brings, is life affirming, the sign of a healthy society.

To enjoy looking dapper for one's age, to exercise and maintain a sensible
diet, to avoid the excessive use of life-shortening pastimes like drinking and smoking . . . these *can* be called life affirming and can be the signs of a creative
approach to one's existence. Having attained the age of, say, 75, one is not automatically required to consider oneself *old* or to obey the rule our society has
adopted for its "senior citizens": look young and act young for as long as possible
and then have the decency not to bother us anymore.

If we had a truly realistic appreciation of age, we would make a clear
separation in our minds between staying healthy and vigorous because we know
how to live and *looking* young and vigorous because society dislikes being reminded of the physical (*and* sexual) deterioration that are part of nature's cycle.
Because of our deep-rooted fear of death we are too often hedonistic—pleasure
seeking—in youth, driven by the philosophy that time is running out on us, engag-

ing in activities that are distinctly life denying, then only later becoming "health-conscious" in a desperate effort to hold time at bay.

Fear of aging is also related to our success orientation. One looks in the mirror, notes the deepening wrinkles, and thinks: "Already here, and what have you got to show for it?" People who in their opinion have not "won," have not been promoted to that longed-for post, have not possessed the symbols of power and success, see the signs of age as visible confirmation of their deteriorating self-image.

The humanities not only have considered this universal characteristic—the fear of aging—but have supplied us with memorable images and prototypes. One thinks of actress Glenn Close in the final moments of the film *Dangerous Liaisons* (1989), playing an aging aristocrat whose only pleasure in life has come from the game of love, especially with the most sought-after and eligible partners in Paris. Without speaking one word, the actress removes every bit of her makeup and stares at the reflection in the mirror of her true physical image: middle-aged, wrinkled, gray-toned, and miserable.

The classic study of the fear of aging is Oscar Wilde's *The Picture of Dorian Gray* (1891), the hero of which is a slim, incredibly handsome, young aristocrat, totally committed to a life of sensuality, leisure, and extravagance. In the opening scene he is observing his portrait, just finished by a major artist of the day:

> "How sad it is! . . . How sad it is! I shall grow old and horrible and dreadful. But this picture will remain always young. It will never be older than this particular day of June. If it were only the other way! If it were I who was to be always young, and the picture that was to grow old! For that—for that—I would give everything! Yes, there is nothing in the whole world I would not give! I would give my soul for that!"[17]

Like Faust, another famous character who barters his soul for a forbidden prize, Dorian has his wish granted by some mysterious power that hears him. He thus remains young while others age, but he loses his innocence: he becomes cruel and sadistic; develops an addiction to every conceivable pleasure, knowing that he cannot do harm to his body; and ultimately, commits murder. His appearance does not change, but the portrait, locked away in the attic, does. It reflects every sordid moment, every horrible deed for which he is responsible. When he stares at the painting, he sees an old, gnarled man with a fiendish look and blood on his hands. Horrified, he seizes a knife and plunges it into the heart of the portrait. His servants at length find him "withered, wrinkled, and loathsome of visage." He has become the very thing he feared most; on the wall, however, is "a splendid portrait of their master as they had last seen him, in all the wonder of his exquisite youth and beauty."

*Those who are reconciled to aging still face the problem of society's fear of the aged.*

For thousands the fear of aging is every bit as great as the fear of death itself. Physiological changes, including the gradual waning of sexual desire, are hard to accept when one has never learned to understand the different rhythms of life.

For still thousands of others who are reconciled to aging—who even find Wordsworth's sober, reflective joys that come from having more time to read, write, and think—there can be the problem of *society's fear of the aged*. Our youth-oriented culture finds age too unpleasant a reminder of what one should not have to think about: "getting old and becoming a burden to the children."

Ad campaigns thus encourage those who are aging to look young and stay independent by taking vitamins and laxatives, investing in the right mutual funds, and finding the right Medicare supplement so they will have peace of mind. In every case the older people are shown living effectively on their own, with no acknowledgment of the fact that they one day may need the love and care of their family, as if this were shameful.

## Models of Life Affirmation

If negative attitudes and negative internal imagery act to dampen people's lives and cause them to "die" many times over before the actual and unique moment of true physical death, then it should follow—and it does—that positive attitudes and positive images are possible. We are not talking here of shallow optimism. The issue is the profound realization that the potential for a productive, exciting life belongs to each of us. *We* control our attitudes—that is, we can if we allow ourselves to. Of course, others—society and the media—will influence those attitudes if we allow *them* to.

*Life affirmation* is recognizing that real death happens only once and, in a sense, does not "happen" to us at all. We will probably no longer be feeling sensation at the exact moment; for most people conscious sensation has terminated considerably before the stroke of death. Even in cases involving sudden death—a plane crash or an automobile accident—it is likely that everything happens too fast for a rational analysis of the situation. We in fact have much testimony from people who have come very close to death and who retain the memory of what they experienced. There are few reports of terror and many reports of a sense of calm and well-being, and even of disappointment at being "brought back."

## The Phoenix

An ancient and enduring symbol of life affirmation is that of the phoenix, a mythological bird of rare and exotic plumage and supernatural powers. The Greek historian Herodotus reported that the phoenix actually existed and was known to have visited the Egyptians every 500 years. The Roman belief was that each era bears witness to the birth of one phoenix, that it lives for a very long time, and that at the moment of its death, it generates a worm that becomes the phoenix for the next age.

Yet another version of the legend is that the phoenix is a bird from India that lives for 500 years and then flies to a secret temple, where it is burned to ashes upon the altar, only to rise from the ashes three days later, young and resplendent.

In folklore, poetry, and song, in fiction, drama, and epic, the phoenix has endured through time as a symbol of rebirth, new growth, regeneration, and redemption. Religions have counterpart symbols: gods who die or descend into the underworld, there to remain for a time and then to rise, reborn and renewed.

The phoenix has given structure to many masterworks, such as Dante's

*In ad campaigns older people are shown living effectively on their own, without needing to be cared for.*

*A Death Model*

*I've already taken the qualifying exam for the third time. Now I'm out for good. I'll never amount to anything.*

*A Phoenix Model*

*I'm obviously not suited for that kind of work. Let me see . . .*

*Divine Comedy*, in which the poet, seeking a vision of God in paradise, must first travel through the very depths of hell before his wish is granted. The phoenix has suggested to many people certain ways of thinking about events. Thus does "I've been through hell" often preface an account of some happier turn of events, or at least invite the listener to effect a happy change for the sufferer through lavish sympathy or some other sign of compassion. People say, "I'm going to pull myself out of this." Even the popular exhortation "Lift yourself up by your own bootstraps" has underlying suggestions of the phoenix myth, for there exists within the bird the creative thrust to soar from its own ashes.

Goethe's *Faust* is for most students of literature the epic of a man's pact with the devil for a lifetime of pleasure, a pact that eventually leads to the loss of his soul and the devil's triumph. One reason for this limited view is that literature courses generally assign only Part 1 of the drama. To add Part 2 would require many hours of reading. It would also reveal the true meaning of the work: the *human* triumph. Goethe's *Faust* in its entirety is the perfect *phoenix model*, a work of ringing life affirmation in the very confrontation of life's harshest realities.

In Part 1 the devil has promised to offer unlimited pleasure so long as Faust agrees to one condition: *he must never come upon a moment that is so satisfying he will wish time could stand still.* Faust has made the pact because he has grown weary of the search for truth. He wants to throw himself into life, existing always for the moment, never sitting back to reflect. He wants continual change. Since nothing amounts to anything, why would anyone ever hold onto a moment?

In Part 2 the protagonist is older and tired of a life that offers nothing but a variety of sense experiences without thought. He is beginning to long for some accomplishment, something to show for his having lived. He is, in fact, tired of serving only himself, and so he becomes the mayor of a village on the North Sea, situated on land so low that the ocean threatens to engulf it. His project as mayor is to supervise the building of a seawall, but he finds that each time the wall is extended a little further, the sea has already begun to erode the completed part of the work. Thus he is faced with an impossible task; the wall will obviously *never* be finished. Yet he is filled with a raging passion to challenge the sea. If he cannot ultimately win, he shall not ultimately lose either. Each day a little more land is made suitable for agriculture, and, though floods will come, the people will have raised food—perhaps a little bit more each year.

The thought that things are worth doing even if the work of one's life is unfinishable strikes him with the force of lightning:

> *He only earns both freedom and existence*
> *Who must reconquer them each day.*
> *And so, ringed all about by perils, here*
> *Youth, manhood, age will spend their strenuous year.*
> *Such teeming would I see upon this land,*
> *On acres free among free people stand.*
> *I might entreat the fleeting minute:*
> *Oh tarry yet, thou art so fair!* [18]

This, then, is the devil's triumph. Faust has lost the bargain, he has found a satisfying moment, but does he care? He has found the truth for which he was searching

*For me, thinking finally came late that night as I wandered through the shattered house by flashlight. I looked up through where the kitchen ceiling had been and saw a clear sky filled with more stars than I ever knew were possible. I realized that those stars were only visible now because there was darkness all around; they were no longer lost in the wash of light from Earth.*

*Leonard Pitts, Jr.*

*[From an article in the* Miami Herald, *August 26, 1992, two days after the devastation of Hurricane Andrew]*

long ago: there is no *one* truth; there are only the many truths that many people find, walking their individual paths. If all these truth-seekers share one common insight, it is that the road to truth is embracing a cause greater than oneself.

The humanities, as we have said all along, teach us to keep an open mind; not everyone will find the truth—and thus life affirmation, the phoenix model—through a selfless mission. Still, reason might suggest that the less we think of our own plight as we grow older, the less worried we may be about aging or breaking the social rules governing age—or even about death itself.

*Reason might suggest that the less we think of our own plight as we grow older, the less worried we may be about aging—or even about death itself.*

## Living Without Dying

As the old baseball philosopher Yogi Berra put the matter: "It ain't over till it's over." Strange how many of us have difficulty accepting the idea that life is life and the moment is always now. Memories and plans for the future notwithstanding, existence is always with us. Life is not slipping through our fingers. The years are not hurrying by. Time, urgency, desperation . . . these are human constructs. They are inside us. At least, this is one message we are at liberty to glean from the humanities.

There is an actress who tells this story about teaching a class to several young people. A girl of 16 was playing a scene in which her character was supposed to be 50 years old. Suddenly the girl entered the room in a wheelchair and spoke in a cracking voice, sounding like the witch in *Snow White*. "What in the world are you doing?" asked the teacher. "Trying to physicalize the woman's age," was the answer. The actress told her to play 50 as she would 16. "But I *am* sixteen," the girl said. "Exactly," said the actress.

To break our illusion of time rushing by to an inevitable aging and death, we can replace pyramids with circles as our dominant inner images. In pyramid imagery, we visualize ourselves as rising through the ranks (in school, on the job, and so on), reaching a peak or a crest, and then being "over the hill." In circle imagery, life is like a ferris wheel, rising, reaching a crest, going back down, and *then* starting up all over again.

*We can replace pyramids with circles as our dominant inner images.*

You can consider that you "lost" a job, or you can say you are beginning another phase of life. You can experience the end of love (the *death* of a romance) or you can be starting another set of experiences, looking forward with excitement to the next love, the new friendship, or the opportunity to be alone for a while and do all the things you never had time to do by yourself.

Of course, taking care of your feelings about time, aging, and death does sound self-serving, doesn't it? What about looking beyond the self? Wasn't that Faust's salvation? The answer here may be that we need to be at peace with ourselves before we are fit company for others. Once we feel confident about who we are *at whatever age*, then we don't *need* to stay wrapped up in our own problems.

Every once in a while, however, it's a good idea to make sure you haven't fallen back into an old rut—to make sure you haven't stopped growing.

One of the authors' dearest friends, a poet who is no longer with us, never had any problem dealing with the fate that stalked her for a number of years. In her youth she had written these lines, and they remained her credo throughout a productive and happy life:

*Ride a wild horse*
*with purple wings*
*striped yellow and black*
*except his head*
*which must be red.*

*Ride a wild horse*
*against the sky*
*hold tight to his wings*

*before you die*
*whatever else you leave undone—*
*once ride a wild horse*
*into the sun.*[19]

## Glossary

*Elysian fields:* In Greek mythology, a special land of immortality for brave warriors, whose spirits go there without having to suffer the pain of death.

*fatalism:* The belief that all events, including one's death, have been predetermined.

*Grim Reaper:* The figure of death in myth and art, usually depicted as wearing a shroud and carrying a scythe to cut down the person appointed to die.

*Job:* The biblical character who lost almost everything as a test from God and who questioned why he, a man who had led a nearly blameless life, should suffer when others no better than he were free of pain. Having taken his agonized questions to God, he was reminded that humanity must not presume to make demands on a power beyond human comprehension.

*life affirmation:* An outlook toward specific events or contemplated actions that sees them as forms of growth and is therefore supportive of them.

*phoenix model:* A model of living based on the mythical archetype of the phoenix, an immortal bird that goes up in flames every 500 years and flies up again, newborn. For us, the phoenix can be represented in a number of symbolic ways, but all have to do with rising from the ashes of something in our lives that has ended or failed.

## Notes

1. J. R. R. Tolkien, *The Return of the King* (New York: Ballantine Books, 1966), 384.

2. *The Apology of Socrates,* tr. Benjamin Jowett.

3. *Phaedo,* tr. Benjamin Jowett.

4. *Hamlet,* II.ii.

5. Ibid., V.i.

6. Edwin Arlington Robinson, "The Man Against the Sky," from *Collected Poems of Edwin Arlington Robinson.* Copyright 1916 by Edwin Arlington Robinson, renewed 1944 by Ruth Nivison.

7. From Alfred, Lord Tennyson, *In Memoriam,* II.1–4, 13–16.

8. From "The Convergence of the Twain" from *The Complete Poems of Thomas Hardy,* ed. James Gibson, 1978. Reprinted by permission of Macmillan Publishing Company, New York.

9. Linnea Parsons, *Separate Paths* (New York: Harper & Row, 1977), 48.

10. Albert Camus, "An Absurd Reasoning," in *The Myth of Sisyphus and Other Essays,* tr. Justin O'Brien (New York: Random House, Vintage, 1952), 3.

11. From "Metaphors," from *The Collected Poems* by Sylvia Plath, edited by Ted Hughes. Copyright © 1960, 1965, 1971, 1981 by the Estate of Sylvia Plath. Editorial material copyright © 1981 by Ted Hughes. Reprinted by permission of HarperCollins Publishers, Inc., and Faber and Faber Ltd.

12. From "Live," in *Live or Die* by Anne Sexton (Boston: Houghton Mifflin, 1966), 87. Copyright © 1966 by Anne Sexton. Reprinted by permission of

Houghton Mifflin Company. All rights reserved.

13. In *The Snows of Kilimanjaro and Other Stories* (New York: Scribner's, 1970), 69.

14. Originally published in *My World and Welcome to It* (New York: Harcourt, Brace, 1942). Now widely available in anthologies of short stories and American literature.

15. From *Long Day's Journey into Night* by Eugene O'Neill. Copyright © 1955 by Carlotta Monterey O'Neill. Reprinted by permission of Yale University Press.

16. From *Long Day's Journey into Night*, 165-166, by Eugene O'Neill. Copyright © 1955 by Carlotta Monterey O'Neill. Reprinted by permission of Yale University Press.

17. Oscar Wilde, *The Picture of Dorian Gray* (New York: Dell, 1977), 33.

18. Tr. Walter Arndt (New York: Norton, 1976), 294.

19. From *Eve's Daughter*, by Hannah Kahn, 1962. Reprinted by permission.

## Suggested Reading

Bowker, John. *The Meanings of Death*. New York: Cambridge University Press, 1991. This important new work challenges what the author calls the "orthodoxies of modernity." These presumably hold the view that the origins of religion can be found in the fear of death and the false promise of life beyond the grave. Bowker finds that early religious documents actually emphasize maximizing the potential of this life because the next life is bleak and undesirable.

Colgrove, Melba, Harold H. Bloomfield, and Peter McWilliams. *How to Survive the Loss of a Love*. Los Angeles: Prelude Press, 1991. The end of a love relationship is a form of symbolic death, one that can cause a longer period of grief than a real death can. The authors take the reader on a step-by-step process of recovering from such a loss. A fine guidebook to have on your shelf— just in case.

Crane, Stephen. *The Red Badge of Courage*. (1895). The short but powerful classic American novel about a young man's romantic view of dying heroically in war, and how he discovers the grim reality.

Fulton, Robert, et al., eds. *Death and Dying: Challenge and Change*. Reading, Mass.: Addison-Wesley, 1978. A series of essays by psychologists and thanatologists (counselors to those with a terminal illness or those who need assistance in recovering from mourning) on every aspect of the dying and grieving process.

Kübler-Ross, Elisabeth. *Death: The Final Stage of Growth*. Englewood Cliffs, N.J.: Prentice-Hall,

1975. The title alone is provocative enough to justify reading this important work. The author's premise is that, far from ignoring the inevitability of death, we should use the event as a starting place for a philosophy of living. Kübler-Ross believes that once we learn to face death calmly and rationally, life suddenly opens up with unlimited options.

————. *On Death and Dying*. New York: Macmillan, 1969. In this her most influential work, the world's most renowned thanatologist analyzes the American neurosis on the subject of death, especially the shameful treatment our society gives to the elderly and the dying.

Menten, Ted. *Gentle Crossings: How to Say Goodbye to Someone You Love*. Philadelphia: Running Press, 1992. The author has worked with terminally ill children and their families. He explains carefully how to cope, what to say to the dying and the bereaved, and how to facilitate peace.

Mitford, Jessica. *The American Way of Death*. New York: Simon & Schuster, 1963. Available in most libraries. The original jacket had a picture of a funeral wreath in the shape of a dollar sign, so you can readily imagine the subject matter. The author is an Englishwoman with none-too-complimentary observations on the funeral industry as *big* business in the United States. The book caused a sensation when first published and led to investigations of some funeral homes.

Tolstoy, Leo. *The Death of Ivan Ilych*. Tr. Aylmer Maude. New York: New American Library/Signet Classics, 1960. A graphic and exhausting study of terminal illness, leaving the reader in a strangely peaceful mood of complete catharsis. We recommend this translation of the 1884 classic.

Wilder, Thornton. *Our Town*. (1940). One of the greatest of all American plays—a simple yet profound statement about the cycle of birth and death and the everlasting fitness of things.

Yehoshua, A. B. *Five Seasons*. Tr. Hillel Halkin. New York: Doubleday, 1989. A moving novel describing the first year following the death of a man's wife and the curious numbness he experiences after having devoted himself to her for the seven years of her illness. The author takes us into all of the shadows of the man's complex and conflicting emotions. We realize that the emptiness following a death can be harder to bear than the loss itself.

*Wendell Minor,* The Last Call *(Courtesy of Wendell Minor)*

# *Nature in the Humanities*

## *Overview*

In 1860, which has been called by some meteorologists and environmentalists the "Year Without a Summer," a minor volcanic explosion in a far-off corner of the globe—so minor as to go virtually unreported—led to drastic climatic changes. Snow fell in temperate zones when people would normally be at the beach; rainfall counted upon for harvests failed to appear. There were crop failures, widespread unemployment as a result, and more than a little confusion for practically everybody who had thought nature was as dependable as . . . well, as the morning sunrise.

Somehow or other that summerless year has been forgotten by all but a few. One reason that the Year Without a Summer may not loom large in human history is that even if the cause of the drastic alteration in climate were remembered, most people would simply say that nature had gone on a rampage and nobody could have done much about it. More than likely, great numbers of environmental catastrophes have taken place over the centuries and have been similarly dismissed.

In 1836, just 24 years before the summer that wasn't, the American poet and philosopher Ralph Waldo Emerson had written these words:

> *Nature*, in the common sense, refers to essences unchanged by man; space, the air, the river, the leaf. . . . The stars awaken a certain reverence, because they are always present, they are inaccessible; but all natural objects make a kindred impression, when the mind is open to their influence.

In all probability this harmless passage escaped profound notice. Anyone who has ever studied Emerson knows, of course, that the sage of Concord found great inspiration in nature and displayed what can be called a mystic reverence for its wonders. Here he is gently inspiring his readers to establish a closer relationship to nature. Had Emerson discovered the elusive Fountain of Youth and lived into our time, he would not be gentle; he would scold us for failing not only to open our minds to nature, but to take responsibility for many of the terrible things happening to nature. He would point out that a volcanic explosion is a *natural* disaster, but that the current dissipation of the protective ozone layer is being humanly engineered. And he would warn us, *You cannot ignore nature while at the same time destroying it.*

Nature has had effects of varying sorts on the humanities ever since there has been a *concept* of nature—a thought that what surrounds us, shapes our lives, nourishes us, and sometimes hurts us is not just an unrelated series of things but a *whole* event, a dynamic and even living system.

Take away the impact of nature on the minds and sensibilities of those who create the humanities, and you find far less to study. Even the Greeks and Romans, who were so clearly centered on understanding what it meant to be human, were not entirely oblivious to nature. The Roman poet Lucretius (c. 94-55 B.C.) wrote a vast poem called *Of the Nature of Things*, in which he ponders how existence began and attributes it to a mighty collision of atoms. Inevitably, he adds, the primal atomic energy will reassert itself, and the world will end in a violent eruption.

The thinking of Lucretius probably terrified many readers. But we cannot say it started a great tradition of awe and respect for nature's fearful power. For many centuries nature was seen as a beautiful cloak (often believed to have been made by God expressly for humanity), one that held and enclosed the world securely.

With the rise of modern science in the seventeenth century and the conceptualization of the Newtonian universe—which operated according to unchanging natural laws, such as those of gravity and motion—the idea of nature as mechanical system took hold. It is doubtful that anyone can trace the precise origins of the popular saying *Let nature take its course*, but it certainly fits the Newtonian view.

The romantic poets, artists, and composers of the nineteenth century *did* look upon nature with awe and respect, but usually not with fear. Instead of Newton's mechanical, clockwork system, they saw nature as a living organism with a mind, a spirit, and a soul driving it, conscious of humanity, its twin—in fact, the lover and lifelong *protector* of humanity.

*A complete recovery from each of the five major extinctions required tens of millions of years. . . . These figures should give pause to anyone who believes that what* Homo sapiens *destroys, Nature will redeem. Maybe so, but not within any length of time that has meaning for contemporary humanity.*

*Edward O. Wilson*

We can only speculate on whether this romantic idea later turned into an unconscious feeling that human beings could do anything they wanted to nature and somehow it would always heal itself, just as a young child may make constant demands on his or her mother, never supposing that the mother's resources are limited.

*. . . an unconscious feeling that human beings could do anything they wanted to nature . . .*

At any rate, the humanities in this century have sometimes been a lone force attempting to feel the mother's fatigue and pain and to warn its audience that what Lucretius predicted thousands of years ago—the end of our world in violent upheavals—may well be coming true, and sooner than even the concerned probably suspect.

## Early Warnings

A number of years ago, when concern for environmental deterioration was becoming significant enough to reach the media, a panel of scientists engaged in a discussion on television, the aim of which was apparently to decide what or whom to blame for the attitude that people had a right to abuse nature without guilt. One participant suggested that the source of this attitude was the Bible itself, in particular, the Book of Genesis.

*One panelist suggested that the Bible gave people the belief they could abuse nature without guilt.*

He believed that in Genesis was planted the seed of a "stewardship" theory, according to which God presumably gave his newly created children the job of supervising the earth. He cited this passage (2:4-5; 7-8) from the book:

> So God created man in his own image, in the image of God he created him; male and female he created them.
>
> God blessed them and said to them, "Be fruitful and increase in number; fill the earth and subdue it. Rule over the fish of the sea and the birds of the air and over every living creature that moves on the ground."
>
> *(New International Version 1984)*

The traditional belief inherited by Western civilization from the Bible, continued the panelist, is that God created the beautiful garden for the delight and use of human beings. This did not mean, of course, that they also inherited the right to trash the garden, but, he suggested, might not the fact of God's absentee ownership have encouraged the human occupants to think *they* were the owners? Suppose a property owner hires a superintendent and then never actually visits the property, even though there are reports that she or he is somehow watching it from afar. How long before the superintendent grows cocky and believes it is his or her property?

The possibility is indeed an interesting one, and perhaps a good case could be made for the fact that much of humanity has conveniently forgotten this line (2:15) from Genesis: "And the Lord God took the man, and put him into the garden of Eden to dress it and keep it."

Thousands of years after Genesis was written John D. Rockefeller I, founder of one of the most powerful financial empires in history (including the globe-spanning Standard Oil), wrote in his autobiography that God was entirely responsible for his success. Since much of that success involved the large-scale depletion of fossil fuel, was Rockefeller implying that God approved of his endeavors? Or at least that a God-fearing man, who benefited humanity through his businesses, had the right to avail himself of the earth's riches?

Perhaps—who knows?—Rockefeller secretly read (or reread) the Biblical admonition that humanity was to "dress" and "keep" its garden. Late in his life he purchased a good portion of Wyoming wilderness, presumably to keep unscrupulous developers from buying it up, and finally willed it to the United States with the proviso that it be kept forever as a natural reserve, where citizens might enjoy the unspoiled wonders of nature. This land became the Grand Teton and Yellowstone national parks. Would God, then, consider Rockefeller a plunderer of the earth or a good steward of it? Was he a good or a bad "superintendent"?

We of course will never know the answers to these questions. We do know, however, that after Adam and Eve have disobeyed God's command not to eat the forbidden fruit, God punishes them by putting death and sorrow on earth and saying (3:17-18) to Adam, "Cursed is the ground because of you; through painful toil you will eat of it all the days of your life./It will produce thorns and thistles for you."

On reflection, we might well consider the Book of Genesis as the first of the warning signals sounded in the humanities—if we do not care for the earth as God commands us to do, we will pay the consequences.

*The Book of Genesis might be considered an early warning signal: if we do not care for the earth as God commands us to do, we will pay the consequences.*

## The Forest of Arden

During the early Middle Ages—from about the sixth to the eleventh centuries—there must have been nature, in the sense of woods and streams, hills and valleys, in abundance. There must have been plenty of vegetation too, for it was at this time that the monks who worked at making the great illuminated manuscripts discovered how to create all kinds of paints from the juices of flowers and berries. But except for necessary forays into the countryside for running errands or traveling or going off to fight a war, medieval people probably did not venture very much outside their villages or their walled fortresses or their monasteries. Medieval nature must have been something "out there," with little direct relationship to human beings. Besides, who need waste time looking at clouds and flowers when nothing in this vale of tears mattered as much as salvation in the next world?

During the eleventh and twelfth centuries there appeared a highly secular form of literature, often written by rebellious young men studying for the priesthood but objecting to the austerity and lack of humor in their daily training. These were poets who in their youth at least took exception to the other-worldly bent of their elders. The author of this poem urges his fellow students to discover the natural world outside:

> *Cast aside dull books and thought;*
> *Sweet is folly, sweet is play:*
> *Take the pleasure Spring hath brought*
> *In youth's opening holiday!*
> *Right it is old age should ponder*
> *On grave matters fraught with care;*
> *Tender youth is free to wander,*
> *Free to frolic light as air.*

Here we have, perhaps, the earliest stirrings of a great poetic theme, which is to return in full force during the eighteenth and nineteenth centuries when the implications of the Industrial Revolution are starting to make themselves felt: *the identification of nature with youth and joy, with all good things*. As the medieval walled fortresses turned into walled cities, as plague and pestilence and poverty snaked along insidiously behind those walls, many sensitive souls looked upon the city as a place of death, decay, and evil. The countryside thus became a place of blessed escape.

Like other Renaissance poets, the young William Shakespeare wrote about imaginary, unspoiled countrysides where the joys of love were experienced, if only briefly. By the time he came to London from Stratford-upon-Avon in the last quarter of the sixteenth century, that city was already a sprawling metropolis—and a place of filth, dire poverty, and crime. The aristocrats who patronized young poets and bought their books could ignore the truth of the city. Why read about the wretched poor when there isn't anything we can do for them anyway?

The popularity of idealized country settings led Shakespeare to capitalize on this form of escapism, both in his comedies and in his serious plays. For the most part, Shakespearean nature is artificial. *A Midsummer Night's Dream* (1594) is set in a Disneyland-like woodland, with charming fairies playing harmless tricks on mortals, who stay forever young in idyllic bliss. Much of *The Winter's Tale* (1610) takes place on the beautiful and fabricated "seacoast of Bohemia" (which, unknown to Shakespeare, *had* no seacoast). His presumed final play, *The Tempest* (1611), takes us to a faraway desert island where humans, a poetry-making fairy, and a strange-looking part-human, part-animal being with a poetic soul all live in a reality of their own.

*Shakespeare capitalized on the popularity of escapist fantasies set in artificial nature wonderlands.*

Earlier, in 1598, Shakespeare had, however, written *As You Like It*, which is not only one of his most enduring comedies but contains a very unexpected, very uncharacteristic, and decidedly premature environmentalism. One can readily make a case against the view that Shakespeare was *conscious* of the implications, but they are there all the same.

*As You Like It contains a very premature environmentalism.*

In the play, an aristocrat, identified only as Duke Senior, has been exiled by his evil brother. He and a small band of followers move to the forest of Arden, Shakespeare's version of the Garden of Eden, where they enjoy a simple existence free of the corruption found in court:

> *Sweet are the uses of adversity,*
> *Which like the toad, ugly and venomous,*
> *Wears yet a precious jewel in his head;*
> *And this our life, exempt from public haunt,*
> *Finds tongues in trees, books in the running brooks,*
> *Sermons in stones, and good in everything.*[1]

So says the Duke in words that could have been written by a late-eighteenth-century romantic poet. This is surely not the last time a writer will suggest that one can receive a better education in nature than in the library!

But these are civilized men, accustomed to the food of city-bred people. Instead therefore of leaving their paradise as they find it, they begin to kill the wild deer, a fact that sorely grieves one of the Duke's attendants, Jaques, a brooding, melancholy person. Jaques, the Duke is told, "swears you do more usurp/Than doth your brother that hath banish'd you."[2] Jaques claims that what they are doing to nature is worse than the court corruption that exiled them in the first place.

At one point, Jaques witnesses the excruciating death throes of a wounded stag:

> *"Poor dear," quoth he, "thou mak'st a testament*
> *As worldlings do, giving thy sum of more*
> *To that which had too much."*[3]

Then he cries out to the herd of still-surviving deer that they should hide themselves from the "tyrants," who have come to destroy the animals in "their assign'd and native dwelling place."

In Shakespeare's time nature and humanity were not considered to be part of each other. Humanity should therefore not, because it cannot, try to meddle with nature, where everything has its rightful place and function. The tragedy of Jaques is that he *feels* the agony of nature without being able to help. All he can do is be seen "weeping and lamenting/Upon the sobbing deer."

His misanthropy, fueled by the corruption of the forest, drives him almost mad. In his delusion he believes he can reform the world:

> *Invest me in my motley; give me leave*
> *To speak my mind, and I will through and through*
> *Cleanse the foul body of th'infected world,*
> *If they will patiently receive my medicine.*[4]

Of course, he will never be successful. At the play's conclusion, when the two brothers are reconciled and the four young couples are to be happily married, Jaques wishes everyone peace and joy, but declares he cannot stay in their midst; he is "for other than for dancing measures." When they beg him to return to civilization for his own good, he answers: "To see no pastime I. What you would have/I'll stay to know at your abandon'd cave."[5]

The traditional critical opinion is that Shakespeare intended Jaques's morose and gloomy character to amuse the audience, who, after all, were from the city and knew no "abandon'd caves" in which to live. At any rate, even without being sure of Shakespeare's intentions, we are fairly safe in assuming that any contemporary actor would play Jaques with empathy for his cynicism. Were he writing today, Shakespeare might well have made Jaques a serious character and his condemnation of humanity's civilized cruelties a central theme.

*By every conceivable measure, humanity is ecologically abnormal. Our species appropriates between 20 and 40 percent of the solar energy captured in inorganic material by land plants. There is no way that we can draw upon the resources of the planet to such a degree without drastically reducing the state of most other species.*

*Edward O. Wilson*

## The Decay of Nature

During the eighteenth century, many decades after Newton had published the laws of motion and gravity and many followers were echoing his idea that nature was as finely tuned as a clock, there came to prominence a pessimistic version of the "grand machine" view of nature derived from Newton. This was triggered by the feeling in some quarters that—to use the clock analogy—even the most well-crafted clock would eventually stop running.

The theory was named the "decay-of-nature" theory, and one of its principal architects was a man named Sir William Temple, a distant cousin and one-time employer of one of the greatest prose writers in English literature: Jonathan Swift (1667-1745), author of *Gulliver's Travels*. As a young man newly graduated from college, Swift worked as Temple's private secretary, in which position he must surely have become familiar with the man's philosophy. Temple, and others of his circle, had been strongly influenced by *deism*, a new kind of religion reflecting Newton's idea of nature as an interconnecting system of natural laws. Deism held that nothing so perfect as this system could have created itself, but there was also no proof that the creator actually intervened in its operations. The parting of the Red Sea by Moses and the ability of Jesus to perform miracles were, in their opinion, mythological stories, not scientific facts. The evidence seemed to indicate that the deity who created the machine must surely have gone away and left it to run by itself.

Thousands of years before, Aristotle, in trying to explain why the sun, the planets, and the stars were kept in apparently endless motion across the sky, had come up with the idea that motion was caused by a "first mover," a being of some sort who was not himself or herself (or itself) moved by anything else. Aristotle does not make clear whether this first mover had to keep on with his or her duties forever or if, once begun, motion would continue indefinitely. Newton's first law had guaranteed that things in motion would continue in motion until acted upon by an opposite force. An apple, for example, falling to the ground is stopped by the earth itself; otherwise it would fall forever. The decay-of-nature philosophers, however, could not imagine that Newton's machine would go on forever. Spin a top, and it will eventually stop turning.

They also believed that as the universe slowed down, nature itself would wither and die and all life would perish. Swift, who eventually became an ordained Anglican priest, appears to have taken his employer's theory and made it apply to the moral condition of humanity. It too was running down, going from bad to worse. The normal course of a person's life was to move from innocence to corruption. We might call his theory the "decay-of-*human*-nature" theory.

In his great work *Gulliver's Travels*, first published in 1726, the hero, finding himself in the land of Brobdingnag, peopled by a race of giants, tells the king about his country and the human beings who occupy it. The king, horrified, replies:

> "My little friend Grildrig; you have made a most admirable panegyrick upon your country. You have clearly proved that ignorance, idleness, and vice are the proper ingredients for qualifying a legislator. That laws are best explained, interpreted, and applied by those whose interest and abilities lie in perverting, confounding, and eluding them. . . . It doth not appear, from all you have said, how any one perfection is required towards the procurement of any one station among you; much less that men are ennobled on account of their virtue, that priests are advanced for their piety or learning, soldiers for their conduct or valor, judges for their integrity, senators for their love of country, or counsellors for their wisdom. . . . But by what I have gathered from your own relation, and the answers I have with much pain wringed and extorted from you; I cannot but conclude the bulk of your natives, to be the most pernicious race of little odious vermin that nature ever suffered to crawl upon the surface of the earth."

Just how serious was Swift's legendary hatred of the human race is anybody's guess, but Temple's philosophy seems to have deeply affected him. If nothing else, *Gulliver's Travels* stands as an enduring condemnation of the moral environment.

Temple and his followers became something of a cult, and they attracted attention for a time from London intellectuals; they must not be regarded as distant ancestors of today's environmental activists, however. Nothing in the decay-of-nature theory indicated that humanity might develop some collective ideas about *saving* nature or that some parts of the world might be better for human habitation than others. Temple himself lived at Moor Park, a sprawling and wooded estate outside of London, but both he and his devoted secretary, Swift, seemed very much at home in urban society. Later in the eighteenth century, however, many artists and writers began to perceive that options existed. The word *nature* began to signify *not* the total Newtonian system, but the countryside, the out-of-doors. In short, it meant that part of the world that human greed had not destroyed with factories, vermin-infested housing, and garbage-strewn streets.

*In the late eighteenth century* nature *began to signify that part of the world that human greed had not destroyed with factories, vermin-infested housing, and garbage-strewn streets.*

## The City Versus the Country

The awareness that *options* existed—that one could choose between urban and rural life—can be traced to the beginnings of the Industrial Revolution during the latter part of the eighteenth century. We need to realize, however, that this extraordinary revolution was not greeted with widespread cynicism, as it often is today. After all, the booming of industry led to the growth of the cities, the proliferation of jobs, and the migration of hopeful workers from the country. Cities were looked at as places of opportunity; a positive attitude toward the city already had a long history in the humanities.

The ancient Athenians probably are responsible for developing the *urban attitude*, though both they and the Romans who followed had poets who sometimes related strongly to the natural world. The first major female poet, Sappho (610?–580? B.C.), endows nature with almost a mystic quality in these lines:

> *Hail, gentle Evening, that bringest back*
> *All things that bright morning hath beguiled.*
> *Thou bringest the lamb, thou bringest the kid,*
> *And to its mother, her drowsy child.*

Sappho spent part of her life in Sicily and the rest of it on the island of Lesbos. The urbanization of Athens took place long after her death, and it was in Athens that Greek humanism, a concern for the products of the human mind, flourished.

The urban attitude of Athens wasn't much different at heart from what we might term the *Manhattan attitude* of today, shared by those whose world is bounded by theaters, galleries, concert halls, high-class stores, elegant restaurants, and uniformed apartment house guards. When asked why he never went for walks in the country, Socrates simply stared and replied that being by himself in lifeless nature could never take the place of a stimulating conversation with his companions. For the Athenians the city meant culture, sophistication, art, and philosophy—little short of life itself. Despite the current centuries-old cynicism toward the cities and the glorification of the natural world that the humanities have contributed since the late eighteenth century, the devoted New Yorker probably still feels as Socrates did.

*The* Manhattan attitude *of today is not much different from the urban attitude of the Athenians: a love of culture, sophistication, art, and philosophy.*

# Up with Cities!

Throughout the nineteenth and well into the twentieth century a popular theme of novels and plays was the melodramatic disaster awaiting innocent young men and women from the country when they ventured into the big city. Popular literature and drama drew a parallel between the natural and the moral world. People raised out-of-doors, on farms, in tiny villages, without "book-learnin'" and a head for business, tended to be morally pure; they were certain to be taken advantage of by the "city slickers" upon alighting from a carriage or, in more recent times, a dusty old bus.

This romantic glorification of nature and naturalness is only about two hundred years old, however. Urbanity is thousands of years old and in many, many minds is still the yardstick by which human progress is measured.

The myth of our own history is an urban one. Settlers of "these United States" were the "trailblazers," brave pioneers who "fought and tamed a wilderness." In early Hollywood westerns, these pioneers and cowboys, aided by the U.S. cavalry, righteously killed the marauding red man, whose sole purpose, so the myth implied, was to prevent the spread of "civilization."

*David Hockney,* The Brooklyn Bridge, Nov. 28th 1982: *There is little question, even in today's environmentally sensitive circles, that living in a big city can still cause excitement.* (© David Hockney)

*The original meaning of* Manifest Destiny *was that superior nations were obliged to civilize the "less-developed" world.*

In 1845 a journalist named John Louis O'Sullivan, defending the annexation of Texas, coined the phrase *Manifest Destiny*. Its underlying implication, as far as many were concerned, was that the superior nation was *obliged* to spread the gospel of civilization to the "less-developed" world.

Despite his adoration of the natural world, Walt Whitman (1819-1892), often called the true poet laureate of America, was caught up in the American love of progress; progress was an urban affair. Whitman celebrated New York City with all of its recognized problems:

> *Rich, hemm'd thick all around with sailships and steamships, an*
>     *island sixteen miles long, solid-founded,*
> *Numberless crowded streets, high growths of iron, slender, strong,*
>     *light, splendidly uprising toward clear skies,*
> *Tides swift and ample, well-loved by me, toward sundown,*
> *The flowing sea-currents, the little islands, larger adjoining islands,*
>     *the heights, the villas,*
> *The countless masts, the white shore-steamers, the lighters, the ferry-*
>     *boats, the black sea-steamers well model'd,*
> *The downtown streets, the jobbers' houses of business, the houses of*
>     *business of the ship-merchants and money-brokers, the river-streets,*
> *Immigrants arriving, fifteen or twenty thousand in a week,*
> *The carts hauling goods, the manly race of drivers of horses, the*
>     *brown-faced sailors. . . .*
> *A million people—manners free and superb—open voices—*
>     *hospitality—the most courageous and friendly young men,*
> *City of hurried and sparkling waters! city of spires and masts!*
> *City nested in bays!    My city!* [6]

Whitman's sweeping lines make the big city sound romantic and exciting, though we have no way of assessing how many were cursing their tiny living quarters or were afraid, even then, to walk the crowded streets at night. Yet the association between the expanding city and the pulsating thrill of American progress was picked up by Carl Sandburg (1878-1967), who in 1914 wrote these lines about *his* city, Chicago:

> *They tell me you are wicked and I believe them, for I have seen your*
>     *painted women under the gas lamps luring the farm boys.*
> *And they tell me you are crooked and I answer: Yes, it is true I have*
>     *seen the gunman kill and go free to kill again.*
> *And they tell me you are brutal and my reply is: On the faces of*
>     *women and children I have seen the marks of wanton hunger.*
> *And having answered so I turn once more to those who sneer at this*
>     *my city, and I give them back the sneer and say to them:*
> *Come and show me another city with lifted head singing so proud to*
>     *be alive and coarse and strong and cunning.*
> *Flinging magnetic curses amid the toil of piling job on job, here is a*
>     *tall bold slugger set vivid against the soft little cities;*
> *Fierce as a dog with tongue lapping for action, cunning as a savage*
>     *pitted against the wilderness . . .* [7]

There is little question that even in today's environmentally sensitive circles, living in big cities is still considered exciting. Sandburg and Whitman are not museum pieces. Theirs is a representative attitude that brings millions of tourists each year into the megalopolises, where hordes continue to gaze in wonder at skyscrapers. Films like Woody Allen's *Manhattan* (see Chapter 5); novels like Ayn Rand's *The Fountainhead* (1943), which glorifies human architectural improvements on nature; and musicals like Leonard Bernstein's *On the Town* (1942) and *Wonderful Town* (1953) are passionate statements by notable artists about the big city. With all its crime and its dangerous fumes and its suspect water supply, the city continues to be, in the opinion of many, the proper abode of civilized humanity.

*With all its crime and its dangerous fumes and its suspect water supply, the city continues to be, in the opinion of many, the proper abode of civilized humanity.*

## Nature as Living, Spiritual Organism

The glorification of the country was hardly limited to romantic fables about the corruption of those who go to the city. During the nineteenth century, on both sides of the Atlantic, the country became equated with nature as a whole, as though somehow the natural world disappeared as soon as you passed through the city gates. The fable was one aspect, in other words, of a much larger myth—a myth we need to pay special attention to because it has done, in its own way, as much damage as environmentalists claim the urban attitude has done.

The innocent farm boys and girls of the "corruption" fables were held to be morally pure because of the underlying romantic assumption that the natural world had a soul and was itself morally uncorrupted. This assumption has something to do with deism, the natural religion we previously discussed, which claimed that God created the world and then left it to run by itself. Though many of the deists believed their philosophy was a scientific one, rooted in Newton's natural laws, the reassuring idea that nature, though self-operating, was nonetheless *divine* still lurked in the back of many minds. As early as 1709 the poet Alexander Pope, reflecting deistic attitudes, wrote, "Unerring NATURE, still divinely bright,/One clear, unchanged, and universal light. . . .[8] "Unerring" is a certain reference to Newton's eternal natural laws, but it is also the hallmark of the morally pure.

The movement in the humanities that we call *romanticism* (already discussed in Chapter 3) tended to view nature as a living organism that was not only morally but physically healthy as well. In this movement lie the roots of those wonderful connotations we still recognize as underlying the word *natural*. We are urged to eat "natural" foods, to have children by means of "natural" childbirth. *As nature intended* is a rubber-stamped approval on anything from real-estate ads for retirees ("Spend your golden years as nature intended") to educational methods ("Have your child taught as nature intended"). *Natural* has come to mean all that is "real" and "legitimate" and "healthful" as opposed to that which is technological, chemical, electronic, medical, and intellectual.

*Natural has come to mean all that is "real" and "legitimate" and "healthful" as opposed to that which is chemical, medical, and intellectual.*

Romanticism tended as well to condemn the intellectual quest for further knowledge, equating intellectual activity with moral corruption. In romantic literature and drama, intellectuals are always from the city and either morally evil or unhappy souls. In this respect romanticism hearkened back to the poems and songs of the medieval secular poets urging young men to leave their studies and have fun outside the university walls. The point here is that *nature and the natural life are seen as taking care of themselves*. They *are* themselves the way a

*In romantic literature and drama, intellectuals are always from the city and either morally evil or unhappy.*

*Worthington Whittredge,* Trout Bridge in the Catskills: *Nature seen as taking care of herself. (In the collection of The Corcoran Gallery of Art, Museum Purchase)*

rose is itself and has no need of human know-how to create it. Human products and the works of the human mind, like complex philosophical tomes, are *not* themselves as flowers are but are superimposed upon the natural world—and never for any good purpose.

As we said in the overview, this idea—nature as a self-generating, self-healing organism with its own mysterious way of knowing what to do and in which direction to move—*may* be at least partly responsible for the belief that somehow nature will pull itself out of its current illness. Yes, perhaps we did much to cause the illness, but everything will be all right. The title song from the musical play *Dear World* (1969) reviews all of the ills from which the world is suffering, but ultimately puts the burden on the world itself, not on us. It urges the world to be a dear and "get well soon."

Like Plato's theory of the Forms (see Chapter 6), the romantic *country* (as opposed to the *urban*) attitude should not be dismissed lightly, for it has had as profound an effect upon humanity as any idea ever expressed. If it has had something to do with a *laissez-faire* policy towards nature—influencing many to believe that nature is immune to any harm we might inflict upon it—the country attitude has also been a rich source of inspiration to humanity. This very chapter, tracing the way nature has been expressed in the humanities, would not have been thought necessary if the authors did not share the view that nature *is* indeed a wondrous thing, vitally connected to the meaning of our humanness. That so many now lament what could be irreversible damage to nature may owe as much to the esthetics of nature as it does to the fear that our carelessness may be jeopardizing our very survival. The romantic poets, artists, and composers helped us to hear the music and see the glories of nature.

Perhaps the major poetic voice of nature has been that of William Words-worth (1770-1850), who, unlike some of his more emotional contemporaries, found the quiet, reflective life of reason as engaging as the sensuous excitements

*The country attitude . . . influencing many to believe that nature is immune to any harm we might inflict upon it . . .*

of the natural world. Nonetheless, Wordsworth preferred the country to the city, spending his time in the still-beautiful Lake District of northwestern England. Many of his most famous poems sing the glories of nature and the joys of childhood, when, free of adult cares and responsibility, one can revel in the miracle of just being alive. In these familiar lines the poet urges the reader never to let go of youth's vitality:

> *My heart leaps up when I behold*
>    *A rainbow in the sky;*
> *So was it when my life began;*
> *So is it now I am a man;*
> *So be it when I shall grow old,*
>    *Or let me die!*
> *The Child is father of the Man;*
> *And I could wish my days to be*
> *Bound each to each by natural piety.*[9]

The life of reason, for Wordsworth, is one of nature's gifts, but it must not be cultivated to the exclusion of the spontaneous emotions that nature inspires in us. All significant thought arises from observing and "feeling" the natural world, and it is to this world that we must always return. In other words, the only valid intellectual life is one spent trying to understand reality, not convoluted abstract ideas that do not relate to the real world. The human mind is nature *aware of itself,* though it does have the power to isolate itself and spin fantasies of an unreal world. The mind is at once humanity's greatest achievement and its most perilous foe. The maturing adult must always return to the natural world, the source of all knowledge, all inspiration, all beauty.

In one of his major poems, "Lines Composed a Few Miles Above Tintern

*The mind is at once humanity's greatest achievement and its most perilous foe.*

*Eugene Delacroix,* Horse Frightened by Storm: *"A motion and a spirit, that . . . rolls through all things." (Hungarian National Gallery, Budapest)*

Abbey," the poet finds himself as a young adult, standing in a particular spot with a spectacular view that excited him as a child:

> *And I have felt*
> *A presence that disturbs me with the joy*
> *Of elevated thoughts; a sense sublime*
> *Of something far more deeply interfused,*
> *Whose dwelling is the light of setting suns,*
> *And the round ocean and the living air,*
> *And the blue sky, and in the mind of man:*
> *A motion and a spirit, that impels*
> *All thinking things, all objects of all thought,*
> *And rolls through all things.*

The attribution of a soul to nature as well as the oneness of humanity and nature has perhaps never been more eloquently expressed.

Later in the poem he confesses that now, as a rational adult, he has obligations and responsibilities that prevent his roaming among the hills and breathing in nature's subtle fragrances, but he prays that all human beings will keep returning to their source, as he does now:

> *and this prayer I make*
> *Knowing that Nature never did betray*
> *The heart that loved her; 'tis her privilege,*
> *Through all the years of this our life, to lead*
> *From joy to joy; for she can so inform*
> *The mind that is within us, so impress*
> *With quietness and beauty, and so feed*
> *With lofty thoughts, that neither evil tongues,*
> *Rash judgments, nor the sneers of selfish men,*
> *Nor greetings where no kindness is, nor all*
> *The dreary intercourse of daily life,*
> *Shall e'er prevail against us, or disturb*
> *Our cheerful faith, that all which we behold*
> *Is full of blessings.*

Nature must be the constant, the only guide to our thoughts. If not, then our thoughts relate solely to our own needs and grow so detached from reality that human reason becomes a villain.

What Wordsworth is advising is to trust in intuition—or, as we defined it in Chapter 1, the Dionysian aspect of ourselves. After all, Dionysus was the ancient god of nature, of the spontaneous earth. For the romantic poets, though they never said it, Dionysus might have been the god of truth. One could trust intuition as one could trust nature to be self-generating and self-healing; nature would never "betray/The heart that loved her."

A distant echo of Buddhism (see Chapter 8) appears to haunt these lines from one of Wordsworth's most popular sonnets:

> *The world is too much with us; late and soon,*
> *Getting and spending, we lay waste our powers:*

*Little we see in Nature that is ours;*
*We have given our hearts away, a sordid boon!* [10]

This is not the young adult of "Tintern Abbey," returning to a secret place in his childhood. This is a weary, burned-out narrator, caught up in what the Buddhists call *samsara*: the marketplace, the endless round of cause and effect, action and reaction, which blinds us to both the natural world and our true place within it.

## Natural Radicalism

"Back to Nature" movements often inspire political radicalism and social activism. Nature enthusiasts, past and present, tend to view government officials as being driven by personal power needs or by purely abstract *Apollonian* schemes for regulating society. Either way, government is divorced from reality, which is often a synonym for the natural world. Leaving the city and returning to the spontaneous joy of living in nature has meant for some finding ways of resisting government power.

Romantic writers in Europe and America who placed intuition above reason urged their readers to follow their hearts in all things, even if this meant dropping out of society altogether. In this country the "natural radicals" were fond of pointing out that Jefferson and his colleagues founded this nation, as they stated in the Declaration of Independence, according to the laws of "Nature and Nature's God" and believed that government's only function was to assist humanity in leading free and happy lives. In the state of nature all people were equal. Controls by power groups were therefore *un*natural.

Henry David Thoreau (1817-1862) was both a political radical and a naturalist. He is best remembered as the author of the essay *Civil Disobedience* (1849) and the book *Walden, or Life in the Woods* (1854).

*Civil Disobedience* opens by amending Jefferson's "That government is best which governs least" to read "That government is best which governs not at all." The essay discusses Thoreau's protest of a state tax for the privilege of voting, a tax he said was being used to support the proslavery faction. Though the poll tax was quite small, the principle outraged Thoreau. He refused to pay the tax, and was briefly imprisoned. Soon after he was bailed out by his friend Emerson, he decided to exercise the right of a free man and seceded from the state of Massachusetts. He then embarked on his famous adventure in natural living, described in *Walden*, an adventure that may have served as the role model for the lifestyle of a good many social dropouts during the 1960s.

In 1845 he took up residence in the woods near the shores of Walden Pond in Lincoln. One can still see the site of the hut Thoreau built for $28.12½, though he would be distressed if he could visit Walden today and see the litter and learn about the pollution of his beloved pond. He did not work or take any part in the social life of Lincoln. He was entirely self-sufficient, living for the most part on wild berries and the vegetables he himself grew. He left after two years, not because he had grown weary of living without any of the city comforts many of us could not do without, but because his free and easy life was becoming too routine and he needed a fresh source of inspiration.

Nature, as Thoreau describes it in his book season by season, is indeed a spirit, a living organism. Like Wordsworth, Thoreau believed that nature could never betray a heart that loved it. Whether we would have the courage to follow in

*The desire to preserve nature has always gone hand in hand with political radicalism and social activism.*

his footsteps and forsake the city altogether, we do well to keep a copy of *Walden* on our night table, if only to help us realize the limitations of *samsara*:

> To him whose elastic and vigorous thought keeps pace with the sun, the day is a perpetual morning.
>
> To be awake is to be alive. I have never met a man who was quite awake. How could I have looked him in the face?
>
> . . . I could easily do without the post-office. I think there are very few important communications made through it. To speak critically, I never received more than one or two letters in my life . . . that were worth the postage.
>
> The mass of men lead lives of quiet desperation.

*Humankind's great challenge is not so much to build the perfect mousetrap, but to subdue and transform its worst instincts . . .*

*Joel Achenbach*

The last sentence is probably Thoreau's most celebrated contribution to the human legacy. During the 1960s it became a battle cry for many who left work, school, marriage, or family to find something better; the rationale was often that they wished to live as nature intended. Substituting the free and natural life for the nine-to-five structure they regarded as *un*natural, many found joy when they joined their peers in campsites hundreds of miles from city conveniences. Some have never been heard from since.

The validity of social rebellion or political activism is not under discussion here, nor is the contention that dropping out is equivalent to the natural life. There is, of course, the possibility that the "natural life" is wanting a clear definition. The point is that the ideology introduced by the romantic writers a long time ago is still with us. It is there when hundreds of protestors gather outside a nuclear plant, or when activists boldly ask why the National Park Service permits the cutting down and sale of millions of trees each year.

## "The Evil That Men Do"

Both Wordsworth and Thoreau agreed the world was too much with us. Both seemed never to have lost the faith that nature as living organism would always be there to reward the person who returned to it. They shared the romantic vision of nature as a self-contained spirit, capable not only of healing itself, but of healing the troubled hearts of people who have lost touch with it.

The idea of nature as its own physician is memorably expressed in these lines from a sonnet by John Keats (1795–1821), a London-born poet who discovered the joys of nature near the end of his tragically brief life:

> *After dark vapours have oppress'd our plains*
> *For a long dreary season, comes a day*
> *Born of the gentle South, and clears away*
>
> *From the sick heavens all unseemly stains.*
> *The anxious month, relieved its pains,*
> *Takes as a long-lost right the feel of May.*[11]

Romantic artists also invested nature with the awesomeness that Dante and Michelangelo gave to God and the angels. A visual parallel to the poetic ecstasy of Wordsworth and Keats is the work of the outstanding English painter of the nineteenth century, J. M. W. Turner (1775-1851), whose often vast canvases depict nature as a force that is both majestically beautiful and terrifying. The most comprehensive collection of his work is in a newly added wing of London's Tate Gallery. There the visitor will find landscapes and especially seascapes in which the furious energy at the heart of nature bursts forth in riotously colored sunsets and monstrous ocean waves—an energy that seems impossible to comprehend and never to be controlled, but always worshipped by humanity, part of but in no way superior to its grandeur.

In the paintings of Turner we find early indications that nature is far more than the gently rolling hills of Wordsworth, though the latter's vision of the "motion" and "spirit" that "rolls through all things" would have been understood by Turner. Nature is gigantic, and the implication is clearly that humanity had better not meddle with it. Interestingly enough, in the very year of Turner's death the American novelist Herman Melville (1819-1891) published his epic novel *Moby-Dick*, containing the verbal equivalent of Turner's wild and thrilling oceans. In the work of both, nature is God, but perhaps not benevolent and caring.

*In the paintings of Turner we find early indications that nature is far more than the gently rolling hills of Wordsworth.*

Yet *Moby-Dick* is not about the awesome power of nature, but the tragic attempt by one human being to destroy a huge whale that for him embodies all of nature's horrors. Captain Ahab is part demon, part hero, destroyed in a futile effort to bring the whale (and thus nature) under his control. Melville is, perhaps without realizing it, a naturalist, sounding a warning against human egotism. We finish the novel fully aware that nature is too mysterious and powerful to be understood and harnessed for human purposes. Nevertheless, humanity constantly tries to use nature when the appropriate technology becomes available. Another nineteenth-century novel cautions against such pride, this time giving its warning to science.

*We finish* Moby-Dick *fully aware that nature is too mysterious and powerful to be understood and harnessed for human purposes.*

## The Frankenstein Monster

*Frankenstein, or the Modern Prometheus* appeared in 1818, in three slender volumes, the work of a 23-year-old woman. The book has become a classic anti-science fable. The phrase *Frankenstein monster* has become a vital part of our mythology, a convenient way to describe any scheme that goes awry and turns on its creator. Certain aspects of our handling of environmental matters have already followed this pattern. For example, earlier in this century a group of meteorologists decided to see whether they could diffuse the powerful force of a hurricane by bombarding the storm clouds with dry ice. The result of the experiment was that the hurricane in question split into two, did twice as much damage, and proved twice as costly in lives and property lost.

The author of *Frankenstein* was Mary Wollstonecraft Shelley (1797-1851), wife of the famous poet and daughter of the radical political philosopher William Godwin. The novelist based her story on the ancient myth of Prometheus, one of an early species of human being that was half-human, half-god. His godly nature caused him to seek unlimited power for the human race, a power equal to that of the gods. He thus attempted to steal fire from the gods, but was caught in the act and sentenced to an eternity of anguish in which he was chained to a rock while a vulture ate his liver, a torture that could never end because the devoured liver always grew back.

Mary Shelley's version of the myth has for its central character Victor Frankenstein, who is not the mad scientist of the well-known movie adaptation but a sensitive, gentle person intrigued from childhood by science (then called "natural philosophy") and eager to learn everything that could possibly be learned so that he might make life happier for all people. As he matures, he finds himself particularly concerned with the way the body functions:

> Wealth was an inferior object; but what glory would attend the discovery, if I could but banish disease from the human frame, and render man invulnerable to any but a violent death![12]

But how is he to find the secret of immortality unless he first learns where life comes from?

Like her husband and other romantic writers, Mary Shelley saw in nature a mystery full of such secrets; the miracles of nature were an all-consuming passion. She and Percy Bysshe Shelley, whom she married at the age of 16, loved especially the grandeur of lakes and mountains. Switzerland, the locale of the novel, was her favorite spot on earth. For her, nature was to be admired, adored, worshipped, but not analyzed; certainly no mere human being had the right to tamper with its workings. The tragic flaw of Dr. Frankenstein is that he wants to be more than a *part* of nature, existing harmoniously with the rest. Not content with merely *understanding* how the spark of life enters lifeless matter—from electricity, he is convinced—he must take a further step. He must assemble parts of cadavers into an eight-foot superman who will represent the perfection of the species and live forever.

The outcome of his experiments is, as everyone knows, not what he expected:

> I had selected his features as beautiful. Beautiful!—Great God! His yellow skin scarcely covered the work of muscles; and arteries beneath; his hair was of a lustrous black, and flowing; his teeth of a pearly whiteness; but these luxuriances only formed a more horrid contrast with his watery eyes, and seemed almost of the same colour as the dun white sockets in which they were set, his shrivelled complexion, and straight black lips.[13]

Nonetheless, the "daemon," as the author calls him since he has no other name, is at first kind and gentle. Once life has entered the being, the miracle of nature goes to work; in other words, nature, undisturbed, is good at heart—a fervent romantic belief. Yet society will not leave the daemon alone. Because of his frightening appearance he is rejected, scorned, and ultimately becomes a vicious killer. "Misery," he explains after he has murdered his first victim, "made me a fiend." Before his transformation, however, he has shown the noblest of feelings. He is a vegetarian, believing it immoral to eat animal flesh. Overhearing an account of how America was discovered, he weeps at the fate of the "original inhabitants." Hiding out in a farmhouse, he stops stealing the food for which he desperately hungers when he observes members of the family sharing what little they have with each other.

*For Mary Shelley nature was to be admired, adored, worshipped, not analyzed; no mere human being had the right to tamper with its workings.*

*In the novel Frankenstein's "daemon" is kind and gentle until society turns him into a monster.*

Yet the daemon is not the only tragic result of an experiment gone wrong. In time Victor Frankenstein's own emotions turn on him. Having elevated mind over feeling, he cannot control the passion that wells up inside him to destroy his creation; in time he becomes deadlier than his monster. In an extraordinary finale, anticipating Melville's *Moby-Dick* by over 30 years, Frankenstein pursues his prey to the very ends of the earth, insanely believing, as does Captain Ahab, that once the monster is destroyed, all evil will vanish from the earth.

In the end it is Frankenstein, not the daemon, who dies. The creature is reclaimed by nature, his true and only parent. Dwarfed by the ice mountains of the polar circle, he sails on a raft of ice into a mist, there to meet who knows what destiny. We feel that he belongs in this primordial limbo, outside of time, deep within which lie the ultimate secrets, glimpsed and even unleashed but never grasped or fully controlled by human intelligence.

Were an adventurous film director bold enough to put the true Mary Shelley novel on the screen, he or she would be advised to take the musical background from the Symphony no. 7 by English composer Ralph Vaughn Williams (1872-1958), appropriately subtitled *The Antarctic Symphony*. Making strings sound like echoes from an untraveled land and using human voices in ways that hypnotize the listener, Vaughn Williams seems to be reaching into the very heart of existence and finding a secret he can hear but not name and which, like the daemon, is "borne away by the waves, and lost in darkness and distance."

If Vaughn Williams and Mary Shelley were living today, they might advise us to hold onto—or, in many cases, to acquire—this sense of mystery that the romantics gave to nature. This mystic reverence for the power behind all existence is well understood by our greatest scientists, those who spend their lives at the boundaries of human knowledge. Mary Shelley's villain was a scientist, true, but he was a scientist who lost sight of his own limitations; those who have harmed nature the most may be people interested primarily in their own glory. The humanities have not been afraid to face this grim possibility.

## The Desecration of Nature as a Sign of Moral Bankruptcy

Ever since Greek dramatists showed the awful consequences that befall arrogant humans who struggle against the fate decreed for them, one of the roles willingly assumed by the humanities has been that of moral guardian. Outcries against the desecration of nature are often underscored by the accusation that it is the fault of the dominant white culture, which has become obsessed with the ideal of economic success at all costs. Many of these outcries have, perhaps understandably, remained in relative obscurity, especially the early warnings. There were, for example, abundant reproofs from native Americans, who saw both land and wildlife plundered for gain.

Crowfoot (1821-1890), a spokesperson for the Blackfoot nation, sees all existence from nature's viewpoint in this haiku-like statement:

> What is life? It is the flash of a firefly in the night. It is the breath of a buffalo in the winter time. It is the little shadow which runs across the grass and loses itself in the Sunset.[14]

*"To the center of the world you have taken me and showed the goodness and the beauty and the strangeness of the greening earth, the only mother—and there the spirit shapes of things, as they should be, you have shown to me and I have seen."*

*John G. Neihardt*
Black Elk Speaks

The difference between those who identify with the earth and those who believe it is their privilege to bend the earth to their will is made clear by a venerable holy woman of the Wintu nation:

> The white people never cared for land or deer or bear. When we Indians kill meat, we eat it all up. When we dig roots we make little holes. When we burn grass for grasshoppers we don't ruin things. We shake down acorns and pinenuts. We don't chop down trees, kill everything. The tree says, "Don't. I am sore. Don't hurt me." But they chop it down and cut it up. The spirit of the land hates them.[15]

*Heart of Darkness: a strong indictment of moral bankruptcy in the dominant culture.*

A strong theme in modern humanities has been that of the exploitation of those once labeled "primitive" or "backward." (Even the recent substitution of words like "developing" still carries the hidden assumption that millions of people are somehow lacking.) In 1889, during a period of economic growth that was frequently spurred by the taking away of lands and resources belonging to such "developing" areas of the world, a novelette was published, the work of a Russian-born writer of Polish ancestry whose original name was Teodor Jozef Konrad Korzeniowski, but who changed it to Joseph Conrad after becoming a British subject in 1886. It was titled *Heart of Darkness*, and it remains one of the strongest indictments of moral bankruptcy in the dominant culture ever written.

Conrad (1857-1924) spent his formative years working on ships that took him to remote corners of the globe, including the then Belgian Congo (now Zaire), a relatively unexplored, largely impenetrable land that nonetheless promised untold wealth in ivory for the intrepid elephant hunter. The narrator of the story is Charlie Marlow, a thinly disguised alter ego of Conrad himself, who used the character in the same role for most of his works. Marlow is hired by a trading company that sends him into the Congo, widely characterized as a dangerous place inhabited by warring savages, to determine whether the company's principal trader, an Austrian named Kurtz, is still alive. Kurtz has not been heard from in some time.

Early in the narrative Marlow describes what it felt like to enter the eerie, forbidding land:

> "Going up that river was like travelling back to the earliest beginnings of the world, when vegetation rioted on the earth and the big trees were kings. An empty stream, a great silence, an impenetrable forest."[16]

On the way he hears legend after legend about the extraordinary Kurtz, reputed to be a wilderness tamer and a man with godlike status in the eyes of the natives. White men in outlying posts refer to Kurtz as "a prodigy . . . an emissary of pity, and science, and progress." Whatever the man is, we know that he is totally European: "His mother was half-English, his father was half-French. All Europe contributed to the making of Kurtz."

What we gradually discover is that Kurtz actually represents all that went wrong with European civilization, beginning with the myth that humanity was the noblest achievement of evolution and that the white man was the noblest of the species. Armed with a belief in the infallibility of white civilization and in the inherent goodness of white "take-overs," Kurtz, we learn, had allowed himself to

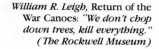

*William R. Leigh,* Return of the
War Canoes: *"We don't chop
down trees, kill everything."*
(*The Rockwell Museum*)

become a god, persuading himself it was in the best interest of the natives. But
what he did not know—and what Marlow comes to see—is that the myth serves
only to mask the *real* heart of darkness that lies within Kurtz himself:

> "But the wilderness had found him out early, and had taken on him a
> terrible vengeance for this fantastic invasion. I think it had whispered
> to him things about himself which he did not know."[17]

In one of the most dramatically anticipated confrontations in all of literature, Marlow and the reader finally meet Kurtz after the latter has been mortally
wounded during an explosive and bloody revolution. "I had immense plans,"
Kurtz insists. "I was on the threshold of great things." What these were to have
been, we never find out. Perhaps in his madness the man thought he was going to
impose the order and discipline of a great civilization upon a people who would
otherwise have never seen the light of human "progress." The many murders
committed by Kurtz were perhaps the result of "savage resistance" to his plan. Or
perhaps they were, more obviously, the evidence of unstoppable power run wild:

> "There was nothing either above or below him, and he knew it. He
> had kicked himself loose of the earth. Confound the man! He had
> kicked the very earth to pieces."[18]

Conrad does not give a full accounting of Kurtz's sins, but we do know
that the man has presided "at certain midnight dances ending with unspeakable
rites"; that he has probably stolen a beautiful native woman from her husband; that

he has been party to the wanton killing of elephants for their ivory; and that he has murdered anyone who stood in his way. Surrounding his house are many poles, each decorated with a shrunken human head. As he dies in Marlow's presence, Kurtz, having looked deep into his soul at the very last, whispers, "The horror! The horror!"

Returning to the civilized gentility of London, Marlow visits the grieving widow of Kurtz. When she asks whether her husband had uttered any final words, Marlow lies and tells her that "his last words were of you." Is Conrad saying that we have gone too far along our chosen course to admit our errors and so must live out the lie? Or that civilization does, after all, have its noble aspects, knowing when to lie to protect this woman from a brutal, and for her ultimately useless, truth? One suspects the latter is the interpretation Conrad preferred. The dominant theme in his writings is the crucial importance of developing a higher ethical consciousness. Only this consciousness will save us.

## Epilogue

Today, when the massive damage that has been and continues to be done to nature—still in the name of progress—is well known, how are the humanities responding?

The reader can see from the frontispiece and the picture on page 433 that our visual artists are responding to the tragedy. We should expect them to be among the first to give expression to their outrage and cynical humor, for those whose passion is to seek beauty in their surroundings may be having a difficult time of it at the moment.

Bookstores are inundated with nonfiction works, such as Rachel Carson's *Silent Spring* (1962), which started the present environmental movement with its startling revelations about the deadly pesticide DDT. Other grim titles include *The Fate of the Earth* (1982) and *The End of Nature* (1989). The authors are sometimes scientists, sometimes humanists, who in other eras might have been talking about love or the breakup of the family or corruption in high places. They are talking now about how an excess of carbon dioxide (from automobile emissions and burning coal) is causing the earth's atmosphere to retain more and more heat from the sun, leading to the so-called greenhouse effect (and thus possibly to the melting of the polar ice caps and an increase in sea levels). They are talking about the double risk we take when we cut down huge repositories of trees, like those in ancient South American rain forests. In addition to sending forth tons and tons of carbon dioxide that has been retained by the trees, those who despoil the rain forests for economic and political advantages are depriving us of a place where much of the carbon dioxide already in the atmosphere can go. From these and other books we discover that trees breathe in as much carbon dioxide as they breathe out oxygen. In *The Next Hundred Years: Shaping the Fate of Our Living Earth* (1990), Jonathan Weiner predicts we could solve the tree problem if every man, woman, and child on earth were to plant a tree tomorrow and never cut it down. One finds optimism somewhat difficult when confronting the unlikelihood of such action.

Nor, we discover, is the tree problem limited to South America. Those of us who have hiked along the nature trails in Yosemite, Grand Teton, or Yellowstone, observed the abundance of trees, and felt a comfortable sense that all was well, would be astonished to learn that our own government has allowed logging companies to cut staggering numbers of trees on federal lands. A forest ranger was recently removed from her position because of her outspoken complaints against the practice.

These books warn us, too, about what CFC (chlorofluorocarbon) gases, expelled into the atmosphere when we use aerosol spray cans or our air conditioners, are doing to the ozone layer. The extinction of the human race from the deterioration of ozone is not imminent, but future inhabitants of the planet may be living mostly indoors (using air-conditioners that will only worsen the problem).

The trashing of our cities through litter and pollution is not as dangerous as these less-visual kinds of damage, but it *is* a sign that the earth is not being cared for. Our artists are sensitive to this sign, as Conrad was to the growing sickness of human behavior. In 1962 Anthony Burgess wrote a novel called *A Clockwork Orange* about a charming cockney youth who plays classical music but also happens to have not one whit of love or compassion inside him. The youth roams the filthy streets of a futuristic London with his buddies, committing acts of violence just for fun, as when they beat up a harmless old drunk:

> So we cracked into him lovely, grinning all over our litsos, but he still went on singing. Then we tripped him so he laid down flat and heavy and a bucketload of beer-vomit came whooshing out. That was disgusting so we gave him the boot, one go each, and then it was blood, not song or vomit, that came out of his filthy old rot. Then we went our way.[19]

*The quest itself is always about seeing and learning. And when the heroine of the great myth returns—Rachel Carson, Joan of Arc, Dorothy of Oz—she bears a vision that is meant to set the world back on its course.*

*Betsy Hilbert*

*Edward Hopper,* Seven A.M. *(1948): Our visual artists are responding to the tragedy. (Collection of Whitney Museum of American Art, New York. Purchase and exchange)*

At first one wonders why the author would create a character like Alex and expect us to care anything about him. But we soon realize that he *has* a soul, that he has human potential, which has been corrupted like the city he lives in, polluted like the earth. The trouble is that nobody will help him find his humanness. People have grown terrified of him. His own parents refuse to protect him. He is captured and made to undergo a "rehabilitation" program that is as sadistic as he was.

Yet, after he is released, facing an uncertain future penniless and alone, Alex is forced to dig far down inside himself for the resources to survive. Burgess is not saying he is morally regenerated, but neither is the author predicting the demise of human civilization. *The spark of civilization is still there.* Alex has turned 18, and, realizing Mozart had already done much significant work by that age, he decides he will get on with his life:

> Tomorrow is all like sweet flowers and the turning vonny earth and the stars and the old Luna up there. . . . A terrible grahzny vonny world really.[20]

Perhaps Burgess was thinking of Conrad's novel, thinking that we are going to have to look deeply and long at the moral and physical evil that has been done to the earth and its people *by* its people, that we have to have the courage to say "The horror! The horror!" before redemption is possible. We may find a measure of hope in the fact that Alex has a vision of his future as "sweet flowers."

No one has yet told us (though some have come close) that it is too late. Jonathan Weiner may end *The Next Hundred Years* with the grim assurance that "the world will never be the same," but both humanity and the natural world have powers yet untapped. Despite centuries of believing it owned the earth or that nature was a self-healing, miraculous organism, humanity has not managed to extinguish the human enterprise. If this light were fading, why write books like *The End of Nature* in the first place? Why have this chapter?

If they teach anything, the humanities teach flexibility of thought, a willingness to learn from the mistakes of the past. If we stand at the top of Pike's Peak and thrill to the wonders of existence, we can also remind ourselves that we have a part to play in the preservation and continuity of both nature and our species. Like Wordsworth, we need to reach a balance between the joy of living and the critical awareness of what it takes to have that privilege.

The humanities tell us that the human enterprise will, because it must, continue. But since each of us is human, how it will continue will be determined by what *we* do.

*"Tomorrow is all like sweet flowers and the turning vonny earth and the stars and the old Luna up there. . . . A terrible grahzny vonny world really."*

# Glossary

*daemon:* A term by which the creature is sometimes called in the novel *Frankenstein*. It should not be confused with the word "demon" because it has no diabolic connotations. One of Mary

Shelley's points is indeed that the creature was made evil by society's diabolic attacks on *him*.

*deism:* A kind of religious philosophy popular during the eighteenth century in which God is said to have created the world, then left it to run by itself.

*Manifest Destiny:* A popular phrase coined in 1845 to support the United States's annexation of Texas. It then came to mean, for some, that the United States had an obligation to become a world leader and a role model for "less-advanced" nations.

*nature:* A word that occurs many times in this chapter and does not lend itself to a generic definition. It has been used as a reference to the world "out there" as perceived by the senses; to

a system of laws governing all the activities and interactions in the universe; to an indwelling spirit or mind that governs the universe and all of the species of life on earth as well as any that might exist elsewhere; and to the environment and the ecosystems within it that are now in critical danger.

## Notes

1. *As You Like It*, II.i.12-17.
2. Ibid., 26-27.
3. Ibid., 47-49.
4. Ibid., II.vii.58-62.
5. Ibid., V.iv.195-196.
6. From "Mannahatta," in the *Calamus* section of *Leaves of Grass* (1891-1892).
7. "Chicago," in *The Complete Poems of Carl Sandburg*, Revised and Expanded Edition (New York: Harcourt Brace Jovanovich, 1969).
8. From *Essay on Criticism* (1711).
9. "My Heart Leaps Up" (1807).
10. "The World Is Too Much with Us" (1807).
11. "After Dark Vapours Have Oppress'd Our Plains" (1817).
12. *Frankenstein, or the Modern Prometheus* (Berkeley: University of California Press, 1984), 24.
13. Ibid., 51.
14. T. C. McLuhan, *Touch the Earth* (New York: Promontory Press, 1971), 12.
15. Ibid., 15.
16. *Heart of Darkness* (New York: Norton, 1971), 34.
17. Ibid., 59.
18. Ibid., 67.
19. *A Clockwork Orange* (New York: Norton, 1987), 14.
20. Ibid., 191.

## Suggested Reading

Burgess, Anthony. *A Clockwork Orange*. New York: Norton, 1987. The novel, written a quarter of a century ago, must be read in the new edition of 1987 because it contains the original ending, omitted in earlier publications. In addition, it has a new introduction by Burgess himself, in which he explains that he wanted to leave the reader with some hope for the future. The antihero, Alex, has been rehabilitated, and presumably will use his aggressive nature for good, not evil. The title, by the way, has much to do with the romantic view of nature as a living

organism. Alex's natural self, with a passion for living that *could* be the source of much good, is altered through behavioral technology and becomes a machine. Perhaps this is a metaphor that Burgess wants applied to our desecration of nature as a whole.

Carson, Rachel. *Silent Spring*. Intro. Paul R. Ehrlich. Greenwich, Conn.: Fawcett Publications, 1970. Originally published in 1962, this seminal work in environmental studies should be read along with Ehrlich's introduction, because by 1970 its influence was beginning to be recorded. The author's intent was to expose the dangers to vegetation and insect life from the pesticide DDT, but the thoroughly documented book triggered a massive reaction from early environmentalists and may have been responsible for getting the movement off the ground.

Conrad, Joseph. *Heart of Darkness*. Intro. Albert Guerard. New York: New American Library, 1950. With our growing concern for the environment and for the violation of human rights, we are confident that there will be a resurgence of interest in this short but powerful book. (If the above edition is not found, you can look for the 1972 Norton publication, edited by Robert Kimbrough.)

Elkington, John, and Julia Hailes. *The Green Consumer*. New York: Penguin Books, 1990. A wonderful catalogue of environmental problems we can still do something about.

Gould, Stephen Jay. *Wonderful Life! The Burgess Shale and the Nature of History*. New York: Norton, 1989. The popular anthropology lecturer and writer turns his attention to the significance of the fossil imprints discovered in British Columbia on a rocky plateau named for the man who found them. These imprints are those of animals extinct for millions of years, which may have been hardier than others that survived far longer. Gould makes the stunning points that Darwin's theory of natural selection (survival of the fittest) may not be accurate after all and that species may survive through random chance. If this new theory holds up, it would give us humans less reason to pat ourselves on the back for being the crowning glory of an evolutionary process.

Krutch, Joseph Wood. *The Modern Temper*. New York: Harcourt Brace Jovanovich, 1957. Written in 1927, this work probably received less attention than it should have in those days of moral liberation and high-flying optimism about the state of the country. Krutch was undoubtedly too pessimistic for the mood of the times, warning his readers that humanity might just be putting itself out of business. In the key chapter, "The Paradox of Humanism," he says that in its self-centered preoccupation with its own achievements and problems, humanity has so detached itself from nature that it no longer knows how to survive in the natural world. Worth reading now in the light of the drastic state in which we find ourselves, especially by those who need a jolt.

McGibben, Bill. *The End of Nature*. New York: Doubleday/Anchor Books, 1989. This is a depressing book (you can tell just from the title) about the undeniable signs that the dread catastrophe about which scientists have been warning us is about to come to pass. There are still steps that can be taken, however.

McLuhan, T. C. *Touch the Earth: A Self-Portrait of Indian Existence*. New York: Promontory Press, 1971. A beautifully edited and photographed collection of Indian wisdom and poetic expressions that appeared during the peak of the "folk" revival of the late 1960s. What the Indian writers have to say about their love of nature and the shameful desecration of it by the white man is so relevant to our growing environmental awareness that the book deserves to be reissued.

Nash, Roderick. *Rights of Nature: A History of Environmental Ethics*. Madison: University of Wisconsin Press, 1989. The author makes two strong points. One is that humanity can best serve its own cause by doing everything possible to save the earth. The other is that nature is a living system and as such has its own rights, among them the right to survive.

Shelley, Mary Wollstonecraft. *Frankenstein, or the Modern Prometheus*. Berkeley: University of California Press, 1984. Mary Shelley is among the many women in the humanities who have been unjustly ignored for a long time. Her novel was the first major work to address the issue of arrogant humanity feeling superior to nature and thus bringing about tragedy. Try to get hold of this beautifully illustrated edition before it disappears.

Steger, Will, and Jon Bowermaster. *Saving the Earth: A Citizen's Guide to Environmental Action*. New York: Knopf, 1990. It's all here—everything you are afraid to find out about the desecration of the planet but secretly know you should know: global warming, ozone depletion, smog, acid rain, fresh- and salt-water pollution, hazardous waste, the disappearance of the rain forests, and overpopulation.

Weiner, Jonathan. *The Next Hundred Years: Shaping the Fate of Our Living Earth*. New York: Bantam Books, 1990. Though this is a detailed and readably scientific analysis of the disasters that have happened or are waiting to happen, one can tell from the title that all is not gloom and doom. The author would not have used this title if he didn't believe the earth was going to last another hundred years. However, one needs to be alerted to the sometimes drastic alterations in human behavior that must come about if this world is going to offer much pleasure to the next generations.

*Henri Matisse,* Piano Lesson *(1916) (Oil on canvas, 8' 1/2" x 6' 11-3/4". Collection, The Museum of Modern Art, New York. Mrs. Simon Guggenheim Fund)*

# *Freedom*

## *Overview*

Though it might seem that, given a choice, everyone would prefer to be free, there is something convenient about a belief that we are not. Without freedom, one can explain a lack of success, happiness, and clear thinking in one's life. Without freedom, the individual is not in control; rather, "things happen" from the outside.

Those who believe that freedom is *not* a human attribute share the assumptions of a great many philosophers, sociologists, economists, and psychologists. More important than freedom, say these commentators, are the accidents of birth: the genetic code, which determines physical characteristics and perhaps intellectual ones as well; family class and income, which can set limits on opportunity; parental success in nurturing children, which can determine whether offspring receive damaging bruises or encouragement to fulfill their potential; and even time itself. The accident of having been born in one year rather than another is clearly a factor beyond one's control. Yet, say those who question the concept of freedom, the attributes admired and needed by one generation may be worthless in another. Thus one may claim that luck or fate is more important than freedom.

An assumption of the humanities is that freedom is vital to the art of being human, which can be described as the art of making free and intelligent choices among significant options. Traditionally, the study of the humanities has shared this assumption, insisting that the freedom to create and the freedom to enjoy what has been created are natural rights everyone should have.

Where these rights are denied, poets cry out in defiance, artists paint their anger in bold colors, composers sound their trumpets—or would if they could. No great art has been created explicitly to defend enslavement or to justify oppression. The poet William Blake expressed the matter simply and incisively:

> *A robin redbreast in a cage*
> *Puts all Heaven in a rage.*

*Man is free. This is at once a heady luxury and also the source of his discontent.*

*Carlton Beck*

On the other hand, even those who claim to believe in freedom are often unwilling to grant it to everyone. The Greeks invented the word and concept of *democracy* and passed on as their legacy the model of the democratic state in which every citizen was "free" to think, to question, to speak out. But "citizens" comprised only five percent of the population. The rest were slaves and women, neither of whom were expected to be rational, responsible human beings. In other words, the Greeks believed that only those should be free who could handle freedom. Even at that, Socrates, surely as rational as a person could have been, was deprived first of freedom, then of life.

That freedom is, or should be, the basic human condition is implicit in our own Bill of Rights, the remarkable first ten constitutional amendments, ratified in 1791. Guaranteed, among others, are the rights to speak out freely, to assemble in groups, to have one's dwelling protected against forcible entry without a warrant, and to remain silent rather than testify against oneself. In our own time the United Nations has passed the Universal Declaration of Human Rights, reaffirming what much of the world already knew but perhaps took for granted.

From a humanistic perspective, the issue is greater than that of liberties denied or the bitter history of cruel inhumanities inflicted upon the innocent—appalling as those issues surely are. What saddens those who have seen loved ones tortured and slain, who have dedicated themselves to a continuing, desperate fight for freedom, is the undeniable fact that *freedom is still being rejected by those who do not recognize its worth*, like so many sparkling diamonds carelessly thrown away.

But before we decide that freedom is ours if we would only reach out for it, we must consider arguments for and against its very existence.

## Determinism: The View That All People Are Limited in Their Choices

First we will consider the many arguments claiming that we are not, or not completely, free. Only when we offer a meaningful challenge to these arguments do the words *I am free* acquire true and powerful significance. Growing up and constantly hearing the phrase *free country* is likely to put our rational faculties to sleep, to lull us into the unexamined assumption that because we live in a "free country," we must obviously be free.

Freedom is the condition of being able to choose between alternatives, particularly those that strongly oppose each other: obeying the speed limit or driving recklessly down the highway; spending one's entire paycheck on clothes and candy or putting a substantial portion aside for a "rainy day"; saying yes to a marriage proposal or suggesting that marriage be shelved in favor of living together. Listing the number of options with which we are faced each day might cause us to think we are indeed free.

Yet stop a moment and reflect on even one of these options. Without an automobile, the first alternatives are reduced to just words. There is a limitation right off. Without the money or the credit we cannot buy the automobile. Another limitation. Without a job we cannot have either money or credit. What kind of job? It has to be a good one if we seek a certain kind of automobile. If we are born with some physical disability or do not have sufficient education, many jobs are out of the question. Of course, money to buy ten cars can be inherited or left by a benefactor, but to qualify, we have to be born in the right place or have been lucky in our acquaintances.

Economic considerations encompass only one class of limitations. Suppose one is born without the coordination that makes driving possible at all: a genetic limitation. In order to go 80 mph on the highway, one must be willing to risk being stopped by the police. Even if this were a first offense, one would be forever deprived of the opportunity to commit a first offense again: a legal limitation. As the offenses mount up, the limitations on choice become imposing.

There exists almost no set of alternatives that are without limitations. Hamlet, contemplating suicide in the "To be or not to be" soliloquy, may think at first that he is free to make the decision; as he analyzes the question, however, he discovers so many reasons *not* to take his own life that we conclude he is anything but free.

The issue of freedom has haunted philosophers for a long time, and our perspective appears to show that there are more arguments *against* freedom than *for* it. *Determinism* is a broad term covering a wide-ranging category of philosophies that seek to prove freedom cannot exist. In its generic form, the word means the belief that one's choices are too severely limited for there to be any question of making a *free* choice, ever.

Determinism originally emerged from the eighteenth-century revolution in philosophy, triggered by science—in particular, the impact of the view that there can be no effect without natural cause. Taking this scientific law and applying it to human behavior, philosophers have argued that all choice is limited by prior condition, limited so severely that it cannot be considered free. Each of us is in fact the product of a chain of cause and effect stretching back to the very dawn of existence.

Let us examine a few of the main categories of deterministic philosophy.

*In all this he always acts according to necessary laws, from which he has no means of emancipating himself.*

*Baron d'Holbach*

## Institutions: Rousseau

One of the staunchest advocates of the philosophy of total and unlimited freedom for all was Jean-Jacques Rousseau (1712-1778), considered by many as the conscious architect of the French Revolution, by some as the indirect architect of

*If there is no natural condition as freedom, then the humanist ideal is open to serious question.*

modern society, and by still others as the individual most responsible for all of the *evils* in that society.

In fanning the revolutionary flames beginning to sweep through a France increasingly outraged at the decadence of the aristocracy and the injustices suffered by the common people, Rousseau constructed a mythical account of the origin of the species to prove that freedom was both a natural condition and a natural right. Called *A Discourse on the Origins of Inequality*, the myth draws a romantic picture of a lost age of innocence, when early people lived in peace and harmony, sharing the fruits of the abundant earth through a common realization that nature provided equal bounty for everyone. At this time no laws or government existed because, obviously, law and government are not necessary when everyone is happy and there is no crime.

Then one day came the *man with the stick*, the first person to take it into his head to grab off more than his natural share of things, the first person to *abuse* nature's gift of freedom by putting it to his own advantage. With his stick he carved out a private piece of territory for himself:

> The first man, who, after enclosing a piece of ground, took it into his head to say, "This is mine," and found people simple enough to believe him, was the true founder of civil society.

The man with the stick was the founder of society because, by creating the model of the exploiter (the inhuman alternative to natural freedom), he and his followers became an ever-present threat to the rights of the others. They therefore had to be suppressed by the gradual development of law, government, and all other institutions dedicated to the curtailment, or the limitation, of all rights. But these "safeguards of liberty," once in place, become despotic in themselves.

Rousseau's position is clearly a revolutionary one. Revolution, even if violent, is a genuine alternative to exploitation and may often be the only means by which to deal with it. The first revolution against the man with the stick would, however, have been a peaceful one had there arisen a daring enough activist

> who, pulling up the stakes or filling up the ditches, should have cried to his fellows: Be sure not to listen to this imposter; you are lost if you forget that the fruits of the earth belong equally to us all, and the earth itself to nobody!

If Rousseau not only explains but justifies revolution in the name of natural rights belonging to all, he does *not* in his myth account for the *origin* of the man with the stick. What made this one man decide to become possessive, when the others were joyously bobbing for golden apples in an age of sun and fun? Or was he merely the first to manifest himself? Did the potential for exploitation lie deep within *every* member of that "innocent" society? If so, when were institutional safeguards ever *not* needed?

Rousseau's anti-institutional bias is based on the assumption that in the "state of nature" (a phrase hotly debated then and since) humankind is decent, tame, moral, and benevolent. Only when held in check, only when threatened with punishment for disobedient acts, do people become hateful, aggressive, and violent—except for periods of rebelling in a just cause. But what Rousseau did not

*I am as free as Nature
first made man,
Ere the base laws of
servitude began,
When wild in woods the
noble savage ran.*

*John Dryden*

know, because he died a decade before the revolution he predicted, was that Napoleon Bonaparte would rise from the ashes of France and, sword in hand, lead forth a new age of exploitation, perhaps even more oppressive than the one it was to supplant.

How shall we ever put Rousseau's assumption to the test? How shall we ever know whether most people, left on their own without law or government, would remain peaceful and willing to share the fruits of the earth with each other, or whether the Men with Sticks would come along and start once again the cycle of exploitation and revolution? What *does* appear certain is that no revolution within human memory has been without its exploiters. We think of Jonestown and its loyal population, led to a remote wilderness in the name of communal love and decency, only to yield up life itself in the name of that very loyalty.

## Self-Image: Nietzsche

Friedrich Nietzsche, who is discussed in Chapter 1 in connection with the Apollo/ Dionysus polarity, was more than concerned—he was *obsessed*—with the problem of the exploiter. For Nietzsche, no god imposed a definite meaning or purpose on life. Existence therefore belonged to the person who could define it and persuade others to follow. All values were relative, and the person who could convince everyone else of certain "truths" would prevail. Whether the truths were "true" or not did not matter, so long as people were willing to accept them.

Nietzsche thus divided society into two classes of people: masters and slaves. The masters were those who assumed they could prevail, and, in the absence of serious opposition, *did* prevail. The slaves were those who were willing to be exploited—would, in fact, *rather* be exploited than live in confusion, without guidelines or direction.

Nietzsche coined the label *übermensch*, or "superman," to refer to the master who proved eminently successful in imposing his own vision of reality, his own value system, upon others. In Nietzsche's view, Jesus Christ was the very model of the superman. Nietzsche never believed that Jesus was a supernatural being, but he marveled at Jesus' ability to sway a crowd. Nietzsche saw that Jesus was able to convince multitudes that he was the son of God, sent down to earth by his father to redeem humankind. What concerned Nietzsche was not the authenticity of the claim but the model that Jesus represented. It could be possible for someone equally visionary to rise up, step forward, and claim to be the vehicle of the Divine Voice.

Nietzsche also believed that people born into a "slave" background—that is, belonging to a group of people having a slave mentality—would develop their parents' self-negation. People would not claim a right to freedom if all they ever heard in the home was that no one in the family deserved much of anything and should be grateful for whatever charity those "better" than they (i.e., the "masters") wished to grant. For Nietzsche, the slave outlook valued virtues such as charity, love, altruism, and caring, but the master outlook valued power, strength, cleverness, manipulation, and all of the characteristics that gave authority to the human enterprise. The master thus honored traits that could restrain the impulses of the slave mentality.

Nietzsche believed no one was necessarily intended to be either a slave or a master. That is, human nature did not automatically place a person in one category or the other. But human nature *did* tend to narrow itself down to two

*Nietzsche never believed that Jesus was a supernatural being, but he marveled at Jesus' ability to sway a crowd.*

*For Nietzsche the urge for freedom is not shared by all. Some people are far happier allowing themselves to be led.*

alternatives. Nietzsche believed the choice was a matter of laziness versus aggressiveness. Some people had sluggish metabolisms, while others were hell-bent on bettering themselves no matter at whose expense. Whether or not the division is as natural as Nietzsche believed, it seems clear that the urge for freedom is not shared by all. Some people are far happier allowing themselves to be led.

## History and Economics: Hegel and Marx

Not humanity, not nature, but money calls the tune—so believed Karl Marx (1818-1883), the economist and philosopher who, in the opinion of many intellectual historians, brought forth ideas that permanently altered the destiny of the human race. As an economist, he developed a theory that explained the behavior of all members of society: the haves, the in-betweens, and the have-nots. As a philosopher, he created a blueprint for a utopian, classless society in which the haves and have-nots would disappear, and, in the words of Rousseau, the fruits of the earth would belong to all. The ideas contained in *The Communist Manifesto*, published in 1843 and coauthored by Marx and his colleague Friedrich Engels (1820-1895), changed the world, though both would have said it was economics that did the changing and all they did was report the facts.

As a young intellectual Karl Marx fell under the strong influence of an earlier German philosopher, Georg Wilhelm Friedrich Hegel (1770-1831), who had developed two massive theories pertaining to the workings of the human mind and human history. Both theories were absorbed and then reinterpreted by Marx.

Hegel developed a logical method of thinking, called a *dialectic*, based on his view of how the mind operates. Like everything else in nature, Hegel believed, the mind oscillates back and forth between poles and strives for a balance between them. First we begin with a *thesis*, the conviction that something is true. Soon the thesis is countered by its own opposite, which Hegel called the *antithesis*, for in testing the validity of a proposed truth, we must determine whether its negation can also be entertained. If the antithesis and thesis can be held with equal conviction but *each negates the other*, then the mind has no choice but to seek a point midway between the two, a point called the *synthesis*.

*Marx applied Hegel's logical method, called the* dialectic, *to the economic progressions of history and came to the conclusion that an economic synthesis was logical and inevitable.*

What interested Marx particularly was the application of the dialectic to the theory of history that Hegel also worked out. In the dialectical method, both poles—the thesis and the antithesis—are limited by what they contain. If the thesis statement is positive—for instance, *He is an only child* (assuming, of course, that we do not *know* whether he is, only that we can entertain such an idea)—we can say that the statement is limited by not including its negation, *He is not an only child*, which, lacking the facts, we can also believe. But the antithesis is also limited by not including its positive form. The synthesis statement, *He is or is not an only child*, is, of course, not limited, since it includes both the positive and the negative versions. Hegel saw human history as an alternation of political and social systems, all in some way limiting the freedom of human beings, as thesis and antithesis were limited. He envisioned a future "synthesis" world in which people were totally free of all limitations—the philosophical model for the Marxian classless society.

*The freedom and independence of the worker during the labor process do not exist.*

*Marx*

Marx saw Hegel's dialectic working through history in economic form; hence the name *dialectical materialism*, by which the Marxian theory of history is better known. For Marx, the future would bring freedom from want, from the one

*Diego Rivera,* Detroit Industry *(1932–33): Not humanity, not nature, but money calls the tune—so believed Karl Marx. (The Detroit Institute of Arts, Founders Society Purchase, Edsel B. Ford Fund and Gift of Edsel B. Ford. Photo: Dirk Bakker, Courtesy the Empire Group)*

important negative factor in the life of ordinary working-class citizens: the lack of enough money to meet their needs and those of their family. His future world developed an *economic synthesis*, in which the balance of power was held not by the affluent (society's positive thesis statement—in short, the haves), nor by the poor (the antithesis—or the have-nots), but by all. *Communism* would be a social structure in which all property was publicly owned.

Dialectical materialism has, of course, an underlying assumption: the meeting of economic needs is what drives human beings, what alone accounts for human behavior. Everything we do has an economic aim, whether we know it or not. If we are rich, we act so as to become richer or at least to preserve what we have. If we are an in-between, everything we do is in the interest of climbing upward. If we are poor, we love, hate, reward, and punish according to the way these actions are likely to affect our pocketbook.

Traditional humanists often find it degrading to suppose that money should be a paramount concern. After all, philosophy, literature, and music are supposed to be *alternatives* to the accumulation of wealth, are they not? Still, finding pleasure in other than material resources is one thing; denying that economic motivation drives enlightened people is quite another.

The art of being human does not entail making a choice between the humanities and money. It *does* require that we observe ourselves in action. If economic motives are not the sole reasons why we do what we do, they *are* sometimes the major ones. Common sense tells us that the poorer we are, the more we look for opportunities to advance. The chronically poor, those who barely survive on the fringes of society, derive values from their economic plight. They may resent the life that passes around them. They probably admire charity

*When the state exists, there is no freedom. When there is freedom, there will be no state.*

*Lenin*

*The inherent vice of capitalism is the unequal sharing of blessings; the inherent virtue of socialism is the equal sharing of miseries.*

*Winston Churchill*

*While all of our choices may not be economically determined, there are times in everyone's life when money is the root of action.*

*In what does the alienation of labor consist? First, that the work is external to the worker, that it is not a part of his nature, that consequently he does not fulfill himself in his work but denies himself, has a feeling of misery, not of well-being . . .*

*Karl Marx*

and a helping hand. But even creative artists, once romantically thought to be "above" the vulgarity of seeking money, retain agents, negotiate contracts, charge high fees for television interviews and college lectures, and go on promotional tours to boost the sales of their latest publication.

We never know when economics will suddenly assume the dominant role in our life. Thirty years with the same company, and now they bring in someone from the outside and make her the general manager. Not fair! But I'll show them. Just see how much loyalty they'll get from me!

We are often constrained by economics, such as when our only options are staying in a job we hate or not being able to meet our car payments. But to be economically determined is not the same as being a Marxist or a crass materialist. The important thing is at all times to recognize the roots of our behavior (a utopian state of consciousness seldom achieved). We are chronically unfree the more we remain blind to reality when it confronts us. We take a step on the path to freedom when we begin to see the things that limit us—or when we impose the limitations on ourselves.

## Character Consistency

*A determinist argument often advanced is that only the insane are always and completely "free."*

Enduring characters in memorable works of fiction—Don Quixote, Becky Sharp, Huckleberry Finn, and Scarlett O'Hara, for example—stay in our minds not because they are amorphous, fluid, and unpredictable, but because they have specific character traits that can be summarized and that readily explain what they do. Indeed, what they do is usually obvious before they act. If they were real people, the determinist would say they lack free will, that they are bound by the very traits that make them come alive to us. A determinist argument often advanced is this: *Only the insane are always and completely "free."*

Suppose that someone stops a stranger in the street and strikes that person in the face. Imagine a panel of experts on human behavior being told this story and asked to predict what the response of the stricken person would be. Their predictions would surely be based on some cause-and-effect view of human interaction, which they would call "rational behavior." But what does this mean? Does it not mean that the stricken person is expected to respond within clear limitations that are accepted and shared by all "rational" persons? Thus, the assaulted person may be projected as (1) striking back out of righteous anger; (2) not striking back, because of pacifist beliefs, but attempting to leave without undergoing further harm; (3) deciding against the use of force on his or her own, preferring to call a police officer; (4) turning the other cheek, because of a strong Biblical upbringing; or perhaps (5) simply staring in disbelief at the assailant, not quite knowing what to do under the circumstances.

But now suppose the victim does not respond in any of these admittedly rational ways but, instead, were suddenly to produce a sword and bid the attacker kneel down and be knighted. There is a good chance that not the assailant but the assailed would be hauled away for observation. Such a response would not fall within any *meaningful* category of behavior. The determinist is likely to argue that of the responses considered, the "King Arthur" action is the only one rightfully labeled *free*. Under these circumstances, who would wish to live in a "free" world?

Of course, if we were bent on finding support for the *libertarian*, or free will, point of view, we could argue back that we are free or unfree according to the terminology we use to think about these states. Advocates of libertarianism are talking about unfettered choices among *rational* options. Certainly, in a rational universe each effect has an antecedent cause, but it is usually one of many that *might* be the cause before the action is performed. The fact that possible causes can be discarded, that a thought or a feeling can be entertained and then become a noncause, supports the libertarian position, or so the libertarians insist.

On the other hand, there are libertarians who not only criticize the character-consistency argument but who urge us not to be bound by the character traits instilled in us during the so-called acculturation process. They tell us we can be rational without being continuously predictable. If such were not the case, how could we explain the creative and the imaginative, the divergent thinkers whose oddball notions have in one way or another altered the shape of human experience? Were all of them insane? And, come to think of it, does any of us want to acquire a hard-and-fast reputation for being always and tiresomely the same?

## Behaviorism: Skinner

Behavioral psychology, founded on the work of B. F. Skinner (1904-1991), holds that we are what we do, and how we behave is determined by a network of rewards and punishments that begins to weave its web as soon as we are born.

If, says Skinner, humanity has a nature, it lies in *the capacity to be conditioned*. Everything we do is the result of a reinforcement of behavior. Those actions that are followed by pleasant consequences tend to be repeated; those followed by unpleasant or painful consequences tend to be avoided.

According to behaviorism, freedom is the effort to escape from the unpleasant consequences of certain actions. We slap at a mosquito that's about to attack to avoid the annoying itching that will follow if we don't. A child who has thrown a tantrum and been sent to bed without supper may cry loudly to escape hunger pangs. There is always a condition acting as a stimulus to a response. No such thing as pure and absolute freedom exists or can be defined.

People often identify the state of absolute freedom as one in which "aversive control" is absent; that is, if there is no apparent oppression, then people imagine themselves to be free. The literature of freedom, such as Rousseau's writings, has always urged people to act against aversive control, against obvious forms of oppression. But after the rebellion, what replaces the former control? The literature of freedom either beckons followers with the false hope that society might be better organized without any controls, or else it fails to point out that there can be new controls that appear less threatening but that nevertheless also condition people's behavior.

Victims of aggression or those who are exploited are actually better off than those being conditioned by nonaversive, nonthreatening controls, says Skinner. The obvious victims are either rescued eventually by some freedom movement, or they themselves rise up and rebel. (Or else they prefer to remain victims.) The people who are badly off are the "happy slaves"—people who are molded by hidden controls and don't know it, believing themselves to be free. In Skinner's words, "The literature of freedom has been designed to make men 'conscious' of aversive control, but in its choice of methods it has failed to rescue the happy slave."[1]

Behaviorism is often rejected by those for whom freedom is likely to be

*According to proponents of behaviorism, if humanity can be said to have a nature it lies in the capacity to be conditioned.*

*and*

*According to the opponents, conditioning reduces human dignity and diminishes the contributions of great artists, writers, and philosophers.*

the most important issue, clearly distinguishing human beings from other animals. Skinner says the desire to hold fast to this ancient and honorable abstraction, "freedom," is tied in with the belief that human dignity is lost if it is shown that humanity is not nor ever can be considered free. What happens to the great artists, writers, and philosophers if they are considered only products of conditioning forces? "We are not inclined to give a person credit for achievements which are in fact due to forces over which he has no control."[2]

But, argues Skinner, *dignity* has no meaning as an absolute abstraction. People do not vibrantly experience an inner something called "dignity" at the thought of being free. Like every other human condition, dignity is a very specific response to a particular kind of stimulus: It is the positive reinforcement given to one who has behaved properly or who has performed some achievement deemed notable. Dignity equals praise. Dignity equals recognition. Robbing people of their dignity is taking away recognition they believe is rightfully theirs.

Praise and recognition represent very positive reinforcements and, as such, are among the most pervasive of conditioning forces. Moreover, we may push Skinner's idea even further and point out that to win praise and recognition, some people would do just about anything required of them. Many have forgiven their own lapses of artistic or intellectual integrity because the stakes were high enough. How many writers and composers have said a fond farewell to the novel in the desk drawer or the sonata in the piano bench in exchange for fame and fortune in films or television?

*Many creative artists, conditioned by the marketplace, are not free, according to behaviorism. Perhaps van Gogh was one of the few who truly achieved freedom, because he did not paint for others.*

There have been many arguments, on the other hand, that dignity is personal integrity and that those who hold fast to their dignity, in this sense of the word, are indeed free. We could cite the example of Vincent van Gogh, an artist who received during his lifetime virtually no praise or attention for any of his work, except from his brother, Theo. Far from doing everything in his power to win recognition, van Gogh continued to paint exactly as he wished. There never seemed to be any doubt in his mind concerning his mission as an artist. He wanted to move people in a very special way. He was often discouraged by his obscurity, but it is probable that he never lost faith in the way he painted. Some might say that van Gogh possessed both artistic dignity and creative freedom.

The title for one of Skinner's most influential works is *Beyond Freedom and Dignity* (1972). We need, says Skinner, to take broad terms that mean very little in themselves—like *freedom* and *dignity*—and redefine them in strictly behavioral language. We need to concentrate on creating what Skinner calls a "technology of behavior." Since people are going to be conditioned anyway, the focus should be on the good controls that *can* exist: "The problem is to free men, not from control, but from certain kinds of control, and it can be solved only if our analysis takes all consequences into account."[3]

*Skinner: Since people are going to be conditioned anyway, the focus should be on the good controls that can exist.*

Skinner is also a kind of modern utopian thinker, believing that eventually an ideal society can be designed in which people develop to the maximum of their abilities through carefully preplanned reinforcements. In such a society there would be no crime, no aggression, no exploitation. *But would we want such a society?*

For many, a "technology of behavior" sounds too precise, too clinical. When "behavioral technicians" realize how much power they have, what will stop them from using those aversive techniques that Skinner wants to eliminate?

What if van Gogh had lived in a behaviorally engineered society? Might he have filed a petition against public indifference, been given a stipend by the minister of culture, and perhaps never painted again? Is this what we would want?

## Genetics

*Genetics*, the science of heredity, studies the role played by innate biological factors in determining reproduction in plants, animals, and human beings. It has not yet become a branch of philosophy or psychology, but its pervasiveness in our culture indicates that theories of existence or human behvior are now almost required to consider the relationship between genetics and the possibilities for freedom of the will.

In the social sciences there has long been a debate about heredity versus environment. This is also known as the nature/nurture dispute. Does biology condition us, or do we owe our personalities and behavioral patterns to the influence of family, peers, education, and the social structure around us? Both sides of the argument imply determinism, you will note.

Of late, heredity has been receiving most of the attention. One reason is surely our increasing knowledge about the DNA molecule and the crucial role it plays *before* the fetus begins to develop inside the womb. We now understand that when the male sperm meets the female egg, a molecular binding of the two cells takes place. The result of this binding has been named the DNA (deoxyribonucleic acid) molecule, which contains genetic information from both parents. This information serves as a code to determine thousands of characteristics, including the color of the child's eyes and hair, the optimum height he or she will reach, the capacity for learning (if not the actual intelligence level), and perhaps even the inclination toward science or the creative arts.

No one can say for sure just how much of what we become is determined by the DNA molecule and to what extent other factors, including environmental influences and the exercise of one's own will, can operate to alter one's genetic destiny. Nevertheless, enough is known for genetic science to press forward in often breathtaking experiments with plant and animal life. Knowledge of how to isolate and then open certain sections of the DNA molecule is increasing almost every day, as is the ability to read genetic codes, to rearrange genetic patterns, to alter the very nature of the molecule *in order to bring about a prearranged result*. The alteration process is called *genetic engineering*, and it already boasts of brighter, longer-lived orchids, for example, and insects that exhibit no undesirable characteristics.

Naturally, there is fear in some quarters that genetic engineering is leading up to an eventual control over the human population. How far off is the day when the genetic coding of human offspring will be hooked up to a computer that has been told what kind of child the parents have requested? If the father's genetic contribution, for example, is deficient in a certain area, one "merely" goes to the storehouse of carefully labeled genes and selects those that will produce the child that is wanted.

Since artificial insemination and test-tube babies are already laboratory realities, the apparently logical next step is DNA interference, a prospect that has many humanists shaking their heads fearfully. Are we closer to the sort of preplanned society of which we were warned in novels like Aldous Huxley's *Brave New World* and George Orwell's *1984?*

*All of us alive today are not products of laboratory precision. We are safe from attempts to induce biological and mental strengths, but are left with the "satisfaction" of having genetic weaknesses. Would we have been better off in a time of genetic engineering?*

But *without* genetic engineering, can we realistically say we are better off? If genetic factors are as powerful as they appear to be, the argument for determinism would seem to be all but won. All of us alive today are not products of laboratory precision, but rather of molecular interaction over which we had no control. We may never be able to free ourselves from the impact of this interaction. In other words, we are safe from attempts to induce biological and mental strengths but are left with the "satisfaction" of having genetic weaknesses.

A new social science called *sociobiology* assumes the absence of free will and studies people in terms of the behavior that genetics makes inevitable. For example, we are destined to favor family members in our dealings because of genetic ties, not out of some spiritual something we might call love. We are less likely to sell a junk car to a brother or a sister than to someone outside the family circle. People fall in love to ensure genetic propagation. "I am not ready to get married" translates into "I am not prepared to make a genetic investment." Altruism is stripped of traditional humane values and becomes an extension of genetic self-interest. A mother sacrifices for her children, but only because they represent the continuing life of her own genes. She would face death to save her child, but not that of another—*except* for cases in which she identifies strongly with the mother. A soldier might die to save his or her battalion, but only after this has become a substitute family.

Why, asks the sociobiologist, do so many persons become depressed when they realize they are both childless and the last of their line? Why do so many childless couples seek to adopt children? Is it not that, lacking real genetic survival, people despair and are willing to settle for what they can get?

Ironically, the widespread use of birth control devices as well as the liberalization of abortion laws may be all we have left that even resembles freedom of will. Those who uphold the "right to life" would, however, argue that the achievement of freedom in this manner is itself a force that prevents a potential human being from having the most basic freedom of all: life.

## Possibilities for Freedom

The literature and philosophy of determinism have always seemed to be greater in quantity and intensity than their libertarian counterparts. Is it easier to tell why we are not free than to find logical support for a belief that we are? You will discover that this chapter has also devoted most of its space to the determinists. One reason is that their arguments are powerful and must be reckoned with. Another is that when the summing up is made, we shall find that much of what they say does indeed apply to many, if not all, people. The state of being a free person is perhaps not equally shared. Perhaps the art of being human includes the art of being free, and like any art, freedom needs to be very delicately and carefully fashioned and preserved.

*Is it easier to tell why we are not free than to find logical support for a belief that we are?*

## Will

The issue of freedom has much to do with the *will*. For centuries philosophers asked, "Is the will free?" More recently they have asked, "Is there such a thing as the will?" B. F. Skinner, for example, argues that the will cannot be detected, cannot be felt. We cannot say, "I have free will" with reference to a specific sensation or emotion. The will, whether free or not, may be only a word.

Arthur Schopenhauer (1788-1860), a German philosopher of the last century, was concerned with the problem of whether the will existed. After much deliberation he came to a most interesting conclusion. Stand, he said, in front of a mirror. Observe yourself. Then think that you would like to raise your left arm. Decide that you *want* to raise the arm. Then do it. There is no doubt that anyone who followed those instructions would see the left arm being raised (assuming no physical impediment, of course). The final observation is that of *the will objectified*. One instant the desire to raise the arm is locked inside the mind, the consciousness. The next instant, it is visibly present in the action perceived in the mirror.

Schopenhauer's simple experiment can be repeated in thousands of different ways, and in each case we experience the will. At this very moment you may decide to stand up or not, turn on the television set or not, hum a few bars of a song or not. We can experience a direct sense that what we are *not* doing is a deliberate act of omission.

When Skinner tells us we cannot feel the will, he *may* mean that most people do not bother to focus their thoughts on the will. At any given moment they cannot say whether they are doing what they have willed to do or are not doing what they have willed not to do.

Classroom students told to close their books in preparation for a surprise quiz may groan and feel at that instant like slaves or prisoners. They may feel they would rather be at the beach, at the movies, driving a car. Instead of groaning, however, they have the option of saying to themselves, "I do not will that I must take a test this morning." If the proposition sounds reasonable—that is, not absurd— they have confirmed the existence of their will. They are withholding their will. If the will were merely an illusion, they could have no rational opinion about the test. It could not be an unpleasantness, an imposition upon them, unless there were other occasions upon which they could say, also quite reasonably, "I will that I am doing this . . ."

Direct consciousness of will, such as in Schopenhauer's suggested exercise in front of a mirror, can have the effect of halting a chain of mechanical actions. That is, if we focus on the very next step, the immediate reality of the next moment—regardless of the circumstances that have brought us to this situation— the possibilities of free choice seem to be there, especially in the split-second flutter of the "afterchoice," when we cry, "Oh, but I meant to do *that!*"

Perhaps some behaviorists are not making sufficient allowance for the play of acute intelligence. Perhaps people can slow down their rate of response to a prior cause and choose not to become robots obediently following the command implicit in that cause. Another exercise is to sit down when confronted with a situation that demands an action and make a list of the cause-and-effect chain that has brought you to the situation. Determine what you *probably* would do and then coolly and calmly do something clearly not programmed. Not a bad exercise in these days of computers and video games, when the programmed response is accepted as the way of all beings, both mechanical and human!

*Perhaps the art of being human includes the art of being free, and like any art, freedom needs to be very delicately and carefully fashioned and preserved.*

*One way to elude determinism: slow down your rate of response to the chain of cause and effect; figure out what you would probably do; and then don't do it.*

## Regret and Relief

The American philosopher William James (1842-1910) reviewed the case for pure determinism as set forth by European philosophers and concluded they were wrong. In fact, James developed a theory he pointedly called *indeterminism*, which presents the world as a random collection of chance happenings. Deter-

*People are able to think back over a hundred choices they wish they had not made.*

*If everything were predetermined, we would not be able to look back and see that genuine alternatives existed, but we were not aware of them.*

minism, for James, was too coldly logical: Cause A leads to effect A. Determinism made people seem like well-run, well-oiled machines. James said, on the contrary, people were indecisive and unpredictable, exactly the opposite of machines.

Regret, he added, was a universal phenomenon. At any given moment people are able to think back over a hundred choices they wish they had not made. But at the same time, regret could not be meaningfully experienced unless there existed an opposite—satisfaction—that gave regret its identity. In other words, within the random collection of happenings, people sometimes make what they consider the right move and many times make what they consider the wrong move. If everything were predetermined—that is, if the will were not free— looking backward could not reveal missed chances. We could not see them unless they had existed, though we may have been blind to them at the moment of choice. How often might murderers think back and realize that they did not *have* to carry a pistol for confronting their enemy? For James, hindsight was proof that genuine alternatives always exist.

If we were to extend the philosophy of indeterminism, we could say that another revealing exercise is to sit back and think of all of the terrible things we might have done last week but refrained from doing, such as

> Having a confrontation with a friend that could have threatened the
> relationship.
> Lying about something that would have involved a whole series of
> other lies.
> Dropping a course in an impulsive moment, a course that is required
> for graduation.
> Taking a chance and driving the old car with two bald tires.

*That we can say we have made many mistakes is an admission that we know ourselves to be free agents.*

We would probably feel relieved that we had not done these things. Thus there is yet another opposite of regret, *relief*. Again it is a matter of intelligence, of focusing the attention on vital matters; we are not aware of relief unless we survey the wrong moves that might have been made but were not.

Our lives are probably split down the middle, with good moves on one side and bad moves on the other. That we can say we have made many mistakes is an admission that we know ourselves to be free agents. That we have sometimes chosen wisely seems to back up the claim.

## Psychoanalysis: Freedom Through the Conscious Self

The study of the mind, which has come to be called *psychology*, is over a century old. It has not traditionally been as concerned with the question of free will as has been philosophy, but much psychology has been based on the premise of a modified determinism: the contention that whatever we think or do is impelled by a previous cause, *which is not of our own choosing*. Psychotherapy thus seeks to free people.

The aim of psychotherapy is to help people integrate their behavior by learning the causes of deviant, antisocial, or uncharacteristic actions. The theory generally is that once the cause is discovered, the subterranean forces driving one's actions can be fully or at least partially controlled. In other words, people go into therapy because they don't like who they are or what they do. Therapy holds out the hope that through understanding and proper guidance, people can change and become less "determined" than they were before.

*Psychoanalysis* is the therapy invented by Sigmund Freud (1856-1939) to assist people toward mental health. It is based on the assumption that because of the suppressed past, many of us have bizarre dreams, make odd statements, and perform actions we cannot comprehend. In other words, our lives are determined by unconscious prior causes: sometimes by guilt-ridden emotions we have refused to deal with; often by desires of the id, that irrational, primitive self human beings possessed long before they developed the rational ego. The aim of the therapist is to analyze the patient's dreams, characteristic use of language, and free associations; to uncover the hidden self responsible for neurotic behavior; and to lead the patient to a happier life dominated by the ego. Presumably the successfully psycho-analyzed patient comes to possess freedom of the will, having been released from the determining phantoms of the past. Will resides in the ego.

In recent years Freud's theories have been reevaluated by many psychologists and historians of ideas. In particular, there is growing skepticism about two of Freud's basic assumptions: the first, that all behavior can sooner or later be traced back to a significant early experience, often in childhood; and the second, that the ego, or the conscious self, is capable of rational, sustained thought once the suppressed secrets of the past are brought to light. For many, human behavior is far more complex than Freud suggests, and freedom is not attainable in the therapist's office.

Nevertheless, Freud has received much recognition in the study of the humanities for having created one of the most prominent and influential myths of the century: *the myth of the liberated self*. Novels, plays, and films, especially in the first half of the century, display the overwhelming impact of Freud. The most popular plot centers on a man or a woman, haunted by nightmarish dreams and held prisoner by past guilt, which the conscious mind refuses to confront. He or she then meets a benevolent, wise (and often very attractive) analyst, who forsakes all personal concerns and works solely to free the prisoner from the shackles of tormenting guilt.

The structure of this generic "therapy plot" is usually that of a detective story. The old question "Who done it?" is replaced by "What did he do?" or "What was done to her that she is afraid to face?" Sometimes we learn that the victim as a young child killed one or the other parent in a terrible accident. Or (very often indeed) that the victim was responsible for the death of a sibling. In one novel that shocked the country in the 1940s—*Kings Row* by Henry Bellamann—the hero falls in love with a very strange girl whose life seems haunted by a terrifying mystery. Suicide is the only freedom that the young woman finds, but the reader eventually discovers that an incestuous father has led to her inevitable doom.

Whether the ending were tragic or happy (often with marriage in the offing between patient and therapist), audiences seemed never to tire of such dramatic premises. Interestingly enough, the popularity of Freudian-based entertainment coincided with the emergence of the American economy from the dismal depression of the 1930s as well as the recognition that the United States must enter World War II to help free those overrun by fascist forces. The need for a literature of freedom was apparently an insatiable one.

Freud-based stories have by no means disappeared, however. Pat Conroy's popular novel *The Prince of Tides* (1988), which became an equally popular 1991 film, hinges on a disturbed man's complex mental journey back to his childhood, under the guidance of a wise female therapist. Since child abuse is a burning issue of our time, the author uses violent rape by an escaped convict as the trauma experienced by the hero long ago. Shame, guilt, and fear of social condemnation have prevented him from being a successful husband and father, but when the truth is finally faced, he is able to return home, his rational self completely restored.

Studying the humanities of this century would be difficult indeed without recognition of Freud's role. We must not, however, go away believing that Freudian theory is all mythical. Many schools of psychotherapy continue to be rooted in his thought, and millions have been restored to mental health through psychoanalytical methods. That Freud's views do not represent an all-inclusive means to human freedom from the determining past should not eclipse the importance of these views to both the arts and to modern psychology.

> *Studying the humanities of this century would be difficult indeed without recognition of Freud's role.*

## Self-Imposed Limitations

It seems fitting to close this book with a theory—and it is just that—by means of which we can apply the word *free* to ourselves in some meaningful sense. First, let's narrow the focus and define freedom in a very specialized way by taking into consideration the determinist argument of causality: If every effect has a cause, there must be many effects *that are caused by oneself*. In strict determinism, one's actions are always the effect of a previous cause. But surely one can be the causer. One can derive a definite sense of being a free agent by saying, "I—and nothing else—have brought this to pass." The price of obtaining freedom in this way is limitation.

> *I know of no more encouraging fact than the unquestionable ability of man to elevate his life by a conscious endeavor.*
>
> Thoreau

If I claim responsibility for an action, I limit the number of possible causes to one. To put the matter in reverse: I limit the number of effects my decision will have. I am late for an appointment. I am driving at night without the glasses I need to see well. Furthermore, I am driving in the rain. As my vehicle careens wildly from one side of the road to the other, I *could* think to myself, "How exhilarating. Anything might happen." Or, placing a limitation on possibilities, I could think, "I am driving irresponsibly. I have no choice but to pull over and stop." Control may be where freedom starts.

The Stoic teacher Epictetus once advised his students to sit and not eat the next time they attended a banquet. Such advice was part of Stoic training, for the Stoic philosophy is built on the idea that we can be happy by controlling our attitudes. Our opinion about occurrences is unnecessary; events cease to be either good or evil. To refrain from eating at a banquet, therefore, means that we were in control of appetite. If something so basic as appetite were within our power to manage, why not everything else? To convert hunger into an attitude and to refuse to hold the attitude—that is, to refuse to allow hunger to enter the consciousness—is true liberation.

The Stoic teachings are among the most enduring influences on the humanist's methods of achieving a clear sense of freedom. We do exactly the reverse of what we might think "freedom" entails. Instead of running about wildly doing whatever comes to mind, we willfully set up certain parameters—including limitations—within which to operate. These, of course, are changed as the situation demands.

People who jog know all about the relationship between freedom and limits. They will tell you about a consciousness of freedom in running, pushing against the wind and feeling their arms and legs equal to the demands made by the will—for runners, in contrast to what Skinner has said, *do* feel their will. When there is a sharp incline, runners must draw upon reserve strength. On the down-ward slope, they know that power may once more be conserved. If they are running against others in a race and there is a need to win, they accelerate; if there is only the need to complete the course, they adopt a more leisurely pace.

*Runners, in contrast to what Skinner has said, do feel their will.*

The vivid experience of will does not happen all of a sudden. In the beginning, jogging is a distinct effort accompanied by pain and soreness. There is the inevitable pulling of muscles, the labored breathing, the tendency to overheat rapidly. In the beginning, joggers stop running for the slightest excuse. After a time they set a goal: to the end of the road and then back. If they are developing into runners, the self-imposed limit is crucial. Gradually the "required" distance is lengthened. Nothing on earth, including wind and rain, will deter most runners from completing their course. The ultimate sense of liberation—the experience of floating on a cloud that all runners know about—occurs only when and if the runner has been faithful to the limitations imposed by the inner self.

Consider a different sort of example—that of a wife and mother who is also the producer of a public television program. The local studio has determined that if viewership does not increase, the program may be canceled or moved to an undesirable time slot. But cheer up! The producer has lined up a world-class interview for this week's program. Her host will be talking with a Nobel prize-winning author from South America. The station manager is delirious with an-ticipation.

On the day of the telecast the woman's son is in the hospital for minor surgery. No matter. She need not be at the studio. Everything has been carefully arranged. But who promised anyone a logical universe? The unthinkable happens. The host also has to be rushed to the hospital. No one else is available to do the interview *except the producer herself.*

Time was (and not too long ago) when the limitation of possibilities worked against freedom for the producer. Her motherly sense of duty would have required that she stay with her child, the author notwithstanding. Even now, the Skinnerian psychologist would probably bet money on the woman's "inevitable" choice of her son's security instead of an interview with a stranger for the sake of her job (a job that, by the way, she *wants* but does not *need*). No doubt many women would do the predictable thing, faced with the same conflict of options.

But it is not impossible for a human being to do the *un*predictable thing by a self-imposed limitation of will. It is not impossible for the producer to decide, for once in her life perhaps, that she will think of herself—that she will be *selfish*, if husband and son decide to give her action that label. The issue is not family morality here. The issue is freedom, for, surely, if the producer forgoes her own desire in the "higher" interest of her family, we can view her as being constrained, her decision determined perhaps by the entire history of marriage.

*Nuns fret not at their convent's narrow room; And hermits are contented with their cells.*

*Wordsworth*

Man's actions are best understood as determined when a person *objectively* observes his own functioning or when he attempts to observe other indi-viduals and seeks reasons for their behavior. On the other hand, belief in freedom is both necessary and possible . . . when a person *subjectively* experiences himself or empathetically experiences another person.

Bruce Shertzer and Shelly C. Stone

Now, assuming that the history of this particular marriage has been one in which the woman's wifely and motherly actions have always received what Skinner calls positive reinforcement, so that the producer has been thoroughly conditioned to give her own job lower priorities, the deliberate absence from the son's hospital room could well be called uncharacteristic by the behaviorists. Most likely she had better be wary of her husband's displeasure! But who is to say that knowing all of this in advance, the woman may not decide to endure the negative reinforcement rather than surrender too easily?

The friend who advises, "Talk to your husband and son; make them understand" is only reinforcing the old, determined pattern. So would the producer herself should she back down at the last minute, cancel the interview, and go to the hospital, her marriage protected against crisis. Many of our actions (or avoided actions) are performed because the easy way out avoids the confrontation and the guilt that can follow. One possibility of avoiding the hassle is, of course, to know that we have *freely chosen determinism*.

Yet the choice of doing what she *really* wants to do represents the free choice of being a free agent. It is a different kind of limitation, one that is imposed by the woman herself, not her family, not society, not tradition. To argue that few women would do such a thing—or that no woman *should*—is to make no real point about freedom. The choice we have suggested is one that could be made. There is nothing in the cosmic scheme of things to prevent it, if that is what this woman is bent on doing.

So we have another possibility: To do what one does not *have* to do may be where freedom begins. Whatever repercussions may follow the producer's decision to go with the interview, the opportunity is there for her to experience a true sense of having broken a rigid pattern of behavior. The number of people who even *want* to be free in this sense may well be limited.

Skinner is probably right, up to a point. But then, William James may also be right, up to a point. Freudian therapy may be quite helpful for some kinds of problems. We can, however, derive a measure of satisfaction from the knowledge that no one has yet been shown to have said the final word for every person on this earth. This knowledge in itself constitutes one road to freedom.

## Epilogue

The message we would like you to carry away from this book is that you, the reader, as a human being possess something the determinists cannot take from you: *the right to see many roads*. All of the art and all of the beliefs we have presented are forms created by our species, but the universal spotlight is on you and *your* forms.

It is your birthright to reach up and mentally redo the Sistine Chapel ceiling if you don't happen to like it. It is your birthright to let go of the past, to reach into the darkness and from it pull forth a new lantern, however unfamiliar the shape, however irregular the beam of light. Not the DNA molecule, not prison doors can deny you the right if you choose to have it.

## Glossary

*behaviorism:* A school of psychology that believes that people are what they do and that what they do is determined by the way past actions have been reinforced (either positively or negatively). Philosophers who accept a deterministic view of life frequently cite

---

*There are only a few things we "must" do. One of them is to blink when someone blows air on our eyes. Most of the other "musts" are "wants."*

*Merry Haber*

*It is not impossible for a human being to do the unpredictable thing by a personal act of will.*

*People very rarely realize the real happening in the arts comes out of the most enormous discipline, because when you've disciplined yourself thoroughly, you know what is possible. That's when you let your imagination move, because you know that by discipline and study and thought you've created the limits.*

*Isaac Stern*

behaviorism for support. Humanists are traditionally antithetical to behaviorism, arguing that one need not be conditioned entirely by external forces.

*determinism:*  The philosophy that holds that free will does not exist.

*dialectic:*  A method of logical thought, developed by Hegel, in which one considers an idea (thesis), its opposite (antithesis), and then achieves a synthesis of the two.

*dialectical materialism:*  Marx's application of Hegel's logical method to what Marx believed were the actual facts of history; a way of interpreting history as an economic struggle between social classes, culminating in a social synthesis, or a classless society.

genetics:  The science of heredity, which believes that physical traits and even certain behaviors are determined by codes that nature places inside genes, infinitesimally small parts of plant, animal, and human cells. In the latest and most controversial phase of this science, experiments are being conducted by which genetic codes are altered, thus giving science potentially powerful control over reproduction.

*indeterminism:*  A philosophy held by William James that says free will is a real possibility; otherwise regret over bad choices would be meaningless. Insofar as in looking back we can wish we had acted differently, we must assume the existence of freedom.

*libertarian:*  One who adopts the view that freedom of choice is possible.

*psychoanalysis:*  A method developed by Freud and his followers of helping patients to a rational awareness of the neurotic basis of abnormal behavior. Freud assumed that once patients understand clearly why they behave in certain ways, they will be liberated. Much psychoanalysis depends upon interpreting patients' dreams.

*sociobiology:*  A relatively new science/philosophy that maintains that the preservation and reproduction of the genes form the basis of all human behavior and value systems.

*übermensch (superman):*  In Nietzschean philosophy, the inevitable product of a human species whose intellect has developed to no avail except to create a subjective fantasy it considers reality. The *übermensch* is the visionary with so powerful a fantasy that others accept it as the truth. In a negative sense, the *übermensch* constitutes a danger to the rest of us. In a positive sense, such a being represents the glory of an otherwise absurd existence.

*will:*  A major term in philosophy, referring to the individual's inward consent that a certain event take place. The crucial argument in this chapter revolves around the issue of whether that consent is self-conceived or whether it occurs because of a long history of causes, making it inevitable.

## Notes

1.  B. F. Skinner, *Beyond Freedom and Dignity* (New York: Bantam/Vintage, 1972), 37.

2.  Ibid., 41.
3.  Ibid., 39.

## Suggested Reading

Brown, Norman O. *Life Against Death*. Middleton, Conn.: Wesleyan University Press, 1959. For the ambitious reader, a brilliant if cynical interpretation of history in terms of Freud's contention that human civilization is essentially neurotic and is the result of the suppression of unconscious drives, particularly the sex drive. The author says that what has been called human "progress" is in reality a long march toward self-destruction, driven by the death wish.

Freud, Sigmund. *The Interpretation of Dreams*. Ed. and tr. James Strachey. New York: Avon Books, 1965. A reprint of the translation used in the standard collection of Freud's work. Though Freud's theory of dreams is now highly disputed, the book is still recommended for two reasons. One is that there is probably much validity to many of the ideas. Some dreams must surely relate to unconscious guilt, anxieties, and wishes. The other reason is the profound influence this work has had on twentieth-century humanities.

Hacker, Andrew. *Two Nations: Black and White;*

*Separate, Hostile, Unequal*. New York: Scribner's, 1992. After many years of research and investigation, the author finds that African Americans still cannot consider themselves free. He compares the two races in terms of sexuality, income, education, and crime statistics, and concludes that racism still underlies our society.

Huxley, Aldous. *Brave New World*. New York: Harper, 1946. The classic novel about a future utopia in which the totalitarian state bans all freedom of thought and keeps the citizenry happily tranquilized so it won't realize all freedom has disappeared. Written in 1932, the novel has many interesting predictions that you will be fascinated to measure against the reality.

James, William. "The Dilemma of Determinism." In *The Writings of William James*. Chicago: University of Chicago Press, 1977. This short and precisely written essay takes the determinist position and turns it back, knifelike, on its supporters. By pushing the position to its logical extreme, James paints a grim picture of a universe that *wills* that disasters occur; chance accidents can happen only in an undetermined world.

Marx, Karl, and Friedrich Engels. *Basic Writings on Politics and Philosophy*. Ed. Lewis B. Fever. Garden City, N.Y.: Doubleday, 1959. A fine selection of the major Marxist statements, including the 1848 *Communist Manifesto*. If you haven't time to read the whole volume, the introduction does a considerable amount of summarizing. In light of the collapse of most Marxist governments, the writings acquire even more interest to the student who wants to know why some ideas work and others do not.

Orwell, George. *1984*. New York: New American Library, 1984. A classic modern novel about a utopian totalitarian state in which freedom of thought is banned. Written in 1948, the book was reissued in the year of predicted doom. The takeover by Orwell's famous "Big Brother," who watches everyone on a TV monitor, had not occurred, but you should be interested in determining whether our society bears any resemblance to the one imagined by the author. Ours is probably not run as efficiently, but perhaps this is the price of freedom?

Schopenhauer, Arthur. *The World as Will and Idea*. Tr. R. B. Haldane and J. Kemp. New York: AMS Press, 1977. A reprint of the 1895 edition, this book is mandatory reading for any student interested in studying philosophy or the history of ideas. Schopenhauer sees all of reality as a projection of will, the force shared by all living entities to grow, move, change, and decay. His theory is a brilliant argument against those who maintain that all motion, all action is determined by a preceding cause. Will by definition is free in the sense that it and only it decides what its results are to be.

Skinner, B. F. *Walden Two*. New York: Macmillan, 1971. Still another classic utopian novel; this one concerns a future society run by principles of behavioral science, that is, by philosopher/psychologists who know how to condition the population through positive and negative reinforcements of behavior. There is no crime, no government inefficiency, no economic distress, and so on, but opponents of behaviorism would also insist that in this society there is no fun, either.

Wilson, Edward. *Sociobiology: The New Synthesis*. Cambridge: Harvard University Press, 1975. The author sets forth the general biological principles that govern social and sexual behavior in all kinds of animals, including humans. Essentially, the motivating force is the necessity for genetic reproduction. In years past, for example, women were not allowed sexual liberties because of the genetic investment at risk in the days before birth control. Now that one has a choice in whether to make the investment, our sexual morality has radically changed.

# Index

INSTRUCTOR'S MANUAL TO ACCOMPANY

*Fourth Edition*

# THE ART
# OF BEING HUMAN

## THE HUMANITIES
## AS A TECHNIQUE
## FOR LIVING

**Richard Paul Janaro**
*New World School of the Arts*

**Thelma C. Altshuler**
*Miami-Dade Community College*

HarperCollinsCollegePublishers

# CONTENTS

# FOREWORD

THE ART OF BEING HUMAN is the broad title for several entities, which are interrelated but can also be discrete. First, it is a humanities text, now in its Fourth Edition, that seeks in non-traditional ways to involve the college freshman or sophomore deeply in the arts, the philosophy, the creative experiences of the human race, then and now.

In 1978, after a long career in teaching general education humanities courses, the authors--Thelma Altshuler and Richard Janaro, colleagues for over two decades--were asked to write a text that would serve as companion to a telecourse in the humanities then being planned by Miami-Dade Community College, for many years a major producer of educational television materials. We welcomed the invitation, for we had been discussing the possibility of doing a text that would not be a chronological history of white European-derived male artists and philosophers. We wanted to try a new approach--one that might reach the general education student with, for the most part, no previous exposure to or curiosity about the humanities; the student who, but for curriculum requirements, would probably not have been in the class at all. The texts then available were largely primary-source anthologies or secondary-source distillations, attempting to cover the entire output of Western man, and generally as distant from our students' lives as Miletus or Byzantium.

The underlying goal of the 1979 First Edition was to focus on the struggle that men and women had experienced in order to create the humanities, a struggle within themselves, within the tradition of art and thought they inherited, and within the society around them. Our hope was that, when students saw that this dreaded course had been the creation of human beings like themselves, feeling many of the same emotions, they would become more deeply involved than otherwise might have been the case. We treated the awesome figures as human beings with human needs which were more intense perhaps than most of us feel, but nonetheless accessible to us: Michelangelo's need to make a seventeen-foot block of marble surrender to his will; Beethoven's need to objectify sounds he himself would never hear as others did; Descartes' need to follow a thought into the uncharted regions of the mind, wherever it might take him. Yet the hoped-for identification was not our sole intent. The idea was to persuade the student that the need to express *whatever and however* was shared by everyone: Beethoven, their teachers, themselves. The fervent wish was that personal explorations and personal expressions would take place during the course, after the course, and for life. We told our own students we could never evaluate the full extent to which the text and the course had benefited them.

We added a cautionary note to the first Instructor's Manual and have been doing so ever since. Now that we are about to launch the Fourth Edition, we repeat the caution and underline it heavily: *Instructors are free to move about the text as they please.* In the following pages you will find possible structures for teaching a humanities course using the text. One is a chapter-by-chapter structure, with suggestions for linking them together. The other is a chronological listing of the material covered, so that, if you chose, you could conduct the course historically as well as in an interdisciplinary manner. Those who have intensely specialized backgrounds in one of the arts or in philosophy will want to augment our generalized treatments with material of their own, and may even wish to assign additional reading in primary sources.

Instructors using the text since the whole enterprise began in 1979 will see how very different it has become. So here's a word on the reason for the many changes. Since 1979 we have received letters and phone calls from hundreds of instructors and students around the country--in many cases, expressing gratitude for a book that, they discovered, was far more helpful to their personal lives than they had originally suspected; in some others, expressing concerns that an issue or an important figure was omitted. We have been highly responsive to this feedback and have made many changes to accommodate those suggestions we thought would improve our book. In addition, both of us have taught from the text in all of its editions and have always asked students what they thought were the strengths and the weaknesses of the text. The questionnaires were always anonymous, so that students could feel free to express their honest feelings.

As might be expected, the Fourth Edition now has many more references to minorities than did the First, though we were always conscious of the need to have a stronger multi-ethnic and dual-gender base than had many of the other texts in the field we had been examining and continue to examine.

Those who want their students to have a sense of history will find better coverage of various periods and movements, though we continue to believe that teaching the humanities chronologically runs the risk of perpetuating the myth that most of the things worth doing have been done by white "Euro-males." Our own preference is for the present structure, which is to divide the course between *Makers of the Humanities* and *Themes of the Humanities*. In this way, the instructor can give as much or as little time to certain figures and movements as is thought desirable and necessary. In short, we wanted our combined middle name to be *Choice*. We hold fast to the conviction that humanists are people who can enhance their lives by making free choices among significant options; who think clearly because they have been presented with many sides of the truth; who sing their songs in different styles because there are so many styles at their disposal; and who will stop to look or to listen whenever there is someone who needs to communicate. They may, having stopped, pass on by; but the significance of the pause is all important.

We said at the beginning that THE ART OF BEING HUMAN was more than one entity. Since that statement, we have talked a great deal about the text and the many changes it has undergone. The question now--for those who will continue to use the telecourse--is: *Can the videotapes continue to be relevant to a greatly altered text that was originally intended to be their complement?*

The answer is a resounding yes. To begin with, the texts of the films generally contain the central ideas of the book. Secondly, the videos never did explicate the book on a page-by-page basis but were always intended to accomplish affectively what we hoped the book was accomplishing cognitively. The videos have never been usable as substitutes for any chapters. A student who misses a number of weeks cannot be told to watch *x* number of films and all will be well. The videotapes enhance the learning experiences; they put matters in a different sort of way. Students have generally found them enjoyable to watch, and the assumption has always been that, without having to take notes or to memorize content, students absorb a great deal. The tapes do NOT constitute the crucial component of your course.

Nonetheless, THE ART OF BEING HUMAN telecourse still exists. A student Study Guide is in preparation with many questions on both the text and the seventeen videotapes that comprise the television component of the course. (The Guide can also be an aid to students in courses that have no video accompaniment.)

In the TEACHING AIDS section of this Manual instructors will find material relevant to the videotape which can be useful in connection with each chapter. This can be safely skipped over if the tape is not available or if the instructor chooses not to use it. The text stands quite on its own. Qualified adopters who are interested can receive videotapes free of charge but need to contact their local HarperCollins representative.

Adopters will also receive an audiocassette containing a variety of unfamiliar music from different parts of the world that instructors may want to use as a supplement to the chapter on music, and a package of art slides compiled by Sandak which illustrate the various styles and art movements dealt with in Chapter 2.

The Manual provides alternate strategies and assignments for each chapter, often asking students to work together in groups to solve a specific problem. There are many essay questions and journal topics worded with specific guidelines to discourage the student from rambling.

The previous editions did not offer such an abundance of auxiliary material, and we are extremely grateful to HarperCollins for the prodigious effort they have put forth in order to make THE ART OF BEING HUMAN, Fourth Edition, more usable than it has ever been and to provide more choices for instructors than has ever been possible. It is our hope that instructors will enjoy the wide range of opportunities to make the course their own.

Richard Paul Janaro
Thelma C. Altshuler

# A POSSIBLE STRUCTURAL SCHEME

The following format represents a *possible* course structure that can be used or adapted for either the classroom or independent study.

Roman numerals represent the units of the course operation. Each one has been given a name, which is sometimes the title of the assigned chapter and sometimes a more inclusive one. Both the names and the units themselves are possibilities only, as is the order in which they appear.

References to videotapes can be ignored by those using only the text.

I.          "WHAT IN FACT *ARE* THE HUMANITIES?"

           Read Introduction, "To Be Human"
           View "The Way of the Humanist"

One suspects that, in their heart of hearts, many who teach courses with the word "humanities" in the title would prefer no definition at all to those which never seem to cover all bases. For, in point of fact, almost any human activity or product of the human mind could be accommodated by the term if the user can make a good case for so doing.

Earlier editions of the text tend to shy away from pat definitions, and the new edition is no exception. We take a very broad perspective indeed: the humanities are "the cumulative expressions of humanity's finest moments." This definition takes in Michelangelo and Beethoven, but it hardly excludes folk tales spoken by an eighty-year-old Seminole storyteller before a campfire, or the reader's own possibly private ventures into poetry or watercolors.

So the introductory chapter more or less guarantees that the so-called humanities are the birthright of every human being born on this earth--whether one is the creator or the appreciator. The stage is set for a discussion of what life would be like *without* the humanities.

The suggested videotape "The Way of the Humanist" does not preach to students that they have an obligation to appreciate the wonderful things the humanities can do for them. Rather, it tells a simple fable of a little girl's meeting with a mystic figure, a mime, who opens her eyes to the miracle of existence. Since the title contains the term "humanist," which often calls to mind a wan scholar or Shakespeare's "bending author," the hope is that students will realize from the outset that the "humanities" are about *them* and the options they have: to let life happen around them or to be alive every minute of the day.

A major theme of this course is going to be *openness to life*.

II.         "APOLLO AND DIONYSUS IN LIFE AND ART"

> Read Chapter 1, "Apollo and Dionysus"
> View "The Sunlit Chariot"

Taking the broadest possible overview of the humanities, can we say that a study of them brings to light a principal secret, a salient *teaching*, an underlying statement that transcends times and cultures? The answer is yes, or we wouldn't have raised the question!

That "secret" appears to be that human development does not occur straight up, like Jack's beanstalk. Rather, both the mind and society are driven by two opposite forces, either of which may dominate at any given time but neither of which can do so indefinitely. The force which we call Apollonian is rational, structured, and verbal; that which we call Dionysian is intuitive, flexible, and less, even non-, verbal. In the humanities, formal philosophy is Apollonian; music is Dionysian. In government, law and order are Apollonian; revolutionary tactics are Dionysian. A textbook that is tightly structured so that one chapter leads inevitably into the next and the order cannot be changed, is Apollonian. *The Art of Being Human* is far more Dionysian in that it allows for a number of different approaches. At any rate, the "secret" appears to be that individuals as well as humanity as a whole must manage to balance these opposing forces. The ideal life is one that has a liberal dose of both Apollo and Dionysus and avoids staying at either extreme.

An opening discussion of the two gods is recommended. Students generally have no trouble comprehending why these names have come to be associated with opposing tendencies in human nature. They like to discuss their own behavioral and personality patterns and seem grateful to find labels for them. Students are glad to find that the fun part of life has some legitimacy in the academic world.

The subject works as a sort of overture for the course. After spending some time on personal relevance of the terms, instructors can continue by showing how the duality is a good launch pad for the study of the humanities.

The "Sunlit Chariot" videotape underscores the duality to be firmly established at the outset. Students have clearly understood the Apollonian origins of the atom bomb as well as its Dionysian consequences. They are also introduced to Golding's *Lord of the Flies* with its contrast between the Apollonian surface of the English schoolboys and the primitive Dionysianism which takes over on the desert island. Housman's poem "The Laws of God, the Laws of Man" ties it all together; human tendencies are Dionysian, but the survival of civilization requires Apollonian controls.


III.         "ART AND THE ARTIST"

> Read Chapter 2, "The Visual Artist"
> View "Art, Tell Me What I Am; Art, Tell Us Who We Are"

Having recognized that a major purpose of the Humanities is to make us more open to the feelings and thoughts of others, no matter how unusual or unfamiliar, and that human expression has its Apollonian and Dionysian sides, we are ready to look in some detail at one of the enduring humanities disciplines: visual art.

In keeping with the open-minded spirit of the book, we begin with the premise that art cannot be defined in any one way. One theory is that artists see with the right brain, that they see both the inner and outer worlds in ways that the rest of us do not and therefore their visual experiences offer us new and exciting ways of being in the world. Another theory is that artists have a need to *imitate* what they see, that the act of imitation is itself a source of inspiration for them and a source or excitement for us. The chapter urges the reader not to have a narrow view of what kind of imitation is acceptable. Imitation does not have to mean reproducing the surface appearance of reality, though it can be just that. The way a work of art approximates the look of reality may not, however, be the most important thing to say about it.

The videotape allows the student to see and hear some contemporary artists talking about what they do in art, and the response has often been one of outrage or derision. ("What makes *them* artists?") At any rate, it prompts a lively discussion and allows for a direct, early confrontation with the underlying attitude of the humanities student--at least in the beginning: why am I in this course? What have the humanities to do with me?


IV.          "MUSIC: THIS IS HOW I SOUND"

             Read Chapter 3, "Music: Sound and Silence"
             View "Jazz/Bach"

The fundamentals of what could be termed "music appreciation" are here. Musical elements such as the scale, harmony, rhythm, and melody are discussed discretely; and there are the contributions of major figures like Bach, Mozart, and Beethoven, as well as contemporaries like Gershwin and Ellington. But the real aim of the chapter is to encourage students not to consider the musical tradition of the humanities as something "educational" and thus apart from them, but rather to explore the possibility that their taste in music reflects *them*, helps them to learn more about what they really are. Therefore, people whose tastes lean toward one--and only one--style of music miss out on the chance to discover aspects of themselves they may not know about. There may be a romantic lurking inside, afraid to come out. Or the blues will provide the ideal outlet for an old sorrow that is almost, but not *quite*, forgotten.

In other words, when dealing with the subject matter of the chapter--musical elements and milestones in musical history--instructors may want to expose the student to as much music as possible, without getting into a discussion of what music *does*, or to combine the historical with the personal. The choice is in keeping with the underlying purpose of the new edition: to have a humanities text that is flexible enough to accommodate a variety of approaches.

The associated videotape "Jazz/Bach" features solo work by jazz renowns Eddie Higgins and Ira Sullivan, talking directly to the students about the inspiration of Bach and what it means for a jazz musician to improvise on a theme, a musical experience which Bach legitimized and which became integral to his legacy, particularly to jazz. (What is especially useful about this tape is that students get to hear wonderful sounds from two eras quite distant from each other *and* come to realize that time is not so very long after all. Bach and Eddie Higgins appear to be quite comfortable with each other.)

# V.    "TRAGEDY AND COMEDY"

Read Chapter 4, "Theater: Two Masks"
View "The Tragic Vision"

If we are to sustain an open-minded attitude toward life, if we are to be tolerant of other life modes which are different and unfamiliar, we need to be as balanced inwardly as we possibly can. That is, we cannot become perpetually involved with our own emotional and intellectual problems--at least to the exclusion of a clear-sighted ability to have at least some semblance of an honest relationship with the world "out there." The tragic and comic arts of the theater provide us with a major means of attaining clear-sightedness. Aristotle's still viable definition of tragedy tells us that, when we witness the fall of the protagonist from a great height, we experience a great emotional release. He does not say so, but in the parlance of modern psychology, we could say that emotional catharsis leaves us, at least for a time, in a state of inner equilibrium. It is also possible that the achievement of such a state, even if it is temporary, helps us transcend a narrow concern with our own problems. (Helping us see beyond ourselves into the minds and hearts of others is one of the major goals of the humanities.)

Much has been made of Aristotle's concept of identification, whereby we tremble at the fall because it is happening to a "person like us." One doubts that the philosopher thought, even in his day, that the citizens who made up the bulk of the audience could really identify with ancient kings and queens personally. What he surely meant was that tragic characters were after all *human* and did not deserve their terrible fate. If we insist that a work of tragedy has validity only when the protagonist is close to us, we are denying ourselves the chance to experience one of the great thrills in life: the joy and the sorrow of witnessing the tragic catastrophe on the stage.

The suggested videotape presents a professional actor in some of the memorable final speeches in the great tragedies, and does indeed offer students the chance to experience and appreciate what tragedy is all about; the chance to comprehend why the sad plays are the most thrilling.

Comedy receives its due, however. The approach taken in the text implies that there is also comic catharsis--a relief of inner tension through laughter. The theory is that for rational people comedy provides a confrontation with the irrational, the illogical, and the morally or socially unacceptable (in short, the *incongruous*), which creates the inner tension; this in turn must be dissipated if one is to maintain mental equilibrium. Laughing or even smiling inwardly (as we do with the cerebral humor of a Shaw) helps us in this all-important survival mechanism.

Comedy exists on many levels--from the wildest sort of farce to satire and the comedy of ideas; from the buffoonery of *commedia* stock characters to the subtle verbal ironies of Oscar Wilde. But we can absorb and profit from all of these, because reality is, after all, more often illogical than otherwise, and the thinking person is almost continually in a state of frustration with the way people are and the way things tend to go. We might say that comic art is a little like getting a vaccination: we are given a sudden dose of the virus itself (incongruity). Our laughing response immunizes us to the daily onslaught of events and behavior that are contrary to our rational expectations. The fault is probably the expectations, not the world, but comic release is a pleasurable cure anyway.

*The Art of Being Human* telecourse contains a videotape called "Knaves and Fools," originally filmed to accompany this unit. Indeed it still can, but we suggest that it can be well used in connection with the following chapter on motion pictures.

## VI.    "FLICKERING IMAGES"

> Read Chapter 5, "The Motion Picture: Art and
> Industry"
> View "Knaves and Fools"

At its best--as art--film gives us an alternate way of viewing experience and *having* an experience, offering an integration of sight and sound that distills life into its essence rather than copies its appearance.

To begin with such a statement could confuse today's students, accustomed as they are to the wide screen and special effects that dazzle the eyes and bombard the ears with intense "realism." Of course we know that exploding buildings, cars careening off cliffs to their fiery doom, and people bursting through plate-glass windows and falling a hundred stories to their splattered deaths . . . these "effects" are NOT real in any scientific sense. They are cinematic illusions that are really illusions; but so are dreams. We would not be damaging our artistic integrity if we were to admit that there is an art to the new cinematic technology and that we have all been entertained by the color-sound-and-rapid-movement spectaculars that dominate the screens today.

On the other hand, students seldom need help in enjoying the bright and loud extravaganzas. For this unit the best strategy is to look at certain milestone achievements in film and at the artistry behind them. It is not necessary to denigrate much contemporary work we feel in our hearts to be ephemeral. Many, many students will see a difference. We should approach this unit on the positive side. *Film indeed is often art, and we shall see why.*

The chapter approaches film historically, and the instructor should have no difficulty focusing on milestone achievements. If *Birth of a Nation*, *The Gold Rush*, *Potemkin*, *Citizen Kane*, and so on, are less attractive than other possibilities, the instructor can easily make substitutions. Some of the cinematic elements discussed--such as Griffith's lingering takes and Welles' use of chiaroscuro--might prove useful if applied to other examples.

The video "Knaves and Fools" can complement the reading, even though its focus is comedy in general, not just on the screen. However, there is a whole section on Charlie Chaplin's art at the end of the film, with excerpts from one of the Little Tramp movies. Students can see the speeded-up action and the very simple, but not ineffective, camera work of early screen art. The important thing is to discourage the view that Chaplin and others are quaint "pioneers" lacking the sophisticated techniques of today's often noisier filmmakers.

## VII.    "THE CHARACTER OF THE PHILOSOPHER"

> Read Chapter 6, "Western Philosophy"
> View "The Problem of Evil"

The text chapter deals with three of the major subjects that philosophers have thought about for centuries: *Mind*, *God*, and *Ultimate Reality*. There are many other issues, of course, including morality, which is the focus of Chapter 7; but the three we have chosen for this chapter offer the student a good overview of what has occupied many of the great minds--and what remains just a little beyond the domain of science.

Our main intent has been to characterize the philosopher as someone with an important function in society and to convince students that they too can engage in speculative thought: in short, to demonstrate the pleasure of thinking by singling out a few outstanding role models.

This unit is crucial to the underlying (if flexible) "theme" of the course--*the human need for keeping an open mind*. The philosopher often comes on strong and gives the impression of having solved the great riddles. This is a privilege we must be willing to grant one who travels so far on an intellectual journey. But the journey started from Point Zero: from a puzzle, a creased forehead, the scratching of the head. Without having an open mind at the outset, no philosopher would ever philosophize. It is this need to question; it is the inability to be satisfied with easy answers that we want to stress.

Bertrand Russell once defined science as "what we know" and philosophy as "what we don't know." With science having pushed further and further past the frontiers of human knowledge, today's student often asks why there is still a need for the philosopher. The final section of the text chapter concerns that question--*reality*--which has preoccupied both kinds of inquiry; and we see that, even though science has traced the origins of the universe back to milliseconds following the Big Bang, there are still unanswered questions, such as "What was around *before* the Big Bang?"

The nature of mind--how we know what we know--and the possibility that there is, or is not, a God . . . these remain legitimate concerns for students who are able to share in the excitement of following thoughts to conclusions. In short, the philosopher--full-time or part-time--must be accommodated, respected, and loved.

The accompanying videotape "The Problem of Evil" demonstrates the philosopher at work analyzing a specific issue, one that has been with humanity for thousands of years. Is there such a thing as evil? If there is a God and God is good, then why is evil permitted to exist? Why do the innocent suffer? In the film a young bride falls to her death while the groom looks on in horror. The young man in sorrow asks a priest to help him understand. From this example, the film goes on to look at a number of answers to the problem. Nothing is resolved, but mighty questions have been asked. The role of the philosopher has been dramatically illustrated.


VIII.        "THE PHILOSOPHER AND THE MORAL ISSUE"

            Read Chapter 7, "The Moral Issue"
            View "The Anguish of Abraham"

Some modern thinkers--and we are talking about a century of them--decided that the speculations of past philosophers into matters such as God's existence or whether human beings are born with a mind (otherwise where do ideas come from?) were no longer appropriate. Sciences like anthropology and biology, not to mention physics, were taking care of many of the old so-called unanswered questions. Please note that not every philosopher subscribed to these views, but in any event, the strong shadow of science in the philosophical arena has brought moral philosophy very much to the fore. The thought of a world in which moral values no longer apply has not been especially palatable; and morality is one area into which science does not venture. No surprise then to find that moral issues dominate the concerns of many contemporary thinkers.

Moral issues are also crucial to a humanities course. Openness to life, the willingness to grow, an insistence upon one's own identity and the right to create one's personal environment . . . all these conditions within the human spirit are what the humanities are about. But there is a limit to the amount of individual unfolding that can take place before one begins to impinge upon the right of another to grow. Human beings live in social groups, and groups need moral laws in order to survive. Even outlaw gangs surely have rules; have a code which must not be broken.

This unit is especially important in a time when many of our students have been taught--or *think* they have been taught--that right and wrong are "up to the individual." Cultural anthropology may have unwittingly been one source of the belief that all values are relative to place and cultural context. But even the philosopher who espouses a moral relativism based on cultural anthropology cannot believe that *individuals* ought to be free to live by whatever values they choose with no concern for others.

Yet where do moral values come from? The chapter looks at a number of possibilities: self-interest, reason, religion, family, education, the workplace, even folk wisdom in the form of popular maxims. No final answer is--or perhaps can be--given; but the student should come away from this unit with the understanding that "Do your own thing" is a facile way of dodging tough thoughts.

The accompanying videotape "The Anguish of Abraham" relates to the discussion of existential morality, which concludes the chapter. The title is the phrase made famous by Kierkegaard, and it is a metaphor for the pain experienced by any mature person who must make a moral decision, who wants to do so with integrity, but who realizes that no one will ever be there to nod with approval and say "Yes, that was definitely the right choice."


IX.          "THE EASTERN OPTION"

          Read Chapter 8, "Western Territory, Eastern Space"
          View "The Still and Empty Center"

This unit suggests that moral dilemmas do indeed have a cultural context, and that many of our values, as well as some of our pain, stem from being born and raised in Western civilization (which used to be considered the king of the roost and which used to be the sole subject of humanities courses). The alternatives offered by Eastern thought are not advocated, merely raised for the student's consideration.

Here we find a very broad dualism between Eastern and Western value systems and beliefs, though the labels are not necessarily geographic ones. The Western mind tends to stress the importance of self, the self's grasp of things, the self's moral dilemmas, and so on; to assume, in short, that solving both the intellectual and emotional problems of the self is the most important thing we do with our minds. But the Eastern outlook, exemplified in Buddhism, denies the separate existence of a self. For the Hindus the whole world is one self, and each of us is part of it. For the Buddhists what Westerners call the self is merely a point at which attitudes, feelings, and thoughts intersect, some of which are those of other people. In other words, each of us is an *interaction*, not a self-comprised entity.

This having been said, we are able to draw several vital conclusions. One is that the death of any one individual is never pivotal in the scheme of things (which do not in fact *have* a scheme--they just happen). Another is that we must strive (through meditation) to overcome the illusion that we are separate entities, opening ourselves to the panorama of life about us. Doing so causes us to behave toward others with compassion; for, in becoming objective about our own illusions of self, in learning to distance ourselves from our *selves*, we begin to see the behavior and internal processes of others in the same way. Understanding why others do what they do makes us more tolerant of them, less likely to be paranoid about them.

The "Eastern option" is thus another means available by which we can become open to life and to the contributions others can make to our own existence. In a sense, they are a *part* of that existence.

The accompanying video encapsulates all that we have said above. In docudrama form, it traces the quest of a young American for self-realization. Trying Buddhism as a possible answer, he discovers that he is approaching an Eastern option with Western expectations; or, as he puts it, "looking for Eastern answers to Western questions." "Self-realization" is a Western ideal--or myth. In Buddhism there are no hard and fast truths. He learns that what he is looking for is the simple acceptance of things as they are. There is no "pay-off" in the Western sense.


X.          "THE CRITICAL THINKER"

            Read Chapter 9, "On Being a Critical Thinker"
            View "The Wonder of Form"

A casual glance at the chapter titles from the text might cause one to think Chapter 9 does not belong where it is or anywhere else in Part One, which is called "Makers of the Humanities." All along we have dealt with the art and philosophical contributions of others: people, movements, schools of thought, artistic and musical styles. Now all of a sudden students find they are dealing with themselves.

First, it is entirely in keeping with the spirit of the book that readers should be part of, not merely appreciators of the humanities. Developing an openness to the experiences and expressions of others does not mean that the student has nothing to offer. Indeed the hope is that, having derived as much as possible from the course, students are then in a position to make their own contributions--if not in art or music, if not in formal philosophy, then surely as a role model of the critical thinker. The humanities soothe the spirit and cleanse the mind, in a manner of speaking, leaving the *amateur*, the lover of creative expression, on an even keel, in a better position to think logically (not in the Aristotelian strict sense, but informally). The critical thinker withholds hasty judgments about people and events; looks for the hidden assumptions behind what people say or what the media report; is not likely to have opinions molded by those media or by teachers or anyone claiming to have authority over the minds of others.

Second, a mistake often made by humanities texts and courses is to overstate the glory of the masters, thus excluding many students and readers from *ever* thinking they are worth something too. To deny the self in the Buddhist sense is at the same time to invite one into the total fellowship of humanity. All of us are interactions; and having been interacting with the humanities, we now belong to the tradition.

The video "The Wonder of Form" does not explicate critical thinking, but strongly invites--*requires*--the application of it. The film states that "form" may be what all art and all thought have in common and indeed that "form" may be what the human adventure is all about. Students should be asked to watch closely, to concentrate, but not to take notes, not to interpret what they are seeing until the film is over and they have had a chance to "digest" it. The instructor should relate the chapter to the discussion of the film, asking, for example, what a literalist would make of it and what critical thinkers can find in it beyond the statements about form. In short, the video allows for a rigorous experience in analysis. Students in the past have shown delight in the process, realizing they have--often for the first time--risen above the literal level of understanding. Possible discussion points are included further on in this Manual when we deal more specifically with each chapter and accompanying video.

XI.        "SOCIETY VERSUS THE HUMANITIES"

        Read Chapter 10 (same title)
        View "The Outer Circle"

The text chapter is new for this edition, and it seems fitting that it should introduce the second part of the book *Themes of the Humanities*. What better theme than one which should have no trouble involving students: the forces which have repressed and continue to repress artists and bold thinkers, forces they know under various names, such as "censorship," "prejudice," "racism," "sexism," and so on? Many important works have been inspired by the struggle between the humanist (using the word broadly, as in the suggested video for the first unit, in which the humanist is portrayed as a little girl looking at the world like Shakespeare's Miranda) and the establishment (often the moral majority). But there are probably more works that were never created, or were never seen or heard--inspired works whose creators were women (when women were not supposed to make names for themselves) or other minorities (when they were supposed to be servants not artists) or people on some authoritative blacklist (like Galileo or those suspected of being Communist sympathizers back in the American '50s).

Students in democratic societies (and one presumes no one else will be taking this course) readily disapprove of repressed art and thought. After all, they are not so far from the age at which their elders were "O.K." and they were not. Recent stormy debates over federal funding of art exhibits with shocking subject matter and court rulings in some states that certain records be taken off music store shelves have given today's student a rallying cause. Experience has shown us, however, that classroom discussions of such cases soon wear thin. The point is too quickly made, and not much learning takes place.

The familiar story is a good starting place, but the instructor will want to move rapidly into a historical overview of repression, which both the chapter and the video provide. There the students will discover much larger issues at stake, deep-rooted hostility toward those with different skin colors and "dangerous" ideas. The point is that some of the recent hoopla over dissenters has to do with politics rather than disturbing human traits which cause lasting enmity between people and which become terrifying weapons in the hands of those with too much power.

Women and racial minorities have been allowed only grudging and token representation in the humanities for a very long time. The authors have discovered that facing the issue of prejudice and sexism head-on is better than shiftily apologizing for the underrepresentation of many people who have always had much to express.

The title of the suggested video "The Outer Circle" is a metaphor for the boundaries of acceptability, which have existed in every age and for varying reasons. The film focuses on milestone cases: the medieval Church and its war against the goliards, rebellious youths who questioned

wandering
student jesters
of 12th & 13th
cents who wrote/sang Latin
satiric verses

Church dogma and wrote irreverent poems and songs; Galileo and his imprisonment and imposed silence by the Inquisition; the 1925 Scopes trial with its enormous implications for the cause of academic freedom. The last segment recognizes that every crusader for free expression is not necessarily a scientist, struggling against religious minds. The meditative student, who is the goliard in modern dress, is opposing the autocracy of science and insisting upon the right to seek other paths to truth.

XII.        "THE REALITY OF MYTH"

     Read Chapter 11, "Myths"
     View "The Collective Dreams of Mankind"

In one respect the title we have given this unit would have been a better one for the text chapter, and we are strongly recommending it to anyone who develops a telecourse, an independent study syllabus, or wishes to structure a classroom course using the text and some or all of the suggested videotapes.

In seeking the goal of openness to life, to new directions, and always new ways of being in this world, we run into an obstacle whenever the word "myth" turns up. For too many people, "myth" means an untruth, a lie, when in actuality most of our lives are shaped and driven by the mythology we inherit. Understanding this force is critical for the free spirit. Myths are not fables we can hear or not hear, or choose entirely to ignore. They constitute much of what we take to be wisdom, and indeed often deserve to be called just that. The reason for the label "myth" can be given with just one example. The tale of how the young Arthur was understood to be the rightful king after drawing forth Excalibur from the stone is part of the legacy of almost anyone born into Western civilization. It cannot be called a scientific fact, for no one has ever proved beyond a shadow of a doubt that a real King Arthur existed, at least not as depicted in the tales of Camelot. So we use the special word "myth." Yet it has had the impact of true history, has it not? The story embodies almost everyone's ideal of the hero, the person born with all those special qualities, who is always there when needed. The hero becomes an idea fixed in our minds, whether consciously or not. It motivates how we approach an election year, for example.

Early in 1992 H. Ross Perot achieved national prominence as an undeclared candidate for the presidency. His legion of followers grew each day, though few people had ever heard of him a year before. He had truly come out of nowhere, an aging version of King Arthur who seemed to arrive at precisely the moment when the national distrust of politicians--of *government*--had reached new heights. When he withdrew from the race, millions protested; many implored him to reconsider, though he had never even stated a platform.

Myths are like Kantian categories. They are pre-sets, or molds, by which the raw material of experience is filtered, shaped, and rendered meaningful to the way human awareness has been developed. Objective reality, without the filter of mythology, is like Melville's white world, which must have the colors we bring to it.

The justification for including a unit on myth in a humanities course is that those who wish to do as much as possible with their time on this earth need to know the forces that are driving them. They reach a better understanding of themselves by knowing to what particular myths they are drawn and recognizing which myth-needs have not been met.

Above all, the unit fits this suggested structure, with its overriding goal of openness, because it seems clear that looking first at the mythologizing process, then at our own mythology, will help us to see more clearly what needs are driving those about us.

The title of the accompanying video is taken directly from the definition of myth given by Carl Jung, whose anthropological and psychological approach is the one we have chosen. Written by a noted scholar of myths and a student of Jung himself, the film summarizes major symbols in the old stories and introduces the student to the all-important term "archetype." This will open the door for a discussion of archetypes the students believe are involved in their own expectations, their own manner of interpreting experience.

Among the archetypes that come to light in such discussions are some that have racist and sexist roots. While one should not change the definition so that myth means "lie" in special cases, one can point out that mythology is often amoral. It explains, but does not justify, some beliefs and some behavior predicated on those beliefs.

XIII.        "THE MYTHS OF LOVE"

        Read Chapter 12, "Love"
        View "Love: Myth and Mystery"

If students are convinced that myths are real forces, influencing our behavior, and not just lies that can be forgotten once they are understood, then the title we are suggesting for this unit should work; should, in fact, greatly support the thesis that myths are real, whether they direct our thoughts and feelings for better or worse. For who will deny that *love* is a universal archetype, one that is likely to dominate our sense of the world for a very large portion of our lives? And what nicer gift may a humanities course give to students than to illustrate that *love* is indeed a very complex archetype, understood in different ways, often by the partners in a relationship that both define as *love* without knowing they are working from different myths?

If most people take King Arthur for the hero who will always appear when needed, one doubts that there could be widespread agreement about, for example, Venus and Adonis. The Greeks, tragedy-prone as they were, probably saw the tale as illustrating what happens when the emotion of lust gets the better of reason. Today's student might decide the brief joy experienced by the lovers was worth the unhappiness that followed. Unless of course that student is coming from a strict religious upbringing!

The unit looks at the subject historically in order to underscore that the substance of a myth can be changed as well as determined by time and place. Generalizations are made, inevitably; and thus a caveat is encouraged before proceeding with the unit. But surely students will agree that it would take many volumes and many courses to do full justice to this subject. Even a cursory look at all the definitions of love that have been and still are possible will serve the purpose of the course; and we don't even have to go outside the humanities to find them.

Students have been particularly interested in the historical roots of romantic love. They are surprised to learn that it has not been around forever, at least as far as we can tell from Biblical and classical writings. They discover that romantic love--that is, love which is not primarily physical, love in which sex may be longed for but is not realized--is first found in the medieval *romances* and may possibly have been a myth created to sanctify tales of extramarital relationships, such as that between Guinevere and Lancelot. (Students who have seen the film version of *Camelot* like to point out that the lovers are in fact in lust as well as in love.) The romances reflect a social order in which marriage among the gentry and the nobility was usually a perfunctory business arrangement. Readers could easily identify with characters who find their true loves but are either denied fulfillment or meet tragic ends like Tristan and Isolde. But whether or not there is tragic consummation, the attraction itself is never in question. Only the *result* is tragic. Hence over time the powerful myth of romantic love was created: love lasting beyond death, love that transcends the flesh and all worldly allures; the love of Romeo and Juliet, Heathcliff and Cathy.

The unit also considers the courtly love model, in which women achieved equality with men, even gaining the ascendancy by requiring that suitors become slaves, worshipping at their feet without promise of tasting the sweet delights of the flesh.

The Victorian model paralleled the growth of business and the business man, who was expected to earn the bread and provide handsomely for a wife with no independent rights--a model which, as students are only too happy to point out, is still very much with us and which feminists of both genders are struggling to lay to rest.

The accompanying video covers much of the same ground, dealing with the attempt of a writer who has lost his companion (exactly how we are not told) to straighten out his thoughts about love. Does it exist? Did it ever for him? Is it a purely biological sensation masquerading as something "spiritual"? Is there any meaning at all to "spiritual"? Is humanity a breed that doesn't like to face the truth about itself, always pretending to be a "higher" species? Or does the pretense become a reality after all?

Instructors may find the ending sentimental, and it may be that it is. But the writer's holding on to the poetic view of romantic love is *his* decision. The author of the film, like the authors of the text, merely raises possibilities--as well they should if the course is to stay on track.

XIV.        "THE MYTH OF HAPPINESS"

          Read Chapter 13, "Happiness"
          View "In Search of Happiness"

For anyone who likes a tight structure the risk of using "myth" once again in a unit title may be well taken. Others may have had enough and will seek a different approach. We recommend the title only if the instructor feels comfortable with the archetypal view of mythology and has been careful to point out that a myth is not a lie but is certainly a relative truth: real to some, totally false to others.

One could begin by presenting an overview of happiness as a super-myth which has gotten so big that its specifics are usually lost. Only the bold outlines remain. All of us want to be happy. Most if not all of us would agree with Aristotle that happiness is the goal of living. Having said that, we realize that any two people, when questioned, would be unlikely to render the same definition. Is happiness, as the saying goes, a "state of mind"? Which one? Is one man's happiness another man's sorrow? Is sorrow necessarily the opposite of happiness?

The text itself divides the term up into various philosophies of happiness, beginning with hedonism, which we believe is dominant in the United States today, for which a humanities course ought to be at least presenting alternatives. We also discuss Epicureanism, Stoicism, and

Aristotle's view that happiness is the condition of a life that has been lived in virtue and wisdom. Students have tended to be intrigued by the Aristotelian principle that happiness is NOT a feeling of pleasure, even that one may be feeling miserable about something at the moment and still know that one's life is happy.

Like the treatments of myth and love before it, this approach to happiness leaves no assumption untested and is therefore another step toward the goal of open-mindedness: in this case, coming to see that one need not after all remain preoccupied with personal problems (excepting unavoidable problems like serious illness) and especially that life doesn't *owe* any of us anything. Of course, we're not saying in this unit that we should just be miserable and keep it to ourselves. We're saying that one is often miserable by misplacing the emphasis--by feeling that one is being "robbed" of the pleasures that others are surely experiencing or that the "good things in life" (usually vaguely defined) are passing one by.

Whether or not the student finds a satisfying approach to a happy life, the unit will at least leave him or her with the realization that happiness should not be considered a lost cause until it has been sensibly and suitably defined. One hint that is not in the text but can be given to a class: *the sensible definition can come first, and more often than not things will fall into place.* One can make up one's mind not to be UNhappy and then go about finding the best road to that destination. Above all, happiness is perhaps not something we should wait around to happen. Another hint: *your happiness ought not to depend upon what other people do.*

The video mainly concerns what the author considers to be misguided efforts to find happiness. The very title "In Search of . . ." says it all. The author sees happiness as a process that is self-generated, not an entity that is to be discovered.


XV.          "DEATH: LIGHT AND SHADOW"

          Read Chapter 14, "Coping with Death"
          View "For Everything, a Season"

In times past the subject of death--or the emergence of death myths--was not part of one's youth. It was not even part of early adulthood, and for many even middle age was too soon to begin thinking about one's mortality. It would have been unthinkable to find such a unit in a humanities course, especially one using a text subtitled "The Humanities as a Technique for Living." How might a discussion of death have contributed to plans for a richer, more satisfying life?

We are now becoming aware that education for death is critically important, and the sooner it begins, the better. Young people have a much easier time of dealing with the subject than do those who have been putting off the confrontation. It holds less terror, and to learn that the fear, once removed, need never return, even when one enters old age, is to have greatly enhanced one's "technique for living."

Besides, the subject of death is found over and over in the humanities from the very beginning. If poets and painters could not help expressing the joy inspired by just being alive, the shadow of death could not have been very far off. A law of human nature appears to be that there cannot *be* light without shadow; and the higher the stakes, the more painful it is to lose. Indeed we should expect that only a species which never learned to be inwardly appreciative of life can ignore death.

Because humanity can think and feel, because it is capable of reaching so many highs, it must also contend with the lows. One can imagine no other form of animal life experiencing the "depths of despair." To teach a humanities course without facing despair is to lie about human life.

Students learn that, as was the case with love and happiness, death means different things. For Socrates, at least as reported by Plato, it was certainly preferable to leading the unexamined life. To Hamlet death was the great leveler, and for many there is comfort in the thought that not even the rich and famous are exempt from the one experience we all share.

The text chapter also looks at the question of suicide, and did not Camus say that this was the *only* valid philosophical issue? We employ the zoom lens and note that for a poet like Sylvia Plath and a writer like Ernest Hemingway self-inflicted death was the only solution for a life that had become unacceptable. Class discussions of this issue have always been filled with energy. Since the purpose of this unit is to suggest that many options exist as counterforces to the shadow of death, students are invited to think of alternatives to suicide. Surely this is better than to let the subject fester in the unconscious!

Of particular interest to students has been the section on symbolic murder and symbolic suicide: ways in which people in real life and fictional characters in the humanities use a form of death as a survival strategy, often with harmful results. Cutting remarks, gossip, and plotting against fellow students or employees are all legal kinds of murder. But we also plot against ourselves; we put ourselves down, compare ourselves unfavorably to others, place ourselves in losing positions deliberately just to have reality confirm the poor self-images we have.

Finally, the Phoenix Model is offered to students as an always available treasure from the humanities, one they can keep for as long as they live. The phoenix bird of legend has to wait 500 years to renew the cycle of death and life, but *we* can learn to rise from our own ashes any time we want to. For the ultimate truth here is that death does not mean just one event, but happens over and over again in the course of life, as we end careers or relationships; and the art of being human includes the power to renew. Having discovered *this*, we may begin to be less concerned about that "one event."

The video opens with a young child burying a dead bird; on the child's face is an expression of peace and understanding, a recognition of the place of death in the scheme of things. It ends with the same sequence as the credits roll, suggesting the cycle of death and rebirth.


XVI.        "DEATH AND LIFE IN NATURE"

        Read Chapter 15, "Nature in the Humanities"
        View "The Man with No Time for Beauty"

Here we have the second of the entirely new chapters, and the subject this time is how the humanities have dealt with, responded to, and helped shape human attitudes toward nature. To be sure, an underlying objective is to reinforce the admonitions students are getting from different sources, that we can no longer afford to take nature for granted.

Looking historically at nature in the humanities, we discover that the Bible itself sounded a very early--perhaps the earliest--warning. The story of Eden is, after all, that of the pristine, unspoiled beauty of this earth, lost forever after the first sin. But the story has deeper implications for today's student. There is the idea that millions have found implicit in the Bible (an idea that is not actually there!): the idea of human stewardship over nature. God presumably gave Adam and Eve the run of the garden, cautioning them to take good care of it. Did "the run of the garden" prove popular, prove irresistible, while the "taking care" became too much bother?

We also find early warnings in Shakespeare. Jaques, it turns out, was something of an environmentalist; and even if his creator intended him to be a comically melancholy fellow, his denunciation of the wanton deerslaying and the corruption of the Forest of Arden have to be taken quite seriously today.

The key to this unit, however, is the discussion of the role of nature in romantic literature and how this became a mythical archetype, still very much with us. That is, the romantic writers saw nature as not only a source of beauty and inspiration but as a godly power that knew what it was about, that, by implication, had only to be left to its own devices and not interfered with. The point is that, though we have greatly interfered with the natural process, too many of us appease our conscience by invoking the myth of nature as self-healer, which may also tie into the old idea of stewardship. We can do anything we want, dump anything on nature, push aerosol buttons all we want, and trust in Wordsworth's "Nature never did betray the heart that loved her." Of course, we lie to ourselves that we do in fact love nature all the while we are trashing it.

The unit ends with consideration of two contemporary, and dark, works of fiction that illustrate with frightening power the moral corruption of humanity that leads to the desecration of the world. In Conrad's *Heart of Darkness* we see the arrogance of white culture laying waste the environment and the inhabitants of what we have come to call the Third World. In Burgess' *A Clockwork Orange* we are given a scary vision of the near future of ruined landscapes, trashed cities, and gangs of amoral, marauding thugs. True, Burgess' hero repents and changes his behavior (at least in the new edition of the novel), but the *deus ex machina* hardly lessens the impact of what has gone before. We know that, unless we do something now, the future may be all too similar to what Burgess describes.

The unit can also be used to underscore an important point: namely, that we cannot expect to open ourselves to life just for our own gratification or "enrichment." Learning to look beyond ourselves, to enter other minds and hearts, comes with an inevitable price. If you keep your eyes open, you have to see what is going on; and that means you can either ignore it (which is closing the mind again) or figuring out what you can do to help.

The accompanying video can also be used--and has indeed in the past been used--as an introduction to the course. Woodrow Tatlock is still mentioned (though not as fully) in the introductory chapter as the prototype of the "nice guy" who retires and then has nothing to do, because he has none of the resources the humanities can provide. The film can also reinforce the subject of this unit, since among Woodrow's sad failings is indifference to the world about him. Cruising along a fjord, he is more interested in telling a fellow passenger about his deceased wife than in observing the awesome landscape. In the final sequence Woodrow sits on a dock fishing, oblivious to the splendor of the sunrise. Woodrow has never taken advantage of what it can mean to be human, has never developed the sensibility that is our human birthright, is now old and self-pitying. The film can tie together many the themes which have already been explored. At what point is anybody officially "retired"? Does this mean one no longer has responsibility toward others, toward the environment? Is one never to experience a new way of thinking and feeling? Are the humanities to be left behind after a curriculum requirement has been met? How did Woodrow get that way in the first place?

# XVII.    "A PORTRAIT OF THE FREE PERSON"

Read Chapter 16, "Freedom"
View "The World Was All Before Them"

If one had world enough and time to actually give the course we have been outlining, with all of the focuses and the implications, and if one's students were miraculously all of a mind-- eager and open to learning and filled with the desire to change things for the better--one would have no trouble coming to the final classes and making a final summation of what the course ought to have accomplished for each participant. The "final product," as some administrators like to say, is the enlightened citizen of tomorrow's world: open-minded, tolerant, com- passionate, even-tempered, rational, ethical, and responsible; able to use leisure time to its ful- lest, enjoying the cultural resources available, but also having created a personal environment of books, artwork, and music that would ensure an unending process of growth.

To become such a person implies a state of freedom. If the course has taught us anything, it is that the art of being human means making good choices from the options we have. If we have no options, we cannot practice this art, but must remain forever at the mercy of whatever table scraps are thrown to us.

So freedom is the inevitable final unit. Does it exist at all? Does it mean liberation? Are all liberated people free? How do they use their freedom? Above all, does everyone really *want* to be free? Everyone wants to be liberated from shackles, but beyond that, what does being free really mean? Perhaps the humanities can offer some answers. The humanities haven't failed us yet!

Two sharply contrasting views emerge from philosophical analyses of the subject: that of the *determinist*, who says that everything we say or do, think or feel is dictated by a preceding cause; and the *libertarian*, who says that free will is indeed a viable concept, not just a human dream.

The authors, in researching the topic, have found far more support for the determinist than the libertarian argument; and this fact ought to be addressed at the outset. Students can be asked WHY determinism appears to be the predominant philosophical view. Perhaps science has some- thing to do with the matter? Ever since Newton, the idea of cause and effect has been difficult to shake. Is free will a concoction of those who fear that a deterministic picture of existence will do away with moral responsibility altogether? Was free will--as has been suggested-- something invented by Saint Augustine, who wanted to find a way to hold God blameless for the evil in the world?

Some determinist positions may strike the instructor as surprising, certainly not traditional. Rousseau, for example, is labeled an "institutional" determinist, and Nietzsche is identified with determinism through one's self-assessment as either a master or a slave. Marx and Skinner are, of course, traditional; and we have added genetics as a major roadblock to those who would still maintain that we have free wills.

The case for libertarianism includes the thoughts of Schopenhauer and William James, as well as that aspect of Freud's work which sees the aim of psychoanalysis as freeing the conscious mind from bondage to the subterranean drives and the repressed (because forbidden) impulses of the libido. While Freud believed society was essentially neurotic, he must have thought *he* was free, along with some of his patients. The Freudian material should be included at any rate, because of the recent reevaluation of it. Students need to learn that a person's contributions are worthy of study even if they may not be supported by contemporary theory. Freud is one of four or five major figures who helped shape the modern mind.

The text closes with the authors' own view that *both* determinism and libertarianism can be applied to the human condition; that, in fact, it is possible to be free, but only if one is willing to pay the price of taking full responsibility for one's actions. The implication is that some few people (among them Gandhi and King) can be considered among the free spirits of this century. But it is a goal to strive for. "Do you WANT to be free?" is always a good question to ask the student. Once it has been answered in the affirmative, the stage is set for a lively and rewarding discussion--and, hopefully, a powerful learning experience.

The final videotape was intentionally made as a course summary, but it can certainly stand on its own in case all of the tapes have not been shown or the chapters read in consecutive order. The narrator, unidentified, is obviously someone observing humanity from a distant vantage point and appears at first very pessimistic about what he sees. But his conclusion is that the one positive trait of this bizarre species is its ability, despite all its mistakes, to start all over again and try something new. Obviously this is a fable with an undisguised message for the student, who recognizes it at once and seems happy that the course has been tied together--and in a song sung by Neil Diamond at that! ("Be" from the sound track of *Jonathan Livingston Seagull*.) The warning is that the film is more affective than cognitive, and the instructor may prefer to do without it, especially if time is short.

# TEACHING AIDS

## INTRODUCTION. *TO BE HUMAN*

*Teaching Overview*

To be human is to have options. One can be whatever biology and genetics decree. One can be whatever one's environment--family, education, religion, companions--decides. One can grow up, reach adulthood, marry, have children, work, play, grow older, and then, of course, die. For too many, this life scheme is all they experience, or indeed expect. It is essential at the outset to let students know that those of us who teach the humanities are not denigrating or condemning the course of life most Americans have as their legacy. For, as surely as an instructor begins by criticizing life styles or warning in advance against the unexamined life, students tend to become hostile. They might--and with good reason--point to areas of the world in which sheer survival is a feat in itself; where to be *completely* human means to be fed, to have at least rudimentary shelter, and to be free of disease. There is no way to overlook these grim realities, to pretend they don't exist, or to argue that music, art, and philosophy are abundant compensation for them.

The introductory chapter treads lightly, many instructors will find. The book, after all, is directed to young people fortunate enough to *be* in college. But the assumption is that they come from divergent backgrounds. Many are working nights and on weekends to afford their tuition. Many already have families. Some may never have to work very hard. Their inheritance is already assured. This is our audience. These are the people for whom our message can make a difference. *To be human can mean so much more than having a good job and a good marriage, and enjoying the material pleasures our society has to offer.* These are the people who need the role model of the humanist, for they are in the best position to be future supporters of the arts, readers of books, buyers of fine paintings.

And we encourage them not just for the survival of the humanities, but for what *their* lives can be. Instructors don't have to be agents for Michelangelo, Beethoven, or Picasso. They have already established their claim to greatness and will manage nicely on their own. The concern of teachers should be the student; otherwise one might as well find another occupation.

You who teach this course, who use this text will be the role models. You love art and music. You go to the theater. You avoid the blockbuster movie hits and go instead to the small houses that are barely making it, but are run by the caring few who want to send the message to Hollywood that film art *will* find its audience. You are a critical thinker and love to engage the students in challenging conversations. You show students how to find assumptions buried deeply under generalizations.

Your first day in class should be devoted not to passing out a course syllabus or announcing how many quizzes there will be and what percentage of the grade will the research paper carry. Students do care about what is going to happen to them in a course, but you can tell them all that information is coming next time. First, they need to know who you are, what kind of person (not teacher) you are, and why you teach this particular course.

It has been our experience that too often humanities courses are the price paid in exchange for the right to teach "in field." Most departments cannot afford to pay a full-time staff of artists, composers, or philosophers so that they may teach majors-only introductory courses and advanced courses with small enrollments. So a compromise has to be made. Teach a few sections of general education humanities, and you can have your studio classes. What often happens is that the general education student senses right from the beginning that the instructor is not "into" the material, is going through the motions: reading old lecture notes, giving the same tests year after year, even telling the same jokes.

THE ART OF BEING HUMAN was not designed to fit into the tried-and-true educational scheme. It is as much about you and your students as it is about the great names in the humanities. It is about creativity--and the pains of living which often inspire the noblest creative efforts. And it says no matter whether you will ever be one of the celebrated few so long as you do as much as you can with your humanness. No two classes using this book should ever be the same. You will inevitably stress different things depending on the chemistry and interactiveness of each class.

Since the book is not written chronologically, there is no set amount of material that must be "covered." Everyone knows the old maxim about teaching students how to fish instead of giving them one fish for supper, The parallel in a humanities course is teaching students that all human beings go through similar experiences, and some leave behind inspiring thoughts and sounds which were their responses, their way of surviving; and some of the students may well add their own someday. Teaching facts is the least important aspect of this book, and hopefully of your course.

**Checklist of Points or Discussion Topics from Text**

1. Defining the humanities. There's an italicized definition on page 4, but perhaps the students can suggest their own? What do we mean by "humanity"? What do we mean when we say that this or that person *lacks* humanity? What do we mean when we say that the arts, etc.--the subject matter of the course--*humanize* people?

2. What does it mean when we say of people that they died without ever having lived"?

3. The subtitle of the book refers to the humanities as a "technique for living." What do the students think this means?

4. Ask around the class to get some idea of what various students have in mind for their futures. Are they primarily interested in "getting ahead"? "Making it"? Are they willing to concede that there's more to life than that?

5. In economics, the law of life is stated as: *Our wants are insatiable, but our resources are limited*. In the humanities, we can say: *Our resources are unlimited, but our wants are too quickly satisfied*. What's wrong with taking advantage of the abundance in the humanities?

6. The text discusses several gifts from the humanities, the first of which is supplying life with some meaning. We remark that for most of us, most of the time, life is whatever it is and does all right without specifically meaning anything. Why then do we prize a sense of meaning when we find it?

7. Hand out entire text of Frost's "Stopping by Woods" and ask the class how the poem serves as an introduction to a humanities course.

8. A second gift is that of form, which is defined as the "significant arrangement of parts." Conduct an informal discussion of where the students are right now on the question of form. What is their idea of significant arrangements?

9. A third gift is that of critical thinking: the art of slowing down, standing back, and looking life right in the eye.

10. We make a pretty outrageous statement at the top of the last paragraph in the chapter: "The humanities have redirected the evolutionary process." Could this possibly be true? What do they think it means?

**Checklist of Discussion Points from Suggested Videotape "The Way of the Humanist"**

1. We have chosen to portray humanism with two characters. One is a young girl in love with the circus and fascinated with the mime. When she grows up, she is a mime herself. What statement about the humanities is being made through the use of the two mimes? (Is it perhaps that the humanist is silent as far as most of society is concerned? Other possibilities? The mime as detached critical thinker?)

2. Provide class with copies of the Keats sonnet "After Dark Vapours." Why would this poem appeal to the girl when nothing else in school excited her? Is there any relationship between the poem and the circus? Why is a "poet's death" the climactically beautiful thought that occurs to Keats?

3. Do we learn anything about the humanities from this poem? (Do they not clear away our own "dark vapours"?)

**Alternate Strategies and Assignments**

Divide class into small groups. Each is given a set of Tinker Toys. Assignment: create an original piece which the group believes has form. Afterwards, hold an "art exhibit" and discuss each piece.

**Suggested Essay Questions on Text**

1. Have you known anyone like Woodrow Tatlock? If he were on trial for violating the spirit of the humanities, could you defend him? If you were prosecuting, what charges would you press?

2. To be considered esthetic form, an arrangement has to seem "right." Illustrate a possible meaning of "right" in reference to something you regard as having form.

3. Describe the "economics of the humanities."

4. Discuss the three gifts of the humanities. Which do you consider the most important? Why?

## Journal Topics

Some instructors may offer the Journal as an alternative to exams or as a means of earning bonus points in the course. One difficulty with Journals, however, is that, if given too vague an assignment, students tend to ramble on and on, especially about their private lives. Without guidelines, they seldom take the time to think through their ideas before committing them to paper. For each text chapter, the instructor will find very specific Journal topics.

A general rule of thumb is to require that students spend between 30 and 60 minutes on a given topic. This will help determine how many topics would be acceptable. (A comment like "This hardly seems to be 30 minutes worth of writing" is seldom challenged.)

1. Define "human being" in as much detail as you can. Try to consider the phrase in both a scientific and a nonscientific sense.

2. Discuss what you think are the major survival skills people need to have. Indicate why you think these are or are not enough to make life worthwhile.

3. Describe a society that has everything but the humanities.

4. Describe the cultural resources of your area. Which ones have you availed yourself of? Which ones have you never patronized? Do you think it's worth trying more of them?

5. Describe how you like to spend your leisure time. Are there ways in which you could make better use of it?

6. If your school has THE ART OF BEING HUMAN videotapes, you might look at "The Man with No Time for Beauty," which is suggested as an accompaniment to Chapter 15 of the text. This early preview will give you a chance to watch an actor playing Woodrow Tatlock on his first and only trip to Europe. Describe his experiences and reactions. Do you think he is typical or atypical of many tourists? Is there anything wrong with his attitude?

# CHAPTER 1. *APOLLO AND DIONYSUS*

*Teaching Overview*

This chapter appeared quite late in the text of the first three editions. Many users have written to us suggesting that it come earlier, perhaps even first. For one thing, students find the subject matter relevant and exciting. For another, the chapter has always seemed easy to read and digest, so much better we thought than starting out with the chapter on visual art with its enormous roster of names students need to know.

This chapter is first and foremost about the students themselves, not about the remote past or famous personalities with whom the beginner has not yet had time to identify. But the instructor has to do a good selling job in order to convince the class that ancient Greek gods are just convenient names which stand for the warring sides of almost every human being. Probably the best approach is to do a yin/yang kind of exercise on the first day of this unit (which is often the second or third meeting of the class.) The students should be relaxed after an informal session or two in which they have talked informally about what esthetic experience is, or form, or Woodrow Tatlock, or how they like to spend their leisure time.

A recommended simple exercise is to ask the class to stand up and walk to whichever side of the room is given a designated identity for which they feel a preference. For example, you point to the left side of the room and say "Stand here if you are a disco"; then you point to the right side and say "Stand here if you are a newsstand." Students will walk back and forth a number of times at the outset, but after a while patterns will begin to emerge. Apollonians will have separated from Dionysians. Other suggested yin/yangs are:

> VW convertibles/Cadillacs
> New Orleans/Boston
> Super Bowl/international chess championship
> a mall/a bank
> liquor cabinet/filing cabinet
> talker/listener
> sandals/shoes
> jeans/prom outfits

The advantage of this exercise is that nobody ever challenges the dualism of it. Then it becomes a very simple task to turn the discussion toward the humanities. Which disciplines seem to be predominantly Apollonian (like philosophy and history); which Dionysian (like music, ballet, abstract art)?

We begin the Fourth Edition with a revised version of the chapter because it is our hope that instructors will indicate that the class will keep returning to these polar opposites as the course moves on. They are going to become part of the course foundation, as indeed learning about "the tug of these opposites in your own personality will become one of the most powerful educational experiences you will ever have."

## Checklist of Points or Discussion Topics from Text

1. Nietzsche's original use of the Apollo/Dionysus dichotomy occurs in his long essay on trage-dy and his contention that it was limiting to see only its rational and moral elements. We should surrender to the passions of tragedy as well.

2. Walking in a forest is a different experience for Apollonians and Dionysians. (We didn't, unfortunately, talk about environmental concerns, but they could be mentioned in class.) Students are prone to side with Dionysus all too readily, and it defeats the whole purpose if there are not some good Apollonian causes around.

3. There is only a paragraph about Apollonian and Dionysian eating habits, but they make for a lively time in class.

4. Classes will enjoy the new section on sex in both its A and D aspects, especially, we think, the pro-life/pro-choice debate, *both* sides of which can be either A or D. Students can be challenged to be up front about whether they tend to be one way or the other as they argue for their belief.

5. The arts are often Dionysian in their assault on the emotions, but it needs to be shown that Apollonian control is necessary if there is to be art. The Housman poem has proved to be an excellent example. The theme (with which students identify) is the need for rebellion that must be curbed by laws, regulations, requirements. It is clear that the poet wishes these Apollonian forces were not necessary. The revelation, however, is how the strict metrical and rhyme scheme acts as an Apollonian "brake" to the poet's passion. If you can get across what tension is--how it comes from the interplay of opposites in a given work--then you will have made the rest of your job a lot easier!

6. Ravel's *Bolero* also works well in this respect--if there is time to play it for the class.

7. In drama, as in other linear forms, we could say that structure is A, and the emotions that come bursting forth FROM that structure are D. (Tennessee Williams is a wonderful exam-ple.) But without the interplay of the two, we have either dull talk or exhausting (and ultimately ineffective) emotional binges.

8. Rousseau wanted the arts to be revolutionary forces, to be didactic and therefore, one sup-poses, Apollonian. On the other hand, a play like *Waiting for Lefty* was strongly Dionysian in its impact. This section can also lead into (though you might be there a long time) NEA matters, censorship, and the need for new works that promote wholesome family values . . . all Apollonian elements. Students, as we've said many times, have no trouble taking the Dionysian position to give 'em hell. It might be worth the time to ask whether there should never be lines drawn.

9. A and D in religion: dogma, teachings, formal ritual; emotional rapture, inspiration, trans-cendence.

10. Education (this is our favorite):

    A. Apollo as administrator. (Should Dionysus take over?)

B. The Apollonian teacher has standards, and memories of great student performances. Students must rise to certain levels.

C. The Dionysian teacher is nonthreatening, willing to curve grades, willing to accommodate him/herself to the latent potential of all students.

D. If one goal in life is to effect a delicate balance between A and D, in the educational system, what would an ideal course be like?

## Checklist of Discussion Points from Suggested Videotape "The Sunlit Chariot"

1. The atomic model as a means of comprehending the nature of the universe has been junked in our time, but the Apollonian belief that the universe *is* ultimately comprehensible remains.

2. The A-bomb. Einstein recommended it at first, then changed his mind vehemently. Question: would the world had been better off if nuclear research had been discontinued?

3. Nuclear power plants (like Three Mile Island or Chernobyl). Is it Apollo vs. a potentially deadly Dionysus?

4. Fra Lippi's work as a nearly perfect balance of A and D in art.

5. Is Protestantism vs. Catholicism a case of A vs. D? Protestant work ethic as Apollonian. Is leisure (idle hands) Dionysian?

6. The Sacco/Vanzetti segment: the use of Apollonian law for a Dionysian purpose? Is all prejudice Dionysian? Point out Vanzetti's expressed belief that some (Apollonian) good would come out of the (Dionysian) tragedy.

7. *The Lord of the Flies*. Is humankind essentially and wantonly Dionysian held in check by an Apollonian surface that is skin deep?

## Alternate Strategies and Assignments

1. If you have done the exercise suggested in the Teaching Overview, you might want to go a step further and ask the Apollonians and Dionysians to perform a little task. Each group is to list only the positive characteristics of themselves and only the negative characteristics of their opponents. The lists are then shared. They should be about the same. What conclusions can we draw?

2. Have students bring in newspaper and magazine ads and then decide what kind of society we are. Of particular value will be those ads which are SUBTLY A or D.

## Suggested Essay Questions on Text

1. Why did Nietzsche draw a distinction between two ways of teaching tragedy? What was he recommending?

2. Contrast the ways in which Apollonians and Dionysians walk in the forest.

3. Is rock Dionysian and jazz Apollonian, or are they both Dionysian?

4. Is love Apollonian and sex Dionysian?

5. Are health food enthusiasts showing an Apollonian control over their bodies or a Dionysian addiction to a fad?

**Journal Topics**

1. Where do you find yourself in the seesaw conflict between A and D? Which side of yourself do you think needs work?

2. Describe an extremely Apollonian class you have had, and an extremely Dionysian one. Which is more fondly remembered? Why?

3. To be completely Apollonian, our legal system would seldom bend. If it were completely Dionysian, it would keep analyzing circumstances until firm decisions would be all but impossible. What do you suggest?

# CHAPTER 2.  *THE VISUAL ARTIST*

*Teaching Overview*

This and the five chapters that follow deal with makers of the humanities: artists, composers and musicians, filmmakers, and philosophers (the last spanning two chapters, one on moral philosophy by itself). To this extent the Fourth Edition, like the Third, is somewhat less interdisciplinary than the first two editions. We have struck a sort of compromise after looking carefully at what many users of the text had to say. One teacher summed it up very well: "You can't be interdisciplinary until students know what the disciplines are."

On the other hand, we did not want the approach taken to be a specialized one. The starting point would still be what it means to paint or write a song or think philosophically. The "greats" would be case histories, or what Emerson called "representative" human beings. We still wanted to aim for an understanding of creativity as a basic human need--more urgent in some than others, but potentially there in each of us.

Of course, specialists in the various disciplines have abundant opportunity to enrich their classes with treatments of the material that is far more in-depth than ours. But the generalist will, we trust, continue to find that the text is nontechnical, inviting discussions of the several disciplines as resources for human growth.

If we were asked to single out the most important goal of Chapter 2, "The Visual Artist," it would surely be to encourage a broad tolerance for the unfamiliar, the newly experienced, in plane-surface art, sculpture, even architecture (though space restrictions have not made it possible for us to include this form of expression in the book). By "unfamiliar" we are referring to all modes of visual art that are not part of the everyday life patterns of the student. These might include a Greek statue, the Sistine ceiling, or Oldenburg's soft toilet sculpture.

In fact, let us reaffirm the underlying goal of the entire text, which is to help bring about a tighter bond between what is available to be experienced and the student's manner of responding to experience.

We talk about the way artists see the world, even as the rest of us might if we tried. This leads into a discussion of what often distinguishes the visual artist: the urgent need to imitate what is seen. But the student is told that imitation does not have to be a literal representation of what is "out there." The artist may also imitate what is inside. (Of special importance is the discussion of whether even ugly and unpleasant pieces, such as we find in Goya, are beautiful because an artist has done them.)

Artists, seeing reality in a certain way, may alter it in their mind and then imitate the alteration. This process accounts for much modern art. Or the artist, like Picasso, may create a new mode, such as Cubism, based on the philosophical idea that so-called realism in art does not truthfully represent the way we actually see.

We have had better luck by not insisting that every art slide students look at is that of a great work (about which they must take our word), but rather is a case in point, something to wonder about, something to *describe*, something that has as much right to exist as they do.

## Checklist of Points or Discussion Topics from Text

1. You might want to spend a few minutes on the four quotations which head the chapter. Students are especially fond of ripping into Robert Thiele's laconic definition.

2. The left brain/right brain chart may take you away from visual art for a bit, if students want to talk about it; but that's what we think is so nice about a text that is not committed to an entire history.

3. The subject of imitation and the need to indulge in it can center on the imagination of children.

4. For this edition, we have added the concept of an artist's *style*, as well as *styles of art*, which we get when a number of artists show similarities in what they imitate and how they do it. The work of Georgia O'Keeffe is used as a case history of what we mean by an art style.

5. Classicism refers to Greek and Roman idealized and geometric art.

6. Realism is given a very broad definition, not confined to a specific time period, and by it we mean "the artist's attempt to imitate what is being seen or remembered or imagined so as to create within the viewer the illusion of a real person or event." Italian Renaissance artists like Raphael and Leonardo can thus be called realists, and one can discuss techniques like perspective and chiaroscuro that help with the illusion.

7. Michelangelo is treated as a style in himself, characterized by *terribilita*, "passion that is somehow frozen by the medium, yet nonetheless is alive and throbbing."

8. Goya is treated as a case history of the artist who wanted to show how ugly and corrupt the real world was, and who painted the emotions which that world stirred in him. Again, we point out the opportunity to discuss whether ugly subjects are still beautiful in art. (As a matter of fact, one can use this unit as a chance to confront the inevitable question, "Why is it art if I don't like it?")

9. Impressionism as an experience in color that was never meant to imitate the real world (by now photography was doing that very well).

10. Picasso as Cubist. Cubism as a complex style based on a new concept of how we see. Picasso as someone with an extraordinary range of styles, someone who contributed far more than his share of new experiences for us.

11. The last part of the chapter lights on a number of moderns: abstractionists, surrealists, superrealists. You can easily introduce whatever and whoever you think will be most likely to intrigue or infuriate.

## Checklist of Discussion Points from Suggested Videotape
## "Art, Tell Me What I Am; Art, Tell Us Who We Are"

1. The script for this video was written by a practicing visual artist who believes that individuals and groups derive their identity from the kind of visual art they produce.

2. The man with the burning need to project himself onto a wall. Should anyone be allowed to paint walls? Or only artists? How do we tell?

3. Art tells us who we are, and is often the only testimony to the nature of an entire culture. Why does it matter that people leave a record behind?

4. Colors are what emotions look like. Orange and yellow are "up" colors, while black and grey are linked to depression and death. Why?

5. Artists often like to juxtapose unconnected and unlikely things obviously because they see connections. Why don't we all?

6. Lines in art: horizontal, vertical, diagonal, curving. Why do they have dramatically different effects?

7. If all you knew about modern art were what the artists in the film have to say, how would you describe modern art?

## Alternate Strategies and Assignments

1. Give each student a sheet of sketching paper after you have asked that a magazine be brought to the next class. Have them find a picture that interests them and try to draw it by turning the magazine upside down.

2. Divide into groups. Give each group a bar of soap and have them, using whatever implements they can find, do a soap sculpture that they think represents the spirit of the class.

3. Send the class to an art gallery (if one is handy) and ask each student to describe one painting as they might to a blind person.

## Suggested Essay Questions on Text

1. Art is often produced from the dynamic tension which develops between an artist's drive, and the resistance of the medium. How can one use different kinds of resistance to good effect in ordinary life?

2. One intellectual historian singled out Picasso as one of the mightiest persons who ever lived, in terms of the amount of change for which he was responsible. Describe some changes made by Picasso in the world of art.

3. Time was when national academies composed of great critics and scholars had the power to decide what did or did not constitute art. Was that a good idea?

4. One modern artist sat inside an air-conditioning vent, audibly taking pleasure in sex fantasies while people in the gallery looked at his work. He claimed the sounds coming from the vent were crucial factors in his art. Is there a limit to what can be art?

5. Does the fact that a piece of sculpture looks exactly like a giant ice bag detract from its being art? Does the subject matter have anything to do with art?

6. Many modern artists consider themselves alienated from society. You are an artist. Are you alienated?

## Journal Topics

1. What reasons can you think of to justify the fact that an enormous curtain, stretched between two mountains, has been widely recognized as art by some critics?

2. A number of years ago the philosopher Peter Bertocci coined the phrase "creative insecurity," by which he meant that people compensate for or transcend personal conflicts and crises by doing wonderful, imaginative things. His idea was that people should be very grateful for all the obstacles life continually throws in their path. If you had your choice, would you like your whole life to be totally fulfilled, or would you prefer a measure of creative insecurity?

3. You are an artist. Tomorrow you will vanish from the earth. What one silent witness would you leave behind that could tell people who and what you were?

4. Would you rather be a relatively stable, modestly successful, but obscure, person all your life, or a genius like van Gogh, even if the price were a lack of recognition, and eventual madness?

# CHAPTER 3. *MUSIC: SOUND AND SILENCE*

*Teaching Overview*

Talking about music is surely as difficult a task as there is in teaching. Many in the humanities never question the wisdom of having students sit there and listen to long passages of unfamiliar sounds. The authors remember well the time they were invited to visit a class in session in a large metropolitan community college. There they found the majority of the students slumped over their desks, apparently asleep. The oblivious instructor was playing an ancient 78-speed recording of Schubert's "The Trout," and waving her arms enthusiastically while she pleaded with the sleeping class to "imagine the happy little fish leaping, leaping in the stream!"

No one can tell students what to hear. Nor can anyone simply assume that, because students are told that the next selection is a great piece of music, they will be instantly respectful and convinced of that greatness.

Experience has taught us that what can work is a delicately balanced blend of discussion and listening. Avoid long pieces. Points made in the text can be brought up relative to the class's general level of sophistication and musical tastes, and short examples of less familiar sounds can be worked into the proceedings. *It is very important to start from where the students seem to be.* One teacher wrote that she began by very honestly confessing that she could make no sense out of heavy metal rock and asked members of the class to bring in some tapes next time so that she could learn something. They willingly obliged, and soon everyone was in the midst of a heated argument over the relative merits of the relentless bass guitars, the deafening percussion, and bewildering (to the teacher) lyrics. She had won the class over by not scorning what was meaningful to the majority of those present. As the class came to a close, she announced that next time "we'll listen to some music that I enjoy, and you tell me whether there's anything in it for you." This teacher was not being condescending or manipulative. Heavy metal sounds were indeed aspects of the students' identity in music, and she found that they were more willing to listen to what she had to tell them after she first heard from them. Some in the class vehemently attacked rock music and provided a very natural transition to "We can see there's no one kind of musical sound that takes care of every need."

More essential than asking students to memorize a lot of names. dates, and titles is the goal of communicating something about the phenomenon that is music and how the abundant varieties of it tell us about the complexity of human nature. Above all, since *you* have explored heavy metal with considerable interest, the moral is that it is only fair for everyone to lend an ear to what may at first seem dull, unpleasant, and irrelevant. Encouraging students not to force an interest is vital. If you play Bach's *Toccata and Fugue in D Minor* and a significant segment of the class fails to respond (which is probably not going to happen, by the way), invite their negative opinions and give them due consideration. Chances are that, as in the above case, opinions will be divided; and you will find that the class opens up the whole subject on its own.

The inevitable question of "Why do we have to know all this?" may already have been asked about the flat surfaces of medieval paintings or the austere geometry of Mondrian. But it may wait for this unit. In any event, be prepared to give an honest but we think *firm* answer-- something like "Because human beings have done these things." This kind of answer holds up in court provided you have not started the course by giving the impression that you have some mysterious wisdom you can't wait to impart.

**Checklist of Points or Discussion Topics from Text**

1. We exist within two kinds of audio environments: one is unplanned, random, and sometimes maddening--especially in densely populated cities; the other is planned, and under the control of people. Music.

2. Music may have come into being as a way of perfecting the art of poetry. Musical accompaniment may have added to the sensuous delight of words in meter.

3. Rhythm probably came before tones, however.

4. Melody is a sequence of lead tones that are distinguished from supporting tones (such as the bass part in a piano piece). The common understanding of melody is that it is beautiful, often repeated, and easy to remember. But if we insist on the definition given, we can argue that melody does not have to sound immediately pleasing any more than what's in a painting has to be immediately identifiable.

5. Middle Ages had plainsong--only melodic line without support. Harmony came in with the Renaissance.

6. Silence is as important a musical element as melody or rhythm. Music can be defined as the *shaped sounds between silences*.

7. Bach:

   A. epitomized baroque style (complexity and improvisation)

   B. illustrates with his work the magnificent tension between the restriction of form and the composer's need for liberation

   C. appeals to jazz musicians because of the flights on which he takes his themes

8. Mozart:

   A. gave expression to "the most prodigious outpouring of music the world has ever received from one human being in so brief a time" (died at 35)

   B. carried the arts of the symphony and opera to new peaks

   C. added the *recitative* to move his plots along, while saving his impassioned melodies for the great *arias*

9. Beethoven:

   A. expanded the range of nearly all concert forms to make them accommodate his enormous passions

   B. enlarged the range of the symphony even beyond Mozart

   C. in his Third, or *Eroica*, Symphony, unified the four movements in a way Mozart was beginning to reach, but not on quite such a scale

D. in his Ninth, or *Choral*, Symphony, added to the orchestra, the size of which he had already enlarged, a huge choir, needing all these resources to objectify the sounds inside him

10. Song is important to us not because it offers insights that have never occurred to us, but as a reinforcement of *network*, a reaching out of souls. It helps to know that others have felt as we do.

11. Folk music endures less for personal than for *group* reasons, as an external anchor for group or ethnic identity. Such is its power that it can create group solidarity even among strangers. There was a revival of folk music in this country during the '60s, and this may be attributed to the need American youth was experiencing for warding off feelings of alienation and isolation.

12. Traditionally considered a truly American musical form, jazz arose out of "churches and fields, brothels and bars." But as it has evolved, it shows a strong influence of older, standard musical structures. Many jazz players admire Bach.

13. Ellington brought jazz to Carnegie Hall, and Gershwin brought it to the concert stages of the world.

## Checklist of Discussion Points from Suggested Videotape "Jazz/Bach"

1. Coincidentally, Bach in German means "brook." The music of both Bach and jazz begins within the confines of formal structure, as a brook is held in by its banks, then flows outward until the brook becomes an ocean, seemingly without bounds.

2. Eddie Higgins, the pianist, acknowledges his debt to Bach by playing the *Air on a G String* "straight," and then as a jazz improvisation. Does the class like both, or prefer one to the other?

3. Bach's improvisatory flights were presumably aimed at heaven, but Ira Sullivan also claims that his music is inspired by God. If a lot of jazz started in the brothels, where and how does it become religious?

4. What have Bach and Scott Joplin in common? Isn't ragtime bouncy music that is held in check by a rigid rhythmic scheme?

## Alternate Strategies and Assignments

1. Divide into two groups or two sets of smaller groups. One side was raised to believe that music is the devil's own work, his means of enslaving our souls. The other side believes that music is the most humanizing of all the arts, that without it there would be no civilization. Each side must make the strongest case possible, then meet and clash.

2. Ask the class to become a symphony orchestra, with one student appointed as the conductor. Following his or her leads, the orchestra must create a new experience in sound. Afterwards, ask people what this did for them.

3. Homework assignment: listen to an hour of music you don't ordinarily like. Write an honest statement of your experience.

**Suggested Essay Questions on Text**

1. Why is it said that, in order to appreciate music, you have to be able to handle silence?

2. In heavy metal rock lyrics are often difficult to understand. Have you an opinion on why this is so?

3. Mention one or two of your favorite songs. Try to explain why they are important to you.

4. Folk music seems less popular today than it was in the '60s. Can you suggest a reason? Do you see a revival coming?

5. Americans are said to be fonder of the bass than the treble, and fonder of brass and percussion than the string section. Why might this be so? Is it true for you?

**Journal Topics**

1. Go through the text and single out any two musical elements you can relate to your own personality and style of life.

2. Are you much given to solitude and silence? Or do you prefer to live amid loud sounds?

3. Why do many people play their car radios at incredible sound levels as they drive by?

4. When many people think of melody, they think of a romantic piece by Tchaikovsky or Rachmaninoff. What do you think of?

5. Of all the composers from the past you have encountered in this course, which one has meant the most to you? Why?

# CHAPTER 4. *THEATER: TWO MASKS*

*Teaching Overview*

In keeping with the overall intent of the book, which is to involve students in an intensive process of discovering the humanities and themselves as well, the title of the drama chapter has a double reference. Not only are the masks of tragedy and comedy the universal symbols of theater art, but they also represent, here, two human needs that must be satisfied.

What do we mean by a need for tragedy? The tragic experience in the theater--the reason so many modern dramatists seek to attain it--is for the audience to become so intensely involved emotionally in the action and the declining fortunes of the protagonist that they leave the theater with the exhilaration that comes from what Emily Dickinson describes as the "formal feeling" which follows "great pain." There are real-life attempts to reach the same point: watching the aftermath of a deadly accident on the freeway or willingly accommodating the misfortunes of others. And presumably there is an added "bonus" in watching catastrophe on the stage, in that we know it is not happening to us.

There is exhilarating catharsis from the comic as well. We laugh to release the tension created whenever our sense of appropriateness, of congruity clashes with the socially, morally, or logically unacceptable. When audience members share the same values, they will laugh together at characters, actions, and statements that violate or deviate from those values. Then we have a comedy that not only satisfies a personal need but helps a social group become cohesive.

To have full tragedy there should be a tight plot structure that brings the protagonist step by step to an inescapable doom. For comedy, there should be a single-minded protagonist blind to his/her follies; characters who are recognizably unacceptable social types, such as the lecherous old man, the vain middle-aged woman unaware that her beauty has faded; the anal-retentive tightwad or organization freak; the sex kitten, and so on; amoral rogue heroes who with wit and charm outfox the dull establishment. Laughter restores our sense of balance--our inner equilibrium, so to speak--helping us to endure atrocities committed in the name of humanity. Both tragedy and comedy keep us civilized and psychologically whole.

## Checklist of Points or Discussion Topics from Text

1. Creon as the prototype tragic figure: of noble birth, a good person, except for the flaw of *hubris*. His downfall is followed by a recognition speech in which he accepts full responsibility for what has happened.

   Now is an appropriate time to go back to Nietzsche's *Birth of Tragedy* and discuss the Apollonian moral lesson ("Fate has brought all my pride to a thought of dust") versus the Dionysian excitement of the unmitigated disasters, which include the destruction of the innocent. Unjust suffering is crucial to the greatest tragedies. Not only must the protagonist's punishment be greater than is deserved, but the impact of the fall must affect others.

   Now is also an appropriate time, if you wish, to compare the classical with the modern. The tragedy of ordinary people--does it work? Can one person's fall matter that much in a democratized world? Or are there tragic possibilities that are not being exploited? Watergate? Marcos? "Only little people pay taxes"?

2. Interestingly enough, Aristotle considered Euripides the most tragic dramatist of the Golden Age that had already passed, despite the fact that his plays end with many loose ends. He is also the most modern. *Medea*, the tragedy of a woman torn apart by jealous rage, can also be seen as a victim: of both sexism and racism.

3. Shakespeare liked the theme of power and its inevitably destructive effects. His characters question whether there can be a God in so wanton a universe, but much of his work shows the tragic consequences when the universal moral order is violated by power that oversteps its bounds. The downfall of the powerful reaffirms this order.

4. In neoclassical tragedy the moral order is really the social order, and plays like *Phaedra* show us what happens when unbridled emotion topples reason and leads to uncivilized behavior.

5. Farce and the comedy of stock characters. The greatest, like Tartuffe, are enduringly relevant and recognizable. Not only that, but they go beyond the two-dimensionality of, say, "the religious hypocrite" to become part of theater lore as themselves.

    Classes enjoy being asked to add to the list of stock figures. TV sitcoms are good starting points.

6. We do not laugh at the rogue hero; we laugh at the stupidity of those around him who are outwitted. We secretly admire his lawlessness, which appeals to our repressed but still strong rebelliousness.

7. The section titled "Sentiment and Psychology" helps get at the heart of what is comic. It faces the fact that comedy can seem cruel and unfeeling, and often the urge to laugh is curbed by considerations of compassion toward others. We merely present the problem, which the instructor may handle or skip over; but the fact remains that underlying the great comedies is the assumption that reason must laugh at human folly.

8. The final section deals with satire and the comedy of ideas, with Shaw quite central. The satirist laughs--or smiles--indirectly, usually pretending to praise what is really being condemned. Satire is a force for social change, but its effectiveness depends upon a homogeneous audience which shares standards and values.

**Checklist of Discussion Points from Suggested Videotape "The Tragic Vision"**

1. Greeks crystallized the tragic experience.

    A. They inherited the super-gods of the Homeric age.

    B. They also developed humanism.

    C. This created a conflict: humanity as godlike, but frail; incomplete, almost but not quite there; mortal, not immortal like the gods; always doomed to inevitable failure.

2. Oedipus as archetypal tragic protagonist.

    A. His is not the tragedy of a man who killed his father and married his mother; it is the tragedy of a man who insists on his own version of reality and is inevitably humbled.

B. Sophocles not for or against the gods. He recognizes their awesome power and knows human aspirations to godliness are pitiable.

3. *Hamlet* is the archetypal tragedy about the loss of innocence.

A. Hamlet has believed in his mother's purity and the king's integrity. Above all, he has believed in himself.

B. His world cracks apart, and he is almost buried in the ruins--but not quite! He is finally equal to the task of revenge. He confronts the king, and though the confrontation destroys him, he is able to rid the state of a cancerous evil.

C. Hamlet is more complex than *Oedipus*. The whole of reality is tragic in this play. Tragedy is the price you pay for maturity. Hamlet becomes a "mighty opposite" to Claudius, and learns to play the king's own game, perhaps becoming corrupted himself in the process (look what he does to Rosencrantz and Guildenstern).

4. *King Lear* is the archetypal tragedy of power.

A. Lear: in power too long--"executive privilege"--vulnerable to his evil daughters' plots in the complacency of his lofty position.

B. Storm on the heath a projection of the psychological storm created within Lear as illusions of his greatness begin to crack.

C. The redemption of Lear: learns charity toward the "poor naked wretches" on the heath.

This is a good place to bring in the ennoblement of character through tragic suffering. (*Oedipus at Colonus*)

D. Lear carrying in dead body of Cordelia--about the most terrifying instance on the stage of unjust suffering. Because of this, the work was considered unfit for the delicate sensibilities of 18th-century audiences.

**Alternate Strategies and Assignments**

1. Ask students to bring to class the daily paper in which they have checked good subjects for tragedy and comedy.

2. This works well. Assign groups to prepare a farcical skit, using stock characters from contemporary society.

3. Instead of "The Tragic Vision" you can rent *Electra*, a Michael Cacoyannis production, with Irene Pappas; either the Fredric March or the Dustin Hoffman *Death of a Salesman*; *Streetcar Named Desire*, Brando and Leigh. There's also *The Importance of Being Earnest*, Michael Redgrave and Edith Evans; *Pygmalion*, Leslie Howard and Wendy Hiller; and Franco Zeffirelli's *Romeo and Juliet*.

**Suggested Essay Questions on Text**

1. Why do you suppose tragedy was the first theatrical art? Why is a sense of tragedy basic to human nature?

2. The text singles out some universal comic types, such as the old man vain enough to think he is appealing to a beautiful young woman. Add some modern types.

3. It has been said that the British do farce better than the Americans, because farce depends upon an audience which admires order and stability and will therefore laugh when things go to pieces. There is certainly less American farce. Do we admire stability less?

**Journal Topics**

1. Outline the plot of a tragic story based on Richard Nixon and Watergate.

2. Do you know anyone who appears to be absolutely without a sense of humor? What is this person like? Do you think he or she is happy?

3. Are the age and the society in which we live better suited for tragedy or comedy? State your reasons.

4. Most people probably like a form of entertainment that is not tragedy or comedy in the classic sense, but something in between. Define what this entertainment is, and give some examples of it.

5. Many people tell jokes about and laugh at the expense of minorities, the handicapped, the mentally slow. How do you feel about this?

# CHAPTER 5. *THE MOTION PICTURE: ART AND INDUSTRY*

*Teaching Overview*

There is too much in this chapter to try to cover everything, but at least there is enough material from which to pick and choose. Some instructors will want to assign the reading, but save class time for the viewing of a contemporary film. Others will assume that the students see plenty of films, even many of the classics on cable, and will want to spend class time on the less familiar information about the pioneer days of films. It would be wonderful to have enough time to show *Citizen Kane* and *Casablanca* (they've all seen *Gone with the Wind* most likely), but this may be asking too much.

A suggestion is to decide on *Casablanca*, having assigned the material on existentialism from Chapter Seven. The Bogart persona is not only vintage Hollywood and legitimately part of the humanities, but it opens the door for discussions of morality in a "crazy world" (which surely hasn't gotten much saner since 1942).

Another suggestion is to use the art vs. industry dichotomy as the theme of the classes on film; show *Kane* or *Casablanca* for the art; and have the class supply examples of the industry (they've seen enough of it).

## Checklist of Points or Discussion Topics from Text

1. Peter Mark Roget, the *Thesaurus* man, is often credited with having sown the seeds of the film medium with his 1824 theory which accounted for the fact that we do not lose visual continuity when we blink our eyes.

2. Magic lantern shows and other animation tricks grew in popularity during the 19th century. In 1889 Thomas Edison's assistant, William Dickson, made a 10-second film in which he both appeared and spoke. Had Edison himself been more interested in the possibilities of film, sound might not have had to wait until 1927.

3. The cut is introduced by Edwin S. Porter in 1903; invented to show simultaneous actions.

4. In 1916 came D. W. Griffith's *Birth of a Nation* with cuts, close-ups, and lingering takes. Griffith also developed the principle of cinematic rhythm--editing so as to create a pace that will involve and affect the audience.

5. Charlie Chaplin was the first major movie star, with box office (and artistic) successes like *The Gold Rush* (1925). Chaplin, who started his career in Mack Sennett's slapstick comedies, moved far away from his mentor with comedies that blended the pathetic and the absurd. His major creation was the Little Tramp, always on the fringe of society and often having to be sneaky and crafty to survive.

6. The art of film editing was advanced by Sergei Eisenstein, whose 1925 classic *Potemkin*, with its famous Odessa steps sequence, introduced the technique of the elongated moment, imitated by Hitchcock in his 1960 *Psycho*. Recent evidence indicates that the massacre never actually took place, but does art depend upon truth?

7. The screwball comedy of the '30s was a popular genre, dealing with rich people whose lives become hopelessly mixed up and trivially complicated--the perfect escape from the grim monotony of poverty.

8. *Gone with the Wind*: film art in full flower, combining an epic tale, a mythic heroine, color cinematography worthy of the Impressionists, and sequences like the burning of Atlanta (old movie sets were set ablaze) that have never been surpassed.

9. *Citizen Kane*: marked the film debut of Orson Welles, who utilized black and white cinematography with the artistry of a Rembrandt to tell the quintessential American myth of the fallen tycoon and the tragic consequences of the American Dream.

10. *Casablanca*: saw Humphrey Bogart carry his persona of the hard-boiled but ethical realist, operating on either side of the law when survival dictates it, to the level of myth in a formula adventure story that suddenly became screen art for reasons that are still being debated. The Bogart integrity may be at the bottom of the mystery.

11. *Auteurism* is the theory, first advanced by Jean-Luc Godard and Andrew Sarris, that certain film directors, with a style and a philosophy of life that are found in work after work, should be treated as authors of their films, even if they did not write the screen plays (though most *auteurs* in fact do). Included in the short list are Frank Capra, Ingmar Bergman, Federico Fellini, Stanley Kubrick, and now Woody Allen.

## Checklist of Discussion Points from Suggested Videotape "Knaves and Fools"

1. A sense of humor is having a keen awareness of the incongruities of life (what happens though reason and common sense would prefer otherwise).

2. Swiftian irony--pretending to approve of something in order to magnify its irrationality.

3. Distinction made between the solemn and the serious. "Mel Brooks is solemn; Woody Allen is serious." Will need some explanation. Is it that Mel Brooks pushes awfully hard but doesn't really have a profound sense of humor, while Woody Allen's humor skips lightly on top of a profound concern for the human condition?

## Alternate Strategies and Assignments

You will, of course, want to show at least one film, if time allows. If you cannot spare class time for this, you might want to require the students to see a current film which has excited controversy or critical comments for one reason or another and ask that they write a mini-review of it.

Suggested Guidelines:

a) What actually goes on in this film? (Not the story by itself, but the kind of viewing experience. "Using many special effects and trick photography, the director takes us into the mind of her central character, and . . .")

b) Does what you saw appear to be very important? ("In *Thelma and Louise*, Butch Cassidy and Sundance have become women. Their actions are often outrageous and morally, not to mention legally, unacceptable. But somehow we allow them the right to be both lawless and sympathetic, as if to compensate for how women have been portrayed in older movies.")

c) What special techniques of screen art did you notice?

WHAT IS IMPORTANT IS THAT THE STUDENT'S GUT-LEVEL EMOTIONAL REACTIONS TO THE FILM SHOULD NOT BE ASKED FOR. It is not that such responses are not legitimate, but they do not have much critical substance and usually tell us about the viewer, not the viewing.

## Suggested Essay Questions on Text

1. Today a major movie costs in the millions to produce and must be concerned with audience appeal. Can you have screen art AND audience appeal?

2. *Gone with the Wind* is continually being revived and remains a popular rental item. If you have seen the film, can you account for its enduring popularity?

3. Orson Welles is a film *auteur* by common agreement. What directors of today command audiences solely on the basis of their names? Why?

4. Michael Curtiz, director of *Casablanca*, has not been regarded as belonging in the same company with the great film auteurs on the basis of one masterpiece that, legend has it, was thrown together and came out right by accident. But some critics are beginning to change their minds. What would it take for Curtiz to be inducted into the auteur Hall of Fame?

5. Screwball comedy was very popular during the Great Depression years of the '30s. During the last 20 years or so Hollywood has made very few films in this genre, and those few have not proved popular at the box office. Why do you think this is so?

## Journal Topics

1. If you became a film producer and had a supporter with no end of money, one who didn't care whether your films paid their way or not, what sort of movies would you make?

2. List and describe specific things that can be done in films but not in plays or novels.

3. If you have seen Hitchcock's *Psycho* (it is easily rentable), discuss two or three specific techniques the director uses to engender feelings of terror in the viewer.

4. Have you seen a recent horror film? Was it horrifying? If so, how did the director work on your emotions? If not, where did the director miss the boat?

5. We have said that the artistic success of *Casablanca* may well have been owing to the complexity of Bogart's screen persona. Is there a star today who has a persona, one that raises his or her films above the level of the mediocre, one who draws crowds because of that persona?

# CHAPTER 6. *WESTERN PHILOSOPHY*

*Teaching Overview*

Generalists or those whose specialization is not philosophy itself should not be intimidated by the title of this chapter. We have added the label "Western" so that readers will not expect a treatment of Hindu or Buddhist thought. It does not purport to embrace an entire tradition. The specialist will find much that needs far more in-depth discussion and will be able to provide this for the students. But the generalist should be able to deal broadly with the philosopher as someone with a contribution to the humanities, and therefore to all of us, though what that is may not be of immediate concern. Is philosophy really worth doing? Would human life be substantially different if nobody did it? What is the value of asking questions that admit to no final answers? Do any of *you* ever ask questions like that? Did you ever wonder why there is anything when there could just as well have been nothing? We know that science is pretty sure the universe started from the Big Bang; but even if we can prove one densely packed cell of matter is what exploded, where did that cell come from?

Students warm up to the subject very quickly when you allow them to think of questions that are interesting to ask, even though the answers may have nothing to do with their lives and their plans for the future. If the charge of irrelevance to real life is levied, a good response is: "All right, let's decide whether life is worth living after all."

Out of all the possible areas of inquiry we decided on three topics for the Third Edition and have kept them, because instructors have apparently had some success with them. They are Mind, Reality, and God. The first is actually epistemology, while the others are metaphysics; but the terms do not appear in the text. We have, however, added empiricism to the section on "Mind," making a fuller discussion of epistemology possible.

## Checklist of Points or Discussion Topics from Text

1. The story of Socrates and his disapproval of the Sophists is given in the chapter Overview. Establish Socrates as the model of the philosopher who believes that somewhere absolute truth exists, and the Sophists as models of the practical viewpoint that truth is whatever works. (After all, they did train lawyers, didn't they?)

2. Plato's Theory of the Forms. The material world, the world of the senses, the world of tangible objects and particular instances gives us impressions, but not knowledge. Truth is what cannot come into and then pass out of existence like the material world. Truth is goodness and beauty; justice and virtue; honor and fidelity. These are the Forms, or the Eternal Verities; and they are in the mind from birth. Experience cannot teach us to recognize the goodness in an action. We have to bring this knowledge *to* the material world. Our innate mind is what causes us to recognize particulars as examples of the general. A virtuous act embodies the Form of virtue. The deed and the doer may be soon forgotten-- may indeed vanish. But virtue does not vanish, cannot vanish, because it exists only in the mind. So, according to Plato, the mind's world is where reality is; and when we die, our minds continue on and migrate to other bodies.

Platonic idealism is difficult for many students to entertain, but a good line of attack is to ask them how they think young minds learn to recognize the general from the particulars. How is "treeness" arrived at from experiences with so many individual varieties that in no way resemble each other?

In other words, there are a good many practical examples of learning that are hard to explain: grammatical syntax, for example, which we learn before we ever begin school.

So the issue of whether we know because we are born with a mind, or we develop a mind as we learn is still very much alive. And it's a good way to teach Plato.

3. Descartes' "Cogito, ergo sum" is not at all difficult to teach, especially if it is made to seem the culminating point of a mystery. What can I really know? Can I doubt everything? Yes, I can, I think. But can I doubt that I doubt? If I doubt that I doubt, am I not doubting? If I do not doubt that I doubt, I am affirming the fact. Either way, I affirm my doubt, which is a thought. Hence I know that I think. And if I think, must I not exist?

4. Descartes is the rationalist--the philosopher who arrives at truth solely through reason. The empiricist denies that reason exists before experience and maintains that all knowledge comes from the senses. But the question is: what is it that makes sense out of the senses? (Even Hume had to use reason to explain how we know some things, such as the missing shade of blue in a color spectrum that has every other shade. We "know" what it must be, even if we have never seen it.)

5. The second section, "What Is Reality, Really?" allows you to talk about early philosophers like Thales and Anaximander, who asked what reality ultimately was; the first atomic theory; and then finally, modern questions about the Big Bang and what may have come before it--to prove that even scientists are engaging in philosophy, that they *have* to when the technology of proof is unavailable.

Note: since the manuscript of the Fourth Edition went to press, we learned that the government has scrapped plans to build the huge multibillion-dollar particle accelerator, which might have brought us closer to understanding what is at the core of our universe.

6. The section on God is essentially unchanged. It goes from Aristotle's theory that reason requires a belief in a First Cause, an Unmoved Mover, to an analysis of the atheist argument. Surprising how exciting Saints Augustine and Aquinas can be for the students, most of whom have never thought about such matters.

**Checklist of Discussion Topics from Suggested Videotape "The Problem of Evil"**

1. It helps to point out before the film that there are three principal kinds of evil: physical, moral, and natural. The film centers on the sudden death of the young bride: physical evil; but it touches on both moral (Nazi holocaust) and natural evil (Moby-Dick).

2. The film asks but does not answer questions. Even the priest is unable to bring comfort to the grieving young man, except to repeat that no one understands God's motives.

3. Interesting question to pose to class: if there were no God, would the problem of evil disappear, even though we may not be able to say why God permits evil to exist?

## Alternate Strategies and Assignments

1. Divide the class into two groups: those who advocate faith and those for whom science is the way to truth. Give the groups a certain amount of time to come up with some ideas on

   a) Have modern investigations into the age and size of the universe diminished the cause of religion?

   b) If there were life on other planets, how might this fact fit in with Biblical views?

   Have the class reassemble for a report from a spokesperson for each group.

2. Divide into a number of small groups. Pose the problem: if Plato's Theory of the Forms is wrong, how can you account for the fact that people all over the world use terms like honor, goodness, beauty, and wisdom as though they had definite meanings? In other words, if we are not born with a knowledge of these abstractions, how do we ever understand them?

## Suggested Essay Questions on Text

1. Children appear to move at some point in their development from the particular to the general: to reach, for example, the concept of "treeness" by which they recognize other trees no matter how dissimilar to the first tree they ever experienced. Does this not appear to indicate that such an ability is inborn?

2. Descartes said that he could not doubt he was doubting and thus he had reached a certainty. Do you think he did?

3. Augustine said emphatically that we have free will and thus are responsible for our sins, even though God has to know in advance what is going to happen. How did Augustine explain the fact that we are responsible for a future we seem to have no control over?

4. We tend to define "skeptic" as someone who doubts or is suspicious. How did Hume use the term to refer to himself?

5. Can you have religion without God? Can you have God without religion?

## Journal Topics

1. Play Descartes. Make a list of statements, beginning with the words "There is no doubt in my mind that . . ." Select two or three of the most interesting and put them in your Journal along with an explanation of why you are so certain.

2. Of Aquinas's five arguments for God's existence, discuss the one which strikes you as most convincing. If none of them do, select one and argue against it.

3. Socrates argued that justice is the same for everyone. Thrasymachus argued that justice was relative to the interests of the people in power. Whom do you agree with?

4. Does it matter what came before the Big Bang? It seems to matter to science and philosophy. Are those people just wasting their time?

# CHAPTER 7. *THE MORAL ISSUE*

*Teaching Overview*

Like many others in this text, the chapter offers the instructor an opportunity to go in a variety of directions and to focus on that aspect of ethics which seems appropriate for the kind of class and for the time allowed. The bulk of the chapter lists and analyzes the sources of moral values: the traditions or assumptions which influence our value system.

A moral value is the basis for a choice among live options. But many people simply choose without being aware that there are reasons for the choice. For many, there is a right way and a wrong way, and that is "how things are." Hence the overall purpose of this unit is to help students clear up their thinking about their values and their behavior. Some of them are going to learn the hard-to-face lesson that they give lip service to one set of values but a totally different set really underlies their actions. Moral integrity is not easy to attain.

The major sources of moral values are self-interest, reason, religion, unexamined assumptions ("Of course"), popular slogans, the workplace, tradition (the public moral conscience--or what Freud called the superego), and zealots.

The chapter concludes by looking closely at two popular moral philosophies of today: situationalism and existentialism. Students need to be told that, with so many systems to choose from, the majority of us may be motivated by self-interest. If this is the case, are all the other moral philosophies simply window dressing?

## Checklist of Points or Discussion Topics from Text

1. If moral values tend to go back to self-interest, we often serve ourselves by assuming that others are in violation of acceptable moral codes. Or: morality is what others do wrong.

2. Glaucon vs. Socrates. Put the question: Would you be honest about something if you could be dishonest without anyone's knowing it? Commentators have for centuries questioned whether Socrates' argument that the just man values the just act for its own sake is either rational or realistic.

3. Socrates also believed that no evil can befall a good man. How do they feel about this?

4. The rational view--that to know the good is to do the good--has historically been in conflict with the view that people act out of self-interest. Can people reasonably be expected to ignore their own concerns when it comes to moral choice?

5. That of Socrates is hardly the only rational approach to morality. Machiavelli can also be considered a rationalist, though arguing from a different direction: enlightened self-interest.

6. Another self-interest philosophy is utilitarianism, based on the assumption that, since people are selfish and pleasure-loving, the moral is that which benefits the most and harms the fewest. Can this view be challenged?

7. Adam Smith is here as a moral philosopher, and capitalism as a moral philosophy, based on the assumption that the good society is one in which the individual must be free to pursue his/her economic self-interest, for this benefits everyone in the long run. Once a free economic market is established, it sets in motion self-correcting mechanisms that prevent greed from devouring all.

8. Now that the Soviet Union has crumbled, ways are being sought to start a free market economy; but there are still those who hold to the view that Communism is the only real answer. Does Communism not work, apparently, because it is rooted in the wrong concept of human nature?

9. Kant's Categorical Imperative is also called the Universal Sense of Ought. Discuss whether the moral sense is truly inborn and therefore universal, or is inculcated through training.

10. Is the Golden Rule the basis of altruism, or a disguised version of enlightened self-interest?

11. Unexamined assumptions, which underlie much moral choice, can be found in statements prefaced by "Of course . . ." Ask students for some of their favorite "Of course . . ." guidelines.

12. How many popular slogans can the class suggest which have influenced the moral thinking of others (not their own, of course)?

13. Most students are not yet working full-time, and it is difficult to imagine that a part-time job would have enormous influence on moral values. But they may have observed such a relationship in their elders.

14. Whenever you teach the course, there are zealots in the news and on TV (or right there on campus). What are the trendy causes at this very moment, and what moral values may they be influencing?

15. Classes are usually hazy about just what existentialism is but eager to find out something about it. Here's a suggested way of explaining it--as easy as ABC.

    A: abandonment, anguish. *One feels alone in a meaningless universe.*

    B: boredom. *One feels that one is simply going through the motions; has no real direction or future; nothing matters.*

    C: crisis. *One reaches a point where some decisive stand must be taken, or there is no reason to continue.* (Camus said the only valid question in philosophy is suicide.)

    D: commitment. *Once one makes a choice of beliefs, one must stand behind them or become a nonauthentic human being.*

16. Kierkegaard's phrase "the anguish of Abraham" is not, however, a reference to the "A" above, but to the agony you go through to remain authentic after you have made your commitment, because you can never really know if you have made the right choice or if others will be adversely affected by it.

## Checklist of Discussion Points from Suggested Videotape "The Anguish of Abraham"

1. Use the story of Abraham and Isaac to explain Kierkegaard's other famous phrase "the leap of faith." Anyone can understand why a father would be unwilling to kill his own son, yet without the leap Abraham would have no God.

2. Revival of Kierkegaard in post-war Paris.

   a) War meant toppling of traditional beliefs and faiths. Quintessential model of abandonment.

   b) In a shattered world, what was left except for the individual to carve out his or her own destiny?

3. Parallels between Abraham and Edouard.

   a) Edouard's faith in himself and chosen life style; Abraham's faith in God and chosen religion.

   b) Edouard: What if my decision costs my brother his life? Abraham: What if there is no God?

   c) Edouard becomes authentic by accepting the guilt. Abraham, by his willingness to accept any consequence of his faith.

## Alternate Strategies and Assignments

1. A good exercise is to have the class comb newspapers and magazines for short articles, headlines, and commercials, bringing in pertinent examples of hidden moral assumptions. E.g.:

   ROBBER KILLS VICTIM FOR ELEVEN DOLLARS

   CONVICTED MURDERER FINALLY KEEPS DATE WITH CHAIR

   POLICE BATTLE VIOLENCE OF PRO-CHOICE MOB

2. Divide class into small groups. Ask each to design its own headlines and ads to push certain values.

## Suggested Essay Questions on Text

1. What is a moral value? Which sources of moral values do you think are most prevalent in our society?

2. Who gives the more persuasive argument: Socrates or Glaucon?

3. If there were someone cheating on this test right now, what would you do about it? Would your action accurately reflect your moral system?

4. What argument would *you* use against someone who did everything solely out of self-interest?

5. Create three "Of course" statements and show how what assumptions are hidden behind each.

6. What do you do if you are existentially authentic and no one else *is*?

**Journal Topics**

1. Political candidates frequently try to win votes by appealing to their listeners' "family values." What exactly are family values? Do you think they are declining in our society?

2. If, as has been said, morality begins in the home, what happens to someone who has been given a strong moral upbringing only to go out into the world and find that it is the clever, not the good, people who get ahead?

3. Should you do unto others as you would have them do unto you, even if they don't?

4. Is the death penalty a just form of punishment? Does it influence human behavior?

5. Discuss three popular slogans that have influenced your moral values.

6. Both lifeboat stories are true. As a member of each jury, how would you have voted? Why?

7. Is there a significant difference between "should" and "would" in your value system?

# CHAPTER 8. *WESTERN TERRITORY, EASTERN SPACE*

*Teaching Overview*

You have a choice. You can guide the students to an understanding of some aspects of Eastern thought that are found primarily in Buddhism, or you can turn the unit into a contrast between Western and Eastern outlooks (as the chapter title suggests).

The West stresses individualism. achievement, upward mobility, possessions, status, and power: i.e., *territory*. The East stresses peace, detachment, nonaggression, the state of egolessness, and, once one has transcended the narrow confines of self concerns, a panoramic, expansive sense of reality: i.e., *space*. The West excludes the many, singles out the great, and venerates super-achievers. The East includes all, recommends humility for those who are made great, and venerates the obscure.

The present edition keeps the chapter fairly intact, even though we have received some letters objecting to what appeared to be a bias toward the East. It was never our intention to advocate either, but rather to describe both as objectively as possible. We mention this, because the instructor might wish to open the unit by advising students that much is to be said in favor of both orientations to life, and that it is healthy to have a knowledge of as many options as possible.

## Checklist of Points or Discussion Topics from Text

1. Buddhism differs from Judaism, Christianity, and Islam in that it has no principle of godhead. It *has* rituals and observances that resemble religious practice. In its mythology there are gods and goddesses, but these represent aspects of the human personality. Finally, it has the Buddha figure, which is praised in myth and widely represented in art works, as if the Buddha were indeed a god; but he was a human being all the same. As a religion Buddhism teaches the ethical views of the Buddha, which are to be followed, not because a god says so, but because they are the only sensible course of life.

2. Relative to the Buddha's (Siddhartha's) enlightenment and attainment of nirvana, some explanation needs to be given that nirvana is originally a Hindu concept, is not an afterlife or a heaven of any sort, but, for the Hindus, represents the blissful passing out of this hellish world where all is pain and suffering. Nirvana in Hinduism is death without the need for rebirth to pay for one's sins in a previous life or lives.

3. The Buddha broke from the Hindu tradition, in which he was raised, by teaching that nirvana is a blissful state of freedom from pain that can be reached during the course of a single lifetime without the need for rebirth.

4. It became the Buddha's mission to show others the path to this blissful state. He chose sharing it with others over staying by himself and enjoying the bliss he had attained.

5. Tibetan Buddhism deemphasizes the life of the Buddha, stressing the importance of sitting meditation as the principal way to bliss, especially sitting within a community of meditators.

6. Tibetan Buddhism also teaches that enlightenment (bliss) is not only attainable within one lifetime, but can be achieved by more than one Buddha in any given era. (This is quite contrary to Hindu teaching, which prophesies one Buddha in an eon, or about 25,000 years.)

7. Zen Buddhism originated in China, but has been developed in Japan. Its meditators spend long hours sitting in order to cleanse the mind of its passions and convoluted thoughts which go nowhere. (In a sense bliss can be defined as complete mindlessness, the absence of a need to think and ponder, because all problems have disappeared.) The serious Zen practitioner lives in a *zendo*, or monastery, in a simple and austere life devoid of material comforts and possessions.

8. Zen Buddhist teachers often use cryptic parables, filled with a wry sense of humor, as a means of confusing the intellect and humbling the ego.

9. In Buddhism, the Dharma is the moral structure behind all existence (similar to the Tao, or the Way, in early Chinese philosophy). By ridding oneself of ego and the need to possess, one understands the unity of all being and has no choice but to behave ethically towards that being. Another way of putting the matter is to say that, by meditating and transcending the preoccupation with self, one achieves deep insights into others. The more insight, the more ethical one becomes.

**Checklist of Points from Suggested Videotape "The Still and Empty Center"**

1. The circle in Buddhism is a symbol of the unity of all existence. "Each blade of grass tells us what the grass is all about." There is only existence, and all the many forms of "it" are still "it."

2. "The center of the circle is everywhere and nowhere." The essence of anything or any moment is what it is. Thus one is always at the center of things, or never at the center of any one thing. This view is in sharp contrast to the Western idea that one has to *go* where the action is.

3. Michael is Western in his quest for a "still center," which for him means a personal identity, without stress--something people go to psychiatrists to find. He tries Buddhism with a specific goal in mind, but Buddhists warn that there are no goals, that goals are Western in nature.

4. Michael's enlightenment is a simple matter of learning to be in the moment and nowhere else.

**Alternate Strategies and Assignments**

Students have enjoyed spending part of a class period learning basic techniques of meditation.

a) Sit cross-legged on the floor (or pillow), in a full lotus position if possible.

b) The back should be erect, not stiff; the hands should be relaxed and allowed to rest on the lap in a comfortable position.

c) The eyes should be open at all times, with the meditator neither attempting to take everything in nor shutting anything out.

d) The mind should just wander, not attempting to "think of nothing." This only creates inner tension.

e) After a few minutes one's thoughts--or mind-chatter--start tumbling and cascading inside one's head. One should simply let it happen. After a time, one becomes distanced from these thoughts.

**Suggested Essay Questions on Text**

1. Distinguish between nirvana in Hinduism and Buddhism.

2. In Hermann Hesse's novel *Siddhartha* a pilgrim finds the Buddha after much searching, throws himself at his feet, and declares himself his slave forever. Siddhartha denounces him. Why do you think he does this?

3. The first Noble Truth of Buddhism is that life is full of suffering. What is its cause? How do we overcome it?

4. As simply as possible, what does the Buddhist mean by egolessness?

5. Define Dharma and samsara in Buddhist teaching.

6. In Zen Buddhism, the meditation pillow is black to encourage boredom. Why?

**Journal Topics**

1. How territorial are you? Do you think you could ever live without a substantial amount of property, money, status, or power? (Whether you have these things now should not affect your answer.)

2. What do you think a "spacious" existence would be like? Would it be satisfying?

3. Buddhists are anti-drugs, yet they speak about altered consciousness and a heightened sense of reality through meditation. In what sense do they use these terms?

4. Buddhists do not say that ego is bad; they say that ego is an illusion. What do they mean?

5. A student objected that Buddhists would be too content to take part in social causes or social change. Do you agree?

6. The Buddhist Middle Way means that to avoid the lows, we have to give up the highs. In your opinion, is the gain worth the loss?

7. Buddhists not in monasteries have to make a living. What kinds of jobs are most conducive to the Buddhist way of life?

# CHAPTER 9. *ON BEING A CRITICAL THINKER*

*Teaching Overview*

While we strongly defend the inclusion of this chapter on the grounds that to produce the critical thinker is surely an admirable goal of the humanities course, we do not deny the difficulty of persuading students of the joys of critical thought. One can, if one chooses, begin with no apology, but simply approach the critical thinker as a philosopher. This would link the chapter very naturally to the three which have come before. Before students realize it, they are being led into the actual *doing* of what the chapter talks about. What better way to conclude Part One than with a discipline of the humanities in which the distinction between writer and reader, maker and appreciator, has become blurred?

A good idea is to begin with simple statements that people actually make, such as a recently published comment denouncing the jury which convicted a professional football player for drug trafficking: *"So this is the thanks he gets for all the pleasure he has given the public."* Students can begin developing general critical principles by finding unexamined assumptions behind such remarks: e.g., *We somehow owe a debt to our professional athletes*; *Star performers need not be bound by the rules followed by the rest of us.*

We have retained Carl Sagan's theory about the three-layered brain, though it may no longer be a "hot" item and surely has been refuted by more than one critic. The purpose is not to teach Carl Sagan, but to trigger discussion and thought. If bottom and mammalian brains do not literally exist, the concerns attributed to them are surely widespread in the everyday thinking of people; and "top" brain skills are surely those of critical thinkers.

Of central import in the chapter is the distinction drawn between thinking and feeling. We are not discrediting emotional reactions, but would have the students not mistake them for critical thought. Or assume that emotions are somehow "better" than thinking.

At the request of more than a few, we have retained the section on literalists and figuratists as was. Students immediately recognize both kinds of people. Literalist responses to figurative statements create an almost instant comprehension of what noncritical thinking is all about; and, what is especially important, students tend to identify with the figuratists!

## Checklist of Points and Discussion Topics from Text

1. The definition is right there on the second page: *Critical thinking is the disposition of the mind to define, describe, and analyze as accurately, as fairly, as dispassionately as possible.*

2. Reptilian (bottom) brain: aggression, territory, ritual Mammalian (middle): intuitions, shelter, family Top: analytical (critical) thinking

3. The section "Exercising the Critical Faculties" provides you with a quick and easy way to determine which kinds of mental activities the students indulge in, especially without having to. Do they, for example, spend time only on those problems with a direct practical bearing on the moment?

4. Before teaching this unit, you might ask the students to listen carefully to the conversations of their friends and unobtrusively jot down hidden assumptions behind what they say. The lists provide a good starting point for discussion.

5. One of the telltale signs of the literalist is the tendency to personalize everything people say. Another is the tendency to hear only the last part of what has been said and respond to that; or to react instantly before the speaker's point has been made and begin to argue against or add to what one *thinks* the point has been. Having two students enact a few of these non-conversations is enjoyable and informative.

**Checklist of Discussion Points from Suggested Videotape "The Wonder of Form"**

(Note: This video was originally designed to complement the Introduction. It can work here as an exercise in critical viewing. What is the film's central theme? What have you learned about form, etc.?)

1. The central theme is not form, but the contrast between the classical and the modern: in history, the humanities, and the human personality. The classical within us seeks forms that are orderly, solid, often serene (Apollonian); the modern seeks forms that are restless, dynamic, experimental, daring (Dionysian). Both extremes are related to the controlling metaphor: the sea, eternal yet ever changing.

2. Since Plato's Theory of the Forms is one example of the classical principle, it is treated in this video; but that portion of the film could be shown as part of the unit on philosophy.

**Alternate Strategies**

1. Divide into pairs, charging each with the task of performing a conversation between a figuratist and a literalist.

2. Give the students till the next class to think about this and bring in a suggested answer.

"Three salesmen check into a hotel and are told a triple room is $90, which must be paid in advance, since they intend to leave early the next morning. Each gives the clerk $30. After they have gone, the clerk realizes he made a mistake. The assigned cost of the room is only $85. He gives the bellhop $5 to return to the men. Realizing the men will leave early and will never see the clerk again, the bellhop decides to pocket $2 for himself. He gives the men the other $3. This means each salesman has paid $29 for the room. $29 x 3 = $87. The bellhop pocketed $2. Problem: what happened to the missing dollar?"
(Answer: The verbal description deliberately confuses the issue. The room actually cost $85. The bellhop took $2 and gave $3 to the men. They really paid $88, not $87, for the room.)

3. Here's a tougher one.

"A professor of logic was listening to the radio and heard a song with these lines.

*Everybody loves my baby*
*But my baby don't love nobody but me*

He realized the lines added up to a logical fallacy. What was it?"

Read the lines to the class; add a third beginning with "Therefore" and see how many can come up with a conclusion that follows but is absurd.

(Answer: Therefore I am my baby. "Everybody" includes "my baby" too. Hence we can rewrite the line to say "My baby loves my baby." But since my baby only loves me, the line can now read "My baby loves me." This makes "me" and "my baby" mean the same thing.)

## Suggested Essay Questions on Text

1. Why are noncritical thinkers literal in their speech habits?

2. Give one reason that there are so few critical thinkers compared to their opposites.

3. A professional critic is someone who is expected to give an objective opinion all the time. What difference would it make if there were *no* professional critics?

## Journal Topics

1. Many complain that professional critics are not really objective; that artistic excellence lies in the mind of the beholder. Discuss one or two reasons *against* that argument.

2. If Carl Sagan's theory of the brain has any validity, we must believe we retain many characteristics of both the reptilian and the mammalian brains. Which traits of each do you think we still need?

3. If you had to wait two hours for a train in a small depot that had no restaurant, no book or magazine counter, and no TV set, how might you use your critical faculties to entertain yourself?

4. Are all of our national leaders figuratists?

# CHAPTER 10. *SOCIETY VERSUS THE HUMANITIES*

*Teaching Overview*

We are glad to introduce this new chapter for a number of reasons. First, we have seen in no other humanities text an indication that the very society which presumably benefits from the humanities can be hostile, unaccepting, even repressive. Second, it provides the best chance we can think of to face head-on a problem which is too often swept under the carpet: *Why are there so few minorities, including women, represented in humanities courses?* The difficulty experienced by minority writers and artists, traditionally and in some cases currently, is a theme in itself; for many have turned their hardships into the subject matter of their work. Granted, this fact does not guarantee that the work in question is great or will be lasting, but neither does exclusion guarantee that some great work is NOT being ignored! In addition, we are adamant in our belief that the themes of repression, moral censorship, and discrimination are so important that they more than outweigh any possible objection that "minor" figures are being studied in a course that should admit only the acknowledged standouts. Besides, the List of acknowledged standouts was drawn up in times past, when very different and now questionable standards were being used.

The section on "The Artist and the Moral Code" puts the issue of moral censorship into a historical perspective instead of dealing solely with immediate problems, such as the decision by the NEA not to fund the Mapplethorpe exhibit. The instructor will surely want to augment our material with current examples.

There is an expansive treatment of Oscar Wilde, his trial for homosexuality, and subsequent imprisonment; a treatment some might find unnecessarily detailed, considering that a fellow Irishman, George Bernard Shaw, is given far less space in the theater chapter. But Wilde is here because of the *issue*, and the *issue* needs to be faced. Is the private life of the artist the business of society? Maybe it is. No attempt is made to make the final pronouncement on the subject.

Cases in point in the long history of "Government Power and Free Speech" should have no trouble engaging the student, many of whom have already experienced what it means to be silenced: on school papers, on yearbooks, in school plays. Students often jump to the defense of all those whose freedom of speech has been denied or curtailed without ever trying to see affirmative possibilities. The opportunity is here.

We wanted to include the McCarthy hearings, because we discovered that many classes had never heard of them. However one feels about the right of elected officials to question private citizens about their comings and goings, what happened in the early '50s is one of the major events of the century.

We're also glad we treated ethnic and gender stereotyping as a form of repression, including the treatment of minorities in Hollywood films of the past. Yes, the traditional concept of the humanities is that of the very best work that humanity does; but the factors which serve to block the very best work need to be understood as well.

## Checklist of Points or Discussion Topics from Text

1. The subject of moral censorship is a good way to link students with the past, for it has always been around. Michelangelo's *Last Judgment* was "censored" after the sculptor's death, and the nude figures were made "decent."

2. The Motion Picture Production Code, which was still in effect, though modified, in 1956, is always interesting to go over with students. You might want to ask them whether a code of some sort is needed.

3. Homosexual artists are not being jailed anymore, but there is still the recent case of Robert Mapplethorpe and the NEA ruling on his photographs.

4. Ask the class to bring in reviews of plays and movies that seem to be requiring that a work have a certain bias.

5. In reference to the "art" of propaganda, are the quotes necessary? Is propaganda legitimate, whether you agree with its intent or not? Was it okay for Leni Riefenstahl to be pro-Nazi in her documentary on the 1936 Olympics?

6. Might there ever have been a legitimate danger from Communist party members working in the film industry?

7. Have we outgrown racial, gender, or other forms of stereotyping in film or television? Are there newer kinds? More subtle forms?

## Checklist of Discussion Points from Suggested Videotape "The Outer Circle"

1. The goliards, or medieval student priests, who composed irreverent songs, were probably victims of moral censorship, though the incident in the film is fictional. Here's a good place to go back to Apollo and Dionysus. Apollo, the moral establishment, seeks absolute control, inviting a revolutionary upsurge from Dionysus.

2. Council of Nicaea, A.D. 325, doctrine of the Trinity becomes dogma. Council of Chalcedon, A.D.451, doctrine of the virgin birth becomes dogma. Do all the students know what dogma is?

3. The imprisonment and subsequent breaking of Galileo's spirit is probably the quintessential example of moral censorship and its effects. The tragic irony, however, is that, though Galileo in fact died in his prison, never having published again, the trial probably did more to advance the cause of science than if the astronomer had been allowed to continue working.

4. The Scopes trial was nearly 70 years ago. Are there issues now with similar significance? What about the teacher who admitted he was homosexual and was immediately fired? What about outlawing prayer in the public school? Same principle?

5. Is the ending of the film dated? Are there still anti-science movements underway? In fact, is there an outer circle for our time?

## Alternate Strategies and Assignments

1. Divide into small groups. Task: come to a group consensus about a recent scandal involving the sexual preference of a celebrity. Does the group think the behavior of celebrities, in the public eye as much as they are, is society's business?

OR

Task: Do recent signs point towards or away from a revival of moral censorship in the arts?

OR

Task: Should anything be permitted on stage or screen? Have group members been offended enough to want a line drawn?

2. You can bring in copies of art works from the past in which a group or representative of a group is depicted in a certain light. See whether the students can determine the views behind the work.

## Suggested Essay Questions on Text

1. Is the present system of rating motion pictures useful? A farce that does no harm? An example of unacceptable moral censorship?

2. According to available information, Oscar Wilde probably would not have been arrested had he not sued the Marquess of Queensberry for libel. Would he have been wiser to have stayed in a closet and ignored the whole matter?

3. Why was John Peter Zenger acquitted of libel charges? On what point did the case turn?

4. Propaganda, it seems, will always be with us. Give examples from recent films or TV shows in which certain groups are depicted either favorably or unfavorably.

5. How did Arthur Miller respond artistically to his experiences before the House Un-American Activities Committee?

6. Why does the text call stereotyping a form of repression?

7. The text has a section on stereotyping called "Are We There Yet?" What does it mean? And are we?

8. Edmonia Lewis "overcame the obstacles of being both black and female." Who was she? Explain what obstacles she overcame. How did she do it?

## Journal Topics

1. Sooner or later somebody's decision that something is obscene and should not be funded is going to reach the Supreme Court after a lawsuit about it. Pretend you are a Chief Justice. What is your decision?

2. You are a juror in the Oscar Wilde trial. How do you vote? Why?

3. Should the sensibilities of minority groups be protected by law? Is the suppression of hate literature and hate graffiti a violation of free speech?

4. Antifeminist views and assumptions go back a long way and may in fact still be influencing people, especially the young. Think back to an early book which had a strong impact on you. In this book was the boy the dominant figure? Did he make all the decisions? Did the girl make mistakes? Was the girl in jeopardy, and did the boy save her?

5. From your early reading or viewing can you recall a stereotype directed at the group to which you belong?

# CHAPTER 11. *MYTHS*

*Teaching Overview*

Mythology, like art or music, is a vast discipline with enough material for several courses, let alone a week! The best attack, in our opinion, is to present as much of the chapter as can be contained in one particular theme. Possibilities are: Learning More about Ourselves from the Mythology That Has Helped Shape Our Consciousness; The Difference between Fairy Tales and Myths (very popular with students); Archetypes of Past and Present. You could easily assign the whole chapter, but advise the students that you are not going to deal in class with all of it. You might want to spend your time on the World Myth or the Myth of the Hero and then get into discussions of our contemporary heroes, or our lack of heroes, or the kind of hero(es) we desperately need at the moment. Pursuing any of these options will allow the class to see mythology in action.

Regardless of your focus, the students should come away from this unit relieved of the misconception that myths are fallacies (even fairy tales are not fallacies), made-up versions of reality, appropriate for children or "primitive" people but not for today's enlightened society. The First Edition included a discussion of the astronaut as hero, but we omitted the section because of what we felt was a waning of general interest in space adventures. Instead--perhaps because we have been working on the latest edition in a presidential year--we ended the chapter with the myth of the Promised Leader. By the time the book reaches you, one of the candidates will be in the White House and people may already be looking forward to the next election. The Promised Leader is an archetype, an abstraction that becomes embodied now and then, here and there, but is always in the consciousness of people whether he or she exists in actuality or not. That is myth.

A final possibility is focusing on the Need for Mythology, what myths do for the psyche. You can ask the students to share their own mythology with the group: everybody's top two hero-types, for example. Get a feeling for the values of this year's young people. Are there common concerns expressed in their hero choices? Common fears? You stand to learn as much as the students. As always, we wouldn't mind hearing about some of your discoveries.

## Checklist of Points or Discussion Topics from Text

1. The approach will be that myths may function in a variety of ways, but they are anything but lies. They affect the way we think and our expectations of life from our earliest years. The chapter will focus on three specific kinds of mythology: Myths of Childhood, Myths as Explanation, and Archetypal Myths.

2. One use of the fairy tale is moral instruction, and opinion is still divided over the long-term effects, especially of the notion that good things always happen to good people.

3. But there is also the factor of "unseen" instruction--what people have told children for centuries without realizing it. A good example, according to Bruno Bettelheim, is the wicked queen-stepmother in "Snow White." Children may have an ambivalent attitude. Yes, she is evil and will be destroyed, but she also represents power, something that fascinates children, since they lack it. He also finds "Red Riding Hood" loaded with sexual symbols and believes children unconsciously absorb a lot of information about sex from the fairy tales.

4. Myths as Explanation deals with early stories about the origins of the universe, human beings, and the various evils which befall them. Students are likely to object here that these stories certainly seem like lies, but what should be stressed is the ongoing human need to account for cosmic beginnings. We're still probing, aren't we?

5. Sexism abounds in early explanations. Evil is often traced to the machinations or curiosity of women such as Eve and Pandora.

6. The Greeks were fond of the family-curse myth, which not only explains why things go wrong but always gets the present generation off the hook. Isn't this still going on in one form or another? Aren't some young people blaming us older folk for despoiling the earth?

7. Jung's theories of universal archetypes and the collective unconscious can be questioned as inborn, *a priori* knowledge; but one can hardly deny that certain models do get into our awareness in our formative years. Students will readily admit the importance of the hero myth and love to offer opinions about contemporary figures who may embody the monomyth. JFK was a choice of Joseph Campbell. The son is now the right age for political aspirations, and perhaps he is the new Arthur.

8. Archetypal motifs like the circle, the journey, and magic are instantly recognizable, but perhaps there are new motifs in newer myths. The Olympic athlete has been a popular hero of modern mythology, and the use of steroids by many athletes seems like an updated version of the curse, the heel of Achilles, or Birnam Wood.

**Checklist of Discussion Points from Suggested Videotape "The Collective Dreams of Mankind"**

1. Opening of the film is a ritual centering on the mandala symbol. It stands for the unity of phenomena and of the inner life; it stands for the oneness of a group or culture. The Nazi party used the swastika, an ancient mandala which for the Hindus symbolized the unity of all being. (Of course, Nazism believed in the oneness of the Aryan race, not of humanity as a whole.)

2. The voyage and the quest as universal mythic structures. This is a good place to bring up *Star Wars*, which is still being viewed by our students. The voyage to find and then protect a beautiful princess is traditional, as is Luke's quest of his father. The Force is localized in a neon lance--an updating of Excalibur and other magic weapons that devastate the bad guys and protect the good guys. It's fun to ask students what the Force really *means* and what the authors are implying. Is it that peace will never come until only the good guys have control of weapons of destruction? Are the good guys *us*?

3. Arthur as the Promised Leader. Who is that nowadays? How shall the Leader be known? We have no birth marks or Excalibur stuck in a rock. (There's usually a mystique about the person chosen to deliver the keynote address at a nominating convention.)

4. Myths of the Garden. The New World; Hitler's Aryan society; Marx's classless society. What about the health spas of today, jogging camps, summer programs for gifted students, retirement communities?

5. The video is a little out-of-date in upholding the astronaut as the myth hero of our time, but the suggestion that space travel may open up new visions of The Garden is still on target, especially as news about the condition of the planet becomes grimmer.

## Alternate Strategies and Assignments

1. Divide into groups. Ask each one to agree on five early myths that influenced their developing consciousness and helped shape their expectations of life: e.g., inner beauty is more important than what's outside; women must wait passively for the inevitable arrival of the prince; evil is a real force and will be conquered by the good. Then have them discuss some of the darker implications, not lessons consciously learned but unconscious, untested, and unexamined information about the world: e.g., it's okay to conquer or even kill those forces that seem harmful; powerful witches, like many evil creatures, can be intriguing figures; the life of the chosen Leader is unhappy and brief.

   The group findings are then shared with the others, and you conclude with a consideration of the question: Should children continue to be exposed to fairy tales?

2. In groups, draw and characterize the ideal hero for our times. Is it a he? A she? A he/she?

3. Each group decides upon a contemporary figure they consider a modern hero, as well as a rating system: so many points for positive characteristics; so many points subtracted for negative traits. What is the score? How much of the hero is left?

   In community, consider the questions: How many heroes of the past might be left if we did the same thing? Is it advisable to do this? Is it better to have a hero than, in some cases, the full truth?

## Suggested Essay Questions on Text

1. Explain briefly the mythology behind the following statements: "The honeymoon is over"; "Knock on wood"; "I'm right back where I started."

2. Many myths and fairy tales are fundamentally sexist in nature. Discuss any two examples.

3. Discuss any two archetypes you picked up early in your development and that you have carried with you. Are they helping you or hindering you at present?

4. Why do you think there is a world myth? What does it tell us about human beings?

5. Is it the purpose of myths to make life bearable or comprehensible?

## Journal Topics

1. Briefly write your autobiography in mythic terms. Describe your birth, your mission in life, the villains you must outwit, your magic powers, your magic weapon, and how you will eventually be recognized as a special person.

2. Take any fairy tale and retell it in updated terms. That is, try to subvert it so that it comes closer to reality than it was when you first heard it. Eliminate sexist attitudes.

3. Luck plays an important part in some myths, and it is usually good. In terms of your own observations, explain this statement: "Luck must exist. How else can we explain the success of people we dislike?"

4. Older myths are not strong on environmental themes. Bad things happen to nature in the stories of Demeter and Dionysus but spring returns and the earth is renewed. In the story from Ghana about the seven-headed serpent there is, however, a long and terrible drought. Perhaps we need a strong environmental myth to wake people up today. Outline the story.

5. Gandhi, Kennedy, and King can be said to have reached the status of myth heroes; and all are tragic. Do you think these myths tend to discourage people from wanting to be in the public eye?

6. How important is magic in your life? Do you have a special object that has a secret power you could not do without?

# CHAPTER 12. *LOVE*

*Teaching Overview*

Here is an opportunity to treat a theme historically. As a matter of fact, we recommend this approach highly; for looking at the chronological development of love definitions will clearly illustrate that 1) the word has no universal "timeless" denotations; 2) its meanings have been influenced by the cultures that use the word; 3) the romantic view of love introduced in the Middle Ages has survived, as has the Victorian idea of marriage, and both of these are colliding with more flexible views that have come in with the sexual revolution of the '60s. The goal of this unit is quite clear: *to help students arrive at realistic expectations without denying the standards they may be setting for themselves.* This is a sensitive subject, and the age gap between student and instructor can loom very large. Educators often make assumptions about the degree of sophistication the students have attained. Yet history is history, and everything we point out exists somewhere in the humanities. Learning to accommodate the truth about an ideal is part of growing up and becoming educated. The subject, however, should be approached without embarrassment, cynicism, or a strong bias. Let the humanities speak for themselves.

## Checklist of Points or Discussion Topics from Text

1. There is nothing cynical about the classical equation of love and lust. It is simply a fact in the history of the humanities, and obviously the equation does not force itself upon us. One can point out that *we* have more options than did our remote ancestors on the Aegean or the Mediterranean. In Graeco-Roman mythology and literature love is often a terrible affliction of mind and body.

2. Platonic love is quite a different matter, though students are inaccurate when they think it is "love without sex." Lust can indeed exist within the context of Platonic love, but the philosopher did indeed believe a physical relationship was a minor goal. Plato thought of love in hierarchical terms. At the top was the highest possible union, when one is in the presence of the ideal, the perfect, or what he calls "absolute beauty." One can be in love with the beauty of another's body as the first step. From this one moves on to find the beautiful in nature, works of art, and works of the mind, and finally reaches the very essence of beauty, loved for itself, without embodiment in anything that is material and impermanent.

3. Biblical love, which may or may not have preceded Plato (since the Hebrew Bible was a very long time in development), introduces something all but unknown in the classical world: the transcendence of self-interest for the group or tribe, the family, significant (ultimately even nonsignificant, even hostile) others, and, finally, God. The New Testament further extends the philosophy of altruism and love of one's enemy.

4. Romantic love is a medieval concept, and is closer to "love without sex," at least in theory, than Plato was. Medieval marriage practice among the upper classes and the nobility gave young people no freedom of choice when it came to a mate for life. The bride or groom, thus sold into matrimony, usually lusted for someone else; and, since sexual relations outside of marriage were sinful, medieval literature idealized love outside of marriage into a vision of nonphysical devotion. The love of Lancelot and Guinevere or Tristan and Isolde typifies the concept. Romantic love usually ends tragically in the stories.

5. The cult of the Virgin Mary, known as *Mariolatry*, plays a part in the history of love. Through the adoration of poets and artists for the Virgin the status of women in general was raised; and woman, having become idealized, became a powerful figure.

6. In the later Middle Ages and early Renaissance the code of courtly love became popular, according to which woman played the role of cruel master, turning man into her slave by holding out the faint promise of sexual gratification (something she was not required to deliver).

7. During the 17th and 18th centuries love is often seen as a game between civilized men and women, who might or might not care for each other romantically. In any event, the woman was not expected to be won without a struggle. The game was less extreme than the requirements of courtly love.

8. In Victorian times love is less important than marriage, and marriage is an economic institution. The rising middle class and the Protestant work ethic demanded a stable home environment with the wife having the responsibility of running the house and overseeing the care of the children, while the husband earned the money. Woman had comfort and security but no human rights.

9. The final sections of the chapter, "Breaking the Code" and "Steps Toward Liberation," focus on efforts, beginning in the last century, to change Victorian role models of man and woman. We find that heroines like Ibsen's Nora, Flaubert's Emma Bovary, Tolstoy's Anna Karenina, and Shaw's Mrs.Warren end up as either tragic victims or social outcasts. As we get closer to our own time, however, we discover that role models have changed dramatically. In Marquez' *Love in the Time of Cholera* the major characters are a pair of elderly lovers. Before this, a succession of strong actresses allowed Hollywood to make films about powerful women, successfully competing in what used to be a "man's world."

**Checklist of Discussion Points from Suggested Videotape "Love: Myth and Mystery"**

1. Story of Eloise and Abelard illustrates the Christian separation of physical and spiritual love, and the conflicts--even tragedy--it caused. Has that separation disappeared?

2. How much has the class discovered about the narrator: his recent past, why he is writing a book with that title, whether he is modern or old-fashioned in his attitude or even his basic problem?

3. In the Bible, one can observe the steady development of the concept of universal love. The New Testament makes love the purpose of life: of God and one's fellow human beings.

4. The separation of the physical and the spiritual is one thing; the belief that sexual love outside of marriage is sinful is found in St.Paul. (Later St.Jerome would say that lusting even for one's wife was a sin.)

5. The medieval romantic view of love was (and has been) around for a very long time. The advent of Freud's theories, however, had a devastating impact. Instead of thinking about Mr. or Ms. Right--or love made in heaven--people had to wonder whether they had fallen in love with parent substitutes.

6. Erich Fromm: We seek love as a means of ending a state of separateness. People cannot bear to be alone.

## Alternate Strategies and Assignments

1. Divide the class into men and women and ask each group to list 10 attributes of the opposite sex in rank order. That is, if you took away #1, you would not have a woman or a man. Then share the lists in community.

   Note: This exercise has been tried many times since the text first appeared. Men tend to be physical and biological in their list and do a lot of heehawing while compiling it. Women tend to rank traits like "gentleness" and "sensitivity" very high. Women almost never consider a man's sexuality as his essence, while men usually give women's sex the highest ratings.

2. As the members of the class enter the room, hand out tags on which they write their first and last names. The men are directed to paste their tags onto their shirts, while the women hold theirs. The men are then asked to stand in a circle in the center of the room, while the women move about inspecting the men with an eye toward choosing a mate.

   When a woman finds a man she wants, she then writes "Mr." in front of her own name and pastes her tag over the man's. She then lays down the rules of the marriage, including her rights and the husband's rights.

   The men then are given 10 minutes to caucus and start a liberation movement. They are allowed to come up with three demands. While they do this, the women caucus and decide what rights they would be willing to give up and what are non-negotiable.

   Community discussion afterwards about marriage, names, rules, rights, and any new concept that might emerge.

## Suggested Essay Questions on Text

1. Do you agree with Morton Hunt's statement that love is any form of relationship between human beings used in conjunction with the phrase "falling in love" or "being in love"?

2. In general, the Greeks and Romans thought of love as straightforward physical desire. Would it clarify matters if you said "I am in lust" instead of "I am in love"?

3. Early Biblical love seems to center on family and tribe. Later the concept of altruism is introduced. Is genuine altruism a tendency of anyone? Or is it a disguised form of self--and family--love?

4. Do you require a Platonic element to exist in a relationship? Define what this is. Or explain why you do not require such a thing, or believe that it exists.

5. Does romantic love continue to define the expectations of people as they think about marriage? If not, does marriage continue to occupy the thoughts of young people? What then is the basis of marriage?

6. Sex roles have undeniably changed now that many wives go to work and many husbands take care of the home. Would you say that the definition of love has also changed?

**Journal Topics**

1. It is frequently said that one cannot love another until one is able to love oneself. Does this make sense to you? Do you agree? Or does loving yourself first negate the whole idea of love?

2. Some say the family is all washed up, that the institution in our society has outlived its usefulness. Others say the family is the very foundation of society. What is your view? If you want the family to continue but believe there is a problem, how do you propose to solve it?

3. The text does not discuss friendship as a form of love. Would you have included it? Or is it a different kind of relationship? If so, which would you rather give up if you had to choose?

4. Do you agree that men have difficulty with outward displays of close friendship?

5. The text looks at the treatment of sex roles in the films of Tracy and Hepburn and in *Kramer vs. Kramer*. There must be a couple of newer treatments you can talk about.

6. In your opinion does the Victorian Model of marriage have any merit at all? Argue for or against, or split your vote.

7. All of us play roles relative to the opposite sex. Single out the roles with which you are most and least comfortable.

8. Suppose you gave a party and everyone you knew came to it. How many different people would you become?

# CHAPTER 13. *HAPPINESS*

*Teaching Overview*

We have always been amazed that there is so little direct contact with the idea of happiness in any area of education. By all rights there should be a Happiness 101 course--and a required one at that! What better gift could educators give to students than to help them think through this complex state that is presumably everyone's goal in life to reach? The ability to analyze the nature of happiness coolly and intelligently before plunging into adult experience and all of its hazards would, we think, be a valuable asset, creating realistic expectations. How ironic that we seldom teach happiness directly when the humanities are so often the passionate expressions of *un*happy people.

We recommend that, before discussing this chapter, you assign the students the task of bringing in their own conceptions of happiness in written form. These can be shared, and most assuredly they will offer a variety of definitions, chief among which will be words like contentment, "making it," "getting ahead," and "self-fulfillment."

Next we recommend asking a question like "How do you know when you are happy?" Again, expect a variety of opinions and a certain amount of confusion. The strategy is not intended as an act of complacent scorn for youthful disorganization. The fact of the matter is that the crucial question is indeed *whether happiness is felt or experienced like the pleasurable taste of gourmet food or is an intangible condition of life that is never directly experienced.*

In order to help clear up the issue, you can say, we will look at a number of the most famous and enduring theories of happiness, and you can choose the one that appeals to you the most or that seems to be most realistic.

## Checklist of Points or Discussion Topics from Text

1. Perhaps a common assumption is that ours is a hedonistic society, yet, if this is the case, one could argue that people do not start off as hedonists. If you took a poll of your class, you might find that their primary goal is not a huge estate with an Olympic swimming pool. Our polls came up with answers like "To finish my degree and get a good job." But having a good job is not in itself a hedonistic ambition. The case may be that pleasure becomes an end in itself as people grow older and become bored with their work.

2. The "big earnings theory" may begin in youth, and it may be the first sign of hedonism. Find out how many students believe they deserve more than they are getting out of life. The big earnings theory could explain the reason for much dissatisfaction or frustration, which for many is the same thing as unhappiness.

3. Epicurus versus the hedonists. Is absence of pain better than the presence of pleasure? Or are certain pleasures *worth* the pain? If students answer yes to this question, then are we still dealing with an economic theory of happiness?

4. Stoicism. Is it better to deny yourself something pleasant, if later the absence of it is likely to cause pain? Do the students think it is better to enjoy life as much as possible and then cope with distress when it comes, or to make careful plans in advance of the distress?

5. Aristotle's theory always seems to come as a surprise to students, who never appear to have thought that their lives can be happy even though they are not consciously having pleasure or are even content with how things are with them; that they can in fact be leading a happy life even though they are existentially miserable at the moment. Aristotle reasoned that a happy life is one filled with all good things and that, if this is true, then the good things exist to promote happiness but cannot be equal to it. (The means cannot be equal to the end.) Hence happiness is not an actual state to be experienced but the abstract condition of a total life.

6. Aristotle did not believe that the goods which we desired for the sake of being happy were all equally capable of promoting happiness. At the top of his list were virtue and wisdom. The students are likely not to agree with this. How can you be happy by doing the virtuous thing if you're missing out on a lot of pleasures? How can knowledge in itself be as good as a new car? Aristotle would probably have answered that only at the end of a good life can one realize what has truly promoted happiness. Till then, the choice is yours. Material acquisitions may appear to promote happiness for a time, but what if you're never satisfied (as is likely to be the case if you keep getting what you want)?

**Checklist of Discussion Points from Suggested Videotape "In Search of Happiness"**

1. Faust's pact with Mephistopheles was a trade-off: unlimited hedonism in exchange for the intellectual pursuit of truth.

2. Old Testament Psalm. Happiness consists of an abundant earth and the sense that God is protecting you.

   Question: Can people, faced with the all-consuming task of making the earth bear fruit, have any view of happiness other than a full larder?

   Question: Are most of us made unhappy because our wants are fairly sophisticated (non-basic)? Are we counting our blessings enough?

3. Ancient Christian view. Life is a vale of tears. We are not here to look for happiness. Or: happiness is the knowledge that there is a better life in store.

4. Marx. Happiness is work, not leisure; and relating oneself to the products of one's work. Factory workers shown here do not seem to be happy. Yet Marxism has failed. Because work alone cannot promote happiness? Can you ever impose on people a "rule" by which happiness is attained?

5. Drugs and alcohol. They offer temporary escape or temporary pleasure, and both, Aristotle might concede, can promote happiness, at least for a time; but then the Stoic would argue that the experience is definitely not worth the after-pain.

**Alternate Strategies and Assignments**

Ask members of the class to create questionnaires to be used as the basis of quick interviews with students, faculty and staff around the campus. The aim of the research is to determine whether people in the college community are generally happy. Suggested questions:

1. If you had to single out one thing that is most likely to make you happy, what would that be?

2. How available is that thing in your life?

3. Do you have a second and third choice?

4. How important to you are the following: a healthy planet; a sound economy; wisdom in the White House; your health; your family; a love relationship; money, etc.?

5. From your answers to the above list, single out the one most important requirement for your happiness.

6. If there is nothing on the list that is in good shape at the moment, would you call yourself unhappy?

## Suggested Essay Questions on Text

1. Consider some of the popular television commercials. What definitions of happiness do they assume?

2. Is the big earnings theory a good explanation for any unhappiness you may be experiencing? If you are not unhappy at all, explain why.

3. Is the absence of pain better than the presence of pleasure?

4. Is the party "before" worth the morning "after"?

5. "Eat, drink, and be merry, for tomorrow you may die" is the hedonist's creed. Is it a sound one? What happens if you *don't* die tomorrow?

6. How would each of the following react to legislation banning the use of automobiles on weekends? The hedonist? The Epicurean? The Stoic? Aristotle?

7. How might Aristotle respond to the objection "What's the good of having a happy life if you don't know that you're happy"?

## Journal Topics

1. Do you know anyone who holds the opposite of the big earnings theory, who believes that he or she does *not* deserve to be happy? Is it possible that some people actually do not?

2. Is it better to pick and choose your deeds with care, so that you are never in a position to feel pain? Or better to take what comes, without worrying about later?

3. Epictetus, a famous Stoic, said "Do not will that things be as you want, but will that they be as they are." Is this a sound philosophy of life? Is it possible for you?

4. Aristotle agreed that happiness was the purpose of life, since all other goals appeared to be sought for the sake of the happiness they would promote. Is it possible there are goals which are sought for a different reason?

5. There are people for whom happiness is integrity: having a strong set of principles and living by them. Often, however, holding to your principles means inviting the scorn and the hostility of others. Would *you* find happiness in integrity even if it meant being fairly isolated from the mainstream? How often do you compromise? Why do you do it?

*Teaching Overview*

Another title we considered for this chapter was "What Is Death?" Then we thought it might be considered facetious--not a good beginning for a serious subject. Looking back, however, we think perhaps that title might have suited our purposes better. Like love and happiness, death has had and continues to have a number of different meanings both in the humanities and society in general.

Death is more than the physical termination of a biological system, though it is this form of death the average person fears most. For many, death is the beginning of another and better life. Or, if not, it can be a welcomed relief from the pain of this one. Or it may not be biological at all. It can be the end of a love affair, a job that has meant one's whole life for a long time, creative inspiration, sexual potency, the end of striving, caring, reaching for what we can never seem to grasp--and, saddest of all, the end of hope.

Physical death we can't do much about, unless it is a contemplated self-inflicted death. The pain--if that must be involved--we have to learn how to bear as best we can. We must say goodbye to loved ones, often long before we consider the time appropriate or reasonable. The other forms of death, however--the *death in life*--are, however, within our power to transcend.

In the humanities death can be accompanied by images of doom and gloom, haunted castles, open graves, creaking coffins, howling wolves, and so on. We are all familiar with the horror story paraphernalia. It is also heroic, as in the glorious deaths of warriors in battle: Hector being dragged around and around the walls of Troy, or Joan of Arc burning at the stake, her faith in God unshaken.

Death is prominent in the romantic literature of the 19th century, and almost always it is connected with resurrection and immortality. In the poetry of Keats, who seems always to have suspected he would die young (and did at 25), death is a gentle, old friend, who holds out a soft and welcoming hand. In Tennyson death is a return to the natural cycle, a reunion with the whole of existence.

Still, our students, young as they mostly are, may not be as moved as we would like by the high-flown phrases of the older poets. Some fear the imminent death of nature. Some see society falling apart, with little hope for the future. Literature, drama, and films of our time paint a generally gloomy picture of existence.

True. So what better class purpose than to cope with this pervasive theme of the humanities and find meaningful, rational ways of putting an end to death in life and learn how to make a new beginning?

## Checklist of Points and Discussion Topics from Text

1. We look first at attitudes toward death--what death can mean to different times, people, and belief systems.

2. Death as personal enemy. The Grim Reaper, waiting somewhere for each of us. Personal death as unthinkable. Some people refuse to use the word in connection with themselves.

3. Using the example of Socrates, who counseled his students not to assume death is the worst fate that can befall anyone, we look at the possibility that, where self-interest is not primary, the fear of death can be greatly mitigated.

4. Many writers and poets have taken a measure of comfort from the image of death as leveler: that is, we all have to die, including the rich, famous, and powerful. *Hamlet* abounds with such sentiments, and there is always Shelley's "Ozymandias."

5. The fear of death is dissolved for many because of the concept of an afterlife. But this takes many forms. Sometimes it is a place; sometimes, another stage of being that cannot be comprehended in our terms.

6. Fatalism is a popular attitude toward death and means of coping with it. If you take the "my number isn't up yet" approach, you may find it easier to handle the thought of an imminent catastrophe. At the same time, the price you pay is the fear that at any moment your number may be coming up. Fatalists, perhaps, think more about death than do those who believe life and death are random accidents.

7. The idea that death can be within one's own control has always been popular, especially among creative people. Albert Camus maintained that suicide is the only real issue in philosophy. We examine the case histories of Sylvia Plath, Anne Sexton, and Ernest Hemingway, all of whom seem to have chosen death over a life that had lost its quality. But if we are to approach life with an open mind, we need to take self-inflicted death very seriously and not believe that only mentally sick people contemplate it.

8. More pervasive than physical death is symbolic death, and this can occur over and over in the lives of some. Symbolic suicide happens to people with poor self-images and oppressive insecurities, and it takes many forms, including martyrdom, compulsive gambling, and deliberately placing oneself in a position to be hurt by others.

9. Symbolic murder often takes the form of gossiping or otherwise undoing someone's reputation and destroying through subtle verbal knife thrusts. Resorting to symbolic murder generally comes from the same root as symbolic suicide: deep-rooted, profound insecurity.

10. Fear of aging is a death-in-life for thousands, perhaps millions. Our culture's youth orientation and poor treatment of the elderly is a major reason that people try to hide their age from themselves as well as others by falling prey to media advertising instructing them how to stay young forever.

11. The ancient legend of the phoenix bird which rises from its own ashes, young and reborn, is a model we can keep with us all of our lives. It involves throwing away the list of what is appropriate behavior at a given age and much risk-taking. But when was growth ever accomplished *without* risks?

**Checklist of Discussion Points from Suggested Videotape "For Everything, a Season"**

1. The Grim Reaper is shown as the major symbol of death as personal enemy, but surely the class can think of other symbols of death that affect us with gloom and fear.

2. Death as cultural enemy. In a success-oriented society, death is seen as ultimate failure. The dead are often mentioned with pity, as we would mention anyone who has just suffered a business loss.

3. The fear of death also inspires the Pompeiian Principle: the sense that mall of us are living at the foot of a volcano which may erupt at any moment, and so we must party to the fullest before it happens.

4. The New Orleans Jazz Funeral is a life-affirming ritual. How do the rest of us bury our dead? From a funeral home and as expeditiously as possible so as not to disturb the familiar rhythms of our lives?

5. The bullfight as a life-affirming ritual. In one sense the bull is death, and the daring matador carries with him the soul of the crowd as he defeats the great enemy.

6. The out-of-body or near-death experience appears to be much more widespread than some of us originally thought. If nothing else, the experience has convinced thousands that death holds no terrors, may be peaceful, and should even be anticipated with an open mind.

## Alternate Strategies and Assignments

1. There are a number of "death exercises" that are effective but may be more appropriate for courses in death and dying. These include filling out one's own death certificate, including cause of death; writing one's own obituary, eulogy, and epitaph (to discover whether the attitude toward oneself is negative or life-affirming); and arranging chairs, symbolic of close friends and family, in chronological order between walls which represent birth and death, and then placing oneself within the chronology.

2. In groups, discuss an organization or institution that is currently suffering from a disease (describe) and is in danger of dying. For example, there is institutional hardening of the arteries when lines of communication become clogged. There may be cancerous cells of office intrigue, gossip, and political maneuvering. Dr. Phoenix then comes to the rescue and suggests ways in which the patient can be restored to full health. Sometimes radical surgery is necessary. Sometimes rehabilitation is possible, especially of damaged brain cells.

## Suggested Essay Questions

1. Lao-Tzu, the Chinese poet and philosopher, said, "The way of life is soft; the way of death is hard." What do you think he meant? Is the hardness of death something we must inevitably face, or can we carry life's softness with us always?

2. Death may be an evil in proportion to the degree of significance given to the self, but minimizing the self is more easily said than done. Suggest one or two ways in which the self can be deemphasized.

3. Is it better to be straightforward and realistic in explaining death to children, or is it necessary to idealize the subject so that they can handle it?

4. Is it life-affirming to say that one ought to have as much fun as possible because life is so short?

5. Writers and philosophers have said that death gives meaning to life. What sort of meaning? Would you rather have endless life even if it had *no* meaning?

6. We could add smoking and drinking to the types of symbolic suicide. Is there an answer to those who maintain that the pleasure of such pastimes more than compensates for any risk involved?

7. Could it be argued that fatalism is a Phoenix Model? That it is life-affirming to believe that one dies when it is time to die?

8. How would you discourage someone from suicide?

9. Do you think it is possible to get ahead in this world without once resorting to symbolic murder?

10. Go back to the Introduction and read, or reread, the story of Woodrow Tatlock. Here is a man badly in need of a Phoenix Model in his life. Provide him with one.

## Journal Topics

1. You are approaching certain death. You think of Socrates, who supposedly spent his final days discussing issues, or at least turning the occasion of his death into the basis for teaching some principles to his young followers. Could you find some issues you considered more important than your personal problem?

2. The death of Elvis Presley drew (and is still drawing) a far greater national response than the death of Albert Einstein. Is this phenomenon attributable to the fact that Einstein was so much older? Or are there other reasons?

3. Years ago the bodies of the deceased were viewed in their own homes. Now, of course, most people use the funeral home. Some thanatologists (psychologists who specialize in counseling the dying and their families) think the earlier practice was better and more life-affirming. Do you agree?

4. Thanatologists also advise that the terminally ill are better off spending their last days at home rather than in a hospital. If the choice of home or hospital were yours to make on behalf of a loved one, which would it be? Why?

5. "Ring Around the Rosy" was originally a medieval game played by children who were used to seeing deaths from the great plague. Now that you know what it means, do you think it is morbid or life-affirming? ("Ashes, ashes; all fall down . . .")

# CHAPTER 15. *NATURE IN THE HUMANITIES*

*Teaching Overview*

If you think this new chapter was written with the idea of encouraging students to worry about the fate of this planet, you are indeed right. At the same time it contains information about artists and writers who were deeply concerned about not only natural decay but the moral decay of a once glorious civilization that is either destroying itself or sitting idly by while destruction is imminent. In this respect the material, we think, is a legitimate part of humanities education. True, most of it is not optimistic, but was *King Lear*? All great creativity is life-affirming in the sense that it puts us in awe of what human genius can accomplish. At the same time the subject matter can be sobering; and when it relates to matters of planetary life or death, it *should* be sobering.

Our strong advice is to teach the material "straight": that is, as further explorations into a given theme of the humanities, in this case the relationship between human beings and nature. Whatever contemporary concerns are there will emerge naturally (no pun intended) and inevitably, without being forced.

The subject is vast, and we knew we were facing an enormous challenge in attempting to deal with so much in one chapter, albeit one of respectable length. To put it into a manageable perspective, you can say that, while nature has always made an impact on human sensibilities to a greater or lesser degree, it has sometimes been seen mainly as a beautiful backdrop for human achievement, sometimes as a titanic force that can be as lethal as it can be lovely, sometimes as a self-generating, self-healing organism (a 19th-century romantic notion that survives because it is comforting), and now as a wounded being that may die unless we drop everything and attend to its needs. Listing the uses of nature in the humanities is better and safer than trying to structure a develop mental scheme of human awakening. Unfortunately, the truth is that artists and writers who mourn the suffering of nature are still in the minority, as are the people who are changing their way of life because of the perilous signs they see everywhere.

## Checklist of Points or Discussion Topics from Text

1. Genesis contains a commandment from God to Adam and Eve that they are to "dress" and "keep" the Garden of Eden. The Bible has sometimes been blamed for introducing the notion that human beings were the stewards of the earth, but there seems no justification for the charge. In punishing Adam, God says "cursed is the ground for thy sake . . . thorns and thistles shall it bring forth to thee . . ." Isn't the Bible saying that humanity is responsible for what has happened to nature?

2. Jaques in *As You Like It* can legitimately be called an early environmentalist, denouncing the wanton killing of deer for food as well as the corruption of the idyllic innocence of the Forest of Arden. One *could* argue that Shakespeare may have intended these sentiments to identify melancholia in the character, almost always the basis for laughter. On the other hand, the melancholia of Jaques, if that indeed is what it should be called, seems justified by the facts and far less absurd than melancholia in, say, Malvolio.

3. Sir William Temple, one-time boss of Swift, has become a somewhat obscure figure--nonexistent in general education--yet his "Decay of Nature" philosophy was fashionable for a time and deserves prominent mention in the history of environmental awareness.

4. The section *The City Versus the Country* allows you to pick and choose from a wide variety of sources, for it is a theme found in the Middle Ages, the Renaissance (all the pastoral literature as well as *As You Like It*), and right up to our own time, when it is being revived in such works as Woody Allen's "I love New York" films and the anti-urban *Local Hero*. Even before environmental activism, there are plenty of artists and writers glorifying country living and relating it to moral purity (even as there are just as many who make fun of country bumpkins).

5. Going back to Pope's "Unerring NATURE" and throughout 19th-century romanticism, we see the growth of the idea that nature is a living spirit with a mind, heart, and soul, the very definite conviction that nature takes good care of us and itself as well. While this can be inspiring, we pose the possibility that the idea has seeped into the unconscious of enough people to perhaps explain why a *laissez-faire* attitude persists about nature. True, much evidence exists to support a belief that nature has performed amazing feats of compensation for natural mistakes and catastrophes, but isn't there a limit to what we can expect?

6. Turner and Melville are introduced as prophetic voices, giving us a vision of nature as terrifying force--not as environmentalists, but as worshippers. Still, the terror should have sent a message that meddling with this force can be disastrous.

7. Mary Shelley's *Frankenstein* is revisited, and a case is made for the super significance of this mythic novel, the tragedy of the destruction of a beautiful, natural being by a society that has steadily grown away from nature. (Perhaps someday it be filmed with its integrity intact.)

8. Native American writings abound with poetic adoration of nature and anger towards the white man for desecrating it.

9. The moral bankruptcy of the white man is the theme of *Heart of Darkness*, which seems so much timelier than its 1889 publication date would suggest. But a century ago there it was: the story of how one human being's greed laid waste another Garden of Eden, killing elephants for profit and killing natives for the joy of exulting in power.

10. Three-quarters of a century after Conrad comes Burgess's *A Clockwork Orange* with its pretty accurate vision of a near future (now at hand) in which cities are garbage heaps and amoral gangs roam at will. (Both Conrad and Burgess see a connection between environmental destruction and moral depravity.) Alex, the main thug, is captured and rehabilitated painfully, and the most recent edition of the novel has a new ending in which there is still a ray of hope for both Alex and the world.

11. Whether that hope has any real basis, whether there will be a tomorrow that Alex is sure will be "all like sweet flowers" may be up to our students.

**Checklist of Discussion Points from Suggested Videotape "The Man with No Time for Beauty"**

This film was originally made as an introduction to the telecourse, but it *can* serve as a video support for this new chapter. Woodrow Tatlock, the main character, rather unfortunately typifies the indifference of many citizens not only to the arts but to issues as well. Is there any indication that Woodrow has had any sensitivity since he was a child drawing the morning with his crayons? In the final scene he is back at his supposedly favorite hobby--fishing. It is early morning, and fanning out before him is a gorgeous sunrise, to which he is utterly oblivious.

Woodrow's problem, stemming from an absorption in his own personal culture, his own past and present, his own memories, makes him incapable of enjoying the *Mona Lisa*, the waltzing park in Vienna, the Hermitage, OR the natural fjords of Norway. Sailing down one of them, Woodrow is too busy talking about his late wife to hear the photographer's cry "But she didn't take everything with her!"

The film can tie the course together as well as this chapter. The arts are, after all, human additions to the natural world. Both have their beauty, and Woodrow has no time for either. Why? Where do people take the wrong step? What happened to the child on the merry-go-round with wide open eyes?

## Alternate Strategies and Assignments

1. Divide into groups, each of which is to pretend it is a travel agency, setting up an itinerary for someone like Woodrow Tatlock. (Even if they haven't seen the film, they may have read about him in the Introduction. Or you can briefly describe him.) The agency is both humanities-oriented and environmentally responsible. Where should he go that will offer him artistic beauty he can tolerate and teach him some lessons about the environment?

2. At an Earth Summit in South America the president of the United States indicated that, while we are concerned about the future of the planet, we give a higher priority to economic development. Find two students who will debate the question:

   *Should our maximum national effort be expended to ensure the highest possible standard of living for each citizen or to do what is possible to save the environment?*

## Suggested Essay Questions

1. Is the 19th-century belief that nature is a strong, vital, self-healing organism still prominent?

2. Jaques in *As You Like It* broods sadly over the death of a wild deer. In the last century Henry David Thoreau told us in *Walden* that he is a vegetarian and that it is unnatural for people to eat animal flesh. Do you think it is okay to raise and slaughter animals for human consumption, or is it more natural for us to eat only what grows from the soil?

3. Sir William Temple's belief that nature was slowly dying led to some pessimistic literature in the mid-1700s. We find that belief today. Is pessimism over the environment finding expression in popular art forms like movies and television?

4. The text indicates that the "Manhattan" (pro-urban) attitude of today isn't much different from the pro-Athens attitude of Socrates' time. Do people who passionately love the metropolitan life of theaters, art galleries, and restaurants contribute in any way to environmental problems; or are the two totally unrelated?

5. Wordsworth is shown in the text to represent the country, as opposed to the urban, attitude. What is Wordsworth's view of nature, and why is it a "country" attitude?

6. In one of his poems Wordsworth assures us that "Nature never did betray/The heart that loved her." What does he mean? Does what he says fill you with optimism or pessimism?

7. Contrast the views of nature we find in the works of Wordsworth and Turner.

8. Do you know enough about the original film version of *Frankenstein* to compare it to Mary Shelley's novel?

9. Conrad wrote *Heart of Darkness* more than a hundred years ago. Is exploitation of less advanced cultures still going on? Give two specific reasons for saying yes or no.

10. Of the two novels, *Heart of Darkness* and *A Clockwork Orange*, which appears to be sounding the stronger warning about danger to the environment?

## Journal Topics

1. Has the ozone hole become larger because of our ignorance or indifference?

2. Aside from the fact that the Book of Genesis clearly predicts the trashing of the earth, would you say that religion today can play a major part in saving the earth? How?

3. What kind of arguments could be used against those who hold that all we have to do is leave nature alone and it will heal itself?

4. Do you tend to hold a city or a country attitude? If your answer is "city," do you think you have any more responsibility toward the environment than do those who answer "country"?

5. Thoreau went to jail rather than pay a tax on the use of the polls. Can you justify a poll tax? Or do you think the state is morally bound to provide voting services free?

6. Of the two novels, *Moby-Dick* and *Frankenstein*, which seems to have a more powerful environmental message?

7. Native Americans in the last century and early years of this century were environmentally sensitive. Check out some of their writings and see if you can find statements that are even more meaningful in our time than the excerpts found in the chapter.

# CHAPTER 16. *FREEDOM*

*Teaching Overview*

We consider the ultimate goal of a humanities course to be that students will learn what resources exist for them beyond those which satisfy their basic needs and those which represent financial security or the path to enviable material possessions. We think students should have learned that they have the power to choose among significant options: whether to devote their lives to the pursuit of money and success or, without scorning these things, to make room for the joys that the arts and critical thinking have to offer.

Yet, having articulated such a goal, we cannot be oblivious to the fact that making a choice among significant options is a cherished human right only if it is a free choice. Living in a part of the world in which the humanities are there just for the rich and the powerful or are hardly there at all, or in which the struggle for survival is a lifetime job . . . one may have no freedom to choose.

In planning the text, we agreed that freedom itself must be the final--because it may be the major--theme of the humanities we wished to consider. The subject abounds in the visual arts, in literature, film, and philosophy. Plato's *Apology of Socrates*, written so long ago, is a ringing cry for freedom of thought and speech. Before Plato, there was the Buddha, preaching the Eightfold Path, the road to liberation from what Blake would have called the "mind-forg'd Manacles" of suffering and despair. Judaism sought freedom from oppression and persecution; Christianity sought freedom from Roman tyranny; the wandering priests of the Middle Ages, singing their irreverent songs, sought freedom from the rigidities of the Church; Galileo sought freedom to tell the truth of what he saw through his telescope; and so on, and on.

The human spirit, it seems, has always refused and will forever refuse to be bowed. This message would be powerful enough in itself as a means of closing the text, of ending the course. But there is more to the subject than to support the rights of human beings to carve out their own destinies. That we must, that we do, goes without saying. But there is a big question that still looms and that is hard to answer; and that is: *What case can be made for or against the belief that human beings are able to be, or want to be, free?* Liberation from oppression is always the first order of business; but this, having been brought about, may not guarantee freedom. This issue is the subject of the final chapter.

The subject of freedom, philosophically speaking, can be broken into an easily explained dichotomy. Do we have free will? Libertarians say yes. Are all our thoughts and actions determined by a long chain of cause and effect, perhaps beginning long before we were ever born? The determinists say yes. Or does the truth lie somewhere in between: despite genetics and all the conditioning factors that help to mold us, is at least a limited kind of "pure" freedom possible? Is this available to everyone, or just those who are willing to work for it?

**Checklist of Points or Discussion Topics from Text**

1. We might as well confess right off that the book has a bias toward free will as a commodity in limited supply, but very real nonetheless. However, anyone teaching it with a determinist persuasion will find a lot of material with which to work. There are, in fact, many more determinist than libertarian arguments around.

2. The first one we present is from Rousseau, and we call it *institutional* determinism, predicated on the philosopher's thesis that the entire system of laws and punishments was invented by society to defend itself against those who took advantage of the unlimited freedom people once enjoyed in a pristine state of nature. That system in place, people had to give up their freedom; and henceforth and forevermore the institutions of society determined human choice.

3. Next we consider Nietzsche's belief that human society is divided into two classes of people: masters and slaves. Your class is determined by your self-image, which in turn has been molded by a long succession of factors. If you are the child of masters, those who like to lead, be in charge, make the rules, you may become one yourself; or, having been made to feel inadequate, you may turn into a slave, someone who is more comfortable being led by others. Nietzsche's argument is not absolute determinism, but the philosopher does postulate that the majority of people prefer to be slaves.

4. The *economic* determinism of Marx, derived from the *historical* determinism of Hegel, is still important despite the demise of the Soviet Union. The failure of a particular kind of government and social structure does not "prove" that people are not driven by economic motives and do not fall into social classes determined by the natural dynamics of wealth and non-wealth. Whether the rich get richer and the poor, poorer without government intervention is still a viable topic of discussion, as is the question of whether we are unable to pursue higher concerns (like the humanities) only after our economic needs are satisfied.

5. Character consistency as a determining force. Can only the irrational, the erratic, the unpredictable be totally free?

6. And, of course, there is still *behaviorism*, by now a classic argument for determinism. It is a philosophy, centering on the belief that our will is shaped by positive or negative reinforcements of our behavior. As a psychology, it believes in behavioral modification techniques as means of changing socially undesirable types (like Alex in *A Clockwork Orange*) or curing us of eating disorders, substance addiction, and so on. You may want to ask the class to project both good and not-so-good possibilities of behaviorism.

7. Since we now know a great deal about the DNA and *genetic* conditioning, we also know either that all bets are off when it comes to the idea of "pure" freedom of will or that we have to accept the fact of an identity with all its genetic luggage as a given and *then* look at whether that new identity can ever be free or is continually being conditioned by other factors.

But students also like to discuss the "playing God" aspect of genetic engineering.

8. Now we come to the many fewer arguments for free will, beginning with *Schopenhauer*, who says we can see our wills objectified by the simple act of deciding to raise our arms or not. The power inherent in all living things to grow and develop and change he called will; and it is free almost by definition. Each of us is aware of the power to choose.

9. Next there is the *indeterminism* of William James, "guaranteed" by the emotions of regret and relief--the one experienced by looking back at wrong choices, the other at correct choices. If we were not aware of the freedom to choose, these emotions could not exist. Of course, you can always ask whether we feel regret *unnecessarily*, without realizing the wrong choice was the only choice.

10. Much of Freud's work is being questioned at the moment, but there is no way to ignore the impact of *psychoanalysis* as well as the staggering number of clinical cases in which patients have been freed from uncontrollable demons of the unconscious mind by being made to understand their source.

Freud is treated here as a philosopher who believed that *some* people are free: those who have not suppressed their guilt and fears.

11. For what it's worth, we finish up with our own modest theory of freedom through self-imposed limitations. That is, once we understand that conditioning factors may have led us to where we are, we can willfully decide to become our own conditioners, taking us to where we want to go. Or to put the matter another way: you can become aware of the power of your free will when you place yourself in opposition to a strong challenge, as when the jogger runs against the wind or bodily fatigue. This powerful push cannot come from any place but the jogger's own determination. Those who don't like to push, who back away from challenges, whose philosophy is to take life as it comes without worrying, and who still say they want to be free . . . THEY may have a hard time proving it's possible.

## Checklist of Discussion Points from Suggested Videotape "The World Was All Before Them"

1. Students have always enjoyed trying to guess who or what the narrator is. Frankly we're not sure ourselves. Is it God? Someone observing us from a distant planet? Someone else?

2. Henry Adams' "Chaos is the law of nature, order the dream of man" may have been amazingly prophetic, considering the gung-ho attitude about science in his time. Many scientists of today suspect that nature is indeed random, erratic, and without purpose.

3. The narrator's main purpose is to review the possible definitions of humanity, and see which ones, if any, work. A humanities course ought to be able to do the same thing.

4. Golding's *Lord of the Flies*. Is civilization just a thin facade, not the wondrous achievement humanities courses are supposed to show?

5. The narrator pays tribute to the human capacity for devising myths, especially the hero myth, but perhaps this is only a fantasy after all.

6. The narrator pays tribute to Einstein, and concedes that the species can indeed create genius. But then he is reminded of what others have done with nuclear power.

7. He says he is moved by what the great artists "among you" have done, but points out how many have been ignored or scorned in their lifetimes.

8. He reviews the goals of the behaviorists who, acknowledging human failings, are trying to create a better society, but he doubts they will succeed, because WHO can fully understand and say the last word about humanity, this baffling species, which has made so many tragic errors and so many false starts, YET WHICH SOMEHOW WILL NOT, CANNOT STAY DOWN, WHICH ALWAYS TRIES NEW BEGINNINGS THAT ARE PERHAPS ITS ONE GREAT STRENGTH. The narrator must close his report "without a final sentence." And so must we, because that sentence is up to the students we have been teaching.

## Alternate Strategies and Assignments

1. If you have a class that is particularly adventurous and doesn't mind some rigorous physical activity, have them arm wrestle or go outside and play tug-of-war or have footraces. Any of these sports can be a powerful means by which they experience their will and determination.

2. Test out the theory that all of our actions are ultimately determined by economic motives. Write on the board or hand out to students a list of actions, such as the following:

> proposing marriage
> choosing a college
> buying a new suit or dress
> ordering dinner in a French restaurant
> deciding where to spend a vacation
> deciding whether to fly or take a bus
> deciding which charity to support
> bottle-feeding the new baby
> repairing the old car
> encouraging Junior to be an athlete or a
> mathematician

Give the class fifteen minutes to write down an economic or noneconomic motive for what is done in each case.

## Suggested Essay Questions on Text

1. Is it true that, if you don't exploit others, someone will exploit you?

2. How important is money to you? Is it the basis of all or only some of your planning for the future? What other factors, if any, are involved? Can you say for certain that these are not somehow economic?

3. What is meant by the observation that only the insane are really free?

4. Do you have to be either a master or a slave? If you say no, how would you respond to a philosopher who argued that, if you refuse to be the master, you *must* be the slave?

5. Can you name three kinds of reinforcement, positive or negative, that were important in your development? As you take stock of where you are at present, would you say that they have played a part in shaping your character and directing your choices?

6. If you were the president and had to decide whether to sign a bill calling for federal funding of experimental behavioral engineering, would you do it?

7. What about experimental genetic engineering?

8. How might jogging help to suggest the possibility of free will?

**Journal Topics**

1. Rousseau's famous position was that, if it were not for the oppressive limitations imposed by social institutions, people would be naturally good and benevolent toward each other. Do you agree that in a state of nature, without any limitations, people would get along? Or is aggression inherent in human nature?

2. Are your tendencies predominantly master- or slave-oriented? Up to now, have you been a follower or a leader?

3. Does the demise of the Soviet Union indicate that Marx's philosophy of economic determinism is unsound or based on an inaccurate view of human behavior?

4. The text quotes B. F. Skinner and his reference to "the happy slave." What is his meaning? Do you in any way fall into that category?

5. The title of one of Skinner's most influential works is *Beyond Freedom and Dignity*. From what you have learned about his theories, explain this title.

6. The time may not be far off when genetic biologists will be able to alter human beings physically and mentally, so that they are in fact no longer themselves. Can you think of any reasons that would justify such actions?

7. Having read the final chapter and examined the arguments for and against free will, you are asked to declare yourself a determinist or a libertarian. Which one will it be?

8. The final chapter has little to do with artists, writers, or composers. What then what is it doing in a humanities text?

# A CHRONOLOGICAL INDEX

The authors wrote the text nonchronologically so that instructors would have a maximum of choice in their presentation of the material. But a historical perspective is possible. For this reason we are including an index of historical periods with a list of the figures treated within each, their dates, disciplines, and the chapters in which they can be found.

## 1ST CENTURY B.C.--2D CENTURY A.D.

New Testament Gospels; ch. 7, 12
Lucretius (94-55 B.C.); ch. 15
Epictetus (1st-2d centuries A.D.); ch. 13, 14, 15

## MIDDLE AGES

Saint Augustine (354-430); ch. 6, 8
Mohammed (570-632); ch. 7
Saint Thomas Aquinas (1225-1274); ch. 6, 8
Dante Alighieri (1265-1321); ch. 7, 14

## RENAISSANCE

Savonarola (1452-1498); ch. 7
Leonardo da Vinci (1452-1519); ch. 2
Niccolo Machiavelli (1469-1527); ch. 7
Michelangelo Buonarotti (1475-1564); ch. 2
Baldassare Castiglione (1478-1529); ch. 12
Raphael Santi (1483-1520); ch. 2

## 16th CENTURY

John Calvin (1509-1564); ch. 14

## 17th CENTURY, ART

Rembrandt van Rijn (1609-1669); ch. 2

## 17th CENTURY, DRAMA

William Shakespeare (1564-1616); ch. 4, 14, 15
Moliere (1622-1673); ch. 4
Jean Racine (1639-1699); ch. 4
William Wycherley (1640-1716); ch. 4
Jeremy Collier (1650-1726); ch. 7
William Congreve (1670-1729); ch. 12

## 17th CENTURY, LITERATURE

Miguel de Cervantes Saavedra (1547-1616); ch. 12
John Milton (1608-1674); ch. 11

## 17th CENTURY, PHILOSOPHY

Rene Descartes (1596-1650); ch. 6

## 17th CENTURY, SCIENCE

Sir Isaac Newton (1642-1727); ch. 15

## 18th CENTURY, ART

Francisco Goya (1746-1828); ch. 2

## 18th CENTURY, DRAMA

Richard B. Sheridan (1751-1816); ch. 4

## 18th CENTURY, LITERATURE

Jonathan Swift (1667-1745); ch. 4, 15
Alexander Pope (1688-1744); ch. 15
Voltaire (1694-1778); ch. 4

## 18th CENTURY, MUSIC

Johann Sebastian Bach (1685-1750); ch. 3
Franz Josef Haydn (1732-1809); ch. 3
Wolfgang Amadeus Mozart (1756-1791); ch. 3

## 18th CENTURY, PHILOSOPHY

George Berkeley (1685-1753); ch. 6
David Hume (1711-1776); ch. 6
Jean-Jacques Rousseau (1712-1778); ch. 16
Adam Smith (1723-1790); ch. 7
Immanuel Kant (1724-1804); ch. 6, 7
Jeremy Bentham (1748-1832); ch. 7

## 19th CENTURY, ART

J. M. W. Turner (1775-1851); ch. 15
Edouard Manet (1832-1883); ch. 2
James M. Whistler (1834-1903); ch. 2
Claude Monet (1840-1926); ch. 2
Edmonia Lewis (1844-?); ch. 10
Mary Cassatt (1845-1926); ch. 2
Paul Gauguin (1848-1903); ch. 2
Vincent van Gogh (1853-1890); ch. 2

## 19th CENTURY, DRAMA

Henrik Ibsen (1821-1906); ch. 4, 12
Oscar Wilde (1854-1900); ch. 4, 10, 12, 14
George Bernard Shaw (1856-1950); ch. 4, 12

## 19th CENTURY, FILM

Peter Mark Roget (1779-1869); ch. 5
Thomas A. Edison (1847-1931); ch. 5

## 19th CENTURY, LITERATURE

Johann Wolfgang von Goethe (1749-1832); ch. 14
William Wordsworth (1780-1850); ch. 15
George Gordon, Lord Byron (1788-1824); ch. 15
Percy Bysshe Shelley (1792-1822); ch. 14
Mary Wollstonecraft Shelley (1797-1851); ch. 15
Nathaniel Hawthorne (1804-1864); ch. 1
Hans Christian Andersen (1805-1875); ch. 11
Alfred, Lord Tennyson (1809-1892); ch. 14
Henry David Thoreau (1817-1862); ch. 15
Herman Melville (1819-1891); ch. 15
Walt Whitman (1819-1892); ch. 15
Gustave Flaubert (1821-1880); ch. 12
Count Leo Tolstoy (1828-1910); ch. 12
Emily Dickinson (1830-1886); ch. 12
Emile Zola (1840-1902); ch. 12
Thomas Hardy (1840-1928); ch. 14
Ambrose Bierce (1842-1914); ch. 14
Joseph Conrad (1857-1924); ch. 15
Edwin Arlington Robinson (1869-1935); ch. 14
Andre Gide (1869-1951); ch. 12
Stephen Crane (1871-1900); ch. 12

## 19th CENTURY, MUSIC

Ludwig van Beethoven (1770-1827); ch. 3
Franz Schubert (1797-1828); ch. 3
Giuseppe Verdi (1813-1901); ch. 3, 12
Johannes Brahms (1833-1897); ch. 3
Peter Ilich Tchaikovsky (1840-1893); ch. 3
Gustav Mahler (1860-1911); ch. 10
Alma Mahler (1879-1964); ch. 10

## 19th CENTURY, PHILOSOPHY

Arthur Schopenhauer (1788-1860); ch. 16
Ralph Waldo Emerson (1803-1882); ch. 15
John Stuart Mill (1806-1873); ch. 7
Soren Kierkegaard (1813-1855); ch. 7
Karl Marx (1818-1883); ch. 16
Friedrich Engels (1820-1895); ch. 16
William James (1842-1910); ch. 6, 16
Friedrich Nietzsche (1844-1900); ch. 1, 16

## 19th CENTURY, SCIENCE

Charles Darwin (1809-1892); ch. 6

## 20th CENTURY, ART

Piet Mondrian (1872-1944); ch. 2
Edward Hopper (1882-1967); ch. 2, 13
Diego Rivera (1886-1957); ch. 10
Marcel Duchamp (1887-1968); ch. 2
Georgia O'Keeffe (1887-1986); ch. 2
Salvador Dali (1904-1989); ch. 2
69th Regiment Armory Show, 1913
Frida Kahlo (1907-1954); ch. 10
Duane Hanson (b. 1925); ch. 2
Edward Kienholz (b. 1927); ch. 2
Claes Oldenburg (b. 1929); ch. 2
Andy Warhol (1930-1987); ch. 2
Christo (b. 1935); ch. 2

## 20th CENTURY, DRAMA

John Millington Synge (1871-1909); ch. 10
Eugene O'Neill (1888-1953); ch. 11, 14
Thornton Wilder (1897-1975); ch. 10, 14
Lillian Hellman (1905-1984); ch. 10
Clifford Odets (1906-1963); ch. 1
Tennessee Williams (1911-1983); ch. 1, 4
Arthur Miller (b. 1915); ch. 4, 10
Neil Simon (b. 1927); ch. 4

## 20th CENTURY, FILM

D. W. Griffith (1875-1948); ch. 5, 10
Mack Sennett (1884-1960); ch. 5
Louis B. Mayer (1885-1957); ch. 5
Charlie Chaplin (1889-1977); ch. 5
Frank Capra (1897-1991); ch. 5
Sergei Eisenstein (1898-1948); ch. 5, 10
Michael Curtiz (1898-1962); ch. 5
Humphrey Bogart (1899-1957); ch. 5
Gary Cooper (1901-1961); ch. 5
Leni Riefenstahl (b. 1902) ch. 5
Katharine Hepburn (b. 1909); ch. 5, 12
Orson Welles (1915-1985); ch. 5
Ingmar Bergman (b. 1918); ch. 5
Federico Fellini (b. 1920); ch. 5
Stanley Kubrick (b. 1928); ch. 5
Jean-Luc Godard (b. 1930); ch. 5
Woody Allen (b. 1935); ch. 5
Francis Ford Coppola (b. 1939); ch. 5

## 20th CENTURY, FILM (continued)

Oliver Stone (b. 1946); ch. 5
Eddie Murphy (b. 1961); ch. 5, 10
Spike Lee (b. 1957); ch. 10

## 20th CENTURY, LITERATURE

Virginia Woolf (1882-1941); ch. 10
A. E. Housman (1859-1936); ch. 1, 9
Carl Sandburg (1878-1967); ch. 15
D. H. Lawrence (1885-1930); ch. 12
James Thurber (1894-1961); ch. 14
Aldous Huxley (1894-1963); ch. 9
Ernest Hemingway (1899-1961); ch. 12, 14
Budd Schulberg (b. 1914); ch. 7
Anthony Burgess (b. 1917); ch. 15
Anne Sexton (1928-1974); ch. 14
Gabriel Garcia Marquez (b. 1928); ch. 12
Sylvia Plath (1932-1963); ch. 14
Isabel Allende (b. 1942); ch. 7

## 20th CENTURY, MUSIC

Claude Debussy (1862-1918); ch. 3
Richard Strauss (1864-1949); ch. 3
Ralph Vaughan Williams (1872-1958); ch. 15
Maurice Ravel (1875-1937); ch. 1, 3
Igor Stravinsky (1882-1971); ch. 3
Duke Ellington (1899-1974); ch. 3
Ferde Grofe (1892-1972); ch. 3
George Gershwin (1898-1937); ch. 3
Aaron Copland (1900-1990); ch. 3
Pete Seeger (b. 1911); ch. 10
Leonard Bernstein (1918-1990); ch. 3

## 20th CENTURY, PHILOSOPHY

Max Weber (1864-1930); ch. 8
Pierre Teilhard de Chardin (1881-1955); ch. 6
Susanne Langer (1895-1985); ch. 6
Mortimer Adler (b. 1902) ch. 6
Jean-Paul Sartre (1905-1980); ch. 7
Hannah Arendt (1906-1975); ch. 7
Albert Camus (1913-1960); ch. 14

## 20th CENTURY, POPULAR MEDIA

Jack Benny (1899-1974); ch. 10
Lucille Ball (1911-1988); ch. 4, 10
Bill Cosby (b. 1937); ch. 10

## 20th CENTURY, PSYCHOLOGY AND PSYCHOANALYSIS

Sigmund Freud (1856-1939); ch. 11, 16
Carl Jung (1875-1961); ch. 11
Bruno Bettelheim (1903-1990); ch. 8, 11
B. F. Skinner (1904-1991); ch. 16

## 20th CENTURY, SCIENCE

Albert Einstein (1879-1955); ch. 6
Rachel Carson (1907-1964); ch. 15

## ON THE REALITY OF THE BEAUTIFUL

by

Donald M. Early

Humankind, says contemporary depth psychology, has an innate capacity to apprehend the beautiful. But what does this mean? To apprehend means "to become aware of, to perceive; to recognize the meaning of . . ." A capacity that is innate must be one that is universal, present everywhere, in every culture. And anthropology does indeed confirm that no human group exists that does not have some form of art--does not both "apprehend the beautiful" and practice it too, by creating some form of beauty of its own.

How shall we explain this phenomenon? Shall we look to psychology for the answer, since it tells us so much about the hidden processes of our minds? No, for both Freud and Jung declare that "psychoanalysis has nothing to say about aesthetics," and that "the problem can never be the object of psychological, but only of an aesthetic-artistic method of approach." It would appear then that the answer lies much deeper, in more ancient soil--in our biology, in the very nature and structure of the world itself.

No one will deny that the world is beautiful. Daily and nightly, season by season, creation unfolds its inexhaustible splendors. And we in our humdrum lives, while unmindful of its beauty, tend to notice it only at favored moments, when we experience beauty as an event: a sunset, a snowfall, the sound of wind and water, the sight and perfume of an orchard in bloom. Yet, the pageant of beauty never pauses, never diminishes, even when we do not attend it. "The Rainbow comes and goes/And lovely is the Rose," the poet would have us remember.

The crucial question seems to be this: is beauty in the thing we behold, or is it in the eye of the beholder? "Is the birdsong in the tree, or in me?" we ask. The philosopher in us may find the question intriguing (remember the old classroom puzzle: if a tree falls in the forest and no one is there to hear it, is there a sound?); but the poet in us may already know the answer.

Surely the world was beautiful long before human eyes were there to witness it. Picture how many eons Earth must have spun in its azure envelope of light in space before the moonshot showed us its breathtaking splendor. Then consider the case of flowers. Loren Eiseley, in his book *The Immense Journey*, tells us that the flowering world as we know it came into being at the same time as the first mammals. Suddenly, it seems, in what can only be described as a veritable explosion of life, incredible numbers of flowering plants appeared, filling the atmosphere with their perfumes, blooming with a prodigality that cannot possibly be accounted for in terms of survival value alone. Such exuberance, proliferating in an infinite variety of beautiful forms and colors, was far in excess of nature's extravagant requirements for preservation. Was this simultaneous advent of flowers and mammals purely coincidental--or were the two related? Can it be that nature, having produced creatures of a higher order capable of perceiving the results, was then inspired to a frenzy of artistic creation--for the sheer joy of virtuosity, for the sheer beauty of it?

Is there, one wonders, a principle in nature that eludes us? Can beauty be a force, a law, a condition of the created world--like gravitation? The scientist may shy away from the idea, but the aesthetician, who studies the nature of the beautiful, and the artist who strives to create the beautiful, will not. Both are convinced that they work according to certain laws of nature, of reality, of their own being; both believe that they are as much in pursuit of Truth as the scientist.

The problem leads back to ourselves, of course. We are creatures of the universe, and whatever universal laws exist must be as evident in us as anywhere else in the cosmos. What then are the laws that guide us in our apprehension of beauty, in the creation of beautiful forms, colors, sounds, odors, sensations?

One of these is the law of sexuality. Beauty attracts, draws us toward a union with itself, whether it be beauty of body, mind, or spirit. In the presence of beauty we are as lovers; and we may find ourselves as dazzled, as swept with delight or terror, as if we were in the throes of a powerful passion. The element of sexuality can never be wholly absent from any experience of beauty. What Nietzsche sagely remarked of the individual can be said as well of the race: "The degree and kind of a person's sexuality reaches up into the ultimate pinnacle of his spirit." This must not be taken to mean that a work of divine aspiration, such as Chartres Cathedral, has overt erotic intent; nothing would be more absurd. Yet the purpose of this great work of art *is* to lead the worshiper through avenues of beauty--some of the sense, others of the spirit--to an eventual union with God.

Nature's laws, says the noted art critic Herbert Read, are the touchstone for all human creativity, though he warns: "We must understand by nature not any vague pantheistic spirit, but the measurements and physical behavior of matter in any process of growth or transformation. The seed that becomes a flowering plant, the metal that crystallizes as it cools and contracts, all such processes exhibit laws, which are modes of material behavior. There is no growth which is not accompanied by its characteristic form, and I think we are so constituted--are so much in sympathy with natural processes--that we always find such form beautiful."

When man creates a work of beauty, he does so intuitively, according to these laws. The "rules" of a work of art are the proportions and rhythms inherent in the universe. The artist perceives these, usually more clearly than the rest of us, though his perceptions may not always be conscious ones. "Artists," explains Read, "are to a considerable degree automata . . . that is, they unwittingly transmit in their works a sense of scale, proportion, symmetry, balance, and other abstract qualities which they have acquired through their purely visual and therefore physical response to the natural environment."

Another critic put it this way: "Things take on the life of their creators, but their spirit derives from a common source which goes back to the origins of the universe, of mankind, of our respective civilizations, back to our birth and are constantly revitalized with the dawn of each new day."

Too many of us have minds so clogged with the impediments of a banal culture, our vision so clouded with falsely ordered impressions, that we have lost the habit of responding spontaneously to aesthetic experience. We have grown dull to what Bernard Berenson calls "the aesthetic moment, that flitting instant, so brief as to be almost timeless, when the spectator . . . ceases to be his ordinary self, and the picture or building, statue, landscape, or aesthetic actuality is no longer outside himself. . . . The two become one entity; time and space are abolished and the spectator is possessed by one awareness." Our lack of awareness of the aesthetic moment is in part the result of our technological culture, our scientific approach to the world. We are conditioned to think analytically, to look for the *elements* of a thing and not at the *thing* itself. The psychologist will tell us that we have emphasized the function of the left (analytical) lobe of the brain to the neglect of that of the right lobe, which perceives things whole. Whatever the cause, true aesthetic experience can come about only when our responses are not impeded by "thinking too precisely upon the event." Beauty asks for a spontaneous union; and when too many clauses and conditions invest the contract, the marriage does not take place.

Spontaneity, however, in no way precludes a knowledge of those natural laws that inform the aesthetic moment. Paleolithic man was not without a canon of esthetics; he already had a highly sophisticated understanding of his art. Indeed, the renowned paleontologist Abbe Breuil speculates that "there were colleges of artists, far from each other, but subject to the conventions and same fashions . . . institutions which directed and . . . created uniformity of expressions." Remains of sketchbooks--bone fragments covered with thousands of beginners' "life studies"-- have been found which lend support to this scholar's assumption.

So the call is not to "return to the primitive" in order to clarify our vision and see things fresh. Quite the reverse. "It takes a mature mind and a great deal of living," says Bruno Bettelheim, "to bear in oneself a vision of the better world for which the real artist (paleolithic or modern) is striving and then embodies in aesthetic form." Growth's direction is always forward, not backward. But growth demands effort; and the man who would have time for beauty must make the effort to get in touch with himself.

A noted architect who designs structures of extraordinary "rightness" has this to say of his own self-awareness: "The pleasurable intensity of my responses to certain buildings, seen for the first time, suggests to me that they must somehow correspond to a model which already exists deep inside me. How else can I account for the sensation so much closer to recognition than to discovery? This, I believe, is the revelation of the self to the self."

The artist who sees more "rightly" than the rest of us helps us to remedy our defective vision, to sharpen our aesthetic sensibilities, to respond more intuitively and *truthfully* to the world of beauty around us. Who, one wonders, every saw--*really* saw--a sunflower, until van Gogh showed us what a sunflower looks like?

We learn, we grow, we increase in awareness and spirit to the degree that we harmonize with nature--all nature--our own most of all. Too many of us lead lives that are discordant, having no real time for beauty . . .

The story is told of a man who died and came before God. And the Creator of the Universe, looking down, inquired, "Well, what did you think of my little world?" The man was silent. "Didn't you find it beautiful?" urged the Questioner. Finally, ashamed to raise his head, the man replied, "I didn't really notice, Lord . . . I never seemed to have the time . . ."

How very sad.

## MASKS: THE KINSHIP OF TRAGEDY AND COMEDY

by

Donald M. Early

Sometimes we will say of a situation: "This would be funny if it weren't so tragic." Sometimes it is the other way round; we think: "This really is tragic, I suppose; but it's all so grotesque and improbable that I want to laugh." Each of us knows these ambivalent moments, when our emotions stand perplexed between two extremes. They seem to occur to remind us again how thin a line separates the tragic and the comic in human life.

The truth is, though we *do* on occasion recognize the ambivalent relationship of tragedy and comedy, our habit is to *think* of them as polarities, opposites, as separate masks experience chooses to wear--now one, now the other--to personify the darker and lighter aspects of the human drama. Objective truth, however, perceives a much more intimate, subtle, and troubling relationship between the two; and here seems the proper place for us to examine that relationship more closely.

> "To know what is serious
> we must also know what
> is laughable."
> --Socrates

We begin with tragedy. The tragedy in life is death. We all know that we must die; this inescapable conclusion permeates the whole of human existence and gives it its somber undertone. It is a thing that cannot be laughed away; it is there. So we begin with that.

If death supplies the ground bass of existence, then the life force is its melody; and the product of their harmonies, their total music, is what concerns us here: the Largo *and* the Scherzo.

The Greeks, who invented the art form of tragedy, never assumed that tragedy told the whole story. They required that each tragic presentation be followed by a comedy, or satyr play, that made irreverent fun of the somber events just enacted. The satyr play said: "Yes, yes, all that is so, and it's grave indeed; but it's funny too. Those pompous gods strutting about, treating men like flies, those blustering heroes daring fate to do its worst! Why all this self-importance? Why can't they relax, enjoy their ambrosia, or their beans and garlic, and make love, and have a good sleep?"

There is nothing in life, or art--or religion, for that matter--that does not also have its comic side. During the Middle Ages, at Carnival time, Christian worshipers celebrated something they called the Ass's Mass. It took place in church, before the altar, where an ass was made to officiate at this most sacred rite. A parody of the Mass was sung, and the faithful brayed their responses: "Hee haw!"

Blasphemous, surely! But it was not thought so, nor was it intended to be. It simply acknowledged that men were but fools in the eyes of God . . . that nothing that miserable humans could do, even in the service of God, was free from sin and the ludicrous. The Ass's Mass served to set man's state in proper perspective, and the comic view of life does it all the time.

William Hazlitt reminds us: "It is a common mistake to suppose that parodies degrade or imply a stigma on the subject; on the contrary, they in general imply something serious or sacred in the originals."

Comedy admires the noble truths of tragedy. It only asks to be allowed to comment as cogently, sharply, even painfully, as needed, in order that the whole truth can emerge and be confirmed. Sometimes, however, comedy cuts so close to the bone of the serious that the truth is too painful to accept. Since it won't go away, it must be subtly transformed, its features made to express what we want them to. Such enforced transformations can be observed in the case of certain works of art whose original intention made people uncomfortable. Chekhov's plays are an example. Chekhov wrote what he insisted were comedies. No one, however, wanted to see them that way: not directors, or critics, or audiences; the plays were "tragic." Now it is true that the characters in Chekhov's major plays *do* see themselves as tragic--but they *aren't*; and that was exactly Chekhov's point. They are poor, bumbling fools who get themselves into ruinous tangles through their own misapprehensions. But so do we, in *real* life. When this truth is exposed, we choose to ignore it, and to see the whole muddle as noble suffering.

Or take the case of Schubert's "Serenade"--one of the best-loved songs in music. We are told that Schubert wrote it somewhat with tongue in cheek, depicting with gentle amusement the extravagant passion of the lovelorn swain. To us latter-day romantics, however, the song isn't at all like that; we hear in its aching strains the very soul of love's longing.

Something similar has occurred with one of Mozart's songs. In the opera *Cosi fan tutti*, two male characters, bereft of their sweethearts, sing of their yearning in a duet. One of the lovers, however, is hungry, and images of food and love get mixed up in the number. The situation invites our laughter. But so beautiful is the music, so meltingly, yearningly sweet, that we cannot respond to it as comedy. We may be moved--to tears, perhaps, but never to laughter.

"Something inside of comedy isn't funny," says Walter Kerr. That "something" is what probes our weaknesses, exposing our peccadilloes and crimes. It also seems bent on exposing our gross subservience to our body's demands--the grumbling stomach, the nagging thirst, the involuntary erection, the need to defecate--even though we try to pretend we're "above" those things. Comedy loves to haul up our bestial origins, our vulnerability, our very mortality for inspection. "Here's what you really are," it says. But often there is no rejoicing on comedy's part. It would rather not have seen the truth; it turns aside--sadly.

Probably nowhere is comedy's ambivalence more clearly epitomized than in the complex image of the clown. The clown, at first glance, seems a figure designed for unalloyed laughter. He has a funny painted face that masks his true features; he wears a ludicrous assortment of hand-me-downs; indulges in slapstick, plays the fall-guy shamelessly, is scorned, tricked, and beaten till he weeps. All of which we think marvelously funny, because, thank God, he isn't us. He isn't our kind, but a different breed, and we can safely make him the butt of our jokes, the scapegoat for our embarrassing failures. Being "outside," he doesn't matter to those "inside."

But something then enters the picture here. The fact that the clown *is* outside puts him in position to view, with disturbing clarity, the actions of those on the inside. God, too, it must be remembered, judges from "outside." So we have to look carefully at what the clown's antics are saying. His crudeness and obscenity--do they pointedly comment on our own? Does he ape us in order to illustrate our own apishness? Is his slyness aimed at exposing our duplicities? When he plays the wretch and whipping boy, is he not acting out our own ignoble self-pity when we think ourselves victims of a malicious universe?

On the other hand, isn't the clown's dog-like love for the beautiful bareback rider, his hopeless dream of enfolding that tinseled loveliness in his arms--isn't that telling us, also, that he understands our impossible desire for the ideal, and shares our despair? Doesn't it seem that at heart he, too, yearns for the beauty, the truth, the perfection that humankind envisions?

Marcel Marceau, the famous French mime, does a scene of a man trying on a series of masks. No actual masks are used, of course; he does it all with that marvelously expressive painted face. One by one he tries them on and removes them, till the comic mask is donned. It won't come off. Embarrassed attempts, then desperate struggles fail. Finally, the truth sinks in, displaying only the agony of the man behind the mask--an agony that will go on and on . . .

Something of this tragic predicament is the clown's. The artist Georges Rouault, who painted such moving, suffering Christs in his stark, stained-glass manner, also painted clowns that were even more shattering in their impact. Another painter, a contemporary named Jonah Kingstein, has done a work he calls "Christ Among the Clowns." It shows the crucified Savior and two grotesque figures flanking the cross. Their clawlike hands reach toward the lacerated flesh. In anger, derision, suffering, love? It must be love--all the wretched, warped, and despairing love of the world, caught in one terrible tragic-comic moment: both mystery and revelation.

Apparently it is this kind of epiphany that certain Christian churches are now seeking by introducing the concept of "God's Fool" into their services. A lay group that calls itself "Clowns for Christ," made up mostly of young people, uses painted faces, mime, and music routines to teach the gospel lessons. Though this kind of evangelism may strike many people as strange, it is not new--as we know from our medieval account. Its very strangeness is doubtless its strength, perhaps jolting people into a new perception of life, where the visions of tragedy and comedy can merge in a single message.

## A CONFLICT FOR ALL SEASONS

by

Joan Cronin

In Western culture a faith/reason dualism appears to have emerged for the first time in the 5th century when St. Augustine attempted to reconcile the fact of evil in the world with Christian belief in a benevolent God. It is a question that has since preoccupied most of the major religions of the world. Briefly stated: we observe that pain, death, earthquake, injustice, and cruelty do exist in the world. If God were all-good, He would not *will* these to be; if He were all powerful, He would not *allow* them to be. Augustine offered a solution in rational terms: evil does not have actual existence; it is the absence of good, but man is free to choose the good. Therefore, the responsibility for evil in the world is man's, not God's.

But part of the problem of evil could not be solved by rational analysis. Augustine taught that God preordained certain individuals to repent and be saved, and others to suffer their just punishment. But a troubling question arises: how can man choose freely if his choice is predestined? Augustine's answer was that the mystery of grace and redemption as revealed in the Holy Scripture is a matter of faith and cannot be rationally understood. The limitation this placed on reason has powerfully influenced religious thought down to our own century; but the enigmas of evil and the suffering of the innocent continue to challenge both faith and reason.

While faith continued for centuries to be an essential source of truth in Christian thought, events in the secular world could not but introduce change in the religious experience. In the 8th century, western Europe was united under Charlemagne in a single Christian empire. Until this time, monasteries had been the only centers of learning, and their purpose had been limited to educating the clergy. In 787 Charlemagne ordered the establishment of schools in connection with every abbey in the realm. Great scholars came together at these schools, and learning took on a far more speculative nature than would have been congenial in the monasteries. An interest in logic and rational values grew up side by side with, but independent of, a reliance on revelation. The minds of Christians became increasingly critical. Attempts to see the universe as intelligible were accompanied by an insistence that God too must be intelligible by reason as well as by faith.

The term "scholasticism" is given to the intellectual movement begun in these abbey schools. The unique characteristics of scholastic thought is that it was able to harmonize faith and reason as compatible sources of knowledge, resting on one absolute truth that transcended both. The scholastic thinkers, by pushing back the limits formerly set on reason, were responsible for the rebirth of philosophy, which had disappeared from European thought since the closing of the philosophical schools of Athens in 529.

In the 13th century, St. Thomas Aquinas represented a synthesis of theology and philosophy that unified medieval thought on every subject of inquiry, natural or supernatural. Aquinas taught that there are mysteries--like the nature of God--that cannot be understood by reason; they are made manifest only by divine revelation and apprehended only by faith. However, he believed that the *existence* of God could be demonstrated by logical inference from the operation of the natural world.

It was also believed that, if the human mind could comprehend God's existence, it could easily comprehend the natural world as well. For Aquinas, reason could not help affirming the existence of a marvelously designed natural universe, one that the Greek astronomer Ptolemy had incorrectly viewed as geocentric.

The earth had been created by God at the very center of the universe, as a fitting home for man, whom He had made in His own image and likeness. Man's whole dignity lay in his crucial position: only one degree below God's angels. The geocentric system of astronomy also provided a model for all the hierarchies of medieval society. The church, society, the natural world were seen as systems in which authority descended from God in fixed and strictly ordered degrees. Thus did reason and faith appear to join forces--to explain both worlds.

Yet out of the synthesis emerged the scientific movement, almost inevitably. Curiosity over the workings of the beautiful design proved irresistible. In 1473 a Polish astronomer named Nicholas Copernicus was born. He was to formulate the theory that the *sun* was at the center of the universe, with earth merely one of the planets revolving around it. Later, in the 17th century Galileo was able to demonstrate the theory with more of science's technology at hand.

Galileo developed a telescope powerful enough to permit observation of the satellites revolving around the planet Jupiter. He recognized in this phenomenon a miniature system that substantiated the Copernican heliocentric theory.

Galileo was forbidden by Pope Paul V to teach or to defend his discovery, but in 1623 he published it in his "Dialogue on the Two Greatest Systems of the Universe," which compare the Ptolemaic and Copernican theories. Galileo was summoned before the Inquisition and condemned as "vehemently suspected of heresy." Under a probable fear of torture he recanted his statements but was sentenced to involuntary confinement to his home. He gradually went blind, but even so, he continued his scientific activity as long as he could.

Galileo's great contribution to the scientific movement was the application of mathematical formulas to a direct observation of nature. He was the first to interpret the heavens as a mechanical system, preparing the way for the Newtonian world view that dominated the 17th and 18th centuries.

Synthesizing the discoveries made from the time of Copernicus to his own age, Newton described an intelligible and orderly physical universe, working with predictable perfection, the so-called World Machine. He discovered the laws of gravitation, light, and motion, but viewed the order in the universe as an indication of the existence of God.

Newton did not believe that his description of the universe was complete, but it was accepted in the following century as a total theory of nature and the God of nature. Eighteenth-century deism was a scientifically oriented religion that held God to be a detached, impersonal power which had created the world, given it physical laws that it might govern itself with perfect regularity, and then withdrawn--never again to interfere with its workings. The most significant aspect of 18th-century philosophy was that these laws of nature were discovered not through revelation but this time by the *exclusive* exercise of human reason.

By the 19th century the discoveries in astronomy, geology, archaeology, and biology were vigorously reinforcing the sovereignty of reason and science. The tenets of old faiths seemed to collapse as even spiritual truths were tested by the language and methods of science. In opposition to the overwhelming impact of science on religion, an intense revival of faith occurred.

In England the revival manifested itself in the Oxford Movement within the Anglican Church. John Henry Newman was one of the central figures in this movement, which was also called "Tractarianism," from the series of ninety tracts published to express its religious views. Believing that reason could not prevent the onslaught of science on religion, Newman urged a return to the dogmatic authority of the Church fathers, to the Bible as a source of revealed truth, and to the medieval color of religious ritual.

Newman especially urged resistance to the exclusive application of reason to religious teaching. Eventually this position was rejected as too conservative for others in the Anglican Church, and Newman believed that the Anglican Church was too liberal for him to find religious certainty in it. He entered the Roman Catholic priesthood and in 1879 became Cardinal.

Newman's contemporary, Thomas Henry Huxley, on the other hand, defended the view that religious truth had to pass the test of scientific thinking. Huxley coined the word "agnostic" to describe his own position: that of one who did not know whether or not God existed. When rational inquiry fails to provide evidence for a belief, Huxley said, the honest course is to suspend judgment rather than to assent on the basis of blind faith. Huxley was a staunch supporter of Charles Darwin in the 19th century's most dramatic conflict between science and faith.

Darwin's theory of biological evolution, published in *On the Origin of Species* in 1859, produced an uproar in European society. Darwin advanced the belief that all forms of life, including the human, have developed from more primitive forms; that chance variations made it possible for some forms to survive the struggle for existence; and that these variations were inherited by descendants. This theory was attacked as a sacrilegious contradiction of revealed truth about the dignity of man and his purpose in the world. People were not prepared to see themselves as descendants of brute beasts in a universe governed by blind change.

Where Newton had been able to reconcile the results of his scientific investigations with the prevalent ethical and religious beliefs of this time, Darwin could not. The conflict reached a climax in 1925 in the trial of John Scopes, a Tennessee schoolteacher. Scopes was arrested for breaking the state law against teaching the theory of evolution. He was defended by Clarence Darrow, a famous attorney who championed freedom of speech and inquiry. The prosecutor was William Jennings Bryan, a former presidential candidate who held firm religious views on the literal interpretation of the biblical account of creation. Scopes was found guilty and fined, but it was not a defeat for Darwin's theory. Darwin had been honored by many of the learned societies of Europe. His ideas were widely influential among scientific thinkers, and many people had come to see in the concept of evolution a promise of unlimited human and material progress.

Today, however, the situation has almost reversed itself; there is a growing distrust of the autonomy of reason and an upsurge in religious faith. Science, many feel, is propelling us not toward a golden age of humanity but toward a technological nightmare. In the early 19th century the poet William Blake expressed his fear that the visionary imagination would be sacrificed in the "dark Satanic mills" of the Industrial Revolution. To many there is ample cause to fear the sacrifice of human values to scientific abstractions. When science insists that the end justifies the means and at the same time divorces itself from a moral responsibility rooted in faith, some argue, the research on human guinea pigs at Buchenwald is made possible; and the holocausts of Nagasaki and Hiroshima, not to mention the agony of Vietnam, become "rational" ways of solving human problems.

# CURRENTS FROM EASTERN WATERS

by

## Joan Cronin

## CONTRASTS IN CONSCIOUSNESS

The culture traditionally considered Western inherits--from classical Greece and the Old Testament--an underlying concept of duality in all existence. God and man are separate realities, as are man and nature, body and mind. In like fashion our individual egos separate us from other people and give each of us a sense of uniqueness. We take pride in the progress made possible by our rational intelligence: the conquest of disease, the harnessing of natural power, the steadily expanding system of information about the universe. And we write books and erect monuments to live after us in defeat of death and oblivion.

Buddhism sees life and death as part of the continuous flow of existence. It denies that there is any duality. There is only existence, and it is totally present in every manifestation of being, whether it is a man or a bird or a pebble in the stream. Buddhism offers a unifying vision, reached by quieting the busy ego-mind and attaining intuitive sources of wisdom. What is important is not to seek success but to live in the present moment with total awareness, to accept with quiet mind whatever is.

This apparent emphasis on passivity and this refusal to deify the rational mind or to engage in competitive striving seems uncomfortable to many energetic Westerners; yet many others claim to have found in the Buddhist approach a source of tranquility, self-acceptance, and enhanced awareness even as they continue to lead busy, active lives. They believe it is possible to effect a synthesis of both Buddhist and Western orientations to life.

## THE TAO

Another unifying concept central to much Eastern culture is contained in Taoism, a philosophy that originated in China in the 6th century before Christ and has influenced the thinking of a number of American writers and artists.

*Tao* is almost impossible to translate in words. It means something like the Way, a formless, eternal principle that flows through all existence and in which all things participate. The Tao is not a thing, but it is not nothingness either.

The joyous life is one lived in harmony with the Tao. This quality of existence is achieved by the practice of *wu wei*, which is a state of quietude that is not really inactive but a source of creative energy. The Chinese philosopher Lao-Tzu (who is credited with founding Taoism and writing the *Tao Te Ching*, sometimes translated as *The Way of Power*), made an analogy between this state of *wu wei* and the qualities we are all familiar with in water. Water effortlessly bears things up and carries them along. One who understands the Tao knows that it, like water, will sustain him if he does not flail about and revel against the fundamental order of things. Like the Tao, the gentle power of water can smooth rocks into pebbles and melt away mountains. In the social order, leaders who have mastered this gentle power can rule without force or strident argument. Finally, water attains clarity by standing still, permitting debris to settle. Thus one does well to wait in quiet for mental distractions to dissipate if one would finally attain clear consciousness.

To the Taoist, assertiveness and competition go counter to the Way. We would not be aggressive toward other people, or toward the natural world, if we followed the Tao in which all participate. This feeling for the totality of existence had a strong influence on the landscape painters of the Sung period in medieval China, and its influence continues among many modern artists. In such paintings the human figures blend quietly with the natural background and are very small in the overall perspective. A general mistiness often obliterates the distinctions between forms, and everything flows together with the utmost harmony.

## HINDUISM: OLD AND NEW

The concept of Tao is expressed as Dharma in both Hinduism and Buddhism. Here too it signifies a universal order. But for the Hindu this order was not always a source of joy and well-being as it was for the Taoist. In the earlier history of India, the idea of Dharma operating in the social order permitted the development of a rigid caste system. The highest castes kept as their privileged possession the sacred writings that taught the Way of justice and virtue. Thus the lower castes could not know what they needed to, in order to avoid wrongdoing. To work off the consequences of their inevitable errors, they saw themselves doomed to an endless series of reincarnations, in each lifetime suffering the consequences of the previous one and accumulating more Karma (the inescapable effects of deeds). They longed to be released from the painful round of life, death, and rebirth; to be absorbed in nirvana, into Brahman, the eternal World Soul. But there was an element of near hopelessness in early Hinduism, for such release could be attained only by the elite castes, and it might take an ordinary person eons of time to work his way up from one lifetime to another.

However, important changes took place in Hinduism in more recent times. During the 19th century, a reform movement known as Ramakrishna began in India. It combined a mystical faith with active concern for human needs. The Ramakrishna group has been responsible for the building of orphanages, hospitals, schools, and universities; it now has work centers all over India and in many of the world's great cities. Mahatma Gandhi, the chief figure of modern Hinduism, exemplifies in his life the doctrine of nonviolence and the social concern implicit in the Ramakrishna movement.

The Hindu belief that desire, the cause of suffering, is the fruit of ignorance was absorbed into Buddhism, which was founded by Siddhartha Gautama in the 6th century before Christ. But Gautama's experience of enlightenment brought to Buddhism a far more optimistic possibility: nirvana is attainable, at least theoretically, for everyone, for the knowledge of the Dharma is revealed not in sacred writings but in meditation on the Four Noble Truths and Holy Eightfold Path, which is really a practical course in systematic habit formation. It has been called the path of common sense, in which one avoids suffering by choosing the middle way between the extremes, for instance, of self-indulgence and self-denial. Through meditation and following the way of the Buddha Dharma, even the simplest person could hope to achieve enlightenment, that is, nirvana.

## BUDDHISM: HINAYANA AND MAHAYANA

However, in practice it was not always so. The earliest form of Buddhism, called the Hinayana, or Narrow Path, taught that nirvana could be attained only if one became a monk, for it was thought impossible to meditate and follow the Path while living an active life in the world, which was full of distractions and temptations. Thus again nirvana was possible only for a limited number, and for them nirvana meant personal salvation with no active concern for the welfare of others.

The Mahayana, or Broad Path, a later form of Buddhism still practiced in both East and West, asserts that salvation (enlightenment) is universally attainable. One who seeks Buddha-mind need not be a monk, but can hope to attain enlightenment while living the everyday life of the world. At one stage a Bodhisattva (or future Buddha) becomes a "great cosmic helper," dedicated to helping mankind to find release. In this way Mahayana Buddhism contains a more humane ethic than Hinayana, and at the heart of that ethic is the quality of compassionate detachment. A Buddhist's conduct--toward himself or his environment or the people he lives and works among--is measured by this quality, for without it, it is impossible to follow the Eightfold Path to enlightenment.

## ZEN

Zen is a form of Buddhism that places very strong emphasis on intensive long periods of meditation as the gateway to the harmony of the Way. By learning through discipline to free the mind of ego-distraction and drawing upon the intuitive wisdom everyone is born with, one can learn to live, attentive to what is going on in the reality of the moment. Some schools of Zen insist upon an almost monastic withdrawal for meditation, but throughout the West there has been a growth of Zen centers, where people live and meditate together, even while holding a variety of jobs outside.

## THE JAPANESE SENSE OF THE BEAUTIFUL

The meditative approach to life that attracts so many people in the West has also produced a uniquely Japanese sense of the beautiful that is evident in many aspects of life. The tea ceremony (known as Cha No Ya or The Way of Tea) is both a meditative and an esthetic experience. It was designed some five hundred years ago by Rikuyo as a way of harmonizing his practical business mind with the awareness he achieved in sitting meditation. The tea ceremony remains much the same today as Rikuyo created it.

When a guest enters the tea hut, he finds tranquil refreshment for each of his senses. He is greeted by a subtle aroma of incense, a sound of water boiling, a beautiful vase or a simple flower arrangement in a corner. Host and guest bow respectfully. The host prepares the tea, and they sip it, savoring its delicacy.

Like all Japanese meals, tea is taken slowly and quietly, and flavors are subtle, even bland. It is not at all like an American meal, where, ideally, brilliant table talk and well-defined flavors create a bright, exciting atmosphere. The host and guests may remain silent throughout the Japanese tea ceremony, or they may converse quietly, admiring some beautiful object in the room like the bowl in which the tea is served. The beauty of the object may not be immediately apparent; the tea bowl may be a plain old one, cracked and mended with gold. What makes it precious is the quality of *Sabi*, a preference for what is simple, even poor, over the pretentious and luxurious. Sabi involves too an awareness of the perishableness of all things. The old tea bowl is beautiful because it speaks of our mortality, and does so with concrete immediacy.

Japanese art forms, like the *Haiku* (a short verse form) and the traditional brush painting, also illustrate the tranquil, meditative approach to life. The Haiku poet is confined to exactly seventeen syllables; he writes of a fragmentary, fleeting moment and relies on a minute concrete detail to communicate somehow the totality of the experience. To appreciate such stark simplicity requires a willingness in the reader to admit that more exists than can ever be put into words. The poet Basho writes of his desire to make the deepest possible contact with the very center of life. To do this, he felt, one must observe minute aspects of things in nature, the seen and the heard, as if there were no separation between them and himself.

Japanese brush painting has many of the qualities of the Haiku. In a few swift strokes the artist may depict a bird or a snow-laden branch. That is all of the picture. The viewer is invited to participate with his or her imagination, to create with the artist. The effect in both these art forms is one of spontaneity and spaciousness, of essential truth caught with the greatest simplicity and directness.

The visitor to a Japanese garden finds a similar experience. A mood of meditative quiet is achieved by the apparently artless arrangement of a single tree, a rock, a slow drip of water from a bamboo pipe. The imagination is given infinite space to create the whole forest, the mountain, the waterfall. No brilliant flower beds distract the eye or the mind. Simplicity, naturalness, a sense of space and tranquility achieved with apparently effortless ease are all qualities that contrast sharply with the ideal of beauty one would find in the formal gardens of Europe, where the visitor's eye is regaled with avenues of statues, polite flower beds, and sculptured shrubbery. At Versailles, for instance, one feels that beauty is achieved by the construction of sharply defined areas, not by the experience of space.

Generally speaking, then, the Japanese attitude toward beauty shares with the meditative approach to life a feeling for quiet harmony with the natural world, for the reality contained in each brief moment and for the mystery underlying existence that cannot be rationally apprehended.

Tea and Tantra
Tea Ceremony is a journey into ourselves--in and out again.
We travel alone with others also alone. We bow, we bend. Bowing
"In Tea" is not just a matter of politeness. It is a way of
yielding to the mystery of being human.

Milly Johnstone

Winter desolation;
In a world of one color.
The sound of the wind.
Basho

If man were never to fade away like
the dews of Adahino, never to vanish
like the smoke over Torobeyana, but
linger on forever in the world, how
things would lose their power to move
us! The most precious thing in life
is its uncertainty.

Kendo


The way of Haiku arises
from concentration and lack
of distraction. Look well
within yourself.

Basho

## FREEDOM AND HUMANISM

by

### Donald M. Early

The conviction persists that freedom and humanity are somehow inseparably linked, and that we cannot hope to understand ourselves until we have some understanding of their relationship. We ask, "Am I free to direct my life, make choices that are genuinely mine, make moral decisions that affect not only me and those about me, but possibly the larger cosmos as well? Or am I without any true volition, simply the tool of destiny . . . perhaps no more than a creature of blind chance?"

Any assumptions we make in these matters--and they can only be assumptions--are of prime importance, for ultimately they affect what meaning, if any, we discover in human life, and in our separate existence.

If we take the position of the determinist, we will say that individuals are *not* free in any way, that the whole enterprise (of which each is the minutest part) is out of their hands. The universe is a system of inflexible laws, and every particle of matter, every spark of life, every thought, every act is nothing but a reflex of those laws. Whatever influence people think they have over events is purely illusory--as if a wave were to think it had stirred the ocean into a storm.

Such concepts have their roots in 19th-century scientific belief, which in turn affected other areas of thought: philosophy, sociology, anthropology, art, and even religion. Determinism is still a valid position for some philosophers, who doubtless find in it the satisfaction of *knowing* beyond any doubt that the universe is wholly without meaning in any humanistic sense.

If, on the other hand, we take the existentialist's view, we will say that humankind, cast adrift on a sea of nothing, and inescapably alone, suffers a terrible freedom--a freedom in which each individual's survival depends upon the ability to "create" self, one's own reality of being. No purpose can be attached to the universe except what one painfully fabricates from fragments of experience that in themselves have no meaning. Humankind is absolutely alone--hence, absolutely free.

The world, in the existentialist's view, is a kind of fortuitous dream, or rather nightmare, beset with all the terrors of undifferentiated possibility. Existentialism is unquestionably the headiest brew modern philosophy has yet concocted, though for some it lacks any soothing, any comforting ingredients. To say "man is condemned to freedom" is to say that he is forced into the terror of choosing, and perhaps choosing wrong.

The determinist and the existentialist occupy extreme positions in philosophy. Most humanist thinkers, on the other hand, tend to avoid the extremes--certainly in areas as clouded with ambiguity as the subject of freedom is--and to assume that in a field of contending forces or opposing views, the truth, or what can be allowed to serve as truth, stands somewhere near the middle. They see a kind of triadic process at work here: from two opposite, interacting elements, a third, synthetic element is born that represents superior insight.

Modern science, which has provided many new insights into humanity's physical and psychological nature, and into its evolutionary history as well, has also provided bases for new speculations on the problem of human freedom. Among such speculations is the idea that freedom may not be something that humanity either has or does not have, but rather something that it may have the capacity to create. Freedom is seen not as a gift (or a gift withheld), but as potentially implicit in the evolutionary venture. Freedom is something to be earned.

It is quite possible that for most of its history humanity has not been free in any positive sense of the word. Human actions and thought may simply have followed guidelines inherent in the human condition, the result of a limited power over the environment and the sequence of events. According to one modern savant (Julian Jaynes, *The Origins of Consciousness in the Breakdown of the Bicameral Mind*) mankind before about 3000 B.C. was not conscious at all in the present sense of the word. Before then, Jaynes tells us, people got their signals from inner voices which they called gods. The inner voices came from the right hemisphere of the brain; the left hemisphere constituted the "human" side of the brain. This meant that ancient people lived psychologically in a bicameral world--that is, their governing faculties consisted of two relatively separate powers. Only the eventual breakdown of this arrangement--and the accompanying decay of the gods--made it possible for people to become conscious in our modern sense--to become *self*-conscious, *self*-aware, *self*-analytical. With consciousness, people gained the ability to deliberate, to pause between stimulus and response, to decide. No longer bound to obey external authority, they now found authority and understanding within their newly conscious self. In short, *they began to be free.*

Such a radical hypothesis, of course, awaits proof. Its value here is as a dramatic indicator of the direction modern thought may be moving toward: a concept of freedom as process, a thing to be achieved when people have reached the stage where they can "deserve" it.

It can be argued that we are at that stage now. For have not the enormous powers conferred by science given us enormous freedom to use or misuse them? Through technology, we now have the power to reshape the environment along artificial, and therefore uniquely human, ways; we find ourselves deciding which species on earth we will or will not preserve; we consider how the atmosphere may be altered, how climate and weather may eventually be controlled. Already we envision our ability, through genetic management, to blueprint our biological future; cloning is only one of the more spectacular possibilities hinted at. Most significantly of all, we possess the terrible freedom utterly to annihilate the world in an atomic holocaust.

Of course, there are those who argue that all these "supposed" freedoms are but stages in a predestined plan to have humanity self-destruct at a certain point. Technology is seen as merely the means of carrying out that end.

Such thinking, however, will strike most of us as the counsel of despair. IF humanity can get past the technological crisis, IF we can avoid annihilating ourselves as well as the planet, then the possibility of almost unlimited freedom emerges: freedom to develop our intelligence by learning to use the now-unused three-quarters of the brain, to achieve new levels of spirit and creativity, to make ourselves what we have always boasted we were--the center of our universe--and perhaps the inseminator of other universes undreamed of, light years away.

# ANSWERS TO STUDY GUIDE SAMPLE TEST QUESTIONS

INTRODUCTION:    4, 1, 4, 1, 5, 3, 1

CHAPTER  1:    2, 1, 3, 5, 1, 4, 4, 5, 1, 5

CHAPTER  2:    5, 2, 4, 1, 1, 3, 3, 3, 1, 2

CHAPTER  3:    3, 3, 5, 5, 4, 1, 5, 2, 1, 2, 5, 1

CHAPTER  4:    3, 1, 4, 3, 5, 2, 2, 3, 1, 2, 1 4, 3, 5, 1

CHAPTER  5:    2, 1, 3, 5, 2, 4, 4, 1, 2, 1 5, 2, 2, 3, 1

CHAPTER  6:    4, 4, 2, 5, 5, 1, 2, 4, 1, 5, 4, 1, 5, 4, 1

CHAPTER  7:    5, 4, 1, 5, 3, 1, 1, 5, 3, 1, 2, 2

CHAPTER  8:    3, 1, 4, 1, 1, 5, 4, 4, 5, 1, 1, 4

CHAPTER  9:    *Sample Test "A"*

1. The first statement, about ballet dancers, is a Craft comment because it tells what the dancers did in relation to the music. Dancers may begin moving before the music starts; they may dance according to the rhythm of the music, or against the beat. Any comment on detail of performers' actions is Craft.

2. This statement is a morality comment because it concentrates on the effect on audiences of what sympathetic characters do. We (the audience) "root for" certain characters; if those characters behave in a lawless way, challenging authority, some moralists worry that audiences will imitate their actions.

3. The information about two artists is factual, telling about what actually happened in their lives. It is not interpretive. It doesn't speculate on how this action indicates dominant ideas of the time, and it doesn't tell what they painted. It is therefore biography.

4. An actor's voice is a major part of his or her skill. It is therefore a Craft comment. To observe the differences in voices of two acclaimed actors is a mark of critical discernment--therefore much better than the general, less observant comment "good." (Looking at two productions of the same play as performed by two different leading actors would be an excellent opportunity to put comparison skills into practice. Even closer observation would occur from comparing the same scene or speech as delivered by two actors.)

5. A comment about the personal life of the viewer is Subjective, mainly because it is idiosyncratic; everyone would not be in the position of being a caregiver for elderly family members. The attraction for or distaste for a particular subject may or may not be true of the populace as a whole. We all have our sensitive spots, along with food preferences and aversions. Sometimes the sensitive spot is hit with a racial stereotype or a particular kind of language (if it affects enough people, it stops being Subjective and reaches the category of "Moral" or "Political.") In this case, the comment is "no interest," but someone in the same situation might be attracted to a story about a familiar topic.

6. Comments on scenery are going to be about Craft. Scenery is often overlooked in favor of comments about actors and plot. When the scenery looks artificial, the cause may be lack of funding for a more natural-appearing background. The reviewer calls it "artificial" for deliberate reasons and ties it to the equally deliberate foolishness of the plot.

7. An attractive heroine finds a reason for supporting unions. Audiences are encouraged to sympathize with the union after they see the working conditions against which the heroine is struggling. (Substitute a less attractive main character, take away the possible love interest--ah, but that's another story.) Anyway, the comment is a political one, because unions--pro or con--represent a political issue.

8. Wordsworth was a poet who lived in a part of England called the Lake District; and that's a biographical fact. His Nature poems may be read and appreciated in light of that information. Comments on the structure and images of the poems would be Craft.

9. What constitutes happy endings is part of the beliefs about happiness in a particular culture. The best response is therefore Historical Context. When the feminist movement urges women to strive for power without regard for the traditional role of subordinating their aims to those of their men, the movement is urging us to challenge previous beliefs.

10. The remark about similarities in a certain kind of film constitutes a statement about the mood of the decade in which the film was produced. Propaganda is designed to urge acceptance of a particular cause--in this case, winning the war. Using people with different accents and different geographical and ethnic origins was a frequent device of war films in the early '40s. The appropriate response is Historical Context.

11. Because the sonnet is a particular kind of poem (14 lines, no more, no less) and because it may be divided in different ways, the reviewer of a poem must notice this structure; and thus the comment is definitely Craft. "Petrarchan" and "Elizabethan" are terms used in the analysis of sonnets, along with rhyme scheme (such as ABBA or ABAB).

12. Noting the length of each episode in a television show before the commercial break is so automatic we might not think it worth mentioning. Those who do so, however, are employing Craft in that their remark deals with the pace of the program. If, however, they want to draw some further conclusion, such as "Modern audiences have a reduced attention span due to the constant interruption of stories, as opposed to the more leisurely pace of 19th century storytelling," they will be adding Historical Context to their criticism.

13. Making a comparison between two works on the same subject by different authors is a Craft element.

14. The *I* is pretty much a dead giveaway that this is Subjective. It belongs in the same category with remarks about the desire for clothing, furniture, a cruise, in imitation of consumer goods displayed on the screen.

15. This is Craft, in the way close observation has picked up on the same shape in two different places. Other Craft remarks about a painting are comments on complementary colors, static versus charged movement, serious and light treatments of the same subject--and a host of other details found in books on Art.

16. This Craft remark recognizes abstract rather than representational painting. The student who insists that every painting must represent an object is likely to make naive remarks about finding light bulbs or lightning when the artist never intended to copy anything from real life.

17. The comment about the sum of money for which a painting has sold is of interest to collectors (but we have no Connoisseur category), and it often reflects the suspicion that artists and dealers are pulling a scam on the unsuspecting public. Because the comment does not deal with the painting itself or the historical background, we must label this one "Subjective."

18. The beliefs of the artist and his patron revealed a clash between Marxism and Capitalism. We can label this one Political or Biographical or Historical Context.

19. Women's roles have changed in many art genres, including dance; and therefore the comment is one of Historical Context.

20. This is a straight statement of Biography, but it is no substitute for describing the painting responsible for the artist's prominence.


CHAPTER 9:     *Sample Test "B":* 3, 1, 4, 2, 5, 3, 5, 4, 1, 3

CHAPTER 10:     3, 1, 3, 3, 3, 4, 5, 2, 5, 3

CHAPTER 11:     4, 4, 4, 4, 1, 2, 5, 5, 3, 1, 1, 3

CHAPTER 12:     3, 1, 3, 1, 4, 5, 1, 2, 3, 4, 1, 1

CHAPTER 13:     3, 4, 1, 3, 4, 1, 4, 1, 1, 3, 4, 5

CHAPTER 14:     1, 4, 3, 4, 2, 1, 4, 4, 5, 2, 1, 3

CHAPTER 15:     1, 5, 1, 2, 3, 4, 2, 5, 4, 4, 4, 1, 5

CHAPTER 16:     3, 3, 5, 1, 5, 1, 4, 2, 5, 1, 2, 3